TWO CHEERS FOR HIGHER EDUCATION

Two Cheers for Higher Education

Why American Universities Are Stronger Than Ever—and How to Meet the Challenges They Face

Steven Brint

PRINCETON UNIVERSITY PRESS

PRINCETON AND OXFORD

Published by Princeton University Press
41 William Street, Princeton, New Jersey 08540
6 Oxford Street, Woodstock, Oxfordshire OX20 1TR

press.princeton.edu

Library of Congress Control Number: 2018941709
ISBN 978-0-691-18266-7

British Library Cataloging-in-Publication Data is available

Editorial: Peter J. Dougherty and Jessica Yao
Production Editorial: Mark Bellis
Production: Erin Suydam
Publicity: Tayler Lord

This book has been composed in Adobe Text Pro and Gotham

Printed on acid-free paper. ∞

Printed in the United States of America

10 9 8 7 6 5 4 3 2 1

For Michele

Lux et Amor

CONTENTS

TWO CHEERS FOR HIGHER EDUCATION

1

The Universities Expansion Made

Even those who are not immersed in the world of higher education are familiar with the litany of challenges facing higher education institutions. We cannot avoid reading about the crushing weight of student loan debt, the dispiriting erosion of state funding for universities, the enrollment declines in the humanities, the seemingly endless expansion of the ranks of adjunct faculty. College graduates in this generation are not always surpassing their parents' standard of living, and so many bright-eyed college entrants leave their intended alma maters disappointed far before they have completed their courses of study. Indeed, passionate critics like sociologist Sara Goldrick-Rab point to the food insecurity experienced by community college students and others who are merely trying to take a baby step toward realizing the American Dream. Especially when set against the cool successes of Silicon Valley, how can anyone deny that these have been some of the worst of times for American higher education?

And yet we need to recognize that despite these very real problems, the narrative trajectory of higher education *as an institution* is utterly different from the one these bleak pictures convey. Beyond the din of the latest protest about sexual violence on campus or the latest controversial speaker whose mere presence on campus provoked an uproar, some remarkably positive trends have left American universities much bigger, stronger, and in a more dominant position—both domestically and internationally—than ever before. I have traced the major contours of American higher education from 1980 through the present, and despite the validity of some of the gloom and doom stories we see every day, a very different picture emerges. I seek to paint this picture, not because I want to sweep the problems of higher education under the rug but to try to set these daily challenges in a broader—and frankly more positive—context.

My focus on the expansion and the growing prominence of universities will come as a surprise—perhaps even as a shock—to many higher education scholars. Higher education scholarship tends toward a deeply pessimistic outlook, and business influence is the primary bête noire of scholars. For many, American universities have come to do the bidding of corporations (Aronowitz 2000; Washburn 2000), transformed themselves into market-oriented, managed enterprises little different from corporations (Engell and Dangerfield 1998, 2005; Gumport 2000; Tuchman 2009), charged exorbitant tuition and fees that put them out of reach of those born in the bottom half of the socioeconomic hierarchy (Haycock and Gerald 2006; Mettler 2014), short-changed matriculated students on quality educational experiences (Arum and Roksa 2011), and created a caste system with low-paid instructors doing most of the teaching and senior professors focusing on their careers, research, conferences, and consultancies (Finkelstein, Conley, and Schuster 2016). Some scholars in this critical stream of thought have argued that the logic of the private sector marketplace is embedded within higher education itself; it is not that universities are directed by business interests but that they have reorganized themselves internally to reflect the market logic of business organizations (Slaughter and Leslie 1997; Slaughter and Rhoades 2004). The view of universities as manifestations of a neoliberalism run amok contains many valuable insights, but it fails to account for the continuing power of relatively autonomous intellectual practices or the dynamic forces that have given universities new prominence for their commitments to economic development and social inclusion.

To an even greater degree, a realistically optimistic appraisal of the future of universities will come as a surprise to journalists and educational technologists who think that higher education as we know it is on the verge of radical reorganization due to the rise of online alternatives (Carey 2012; Kamenetz 2010), the unbundling of practices that have little efficiency value when bundled together (Selingo 2013), and the potential of alternative credentialing systems, such as the modular "badges" promoted by online entrepreneurs (Young 2012). It would be a serious mistake to dismiss these possibilities, but they are less likely to come to fruition than their advocates suggest if higher education can take effective measures to contain the threats they pose. This containment is warranted to prevent these antici- pated reorganizations from reducing the possibilities students have for a better life.

Many of the criticisms of higher education have merit. But they miss the big picture: American research universities have grown stronger, both finan- cially and intellectually. They have done so by incorporating multiple growth logics in an interconnected and flexible way. One is the logic of intellectual advance, and it still informs the activities of most scientists and scholars. It determines many of the fundamental structures of the academy such as the centrality of academic departments and the status acquired through journal and book publication. The second is a market logic that leads colleges and universities to work with industry on new technologies, to create new ap- plied degrees, to cultivate patrons, and to manage the enterprises in ways that are familiar to corporations. The third is a logic of social inclusion that leads universities to hold themselves out as the single best option for the members of disadvantaged groups to gain skills that can lead to upward social mobility.

These logics and the practices they animate comingle in the life of univer- sities. The dean of the engineering school finds that she promotes colleagues who make fundamental advances, but also encourages those who work with industry and sponsors programs for minorities and women in engineering. The chair of the sociology department finds that he celebrates scholars who accumulate influence through the citation of their research, while at the same time seeking to diversify his faculty and graduate student body and adding new "self-supporting" (that is to say, moneymaking) master's degree programs in applied social statistics or human resources management. When we step back from the daily struggles that students and faculty experience, we can see that as an institution colleges and universities have found ways to maintain a high degree of autonomy while becoming ever more closely con- nected both to the most powerful organizations in society and to students from disadvantaged backgrounds who seek a better future. Universities have always been about peeking over the horizon. The contemporary progress- oriented score contains competing, sometimes dissonant, but ultimately compatible themes: the search for as-yet undiscovered knowledge, the pursuit of new market opportunities (most notably through economically relevant innovations and new degree programs), and the movement for ex- panded social opportunities.

The Argument of the Book

The argument of the book follows from these observations.

The traditional structures and purposes of colleges and universities are intended to produce two outcomes: the expansion of knowledge, principally in the disciplines but also at their interstices, and the development of students' cognitive capacities and subject matter knowledge. Colleges and universities have long embraced a large number of ancillary activities, ranging from hospital enterprises to student clubs and organizations to intercollegiate athletics. But these two objectives have remained, in principle, fundamental. During the period I consider in this book two movements hit colleges and universities with great force: one was the movement to use university research to advance economic development through the invention of new technologies with commercial potential. The other was to use colleges and universities as instruments of social inclusion, providing opportunities to members of previously marginalized groups, including women, racial-ethnic minorities, and members of the LGBTQ community. They were driven both by external parties, such as the Business-Higher Education Forum and the great philanthropic foundations, and by campus constituencies who benefited from their advance.

My argument is that these movements created a special kind of dynamism because of the strength of partisan commitments to them, backed up by high levels of patronage. The innovation movement fostered a stronger embrace of entrepreneurship; the rise of engineering and medicine as the two centers of exceptional dynamism in universities; new ideas about economic development related to partnerships between universities, industry, and government; and the creation of new high-tech clusters of firms surrounding universities. It also contributed to the growth of interdisciplinary initiatives on campus, as a result of the underlying assumption that the solution of technological problems required the skills of investigators from many disciplines. The inclusion movement fostered the expansion of the curriculum to include the experiences of marginalized peoples from the United States and those from non-Western cultures; commitments to the diversification of the student body and the faculty; attention to intergroup relations on campus as a measure of the new concept of "campus climate"; and interventions intended to help disadvantaged groups succeed. It too contributed to the growth of interdisciplinary initiatives on campus as means to knit together networks of colleagues with common interests in diversity and social change.

The rise of these two dynamic forces created a contest in which the traditions of academic professionalism both encompassed and resisted pressures to shift attention toward technological innovation and social inclusion. Even as they accommodated the growing interest in use-inspired research, the majority of faculty research continued to focus on the solution of problems identified by colleagues in their disciplinary communities. The proliferation of specialties and subspecialties continued and academic professional culture thrived. Even as they accommodated the push for social inclusion, colleges and universities also found means to preserve their traditional role in the identification of talent, most often found among socially advantaged students, and in the cultivation of students' cognitive capacities and subject matter knowledge. They did so through selective admissions, through the elevation of the more difficult majors, and through the encouragement of motivated students to go on for graduate degrees, as well as through the traditional machinery of course-based assessments. Accommodation was the norm, but occasional tensions also arose, as when faculty entrepreneurs seemed to flout their academic responsibilities in favor of building their enterprises or when the racial or gender backgrounds of candidates seemed to supersede their scholarly achievements as a basis for advancement.

The hierarchical structure of the system reduced the pressures on research universities to manage these tensions. Commitments to new technology development were, not surprisingly, concentrated at research universities. Commitments to social inclusion were also evident at these institutions, but they were constrained by rising prices and higher levels of selectivity. Comprehensive universities—those emphasizing teaching over research—consequently carried the primary responsibility for expanding social inclusion, and this was particularly true of comprehensives dependent on state funding. Even so, inherent tensions existed in the simultaneous pursuit of disciplinary knowledge, technological innovation, and social inclusion. Those engaged at the highest levels in disciplinary knowledge creation or technological innovation often found the university's aspirations to expand access irrelevant to their interests—even as an impediment—while those committed to democratic access just as often viewed the elitism of the leading disciplinary professionals and innovators with skepticism, if not downright antipathy.

The dynamic forces of technological innovation and social inclusion have not been the only fuel for expansion. Universities are voracious; they search for resources wherever they can find them so long as they can justify them on academic grounds. Many of the other sources of the great expansion are well known. In the sphere of research, they included the largesse of the federal government, philanthropic foundations, and individual donors who have spotted in university researchers reliable guides to the as-yet unknown. In the educational arena, they included the value of higher education credentials in the labor market, a value inflated by the near collapse of opportunities for young adults with only high school educations. And of course they also included employers' and students' interest in the contributions to skill development that colleges can deliver.

The often surprising consequences of expansion are not as well known. I argue that as students and patronage poured into colleges and universities, the institutions gained unexpected new powers. The growth of graduate populations funneled tens of thousands of analytically competent personnel into the country's "knowledge intensive" industries. These four dozen or so industries—ranging from aeronautics to wireless communications—did not dominate the economy as theorists of postindustrial society predicted, but they did by the end of the period contribute as much as half of GDP. Those with graduate and professional degrees formed a cognitive resource of more than twenty-five million people, with PhDs alone outnumbering the population of Los Angeles. The expansion of this stratum of highly educated professionals helped create the conditions for looser boundaries between universities and other institutional sectors. University researchers provided testing grounds for new ideas and new technologies developed outside their walls, even as they continued to produce their own at a startling rate. At the same time, the country's divisions by educational level and high-tech industry location created powder-keg conditions; the advance of the educated group, with its commitment to diversity, contributed to the uneasiness and reaction of whites with less education and dimmer prospects.

The boom in undergraduate education created opportunities for mobility for many, a time for maturation for many more, and high-level skills for a motivated minority. It also had a number of less salutary effects. Contained within the burgeoning enrollment statistics were hundreds of thousands of students who lacked either academic or developed professional interests. Colleges and universities accommodated these students mainly by expecting little of them. The keenest observers no longer understood college as principally a place for building academic knowledge and skills but rather as a mechanism for producing adaptable and flexible people, sufficiently conscientious to prove themselves relatively quick studies in a variety of roles. Expansion encouraged the rise of the "practical arts"—applied fields of study connected to the power centers of the American economy: business, technology, health, media, and government. And it led to a romance with basic fields reflecting the culture of upper-middle-class progressives, stimulating enrollments in the arts, the environmental sciences, cognitive and neuroscience, fields embracing an international perspective, and those focusing on social inclusion. The preferences of patrons opened large opportunity gaps between the quantitative and interpretive disciplines, cementing and widening the status division within the faculty ranks.

The growing complexity of the environment surrounding higher education—encircled by regulations, dependent on constituency relations, and buffeted by rising expectations—created the conditions for a tremendous growth of management. The salaries of the administrative staff were offset by the hiring of armies of low-paid part-timers, an academic proletariat that comprised nearly half of the instructional staff by the end of the period. The scope of the vulnerabilities of U.S. colleges and universities extended also to the deep incursions of online and competency-based programs and the escalating costs of attendance. The future of the country's intellectual base turned on how effectively colleges and universities would confront the challenges of instructional quality, cost, and online competition that seemed to be building to a crisis point during the period, at least for the more vulnerable regional colleges and universities.

As this overview of my argument suggests, *Two Cheers for Higher Education* considers both the institutional strengths that growth has allowed universities to develop under the influence of the "three logics" (chapters 2–7) *and* the contradictions that have developed between these logics in the context of resource constraints of various types (the last section of chapter 7 and chapters 8 and 9).

My work stands in contrast to the major works of sociologists who have written about higher education and its role in American society. I cannot, for example, agree with Daniel Bell's (1973) prophecy that universities will become the axial institutions of a postindustrial "knowledge-based" society.[1] The "knowledge sector" of the economy, while growing, does not dominate. Nor does it include all of the most dynamic industries in the country. Corporations will remain the axial institutions, but universities do not need to become the axial institutions to influence the ways corporations work or the way large segments of the public think. They have a far broader influence in the public realm of discourse than corporations, and they have gained influence in part by becoming more porous—working with state, industry, and local communities instead of holding them at arm's length. Richard Florida's (2002) evocation of the "creative class" linked high-tech scientists and engineers, entrepreneurs, and arts creators as the generators of regional economic development and found this core forming most often in university towns. Florida's analysis is closer in spirit to the orientation of this book, but it fails to appreciate the continuing essential contributions of "garden variety" scientific and scholarly specialists or the prosaic but fundamental production of credentialed workers. As originally stated, Florida's theory overlooked the educational and regional divisions that surfaced with the rise of the "creative class" due to gentrification and brain drain, on one side, and stagnating or declining employment prospects, on the other.[2] Indeed, those who are not part of the "creative class" have made their presence known electorally, in no uncertain terms, and universities are grappling with ways to respond.

Nor is my analysis of the social stratification role of universities consistent with the classic works in sociology on this subject. Inequalities by social class and race-ethnicity certainly remain deeply embedded in U.S. higher education, as I will discuss in chapter 5. But Pierre Bourdieu and Jean-Claude Passeron's (1977) emphasis on the "reproduction" of social advantage by universities is belied by the extraordinary gains made by white women and Asian Americans under the influence of social movement organizations, government compulsion, and the university's own commitments to social inclusion. (These gains have extended in much less impressive ways to members of non-Asian minority groups.)

My studies of university organization lead in a different direction than the classic works in this area as well. Christopher Jencks and David Riesman's (1968) "academic revolution," which put academics in the catbird seat relative to university administrators, can no longer be treated as credible; administrators have regained control (if indeed they ever lost it!), and their budgetary decisions have led to spectacular growth in their own ranks, creeping disinvestment in academic departments that cannot raise external funds, and the creation of a huge academic proletariat of part-time instructors.

DATA SOURCES

I draw on a range of materials. These include the studies that my *Colleges & Universities 2000* (C&U 2000) research teams conducted between the years 2000 and 2015. C&U 2000 data are composed of the Institutional Data Archive (IDA), a compendium of data on 385 U.S. colleges and universities collected at five-year intervals between 1970 and 2010; the College Catalog Study (CCS) database, a coding of college catalogs from a subset of 292 IDA institutions at five-year intervals beginning in 1975 and ending in 2010; and the Great Recession database, a coding of all newspaper stories about 300 C&U 2000 institutions during the recession years 2008–12.

My data sources also include the American College Faculty and American College Freshmen studies conducted by the Higher Education Research Institute at UCLA, the Baccalaureate & Beyond longitudinal study, the Cluster Mapping Project of the Harvard Business School, Current Population Survey data from the Census Bureau, the Delta Cost Study database, the Integrated Postsecondary Education Data System (IPEDS), the National Longitudinal Survey of Youth (NLSY), the National Survey of Student Engagement (NSSE), the Student Experience in the Research University and UC Undergraduate Experiences Surveys (SERU/UCUES), the Thomson-Reuters' Web of Science database (WoS), and Lexis-Nexis searches on numerous topics. I also draw on interviews with hundreds of university administrators and faculty members, as well as a number of targeted, small-scale studies, or probes, of worthy topics that I could not engage systematically for lack of time or resources.

EVIDENCE OF GROWTH AND GROWING PROMINENCE

Some writers may long for an imagined golden age in which universities stood apart from—or were in some real or imagined way superior to—the rest of society, but the evidence suggests that the true golden age coincides with the period about which I write. Between 1980 and 2010, for example, research expenditures grew by more than nine times (in 2010 dollars), high-quality publications catalogued in the Web of Science grew by nearly four times, and Web of Science citations grew (measured in 2005) by at least 2.5 times (Brint and Carr 2017). Few sectors were as important to the emerging knowledge society as universities, and the federal government supported their development with high, if never fully sufficient, funding. Federal funding, estimated at approximately $30 billion in 2015 (AAAS 2016), is largely responsible for the research activities and infrastructure on university campuses. So too is the financial aid system, the essential fuel for growth, which expended approximately $65 billion in grants, in loans, and, indirectly, through tax benefits in 2015 (College Board 2015). Both support systems have trended sharply upward in constant dollars since the 1980s, including during recessionary periods.

Other measures of university impact show a similar picture. Universities do not hold a monopoly on knowledge production—far from it!—but the research they produce has contributed to uncountable improvements in economic development and human understanding. Former Columbia University provost Jonathan R. Cole (2009) provided what may be an unsurpassable overview of the most fundamental of these contributions. Among those he highlights include the gene-splicing technology of Herbert Boyer and Stanley Cohen that led directly to the creation of a multibillion-dollar biotechnology industry. Their gene-splicing technique, patented in 1980, has already led to the creation of drugs to treat heart disease, strokes, hemophilia, rheumatoid arthritis, thyroid cancer, asthma, non-Hodgkin's lymphoma, and diabetes, among others. Other biomedical discoveries discussed by Cole have led to new ways to suppress cancer tumors, to prevent smoking (through the nicotine skin patch), to replace broken or damaged joints, to improve hearing through cochlear implants, to allow damaged hearts to beat regularly (through the invention of the pacemaker), and to detect previously undetectable bodily ailments (through the invention of magnetic resonance imaging). New industries related to breakthroughs in the physical sciences include the development of lasers, whose applications range from eye surgery to the creation of audio CDs. Such familiar products as light-emitting diodes (LEDs), bar codes, radar, and transistors were developed by university researchers. Many of the advances in information technology were also the product of university researchers, ranging from the design of the first high-powered computer (Mark I), developments that led to computer-aided design and computer-aided manufacturing, the first web browsers, and packet-network switching that created the architectural foundation for the Internet.

Some other university-initiated projects, such as the search algorithms that led to Google, have become an essential component in the daily life of Americans. Another entirely new industry may be in the making as a result of university researchers' breakthroughs in creating much more flexible and lighter materials through nanoscale technologies, which makes possible the manipulation of individual atoms. Already materials scientists are seeing the potential to manufacture hardware a hundred times lighter but just as strong as hardware manufactured with current materials. Other potential applications include, as Cole recounts, "nanoparticles that can deliver drugs to specific diseased cells in the body; waterproof, tear-resistant cloth fibers; combat jackets that are ultra-strong; sturdier concrete; more durable, lighter sports equipment; and stronger suspension bridges" (2009, 292). Such a list is likely to be out of date the moment it is formulated because new discoveries arrive daily.[3]

The deepening engagement of universities with their societies does not of course end there. As Mitchell Stevens and his colleagues have put it, "higher education systems are key sites where institutions intersect" (Stevens, Armstrong, and Arum 2008, 135). Some have emphasized community service activities of various types as another important channel of interconnection between universities and the wider society. Intercollegiate athletics may be the most important of the community outreach activities provided by universities, because sports like football and basketball connect populations of entire regions and states to pride in "State U" (see Clotfelter 2011). But of course artistic and cultural events also play an important role in community engagement, as do student and faculty volunteering. Urbanists have heralded the rise of high-growth cities and regions built around vibrant and creative university centers (Florida 2002). In most cases, these visions have not been fully realized or have come with unintended consequences for those who are not members of the "creative class." Yet many examples exist of regions that have depended on universities as a centerpiece for development, and these examples help us see the potential that remains to be fully realized. Silicon Valley and Route 128 near Boston are well known; other university-based development economies have popped up in such unexpected spots as Ann Arbor, Michigan; Boulder, Colorado; and Salt Lake City, Utah.

We can add to this sense of the university's growing importance the weight of the tens of thousands of leaders it has helped prepare for positions of responsibility and the tens of millions it has helped equip for occupations requiring well-informed judgment and cognitive skills. When we consider the possibilities for more complete personal development—for the time and challenges to become deeper, more creative, more reflective people—our thoughts naturally turn to the transformations we hope higher education can produce. In a society with few other avenues for social mobility, higher education is also the path that leads out of economic marginality for hundreds of thousands of young people every year.

These contributions could not have been possible without the strong demand for a college education among young people. One important reason for this strong demand is that the market for high school–educated labor has very nearly collapsed—at least in so far as well-paying and stable jobs are concerned. College has become nearly a necessity in the minds of most Americans as the only good option for young people hoping to secure good jobs. The growth in both undergraduate and graduate enrollments was steady from the 1990s on, though recession and prosperity alike. Nor did the rate of increase slow in the face of rising tuition costs. Postsecondary enrollments grew from 15.3 million in 2000 to 20 million in 2010, accelerating through a time when tuitions continued their steady climb upward (NCES 2012a, table 223). These 20 million students represent a college-going group nearly one hundred times larger than in 1900 and nearly ten times larger than in 1950 (NCES 2014, table 303). In 1920, only 5 percent of young adults age 25–29 had finished four years of college. That fraction grew to 8 percent by 1950 and surged thereafter, reaching one-third by 2012 (NCES 2014, table 104.20). One consequence of the larger population of baccalaureates was that postbaccalaureate degrees also became more common. Nearly 25 million Americans held advanced degrees (master's and above) by 2012, the combined size of the five largest American cities.

The Fundamental Challenges

Although higher education is an important sector in American society, universities have also faced formidable economic challenges beginning as early as 1970 in the form of state disinvestment and continuously rising costs (see, e.g., Cheit 1971). The higher education historian Roger Geiger described the characteristic pattern of budget cutting during recessionary periods combined with progressively weaker restorations during times of prosperity:

> The recovery from the recession of 1990 was long and shallow. Additional years passed before tax revenues grew sufficiently for states to expand their budgets. Still, the restoration phase of the budget cycle was unusually weak. . . . A pattern became established in which good economic times brought less restoration and bad times brought greater deterioration. The latter scenario was replayed with a vengeance after the mild recession of 2001. Many states reduced university appropriations, some repeatedly. (Geiger 2004, 44–45)

Most governors would have liked to keep tuition prices as low as possible, but they recognized that tuition provided an alternative source of funding for higher education institutions when state budgets required cutting—and one that was especially attractive because of the countercyclical nature of demand for higher education credentials. Public higher education in this way served as a "balance wheel" in state budgets, allowing states to navigate more effectively through business cycles by cutting higher education spending in bad times and restoring a higher share in good times, though typically not to prerecession levels (Hovey 1999; see also Delaney and Doyle 2007).[4]

With declining state investment came much higher tuitions to make up the difference and to pay for continuously increasing costs. Starting in the early 1980s, following each recession the percentage of educational expense covered by net tuition increased. As the economists Gary C. Fethke and Andrew J. Policano showed, in 1985 net tuition amounted to less than one-quarter of total educational expenses in public higher education; by 2000 it had increased to just under 30 percent, and by 2010 it accounted for more than 40 percent. They concluded, "Many state legislatures have now acquiesced to large tuition increases, essentially abandoning the philosophy that higher education is primarily a social responsibility" (2012, 13).

Higher tuition and fees brought more borrowing to pay for college. Student loans were a backbone of the postwar expansion, but the average student owed relatively little. At the end of the 1970s no public college in the country charged more than $2,500 for annual in-state tuition. By the end of the period under discussion in this book, the costs of tuition and residence halls approached $30,000 per year in public research universities and double that in the leading privates. The average private college student could expect to leave with a degree and $30,000 of student debt to pay. Those who attended public universities were on average just a little better-off in their debt obligations. Most students accepted debt as the inevitable price of a degree that remained a very good investment over the course of a lifetime. Still, this was a tough way to begin adult life, and public opinion polls showed a persistent questioning of the cost of college. Muck-raking books like *Generation Debt* (Kamenetz 2006) and *The Student Loan Scam* (Collinge 2010) stirred debate about whether college was worth the cost and how it could be made more affordable. In 2010, student debt, then approaching $1 trillion, exceeded credit card debt as the second largest category of debt in the country (behind mortgages). The higher education industry promoted the value of the college degree, paying comparatively little attention to its cost.

Private colleges had distinctive reasons for raising tuitions. They were intent on "buying the best" and "offering the most," and these aspirations were expensive. Price increases in the private sector put additional pressure on the publics, ever concerned about falling behind in the competition for top faculty talent, to keep up. In both private and public institutions, college prices grew steadily, by four times the rate of inflation between 1980 and 2012, with a big jump in public tuitions following the recession of 2001. During the same period, the median inflation-adjusted family income increased by less than 20 percent. A family at the median would have had to pay nearly half of its annual earnings to afford an average-priced private nonprofit four-year university, or two and one-half times the proportion it would have spent in 1980. The proportion of the median family's income required to pay tuition in public universities rose even faster, increasing more than three times, from 4 percent of the median family income in 1980 to nearly 20 percent in 2012 (Geiger and Heller 2011; Lowery 2014). By 2016, Americans' concerns with the cost of college had reached a tipping point, with majorities saying for the first time that there were many ways to achieve success in life without a college degree and most Democrats and independents saying that it was a good or somewhat good idea for college to be free for students from lower- and middle-income families (Schliefer and Silliman 2016).

Higher education economists sought to explain why tuition increases continued to far outpace inflation. At private universities, instructional costs were clearly part of the equation; to remain competitive, the leading private colleges and universities had to pay premium salaries to professors who were in high demand. Generous financial aid policies also contributed. To return some tuition dollars to enroll students from the bottom half of the income distribution, higher charges were required for those families who campus financial aid officers determined could afford them (Clotfelter 1996; Ehrenberg 2000). By contrast, instructional costs remained fairly stable at public institutions. Instead, the number of administrators and their salaries grew. So did student affairs budgets (for supporting student clubs, campus arts and entertainment events, state-of-the-art fitness centers, health and counseling centers, dorm renovations, food courts, and the rest of the amenities residential college students expected to balance the time they spent on study). Campuses also continuously added staff to a range of offices required to maintain donor and constituency relations, regulatory compliance, and economic development opportunities (Ehrenberg 2012).

Facing these fiscal challenges, the first prong in the strategy of virtually all universities has been to raise tuition dramatically and to redistribute a significant share of the increase to cover the costs of students from financially needy families. This high tuition/high aid policy has allowed universities to cope with cost increases, while forcing them to consider the value (or in many cases the necessity) of higher enrollments. International and out-of-state students have been a significant contributor to tuition revenues at many institutions. These students typically paid much higher tuitions and were not eligible for financial aid.

The second prong of the strategy has been to focus aggressively on increasing yield from donors. Campus advancement offices have been the backbone of the private university economic model since the early twentieth century. But growing the size of endowments in public universities became an important source of revenue only following the first episodes of state budget cutting in the 1970s.

Because federal research dollars have not risen as fast as the demand for them, a third prong in the strategy has been to build out grant awards from corporations and philanthropies as a complement to federal spending. This has led to a proliferation of efforts to improve entrepreneurial success, from hiring media consultants to help professors pitch projects to offering courses on entrepreneurship to university researchers. Thus universities' interests in growing enrollments and reducing barriers to interaction with the broader society stem from economic imperatives as much as or more than they stem from service ideals.

QUALITY AND AUTONOMY ISSUES

Apart from cost, the quality of undergraduate education has received the most criticism from the public (see, e.g., ETS 2003; Immerwahr 2004; Schliefer and Silliman 2016).[5] The first sentence of Arthur W. Chickering and Zelda Gamson's call for reform in undergraduate education spelled out the dimensions of the problem: "Apathetic students, illiterate graduates, incompetent teaching, impersonal campuses—so rolls the drum-fire of criticism" (1987, 3). In 2003, the National Assessment of Adult Literacy found that only about one in three college graduates could draw accurate inferences from two editorials with contrasting content or could accurately read a three-variable graph relating age, exercise, and blood pressure (Kutner et al. 2007). Theories of the time focused on the more varied composition of college-going populations, the popularity of fast-moving images over slow-moving texts, and the rapid decline among students in reading for pleasure.

A 2011 study published by economists Philip Babcock and Mindy Marks found that undergraduates studied about half as long per week in 2008 as they had in 1962. Students at elite colleges continued to report more study than students at state colleges and engineering majors continued to report more study than education majors, but in all groups self-reported study time fell by proportionate amounts. The average college student attended class and hit the books for more than forty hours per week in the 1960s but just over twenty-five at the end of the Babcock-Marks time series. Judging from University of California data, students were spending most of their found time socializing with friends rather than working or taking care of families (Brint and Cantwell 2010).[6] And these results may greatly overstate the amount of studying undertaken by most undergraduates. Smartpen technology automatically records and time stamps every pen stroke made by a student. Sophisticated studies of time use employing this technology have found much smaller increments of time spent studying course materials, including in difficult courses in which passing grades are necessary to continue in a desirable major (Rawson, Stahovich, and Mayer 2017).

Some suggested that better tools for information retrieval permitted students to study less, but an obvious implication was that college faculty may have adjusted to lower student interest in study by reducing requirements. Richard Arum and Josipa Roksa's (2011) higher education best seller, *Academically Adrift*, found that only about half of students made significant gains on a well-validated test of critical thinking between the beginning of freshman and the middle of sophomore year. A year later, with senior data in hand, they concluded that more than a third of college students failed to make significant gains on critical thinking between freshman and senior year (Arum, Roksa, and Cho 2012). Students did not develop much because many faculty members did not require much. Those students who failed to make significant gains on the test were likely to have lower requirements for reading and writing in their classes.

Online courses and degree programs boomed during the period, and the research showed clearly that well-designed online courses could yield equal learning gains, though such courses were not inexpensive to create and did not save on faculty time. Indeed, the amount of time faculty spent interacting with students often increased in online settings (van de Vord and Pogue 2012; Worley and Tesdell 2009). And no one was sure whether inexperienced and less mature students were well served in online formats. The benefits of the physical campus—from serendipitous conversations to trust-building relationships to the social capital created in student clubs and organizations—were rarely fully "expensed" in the many paeans to online education. And few considered the possibility that the seed corn of the country's intellectual life could be eaten by online companies working for profit rather than knowledge creation and dissemination.

Other issues raised by growth have received less attention but may be no less important. These include questions about faculty autonomy and university management in an age of greater porousness. If universities focus on use-inspired research, which institutions will focus on the basic science and scholarship that has until now been the stronghold of their autonomy and a large source of their authority? If universities draw away from disciplinary organization to focus on interdisciplinary problems, what bodies will protect and advance the principles and insights that have been the product of disciplinary organization? If universities follow the lead of business-oriented administrators and external funders, how will faculty autonomy in the choice of projects, perhaps the most important source of intellectual progress, be maintained and fostered? If shared governance falters, who will protect the university from decisions that do not sufficiently weigh contributions that grow out of departments and specialized knowledge bases? If the state and foundations become much stronger arbiters of universities' agendas, what will prevent universities from becoming not just servants of society but increasingly servile in the face of their powerful benefactors and regulators?

THE HETERONOMY-AUTONOMY PUZZLE

The growing centrality of the university creates unprecedented opportunities. But the problems that have arisen in the wake of growth can prevent the university from giving sufficient attention to the values and practices that brought them to this enviable position in the first place. New approaches to the cost and revenue problems will be essential. To thrive, universities of the future will need to become even more porous to external actors than they currently are. They will do so to increase the two-way traffic between themselves and other institutions in society. They will also need to do so because state governments are receding as a source of funding and the federal government and Congress have not shown a willingness to step in to fill the gap. But, just as importantly, they will need to do a better job of protecting the basic scholarly and scientific values that provide autonomy from external actors who traverse these porous boundaries. To increase public support, they will need to focus more than they have on educational quality and student learning. And they will need to develop self-correcting mechanisms that allow them to identify and address essential pursuits that are in need of attention and resources. In many universities these pursuits include the liberal arts, undergraduate education, and even basic research in the natural and social sciences. What is at stake is not the survival of universities; for the top tier, at least, that is assured. Instead, the difference is between an influential institution subservient to corporations, government, and philanthropies, as compared to a true radiating center of the country's growing knowledge sector. These are facets of the "heteronomy-autonomy puzzle" facing universities, and I will suggest approaches to addressing this puzzle at several points in the book and a fully framed method for sustaining balance in the concluding chapter.

Beyond the Multiversity

This book focuses on the years 1980–2015, a period in which both the opportunities and problems of growth became defining. But it is necessary to go back to the early 1960s to capture the essence of the postwar research university as an organizational structure and cultural ethos. At the time that he gave the Godkin Lectures at Harvard University, Clark Kerr was president of the University of California. In the lectures, published as *The Uses of the University* (1963), he provided a now classic portrait of the new kind of university that was coming into focus at the time of his presidency. He called this new institution the "multiversity." Kerr envisioned the multiversity as a kind of service station to society. It was connected to every important institution in the state and nation, and it provided research and expert advice to help these institutions solve problems. The university was run by the leading researchers who brought renown to the university and, not incidentally, had the option to leave to take up better offers. These researchers were one-part entrepreneur, one-part research manager, and one-part working scientist or scholar. The emphasis on service was central to Kerr's vision. Most university researchers stayed on campus much of the time to work on publications and grant proposals. Others launched themselves out into society to help solve problems either as private consultants or as members of national commissions. As Kerr conceived it, this was essentially a one-way traffic. Neither representatives of social institutions nor the ideas they generated launched themselves into the university to reconfigure research agendas or to engender new research programs.

Senior administrators did not hold the power to direct the enterprise; although increasing complexity brought them close to the center of action on most issues, they were, in Kerr's view, mostly mediators, trying to find common ground among competing faculty, staff, and student interests.

Kerr's multiversity was already in 1963 a very large operation:

The University had operating expenditures from all sources of nearly half a billion dollars with almost another 100 million for construction;

a total employment of over 40,000, more than IBM and in a far greater variety of endeavors; operations in over a hundred locations, counting campuses, experiment stations, agricultural and urban extension centers, and projects abroad involving more than fifty countries; nearly 10,000 courses in its catalogues; some form of contact with nearly every industry, nearly every level of government, nearly every person in its region. (Kerr 1963, 7)

The multiversity in Kerr's view suffered from the problems of its successes. Students often felt lost in the anonymous environment of the large multiversity campus, a situation made worse by the research interests of the faculty; in Kerr's words, "[One of our more pressing problems] is [h]ow to escape the cruel paradox that a superior faculty leads to an inferior concern for undergraduate teaching" (1963, 65). Professors in the humanities were in Kerr's time already feeling alienated from the aspirations of the multiversity, while natural scientists were for the most part highly satisfied with it and prospering. Dependence on the federal government for research funding "substantially reduced" the autonomy of the university, as leading researchers responded with "fidelity and alacrity" to the federal government's priorities (58). But it was not as yet challenged by legions of outside parties, from corporate partners to billion-dollar foundations, seeking to align the interests of the university with their own. In his mind's eye, Kerr may have been thinking of the prospects of the sixty members of the elite Association of American Universities or, more likely, a subset of that membership. Certainly his vision seems more closely aligned to the aspirations of public than private universities.

Today the number of large research universities would extend at least to the 100-plus institutions classified by the Carnegie Foundation as having "very high" research activity. These are the institutions with which I will be principally concerned when I discuss the research activities of universities, though some of my analyses will include the top 200 research producers. By contrast, my discussions of enrollment, curriculum, and staffing will extend to the broader population of four-year colleges and universities, more than 3,000 in number. I have split the frames of research and instruction self-consciously. Discussions of research should be focused on the institutions that produce the great majority of it, while discussions of enrollments and programs should extend to a broader range of institutions. Two-year community colleges are an important but very different type of postsecondary institution, and I will not discuss them in this book except in passing.[7]

"NEOLIBERAL" UNIVERSITIES?

The era analyzed in this book has been described by some social scientists as "neoliberal" (see, e.g., Hall and Lamont 2013; Harvey 2005; Wacquant 2009). I have strong reservations about the use of this term because it has been employed so loosely and so pejoratively that its implications and connotations can become an impediment to understanding (Boas and Gans-Morse 2009; Jones 2012). Those who use the term sometimes seem to minimize the spillover effects of the dynamic industries that lead economic growth and the positive, if unevenly distributed, social changes produced by growth. They have little interest in the ways organizations balance preexisting institutional priorities and new market incentives. Instead, they focus on the social dislocations and social injustices they see as the by-product of neoliberalism and, frequently, on social movements as the most effective—perhaps the only effective—way to confront them. But if the term "neoliberalism" is constrained to focus solely on the transformation of institutions in the direction of greater (though incomplete) responsiveness to market signals and the rise of managers attuned to performance metrics compatible with those signals, then the post-1980 Thatcher/Reagan era certainly merits the designation "neoliberal"—and the label, so revised, also applies to the assumptions and practices of a large proportion of university managers during the period.

There is nothing magical about the year 1980 itself as a marker of a new era. Many of the trends I will discuss had their origins in the decade of the 1970s. President Jimmy Carter began deregulating industries in the late 1970s, though many associate deregulation with his successor, Ronald Reagan. The introduction of heightened concerns for efficiency in the delivery of services and the use of metrics to measure effectiveness of service delivery were also beginning in the 1970s to creep into discussions about how to reform government agencies (Osborne and Gaebler 1992). At universities, too, the trends toward a more utilitarian and entrepreneurial attitude were evident in the 1970s, with higher rates of patenting and industry-sponsored research (Berman 2012). The tax revolt in California led to declines in state spending on higher education beginning in the 1970s, not the 1980s, and the accompanying search for new sources of revenue (Lo 1990). The sociologist David Riesman (1980) published a book on the consequences of rising student consumerism based on observations made about student culture in the 1970s. The National Science Foundation began to experiment with large-scale research centers to contribute to social and economic development under Director Richard Atkinson in the late 1970s (Cole 2009, 162).

The year 1980 is a convenient and symbolically meaningful date because of the election of Ronald Reagan as president and the passage of the Bayh-Dole Act, which encouraged deeper ties between universities and industry. But the era I discuss in this book is best understood as a time when seeds planted in the decade before began to bear fruit—not at a few institutions but at a great many.[8]

POST-1980 GROWTH NARRATIVES

The new visions of research universities that emerged after 1980 lacked Clark Kerr's humane consciousness of institutional weaknesses as a balance to his appreciation of the strengths and contributions of the multiversity. But they did clearly expose the assumptions of the historical period out of which Kerr's vision emerged, and they identified paths that ambitious institutions followed in their pursuit of growth and prominence. When we consider the new visions as responses to a common set of organizational challenges, we can see more clearly the aspirations of managers of already powerful institutions seeking to break out of the constraints of Kerr's nationally focused, federally dependent, and disciplinary-based "service station" into something more encompassing, more accessible, more porous, and more central to the economic and social development of the country.

Each of the new visions can be interpreted as a growth narrative. Each was aware of the contributions of the multiversity and convinced of its service to society. Each anticipated still greater contributions and service in the future. Each was predicated, explicitly or implicitly, on the pursuit of additional sources of funds to allow for greater flexibility and more impactful contributions. They differed, however, in the new sources of revenue they identified and the new types of service to society they anticipated. To put the matter perhaps a bit baldly, universities needed additional revenue to support their complex and far-flung operations—in the public universities this search was hastened by declining state subsidies—and they needed new conceptions of service to society to justify the expansions required to support these operations. For most, motivations for greater service were undoubtedly sincere but brought to speed along the tracks of organizational interest.

The "global university" is an umbrella term encompassing disparate efforts by universities to expand their global status and presence (Marginson

2011). The global university strove for ranking as a "world-class" university in one or both of the two major ranking systems, the *Times Higher Education Supplement* ranking and the Shanghai Jaio Tang ranking (Salmi 2009). The global university also developed one or more international branch campuses to educate its own and foreign students abroad. The development of stronger international ties, both diplomatic and intellectual, justified these engagements as an expansion of the universities' service to society, as of course did long-standing aspirations for students to become "citizens of the world." The economic incentives were clear for foreign governments: they could hope to keep academically talented students in the country rather than pursuing study and careers abroad. Accordingly, foreign governments frequently provided generous subsidies for building and staffing international branch campuses—in the case of NYU Abu Dhabi $50 million (Redden 2013). Although the management issues were formidable (Lane 2011), economic incentives were also evident for U.S. partner institutions: overseas programs could raise the status of American universities, could build potentially beneficial relationships with foreign governments and entrepreneurs, could attract new research talent, and could provide access to a new pool of tuition-paying students. They also allowed universities to increase enrollment by placing a sizable number of home-country students in global satellite campuses.

The "entrepreneurial university," as articulated by Burton Clark (1998), anticipated a wide variety of expanded "third-stream" revenues (i.e., revenues coming from sources other than tuition and research grants). For the entrepreneurial university, the goal was to generate as much third-stream income as possible as a prerequisite for greater adaptability and opportunity. These sources included contracts with corporations, contracts and grants from state and local governments, grants from philanthropies, royalty income from the licensing of intellectual property, and a vast expansion of fund-raising from alumni and other donors. Of course, many of these sources of revenue were familiar at the time of Kerr. The most important new elements were increasing interactions with for-profit businesses and the generation of revenues from the patenting and licensing of intellectual property. The idea of social entrepreneurship also arose to foster problem-solving engagements with community organizations. Clark proposed that universities protect their "academic core" of basic science and scholarship while encouraging professional schools and auxiliary service units on the "academic periphery" to pursue entrepreneurial activities in an aggressive, strategically guided way.

The "interdisciplinary university," a favored project of the Association of American Universities (2005), the National Academies (2005), and many university patrons foresaw the potential for larger grants from federal agencies and major donors based on the universities' capacity to mobilize and integrate larger teams of researchers to address complex problems requiring the skills of many different types of researchers (Gibbons et al. 1994). It justified greater attention to interdisciplinary organization for its capacity to address "grand challenges," such as deceleration of climate change, mapping of the brain, and solving global health problems. The underlying model was the corporate R&D facility, as a complement to the "invisible colleges" uniting researchers with shared interests across disparate institutions. Federal agencies remained the primary sources of funding but with increasing support from private philanthropists who saw the solution of problems largely ignored by academic departments but embraced by interdisciplinary units. The service to society anticipated in these visions amounted to changes in scale as a necessary response to the emergence of complex and highly consequential problems that required the coordinated activity of large teams composed of people with different types of expertise. This was, in essence, the "big-science" model expanded into many more areas of the scientific and scholarly enterprise.

The "broad-access university," a keystone project of the leading higher education philanthropies (see, e.g., Gates 2010; Merisotis 2010), as well as Democratic politicians (see Obama 2010), created opportunities for augmented revenue through higher enrollments, from philanthropy, and from federal and state financial aid as a reward for broadening the demographic makeup of the undergraduate student body. Here the university's expanded service to society was a product of the inclusion of students whose families had for generations lacked opportunities to benefit from a higher education. For the advocates of the broad-access university, elite institutions gained prestige at the expense of meeting national needs to expand access to high-quality higher education experiences. The broad-access university, by contrast, reversed this logic and made inclusivity, rather than exclusion, the watchword. Service to society was based on human capital development among qualified but low-income students and the consequent improved economic prospects of students from these backgrounds. This expansion was in line with the aspirations of U.S. higher education policy under the Obama administration, which called for the doubling of the proportion of eighteen- to twenty-four-year-olds with postsecondary credentials (Obama

2010). Very often advocacy of the broad-access university went hand in hand with support for shifting a large share of enrollments to online courses and degree programs as the most efficient way to accommodate much larger student bodies (see, e.g., Carey 2012; Christensen, Johnson, and Horn 2008; Christensen and Eyring 2011; Smith 2012).

DESIGN FOR A "NEW AMERICAN UNIVERSITY"

Michael M. Crow's New American University stands out as a synthesis of the post-1980s growth narratives in so far as it integrated the themes of entre-preneurialism, interdisciplinary organization, and broad-access into a coherent design plan. (Global reach was included in Crow's vision as well, but received comparatively little attention.) As president of Arizona State University (ASU), Crow worked to shape the New American University design following his arrival in 2002. His *Designing the New American University* (coauthored with William B. Dabars) is a brief for redesigning universities into organizations that are both much larger and much less separated from the communities that surround them. Crow and Dabars's primary complaints about American research universities were that they have not "educated citizens in sufficient numbers" and that they have not adequately addressed "the challenges that beset the world" (2015, 7). They were particularly critical of private research universities whose status is derived, in large measure, by the number of prospective students they reject rather than the number they accept. For Crow and Dabars, the (old) "gold standard" universities include the Ivy League universities, the leading public flagships such as Berkeley, Michigan, and Wisconsin that grew up in the wake of the Morrill Act, and the private universities, such as Johns Hopkins, the University of Chicago, and Stanford, that were founded in the nineteenth century by wealthy industrialists. These universities are excellent at what they do, Crow and Dabars wrote, but "design limitations . . . restrict or subvert their vast potential to contribute to knowledge production as well as societal well-being" (18). Most research universities tried to emulate gold-standard campuses such as Harvard, Stanford, and Chicago, in so far as they were able. Crow and Dabars thought this was both a major mistake and a lost opportunity.

To show why, they contrasted gold-standard universities with "the New American University" (NAU): like other leading research universities, the NAU "expressed competitive interest regarding the intensity of discovery and knowledge production" (60). In other respects, the differences between the two were stark: whereas gold-standard universities were exclusive, the

New American University was inclusive and accessible; it sought to enroll not the top 2 to 5 percent nationally but the top 25 percent of students in its region or state. Where the gold-standard university was oriented to the production of scholarly and scientific knowledge meeting the highest standards of the academic disciplines (with confidence that these achievements would in due course have practical benefits), the New American University was explicitly oriented to the needs of the broader society, with a focus on knowledge that could be applied to solve its problems and contribute to its economic development. Its faculty members and graduate students pursued research and discovery "that benefits the public good," assuming "major responsibility for the economic, social, and cultural vitality and health and well-being of the community" (61). Where gold-standard universities retained the structural integrity of discipline-based academic departments, interdisciplinary and transdisciplinary arrangements were the primary mechanisms through which the New American University's contributions to the community were created. The New American University "creates a distinctive institutional profile by building on existing strengths to produce a federation of unique transdisciplinary departments, centers, institutions, schools, and colleges," and it does so by consolidating "a number of traditional academic departments, which henceforth no longer serve as the sole institutional locus of . . . disciplines" (62).[9]

Crow recounted that research expenditures increased by over 250 percent during the first twelve years of his presidency at Arizona State. Enrollment increased by nearly 50 percent and degree production by more than that. At the same time, ASU became one of the most diverse campuses in the country, with minority enrollments, now one-third of the total, growing by more than 120 percent. ASU is the largest research university in the country with more than 90,000 students on four campuses (including more than 10,000 students enrolled in fully online programs). ASU's six-year graduation rates (58 percent) may not have been impressive, but they showed considerable improvement during Crow's presidency at a time when the student body had grown more diverse and the faculty had not increased dramatically in size (Crow and Dabars 2015, 255–57).

A foundation of Crow's design strategy was to attract highly productive scholars and scientists capable of competing effectively for research grants. ASU's upward trajectory in R&D expenditures, publications, and citations began in the 1980s but continued apace under Crow's administration.[10] The vast expansion of enrollments supported the generous pay and state-of-the-art working conditions of these scholars. Among the augmented senior stratum of scholars and scientists, Crow hired four Nobel Laureates, three Pulitzer Prize winners, and two MacArthur Fellows. Thus rapid enrollment growth was a prerequisite for ASU's capacity to compete for research dollars, because student tuition, when managed using least-cost principles, provided a surplus that could be used to support expensive but productive faculty members. As is true in many private and public universities, the light teaching loads of research-productive scholars were purchased, in part, through increased teaching loads among adjunct faculty. Undoubtedly, Crow's commitment to inclusiveness was genuine, and he pioneered a number of new technologies to produce efficiencies in degree production, including extensive online materials and an "E-Advisor" system that helped students keep on track for timely graduation by displaying current and future required credits and availability of classes for accumulating these credits. Yet ASU had one of the higher student-to-faculty ratios in the country at 22:1 compared to the national average of 15:1. Forty percent of faculty were part-time, or full-time but not on tenure track (College Factual 2015).[11] Writing instructors, for example, were increased to a five-course load per semester and expected to teach double the number of students recommended as a maximum by the National Council of Teachers of English (Warner 2015).[12]

DESIGN LIMITATIONS OF THE "NEW AMERICAN UNIVERSITY"

The question is whether the new models advanced by these visionaries suffered from their own design limitations. As states disinvested, public research universities required greater interaction with external resource providers, and they were driven in this direction in any event by their ambitions for greater centrality in the knowledge society of the future. The New American University model was attractive for its frank recognition of those needs and its embrace of those ambitions. It was an attractive model also because it was not merely a blueprint; through his work at ASU Crow had shown that it could be achieved.

But for many in academe it seemed an unattractive model in so far as it began to blur the lines between universities and other large knowledge-producing organizations. Crow and Dabars emphasized that discovery-based research remained at the heart of the New American University, but discovery-based research no longer distinguishes universities from other enterprises, such as the research arms of pharmaceutical firms, biotechnology firms, Internet service providers, or government R&D facilities. Discovery is essential, but, in addition to discovery, faculty autonomy, faculty participation in governance, commitments to educational quality, and a continuing focus on basic knowledge production are at the heart of the university's capacity to self-direct and ultimately to add value to the individuals and organizations with whom it interacts. From the evidence of Arizona State, as described in *Designing the New American University*, faculty autonomy and participation in governance were of minimal, if any, interest to Crow. Crow and his senior staff were the architects of the New American University design strategy. The faculty were sometimes consulted, but in the end they either adapted to the new strategy or left for other employment. The term "autonomy" rates a few scattered mentions in *Designing the New American University* but no index entries. Educational attainment receives dozens of entries in the index, but neither education as a primary purpose of the university nor educational quality merits an index entry. Use-inspired research receives a warm embrace throughout but basic research only a single passing reference. It is difficult to escape the conclusion that the model may be a prescription for the diminishment of key value-added features and organizational principles of research universities in the guise of a bold plan for the vast expansion of their societal impact.

When we compare the discovery-oriented research arms of corporations and government agencies with research universities, we can see that the soul of a university's distinctiveness stems from the pursuit of self-chosen purposes by faculty researchers, faculty influence in the management of the enterprise, basic science and scholarship as fundamental contributions to both culture and economic development, and a commitment to depth of undergraduate and graduate education. Thus, the key questions are: How can universities solve the heteronomy-autonomy puzzle in a way that preserves a working balance between the two? And how can universities grow in both size and centrality and create more porous boundaries without sacrificing the distinctive features and values that have allowed them to flourish as independent, creative entities?

The Sociology of Educational Expansion

Beyond the big macrolevel pictures of the relationship between universities and American society produced by theorists such as Daniel Bell, Richard Florida, and Pierre Bourdieu, a narrower literature on the causes and consequences of educational expansion has also yielded insights relevant to the argument of this book. Sociologists have been interested in exploring the causes and consequences of educational expansion for more than 150 years. They have frequently told overly simple stories about it.

The earliest sociological narrative conjured an image of the civilizational progress afforded by the spread of higher learning. The post-Napoleonic visionaries of industrial society expected commercial development to bring an era of greater rationality, what Auguste Comte called "the positive stage" of social development, as the knowledge made possible by the flourishing of industry and commerce diffused throughout society, aided by the concomitant growth of scientific understanding. This narrative was adopted, with few reservations, by the late nineteenth-century builders of research universities, such as Andrew White and Daniel Coit Gilman, who replaced Comte's emphasis on industry and commerce with an emphasis on universities as the principal agents of increasing societal progress, and it was carried into the postwar era by those who described an economy and society led by people with advanced degrees (see, e.g., Bell 1973; Drucker 1969; Galbraith 1967).[13] The influence of the Comtean theme will be obvious in this book, though my analysis rests on a much stronger appreciation of internal contradictions of universities and the specific pathways that knowledge advance has taken under the influence of patrons and consumers.

Another of the early sociological narratives about educational expansion focused on the role of institutional differentiation as a means for maintaining social equilibrium in the face of population growth (Durkheim [1893] 1964). In education, this became a story about the differentiation of tiers of varying prestige levels and more and less demanding curricular tracks. Differentiated tracks have been promoted, both in secondary schools and higher education, since the early nineteenth century to maintain high standards at the top and training for a wider range of destinations below the top in the face of increased demand. In the early twentieth century, the Russian sociologist Pitrim Sorokin added a corollary emphasis on vertical channels for the upward circulation of the talented as a necessary complement to legitimize these hierarchically differentiated tracks (Sorokin 1927). Echoes of these functionalist themes will be evident in this book as well but in a form attentive to such new structures of differentiation as quantitative fields, honors programs, and professional master's degrees, as well as the impact of credential inflation in the shaping of educational hierarchies.

Other sociological analyses have emphasized the state's interest in a well-educated labor force and citizenry. This interest derives from education's capacity to build economically valuable skills, thereby contributing to the creation of more productive workers and more numerous taxpayers. It also derives from the host of socially beneficial characteristics associated with higher levels of educational attainment; those most relevant to the state include higher levels of trust in institutions, greater community involvement, and fewer social problems, such as criminal behavior and drug use, that require state expenditures (Fuller and Rubinson 1992). Education is involved in nation-building in so far as schools and universities socialize "modern actors," who are expected to have plans and opinions and whose thinking is at least putatively associated with cognitive rationality (Meyer 2008). The state also has a substantial interest in research that leads to economic and social development. These interests help explain why state subsidies for higher education enrollments are substantial throughout the world and why in the United States enrollments in public universities account for more than 70 percent of the total. But it fails to account for the declining role of the fifty states in funding the basic educational activities of public universities in the United States or what universities have done to make up for the weakened support their states have provided.

MARTIN TROW'S CONTRIBUTIONS

The UC Berkeley sociologist Martin Trow was undoubtedly the most important theorist of higher education expansion.[14] Trow developed a conceptual model that shed light on a wide range of changes associated with the sheer expansion of the proportion of young people pursuing higher degrees (see, e.g., Trow 1970, 1973, 2000, 2005). Trow divided the history of higher education systems into three stages: "elite," "mass," and "universal." Elite systems reach their apogee when no more than 4 to 5 percent of the relevant age cohort attends college. Elite systems are characterized by a sense of common culture, in the West typically focusing on the liberal arts; an emphasis on character and intellectual development; and boundaries between academe and the rest of society, marked off by physical separation of campuses as well as many traditional rituals and ceremonies. Those who receive a college education can recognize one another as members of a distinct status group. In the United States, Ivy League colleges are the archetypal institutions whose origins date to the elite era.

According to Trow, when the proportion of students attending colleges and universities reaches beyond 15 percent or so of the age cohort, the system is moving toward the "mass" stage of higher education development. The mass stage reaches its zenith when about 25 to 30 percent of the age cohort attends colleges and universities. In the mass stage, higher education becomes much more bureaucratically organized with well-defined courses of study and specialized faculties. The dominant ethos shifts from character development to specialized skills development. No longer is the training function of universities subordinate to liberal education for leadership or, in so far as occupational training is involved, focused on preparation for the classical professions of medicine, law, and theology. Instead, training stretches out to embrace an ever-widening range of occupations.

In Trow's account, the transition from elite to mass higher education was triggered by an increasing number of high school graduates seeking credentials to help raise their educational status above their peers. Egalitarian sentiments about access began to spring up and the boundaries between colleges and the rest of society loosened. In the United States, the Morrill Act was one signature expression of a society moving from the elite to the mass stage of higher education development. No longer an institution apart, universities were expected to admit undergraduates from all walks of life and to participate in the development of agriculture and "the mechanical arts." The founding of metropolitan universities beyond the traditional northeastern centers of learning, in cities such as Louisville, Cincinnati, and Detroit, provided further impetus. The idea that higher education is engaged with institutions in the surrounding society became a popular notion at the turn of the twentieth century—and outreach activities, such as agricultural extension and product-testing laboratories, began to develop.

For Trow the "universal" stage—one can quibble with his terminology—arrives when 50 percent or more of the age cohort attends a postsecondary institution. Here we see the growth of short-cycle (one- or two-year) programs in occupational fields. We see more emphasis on engaging students' energies than meeting rigorous academic standards. Higher education is no longer a privilege or even a right but an expectation, even an obligation, for those in the middle and upper classes. The sentiments of democratic egalitarianism permeate the system, not just in two-year colleges but even in "mass" and to some extent in "elite" institutions. Highly structured courses of study begin to weaken in universal-stage institutions, and students may sign up for just a course at a time or a few courses leading to a certificate valuable in the labor market. Boundaries between universal higher education institutions and the rest of society all but disappear. The student role is just one among many experiences that those attending school value. They may spend equal or greater time on their work or family life—and the proportion of students who are working full- or part-time grows dramatically and may reach well above 50 percent. The idea of higher education as a special time in life also fades in another way; instead of formal education ending at a prescribed time, learning may be conceived as a lifelong endeavor, with refreshers common or required throughout the lifetime. In the United States, community colleges are the archetypal institution of the universal stage. Trow was clear to include corporate training programs as another characteristic institution of this stage, and he would undoubtedly include online universities if he were alive today.

In Trow's view, the institutions most characteristic of their age do not supplant those characteristic of earlier periods. Elite education persists during the mass stage—Ivy League colleges do not lose their luster—just as both elite and mass institutions persist during the universal stage. Indeed, within institutions, new structures may reproduce, in an attenuated form, characteristics of higher education during earlier stages of its development; a good example is the development of honors colleges and leadership programs in land-grant universities to reproduce in so far as possible the elite education experience within a mass institutional setting. Although older institutional structures are not supplanted, they may be decisively influenced in important ways by norms and practices characteristic of the current stage of the system. Thus the sense of education as a preparation for work influences ideas and actions even in elite institutions, where engineering and business programs may be added to the undergraduate curriculum. Even where such curricula are not added, students may see their college years less as a life-shaping passage into adulthood than as an essential investment to gain a middle-class income and lifestyle. Similarly, the sense that everyone should be eligible for higher education opportunities, a characteristic of the universal stage, affects admissions in elite and mass institutions by raising new questions about eligibility and the bases of selection. Democratic-egalitarian sentiments, fully in bloom during the universal stage, lead to searches for students from underrepresented groups and give rise to ideologies celebrating diversity, inclusiveness, and civic engagement. Academic study competes for space with other undergraduate priorities.

Who before Trow would have thought that being "engaged" in and beyond the classroom could become a dominant feature of higher education, superseding the traditional emphasis on study and learning? Yet under the influence of the sentiments of universal higher education, including for those who are not at all academically motivated or prepared, "engagement" has in fact become a substitute logic for the older logic of classroom-centered cognitive and skill development characteristic of higher education during the mass stage. And who before Trow would have seen the likelihood that institutions at the bottom of the academic hierarchy would increasingly set the tone for those closer to the top? Indeed, most post–World War II social scientists assumed that the continuing effort of faculty members and institutions to gain status by emulating colleagues at elite institutions would eventually lead to institutions whose values and practices paralleled, to the extent possible, those of elite institutions (see, e.g., Riesman 1957). But Trow was right; "trickle down" did not continue long beyond the immediate postwar era in the hierarchical, market-oriented system of American higher education; instead the blurring of boundaries between academe and the outside society, the rise of vocational subjects, the aggressive recruitment of nontraditional students, student consumerism, and lower academic standards all "trickled up" from community colleges to four-year universities. Only the elite private colleges and universities and a few "public Ivies" remained largely immune to these trends.

A New Perspective

Something valuable can be gained from each of these approaches to the study of educational expansion—and obviously Martin Trow is destined to be an important influence on any sociologist who writes about higher education expansion. The social changes created by knowledge diffusion, the differentiation tracks and tiers under pressure of cost and population growth, state interests in educational expansion, and the changing culture of universities under the aegis of demographic transformation are all relevant to the story I will tell. But these approaches also leave out much. With their deficiencies in mind, I have developed—in some cases refashioned— concepts to aid in making sense of the specific form that expansion took in the United States, the consequences it has had for the broader society, and the contradictions that threatened to undo the accomplishments of these indispensable institutions.

They include:

The System of Academic Professionalism. This is the prevailing dominant system in the organization of academic life. It is organized around discipline-based departments whose scholars are oriented to solving problems identified by colleagues in the disciplines and subdisciplines. The system of academic professionalism is supported by the academic disciplinary associations, such as the American Chemical Society and the Modern Language Association. It is also supported by norms of peer review in academic journals and government research funding panels. It leads to a focus on contributions to knowledge as defined by elites in the disciplines, many of whom are attentive to the interests of scholars in neighboring disciplines as well. It has been the primary form of faculty organization in the United States since the late nineteenth and early twentieth centuries. Its continuing influence is sustained by discipline- and department-based control over hiring and promotion and organization of curricula. It is the backdrop against which the sponsors of technological innovation and social inclusion sought accommodation and greater influence.

The System of Academic Innovationism. This is an ascendant system in the organization of academic life. It is organized around use-inspired research and particularly research that has commercial potential. Its rise has been fueled by national competitiveness policy and the dense ties between business corporations and leading researchers in the natural sciences, engineering, and medicine. Researchers in the system of academic innovationism continue to publish and teach, but they are mindful of opportunities to consult with and start businesses and to place their students in firms aligned with their research. Major vehicles of the system are university offices of technology transfer, entrepreneurship, and economic development, as well as interdisciplinary initiatives and cluster hiring strategies oriented to the invention and marketing of new technologies. The new system can be considered more an accretion than a rival to the dominant system of academic professionalism, but it has become a dynamic force with the power to direct a large portion of the research effort at many universities and to rearrange status systems on campus.

Porousness. This is the idea that universities are open to the outside world in new and enhanced ways. The idea of porousness emphasizes that ideas and research can develop in many institutions outside of academe. In addition to serving as idea suppliers as Kerr emphasized, universities become all-purpose cognitive processing plants, taking in ideas and research generated in other institutions and subjecting them to testing, rejection, or refinement. Conceptual structures generated elsewhere can provide the raw material for academic work, just as academic work can be appropriated for use in institutions outside of academe. The shape of our world is produced in large part by the traffic and direction of these interactions—and what happens to cultural goods while they are in transit. Universities and corporations have developed a fruitful bidirectional exchange that has led to the development of thousands of new technologies and firms. An analysis of the institutional geography of knowledge exchanges leads to a partial dethronement of academe as the center of empirically grounded knowledge structures, but it also brings into sharper relief the distinctive contribution of academe as a cognitive court of last appeal, as well as its continuing role as an idea and research generator.

Market Penetration. If we think of higher education expansion not as the extension of a social good but rather as an (often unacknowledged) industry objective to fully encompass the potential market for higher-level educational credentials, we can see more clearly the reasons why issues of cost and quality are often of secondary interest to university administrators when compared to enrollment statistics. The industry as a whole thrives when the entire population is certain of the necessity of holding educational credentials and, of course, so do individual institutions that have capacity for and interest in enrollment growth. Unlike many consumer product industries in which adaptive upgrading of products is required for firms to stay in business over the long run, higher education can pursue market penetration without industry-wide adaptive upgrading simply by setting up incomparable quality levels through selective and open admissions and by granting baccalaureates to those at lower levels in the system whose performance would not pass muster in the more demanding universities or fields. In the context of selective admissions and missing industry-wide standards for baccalaureate level performance, the paradox of market penetration is that it provides real opportunity for many students who would otherwise be excluded, while at the same time ensuring that many college degrees lag in educational quality and labor market opportunities.

"Creative" and "Industrialized" Universities. The resources available to the top 30–40 U.S. research universities have allowed them to extend the distance between themselves and the remaining 2,500 four-year colleges and universities in the country. Drawing on large endowments (Harvard's has topped $30 billion), extraordinary grant funding (Johns Hopkins received more than $2 billion in federal research funds in 2013–14), and high sticker-price tuition charges (running at more than $40,000 per year in highly selective private universities), the top of the system is remarkably dynamic, both in its research accomplishments and in the educational opportunities it provides. By contrast, with limited funds for the employment of instructors and graders, the middle and bottom of the system has become increasingly mechanized. In a public institution like Central Florida University, a leading case, students can choose from among sixty fully online degree and certificate programs and hundreds of individual online classes. Even those that are taught face-to-face often feature assessments based on machine-graded examinations. Where the expert, or professional specialist type of person,

prevailed as an ideal in universities for most of the twentieth century, new ideals feature, in addition to the specialist, the creative type of individual who combines multiple talents across several disciplines and clubs and the mass-produced technician who can perhaps demonstrate measurable competencies but is not expected to show interpersonal skill, professional judgment, or command of a field of knowledge.

Disciplinary Divergence. When college going was rare, the prestige of the disciplines mattered comparatively little. Science and engineering were prestigious because of their association with industrial and technological progress, but the humanities were also prestigious because of their association with wealth and cultivation. The arrival of mass higher education challenged and finally eroded that rough equality. Academic status became associated with perceptions of rigor and capacities for abstraction as well as the excitement of fundamental discoveries. Mathematics and physics stood atop this hierarchy, but the biomedical and life sciences have now contested for status due to their technological accomplishments during the period. A parallel hierarchy of labor market opportunities undoubtedly impressed students and their parents more—with engineering and business students having the best chance at good salaries, followed by those in physical and life sciences, the social sciences, the humanities and the arts, and, finally, education and human services. These hierarchies are the result of not only the relative demand for educated labor but also the elimination through academic failure of many prospective majors in the more advantaged fields. While providing a relatively stable prestige order, useful to university administrators in the allocation of resources, the hierarchy and the elimination process also created awkward imbalances in university life, including the reliance of universities on nonquantitative fields with large student enrollments to subsidize quantitative fields with small student enrollments, and the development of large differences in expectations and racial composition between quantitative and nonquantitative fields. Asian and white students tended to gravitate to the advantaged fields, while women and members of underrepresented minority groups disproportionately populated nonquantitative fields, reproducing, in an attenuated form, inequalities in the larger society.

Accommodations between Social Inclusion and Status Locations. Most students who attended Clark Kerr's multiversity were white. A primary purpose of undergraduate education was to identify students capable of succeeding in graduate programs. Professors looked favorably on students who most closely resembled their young adult selves. The civil rights and women's movements created the conditions for a new legitimation of college education as a means for the social incorporation of socially marginalized groups. Undoubtedly, outreach to underrepresented, first-generation, and low-income students has contributed to expanding the social frame of knowledge. It has also made possible the identification of academically talented students who would never have had the opportunity to attend college in the past. In this respect diversity and academic excellence are mutually supportive. At the same time, the identification and nurturing of talent remains an important feature both of the system as a whole and on every university campus. On campus, inclusive admissions and sensitivity to campus climate issues have consequently been accompanied by the expansion of high-status locations, promoting, for example, the growth of honors programs, leadership programs, entrepreneurship programs, and undergraduate research opportunities.

Forms of Patronage. Universities require ample patronage to expand. Students are the primary patrons at most institutions, and it is no surprise that universities have come to cater to students as a critical source of revenues. The federal government, the states, and private donors are the other key patrons. The federal government supplies the great majority of research funds and financial aid that allows research universities to operate effectively. The states are most important for general appropriations supporting education and related activities, and they also contribute significantly to financial aid and, in a modest way, to academic research activities. Private donors have shown a strong preference for fields that are closely connected to power centers in American society, to research that can lead to technological innovations, and to rewarding high-achieving students rather than those most in need of financial aid. By contrast, professors tend to identify with academic disciplines and social inclusion. The preferences of professors and patrons, while in seeming contradiction, contribute to the dynamism of the system as a whole by providing committed support both for disciplinarians and for innovators and both for student market expansion and student talent recognition.

Agenda-Driven Policymaking. As higher education became a more central institution in American society, it attracted the attention of those who wished to use it to advance their conceptions of national priorities. Of course, agendas had always impacted federal mission agencies, but during the period agenda-driven policymaking entered also into basic science policy, competitiveness policy, college completion policy, and other policy domains. Competitiveness policy provided funds to support the work of thousands of researchers engaged in new technology development. The federal government drove agendas even in basic science by sponsoring "grand challenges" and large-scale research initiatives to map the brain, defeat cancer, protect cybersecurity, and stabilize climate change, among other priorities (Office of Science and Technology Policy 2013). Two large philanthropies, the Bill and Melinda Gates Foundation and the Lumina Foundation, dominated a new "college completion" agenda that focused on mechanisms, including digital technologies and competency-based credentials, to raise the proportion of young people obtaining postsecondary credentials. Although they fell well short of the goals they set, they too launched the efforts of thousands of researchers and reformers (Chronicle of Higher Education 2013a).

The Accumulation of Administration. As the size and complexity of universities increased, so did the administrative cadres responsible for steering the institutions. Administrators used a distinctive set of tools to help steer their institutions, reflecting the unusual structural characteristics of universities. As a rule, senior managers have invested discretionary funds in units with strong research records, in interdisciplinary developments, in revenue-centered budgeting, and in cross-subsidizations that shifted funds away from lower-division students and large, high-enrollment fields to graduate students and research-heavy fields, from those who taught introductory courses to those who taught mainly graduate courses, and from discipline-focused units to society-focused units. Just as mayors provide tax breaks for businesses that promise to bring jobs, so university administrators provided what amounts to tax breaks to units that promised to bring prestige and, hence, indirectly attract high-quality faculty and students. The growth of administrative staffs has been subsidized, in part, by the vast expansion of poorly paid part-time instructors who constituted nearly half of the instructional force by the end of the period.

These concepts provide entrée into a new understanding of the trajectory of American higher education during a period in which technological innovation and social inclusion became important drivers of expansion—and the largesse of university patrons multiplied. They also reveal the outlines of important contradictions that emerged as universities sought to balance traditional aims with new sources of revenue and reputation.

2

The Academic Professions and American Society

Higher education is in many ways like other expanding industries in the United States: a service provider regulated by the state, run by energetic chief executives and their staffs, and employing a highly trained professional workforce. It is market oriented in so far as senior administrators are sensitive to the preferences of patrons, student demand, and other market signals. Without being explicit about it as an industry goal, the industry seeks more complete market penetration among potential consumers. Higher education is not as weighty in national accounts as a number of other service industries. It contributes less than one-fifth as much as health care, for example, and only one-third as much as finance to national GDP—and employs comparably fewer workers. No one would consider it a powerhouse on the basis of these numbers alone.

Nevertheless, it is a vast enterprise. The now more than 3,000 institutions that comprise the population of four-year colleges and universities enroll some 14 million students every year. Colleges and universities graduate nearly two million undergraduates annually with baccalaureate degrees— and about one million with advanced degrees (NCES 2016b, table 310). Both undergraduate and graduate enrollments nearly doubled between 1980 and 2015. Undergraduate enrollments grew from under 6 million to over 10.5 million (NCES 2016b, table 303.70), while graduate enrollments increased from a little over 1.5 million to nearly 3 million (ibid., table 303.80).

It is also a highly stratified and multiply segmented enterprise. The top 200 research universities—less than 5 percent of all postsecondary institutions—conduct more than 80 percent of published peer-reviewed research. All other colleges and universities are primarily oriented to teaching, and for most of them undergraduate teaching dominates. At the base of the structure are several hundred financially insecure, low-enrollment, for-profit colleges. The ascending layers include: public two-year community colleges followed by non-elite (and often religiously affiliated) baccalaureate-granting institutions, followed by master's-granting universities, and, closer to the top, doctoral-granting institutions that produce comparatively little research. The structure is capped by one very small peak of the wealthiest and most selective private liberal arts colleges (such as Amherst, Swarthmore, and Williams) and a larger peak composed of the nation's top research universities, the majority of which are members of the Association of American Universities—household names such as Harvard, Stanford, Yale, Berkeley, Michigan, and Virginia. Many of the stronger institutions at each of the lower levels aspire to climb higher in this structure, lending a dynamic quality to the system. Private, nonprofit colleges typically hope to do so by becoming more selective in admissions, and public institutions typically hope to do so by adding higher-level degrees (Brint, Riddle, and Hanneman 2006). The stronger for-profits and the specialized institutions (such as art schools, business colleges, and seminaries) occupy distinctive niches of their own.

The most important structural divisions within the system are based on the highest degree awarded by the institutions, the level of selectivity in their admissions, and whether governance control is public, private and nonprofit, or for-profit (ibid.). About 70 percent of students attend public colleges and universities—most are far from selective and enroll the largest proportions of minority, first-generation, and low-income students. About 20 percent attend private, nonprofit institutions. These tend to be favored by more affluent families. No more than 5 to 7 percent of undergraduate students attend highly selective institutions, those in which less than half of applicants are admitted. The final 10 percent of college students attend for-profits catering to working adults (see table 2.1).

Meaningful identities also traverse these major structural divisions. College administrators, faculty, and students identify with (and often compete against) others of the same religious affiliation (such as fellow Jesuit or evangelical Christian colleges), other branch campuses in the same state systems, universities in the same athletic conferences, and campuses enrolling

TABLE 2.1. Size of Strata in U.S. Postsecondary Education System

Stratum	Approx. Proportion: Undergraduate Students	Approx. Proportion: Graduate Students
For-Profits	< 10	–
Community Colleges	30	–
Master's-Granting Universities	15	15
Doctoral-Granting/Limited Research Universities	20	20
Selective Liberal Arts Colleges	2	–
Highly Research-Intensive Universities	10	60
Specialized Institutions	2	< 2

Source: Calculated from AAU 2015; NCES 2015, table 303.70.

student populations similar to their own (such as the historically black and women's institutions and the military academies).

This chapter is intended to provide a portrait of the dominant system for organizing and pursuing knowledge and the contributions of that system to American life. By doing so I hope to convey some of the hidden strengths of the current system while revealing several of the vulnerabilities that have made it a target for those who would like to use it for more exclusively utilitarian purposes. While it is true, for example, that much academic research is intended for other academics—arguably a forfeiture of broader societal impact—it is easy to miss the many unheralded ways that academic research informs public discourse, public policy, and organizational processes. Similarly, while it is true that many college graduates do not use much—sometimes none!—of the formal subject matter knowledge they learn in college, it is easy to miss the economically valuable qualities of mind that academic study can impart or deepen: the capacity to work with abstractions, to effectively engage novel situations, and to exercise judgment. I will attempt to provide a more rounded picture of the contributions made by university researchers and educators than can be found in the critical literature.

The Structure of Academic Professionalism

Beyond the leafy confines and stately buildings, beyond the busy quads filled with students passing to and from classes and stopping to chat with classmates, and beyond the bulletin boards crowded with announcements of campus events lies a system for organizing knowledge that governs the work of four-year college and university faculty members regardless of their institutional location. I will call this *the system of academic professionalism*. It is the system that lends to colleges and universities their distinctive strengths and weaknesses. During the period examined here, the years 1980 to 2015, technology entrepreneurs, diversity advocates, student consumers, and wealthy patrons pushed for universities to evolve in ways that more completely matched their interests. The determination of faculty members to maintain the system of academic professionalism against these powerful constituencies for change represents one of the major themes of this book. In most institutions, accommodations and accretions worked to halt the disruptive transformations advocated by the protagonists of change, but these adjustments also created sizable cracks in the once-sturdy foundations of the discipline-based system.

The strengths and weaknesses that universities show in relation to the production of research and educated graduates are closely connected to the system that organizes knowledge in universities. Both research and education are directed by the academic priorities and disciplinary boundaries that are at the heart of this system. For those enmeshed in it, my exposition will seem old hat—skim it if you wish. But not all readers are so enmeshed. Table 2.2 lays out the principal aims and organizing structures of the system of academic professionalism.

In research universities, the central orientation has been to advance knowledge, not to serve society or the economy in a direct way. On campus, the main intellectual structures are disciplines, as they take root in departmental organization and organized research units. By the first decades of the twentieth century, the department became the most important organizational mechanism in the recruitment of new faculty members and in the construction of curricula for undergraduate and graduate students to engage. Departments in turn have been linked to disciplines with distinct foci on features of the natural, social, and cultural worlds.

The disciplines may seem to be the products of a logical system of Aristotelian classification, but they are not.[1] Instead, the intellectual history of the disciplines must take into account accidents of history and subsequent competition over jurisdictions and efforts to monopolize or infringe on those jurisdictions. There is no logical reason, for example, why anthropology and sociology should have developed as separate disciplines, but their founders had distinctive interests and backgrounds, and the colonial administrators and cultural preservationists who started anthropology went their own way from the grand theorists of history and the social reformers who gave birth

TABLE 2.2. The System of Academic Professionalism

Orientation	to Academic Peers
	to Unsolved Problems in Field
	to New/Refined Methods
	to Established/Emerging Theories and Paradigms
Main Intellectual Structures	Disciplines
	Subdisciplines
	Organized Research Units
	Professional Associations
	Academic Journals
	Academic Book Publishers
Scope	All Academic Fields
Research Funding	Primarily Federal
	Limited Funding by Donors, Corporations, States
	Significant Self-funding
Relation to Economy	Limited in Relation to All Research
	High in Relation to Research in Selected Scientific Fields
	High in Labor Force Preparation
Key Relational Institutions	Professions
	Cultural Organizations
	News and Opinion Media
	Public Officials
	Knowledge-Sector Industries
	Community Organizations
Key Actors in Production	Tenured and Tenure-Track Faculty
	"Soft Money" Researchers
	Postdoctoral Researchers
Metrics	Publications
	Citations
	Academic Honors
	Research Grants

to sociology. The history of the disciplines must also take into account opportunities for new knowledge creation, a cause for the breakup of biology into micro (cell and molecular) and macro (ecological) wings, with all manner of investigation in between. New specializations and subspecializations have developed either as intellectually fruitful offshoots of originating disciplines, as happened in biology, or as a result of combining methods, theories, and findings from more than one discipline, as happened in the case of cognitive and neuroscience. The principal benefits of disciplines, as Stephen Turner observed, is "communicative competence":

The fact that a lot of people are trained in fundamentally the same way makes it possible for them to effectively make judgements about the quality of the work done by other people and for regimes of training to themselves be evaluated for their rigor. (2000, 52)

In the system of academic professionalism, professors and graduate students are oriented to solving problems in their fields, as identified and evaluated by their academic peers through conference proceedings and journal and book publication processes. Some of this work focuses on developing and refining methods to provide more secure analyses, and some on elaborating and critiquing theory. But most of it is constituted by empirical work to better explain phenomena of the natural, social, or cultural and artistic worlds. Professors and graduate students gain renown through the recognition of their disciplinary colleagues, by accumulating citations to their work, academic honors, and research funding.

Three decades ago, the higher education scholar Burton Clark wrote, "The discipline [and the professional area of study] is a domain of knowledge with a life and dynamic of its own. . . . These going concerns are not organized to carry out the will of nominal superiors in organized hierarchies; instead they develop their own incentives and their own forms of cooperation around a subject matter and its problems" (1987, 381).

Making a scientific or scholarly contribution is uppermost in the minds of the academic professionals who set the tone. Based on interviews with sixty physicists in the 1990s, sociologist Joseph Hermanowicz concluded:

The presumption is that by carefully selecting "important" problems and following through with "good" work, scientists may carve a path toward major scientific breakthroughs. They seek to unravel long-perplexing mysteries of nature and the structure of the physical universe. . . . Part of the responsibility of playing the scientific role involves pledging allegiance to its institutional purpose: the development and extension of certified knowledge. (1998, 70)

This objective is closely tied to the reward system in academe, as illustrated by the pseudonymous Geoff Silverman in Hermanowicz's book: "The dream is to discover some fantastic new effect that knocks the socks off my friends and colleagues, that knocks the socks off the community . . . I want my Josephson effect, my fractional quantum pull effect" (110). This goal of producing important work persists among those working at elite institutions or aspiring to elite status throughout their careers, even as those working in less prestigious institutions often redefine their aspirations toward more personal or less ambitious occupational goals.

The power of the professorate stems from the contributions of disciplinary organization—now more than 120 years old—and is enhanced by the mobility opportunities provided by disciplinary associations to faculty members through recognition by their peers. As Christopher Jencks and David Riesman wrote in *The Academic Revolution*:

> Most university presidents . . . see their institution primarily as an assemblage of scholars and scientists, each doing his own work in his own way. . . . The typical president's greatest ambition for the future is usually to "strengthen" his institution, and operationally this usually turns out to mean assembling scholars of even greater competence and reputation than are now present. (1968, 17)

The scope of academic professionalism is very wide—at the most detailed level nearly two thousand separate fields are coded by the National Center for Education Statistics (2010)[2]—and recognized subfields include many thousands more areas of organized study.

The system of academic professionalism is buttressed by the tenure system, which virtually guarantees lifetime employment for those who are advanced, and the near-monopoly that disciplines hold over two vital responsibilities. Through their professional associations and collegial networks, they control nearly all faculty hiring, and through their departmental organizations on campus they control nearly all of the curricula that undergraduates are required to study in order to graduate with a major. Unless these responsibilities are lost, the discipline-based system of academic professionalism remains in a strong position to reproduce itself (Abbott 2001, 126–31), albeit under the influence of student demand for popular majors and patrons' preferences for research that contributes to economic growth or to the solution of societal problems (Brint et al. 2012b).

The Research Output of Universities

Research is one of the two main products of universities, the other of course being education and credentialing. Statistics on the growth of scientific and scholarly production provide a sense of just how extensive and expansive the system has become. Researchers estimate a doubling of scientific publications every nine to ten years (see Van Noorden 2014). As of 2014, the

Web of Science, the most widely used citation source in the sciences, indexed 12,000 journals and 160,000 conference proceedings in more than 250 disciplines. The index included a total count of 90 million records and more than one billion total citations.

But, as vast as these totals sound, Web of Science (WoS) is just the most visible feature of a larger mass. It only indexes high-quality journals and conference proceedings as indicated by citation impact factors. Researchers estimate 24,000 to 28,000 peer-reviewed journals are published worldwide, at least double the share in WoS (Larsen and von Ins 2010; Ware and Mabe 2015)—and the number of non-peer-reviewed journals is estimated to be ten times larger still (Larsen and von Ins 2010). Estimating the growth rate of publications and citations is consequently highly sensitive to the sources used. A comprehensive study of a wide range of sources on peer-reviewed journals and conference proceedings by Larsen and von Ins (2010) estimated a growth rate of 2.7 to 13.5 percent per year for 1997–2006 for all types of publications and a growth rate of 2.2 to 9 percent per year for journal articles only. Engineering and computer science are rapid discovery disciplines, where publication rates are very high (and in which publications more often appear in conference proceedings). Publication in traditional scientific disciplines such as chemistry, mathematics, and physics has grown more slowly, though still explosively. On average, social scientists publish significantly less than natural scientists, and arts and humanities scholars significantly less than social scientists (Ware and Mabe 2015).

One reason for the lower output of arts and humanities professors is that they favor book publishing over article publication. A book may take many years to complete and each chapter could in theory be considered roughly the equivalent of a journal article. In 2009, a survey of academic publishers found 24,000 new titles with a backlist of nearly 350,000 titles (Ware and Mabe 2009). Most of these books are written by professors in the humanities, social sciences, and related fields and can be classified as monographs about relatively obscure topics—everything from the interaction of miners in southern Mexico with transnational corporations to the observances of monks in eleventh-century Poland. These monographs once sold at least two thousand copies because purchase was more or less mandatory at self-respecting libraries. Those totals are now much lower, as library consortia have shared resources to save money—a major reason why humanities scholars now are beginning to publish more often in journals. Textbooks make up most of the academic best sellers; they can accumulate sales in the millions of dollars and, in rare cases, tens of thousands of citations (Brint 2017).[3]

This large volume of academic research supports a literate, refined, scholarly, and scientific culture—and the multiple conflicting viewpoints found within it—but most of it is not directly relevant to economic growth or the solution of societal problems, a situation many reformers during the period found problematic. Much of the research produced in universities could be considered "purely academic" in the negative sense of the phrase—it concerns issues of limited importance, chosen by scholars searching for a small opening in which to make their mark, and very few may read or care about it. This is, arguably, a major problem with the academic system; the median research publication catalogued in the Web of Science receives all of one citation!

The rapid growth of peer-reviewed journals and peer-reviewed articles published annually is very highly correlated with the growing number of research workers worldwide. However, this correlation does not tell the full story. Although academics comprise only 10 to 20 percent of the total scientific workforce, they are responsible for about three-quarters of publications. This suggests new mechanisms for increasing output within academe. Contributing factors include labor-saving technologies, such as computer software; the growing size of scientific teams, allowing for enhanced productivity through division of labor; and the changing norms of graduate student publication. Graduate students in the sciences are now expected to publish prior to receiving their degrees, and some newly minted PhDs have publication records that would have been sufficient for advancement to tenure in previous generations. The growth of "salami publishing," the chopping up of research into "least publishable units" (or LPUs), is another, unfortunate influence on publication growth statistics.

THE RESEARCH PRODUCERS

Research productivity is highly concentrated among a very few of the 3,000-plus four-year colleges and universities in the United States. In 2010, the 108 Carnegie "very high research" institutions accounted for some three-quarters of the papers catalogued in the Web of Science, and the 99 Carnegie "high research" universities accounted for most of the remaining 25 percent (Brint and Carr 2017). The research peaks among universities are comprised of the majority of the 60 U.S. universities that are members of the Association of American Universities (AAU)—a few have become laggards—plus a handful of other high performers, such as the University of Alabama-Birmingham and the University of Massachusetts-Amherst, that are not yet members of the AAU. These high-level performers also include a number of medical schools, such as the University of California-San Francisco and the M. D. Anderson School of the University of Texas, that are not eligible to join the AAU because of their concentration on medical education and research rather than a larger number of fields.[4]

The period covered in this book was one of steady and impressive growth in the research output of the leading universities. Cynthia Carr and I examined the productivity of the top 194 research universities (including medical institutions) as rated in 1979 (see Geiger and Feller 1995) over the thirty-year period, 1980–2010. We measured productivity in relation to the metrics that are most important in the system of academic professionalism: research expenditures, research publications, and citations.[5] In constant 2010 dollars, total research expenditures in our sample of 194 increased from $4.4 billion in 1979 to $46.8 billion in 2010, a tenfold increase. Increases were evident in every decile of institutions during each decade we studied. Research publications grew from about 191,000 in 1979 to about 555,000 in 2010, a 190 percent increase over the period, and here too growth was evident in every decile of institutions during each time period. We measured citation count as the number of times a publication catalogued in the WoS cited an article produced by a target institution in a target year and proceeded with the same process at five-year intervals.[6] Citations grew from 4.3 million in 1980 to 10.7 million in 2005, a 146 percent increase. Here too increases were evident in every one of the 19 deciles during each period studied.

Perhaps even more impressively, the great majority of the individual campuses in our sample also increased their productivity over each decade studied. Only 23 of the 188 sample institutions reporting data throughout the period experienced declines in publication counts in *any one* of the three decades studied. Only eight institutions experienced declines in constant dollar R&D expenditures, and only ten showed declines in citations in any decade over the period we counted.[7] The robust growth of research output suggests that the golden age of research may be now.

Researchers at virtually all of the institutions we studied increased their output, but the hierarchy of top research producers did not change much. Following a period of dispersion between 1980 and 1990,[8] as measured by the Gini coefficient, inequality in all three of our measures stabilized in the years between 1990 and 2010 and remained at a high level. The rich did not get richer relative to other research institutions, but they effectively maintained their standing. The competitive advantages of the top thirty-five research universities enabled them to maintain their leadership and leverage greater successes in science (including entrepreneurial science) to add to their wealth and prestige. Carr and I found very limited long-range mobility within the system; only 8 percent of the institutions in the sample moved up the ranks *more than one decile* during the entire thirty-year period in either publication or citation counts. Upward mobility was only slightly more frequent in R&D expenditures rankings. It seems likely that competition for place may contribute to the overall productivity of the system, even if it fails to produce many universities whose positions improve dramatically over time (Brint and Carr 2017).

No one will be surprised that within this system the natural sciences, engineering, and medicine were the heavyweight contributors to research productivity; all but one of the top ten publishing fields were from these fields. Between 1980 and 2015, chemists, engineers, and physicists each published more than three million WoS-catalogued journal articles. Biologists, medical researchers, and biochemists/molecular biologists followed, each with more than one million WoS-catalogued publications during the period. Computer science and mathematics also placed on the top ten list. Psychology was the sole non-STEM field on the top ten list, but the designation of psychology as non-STEM may soon become contestable given the ascendance of cognitive and neuroscience in psychology. Although not in the top ten, environmental science also scored high on the publication list at more than 650,000 publications over the period.

Several of the larger subfields within these STEM disciplines published at a rate that would put them among the top twenty publishing fields. These include electrical and electronics engineering, condensed matter physics, organic chemistry, and cell biology—each with more than 500,000 WoS journal publications during the period. The volume of peer-reviewed work in such applied sciences as medical research, computer science, and electrical engineering is, moreover, greatly understated by these figures, given that many discoveries and research results in these fields are published in conference proceedings rather than journal articles. (Publication rates nearly double when conference proceedings are included for these fields.)

Social science fields and human-centered professional fields dominated at the next level—those with 100,000 to 400,000 journal article publications in WoS during the period. Economics, political science, geography, and sociology are included in this tier among the social sciences, as well as education, management, architecture, and law among the applied fields. The larger humanities disciplines—history, literature, philosophy, and religious studies—also appeared in this second publication tier. The third tier—disciplines with fewer than 100,000 publications during the period—was composed of a mix of cultural studies (e.g., area studies, classics, women's studies, and ethnic studies); arts (e.g., art, music, theater, dance); more qualitative social science fields, such as anthropology and communications; and smaller professional fields, such as public policy and social work. It also included a few small natural science fields such as geology and agricultural science. Judging solely by WoS journal publication counts, over the thirty-year period fields like chemistry and physics were approximately fifty times more active in publication than fields like anthropology and communications and approximately one hundred times more active in publication than fields like classics, art, dance, and theater. Of course, the importance of book publication in these latter fields partially makes up for the relative paucity of their journal publications.

It is a reasonable expectation that the strongest and most pervasive commitments to the research mentality will be found at the intersection of two sets of locations—among professors and their graduate students in research-intensive fields located in highly research-productive institutions.

RESEARCH OUTPUT AND FUNDING OPPORTUNITIES

These differences in research outputs were strongly associated with differences in access to external funding. The federal government's largesse is heavily weighted toward the natural and applied sciences. The top disciplinary recipients of nondefense R&D spending in fiscal year 2014, for example, overlapped almost completely *in the aggregate* with the top research producing fields. These federally favored disciplines were: biology ($15.3 billion), engineering ($11.9 billion), medical sciences ($11 billion), physics ($3.6 billion), computer science ($2.6 billion), other life sciences ($2.5 billion), psychology ($2 billion), astronomy ($1.2 billion), chemistry ($1 billion), and environmental sciences ($1 billion). Of those receiving at least $1 billion, only agricultural science could be considered clearly anomalous given the low publication rate of agricultural scientists (NSF 2016a, figure 5-1). By contrast, all arts fields taken together have received approximately $150 million annually in recent fiscal years (NEA 2016), and all humanities fields have received approximately the same amount (NEH 2017)—each 100 times lower than the single discipline of biology.[9]

The funding allocations that focused on basic research, peer review, and individual principal investigators all tended to support a continued focus on problems defined by researchers in the disciplines, rather than a focus on

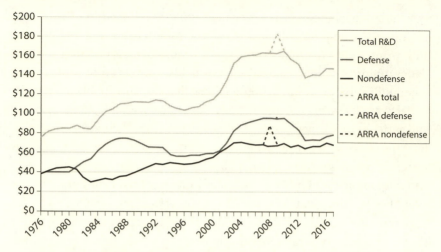

FIGURE 2.1. Trends in Federal R&D, 1976–2017.
Source: American Association for the Advancement of Science analysis of historical agency data and FY 2017 requests, with permission from AAAS.

problems prioritized by government mission agencies or industry groups only. They enhanced the contributions of universities to the culture of academic professionalism rooted in the disciplines and supported their relative autonomy from state and industry (see figure 2.1). Indeed, their impact was strengthened by the near-tripling of federal science and engineering R&D spending in constant dollars between 1980 and 2015 (NSF 2016a, figure 5.2). However, as I will show in chapters 3 and 6, the priorities of patrons, including the federal government, began to shift during the period toward a focus on use-inspired research, "grand challenges" to make progress in government-identified national priority areas, and large team science to meet these objectives.[10]

INFLUENCES ON PUBLIC DISCOURSE

Economic impact is hardly ever a priority among professors of arts, humanities, or social sciences. Nevertheless, the findings of scholars in these latter fields can have a major impact—on public discourse and practice. For all of the conflict that ensued (and has by no means ended), the post–civil rights era interest of humanities scholars in the histories and literatures of non-Western, racial-ethnic minority, and female actors has certainly influenced the cultural incorporation of these groups and the expansion of the social coordinates of knowledge (see, e.g., Frank, Schofer, and Torres 1994; Gates 1992; Oakley 2005). It has contributed to the social incorporation of these groups into the university and the professions, albeit with considerable pushback during periods of conservative ascendance. (See the discussion in chapter 9.)

Other, less publicized contributions to public culture can also be identified. In a recent study of highly cited articles and books in social science, I found that many concepts that have become familiar ways of understanding the world originated in the minds of social scientists who published during the period 1980–2010. The influence of these concepts is so pervasive in discourse that it is easy now to forget their origins in social science. They include: stakeholders (as opposed to shareholders), relationship-based (as opposed to principle-based) moral reasoning, social capital and cultural capital, network embeddedness, communities of practice, self-efficacy (as a feature of elevated performance), emotional intelligence, coping strategies, and decision biases (see Brint 2017). In some cases, these social science concepts have found their way into broader realms of social life (as in the case of stakeholders, communities of practice, network embeddedness, and self-efficacy). But their primary objective has been to illuminate: to help literate people understand the world in new ways and to make previously invisible phenomena of social life visible to the conscious mind.[11]

Indeed, the role of academic research as an influence on literate public discourse may be as significant as its contribution to economic development, though it is of course much harder to measure. Every week dozens of academic studies become fodder for discussion on topics ranging from the consequences for brain function of the constant collisions in football to the reasons for the wave of ethnonationalist protest voting in the Western democracies. In a probe of authorities cited in every article in the *New York Times* over the course of a single week in late January 2017, I found that professors were more likely than any other occupational group to be quoted and cited as authorities. Only government officials (including politicians and former government officials) were quoted and cited at nearly the same rate as professors.[12] Members of both groups were cited well over a hundred times during the week. From these two occupational groups, I found a steep drop-off to the next level: directors and staff of nonprofit organizations, businesspeople, and directors and staff of think tanks—all with fewer than half as many appearances as expert commentators. The use of university

professors for expert commentary spanned a wide range of fields and topics. In the *New York Times* that week they commented on everything from
investment in robotics technology to the history of popular music.[13]

It seems very likely that the breadth of university research is one reason
why professors so commonly appear as authorities. Of course, there are
many other media outlets, and it is unclear whether professors' views are
as favored in these other outlets as they are in the *New York Times*. One
imagines that professors are only very infrequent sources in media with a
regional or local reputation only. But at a minimum this probe suggests that
professors are an important source of expert authority in America's newspaper of record. It would not be surprising if other national media also
relied on their expertise; the reputation of professors for objectivity and
careful and critical discourse is a form of symbolic capital that makes them
obvious choices for expert commentary on public and cultural affairs.

ECONOMIC VERSUS CULTURAL CONTRIBUTIONS

It is true of course that some research work that is for a long period considered of purely academic interest will find its way into practice. A famous
example is the article by the sociologist Mark Mizruchi and colleagues
(1986) on disaggregating centrality scores in social networks. The concep-
tualization introduced in this otherwise fairly obscure article was one of
the sources for the algorithms underlying the Google search engine and
was cited in the first patent application of Google founders Larry Page and
Sergey Brin.

More commonly, many industrial practices have been subjected to
deeper scrutiny by university researchers, leading to improved processes.
For example, frameworks and methods for separating compounds developed in university laboratories when it became clear that batch processing
used in industry could not provide the quality or efficiency that would be
desirable for many bulk goods. In some cases, these separations require
total purification, as in electrolysis refining of bauxite ore for aluminum.
In other cases, the separation process splits mixtures into other more valuable mixtures, as in crude oil refinery. Different techniques are suitable depending on differences in chemical properties or physical properties such as
shape, mass, density, or chemical affinity (Wilson et al. 2000). Today dozens of separation techniques exist, and most were developed in university
laboratories.

Academic research also influences professional life. If they wish to stay current, doctors will refer to the medical literature in their specialization, together with guidelines on standard treatment practices and their patients' charts. Indeed, practice guidelines in medicine are built around the cumulative evidence produced by published academic studies, particularly those considered to be "high quality" because they meet the rigorous standards of reviewing forums such as the Cochrane Collaboration (Green et al. 2011). Similarly, improved scales for measuring affect, depression, or stress developed by university psychologists are quickly incorporated into mental health diagnosing practices if they have proven their value in tests with many hundreds of subjects. Some highly specialized and scholarly minded lawyers consult relevant law journal articles as well as case law. Engineers in fast-changing technical fields will do the same. No studies have been conducted about how often working professionals consult the academic literature relevant to their fields of expertise. For the few professionals who are required to be scholarly by the nature of their work—advisors to government, federal judges, leading medical practitioners, art appraisers working for the leading museums—the traffic with academic research is undoubtedly heavy.

Yet, as I have noted, most scholarly and scientific articles *are* primarily intended for other academics. These are the people who read and cite their work, and these citations are the stuff out of which academic careers are built. The goal of most research is to contribute to the solution of issues in a field of study by comparing or connecting different approaches to a problem, by investigating a thesis in a new population, by introducing new methods for analysis, by reporting new results related to problems in the disciplines, by raising controversy with existing interpretations or explanations, or by applying concepts drawn from the literature in the same or another field to a new problem.

Take one example: A vexing problem in the sociology and social psychology of education has been the lower academic performance of African American students matched for social background and academic aptitude to students from nonminority backgrounds. A lively literature has ensued about whether African American male students have developed a self-defeating oppositional culture that leads them to underperform in school (a view not strongly supported by the evidence); whether they seek affirmation from their peer groups by employing nondominant "cultural capital" (such as dialect) that is at odds with the expectations of schools (apparently true of many students); whether males see schools as feminized environments (seemingly true for some); whether they suffer from "stereotype threat" in high-stakes testing (the evidence is strong that many do); and/or whether subtle microaggressions may affect their performance (not yet established through credible research). Improving the school performance of African American males could help build capacities that contribute to their mobility opportunities and the strength of their communities. But the academic community has not reached any sort of consensus about the nature of the problem or what can be done to counter the problem, if consensus can be reached. Nor does research necessarily translate into policy. That depends on problems coming into prominence on the political agenda and policy entrepreneurs who can effectively promote solutions.

And of course much academic research is less relevant to the economy than the example of African American males' educational performance. The question of the extent to which Christians in the Western Roman Empire borrowed from pagans in the construction of their religious and charitable practices is utterly divorced from contemporary economic development, but it nevertheless galvanizes contending camps in religious and historical studies. Ultimately, questions like these are relevant to the interests of university humanities faculty in reconstructing and reimagining human civilizations: How did people at other times and in other cultures think and feel? How did their institutions work? What stories did they tell and why were those stories meaningful? Why did turning-point events happen as they did? The phrase "the matter is purely academic" is a put-down, but it is no put-down to academics who are immersed in their fields, trying to answer important questions about the contours and trajectories of human societies and cultures.

Research that is of "purely academic interest" has practical consequences for the careers of professors, their graduate students, and the communities of which they are a part. It holds many lessons for those who are open to appreciating those lessons. Yet it seems possible that research in liberal arts fields may be as important for the qualities of mind and practice it instills in students as for the light it shines on matters of academic interest and debate. In well-designed courses, these qualities include: problem assessment, thinking through approaches for addressing problems, analyzing results of approaches taken, and drawing conclusions based on the evidence, taking into account the limitations of the materials available. They include also weighing the explanatory power or contributions of different interpretations of the same material and craft care in the preparation of citations, notes, and references. These are habits consistent with success in professional, technical, and managerial occupations, even if they do not guarantee it.

The Institutional Geography of Knowledge Exchange

One consequence of producing a large number of people with higher-level degrees is that university researchers now share a similar mentality and a shared responsibility for idea production with workers in nonacademic organizations. Sociologists have speculated that one of the important outcomes of the growth of a knowledge sector populated by people with advanced degrees is a change in dominant thought styles. The sociologist David P. Baker has described these changes as "an epistemological revolution":

> The growth and intensity of science, rationalized inquiry, theory, [and] empirical methods [are] all influenced and reinforced. . . . [These changes can be] understood as . . . at the core of an epistemological revolution. (2014, 189–90)

If Baker is even partly correct, we should see a growing capacity, found primarily among those with advanced degrees, to think abstractly and to gather and weigh evidence in support of abstract conceptual frameworks and thereby to order the world by these empirically anchored abstract conceptual frameworks (see also Lamont 2009). The ecology of knowledge production should change with the growth of a highly educated stratum of workers; universities would remain central, but they would share the stage and part of their work would be to refine and correct ideas produced by thinkers outside of academe.

We know that this sharing of responsibility must be true, given that many discoveries are made by federal government or corporate researchers rather than by university researchers. A famous example was the race between the for-profit company headed by Craig Vetter and the government-funded team of scientists headed by Francis Collins to be the first to map the human genome. In chapter 3, I will provide many more examples of the competition between and interaction of researchers from universities, government labs, and corporations. But what about the concepts we use to explain the social world? Shouldn't they be more exclusively the province of university researchers? My research suggests that the answer is no. Here too we see an increasing porousness between universities and other institutional arenas.

I conducted a probe intended to provide examples of the phenomenon of empirically verifiable concept development that occurs outside of academe. I also investigated the role of academics in subjecting these "knowledge structures" to refinement and revision. As I will use the term, "knowledge structures" are akin to Thomas Kuhn's (1962) paradigms; they provide a framework of interrelated concepts, results, and procedures within which subsequent work is structured and they are subject to empirical verification or disconfirmation. (I do not like the term "conceptual structures" to describe what I have in mind because conceptual structures may or may not be subject to verification or disconfirmation.) The "balanced scorecard," for example, is a knowledge structure that provides a framework for managerial accountability in use by tens of thousands of businesses. It is based on abstract thinking about the key criteria for effective unit performance: financial stewardship, customer satisfaction, internal business processes that encourage efficiency, and organizational capacity for sharing knowledge and creating innovation. The concept is that an effective organization attends to each of these criteria in a balanced way. The balanced scorecard encourages the development of metrics for scoring how well a manager is performing in relation to these key criteria (Kaplan and Norton 1996). Moreover, the potential exists for empirical verification of the balanced scorecard as a contributor to unit effectiveness.

Good samples of knowledge structures like these can be identified and studied more easily than the nearly limitless volume of knowledge "bits" that flow across conversations and the Internet every day. I will discuss the very dense traffic around new technologies in greater detail in chapter 3. For purposes of illustration I will dwell here on just a handful of non-technology-based cases of the circulation of knowledge structures that originated outside of universities.[14] My point is to show the porousness of universities—the cross-institutional traffic that has thickened over time, even in areas that do not involve technological innovation.

Within the film industry, for example, formulas have long existed for predicting a film's success. One set of formulas makes predictions based on business variables, such as number of screens contracted, marketing budget, genre, release date, success rate of producers, and marquee value of directors and stars. Another set of formulas makes predictions based on the "emotional torque" of narratives (Anders 2011). Academics have examined the business formula for film success, throwing doubt on the importance of star power while affirming the significance of budget summer and holiday release and the popularity of the historically highest-grossing genres (Brewer, Kelley, and Jozefowicz 2009), or concluding that because of the heavily right-tailed distribution, with infinite variance, no predictions of exceptional box office success are possible (De Vany and Walls 1999). In recent years, more sophisticated modeling has developed in which much finer-grained story elements are considered, using neural network methodologies, including, for example, locale of the setting, how well the film takes advantage of the dramatic potential of the setting, and whether or not a woman is brought into peril. The specific features of these empirically derived predictive models are closely held by commercial firms, some founded by former academics and most drawing on the statistical expertise of academics or former academics (Barnes 2013; Gladwell 2006). A parallel case exists in the popular music industry, where firms, such as Music Xray, measure the mathematical relationships among melody, harmony, beat, tempo, rhythm, octave, pitch, chord progression, cadence, sonic brilliance, and frequency to identify "hit" clusters and to predict the probable success of new songs by their closeness to one of these clusters (Gladwell 2006). Although academics have not yet subjected the results of musical hit prediction to verification or disconfirmation, the possibility is there for doing so.

Another provocative example comes from the world of spiritual practices. Maharishi Mahesh Yogi introduced transcendental meditation (TM) into the United States in the late 1950s as a mental calming and spiritual development practice. The first tests of the physiological effects of TM were conducted in the early 1970s by Herbert Benson and his associates at the Harvard Medical School (Benson and Associates 1975). Since then, the transcendental meditation movement has gained traction throughout the Western world, with practitioners using it to reduce anxiety, improve health, and achieve a heightened level of spirituality. Hundreds of academic tests of the effects of transcendental meditation have yielded mixed results. A consensus has developed that regular practice can have benefits for stress/anxiety relief, can have modest benefits for cardiovascular health, and can be prescribed for hypertension (see, e.g., Bai et al. 2015; MacLean et al. 1997; Zamarra et al. 1996), though its benefits do not typically exceed those of other relaxation techniques or regular exercise. This medical support, while mixed, has helped legitimize and expand the popularity of a practice that once appealed in the West only to a small population of countercultural young people.

The evolution of user- (or human-) centered design (UCD) provides an example of the interplay of an early influential idea from industry and its refinement and formalization by academic researchers. In UCD the needs, wants, and limitations of end users are given centrality at each stage of the design process. The first seminal publication on the topic, by IBM engineers John D. Gould and Clayton Lewis (1985), identified several elements of user-centered design that remain central: early and continual focus on users; empirical measurement of usage; and iterative design. Subsequent work by academic researchers led to elaboration of methods for understanding users, for prototyping, and for validating design. Affinity diagrams (compilations of user insights), personas, mental models, and use scenarios have been identified by academic researchers as valuable methods for probing the minds and practices of users (Wallach and Scholz 2012). Drawing on these developments, the engineering professor Donald Norman (1988) provided a conceptual frame that focused on the broader world of design of "everyday things." In Norman's scheme, human-centered design focused on simplifying the structure of tasks, making things visible, getting the mapping of the product right, exploiting the powers of constraint, designing for error, exploring affordances (such as the historical connection between handles and pulling), and standardizing when "all else fails." Academic researchers such as William Rouse (2007) extended similar ideas to organizational systems and processes.

Similarly, scenario planning methodologies were imported into academe from the military and industry, where they were subsequently formalized and exported back to the military and industry, with mixed reception. Scenario planning is used as a strategic tool for individuals and organizations to imagine realistic possible future developments in order to improve planning and decision-making processes with different prospects in mind (Chermack, Lynham, and Ruona 2001; Varum and Melo 2010). Scenario planning originated in war game planning, led by the military strategist Herman Kahn, and was quickly adopted by the oil industry as an aid to think through and cope with uncertain national political environments (Schwartz 1996). The theoretical framework of scenario planning was researched, refined, and formalized by academic thinkers from RAND, the University of Pennsylvania's Wharton School, and the University of Strathclyde (Georgantzas and Acar 1995). These scholars helped introduce alternative approaches to the generation of scenarios, such as mathematical models and algorithms, which did not rely solely on judgment and intuition (ibid.). One of the pioneers of scenario planning, Kees Van der Heijden, moved from the Shell Oil Company to a university appointment in Scotland where he formalized principles of scenario planning in a prize-winning book on strategy (Van der Heijden 1997). Although the methodology of scenario planning has become more sophisticated as a result of the work of academic researchers, the jury is still out about whether it contributes to organizational learning or long-term stability (Chermack, Lynham, and Ruona 2001; Varum and Melo 2010).

These few examples suggest the need for a revision in conventional thinking about the interaction of universities with institutions outside their walls. Clark Kerr (1963) wrote of postwar research universities as "the service stations of society," meaning that universities generated knowledge and expertise that helped direct and improve a wide range of organizations in their environment. Research on the institutional geography of knowledge exchange leads in the direction of thinking about universities not as service stations but rather as all-purpose cognitive production and processing plants. They create knowledge products on their own, while at the same time taking in conceptual material from a variety of outside sources, rejecting some of this material as empirically incorrect, and in other cases feeding back tested and refined ideas and principles, with greater or lesser impact, to the source institutions.

The Educational Output of Universities

The other central purpose of universities of course is to prepare students for work in occupations that are thought to require higher-than-average levels of education. If we are interested in higher education's contribution to economic development, its work in training and credentialing is arguably more important than its research production, given that so much research contributes solely to problems identified by the disciplines. Indeed, the most important (near) monopoly universities enjoy is over the awarding of higher-level educational credentials.

The sociologist Harold Wilensky (1964) was the first to identify the process by which occupations become professionalized and thereby to require employees with college or postgraduate educations. First, of course, practitioners start doing something full-time that needs doing, whether that is healing, pleading, professing, or building. Second, in the common pattern, they establish a training school. This school need not be associated at first with a university, but, Wilensky showed, within two to three decades, the more ambitious practitioners within a professionalizing occupation make contact with universities to offer specialized curricula. Third, the leading practitioners form a professional association to allow for the sharing of new knowledge and the setting of practice standards. Often this includes efforts to separate the competent from the less competent and to restrict entry into the profession to those with prescribed training. Fourth, the professional association seeks to win the protection of law for its standards through the construction of state-regulated licensing and other practice regulations. Finally, efforts to eliminate the unqualified and unscrupulous and to protect clients become embodied in codes of ethics (1964, 141–43). Thus the higher education credentialing system has been a co-construction of universities, professional associations, and states, a co-construction whose origins lie in the reforming and rationalizing spirit of the Progressive Era of the late nineteenth and early twentieth centuries. These institutions were aided in the early days by philanthropic foundations that hoped to drive out pseudo-professional enterprisers, or "quacks," as they were known in the medical profession. They are vouchsafed today by educational and occupational accrediting associations.

Employers had their own reasons for preferring college graduates for managerial positions. In the early twentieth century these reasons had very little to do with the technical qualifications of graduates. Instead, as David Brown (1995) showed, college graduates were preferred because of their "mental resourcefulness," "sound judgement," and "interpersonal skills." Compared to other employees, managers were expected to deal with many more situations in which the proper course of action was uncertain and consequently required assessment of alternatives and good judgment in choices of action (Brown 1995, 151–52). Written and oral communication skills were the only "technical" skills mentioned frequently in studies of managerial hiring in the early twentieth century (see, e.g., Bossard and Dewhurst 1931, 106–7).

Occupational closure based on educational credentials was slower to develop than many people assume. Scholarly discussions described the shift from elite to mass higher education as beginning in the early twentieth century (see, e.g., Trow 2005), and many works on occupational closure through higher education credentialing appeared in the 1970s (see Berg 1970; Collins 1977; Sarfatti Larson 1979; Parkin 1979). But in the United States college degrees were in fact not required for access to most Census-identified professional occupations until the last decades of the twentieth century, and they are still not always required at front-line levels of management.

The *Colleges & Universities 2000* research team examined these links between higher education and occupations. In this work, we defined "fully enclosed" occupations as those for which the baccalaureate or a higher-level degree was required, with rare exceptions, for occupational entry. There were only a few of these fully enclosed occupations prior to 1980. They included medical doctors, lawyers, university professors, schoolteachers, and some non-university-based physical and life science specialists. We defined "partially enclosed" occupations as those in which most employees have college degrees but for which a college degree is not essential for entry. They can be defined, in quantitative terms, as occupations in which 50 to

80 percent of incumbents have at least baccalaureate degrees. In 1980 partially enclosed occupations included many in scientific and technical fields (atmospheric and space scientists, naturalists and conservation scientists, mathematicians, agricultural and food scientists, electrical engineers, mechanical engineers, civil engineers, materials engineers, and computer scientists). They also included many in health professions (health administrators, occupational therapists, dieticians, and nutritionists) and many in business service professions (accountants and auditors, management analysts, and operations and systems researchers). They included several in communications fields (reporters, editors, archivists, and librarians) and some in social science related fields (social workers, economists, market researchers, sociologists, and other social scientists).

We found that the nearly 300 colleges and universities in our study base were very likely during the period 1980–2000 to add curricula for training students who desired to enter these partially enclosed occupations (Brint et al. 2012b, 296). Bureau of Labor Statistics data indicate that most of these partially enclosed occupations had become fully enclosed (80 percent or more with at least baccalaureate degrees) by 2015 (BLS 2015, table 1.11). Postsecondary credentials, typically at the associate's level, also became required for police officers, firefighters, emergency medical technicians, and even cosmetologists during this period.

Managerial occupations, by contrast, remained comparatively open to those without degrees, with only 55 percent having obtained baccalaureate degrees, according to the annual average of the Current Population Survey in 2015 (BLS 2015). In large corporations, however, the college degrees became all but compulsory for mobility into upper management (Useem and Karabel 1986). Sarah Yoshikawa and I found that 92 percent plus of senior executives of Fortune 1000 firms in fifteen industrial sectors could be verified as having obtained bachelor's degrees in 2014, and two-thirds could be verified as having obtained advanced degrees, usually in either business or law (Brint and Yoshikawa 2017).

A shift toward occupationally relevant curricula was clearly evident in the 1970s, and it accelerated through the mid-1980 and 1990s. Even liberal arts colleges added occupational programs to stay competitive (Kraatz and Zajac 1996). Smith College's engineering program was an early successful example. Business was the big gainer during the period with more than one in seven college majors by the early 1990s (Adelman 1999). By the early 1990s the proportion of students studying occupationally relevant fields plateaued at about 60 percent, where it has remained since, with the remainder majoring in what are often called the "basic" fields in the arts and sciences—those claiming no direct connection with jobs (see Brint et al. 2005 and chapter 4).

Nevertheless, one might say that baccalaureate-level study remained tilted ever so slightly in favor of "liberal education." This conclusion would be based on the 40 percent of college students still majoring in the arts and sciences and the persistence of general education in the first two years, an education intended to broaden students' understandings of the world in which they live, most often through sampling courses in the natural sciences, the social sciences, and the humanities (Brint et al. 2009). Since the time of the philosophical academies in ancient Greece, the ideal of a liberal education has played a decisive role in Western understandings of higher education. The term "liberal," in this context, means freedom of the mind and is opposed to the "servility" of following others blindly. The values of liberal education persist, albeit in an enfeebled form at most universities— and in stiff competition with the ideal of occupationally relevant learning.

Why have occupational curricula not become still more dominant than they are? One reason is that students do not always want to study fields that are in high demand or deemed to be practical. Students have been less interested, for example, in engineering majors than the pay for engineers suggests they should be. All but one of the ten college majors with the highest pay in mid-career, according to PayScale, are engineering degrees, with petroleum engineering at the top and systems engineering next (PayScale 2016). But in recent years less than 5 percent of bachelor's degrees were awarded in engineering. Part of the explanation for this apparent mismatch has to do with the difficulty of engineering majors—a conclusion that extends in a more limited way to all quantitative majors. Nationally, about 40 percent of entering freshmen declare an interest in majoring in STEM subjects, but only one-third actually complete a STEM degree (National Science Board 2016, chap. 2). In addition, many students, it turns out, want to study subjects that interest them, whether or not they align closely with demand in the labor market or expected salaries. The *C&U 2000* research team found that quite a few fields grew significantly faster in degrees awarded during the period 1980–2000 than market demand seemed to warrant. These included communications, environmental studies, ethnic studies, psychology, recreation and leisure studies, visual and performing arts, and women's studies (Brint et al. 2011).

The situation is quite different for advanced degrees. Apart from the rare intellectual adventurer, those studying in graduate programs are intending to use their educational credentials for access to professional careers closely linked to their fields of study.[15] Professional degrees are essentially universal among lawyers, doctors, and dentists and nearly as common among college professors (not counting junior colleges who hire many practitioners) and psychologists/psychiatrists in practice. More than 50 percent of physical and life scientists, nuclear engineers, urban and regional planners, secondary school teachers, and clergy have advanced degrees (BLS 2016a, table 12).

The growth of professional master's degree programs was arguably one of the most important changes in higher education during the period. The professional master's degree combined academic study with practical applications (including internships). It had had a long history in accounting, business, education, engineering, and public administration. The degree showed phenomenal growth through the 1990s and 2000s, with more than 700,000 master's degrees conferred by 2010, greatly exceeding government projections from a decade before. Business, education, health professions, engineering, and computer science represented some two-thirds of the total of master's degrees awarded (NCES 2017, table 323.10). Master's candidates expanded in such specialized health fields as physical therapy, physician's assistant, and nurse anesthesia and later in data-based fields like cybersecurity, data analytics, and health informatics. Universities grew these programs not only to respond to student and employer demand but because they could price them at rates that made them self-supporting and, prospectively, to protect potential revenue sources from the designs of institutional competitors (Glazer-Raymo 2005).

In 1997, the Sloan Foundation began to promote the professional science master's, a degree intended not only to augment the STEM workforce but to provide business skills as a central component of training. Though enrollments gained ground slowly—remaining well below 10,000 by the end of the period—advocates argued that the degree would eventually become "the MBA of the 21st century" (Tobias 2009). Also notable was the growing prominence of science and engineering in the production of new doctorates. According to the 2015 *Survey of Earned Doctorates*, more than two-thirds of doctoral degrees awarded to men were in science and engineering fields, as were nearly half of doctoral degrees awarded to women (NSF National Center for Science and Engineering Statistics 2015, table 14).

A Knowledge-Based Economy?

The system of academic professionalism persists in part because theorists have convinced journalists and policymakers that it produces the research and advanced training required by a putatively "knowledge-based" postindustrial society and economy. In 1962, the Princeton economist Fritz Machlup published the first estimates of the size of what he called the "information economy." Machlup counted the gross output of industries he classified as "intending to create an impression in human minds" (30). For Machlup, these industries included education, research and development, mass media and communications, information machines (such as computers), and professional services. Machlup provided what became an important estimate of the size of the knowledge economy—nearly 30 percent of GDP by the end of the 1950s. A year later, citing Machlup, Clark Kerr wrote:

> Knowledge has certainly never in history been so central to the conduct of an entire society. What the railroads did for the second half of the last century and the automobile did for the first half of [the twentieth] century may be done for the second half of this century by the knowledge industry: that is, to serve as the focal point for national growth. And the university is at the center of the knowledge process. (1963, 88)

From Machlup and Kerr, it was but a short step to the appearance of widely cited works on "the new industrial state" (Galbraith 1967), the "post-industrial society" (Bell 1973), and the "knowledge-based economy" (Drucker 1969). These theorists shared the belief that knowledge was transforming economic development and social relations but differed as to whether this transformation should be considered primarily in terms of control and innovation within large organizations (see Galbraith 1967; Drucker 1969) or in terms that encompassed both organizational control *and* sectoral development in an economy whose shape was being transformed by high-tech industry, the rise of business services, and the expansion of services connected to quality of life (see Bell 1973; Stanback et al. 1981).

The knowledge economy idea provided the strongest possible justification for the perpetuation and growth of the research and educational enterprise of universities, and it was naturally popular among university professors. The idea came to be widely accepted among progressive-minded journalists, politicians, and policymakers. A count of new stories through Lexis-Nexis showed more than 10,000 mentioning "post-industrial society" beginning in the early 1970s (author's calculation). In 1996, the OECD released a report that echoed and strongly reinforced the emerging consensus. The first paragraph of the report observed:

OECD . . . policies should be formulated to maximise performance and well-being in "knowledge-based economies"—economies which are directly based on the production, distribution and use of knowledge and information. This is reflected in the trend in OECD economies towards growth in high-technology investments, high-technology industries, more highly-skilled labour and associated productivity gains. (OECD 1996, 1)

In more vivid prose, former Cornell University president Frank Rhodes wrote:

A nation's present well-being and future destiny are no longer constrained only by its [geography, population, and natural resources]. Knowledge has become the prime mover; science and technology represent the new driving force. Economic prosperity, energy supplies, manufacturing capacity, personal health, public safety, military security, and environmental quality—all these and more will depend on knowledge. (2001, 229)

Most social scientists who are interested in higher education attributed the growing prominence of universities to their role in supplying research and credentialed personnel to an economy that was becoming more and more dependent on knowledge to produce growth. The question is: To what extent were these contentions right? The circular reasoning that the economy must be more knowledge dependent because it is employing more college graduates will not suffice as an answer to this question because credential inflation can produce the same effect and because, we know, many college graduates do not actually use much of what they have learned in college in their work lives—whether in terms of subject matter or thinking skills.

HIGHER EDUCATION AND KNOWLEDGE-IN-PRACTICE

Some early theorists of the knowledge society emphasized the mastery of formal subject matter as the precondition for success in the professions and management (see, e.g., Bell 1973; Freidson 1985, chap. 4). Contemporary work on knowledge as an economically valuable resource has continued to emphasize the manipulation of symbolic content but has elevated practice-based insights and judgment over classroom-based abstraction and formalization. The experience of study (and the associated experiences of thinking through problems, reading scholarship, and conducting research) is relevant to work practice in the professions and management, but the frequent utilization of formal knowledge per se is not necessarily common. Instead, adequate mastery of curricula is important for obtaining educational credentials and professional licenses. Only the latter are directly relevant to gaining privileged access to professional and managerial positions (Freidson 1985, chap. 4).

Knowledge-in-practice in this stream of thought is more like improvisational jazz than a composition based on formal music theory. Working knowledge is the capacity to marry new information to formal knowledge, developed skills, past experience, and tested judgment to produce valuable and efficient action. The management scholars Thomas Davenport and Laurence Prusak, for example, defined "knowledge" as "a fluid mix of framed experiences, values, contextualized information, and expert insight that provides a framework for evaluating and incorporating new experiences and information" (2000, 5). It is also important to note that knowledge is not a fixed resource, because those who have it can share it through documents or interactions to expand the knowledge base within their organizations.

People who are experienced in the manipulation of symbolic content compare what is known about the current situation to other situations experienced in the past. They think through the implications of information for decisions and actions. They connect new bits of knowledge to previous bits, and they converse with others about what they think about the information, refining approaches to action in the process. Those who use and manipulate symbols for a living engage in the following typical activities: collecting, analyzing, and reporting data; communicating through the construction of texts and expressive work; diagnosing and treating based on consultation and questioning; solving organizational and client problems; developing and implementing new ideas and products; collaborating and convincing others based on evidence; creating scenarios and models; monitoring relevant contexts; planning for the future; and evaluating the outcomes of actions taken.

For Davenport and Prusak, knowledge is valuable because it is close to action. It can be evaluated against the decisions and actions to which it leads. It can lead, for example, to measurable efficiencies in product development or production. It can be used to make better decisions about how to do work, projects to take on or to avoid, how to evaluate outcomes, and broader strategic directions. Working knowledge contains judgment and is in this sense opposed to the automatic decision making produced by algorithms or in highly scripted routine labor. Other theorists have taken a similar approach to understanding knowledge in practice. The learning theorist Donald A.

Schoen (1983, 1987), for example, emphasized that effective action in new situations typically requires not the application of theory but informed improvisation based on experience, practice, learning, and judgment.

How, then, does a college or postgraduate education contribute to effectiveness at work? One fundamental issue is whether most non-college-educated workers could handle the level of abstraction required in the jobs of college-educated professionals and managers. Some undoubtedly could, but an unknown, presumably large number could not. An example: it is tempting to consider coding variables on spreadsheets as routine work, except that many people lack the capacity for abstraction that would allow them to understand the meaning of a variable, the variety of ways a variable can be coded, and how to choose from a set of options for coding variables. (The patience for learning how to do these things is also a big factor, of course, and is created in large part by the volume of learning activities college students must engage in.) To take a second example, something similar is undoubtedly true for preparing complex budgets. These may follow a fairly standard form, but what seems like relatively routine work could not be accomplished satisfactorily by most people, even if they had prior training. Those who prepare budgets need to know many conventions, many exceptions to these conventions, and ways of justifying expenditures.

Novel situations that do not fit established scripts are another pivot point. Many people operate under scripts that we can label "standard operating procedure" but nevertheless occasionally encounter individuals, situations, and projects that do not fit the script. A patient may present to a doctor with symptoms that are not at all standard. At this point, research and specialized experience come into play (at least for doctors who are paying attention). According to Sarfatti Larson (1979), the optimal circumstance for professionals is one in which outcomes are not so unpredictable that they defy the application of expertise, nor so patterned that they can be reduced to standard operating procedures or off-the-shelf commodification. Paul Adler (2015) has discussed the case of computer programmers in a large company whose work has been highly standardized by the company but begin to complain about constraints when more ambitious projects are sent their way with the expectation that they will employ standardized tools. New projects require problem assessment, design, planning, and evaluation—activities that require the capacity for independent thought based on knowledge-in-practice. These examples suggest that novel situations are episodic rather than continuous. Jobs, however, can be classified in terms of the frequency with which judgment that departs from standard operating procedure is required. Most highly educated professionals (and managers) would presumably rank comparatively high on this measure—this is a large part of what we mean by expertise—but standard operating procedure would nevertheless apply in many, if not most, circumstances.

Novel situations require the exercise of judgment. So too do problems that are complex and have a range of possible solutions. For example, when a social scientist considers which analytical techniques to employ on a data set, a range of considerations come into play concerning the objectives of the inquiry, the size of the sample, the quality of the data, the distribution of the key variables, possible selection effects and what to do about them, control variables, interaction terms that theory suggests may be important, and many other possibilities. Judgment in the face of complexity is a clear feature of many technical jobs. Complex managerial jobs have their own distinctive sets of judgments concerning such matters as allocation of resources, how to improve organizational effectiveness and work processes, how to improve the work performance of direct reports who seem to be underperforming, when and how to take on new projects, and how to allocate time in the face of competing priorities.

Available data on the work lives of highly educated professionals and managers, relative to those of other workers, affirm these emphases on comfort with abstraction, non-routine events and the application of informed judgment. Professionals can realize the valued goal of fulfilling work more often than other workers because they are more frequently employed in jobs designed with high levels of flexibility. These jobs combine high levels of multitasking, discretion, capacity to use intellectual abilities, and unregulated coordination with others (Applebaum and Batt 1994; Zoghi, Levenson, and Gibbs 2005). They are most likely to be found in industries, such as finance and research, that produce complex products or involve complex work processes (Zoghi, Levenson, and Gibbs 2005). The volume and speed of information that must be processed at work also matters. It is now common to see upper-level professionals and managers working on several screens at once on their computers or checking for information on their smartphones during their spare minutes.

THE SIZE OF THE "KNOWLEDGE WORKER" STRATUM

College graduates end up in a wide variety of jobs; indeed, according to the New York Federal Reserve, more than 40 percent of recent college graduates take jobs after graduation that do not require college-level skills—jobs such

TABLE 2.3. Largest Professional Occupations, 2015 (rounded to nearest thousand)

Occupation	Number Employed (age 25 or older)
Schoolteachers (not incl. preschool)	4,073,000
Registered Nurses	2,845,000
Engineers	1,992,000
Accountants/Auditors	1,653,000
Software Developers	1,278,000
Professors and College Instructors	1,233,000
Lawyers	1,157,000
Physicians	1,005,000
Financial Analysts/Advisors	832,000
Designers	829,000
Management Analysts/Consultants	819,000
Counselors	740,000
Social Workers	725,000
Natural Scientists	697,000
Computer Scientists/System Analysts	616,000

Source: Adapted from BLS 2015, table 12.

as waiter, cashier, and construction worker—and about one-third of all college graduates—not just recent graduates—are underemployed in this way, even if most achieve decent incomes (Cooper 2017). These estimates may be grossly inflated—much depends on how one measures a "college-level job" and there is a vigorous debate about whether existing measures are adequate. The majority of college graduates do sooner or later flow into professional, managerial, or technical occupations. Professional occupations are the most frequent landing point. According to the Current Population Survey, as of 2015, the fifteen largest occupations classified as professional were schoolteachers, nurses, engineers, accountants and auditors, software developers, professors, lawyers, physicians and surgeons, designers, management consultants, counselors, social workers, natural scientists, financial analysts and advisors, and computer scientists and systems analysts. College and graduate degrees are the norm in each of these occupations (see Table 2.3).

As I have noted, managers are a more diverse category. A majority of them, including most first-line supervisors and small business owners, do not have college degrees. But the 45 percent who do have college degrees make up another 4 million workers (author's calculations from U.S. Bureau of the Census 2016a).

We cannot be sure that most college graduates use subject-related knowledge in their work, or even that they are required to display comfort with abstraction, capacity to handle novel situations, or exercise of judgment. A sizable proportion undoubtedly do, but many do not. The situation for those with advanced degrees is different. Here retention of subject-related concepts, principles, and skills is more likely to impact practice. People with advanced degrees are also more likely to experience the work practice requirements for a professional outlook and demeanor.

If we are thinking about the core of the professional-managerial stratum, then, a reasonable constraint is to focus on people with advanced degrees, not on those with baccalaureates only. In 2015, approximately fourteen million people age twenty-five or above were classified by the Census Bureau as professionals with advanced degrees, or 11 percent of the labor force. We add another 1 percent to this total by including managers with advanced degrees. Thus, by the end of the period, about one out of eight employed Americans over the age of twenty-five constituted the core stratum of "knowledge workers," or experts. These people can be considered the most important educational "products" of universities. (The broader stratum of all professionals and managers with at least baccalaureate degrees was twice as large in 2015, constituting about one-quarter of the labor force.)

KNOWLEDGE-SECTOR INDUSTRIES

A different approach is necessary to estimate the size of the "knowledge sector" of the economy, the most important concept for partisans of the knowledge economy idea. A synoptic view of knowledge-sector industries requires integration of the insights of the theorists who have attempted to identify these industries. At least the following factors are involved: (1) Large firms with extensive and highly differentiated markets rely on technologies that reduce uncertainty in their environments and create the capacity for innovation and strategic growth. These innovators and planners are the core of the Galbraithian (1967) "techno-structure." (2) These incentives for planning and data-based control encouraged the development of "producer services," supplying business expertise both in-house and out-of-house. Most notably, business service professionals supply necessary resources in the form of contributions to corporate capitalization and advice in the form of management consulting, accounting, and legal services (Stanback et al. 1981). (3) In addition, some industries relying on new and rapidly developing technologies (the computer software and biotechnology/bioengineering industries are among the more important contemporary examples) employ high proportions of scientists and engineers who can keep their firms competitive during what amount to continuous periods of technological change (Bell 1973). (4) With the increase in national income characteristic of relatively affluent capitalist economies, services in the so-called "quinary sector" (health, education, arts, and recreation) become important as means of access to the "good life" that more and more citizens expect and can afford (ibid.). (5) In a more highly developed and complex economy with a strong private sector and citizen interests in security and human capital development, government takes on expanded regulatory and social welfare activities. These too rely on expertise in the formulation, implementation, and evaluation of initiatives. Taken together, these developments make for impressive tributaries flowing into a river of socioeconomic development.

The knowledge-intensity of an industry can be measured by the ratio of employees with graduate degrees to the entire labor force in the industry. As I will show, this approach leads to a categorization of knowledge-sector industries that aligns very well with the five streams of economic development identified by the major theorists of postindustrial society. We can then develop a sense of the size of the knowledge sector and its contribution to GDP over time by summing the industries identified as employing a high proportion of workers with advanced degrees and then examining their combined contribution to GDP.[16]

Unfortunately, no single data set can provide the comprehensive overview that is necessary to understand the size and composition and the trajectory of knowledge-sector industries. To classify industries, I used the General Social Survey (GSS) cumulated over multiple years. The GSS provides evidence on educational distributions within industries and allows researchers to combine industries to bring out meaningful distinctions based on theory. To estimate the contribution of knowledge-sector industries to GDP, I used U.S. Department of Commerce Bureau of Economic Analysis (BEA) data. To examine growth rates for knowledge-sector industries I used U.S. Department of Labor Bureau of Labor Statistics (BLS) data. Given the different industrial classifications used in these data sets, I have had to group industries slightly differently for different analyses.

I initially used the criterion of 5 or more percent of employees holding advanced degrees (master's and above) to identify knowledge-sector industries. I found it necessary to raise this criterion to 10 percent or more by the very end of the period, in deference to the continued growth of workers with advanced degrees.[17] As Table 2.4 shows, the knowledge sector,

TABLE 2.4. U.S. Knowledge-Sector Industries, 1990–2010

Industry	1990–2010 Cumulative Percent w/Graduate Degrees	GSS N 1990–2010
Offices of Health Practitioners	50	42
Colleges & Universities	40	723
Legal Services	35	297
Noncommercial Research Firms	31	61
Elementary & Secondary Schools	30	1,904
Commercial Research & Testing Firms	29	52
Museums, Art Galleries & Zoos	24	34
Educational Services	23	74
Engineering & Architectural Services	23	203
Misc. Professional Services	22	95
Social Services	22	310
Offices of Physicians	20	260
Religious Organizations	20	183
Management Consulting	19	184
Computer & Data-Processing Services	18	268
Security & Investment Companies	18	170
Pharmaceuticals	17	91
Libraries	15	59
Offices of Dentists	15	126
Electronic Computing Equipment	15	141
Guided Missiles & Space Vehicles	14	57
Human Resources Administration	14	163
Agricultural Services	13	87
General Government	12	347
Misc. Communications Services	12	82
Economic Program Administration	12	117
Scientific Instruments	12	26
National Security & Int'l Affairs	11	468
Environmental Quality Administration	11	100
Broadcasting	11	74
Health Services	11	455
Job Training Services	10	29
Accounting & Auditing Services	10	138
Residential Care Facilities	10	91
Electrical Machinery & Equipment	10	51
Hospitals	10	1,226
Photographic Equipment & Sales	9	32
Business & Vocational Schools	9	33
Membership Organizations	9	102
Petroleum Products	9	46
Public Finance & Taxation	9	81
Justice, Public Order & Safety	8	519

TABLE 2.4. (*continued*)

Industry	1990–2010 Cumulative Percent w/Graduate Degrees	GSS N 1990–2010
Theaters & Motion Pictures	8	155
Banking	8	470
Optical & Health Services Supplies	7	83
Aircraft & Parts	7	125
Printing & Publishing, except Newspapers	7	272
Advertising/Marketing	6	78
Book & Stationery Stores	6	47
Real Estate, incl. Real Estate Law	6	509
Newspaper Publishing	6	116
Insurance	6	452
Air Transportation	6	155
Credit Agencies	6	156

Source: Calculated from the General Social Survey, 1990–2010.

so defined, includes: agricultural services (but not agriculture itself), mass media industries, museums and other arts organizations, chemicals, plastics, pharmaceuticals, computers and electronic equipment, scientific instruments, banking and investment, accounting, consulting and other business services, health services and hospitals, education services, legal services, nearly all of government, and religious and membership organizations. Clearly, the great majority of industries are *not* part of the "knowledge sector," including virtually all of farming and mining, manufacturing, wholesale and retail trade, warehousing, transportation, and consumer repair and amenity services (such as eating and drinking establishments). In the later study encompassing the years 1990–2010, Jacob Apkarian and I found that approximately 85 percent of all workers with advanced degrees were employed in 54 "knowledge-sector" industries we identified in the GSS; the remaining 15 percent were scattered across the 180 industries not included as part of the knowledge sector.[18]

Using this strategy for categorizing industries by the proportion of workers with advanced degrees, we can estimate the contribution of the knowledge-sector industries to GDP.[19] Using BEA data (see BEA 2016), I found that industries in the knowledge sector accounted for approximately 37 percent of GDP in the last quarter of the twentieth century, growing from just one-quarter in 1959 to nearly two-fifths in 1997 (Brint 2001, 120). Knowledge-sector industries continued to be among the most dynamic in the economy from 2000 through 2010. Taken collectively, by 2010 they still did not constitute the majority contribution to gross domestic product, but they were edging much closer—at 43 percent of GDP.[20] By 2015, knowledge-sector industries accounted for 43 to 51 percent of GDP. (State and local governments are difficult to classify because of the variability in their staffing from state to state and locality to locality. If the contribution of state and local government to GDP is weighted as part of the knowledge sector, the higher figure is the better estimate; if state and local government is not weighted at all, the lower figure is the better estimate.)

The results of these analyses yield a split decision about the significance of knowledge- sector industries. Manufacturing of durable and nondurable goods, warehousing and storage, transportation, and sales in wholesale and retail trade are large contributors to GDP and none of these industries should be included in the knowledge sector, according to my classificatory criteria. But software, business services, health, education, and many other professional services are also large contributors, and these industries can, using my criteria, be properly classified in the knowledge sector.

The average growth rates of industries provide another perspective on the dynamism of knowledge-sector industries relative to others. BLS data for the period 1997–2015 show that of 71 industry groups in which very accurate gross output data exist, 30 exceeded the average growth rate for the economy as a whole over the period. About half of the 30 were knowledge-sector industries, including information services (such as data processing and Internet publishing), computer software design, computer hardware and electronics, securities and investments, funds and trusts, health care, educational services, miscellaneous scientific and professional services, nondefense government operations, broadcasting and telecommunications, publishing, and performing arts. The remainder of the fast-growing industries were located outside the knowledge sector (see Table 2.5). I include only 28 of the 30 industries in the table because of ambiguities about the meaning or classification of two industrial categories in the BLS data.[21] I have also italicized two industries, insurance and real estate, that barely make the cutoff I have used to classify knowledge-sector industries.[22]

IS POSTINDUSTRIAL SOCIETY A DISTORTING LENS?

Thus, one reason for concern about the knowledge-economy idea is that it seems to be, at best, a half-truth. Knowledge-sector industries contributed heavily to GDP growth, but by the end of the period the U.S. economy

TABLE 2.5. 29 Fast-Growing Industries, as Measured by Gross Output, 1997–2015 (in constant 1994 dollars)

Knowledge Sector	Growth Rate	Other Industries	Growth Rate
Information Services[1]	333%	Warehousing/Storage	196%
Computer Software Design	172%	Mining Support Services	125%
Broadcasting/Telecomm.	132%	Admin. Support Services	90%
Computers & Electronics	109%	Rentals & Leasing	78%
Management Consulting	106%	Misc. Retail Stores	74%
Securities & Investments	106%	General Merchandise Stores	71%
Insurance Carriers	*89%*	Wholesale Trade	58%
Health Care	80%	Water Transportation	53%
Performing Arts	68%	Misc. Transportation	52%
Misc. Science/Prof. Services	66%	Recreation Industries	52%
Funds & Trusts	66%	Oil & Gas	50%
Real Estate	*66%*	Motor Vehicles & Parts	43%
Educational Services	62%	Waste Management	43%
Nondefense Government	52%		
Publishing	40%		

[1] Includes data processing, Internet publishing, and other information services.
Source: BLS 2016b.

remained no more than half a knowledge-based economy. And not all of the most dynamic industries were in the knowledge sector. It seems very likely that knowledge-sector industries will eventually become the largest part of the economy, but that has not yet happened.

I have more fundamental concerns about the idea in so far as it is intended to describe the fundamental contributions of universities to their societies. The idea diminishes not only the very broad scope of economic activity that has little to do with universities but also the very broad scope of what universities do that goes beyond their economic import. It can be a perverse misunderstanding, too, because it fails to recognize one of the central sources of universities' influence in society: their simultaneous connection to and distance from the sphere of production. The knowledge-economy idea encouraged a self-regarding myopia. It has created, among intellectuals and professionals, a misunderstanding of the size of the sectors of the economy that are not "knowledge-based" and, in a closely divided polity, an underestimation of the power of the less educated, those who have not typically performed well in school and do not perceive themselves as having benefited particularly from the expanding influence of universities or knowledge-sector industries.

As I have shown, the relationships that universities build in the world outside their gates are much wider than a purely economic analysis can encompass. They include the cultural organizations (museums, performances, magazines) that the highly educated support, the news and opinion media that rely on professors for authoritative commentary, the public officials and industry groups who consult with professors on research and policy issues, and the community organizations supported by students and faculty members. They are important vehicles for the upward mobility aspirations of underrepresented, first-generation, and low-income students. In addition, universities are typically among the largest employers in their towns and cities, and their contribution to the quality of life of the communities in which they are located is high through arts and lectures, sporting events, engagement with civic groups, and support for local businesses. In order to properly situate universities and to understand the true sources of their influence, a more rounded picture is required, one that is less exclusively oriented to the economic value of university research and training.

Figure 2.2 provides a schematic depiction of the relationships I have described in this chapter. It depicts a larger flow of university-credentialed people (labeled "students") into the several dozen industries that employ large percentages of workers with advanced degrees, labeled here as "knowledge-sector industries." It also depicts a smaller flow of university-credentialed people into other sectors of the economy. So far, so good for the knowledge-economy idea. But the idea begins to fail when we shift attention to research. While it is true that a sizable share of university research is relevant to and used by industry and the professions, most of it is not. It is of interest primarily to other academic specialists. Accordingly, the figure depicts the larger flow of research into academic professional culture and smaller flows into the economy and public discourse.

The diverging purposes between universities and corporations constitute a mismatch only if one supposes that the primary purpose of universities is to serve economic development. They do not constitute a mismatch if one supposes that the primary purpose of universities is to preserve and extend the accumulated knowledge and understanding of the scholarly and scientific disciplines—in other words, that their cultural contributions coexist with and, institutionally, take precedence over their economic contributions. A different mix of commitments is of course possible. Indeed, a principal project of university patrons throughout the period was to encourage this different mix—one more heavily weighted toward research with economic and societal impact.

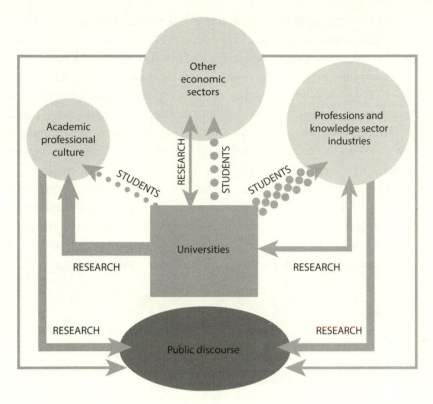

FIGURE 2.2. The Relationship of University Research and Credentialing to Other Social Institutions.

TOWARD INNOVATION-CENTERED UNIVERSITIES?

Bubbling under the swell of support for the postindustrial society idea was a counternarrative focusing attention much more closely on the role of universities in technological innovation. Edward Denison's (1985) calculations, for example, placed a very large emphasis on technological innovation as a driver of economic growth. Denison argued that, in cross-national studies, about two-thirds of the economic development residual not accounted for by land, labor, and capital should be attributed to technological innovation and only one-third to human capital development associated with longer periods of schooling. Analyses like these contributed to new policy thinking about the formation of a more powerful national innovation system in which universities played an enhanced role as generators of discoveries with commercial potential.

Under the influence of analyses like Denison's, the system of academic professionalism came in for stiff criticism at the dawn of the neoliberal age. Critics assailed the practical irrelevance of much academic research. They also assailed the mismatch between academic organization, with its embrace of the widest possible range of scholarly fields, and the increasing dependence of the economy on new technology development that could be produced in part by university researchers. Some universities, such as the Massachusetts Institute of Technology and Stanford University, helped create the new policy environment through their successes in seeding new firms and even entirely new industries. Others, such as Arizona State University, provided a model for an alternative form of organization focused not on the traditional mix of basic and applied disciplines but on interdisciplinary work intended explicitly for social and economic impact. It is to the rise of this alternative system of "academic innovationism" that I now turn.

3

The Rise of Academic Innovationism

Beginning in the 1980s, a second system arose as a complement and some-times competitor to the system of academic professionalism. I will call this second system *academic innovationism*, a slightly awkward term I know, but one that captures the dynamic quality of the new system and its distinctive differences from the dominant system for organizing knowledge acquisition and transmission.[1] This second system was predicated on the idea that university-based science and engineering had the capacity to generate new jobs and wealth when harnessed to work on new technologies with commercial potential. Investments by the federal government, corporations, and universities themselves focused on a handful of fields—computer science, engineering, medicine, physics, chemistry, and the life sciences. The objectives of the innovation system were different—not so much solutions to problems identified by disciplinary communities as practical applications of those solutions. A different set of institutions arose to foster the universities' role in innovation. These institutions included: research centers revolving around use-inspired research; research parks that housed entrepreneurial academics and in some cases the firms with whom they worked; offices of technology transfer; start-up companies formed around the discoveries of university researchers; poster sessions and conference presentations that supplanted publications in some rapid-discovery disciplines; and consulting relationships with high-tech firms. The new system was entrepreneurial, but more than that it was oriented to the transfer of new technologies as quickly as possible into the bloodstream of the economy.

In Table 3.1, I provide an analytical contrast between the two systems for organizing research and education, the system of academic professionalism and the system of academic innovationism.

Under the impetus of academic innovationism, universities became more porous to the outside world and reciprocal relations of knowledge exchange grew denser. On balance, the new system contributed significantly and positively to the research prowess of universities. It was responsible for a number of transformative technologies, including new drug therapies, new manufacturing processes, and new scientific instruments that greatly improved the quality of life. It helped universities grow beyond the limitations of Clark Kerr's multiversity model to think in more global and reciprocal terms and to look beyond the federal government for research support. But it has also yielded a spotty record—some extraordinary successes but also many short-lived, troubled collaborations. Some universities invested heavily in the infrastructure to foster academic innovation and had little to show for their investments. Moreover, the momentum slowed toward the end of the period. For research universities, the challenge for the future will be to expand the possibilities to contribute more to the national innovation effort by learning from both the successes and failures of post-1980 entrepreneurial science.

Ideas and Policies That Launched a Movement

The era of entrepreneurial science had its origins in the dismal state of the U.S. economy in the mid-1970s. After-tax profits fell from a high of nearly 10 percent in 1965 to lows of near 4.5 percent in the mid-1970s, and between the late 1960s and mid-1970s productivity gains plateaued at below 1 percent annually (Slaughter and Rhoades 1996, 309). Declining U.S. profits and sluggish productivity gains signaled a more competitive world and one in which surging East Asian economies, in particular, represented a threat to the U.S. economic position. By the late 1970s, Japanese firms were gaining large chunks of market share in industries formerly dominated by the United States, including steel, automobiles, machine tools, and consumer electronics (Nester 1993, chap. 3). Influential commentators heralded the age of "Japan as Number One" (Vogel 1979). The rise of tighter connections between universities and industry grew out of efforts to improve the

TABLE 3.1. Two Academic Systems

	Academic Professionalism	Academic Innovationism
Orientation	to Academic Peers to Unsolved Problems in Field to New/Refined Methods to Established/Emerging Theories/Paradigms	to New Technology Development to Use-Inspired Research to Marketable Discoveries
Main Intellectual Structures	Disciplines Subdisciplines Organized Research Units Professional Associations Academic Journals Academic Book Publishers	Interdisciplinary Teams Centers and Institutes Connected to the Economy Academic Journals Rapid-Discovery Conferences
Scope	All Academic Fields	Applied Science and Engineering

Research Funding	Primarily Federal
	Limited Funding by Donors,
	   Corporations, States
		State-Industry-University
		   Partnerships
		National Priority Fields
		"Grand Challenges"

Relation to Economy	Limited in Relation to All
	   Research
	High in Relation to Research
	   in Selected Scientific Fields
	High in Labor Force
	   Preparation
		Targeted to Discoveries with
		   Commercial Potential
		STEM-Centered in Education

Key Relational
   Institutions
	Professions
	Cultural Organizations
	News and Opinion Media
	Public Officials
	Knowledge-Sector Industries
	Community Organizations
		High-Tech Firms/Industry Groups
		State Economic Development
		   Offices
		Technology Transfer Offices on
		   Campus

Key Actors	Tenured/Tenure-Track
	   Professors
	"Soft Money" Researchers
	Postdoctoral Researchers
		Top 1% of Scientists/Engineers
		Faculty Entrepreneurs
		Vice Chancellors for Economic
		   Development
		STEM Graduate Students/
		   Postdoctoral Researchers

Metrics	Publications Citations Academic Honors Research Grants Institutional Reputation	Patents Licenses Start-Ups Industry Cluster Formation

U.S. competitive positions in the face of this East Asian challenge (Berman 2012; Etzkowitz, Webster, and Healy 1998; Hackett 2000; Slaughter and Rhoades 1996).[2]

The problems of the economy created a policy window in which new ideas had an opportunity to gain a hearing. Beginning with the work of Robert Solow in the 1950s (1956, 1957), a series of economic studies had established that a very large residual in growth rates across countries remained after the main factors of production (land, labor, and capital) were taken into account. Solow had proposed that technical advance, broadly conceived, accounted for this residual. As policymakers puzzled over how to reverse sluggish growth, the Solow school's prescriptions gained a new hearing. In the late 1970s, a consensus began to form that the United States needed to shore up its "national innovation system." Economists such as Edward Denison (1985) presented evidence that Solow's "technical advance" could be divided into two components: technological innovation per se and contributions to human capital through increased schooling. Denison argued that technological innovation was about twice as important for producing growth as human capital development. The problem of sluggish growth had found a promising solution, and the race to stimulate new technologies through any means possible was on.

For Ronald Reagan's science advisor George Keyworth II, the isolation of American science from industry was a central failing of the American innovation system. In 1983, he wrote,

> American technological progress suffers badly from the artificial barriers between industry and the bulk of the basic research establishment. Most academic and federal scientists still operate in virtual isolation from the expertise of industry and from the experience and guidance of the marketplace. One can make a convincing case that this separation is a root cause of our sluggishness . . . in turning research into products. (1983, 1123)

The Business-Higher Education Forum, an organization comprised of corporate chief executive officers and presidents of leading universities, helped build a consensus for legislative changes that made possible the faster transfer of technology from universities to corporations and created more opportunities for universities in a wide range of for-profit activities surrounding intellectual property. The ideas discussed in the forum and other institutions[3] concerned about threats to U.S. economic power provided the foundations for key competitiveness legislation, the Bayh-Dole Act and Stevenson-Wydler Act of 1980, which encouraged universities and federal laboratories to license new technologies to private firms and allowed universities to retain equity interests in companies started by staff and students. The U.S. Council on Competitiveness, founded in 1986 and composed of CEOs, university presidents, labor leaders, and directors of national labs, provided research studies to support a continued policy emphasis on competitiveness. In a series of reports published in 1991, the council showed the slipping position of American industry in nine major sectors of the economy and in ninety different "critical technologies."

Democrat Bill Clinton (1992) also championed policies to harness university science and engineering to national competitiveness goals:

> Technology has accounted for the bulk of U.S. productivity gains during the past half-century, spawned entire new industries, created millions of jobs, and been a primary source of America's ability to maintain a high standard of living for its citizens. We are the world leaders in biotechnology, information technology, aerospace technology and many other fields on the frontiers of science applied to human life. As a result of intense international competition, however, the U.S. technology edge has eroded in some of our prominent industries. . . . The United States must act now to establish a technology policy that will help U.S. companies to succeed in world markets and help American citizens earn a good living in the global economy.

The breakthrough idea for universities was that the federal government and industrial leaders concluded that they could be used to intensify new technology discovery and thereby to fuel economic growth. This realization had been impeded for many years by the cultural gulf that separated academic scientists, whose outlook was oriented to the scientific community, and businesspeople, whose outlook was oriented to their firms and competitors. The support for academic innovationism quickly spread beyond the federal government to include the fifty states and virtually all research university campuses, as well as their industry partners. The dynamism associated with academic innovationism created a new centrality for universities based on their potential as engines of economic development.

Federal competitiveness policy unfurled in three waves. The objective of the first wave (1980–87) was the effort to foster the rapid diffusion of new technologies from universities and federal labs to industry by allowing universities and the federal labs to patent inventions and license them to industry, retaining the profits from these licenses for themselves. This first wave also fostered the development of cooperative research agreements between recipients of federal funds and private industry. These agreements encouraged and facilitated more extensive collaborations. The objective of the second wave (1992–98) was support for technology development in small business through small business research innovation grants. Many of these grants included academic researchers as consultants or co-developers. The third wave (2007 and beyond) cannot be characterized by a singular theme. Legislation emphasized improvements in science and technology education and investments in national priority research. The Obama administration greatly enhanced funding for big-science projects in identified priority areas such cancer research and clean energy. The idea of solving "grand challenges" of many types rippled through government and industry (for industry examples, see XPrize, n.d.).

IDEOLOGICAL INNOVATION

The waves of competitiveness policy were accompanied by new cultural frameworks supporting partnerships between universities, government, and industry.[4] Political economists use the term "corporatist" to describe joint decision-making bodies involving representatives from several institutional sectors, and I will use the term in this sense, rather than in the sense of decision making by corporations. The idea of building a national innovation system stirred the imagination of policymakers more than the careful academic analyses (see Nelson 1992) that attempted to understand the complexity of new technology development using case studies. Individuals working at the intersection of industry, government, and academe spoke with increasing assurance of the value of multiplying the forms of partnership that connected actors in the three spheres (see, e.g., Branscomb and Keller 1999), replacing the old style of European corporatism in wage setting (involving business, labor, and government) with a new style of corporatism in technological advance. Shortly after taking office in 1993, President Bill Clinton and Vice President Al Gore called for a shift in American technology policy toward an expansion of public investments in university partnerships with industry, precisely the position advocated by the new corporatists.

Not long after, Leydesdorff and Etzkowitz (1996) introduced a network theory of innovation in which expanding communications and changing expectations resulting from interactions between universities, governments, and industries—the "triple helix"—reshaped institutional relationships, while creating new "trilateral networks" and "hybrid organizations" capable of continuous innovation. As they interacted, Leydesdorff and Etzkowitz argued, individuals in each of the three "helices" learned to communicate in terms of each other's understandings and to take the role of one another "to a certain degree," creating "an endless transition" to new technological frontiers (Etzkowitz and Leydesdorff 2000, 119). In its vision of multiplying institutional fusions, the triple helix model can be interpreted as representing an apex of late twentieth-century utopian thought concerning the shared interests of industry, government, and academe. The actual results of these tripartite interactions were sometimes spectacularly successful, but, as I will show, many failed to match the theorists' dreams of corporatist-induced bounties.

MOBILIZATION IN THE FEDERAL AGENCIES

Most federal agencies had been mission oriented from the beginning, and some of the technologies they developed spilled over into commercial production. The Department of Defense was a leader in this area. The jet airliner, GPS, the Internet, semiconductors, and unmanned aerial vehicles are among the commercial technologies that had their origins in military research. The first computers were also built for military applications. Economic applications became much more important during the period. Yet the notion of a "regime change" toward competitiveness policy, as a substitute for national defense priorities, is not credible. National security (and treatment of diseases) remained the dominant concern of federal research policy. Instead competitiveness policy stood alongside the traditional aims of U.S. research policy and cross-cut these aims by encouraging technology transfer; cooperative ventures between government, universities, and industries; and the solution of high-profile problems through concerted scientific effort.

The new note was the mobilization of the federal basic science agencies— the National Science Foundation (NSF), the National Institutes of Health (NIH), and, later, the Department of Energy (DOE)—in support of competitiveness policy. At NSF, plans to open Engineering Research Centers to jump-start new technologies started under director Richard Atkinson in the late 1970s. Erich Bloch, Atkinson's influential successor, had served on a National Academy of Engineering Committee that offered NSF guidance on creating engineering research centers (ERCs). Bloch came from the world of corporate research as a top manager at IBM and held an unwavering conviction that academic science needed to become more like industrial science (NSF, n.d.). The first six ERCs were funded shortly after he arrived at NSF. As reported in his obituary, Bloch's support for large-scale centers was resisted by many academics: "Many feared that centers would siphon money from bread-and-butter research grants and were dubious of what they saw as industrial-scale science as antithetical to the traditional model of having a single investigator direct a few graduate students" (Mervis 2016b). ERCs grew rapidly, and they were soon followed by the still-larger Science and Technology Centers (STCs) that funded similar work in *all* fields that NSF supported. In the early 1980s, NSF also began to support Industry-University Cooperative Research Centers.

Center support continued to grow in the 1990s and 2000s. During the fiscal year 2002–3, for example, the NSF funded 275 research centers from a base budget of $365 million (with many additional millions going to the individual projects of scientists associated with the centers). These included 82 Information Centers, 34 Centers of Environmental Research, 33 Materials Research and Engineering Centers, 29 Chemistry Centers, 29 Plant Genome Virtual Centers, 20 Engineering Research Centers, 11 Interdisciplinary Science and Technology Centers, 8 Nano-scale Science and Engineering Centers, and 5 Physics Frontier Centers (Brint 2005). The 80 Industry-University Research Centers, the first of which were established in the Carter administration, required fees of $30,000 on average from industry partners. They supported 600 faculty members and 1,000 students, attracted 600 industry partners, and generated an annual budget of $60 million (Gray and Walters 1998, xvii). Even so, center funding remained under 10 percent of total NSF funding (calculated from NSF 2015, table 23).

Centers were funded on five-year awards. Many of the centers started strong but were not able to sustain their productivity. NSF began to shift funding in the direction of identified national priority initiatives with the announcement of the National Nanotechnology Initiative in 2000 (Roco 2011). The total center budget declined to $268 million by 2015. Cross-agency major initiatives, by contrast, totaled more than ten times as much, at nearly $3 billion. These included large-scale investments in networking and information technology (primarily for big data activities), nanotechnology, and climate change. Altogether, center grants and cross-agency initiatives constituted nearly half of the $7.4 billion NSF budget in FY 2015 (NSF 2016c).

The idea also took hold that basic science research should serve not only the interests of academic communities but broader social and economic purposes. The idea informally influenced panel decisions in the 1980s (NSF

1989). In 1997, NSF institutionalized the expectation that use-inspired research would become the norm when it simplified its review criteria to just two categories: intellectual merit and "broader impacts" (NSF 2007). In 2014, NSF director France A. Cordova summarized the position of the agency in words that sounded quite unlike those of Vannevar Bush: "As a public agency we need to stay relevant with those who entrust us with taxpayer funds" (NSF 2015, 3).[5]

The two other basic science agencies, the National Institutes of Health and the Department of Energy, also ramped up their efforts to fund research in the national interest, shifting dollars away from individuals and small teams working on problems of the disciplines and toward problems identified by national science leaders and agency heads as having the potential for fundamental breakthroughs and new therapies and technologies with commercial potential. NIH used its Common Fund as a primary mechanism for funding research in the national interest, while DOE focused on innovation hubs and other mechanisms to bring teams of researchers together to solve problems of energy distribution and storage, and new materials. (These initiatives are discussed in greater detail in chapter 6.)

THE STATES JOIN IN

The states joined the competitiveness bandwagon as early as 1983, with the founding of the first of the New York State Centers for Advanced Technology. The Georgia Research Alliance (GRA) was one of the most successful of these efforts. It was initiated in 1990 after Georgia lost its bid to host the Microelectronics and Computer Technology Consortium to a competitor with strong public-private organization in Austin. The program is organized around the recruitment of leading scientists at eight Georgia universities. GRA claims to have leveraged $600 million in state funding into $4 billion of direct federal and private investment, 150-plus new companies, and a large portfolio of inventions, processes, and technologies, as well as the development of more than 5,000 high-wage jobs (GRA 2010). Each of the eight strategic areas it identified was supported by at least five university researchers who had identified ties to firms in its focus area. These focus areas included: agricultural science and genomics, biomedical engineering and regenerative medicine, cancer and human genomics, computing and networks, electronics and optics, energy and environmental engineering, immunology and vaccines, and informatics and system biology (GRA, n.d.).

By 2015, the roster of the Eminent Scholars Academy included 63 university researchers. Several other states, including Louisiana, Missouri, Tennessee, and Utah, enacted Eminent Scholars programs on the Georgia model.

Centers of Excellence were another popular approach to stimulating economic growth through university-based research. One notable example comes from the country's largest state. The four California Institutes of Science and Innovation (Cal ISIs) were founded in 2000. Each is organized as a multicampus consortium, with a primary location at one of the University of California campuses. The institutes address distinct technologies: biotechnology in the case of the institute located primarily at UC San Francisco and UC Berkeley; computer and wireless technologies in the cases of the institutes located primarily at UC Berkeley and UC San Diego; and nanotechnology in the case of the institute located primarily at UC Santa Barbara. The institutes were funded by the state at $100 million each with the expectation of a 2:1 industry or federal government match. The CalIT2 information technology center, located primarily at UC San Diego, lists more than 130 corporate partners and an ambitious research agenda of "enabling technologies" in the interconnected fields of wireless communications, photonics, and cyberspace, as well as nanotechnology and micro-electro-mechanical systems. The institute develops "living laboratories" and research spaces to house multidisciplinary collaborations to facilitate the development of new technologies, systems, and expertise. CalIT2 leaders describe the institute as identifying the necessary expertise across the range of disciplines involved, forming teams typically including industrial representatives themselves, and applying the team to solving the problem posed by the client. CalIT2 faculty focus on "address[ing] industry's needs in a meaningful way" (CalIT2, n.d.). The quantitative biology center at UCSF has partnered with dozens of biomedical industries and has also given rise to several successful spin-off companies.

Every state maintained a profile in technology-based economic development. A report from the National Science Foundation (2016b) found that states were spending $2.2 billion on research and development programs. Five states—California, New York, Florida, Texas, and Ohio—accounted for more than 60 percent of the total, with some surprising states, such as New Mexico and Utah, also appearing in the top ten. As manufacturing industries have continued to experience decline, high-tech industry has risen as the hope of all states for improved economic fortunes. The old days of smokestack chasing through the provision of tax holidays and other benefits have been replaced or supplemented in many localities by the hope for seeding new technology clusters. These efforts are often still accompanied by tax benefits for relocating firms but they now placed universities in a much more central role as magnets for firm relocation and generators of technological breakthroughs that could be exploited for commercial value.

All states hoped to reproduce the successes of Silicon Valley and the Massachusetts High Tech Corridor along Route 128, at least in a limited way. To do so, some placed large bets on specific new technologies. These include broadband technologies through the Yamacraw Project (later the Georgia Electronic Design Center) organized by the Georgia Institute of Technology; stem cell therapies through the Institute for Regenerative Medicine in northern California and led by UC San Francisco; new materials research in the Albany Nanotech Corridor located adjacent to the State University of New York at Albany; and a variety of biosciences initiatives in Arizona whose leading force has been Arizona State University's Michael Crow (see Geiger and Sa 2008, 84–116).

CAMPUS INFRASTRUCTURES FOR INNOVATION

Following the passage of Bayh-Dole, every major research university added Offices of Technology Transfer to move inventions from campus quickly into the bloodstream of commerce. They helped faculty inventors with patenting and negotiated licenses so that companies could make use of these patents. Many also provided incubators and accelerators for faculty members who were considering starting companies of their own. "Pitch contests" became staples of campus life, involving not only faculty members but also graduate students and even undergraduates. Everyone with an idea that had commercial potential could find mentors on campus to help materialize the idea.

The sense of excitement about new opportunities was palpable in the words of university administrators. As a vice chancellor for research of a midlevel research university told me, "We try to allocate discretionary resources in thematic areas—nanotechnology, info technology, biotech, environment—the same as everyone." He was keenly interested in matching agency priorities to campus strengths: "Our materials research area is supported by NSF and Department of Defense. It emphasizes spin electronics and is led by the Department of Physics with support from engineering. We've had some spillover into the homeland sensors' bandwagon" (quoted in Brint 2005, 31–32). Many university managers began to describe academic departments as "silos" or "stovepipes" and criticized them for being too narrowly specialized to adapt to new research policy environments.

Outreach to industry was fostered both by federal agencies and by university administrators. When Wesley Cohen and his colleagues surveyed university campuses in the late 1990s, they found more than 1,100 university-industry research centers in operation, some supported by federal funds and others funded entirely by corporations and universities themselves. A widely emulated model was MIT's Polymer Processing Center, which had created a string of innovations for plastics degradability and improved manufacturing processes. Following Stanford's example, many universities also started affiliate programs to make faculty expertise available to firms willing to pay fees for access. Consultancies proliferated. By the late 1980s, relationships between academic researchers in the life sciences and private firms were pervasive; nearly half of 800 scientists surveyed by Blumenthal et al. (1986) said they consulted with firms, nearly one-quarter said they held industry contracts or grants, and 8 percent reported that they owned equity in a firm (see also Blumenthal et al. 1986).

Discipline-based scholars began to experience the push for interdisciplinarity as a competing project for advancing knowledge.[6] In its *Crossing Boundaries* report of 1988, Duke University was the first to pioneer the idea that interdisciplinarity should be central to the academic mission of research universities. In 1994, the University of Southern California vowed to develop a more "creative profile" by upgrading its curriculum by encouraging "innovative interdisciplinary research and education in selected areas that reflected the special characteristics of Southern California and Los Angeles" (notably, decentralized urbanism, cultural diversity, and technological innovations for the arts and entertainment industries). In its four-year assessment of its new strategic plan, the university committee wrote: "The most interesting and important problems facing society today are highly interdisciplinary. With our complementary research strengths, we have the potential to be a leader in addressing selected interdisciplinary problems of importance to society" (USC 1998, 7). In 1998, the University of Wisconsin-Madison launched the first large-scale cluster hiring program, including several, such as those in agricultural ecology and women's health, that brought in millions of dollars in new grants (see University of Wisconsin-Madison 2003, 2008). Through 2015, at least eighty-four universities had followed the University of Wisconsin's lead by introducing cluster hiring as a complement to traditional processes of departmental hiring. To a greater or lesser degree, each of these campuses was challenging the premises of academic professionalism.

The Fruits of Innovationism

The ethos of academic science revolving around the norms of communal sharing and responsibility, disinterestedness, and organized skepticism was articulated in classic form by the sociologist Robert K. Merton (1942).[7] The potential for violating these norms is clearly greater in entrepreneurial science than in publicly oriented science. A commercial stake in a discovery changes the dynamics of sharing characteristic of public science; sharing continues, but at a price. Most firms require delays in publication and data sharing to provide sufficient time for patent attorneys to make applications in cases of potentially valuable discoveries made using corporate funds. These restrictions have created secretive atmospheres in some university science and medical departments. Studies have found that a surprisingly low proportion of scientists disclosed potential conflicts of interest to editors of journals, even when they were required to do so (Krimsky and Rothenberg 2001). Others have found industry sponsorship to be significantly associated with pro-industry conclusions. Bekelman and his colleagues summarized the results of studies conducted on biomedical research through 2000 and concluded, "Strong and consistent evidence shows that industry-sponsored research tends to draw pro-industry conclusions" (Bekelman, Li, and Gross 2003, 463). In addition, a few spectacular cases of conflict of interest have periodically cast corporate sponsorship in a dim light. These cases involved pressure from companies to suppress findings that reflected poorly on their products (see, e.g., Krimsky 2003, 132–34; Washburn 2000, chap. 5). The scientific community has worked to contain these pressures through tougher disclosure policies, stricter contractual language in collaborative agreements, and wide dissemination of incidents of scientific fraud.

The tensions between scientific community norms and entrepreneurial science are matters for continuing concern and regulation. Yet these tensions do not, in my view, begin to overshadow the benefits of academics' work with industry. As I showed in chapter 1, drawing on the work of Cole (2009) and others, it does not take much investigation to find university researchers whose discoveries have transformed the quality of life while contributing to the creation of new firms that have brought millions (and occasionally billions) of dollars of new wealth to the United States. Such powerhouses of the American economy as Google and Broadcom began in academic research. Moreover, the pace of academic innovation shows few signs of slowing down and includes over the last decade alone the invention of CRISPR technology for the rapid editing of genomes, developed by the biochemists Jennifer Doudna (UC Berkeley) and Emmanuelle Charpentier (Max Planck Institute for Infection Biology) and first used to edit human cells by a team led by Feng Zhang of MIT. It also includes the extraordinary advance in computer power promised by quantum computing, conceptualized and designed by a team led by the Yale physicist Robert Schoelkopf.[8]

At the same time, for every technological breakthrough produced by university researchers it is not challenging to come up with two or three produced by entrepreneurs or in government and corporate research units. The Internet may have helped produce Jeffrey Bezos's Amazon, but his company created the complex networks of mechanization and distribution that made rapid delivery of merchandise on a grand scale possible. The government operates the satellites that allow global positioning systems to work, but private firms like Android and Magellan were the ones that put millions of GPS units in the hands of consumers. Apart from Linux, the operating systems that run personal computers were produced exclusively by private firms. The great majority of drugs on the market from Abilify to Zetia were developed by researchers in pharmaceutical firms, not in university laboratories. One might legitimately wonder whether cherry-picking the top results of academic innovationism gives entrepreneurial scientists more credit than they deserve relative to the behemoth of corporate R&D.

THE ROLE OF UNIVERSITIES IN 50 TOP INVENTIONS, 1955–2005

We can begin to gain a more balanced view of the role of academic researchers in innovation thanks to the magazine *Popular Mechanics* (*PM*), whose editors polled a group twenty-five experts about the fifty "top inventions" between 1955 and 2005 (see Hutchinson 2005). As far as I can tell, this is the only poll of multiple experts that has been published. One can debate the criteria and method used to identify these top inventions,[9] but I believe analysis of the inventions nevertheless provides insight as to the role of universities in important technological breakthroughs of the late twentieth and early twenty-first centuries.

In alphabetical order, the *PM* list of top inventions included: ARAPANET (the forerunner of the Internet), the Automatic Teller Machine (ATM), birth control pills, carbon-fiber composites, the cell phone, the charge-coupled device, communication satellites, the computer mouse, cordless tools (I included the lithium-ion battery as an essential element), coronary bypass surgery, digital music, DNA fingerprinting, electronic ignition, fiber optics, float glass, fuel cell vehicles, genetic engineering, genetic sequencing, the global positioning system (I included GPS receivers as an essential element), high-yield rice, HIV protease inhibitors, HTML (the mark-up language used initially on the World Wide Web), the hybrid electric car, the industrial robot, the integrated circuit, in vitro fertilization, the jet airliner, Kevlar, the laser beam, the light-emitting diode, the microwave oven, the MP3 player, the Magnetic Resonance Instrument (MRI), the music synthesizer, the pacemaker, the personal computer, polio vaccine, polymerase chain reaction (PCR), Prozac, the scanning tunneling microscope, the smoke detector, the Sony Walkman, superglue, the three-point seat belt, the television remote control, unmanned aerial vehicles, Velcro, video games, waffle-sole running shoes, and the World Wide Web.

In the study I sought to determine how important university researchers were in each discovery and invention.[10] I attended only to developments that occurred following the end of World War II in the spirit of the *PM* inquiry. I also set out to identify whether the contributions of university researchers were concentrated among those employed at the top fifty universities worldwide or whether these researchers were spread out among a wider range of universities. Finally, I was interested in whether university researchers were involved mainly at earliest upstream research stages or whether their involvement was common throughout the process of research and development.

Here's what I found: academic researchers were significantly involved in at least one stage (early research, refining research, or development) in three-quarters of the cases (37 of 50). I identified academic researchers as playing "the most important" role in 8 of the 50 cases: coronary bypass surgery, DNA fingerprinting, fuel cells, genetic engineering, genetic sequencing, in vitro fertilization, MRI, and the polio vaccine. I identified them as playing a "very important" role (competing with or working jointly with government, industry, and/or nonprofit researchers) in another 12 cases: ARAPANET, fiber optics, high-yield rice, HIV protease inhibitors, HTML, industrial robots, the laser beam, the MP3 player, the pacemaker, the personal computer, video games, and the World Wide Web. In addition, the first relatively crude version of the computer mouse was invented at SRI International, a nonprofit with very close ties to Stanford University and later perfected at nearby Xerox PARC.

Given that many of the inventions on the *PM* list are consumer products that have their origins in industrial research or the work of independent entrepreneurs, it is an impressive achievement for academic researchers to have contributed so significantly in 40 percent of the inventions. The achievement is more impressive given that investments in academic R&D have run between 0.2 percent and 0.4 percent of GDP in recent years (Kennedy 2012). Fourteen of the 50 inventions originated outside of the United States; nevertheless, these figures suggest how extraordinary the return on investment has been for U.S. academic science and engineering—a very small part of GDP yielding a sizable portion of important new technologies.

The findings of this research challenge some common perceptions about academic researchers' role in technological innovation. Contributions tended to come from a wide range of universities rather than only those that could be classified as in the top 50 worldwide. This was true, by my count, in 28 of the 37 cases in which academic researchers were involved in research or development of a *PM*-identified top 50 invention. For example, neither of the pioneers of the polio vaccine, Salk and Sabin, came from one of the most prominent research universities—the University of Pittsburgh in the case of Jonas Salk and the University of Cincinnati in the case of Albert Sabin. The inventor of DNA fingerprinting, Alec Jeffreys, worked at the University of Leicester in England. The touch screen for smartphones was invented by Wayne Westerman, a graduate student at the University of Delaware. One of the key researchers responsible for the development of high-yield rice, Yuan Longping, conducted his work at the obscure Southwest University in China. Nor were the contributions of university researchers concentrated primarily at the upstream, early research stage. Instead, the modal pattern is for university researchers to be involved at all stages in discovery and invention, except of course production. University researchers were as likely to be contributors at the development stage as at the early research stage.

In about 60 percent of the cases (29 of 50), I was able to identify that funding for research and/or development came from the U.S. federal government or a foreign government. Defense spending was arguably responsible for a higher proportion of breakthroughs than nondefense spending. Spin-offs from defense spending included the Internet, carbon fiber, the cell phone, communication satellites, the computer mouse, electronic ignition, fuel cells, the Global Positioning System, the jet airliner, military-grade Kevlar, the three-point seat belt, and unmanned aerial vehicles. (For further evidence on federal funding of major inventions, see Singer 2014.)

Many know the story of Herbert Boyer and Stanley Cohen, whose gene-splicing technology launched the biotechnology industry. But few know the stories of other academic researchers on this list whose discoveries and inventions have had large impacts on how we live. One is Alec Jeffreys, who discovered that the complex variable patterns in DNA could be used for genetic fingerprinting with applications to solving crimes, paternity contests, identification of twins, and conservation of human species. Another is the above-mentioned Yuan Longping, an agronomist laboring in southwest China who discovered the genetic heterosis in rice and thereby methods for reproducing high-yield hybrid rice. His work allowed China's total rice output to increase fourfold between 1950 and 2000. A few have won Nobel Prizes, including Richard Ernst, Paul Lauterbur, and Peter Mansfield (for the MRI) and Charles Townes (for the laser). Some like Robert Edwards (for in vitro fertilization), Vasilii Kolesov (for coronary bypass surgery), and Jonas Salk and Albert Sabin (for the polio vaccine) have helped create or save lives. Others like Tomislav Uzelac (the inventor of the first MP3 player) and Vinton Cerf (the co-inventor of the protocol for packet network interconnection underlying the Internet) have succeeded by making the world a far more interesting and enjoyable place.

Corporate researchers were the only actors more frequently involved than academic researchers in these high-profile inventions; they were involved in at least one stage 95 percent of the time (47 of 50 cases).[11] The great majority of corporate researchers who played key roles in discovery received graduate training at leading research universities. It is clear that without the outstanding graduate training they received, Gregory Pincus would not have made the synthesis that led to the birth control pill, Kary Mullis would not have discovered the polymerase chain reaction, and Gerd Binning and Heinrich Rohrer would not have invented the scanning tunneling microscope that has become essential to nanoscale research—to name just three of the dozens about which the same statement could be made.

THE MAGNETIC QUALITY OF STAR RESEARCHERS

The largest academic contributions to the national innovation system have come from star researchers who have either invented transformative processes or products or have seeded the creation of industrial clusters around the universities in which they work. Research by Lynne Zucker and Michael Darby has made this point through meticulous empirical study. In work that began with biotechnology but extended to six areas of science and technology, Zucker and Darby established that the location of star scientists and engineers in a U.S. region has a "consistently significant and quantitatively large positive effect" on the probability of firm entry in the same region and area of science and technology (Zucker and Darby 2014, 137; see also

Zucker and Darby 1996; Zucker, Darby, and Brewer 1998; Zucker, Darby, and Armstrong 2002).[12] The effect of star scientists on firm entry was significant in four of the six science areas studied, with semiconductors and computing being the exceptions (Zucker and Darby 2014).[13] The effect of the personal presence of these star scientists and engineers—the top 1 percent of all scientists and engineers—was much greater than other possible university influences on firm location (such as volume of highly cited publications or patent volume). Moreover, star scientists tended to concentrate in universities where many other star scientists were employed, creating "agglomeration effects" that help initiate and maintain high-tech clusters. These findings held after controls for total population and the average wage of workers in the region. At the same time, star scientists were clearly only one draw for new and relocating high-tech firms.[14] The effects of population size and average wage were quite a bit larger than the effects of star scientists (see Zucker and Darby 2014, table 2).

THE PUSH TO DEVELOP INDUSTRIAL CLUSTERS

The seeding of new industrial clusters by university research was another signal achievement of the era. "Industrial cluster" is the term used to describe a geographic concentration of interconnected companies and institutions in a particular field (Porter 1998). Much of the economy—from Hollywood to Wall Street—is organized in these agglomerations of firms working in the same business. "Old economy" theories of regional economic development emphasized the importance of large anchoring firms, market creation, and state support through tax breaks and infrastructure support. "New economy" theories focus on the generation of clusters of firms focusing on similar or related technologies and generated, in large part, by accessibility to leading university researchers and, perhaps more importantly, by the students they train.[15]

The technology clusters produced in large part by proximity to Stanford and the Massachusetts Institute of Technology (MIT) are the *ur* cases that other regions have hoped to emulate. Stanford has kept track of the companies the members of its community have founded since Hewlett-Packard began in 1939. By 2010, these numbered over 5,000 and included several of the largest companies in the country: Cisco Systems, Google, Hewlett-Packard, Sun Microsystems, E-bay, and Agilent Technologies. The 53 largest firms generated sales totaling more than $267 billion, or nearly half of the total reported by the top 150 firms in Silicon Valley. The same 53 reported income totaling more than $34 billion, or 40 percent of the total income of the top 150 in Silicon Valley. The total market capitalization of these firms was nearly $650 billion—and of course just a fraction of the capitalization of all firms whose founders had at one time or another been affiliated with Stanford (Stanford University, n.d.).

The accomplishments of MIT have been still more impressive. According to research funded by the Ewing Marion Kauffman Foundation, as of 2014 MIT alumni had founded tens of thousands of firms. The rate of founding accelerated during the 1980s and 1990s and the age of founders declined (Roberts, Murray, and Kim 2016). Nearly one-third of the companies founded by MIT alumni have been located in Massachusetts—a principal reason why Massachusetts often ranks first on lists of the leading technology states (Milken Institute 2016). The fruits of university-based innovation have included the founding of such successful firms as Akamai Technologies, Biogen, Delphi Communications, and Genome Therapeutics by Cambridge-based faculty entrepreneurs (BankBoston 1997, 2003).

Technological innovation concentrated in geographical regions has spill-over effects (Krugman 1991; Moretti 2013). Those working in the innovation economy want to be surrounded by others they find stimulating and from whom they may be able to obtain valuable advice and referrals. This is an important reason why tech firms are regionally concentrated, even though land and rental prices are much higher than could be found in outlying areas (Bresnahan, Gambarella, and Saxenian 2001; Lucas 1988; Moretti 2013). Moreover, profitable, innovative companies clearly produce spillover effects on the earnings and quality of life of less educated workers. Everything from haircuts to restaurants costs more in cities like San Francisco and Seattle that have high-tech dominated economies, creating more jobs and higher standards of living for those who supply these services (Moretti 2013).[16]

In addition to the well-known cases of Silicon Valley and Route 128 outside Boston (O'Mara 2005; Saxenian 1994), prominent examples of industrial clusters include Research Triangle Park in North Carolina (Link and Scott 2003; Weddle, Rooks, and Valdecanas 2006); the Northwest Austin Tech and Start-Up Corridor also known as "Silicon Hills" (O'Brien 2016; Zimmerman 2013); the Ann Arbor Life Sciences Corridor (Paytas, Gradek, and Andrews 2004); Silicon Beach outside of Los Angeles (Gammon 2016); San Diego's telecommunications and biotechnology clusters (Casper 2014; Walshok and West 2014); and Silicon Alley in New York City (Metz 2012; Zabusky 2015). Some other university-led developments can be found sprinkled around the country, including in Boulder, Colorado, where the

University of Colorado has generated nearly 100 tech start-ups in aerospace, bioscience, information technology, and clean energy (Boulder Economic Council 2017), and Seattle, where the University of Washington is now beginning to become an important player in the high-tech community that grew up around Microsoft, Boeing, and Amazon (Haug 1995; Partovi 2015).

The University of Utah presents a striking case of university leadership in cluster formation. Located in Salt Lake City, a small city of under 200,000 (and not among the 100 largest cities in the United States), the university was the leading producer of patents in the region during the period 2009–13. In the two decades between the mid-1990s and mid-2010s, University of Utah researchers spun off 180 companies, the ninth highest rate in the country, according to state statistics (UStar 2017). The patents and companies produced by the University of Utah helped create regional clusters in information technology, aerospace, medical devices, and biopharmaceuticals (CMP 2017). In 2006, the state government pledged $180 million in support for hiring eminent scholars interested in commercialization and for setting new priorities for future technology-based development in the areas of medical therapies, clean energy, and sensor technologies (UStar 2017).

Nearly all of these successful new-economy developments began around anchor firms or industrial consortia that attracted other firms to the area. The Research Triangle Park in North Carolina is a canonical case. By 2013, the Park housed 170 companies employing more than 39,000 full-time researchers (RTP Media Resources 2013). But these impressive accomplishments depended on initial investments of the state and local business communities to build infrastructure and sponsor firm recruitment activities. The idea to build around university research was part of the plan from the beginning, but large organizations created the anchors around which sustainable development eventually occurred (Link and Scott 2003; Luger and Goldstein 1991). The results were far from immediate. Six years after the founding of the Park, IBM announced that it would locate a 400-acre research facility in the Park. Also in 1965, the U.S. Department of Health, Education, and Welfare decided to locate its new $70 million National Environmental Health Science Center at the Park (Weddle, Rooks, and Valdecanas 2006). A decade later, in 1974, the three local research universities (Duke University, the University of North Carolina-Chapel Hill, and North Carolina State University) set up the Triangle Universities Center for Advanced Study, designed to create an environment in which faculty and students could collaborate with the Park's scientists and engineers. This addition contributed to the Park's solvency and its power to attract new firms, but it occurred fully twenty years after the initial idea for the Park was proposed by a local financier.

Many other industrial clusters received jump starts with an infusion of government cash, as in the case of the $1.5 million in investment funds generated by the state and local businesspeople that attracted the first tenants to Research Triangle Park (Link and Scott 2003) and of New York City's much later and much larger $400 million investment in Silicon Alley (Metz 2012). Leading universities in regions built on "new-economy" industries may not be remotely close to top performers in technology patents and yet contribute centrally to regional economic development because of high-value patents or spin-offs. Stanford University, for example, produced some 6,500 fewer patents than Google between 2009 and 2013, but, after all, its computer science program gave rise to Google in the first place. The same is true for UCLA, a prolific producer of patents but far behind the leader in its region, Broadcom, whose founder was, however, at one time a professor at UCLA.

The Ecology of Innovation

The disproportionate importance of star scientists leads to questions about the other instruments of academic innovationism. Have academic patenting and licensing, academic start-ups, industry-university research centers, or campus interdisciplinary initiatives contributed as much as expected to the strength of "the national innovation system"? If we look at the instruments of competitiveness policy as part of an ecology of innovation, the record is stronger than if we look at them as a rival to the contributions of researchers in the private sector. That is because the contributions of the latter remain far more important to economic development.

The contributions of universities do not primarily lie, as many believe, in the patents and licenses generated by university offices of technology transfer or in the start-up companies founded on the basis of campus discoveries. Instead, they lie in the diverse relationships that scientists and engineers have formed with industry. These include: research collaborations, consultancies, training of graduate students, and in some cases overseeing industry-wide improvements through open science collaborations. Perhaps most important of all is the capacity of industry-based scientists to draw on the research literature produced by academics to advance the development of new technologies with commercial potential.

PATENTS, LICENSES, AND START-UPS

At the time of the passage of the Bayh-Dole Act in 1980, U.S. universities were generating fewer than 300 patents a year (Slaughter and Rhoades 1996). In 2014, they generated nearly 6,000, a twentyfold increase. The rate of patenting increased dramatically following the passage of the America COMPETES Act in 2007; patents in biotechnology, medical technology, organic fine chemistry, computer technology, semiconductors, and clean energy all increased significantly (National Science Board 2016, figure 5-38). But their contribution pales in comparison to the activity generated by private firms. University-owned patents accounted for just 4 percent of all U.S. patents awarded, for example, in 2014 (see figure 3.1).

Universities' contributions to new inventions can be placed in a stronger light if we look at citations to work in approved patents. The front pages of patent applications include key citations, and this work can be considered an important way that research contributes to the development of inventions. In 2013, more than 300,000 science and engineering articles were cited in U.S. approved patents. (Some of these articles are cited by multiple patent seekers.) Among those citing U.S.-based work, academic citations dominated, representing nearly two-thirds of the total and more than 205,000 articles (calculated from National Science Board 2016, appendix table 5-64).

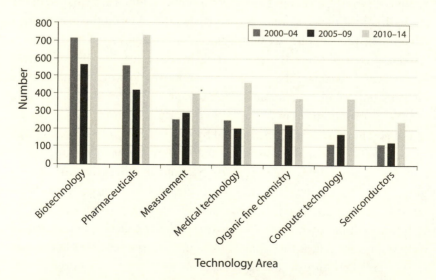

FIGURE 3.1. U.S. Academic Patents, by Technology Areas, Selected Five-Year Averages. *Source*: National Science Foundation, Science and Engineering Indicators (2012).

In an early study of the role of academic citations on technology development, Narin, Hamilton, and Olivastro (1997) found that cited U.S. papers on approved patents were "from the mainstream of modern science." Most were findings from basic research, published in influential journals, authored by professors at leading universities, relatively recent in appearance, and supported by grants from NSF, NIH, and other federal R&D agencies. Citations to U.S. articles in 2014 patents were dominated by biological sciences, medical sciences, computer science, engineering, physics, and chemistry. These six fields accounted for 98 percent of the total citations (National Science Board 2016, figure 5-35).

Nor are the data on university-owned licenses and start-ups particularly impressive when compared to the contributions of the private sector. In fact, only about 16,000 revenue-generating licenses were active in university offices of technology transfer in 2014 (National Science Board 2016, appendix table 5-68), a considerable increase over time but a drop in the bucket relative to new commercial activity in the economy as a whole. The group of universities that generated revenue through technology transfer is also surprisingly small. In 2014, only six universities earned $100 million or more in licensing revenue. All six were large, wealthy institutions (Northwestern University, New York University, Princeton University, Columbia University, the University of California system, and Stanford). The seventh in rank, the University of Texas system, earned $49 million. The net returns to the institutions were much lower once legal fees, other expenses, and receipts to faculty inventors were deducted from earnings. The University of California, for example, earned approximately $108 million on licensing revenue in 2014 but netted just $58 million. This net amount represented about 0.2 percent of UC's $26 billion operating budget (Gordon 2015). Figure 3.2 reports cumulative licenses executed and cumulative licensing income from 1991 through 2015. Note that licensing income stagnated relative to the continued growth in licensed technologies.

Universities like Northwestern, Columbia, Princeton, MIT, and Stanford and New York University, the University of California system, the University of Texas-Austin, the University of Wisconsin-Madison, and the University of Washington-Seattle usually topped the annual licensing income lists (National Academies 2011b, chap. 1). For these elite institutions, entrepreneurial success created another, if comparatively nominal, income stream on top of endowment and tuition revenues. Only a few of the significant income producers in entrepreneurial science, such as Wake Forest and the University of South Florida, stood outside the group of top research universities.

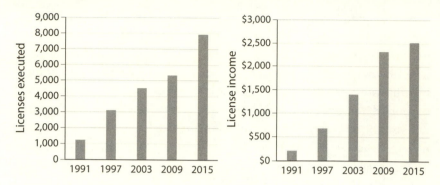

FIGURE 3.2. Cumulative Licenses Executed and Cumulative Licensing Income, 1991–2015 (in millions).

Source: Adapted from Association of University Technology Managers (AUTM), 1991–2015.

In 2001, there were fewer than 2,000 operational university-generated start-ups with formations of about 400 a year. In 2013, the number of start-ups had doubled to nearly 4,000 and annual formations had also grown to more than 750 (National Science Board 2016, appendix table 5-68). This rate of formation is obviously a sizable increase, but it represented approximately 0.2 percent of the more than 410,000 start-ups with at least one employee and business activity for more than a year counted in 2012 by the U.S. government sources and reported by the Ewing Marion Kauffman Foundation (Fairlie et al. 2015). Google, with its worldwide influence, tens of thousands of employees, and hundreds of billions of capitalization, is the limiting case. Stanford held equity in the company started by two of its graduate students but sold the equity for $336 million in 2005, shortly after the initial public offering, to avoid conflict of interest. A few of the other university start-ups, such as Broadcom and Akamai Technologies, have generated businesses with thousands of employees and hundreds of millions of dollars in revenue. But hundreds and perhaps thousands more nonacademic start-ups have achieved these benchmarks of business success.

Birch Bayh and Robert Dole imagined that incentives to capitalize on the knowledge that resulted from federal funding of basic research would, in Dole's words, no longer "delay innovations and deny the benefits of further development, disclosure, exploitation and commercialization to the American people" (Dole 2006). The act was successful, but it did not transform academe. Professors continued to excel in the ways that they had long excelled, by producing research that corporations and entrepreneurs discovered had applications to the development of new technologies. The primary objective continued to be to advance knowledge, not to generate marketable technologies. Technology transfer was intended to be a public service more than a revenue enhancement activity, and that is precisely where its value lay. Most university technology transfer offices operated in the red (Loise and Stevens 2010). Those that made money were typically buoyed by a very small number of "big hits," such as Northwestern University's compound to ease neuropathic pain and the improved strawberry UC Davis plant scientists developed (Gordon 2015).

CORPORATE ANCHORS AND REGIONAL DEVELOPMENT

Nor are the roles that universities play in regional economic development well understood. Those writers who emphasized the centrality of business and engineering deans in the creation of industrial clusters usually had the origin story backward. This is evident even in the most famous case of all. It is true that Stanford Engineering dean Fred Terman was central to the development of Silicon Valley, but he was not the progenitor. Sensing opportunity, Terman sent out faculty members to learn about semiconductors from the leading firm in the industry at the time, Fairchild Semiconductors. He also made contacts with another important Valley firm, Hewlett-Packard. His scouts returned with the knowledge that allowed Terman to organize graduate programs in computer and software engineering, developing the seeds for cluster development (O'Mara 2005, chap. 3).

Indeed, most of the successful university-connected clusters grew out of the R&D activities of anchor firms or consortia. This was the pattern also in Austin, where the semiconductor technology consortium SEMATECH fostered cluster development (Anderson 1988); in Seattle, where Microsoft and Amazon were the major initial attractors of high-tech talent (Partovi 2015); and in San Diego, where Hybritech and later Eli Lilly set the creative pace in biotechnology and Qualcomm anchored developments in telecommunications (Walshok and West 2014). Substantial state investment has been a second source of cluster formation, as the cases of Austin, Research Triangle Park, and Silicon Alley illustrate.

Neither world-class science nor streams of doctoral students were sufficient to generate industrial clusters. In addition to the existence of major firms that served as anchors for future cluster development, the most important factors appear to have been the availability of venture capital, alignment of university programs with existing industry concentrations, a developed transportation infrastructure, and a skilled labor force (Allen and

O'Shea 2014; Fitzgerald and Leigh 2002; Lyanages 2006; Porter 1998).[17] Venture capital was highly concentrated in the leading tech cities—San Francisco, Boston, Seattle, San Diego, and Raleigh-Durham (Wu 2005; Chen et al. 2010)—and even some of the strongest university performers oriented toward industrial applications, such as Georgia Tech, have had to look outside of their home state for venture capital funds (Georgia Institute of Technology 2007).

Even so, by the mid-2000s, virtually every major research university had created innovation centers with the idea of generating start-ups and, if possible, industrial clusters. A large literature exists on the success stories. Less is known about those that failed to leverage the research prowess of academic scientists. Large investments in the high-tech corridor along Route 315 failed to yield strong results in Columbus, Ohio, the home of the Ohio State University (Montieth 2010). Nor did those along route I-99 near Pennsylvania State University (Hamill 2008) or those for Progress Research Park or Innovation Square in Gainesville, the home of the University of Florida (McDuffie 2012). Modest successes were far more common than the urban transformations envisioned by "new-economy" visionaries. The University of Minnesota generated a small medical devices cluster (Puri et al. 2011) with fewer than 40 companies listed as of 2014 (Bizlistr 2014). University of Wisconsin administrators and faculty worked hard to generate a Health Tech cluster but had yielded only 43 companies by 2015 (Engel 2015). After hundreds of millions of dollars in state investment, Yale's much-heralded Bioscience Cluster had produced approximately 60 firms by 2016 (Seay 2016).

Some top research universities showed little, if any, significant impact on new firm formation in their cities and regions. Johns Hopkins University represented a famous and well-studied case. Hopkins is the university with the highest annual levels of federal R&D support (counting its applied physics laboratory, which closely resembles a federal research and development lab), but it failed to contribute significantly to the generation of new firms, much less industrial clusters, in its home city of Baltimore. University scientists, oriented toward the system of academic professionalism and the Department of Defense, chose to remain largely enclosed within their professional communities and federal patron circles rather than interacting with the city of Baltimore, which many regarded warily because of its low-skilled labor force and persistent urban problems (Feldman 1994; Feldman and Desrochers 2004).

Other prestigious private universities continued to pursue "truth for its own sake" more avidly (or more effectively) than a regional economic contribution. Though representatives of the universities may dispute my assessment, I categorize Boston University, Emory University (apart from its medical complex), the University of Chicago, Princeton University, and Vanderbilt University among this group of universities with limited entrepreneurial success.[18] Others expressed great interest in economic development but failed to generate a proportional impact. The University of Pennsylvania tried for many years to generate momentum for high-tech jobs in Philadelphia but had limited success due to persistent town-gown conflict and protest over Penn's real estate ventures (O'Mara 2005, chap. 4; see also University of Pennsylvania 2014, 2015). Quite a few other institutions—including Cornell University, Indiana University, Pennsylvania State University, the University of Florida, the University of Illinois, and the University of Massachusetts-Amherst—were hampered by their locations in remote rural areas and inadequate transportation networks to major sources of venture capital.[19] Largely unsuccessful in building up the greater Syracuse area (see Cornell University 2011), Cornell decided to look for economic impact (and new opportunities) in New York City, founding Cornell Tech with the Technion University of Israel in 2012 (Cornell Tech 2017).

My analysis of data collected by the Harvard Business School's Cluster Mapping Project indicates that thirty of the top 40 universities in the United States were among the leading producers of patents in their regions during the period 2009–13. In five cases (the University of Wisconsin, the University of Illinois, the University of Florida, the University of Utah, and Pennsylvania State University), they were *the* top producers of patents in their regions. But in each of these cases, except the University of Utah, the economic composition of the region has not aligned well with the patenting of university researchers. I found a moderately high correlation ($r = .47$) between the median income of economic areas and the gap between the number of university patents and that of the most active patent awardee in the region. In wealthy regions, large firms produce the most patents and, however active universities may be, they typically run well behind the leading firms. The opposite tends to be true in economically depressed regions; universities are more likely to be among the leaders in patenting. These tend to be agricultural or traditional manufacturing regions that have not yet joined the "knowledge economy."

BIDIRECTIONAL INFLUENCES

Research on universities' contributions to regional growth has moved away from a focus on the unidirectional movement from university-based research into firm-based production and now emphasizes the bidirectionality of influences between universities and firms and the ways that preexisting regional organizational environments influence the interests of university researchers (Kenney and Mowery 2014; Powell et al. 2005). Bidirectionality takes many forms: in some cases, university researchers consult with firms whose scientists are interested in exploiting the tacit knowledge they have attained in the course of their work. In other cases, corporate researchers spend what amount to sabbaticals in university laboratories to gain skills that can translate into product development. Established firms or consortia can help fuel university research agendas, as happened when the Microelectronics and Computer Technology Corporation (a consortium of computer industry companies) and SEMATECH (a consortia of semiconductor technology companies) located in Austin, Texas, in the 1980s, after successful courtships by Austin and Texas business and civic leaders. These consortia created close ties with both the business and engineering schools at UT.

From these studies it is clear that university researchers also adapt to the opportunities in their environments. Comparisons of the contributions of University of California researchers to new communications technologies show the extent to which environment shapes opportunity. UC Berkeley capitalized on its nearby location to Silicon Valley and focused on silicon integrated circuits. UCLA, by contrast, fed off the defense industries in Southern California and developed strengths in broadband communications chips. A later developer, UC Santa Barbara faculty concentrated on semiconductors using materials other than silicon, a field not yet fully occupied by other researchers (Kenney and Mowery 2014, 14; Lecuyer 2014). Similarly, a study of biotechnology in two California regions emphasized the role of managerial entrepreneurialism in the aftermath of Eli Lilly's purchase of one of the original San Diego biotechnology firms and the role of firms in "pulling in" leading scientists. Lacking the entrepreneurial networks encircling Lilly, UC San Francisco compensated by creating an entrepreneurial culture that attracted biotechnology firms to its researchers (Casper 2014).

The wine industry in California provides an illuminating example of the importance of the potential of open science collaborations. When fruit disease wiped out the existing rootstocks, growers in Napa County began to look to UC Davis researchers to create conditions for more resilient grapes and the higher-quality wine the American public was beginning to support. A long tradition of agricultural extension, dating from the Morrill Acts, created the conditions for industry-wide concerns. Davis scientists shared their research on the qualities of grape varieties and rootstocks with local growers, as well as their findings on canopy and irrigation management. The first analytical laboratory was not established by UC Davis but rather by a French-trained winemaker who had relocated to Napa in the 1940s. He organized the Napa Valley Technical Group as a forum for sharing technical information learned from experiments. The group became a forum for UC Davis viniculturalists and enologists to share the fruits of their research with firm representatives. Patenting and licensing would only have slowed the dissemination of valuable research findings; the open science model adopted in Napa made continuous cross-regional improvement possible (Lapsley and Sumner 2014). Davis researchers, funded in part by the wine growers, ran experiments on trellising, vine spacing, and pruning levels. Later experiments examined such practices as shoot thinning, leaf removal, and timing of hedging for their effects on wine quality and led to the discovery of the value of limiting the water to vines now referred to as "deficit irrigation." The researchers also developed new technologies to quantify light penetration and to predict wine quality. As Lapsley and Sumner wrote, "University research was unraveling the relationship between grape environment and wine quality" (199). The involvement of Davis agricultural scientists with the wine industry paid off handsomely for the campus, too, in the form of donations of new buildings, such as the Mondavi Center for the Performing Arts, and other contributions to campus fund-raising campaigns.

The Napa case is a reminder that collegiality can yield collective advantages that commercialism cannot offer. Open innovation communities, like that found in the wine industry, very often work more efficiently than proprietary communities. Imagine how different the world would have been if Tim Berners-Lee and his colleagues had developed the World Wide Web for commercial gain rather than as a public resource. We might find that every bit of information retrieval would bring a small charge against our Internet account, pricing many out of the information market. Or imagine how few bugs and how little expensive obsolescence users would have had to endure if the major commercial operating systems for computers were developed as public resources rather than for private gain. Open innovation communities have produced strong results in source software, gene transfer technologies, medical innovation, and of course encyclopedia publishing (Goetz 2003). However, these communities typically require a strong integrating organization to mobilize volunteers and to avoid the dangers of fragmentation, balkanization, and diverging standards (Fleming and Waguespack 2007).

Recurrent Obstacles

The most important obstacles limiting the achievements of academic innovators are the relatively short time horizons and budgetary pressures experienced by state and industry partners. In all but the wealthiest or most
committed of the fifty states, contributions to university-based technology
development initiatives have been too low or too unstable to reproduce
the impacts of standout programs like the Georgia Research Alliance.[20]
Pressures on state budgets have made low-achieving university R&D funds
attractive targets for reduction or elimination in many states. The Ohio Edison Technology Centers, founded in 1984 and supported by the State of
Ohio's economic development authority, were a notable example as one
of the first of the state-supported tech business services programs. In early
incarnations, the regional centers played a "bridging role" linking academic
research and industry (Braunerhjelm and Carlsson 1999). The Edison Centers were cut back dramatically in the late 1990s and terminated in the early
2010s. Similarly, in states such as Maryland and Illinois, large investments
in technology-based economic development programs were curtailed when
reports showed lackluster performance or weak returns on investment (Ad
Hoc Committee 2010; Riggle and Stough 2003). In Texas, suspicions arose
that the new technology investment fund of Governor Rick Perry was being
use to reward campaign contributors, and the program was scrapped when
a new governor was elected.

Work with industry is always challenging for universities owing to firms'
restrictions on open science, their short time horizons, and their changing priorities. As Roger Geiger and Creso Sa have noted, "For universities,
the tenuous nature of industry commitments represent[s] the weak reed
of [partnerships]" (2008, 60). Industry too has often failed to achieve the
gains it has hoped to make from large-scale investment in university research. When Novartis signed a $25 million contract with the Department
of Plant and Microbial Biology at UC Berkeley for the rights to discoveries
with commercial potential, faculty members criticized the contract on the
grounds that it seemed like a corporate takeover of the department. But Novartis licensed only two discoveries during its five-year association with the
department, and the agreement ended benefiting the Berkeley department
far more than the much-maligned company (Price and Goldman 2002). Similarly, BP provided funds for a new building on the Berkeley campus and for
rights to collaborate with Berkeley scientists over a five-year period, but the
gains seem again to have enriched the university more than the firm, and BP

ended the relationship after the first five-year contract elapsed. An argument can be made that relatively small fees for center affiliate status have served corporations better than large-scale investments, but even those small fees have proven difficult to sustain in the absence of perceived value-added for access to cutting-edge researchers.

In spite of these persistent difficulties, some university-industry research centers have shown spectacular results, as in the canonical case of the Polymer Processing Center at MIT, which contributed major improvements in the compounding process for chemicals used in plastics, manmade fibers, adhesives, surface coatings, and many other products. The Mid-America Earthquake Center headquartered at the University of Illinois main campus is another well-documented case of multilevel success. It has contributed new geotechnical engineering designs and sensing equipment while greatly increasing the scientific research output of participants as compared to their earlier career achievements (Ponomariov and Boardman 2010). Nevertheless, data on NSF-funded interdisciplinary research centers suggest high levels of variability in the accomplishments of centers involving both academics and industry researchers. Academics want primarily to publish research results and to train students and postdocs, while industry partners want to make practical advances that will help their firms in the marketplace. Such potentially incommensurate goals can lead to persistent difficulties in collaboration (P. Craig Boardman, personal communication).

The same variability emerges in the case of campus-based interdisciplinary centers. Geiger and Sa (2008, chap. 5) provided examples of interdisciplinary centers in the life sciences that delivered a stream of breakthrough science discoveries. These include Bio X at Stanford, computational biology at Berkeley, genomics at Duke, and life sciences technology at Cornell. Some cluster hiring initiatives have also done well. At the University of Wisconsin-Madison, the agro-ecology cluster, for example, had produced more than 100 publications and $6.5 million in external grants by 2015 (Patton 2015), and the women's health cluster has been credited with multiple improvements in medical practice (Greenberger 2002).

But interdisciplinary centers and hires run into problems when intellectual and organizational leadership is lackluster, when a common focus for collaborative work does not exist, and when researchers have independent sources of funds that make deep engagement in the work of the group less attractive than full commitment. Diana Rhoten (2004) studied six interdisciplinary research centers and found that none was producing breakthrough collaborative work. Instead, the typical pattern was for researchers to conduct their respective pieces of the research "in near isolation from one another." She also reported that 30 percent of the researchers felt that interdisciplinary research had not helped their careers. The centers typically lacked a well-defined problem definition and consequently became a "nexus of loosely connected individuals searching for intersections, as opposed to cohesive groups tackling well-defined problems" (9). Geiger and Sa (2008, 116) reported that only two of thirteen interdisciplinary initiatives launched by Duke University in 2001 were still on the books five years later. Similarly, in recent years USC, another early proponent, pulled back on the interdisciplinary initiatives it launched in the mid-1990s because of the failure of many of them to gel (William Tierney, personal correspondence). In a few cases, interdisciplinary hiring initiatives have turned into full-blown fiascos due to poor planning, disorganized processes, and lack of sufficient consultation with deans and departments prior to launch (see, e.g., McMurtrie 2016).

The most illuminating studies of interdisciplinary hiring so far have been conducted by the Stanford sociologist Daniel McFarland and his colleagues. McFarland and his colleagues were given full access to Stanford records over several decades. They found that those who were hired in interdisciplinary clusters took longer to publish and were more likely to not receive tenure or to leave the university, even if they did receive tenure (Evans 2016). The most productive clusters were built around one or two existing highly productive scholars who were capable of mobilizing the energy and talents of the group around leading-edge research questions (Dahlander and McFarland 2013; Rawlings et al. 2015). Interdisciplinary clusters that included researchers who had published together or cited each other's work extensively prior to cluster formation had a higher probability of success (Dahlander and Mc-Farland 2013; Rawlings and McFarland 2011). And interdisciplinary initiatives in natural science and engineering fields had a better record of success than those in social science related fields where the team science approach is less familiar and not yet a dominant feature of academic production (Daniel McFarland, personal communication).

Capturing Lightning in a Bottle

The innovation system has as yet neither displaced nor overshadowed the discipline- and department-based university. Indeed, the most commercially successful academics have usually been among the best published and most highly cited researchers on campus. Stanford biosciences professor Leroy Hood is an outstanding example of this dual eminence. Hood invented a much faster process for gene sequencing, an invention that contributed significantly to mapping the human genome. In addition to this singular invention, he has published 750 papers, has been awarded 36 patents, has held 17 honorary degrees, and has received more than 100 major awards and honors. He is one of 15 people to have been elected to all three National Academies—Science, Engineering, and Medicine. He also founded or cofounded 15 biotechnology companies including Amgen and Applied Biosystems (Institute for Systems Biology 2017). MIT professor Robert S. Langer, a pioneer in drug delivery technology and tissue engineering, is an even more astonishing example of dual eminence. Langer is likely the most widely cited engineer of all time. He was the youngest person to be elected to all three National Academies, and he has been the recipient of more than 220 major scientific awards. He has also been involved in the founding of at least 25 companies, many based on one of his more than 800 patents. His lab at MIT manages $10 million in annual grants and employees as many as 100 researchers (Langer Lab 2017; Seligson 2012).

These exceptional individuals differ only in degree from many other star scientists. Among the fascinating findings of the Zucker-Darby research on academic stars is the degree of entrepreneurialism typical of the 5,400 scientists and engineers included in their study base. Remember, these are people who stand in the top one-half to 1 percent of highly cited researchers in their fields; they are the most eminent people in their fields as defined by the standards of academic professionalism. Nearly three-quarters (72 percent) had identified a relationship with at least one firm at some point in their career, through copublication and/or patent assignment. More than three-fifths of their patents were filed with a firm and only 11 percent listed a university among the patent assignees. The conflict between academic professionalism, as indicated by very high citation counts, and academic innovationism, as indicated by firm relationships, simply does not exist for most of the scientists in the Zucker-Darby database (see Zucker and Darby 2014).

Along similar lines at the institutional level, Cynthia Carr and I found that universities and medical schools that experienced the greatest upward mobility in publication and citation counts were often those closely associated with entrepreneurial science. The University of California-San Francisco, the University of California-San Diego, the M. D. Anderson Medical School, the Georgia Institute of Technology, and Arizona State University were among these upwardly mobile, highly entrepreneurial institutions (Brint and Carr 2017).

The most important reason for the compatibility between academic professionalism and academic entrepreneurship has to do with the verification of discoveries. Even if they are primarily interested in commercial opportunities, most scientists must publish to make sure that they are not wrong about their discoveries. Accurate science requires feedback from specialists drawn from among the world's leading authorities, something that obviously is not possible within the confines of proprietary research. The race to discover the HIV protease inhibitor provides a valuable example of how dangerous it can be to be wrong. Three teams were working simultaneously on the problem: Thomas Blundell's group at Birkbeck College in England; Alex Wlodawer's group at the U.S. National Cancer Institute; and a group led by Manuel Navia at Merck Pharmaceuticals. In February 1989, the Merck group was the first to publish its findings (in *Nature*), but Blundell correctly saw an inconsistency in the C-terminal of the protease, and his correction was confirmed by the Wlodawer group in a widely cited article in *Science*, which appeared six months after the Merck group's article.

Firms can delay publication, but the utilitarian value of publication supports the traditional communitarian orientation of scientific publication. Scientific reputation provides opportunities, both in the professional and the commercial realm, and scientific reputation requires publication. It is therefore not surprising that researchers have failed to find a negative relationship between academic activities, such as publishing, and commercial activities, such as patenting. In general, the more prolific publishers are also more actively involved with entrepreneurial science (Zucker and Darby 2014). Many years ago, Jason Owen-Smith and Walter W. Powell concluded, "Growing commercial engagement has not, thus far, altered the research culture of universities so as to privilege applied orientations at the expense of basic science" (2003, 1695). Today it would be more accurate to say that commercial engagement *has* privileged applied orientations but has not seemed to harm basic science.

Has Academic Innovationism Reached Its Limits?

The limits of academic innovationism have not been reached in so far as academic researchers are concerned. They have continued to make discoveries that have the potential to improve the quality of life through new drug therapies, improvement in new energy sources, the invention of new materials, new ways to use computer code, and many other ways.

The question is whether the contributions of academic innovators are reaching their quantitative limits as a result of stagnation in government funding and declining marginal returns for industry. Many of the indicators suggest as much. The average number of new patents and licenses fell following the Great Recession and would have tailed off significantly if not for the tendency of foreign academics to pursue U.S. patents (Leydesdorff, Etzkowitz, and Kushnir 2016). Nor has the number of new start-ups climbed in ways that suggest the era of academic entrepreneurship is just beginning. Federal spending on basic science grew dramatically through 2003 but stabilized thereafter at $38 billion (in 2005 dollars) (Press 2013). As a proportion of total funding for academic research, corporate funding reached its high point in 2000 and has fallen since that time from over 7 percent to slightly under 6 percent. In spite of the billions that have been poured into STEM education, the proportion of students majoring in these disciplines has barely budged over time.

Most large high-tech firms prefer to do their own R&D work. Industry remains by far the largest funder of R&D in the United States at about two-thirds of the total. Quite a bit of variation exists across industries, however, in preferences for embedding or outsourcing basic research. Information technology and Internet services firms such as Apple, Google, Amazon, and Facebook have continued to make long-term in-house investments in basic research. But many life science firms, in particular, have cut back on internal R&D and often license discoveries made by academic and nonprofit researchers. These firms included many of the largest in the pharmaceuticals industry: Pfizer, Novartis, Merck, AstraZeneca, Eli Lilly, GlaxoSmithKline, and Bristol Myers Squibb. Other industries, such as semiconductors and chemical products, have also cut back on basic science R&D (Industrial Research Institute 2016). DuPont R&D, the inventors of nylon, rayon, Teflon, and solar cells, announced cutbacks in R&D in 2015 following a merger with Dow and capitulation to activist investors with short-term horizons (George 2015).

Universities are consequently in a position to benefit from cutbacks in industry spending on basic research. As the Industrial Research Institute observed, "For many years now, academe has been the go-to organization for performing advanced basic research and even applied research when government or industrial organizations are looking for cost-effective ways to perform a development program" (2016, 12).

The age of academic entrepreneurship has arrived, and there are no persuasive reasons for universities to turn back to an age of lesser influence and more singular dependence on the public purse—particularly not when state governments have failed as reliable partners during economic downturns. But the capacity of the federal government and the interest of high-tech industries in supporting entrepreneurial science at higher levels remain in doubt.

These relationships can be strengthened if those who fund entrepreneurial initiatives learn from both the successes and the failures of intersectoral and multidisciplinary initiatives. Based on the existing evidence, the characteristics of successful interdisciplinary collaborations include: very strong intellectual and organizational leadership; researchers who have worked together successfully prior to formal affiliation; clear project foci; early success in enhancing affiliates' levels of publication and grant support; and clearly communicated arrangements with departments for evaluating affiliates' performances. The safest approach for universities is to build around one or two highly productive researchers (Rawlings et al. 2015), adding carefully to build in complementary personnel. Distinct roles include "star scientists" who provide creative ideas and "connectors" who can build group social ties and translate across disciplines (see Collins, Evans, and Gorman 2010). Some have found that building around expensive shared scientific instrumentation can be a better and more flexible strategy than building around particular topics (Paul Alivisatos, personal communication).[21]

Work with industry is in the public interest if one judges by the quality of life improvements that come from new technologies and medical therapies. But the public interest extends well beyond products that can yield a profit for companies while improving quality of life for consumers. Unless they have no choice, business leaders will not criticize their own firms or one another for despoiling the environment, skirting regulation, creating unsafe working conditions, exploiting labor, or any other action that harms a community but pleases shareholders.

By contrast, universities are places where criticism is essential, not only to advance knowledge but to shed a spotlight on problems that require repair. Concerns about crime, environmental protection, declining opportunities for social mobility, health and safety regulations, government corruption, the rise of pernicious ideologies, just to cite a few examples—all of these are legitimate public interest topics for university research. No corporation would support them unless they sensed commercial potential from the inquiry; any university worth its salt would. The ultimate value and power of the university therefore lies in the range of public-serving fields it covers. By providing education and research in a range of scholarly and scientific fields, regardless of their commercial potential, the university ensures that it is a hub for activity reaching out to every important occupation, group, and institution in society. A few specialized research institutes can survive by focusing their energies on science and technology with commercial po-tential. Universities would fail to serve if they shrank to do so.[22]

Research, of course, is only one of the drivers of the expansion and in-creasing prominence of American universities. In chapter 4, I turn to the other great driver: the enrollment of a larger and more diverse student body.

4

College for All

Many who teach in colleges or universities have met students like Denise Adams. Denise (not her real name) is the daughter of a single mother who grew up in a hardscrabble community in inland Southern California. Her mother encouraged her toward study, and she achieved a strong record in secondary school. She was also a champion middle-distance runner. She was accepted at several colleges but chose one close to home so that she could be near enough to pitch in at home. At college she ran for the women's track team and majored in political science and law and society. I taught her in a class on leadership and organizational effectiveness where she stood out for the quality of her writing and for her poise when answering questions during class discussion. She moved on to law school in New York. Today she is working as an attorney in the military, having passed the difficult New York bar examination on her first try. Two generations ago Denise would likely not have attended college at all. Expectations for women were not as high and college might well have seemed out of reach to Denise's mother. Denise's story, repeated tens of thousands times every year, is the signature story of the college-for-all system.

Social inclusion—the mechanisms that allowed Denise Adams to attend and succeed in college—is another primary driver of the expansion and increased prominence of U.S. higher education institutions. Like academic innovationism, it is also a disruptive force because it challenges the traditional structures of higher education. It puts pressure on colleges and universities to make accommodations beyond their default preferences for academically well-prepared students. At the same time, social inclusion is far from contradictory to the interests of higher education as an industry; it brings in new resources and students to fill the classes of a wide range of specialties.

The idea that colleges and universities should be used to foster social inclusion has been a high priority in the United States for so long a time that it is difficult to appreciate the extent to which it remains a propulsive force. The value of social incorporation could hardly be higher from the perspective of societal mobilization. By creating expanded opportunities for upward mobility, colleges and universities energize large populations to aim higher than they would otherwise have thought possible. And yet the push for inclusion also means that an elitist approach to what undergraduate students should know is no longer possible, except in rarefied corners of the system. Learning itself must often contend with the far less ambitious goal of student "engagement," whether that engagement be through campus social life, cocurricular activities, or community service.

In chapter 3, I wrote of the challenges research university administrators face in managing commitment to the dominant system of academic professionalism while at the same time encouraging the rapid expansion of technological innovation. The sociologist James E. Rosenbaum (1998) coined the term "college for all" to describe the aspirations of policymakers and college and university administrators to extend college opportunities as widely as possible. College for all similarly poses one side of a dialectical tension that colleges and universities must find ways to manage. This tension surrounds the maintenance of high-status tracks and opportunities in the face of demand for broader access to educational credentials. Access and completion are the drivers of the educational revolution that has made college seem less like a choice than a necessity, but the revolution could not have occurred unless it had preserved and indeed added ways for ambitious students to acquire status at college and beyond graduation. The college-for-all system is therefore also the "much-more-valuable-college-for-some" system.

In this chapter, I will discuss the processes and discourses of enrollment expansion, as well as the mechanisms colleges and universities have used to help improve the prospects of students who are most at risk of noncompletion. I will also discuss the effects of higher education expansion on the curriculum and undergraduate student culture. In chapter 5, I will discuss the ways that colleges and universities have preserved and added to high-status locations on campus, matching advances of the college-for-all system with a mix of old and new approaches to conferring social and academic distinction.

The Higher Education Gold Rush

The most important power held by colleges and universities is their monopoly over accredited higher education credentials. This is a monopoly that all college and university personnel have an interest in preserving. Some private corporations have attempted to substitute alternative credentials for postsecondary degrees, such as badges for completion of learning modules (see Olneck 2018). These efforts have not as yet proven successful because the credentials have not demonstrated significant attraction to employers. Unless and until they do, degrees and certificates from accredited postsecondary institutions remain the tickets required for access to the great majority of the better-paying jobs in the American occupational structure. It is a near-monopoly position that has only increased in importance over time (see Brint et al. 2012b).

WHY HAS DEMAND GROWN?

College for all is very nearly a reality with respect to campus entry. About two-thirds of high school graduates enroll in college right after high school. According to research conducted by Rosenbaum and two colleagues on a 2004 cohort of high school graduates, including those who delayed college entry, nearly 90 percent of on-time high school graduates enrolled in college (including community colleges) within eight years of high school graduation (Rosenbaum, Ahearn, and Rosenbaum 2017, 1, 26). Moreover, the rates of college entry were very similar across racial-ethnic groups. The rates of college entry among African Americans, the least likely to attend, were, for example, well above 80 percent.

College completion is where the idea of college for all breaks down. Fewer than half who enter college—again including community colleges—obtain a credential, and only about one-third complete a bachelor's degree. Of those who complete a bachelor's degree, about half now go on to a postgraduate program, and of those more than three-quarters eventually obtain a postgraduate credential. About 5 percent obtain one of the more prestigious postgraduate degrees (medicine/dentistry, law, or the doctorate). The college-for-all system winnows at every stage (see table 4.1).

Yet for all the siphoning that occurs, the growth in the system is unmistakable and impressive. At both the undergraduate and graduate levels, enrollments nearly doubled between 1980 and 2015 (NCES 2015, table 303.20). The number of undergraduate degrees awarded annually

TABLE 4.1. U.S. Educational Attainment, 2015

	Proportion of 18–24 Age Group
Graduation from High School	92%
HS Graduates Who Enroll in a Postsecondary Institution within eight years of high school graduation	88%
Graduation from a Four-Year College	34%
Enrollment in a Postgraduate Program	17%
Graduation from Any Postgraduate Program	14%
Graduation with First Professional or Doctoral Degree	5%

Source: Author's estimate from NCES 2015, table 104.20; Rosenbaum, Ahearn, and Rosenbaum 2017, 1, 26; Ryan and Bauman 2016, table 1.

nearly doubled during the period, and the number of advanced degrees awarded more than doubled (NCES 2015, table 318.10). By 2014, there were some 13.5 million students enrolled in baccalaureate-granting institutions, with nearly two million students graduating with baccalaureate degrees annually and nearly another million graduating with master's or higher-level degrees (NCES 2015, table 301.10).

We should pause to consider what an accomplishment this is. During a period in which tuition and fees at public universities increased by more than four times the rate of inflation, college and graduate school enrollments nevertheless climbed steadily. It is as if car manufacturers quadrupled the cost of their brands, without clear evidence of greatly improved quality, and instead of facing plummeting demand found that twice as many people wanted to buy their vehicles. Of course there are important differences between consumer demand for automobiles and college degrees. Higher education remained a very good investment—unlike cars college degrees do not depreciate over time. Indeed, the mid-career income gap between high school and college graduates widened. Colleges also subsidized costs for lower-income students in ways that car manufacturers would never dream of doing. And lower-cost postsecondary options—notably community colleges and some online programs—did grow quite a bit faster than higher-cost options. Even so, the vigorous growth of four-year college enrollments belies the argument of would-be disrupters that the higher education market was teetering on the brink of a cost-driven restructuring.

I have emphasized the importance of social inclusion as a driver of enrollment growth. Inclusion has been interpreted, by most university administrators, to mean extension of educational opportunities to previously marginalized groups, particularly women and underrepresented minorities. And indeed the results of mobilization and demographic change can be seen in the growth of women and minorities in undergraduate student bodies. Women increased in representation from 42 percent in 1970 to 57 percent in 2010, without much additional change through mid-decade, while underrepresented minorities (i.e., African Americans, Hispanics, and Native Americans) increased from 14 percent of the undergraduate student body in 1980 to nearly 28 percent in 2010 and to 32 percent by mid-decade (NCES 2015, tables 303.70 and 306.10). Female undergraduates exceed their proportion of the eighteen- to twenty-four-year-old population, while underrepresented minorities equaled their proportion of the age group (Musu-Gillette et al. 2016).[1]

Why have so many young people pursued baccalaureate and higher degrees? The answer may seem obvious: because college and graduate degrees are rewarded in the labor market. And clearly the demand side of college attendance and completion *is* a major part of the story—as the system has matured, it has become the most important part of the story. The Georgetown University Center on Education and the Workforce is a leading source on "the college payoff." Over the course of a working life career, in 2011 the center estimated, the median college graduate earned 68 percent more than the median high school graduate—the difference between $2.2 million and $1.5 million in average lifetime earnings. Those with professional degrees (including, notably, doctors and lawyers), in turn, earned 59 percent more on average than those holding a bachelor's—the difference between $3.7 million and $2.2 million in lifetime earnings at the median. Although workers with different levels of educational attainment start their careers fairly close in earnings, later career earnings trajectories are much steeper for those with higher degrees (Carnevale, Rose, and Cheah 2011, 3).[2] A complete accounting would require adjustments of expected earnings for opportunity costs of attending college. The complexities of arriving at lifetime expected earnings net of opportunity costs do not, however, diminish the consistent conclusion of those who have looked into the relationship between education and earnings over many decades. As the authors of the Georgetown study put it, "No matter how you cut it, education pays" (Carnevale, Rose, and Cheah 2011, 20).

The most common reason given for the higher pay of college graduates is that by investing in institutions of higher learning, graduates have improved their "human capital," the mix of cognitive and noncognitive skills that makes them more efficient and effective workers. This view is contested because higher education credentials can serve as status signals without necessarily saying much about students' development during their college years (see, e.g., Bills 2003). Although a sizable minority of students make little or no progress in developing their cognitive skills during their college years, the majority do make gains in their knowledge of specialized fields and in their thinking and communication skills (Arum and Roksa 2011; Pascarella et al. 2011). Moreover, additional years of attending classes, reading and doing homework, studying for exams, and writing papers can hardly help but improve the conscientiousness of students, their responsiveness to authority, their capacity to dress and speak like middle-class professionals, and their ability to manage several tasks at once (Brint, Cantwell, and Saxena 2012). A long line of studies suggest that these traits are valuable in organizational life. Economists have argued that a way to suppress the growth of inequality is to "outrace" technological change by training students for jobs whose productivity can be increased by technology rather than made redundant by it (Goldin and Katz 2008).

Others attribute the college wage advantage less to qualities of the highly educated than to the virtual collapse of the labor market for young adults with lower levels of education. The labor economist Annette Bernhardt and her colleagues (1999), for example, emphasized the extent to which wages associated with the high school labor market have fallen in real terms, leaving students who wish to escape a life at the margins of society with little alternative but to attempt college. Human capital development is largely beside the point for labor economists like Bernhardt; it is low-income jobs that are expanding fastest in the U.S. economy (see also Bernhardt 2012). Employers are happy to fill many of these jobs with college-educated labor, particularly when they have reason to be wary of workers who lack the motivation to attempt college. Few scholars doubt that part of the demand for postsecondary credentials has to do with the reduced prospects of those without postsecondary credentials. But the impact has been greatest for those who pursue two-year rather than four-year degrees.

When students think about the benefits of college, they may also have at least some awareness that the opportunities for a better life extend beyond the labor market opportunities colleges provide. More highly educated people are on average healthier and exercise more than people with less education. They say they are happier and, if as proof, they live longer. They read more books and newspapers than other people and are more likely to be well informed about current events (even if they are not very well informed, alas). Their marriages are more likely to last. They participate more actively in the political and civic life of their communities. They are more cosmopolitan and more accepting of cultural differences. And they express higher levels of trust in others. Not surprisingly, they are much less likely to be involved with drugs or to be in trouble with the law than those with lower levels of education. (However, they do seem to drink and gamble about as much on average as the less educated.) Educated people show these socially desirable attributes, even when their class backgrounds and current incomes are statistically controlled in order to more accurately isolate the effects of educational differences alone. Preexisting unmeasured differences in motivation or outlook are undoubtedly important factors separating college graduates from others on these desirable social attributes, but, at a minimun, college is an industrial-strength reinforcer. Educational differences in each of these domains have been remarkably consistent since social scientists began studying them in the 1950s (see, e.g., Bowen 1977; Davis 1982; Hyman and Wright 1979; Hout 2012; Kingston et al. 2003; Stouffer 1958).

Studies of the college "payoff" typically ignore the supply side factors behind the expansion of postsecondary opportunities. But the supply side is, if anything, a more important part of the story—at least it was at the beginning of the postwar era of expansion. One by one, the GI Bill, the War on Poverty, and the Higher Education Act of 1965 singled out education as *the way* of national and personal advance. "The answer to all of our national problems," as Lyndon Johnson put it in 1965, "comes down to one single word: education." The interests of the states and federal government were both altruistic and prudential. They saw college graduates as contributors not only to economic development but also to the state's net financial balance sheet. Graduates contributed much more than their share to federal and state tax rolls, without drawing much from state resources for social welfare or criminal justice. For the federal government and the states too college was a good investment.

One result of the rise of educational credentials as exchangeable for access to higher-level jobs has been the proliferation of specialized occupational jurisdictions off limits to anyone without the accepted educational credentials. Professional associations, governments, and educational institutions themselves have each played a role in carving the job structure into this jigsaw puzzle of occupational jurisdictions controlled by the holders of specialized credentials. Each of these institutions had a stake in the expansion of the credential society: professional associations are evaluators in the accreditation process and, indirectly, in the licensing examinations in their jurisdictions because they contribute to the composition of licensing examinations. They want to guarantee to the extent possible high-quality performance to maintain their respectability. Governments have a stake in the regulation of occupations and colleges, and they provide the financial aid funding that allows them to continue operations. Of the approximately 20 million undergraduate students enrolled in higher education institutions in AY 2013–14, close to 12 million students, or 60 percent, borrowed to cover their costs. Federal student loan programs were the largest source of financing for students who needed loans to attend college, though private banks also provided loans for those whose need exceeded what the federal government would meet. As of 2013–14, approximately $864 billion was outstanding in federal student loans, while another $150 billion was outstanding in private student loans (American Student Assistance 2014). Many states supplemented these federal programs with grant programs of their own (see chapter 6). It is rarely acknowledged but certainly true that governments have a strong stake in keeping many young people in college and graduate school so as not to flood the labor market with workers who would put downward pressure on wages. And educational institutions provide the medium of exchange—degrees and certificates—that keep the wheels of the system turning (see Abbott 1988; Brown 1995; Collins 1979, chaps. 1 and 2).

Just as the smartphone industry looks to the day when everyone has a smartphone, so too do many in the higher education industry (and those connected to it) look to the day when everyone has a college degree. Individual campuses may have interests in heightened selectivity, but the industry as a whole has an interest in more students with more degrees. University administrators believe in the power of higher education, of course, but whenever a higher education leader discusses the demands of the "knowledge economy" for more highly trained college educated workers, it is wise to hold in mind that this phrase may simultaneously reflect a real belief *and* the marketing aspirations of the higher education industry (see also Kirp 2003). In a system (including two-year colleges) that eventually enrolls more than 70 percent of those who graduate from secondary school, 100 percent market penetration is the logical end point. Expansion of the number of completers becomes another objective. Dollars are lost to the system both from those who fail to enroll and from those who fail to complete. The idea that postsecondary education is the key to a better life—perhaps the only important key for those not born to wealth—should be seen not only in light of the probabilities that this proposition holds true for individuals but as a powerful instrument supporting the expansionary interests of higher education leaders as representatives of an industry with considerable remaining growth potential.

Enrollment-conscious administrators—those working in the broad-access sector—consequently see the economic interests of their institutions much better supported by egalitarians than by advocates of meritocracy, and it is common to hear them speak essentially the same language of social justice that campus progressives do. Of course, many such administrators are attracted to work in broad-access institutions because of personal experiences of economic hardship or convictions about the importance of equality of opportunity, rather than because they are motivated by the pecuniary interests of their institutions. Nonetheless, dependence on enrollment revenues can hardly help but reinforce these experiences and convictions, when they do not determine them.[3]

THE PROCESSES OF GROWTH

The tension between access and status, egalitarianism and meritocracy is inescapable in a system that was founded to prepare students for a few learned professions but now includes preparation for virtually every white-collar occupation that requires more than routine paper or people processing. As the creators of the American hierarchical system of colleges and universities hoped (Brint and Karabel 1989, chaps. 1 and 2), most of the growth in enrollments has been funneled into the less expensive lower tracks of the system (see Astin and Oseguera 2004; Bastedo and Jacquette 2011; Posselt et al. 2012). These tracks absorb students with lower levels of academic preparation and include high proportions of low-income, first-generation, and underrepresented minority students. But this disproportionate growth at the bottom of the system is not the only process by which the system has managed demand. Nearly every campus has also grown larger, and ambitious administrators have vied with one another to add programs and degrees to facilitate further growth.

Disproportionate Growth at the Bottom of the System

The most secure way to allow wider access while maintaining high-status tracks is to encourage price differentiation and selective admissions. Price differentiation supports selection at the top of the system while opening access at the bottom. Down-market expansion preserves the four-year colleges and universities for a somewhat more academically inclined (and generally

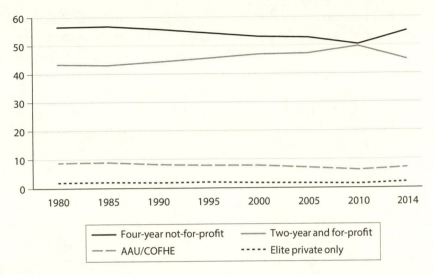

FIGURE 4.1. Undergraduate Enrollment in the United States by Control and Level, 1980–2010. *Sources*: Adapted from NCES 2012a, table 240 and NCES 2015, tables 303.50–303.60. Data on Association of American University (AAU) and Council on Financing Higher Education (COFHE) institutions computed by author using IPEDS Data Center online tool.

more affluent) stratum of students. And it maintains the most selective private institutions as a world apart. The most immediate result of the college-for-all era was the direction of most of the growth in student numbers into the "people's colleges": two-year and for-profit colleges. As the educational historian David F. Labaree has written,

> What students find when they enter the educational system . . . is that they are gaining equal access to a sharply unequal array of educational experiences. . . . [T]he system balances open access with radical stratification. . . . Almost everyone can go to college, but the institutions that are most accessible (community colleges) provide the smallest boost to a student's life chances, whereas the ones that offer the surest entrée into the best jobs (major research universities) are highly selective. This extreme mixture of equality and inequality, of accessibility and stratification, is a striking and fascinating characteristic of American education. (2011, 193)

As figure 4.1 shows, public and private four-year colleges and universities enrolled nearly 70 percent of undergraduate students in 1970. By 2010, their share had declined to just over 50 percent. By contrast, two-year colleges and for-profits enrolled about 30 percent of undergraduate students in

1970. By 2010, they had reached nearly 50 percent of enrollment. This sharp shift in market share was more remarkable given the 150 percent growth of enrollments during the period. Public community colleges rivaled public four-year colleges and universities as the largest single sector in American higher education for two decades, from the 1990s through 2010. And for-profits were the fastest-growing sector during the period, up from just 0.2 percent in 1970 to 10 percent of undergraduate enrollments in 2010 (NCES 2015, table 303.25).

In chapter 5 I will show the extent to which enrollments in selective and nonselective institutions varied by students' socioeconomic status and racial-ethnic backgrounds. These distributional gaps were much wider than most people imagine; they can be seen as a statistical rebuke to those who allege that the system is stacked in favor of minorities through affirmative action and other preferences. For now, I will only note that the vigorous enrollment growth of the period showed a distinct color and income gradient by selectivity level.

The less expensive alternatives of community colleges and four-year comprehensives have had the consequence of protecting the value of higher-status degrees. Indeed, the prototype for this approach was invented before the twentieth century when leading educators and university presidents championed the growth of two-year colleges—then called junior colleges—as a mechanism for protecting the leading state and private universities from what they feared would be a deluge of ambitious but unqualified students (Brint and Karabel 1989, chap. 2). Then too beliefs in social progress and democratic opportunity, as well as low prices, fueled the growth of broad-access institutions at the bottom of the stratification structure. Like community colleges, regional public universities play the role of sieve today for many flagship state universities. One vice president of research at an AAU public university told me that the regional campuses in his system absorbed, to use his term, "the run-off" of students who would like to attend his institution but were not academically strong enough to do so. They played an important role by offering practical training more suited to these students' eventual destinations in the labor force. Indeed, with the continuing growth of community colleges and regional comprehensives, state flagship universities that once maintained relatively low admission standards have shifted toward admitting only the most highly qualified students in their states (Haycock, Lynch, and Engle 2010).

The decades of shifting enrollments toward the bottom of the higher education system ended, at least temporarily, as the impact of the Great

Recession wound down. Students who would have enrolled in community colleges or for-profits left the system entirely to seek employment and others enrolled in four-year institutions. The federal government's crackdown on the abusive loan practices of for-profits undoubtedly accounted for a large share of their dip in enrollments. By fall 2014, four-year colleges were enrolling 55 percent of undergraduates (NCES 2015, table 303.50). This change did not augur an end to policymakers' aspirations for college for all—but it did shift growth, at least temporarily, to higher levels in the system. Enrollments at four-year colleges and universities, both public and private, continued to increase at a steady rate during the period following the recession; these institutions added nearly 500,000 new students per year between 2010 and 2014 (NCES 2015, table 303.70).

Most Institutions Grow Larger

At the same time, undergraduate enrollments in virtually every institution have grown over time, including even in elite institutions that would seem to have everything at stake in remaining as small and exclusive as possible. Among a set of nearly 1,100 four-year institutions that continued to operate under the same name between 1970 and 2010, the *Colleges & Universities 2000* research team found a near doubling of the average size of both doctoral-granting and master's-granting universities. The average university with very high research activity, for example, enrolled about 16,500 students in 1970 and nearly 27,000 in 2010.[4] Even the leafy confines of baccalaureate-granting colleges expanded moderately to accommodate more students (see table 4.2).

A common view from the 1960s was that economies of scale could be reached at research universities by adding enrollments up to 20,000 but that beyond that point quality suffered and no additional economies of scale could be realized (Cartter 1966). By 2010, the 20,000-student rule of thumb had been superseded by 140 colleges and universities, led by the University of Phoenix in the for-profit sector (308,000 mostly online students in 2011–12), Arizona State University among four-year institutions (90,000-plus students), and Miami-Dade Community College among two-year institutions (61,000-plus students) (NCES 2012b, table 249).[5] The presidents of tuition-dependent public institutions can hardly help but be interested in expanding the student body, if they want disposable funds to be used for purposes of institutional improvements.

Modernization plans focusing on higher education expansion continue to stimulate foundation elites and sympathetic politicians. During the Obama

TABLE 4.2. Average Fall Enrollment and Standard Deviations, 1970–2010

Carnegie Expanded Classification (n = 1,083)

	1970	1980	1990	2000	2010
Research U. (v. high activity)	16,505	20,124	22,053	22,747	26,799
(N = 99)	(13,054)	(11,195)	(11,576)	(11,690)	(11,458)
Research U. (high activity)	11,384	13,657	15,474	15,426	18,281
(N = 79)	(8,071)	(6,601)	(7,194)	(7,232)	(7,180)
Doctoral/Research U.	5,332	7,140	8,204	8,859	10,787
(N = 54)	(6,483)	(5,463)	(5,015)	(4,888)	(4,400)
Master's	3,600	4,394	5,169	5,482	6,596
(N = 484)	(5,472)	(4,659)	(4,916)	(4,421)	(4,350)
Baccalaureate	1,202	1,382	1,564	1,646	1,840
(N = 367)	(1,503)	(1,199)	(1,221)	(965)	(721)

Source: Calculated by author from IPEDS 1970–2010 (constant set of institutions). Standard deviations are in parentheses under average enrollments.

years, the federal government's goal of increasing to 60 percent the proportion of the 18–25 age cohort completing college placed new pressures on colleges and universities to enhance what is now sometimes unselfconsciously referred to as "throughput." Higher throughput frequently translates into larger face-to-face and more online classes. The push for throughput dovetailed with the rhetoric of equal opportunity, because progress toward the 60 percent goal required much higher completion rates, in particular, among first-generation students, those from the bottom half of the income distribution, and those from underrepresented minority groups.

The Ambitions of Administrators

The ambitions of administrators are one of the hidden propellants to growth. My research on *C&U 2000* data with Mark Riddle and Robert A. Hanneman (2006) confirmed a high degree of restlessness among university presidents. We asked presidents of *Colleges & Universities 2000* institutions not only about the institutions they currently resembled but also about those they aspired to resemble in ten years' time. When asked to list institutions in their current reference groups, presidents sorted themselves mainly along the lines of selectivity, the highest degree their institutions awarded, and whether they were under public or private, nonprofit control. The answers shifted when we asked about aspirations. Those at the top of the institutional hierarchy were content with their place in the order—who wouldn't be? But below the top, presidents of the financially stronger institutions in each of the six strata we identified very frequently aspired to occupy higher positions in the institutional landscape. Judging by their choices of aspirational peer institutions, ambitious presidents of public colleges and universities usually hoped to climb the ladder by adding higher-level degrees or greater research intensity, while presidents of private institutions typically set their sights on becoming more selective. Only the presidents of the financially weaker institutions in each stratum tended to be content with their current peer institutions. This restlessness contributes to the growth of the system by encouraging the stronger institutions at each level to work toward emulating not their peers but those above them in the institutional hierarchy.

The Discourses of Educational Opportunity

The discourse on equality of opportunity changed in important ways during the period, from a lingering focus on undiscovered talent to a more concentrated emphasis on the prospects of groups mobilized during the civil rights era—notably, women and minorities (followed in the later 1980s by lesbian and gay students). A final, partial shift in discourse occurred at the end of the period, when a foundation-led class-based discourse sought to realign the interests of the college-for-all system with those of students whose family incomes fell in the lower half of the income distribution, including both whites and minorities. The advocates of race-based affirmative action continued to push back on these class-based approaches to inclusion because, they feared, with good reason, that such a shift would yield fewer slots for minorities at selective institutions (see, e.g., the analyses in Ashkenas, Park, and Pearce 2017; and Espenshade and Radford 2009).

TALENT LOSS

The deep background to higher education expansion derives from the focus of postwar planners on the issue of "talent loss." Often linked to international competition in science and technology, the discourse of talent loss had, at times, a distinctly masculine orientation. Planners assumed that men were the ones who would be most attracted to scientific careers. But the discourse was even more clearly focused on the discovery of talent among high school students of limited economic means. They were seen as the untapped resource who could help meet national priority needs in science and engineering. This discourse was evident in the 1947 Truman Commission report: "The present state of affairs is resulting in far too great a loss of talent—our most precious national resource in a democracy" (36). It intensified following the successful launch of the Soviet satellite *Sputnik* in 1957: as one of the postwar planners, Dael Wolfle, the executive officer of the American Association for the Advancement of Science, wrote in 1958:

> How much talent there is in the nation, no one really knows. But it seems to be true that the harder one searches for it, the more one finds. If by educational waste we mean . . . the failure to educate young people to as high a level as they might attain, certainly there is waste in our failure to identify and encourage the bright children who grow up in homes and environments that are not providing that encouragement. (366)

The idea that talent is generously spread across the social spectrum led to optimism about the extent to which the country could be reenergized by the discovery of academic (and especially scientific) talent where most colleges and universities had never previously thought to look very deeply. Postwar planners, beginning with the Truman Commission, anticipated a vast expansion of financial aid resources to provide equality of opportunity. Many sociological studies of the period contributed to the pursuit of equality of opportunity by showing that college access for high socioeconomic status (SES) students in the lowest ability quartile equaled or exceeded that of low SES students in the highest ability quartile (see, e.g., Sewell and Shah 1967), a shocking demonstration of the extent to which social class mattered for college-going opportunities.

During the period covered by this book, talent loss remained a minor theme in the discourse on inclusion, and one that continued to be of interest mainly to scientists and engineers. Rita Colwell, a former director of the National Institutes of Health, for example, brought a hint of talent loss thinking into speeches that focused primarily on the social fairness foundations of the push for greater diversity: "Diversity gives greater scope for adaptation and innovation—traits our social systems, our nation, and our economy also need. A more diverse science and engineering workforce will bring in different talents, approaches and experiences" (Colwell 2002).

THE DIVERSITY ERA

Colwell's statement reflects the shift in emphasis from the costs of talent loss to the benefits of diversity. As a result of the civil rights movement of the 1960s, the discourse on college access shifted toward a concern for the diversification of student bodies (and faculties) as a matter of "social justice" and equity.[6] Working in tandem with civil rights activists, the federal government demanded this shift in orientation. Title VI of the Civil Rights Act of 1964 banned discrimination by race, color, or national origins. Title VI also banned discrimination by religion and sex. Title IX of the Education Amendments of 1972 expanded protection against discrimination by sex. These acts were important symbolically because they put the force of state power (as well as relatively small amounts of funding) on the side of legally protected groups.

But the laws did not in themselves create the new association of equality of opportunity with opportunities for minorities and women. If law alone had mattered, military veterans and students with disabilities would have become greater forces than they became during the period, because they too enjoyed legal protections. Instead, the civil rights and feminist movements of the 1960s and 1970s gave rise to a mobilized "party of change" on university campuses. Only women and minorities (and later gay and lesbian students) showed the capacity for continuous mobilization on campus during the post–civil rights era. They established a watchful presence over admissions and faculty hiring. They monitored campus discourse for evidence of insensitivity and discrimination. And they took on a protracted, and ultimately successful, critique of white and male-dominated "Eurocentric" curricula in the arts, humanities, and social sciences (see, e.g., Gates 1992; Oakley 1997).

The language of diversity was an important feature of this reorientation in college opportunity rhetoric. Although the term "diversity" could, in theory, denote representation by family income, national origins, religion, political views, or any number of other characteristics, in practice it came to refer to representation by gender, race, and, later, sexual orientation. The term gained currency following Supreme Court Justice Lewis Powell's opinion in the *Bakke* case (1976), in which a white student had sued the University of California-Davis because he had been denied admission to its law school though his academic qualifications were stronger than some minority students who had gained admission. Powell used the term "diversity" to justify the employment of differential admission criteria, arguing that the attainment of a diverse student body broadens the range of viewpoints collectively held by students and subsequently allows "an institution to provide an atmosphere that is conducive to speculation, experiment, and creation—so essential to the quality of education" (quoted in Chang, Chang, and Ledesma 2005, 25).[7]

Following *Bakke*, "diversity" became the term of choice for promoting equality of opportunity aimed specifically at improving the life chances of women and minorities. The Court's decision seemed to promise greater economic diversity on college campuses, but selective institutions instead recruited heavily among upper-middle-class blacks and Hispanics rather than among the disadvantaged (Giancola and Kahlenberg 2016). Subsequent Court rulings involving student complaints against the University of Michigan and the University of Texas narrowed the scope of affirmative action but retained the principle that campuses could use race as a "plus-factor" in admissions in so far as racially sensitive admissions contributed positively to the educational environment.

Beginning in the 1970s, major philanthropies encouraged responses to the diversification of college campuses through curricular reform aimed at increasing the representation of women, minorities, and non-Western cultures. Early philanthropic supporters for expanding cultural representation in the curriculum included the Carnegie Corporation, the Ford Foundation, and the Mellon Foundation (Shiao 2005, 159–77). These philanthropies sponsored conferences, and they funded projects to study the consequences of curricular change for student learning and student attitudes related to "cultural competence." The Ford Foundation, in particular, pushed for the greater diversification of student bodies and faculties (ibid., 111, 198–99).

The Association of American Colleges and Universities (AAC&U), the only major national organization focusing on liberal and general education, added the theme of diversity to its mission in the early 1980s and became one of the most important national agents of change in the discourse on equality of opportunity. During the 1980s and 1990s, the vision of AAC&U focused on reshaping the liberal arts to bring diversity within the compass of its fundamental commitments. In the early 1990s, AAC&U effectively advocated the addition of courses on gender, race, and non-Western cultures into the general education curriculum (see, e.g., Brint et al. 2009; Cornwell and Stoddard 1999; Musil 1992). The organization saw itself as a "leading edge of change" whose goal was to "amplify what it [saw] in the field" (D. Humphreys, personal communication). This work culminated in the American Commitments initiative (1993–2001), funded by the Ford Foundation, the Hewlett Foundation, and the National Endowment for the Humanities. The hopeful but unproven connection between expanded diversity and stronger democracy provided a signal theme for this work. AAC&U drew on familiar images of pluralism but with a new twist: "Higher education," it wrote, "can nurture America's commitment and capacity to create a society in which democratic aspiration becomes democratic justice. Diversity provides a means of forging deeper civic unity" (Beckham 2000).

The AAC&U used a wide variety of organizational tools to foster the association of democracy with diversity. These included the formation of a national panel, composed of prestigious academics, modeled on the blue-ribbon commissions that had long been used by the federal government as a means for focusing support on policy initiatives. They also included Diversity Leadership Institutes, held during the year and, more intensively, during summers for twenty to thirty member institutions. These institutions disseminated "best practices" for reforming general education as a vehicle for teaching about diversity and promoting "global social awareness." They also included seminars "to discuss and re-imagine what it means to be a citizen in a multiracial society." AAC&U was one of the first national higher education associations to find effective use of the Internet for creating compendia of campus practices and resources to promote diversity and for highlighting successful efforts to implement change in organizational practices. Its flagship magazine, *Liberal Education*, highlighted diversity initiatives on member campuses and the connection between diversity and democracy. The association claimed that 160 campuses were involved in at least one of the face-to-face programs and that 100 institutions undertook efforts to rethink curricula and to provide opportunities for students to consider "critical questions about American pluralism" (Brint 2011, 53–54).

During the period virtually every four-year college and university also found ways to recruit and support minority students and women. In selective institutions, this meant a degree of preference in otherwise comparable cases for minority candidates (Espenshade and Walton 2009), with the understanding that failure to provide preference would lead to a significant decrease in minority enrollments. Campuses relied on a variety of connections to encourage minority admissions, from groups like the Posse who mentored upwardly mobile minority high school students to alumni contacts and organized parents' groups in minority communities. It meant encouragement of cultural affinity clubs and organizations on campus. Support for diversity also meant the funding of offices of equity and diversity to monitor compliance with federal law and university aspirations for fair treatment of women and minorities. Indeed, the sword of Damocles hovered over colleges and universities in the form of Equal Employment Opportunity Commission (EEOC) audits of hiring practices intended to create a more level playing field, and dozens of universities were sued by the EEOC for failing to comply with federal law on equal treatment (Wallace and King 2013). It also meant hiring student affairs vice chancellors and staff who were keenly aware of the obstacles minority students faced in adjustment to the college experience and developing mentoring, early research experience, and scholarship programs to provide support for minority students. When I examined eighty-four strategic plans of U.S. research universities in the early 2000s, the *only* theme each one shared in common was a stated and seemingly heartfelt commitment to diversity (Brint 2005). And, of course, they all aspired to "excellence" as well.[8]

The social movements promoting organizational change gained support from demographic transformations on campus. By the early 1970s, white males had become a numerical minority on American college and university campuses, and twenty years later they represented just one-third of college students. Most observers at the time did not foresee that underlying demographic trends would soon have a large influence on higher education. By the 1990s, these consequences were clear. In 1993, the sociologist Neil J. Smelser noted that conflicts over "legitimate culture" could not be expected to fade away. "The political forces of the nation are," he wrote, "such that the march of diversification in universities will become an established social fact" (53).

The affirmative action policies of the era were focused more or less exclusively on women and underrepresented minorities. Few gave attention to low-income students as candidates for affirmative action. Data on the proportion of college students from the bottom half of the income distribution indicated that lower-income students, whether white or minority, were significantly underrepresented in four-year colleges. The college entry gaps between students coming from top quartile families and those coming from the bottom half of the income distribution actually increased between the late 1970s and the mid-1990s (Bailey and Dynarski 2011, figure 6.2). At selective colleges and universities, the proportion of students from underrepresented minority backgrounds reached parity with their population proportions in the early 2000s, even as striking class divisions remained. Students from the bottom 50 percent of the income distribution hardly ever surpassed 20 percent at leading liberal arts colleges, elite private universities, or even the most prestigious state flagship universities. More often, their proportions were in the range of 5 to 15 percent (Carnevale and Strohl 2010; Chetty et al. 2017). Between 1999 and 2013, more students from top 1 percent families were enrolled in "Ivy League-plus" institutions (14.5 percent) than were students from the entire bottom half of the income distribution (13.5 percent) (author's calculations from IPEDS data; see also Chetty et al. 2017).

White working-class students did not mobilize to pursue their group interests in expanded admissions. As Ann Mullen's (2010) ethnography of working-class white males on two Eastern college campuses makes clear, most felt at least mildly alienated from an undergraduate culture that seemed not to be built for them. They saw campuses as organized to benefit wealthy students and minorities, and they also found many of the requirements of college unnecessary obstacles to the acquisition of valuable training and credentials. The mobilized few sought to press their views through conservative political action groups, such as College Republicans, rather than as a networked social movement with vocal faculty allies. The divergent trajectories of upwardly mobile minorities and precariously situated low-income whites introduced a source of tension between colleges and universities and those who felt left out of the circle of their concern.

This tension reflected broader trends in national politics. Seeing a reduced place for themselves in the Democratic Party (and the institutions aligned with it), less educated white workers identified more often as independents or Republicans, and their resentments about special preferences for minorities were episodically and skillfully exploited by Republican politicians and media personalities (Binder and Wood 2014; Edsall and Edsall 1992; Gross 2013). In a fashion that proved effective in stimulating backlash, the academic left contributed to this alienation by promoting ideologies that elevated "social justice" for women and minorities as a goal of greater importance than other campus objectives, including academic excellence and measurable contributions to student learning.

A NEW CLASS-BASED DISCOURSE?

In the late 2000s philanthropic reformers began to argue that future gains in college enrollment and completion would necessarily come disproportionately from the bottom half of the income distribution, including from among lower-income whites. This expansion of recruitment would be the only way to accomplish their philanthropies' "big goal" of doubling the proportion of college students with postsecondary credentials by 2025. A new discourse of opportunity highlighting the struggles of first-generation and low-income college students gained ground as a result of the efforts of these foundation heads and the organizations they funded. Underrepresented minorities remained part of the discourse, woven into a broader class-based analysis, allowing for a degree of continuity with the still-dominant diversity discourse. Unlike the postwar discourse on talent loss, themes of economic decline and lives uplifted from poverty drove the new narrative, not worries about undiscovered greatness.[9]

The interest of the foundations in college graduation began with studies commissioned by Microsoft founder Bill Gates that showed higher education to be the most feasible antidote to poverty, given the country's aversion to wage regulation or wage support. This led the Bill and Melinda Gates Foundation to launch a series of programs to bolster college graduation rates in association with other major philanthropies, most notably the Lumina Foundation and its president, Jamie Merisotis. In op-eds and speeches, Merisotis worked energetically to promote this goal and to explain why it was necessary if the United States was to retain world economic leadership. The "President's Corner" on the Lumina website contained ninety-eight speeches given by Merisotis between February 2008 and June 2014 to business leaders, boards of trustees, legislative committees, scholarly audiences, and policy forums—and twenty-eight op-eds that he and his staff had written for newspapers around the country. The underlying message was remarkably consistent: meeting the "big goal" is the only way to ensure that America's workers and citizens have the knowledge and skills they need to succeed in a globally competitive environment.

Organizations funded by these philanthropic giants worked hard to achieve their "big goals." Marc Parry and his colleagues at the *Chronicle of Higher Education* found that between 2006 and 2011 the Gates Foundation provided $472 million to 185 recipients; the Lumina Foundation provided $237 million to 314 recipients; and the Kresge Foundation provided $73 million to 86 recipients—all in all, more than three-quarters of a billion dollars to more than 500 individual recipients (Parry, Field, and Supiano 2013). Although they received less funding, organizations with the goal of changing policy in the fifty states may have been more important still. These organizations included, notably, Complete College America, which received more than $10 million in philanthropic funding during the period and could be considered an arm of the Gates and Lumina foundations (as well as the National Governors Association). By the mid-2010s, it had convinced thirty-six states to "pledge to develop and implement aggressive state and campus-level action plans to meet college completion goals" (quoted in Mangan 2013).[10]

Consistent with the turn toward advocacy of a class-based approach to college access and completion, the "first-generation college student" entered public discourse as a subject worthy of praise (see figure 4.2). These students, admired for their grit and determination, became an identifiable status group on some progressive-minded campuses. The University of Cincinnati, the University of Kentucky, and Southern Connecticut State University

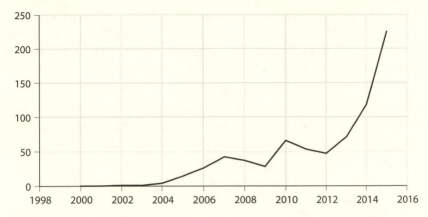

FIGURE 4.2. Lexis-Nexis References to First-Generation College Students, 2000–2015. *Source*: Author's calculations from Lexis-Nexis.

were among the campuses that started learning communities geared toward "first-gen" students. The University of North Carolina-Asheville paired first-generation college students with faculty member mentors who were themselves the first in their families to attend college (Opidee 2015). On some University of California campuses, professors were encouraged to publicize their own first-generation status with stickers on their office doors or on websites directed toward first-gen students. Women dropped out as an essential constituency of the reformers; by the end of the period, they were greatly outperforming men on virtually every measure of academic achievement (DiPrete and Buchmann 2013), even as their labor market outcomes continued to lag behind men's.

Opportunity Engines

It is important to recognize the many students from first-generation and lower-income families who come to campus with little or no family experience in higher education and yet find the spark within themselves, supported by their friends and families, to achieve impressive accomplishments. Nearly everyone who has taught in college recently has encountered students like Juan Bautista, Ivie Eigebor, and Sang Nguyen, three undergraduates I came to know of from my work as a university administrator. Juan, a first-generation college student from one of the poorest cities in Southern California, won a "great minds" fellowship to work at the Johnson Space Center in Florida, where, among other activities, he has worked on developing organic light-emitting diodes to replace costly and heavy cathode ray tube technology on the NASA *Orion* spacecraft. Ivie, whose family emigrated from Nigeria, achieved honors grades in one of the toughest majors on campus, biochemistry, while minoring in public policy, and subsequently enrolled in medical school pursuing a career as a pediatrician. Sang came to the United States from Thailand as a high school student so that his family could seek treatment for his leukemia. Having beaten leukemia and learned English in adolescence, he devoted himself to understanding the molecular processes underlying the spread of cancer cells. He has now worked with researchers at both Harvard and Cal Tech studying the RNA-binding proteins that may help unlock the molecular basis for control of many forms of cancer.

The Stanford economist Raj Chetty and his colleagues have put statistical meat on these anecdotal bones. They gained access to IRS records on parents' and children's pretransfer incomes and examined colleges that are mobility accelerators for those born into disadvantaged circumstances. Their calculation focuses on bottom-to-top mobility. The calculation is based on multiplying "access" (the proportion of students from low-income families) by "success" (the proportion who attain top quintile earnings). Some selective colleges and universities, such as Pomona College and Princeton University, have made efforts to enroll more students from lower-income backgrounds, but these institutions are too small to generate large numbers of graduates who achieve bottom-to-top mobility. Instead, the Stanford group draws attention to what we might call "the people's colleges" because these are the colleges that enroll many more low-income students than Ivy League-plus institutions do. Several California State Universities were mobility accelerators in this study, including Cal State Los Angeles and Cal Poly Pomona. The City University of New York campuses and two of the regional campuses of the University of Texas were also among the leaders. One private college, Pace University, and one for-profit, Technical Career Institute, both in New York City, also scored high. Only one major research university, SUNY Stony Brook, made the top 10 list. Each of the top 10 in the study had bottom-to-top mobility rates of 6.8 to 10 percent, representing tens of thousands of modern Horatio Alger stories—stories in which study rather than luck plays the facilitating role (2017, table 4). Altogether, 39 colleges achieved a bottom-to-top mobility rate of 5 percent or more, with two-thirds of these institutions located among public four-year colleges and universities (Chronicle of Higher Education 2017b).

Slightly different configurations of high-performing colleges emerge when different cut points are adopted—for example, mobility from the bottom 40 percent into the top 40 percent of earners. And naturally Chetty's team found much higher mobility rates when they focused on the shorter social distances like these that students can climb using their college degrees; in a few colleges 33 percent or more of students attained bottom 40 to top 40 percent mobility. Yet the same types of colleges—those that enroll large numbers of low-income students—emerged as mobility generators over shorter social distances as well (New York Times 2017).

In whatever way one cuts the data, the results show that the college-for-all system is populated by dozens of institutions that are making a sizable contribution to bringing students from poverty (or near-poverty) to economic security.

The consequences of attending and graduating from college may be most important for the least advantaged students. Sociologists Paul Attewell and David Lavin followed up a representative sample of minority women who had attended the City University of New York during the brief open-admissions era in the early 1970s to see how they and their families were faring thirty years after they had first enrolled. The results, comparing women who eventually completed college and those who did not, were, as the authors wrote, "startling" (2007, 4). In addition to securing more stable and better-paying jobs, the college graduates tended to talk to their children far more often about their days and about their classes. They tended to provide much more emotional support to them when they needed it. The children of the college graduates also read more books and were more likely to have computers in their homes. They were more likely to take outings for educational purposes, attending art exhibits, listening to musical performances, and visiting zoos. The college graduates were also much more likely to know their children's friends and their parents. They volunteered in community organizations and they took their children to church more often than women who failed to complete college. All of these parenting qualities influenced children's success in school and their likelihood of staying out of trouble. What is particularly impressive is that nearly all of the statistical relationships held up, though often diminished in strength, after the authors controlled for a battery of background factors, including the women's social class background, race, measured IQ, and high school academic preparation.

The Preparation Gap

Nevertheless, a tension exists between higher education expansion in a highly unequal society like the United States and the capacity of the system to realize its aims to develop human capital to a high level. Tens of thousands of students like Juan, Ivie, and Sang graduate from college every year, but hundreds of thousands from similar backgrounds start but do not complete degrees. Very often students' problems in college arise from a tangle of financial difficulties, family hardships, poor grades, and underdeveloped time management skills. The role that poor academic skills play in this tangle can be difficult to distinguish clearly. The economists John Bound, Michael Lovenheim, and Sarah Turner (2010) have argued that the most important cause of noncompletion among community college students is their lack of adequate secondary school preparation. Although they attribute noncompletion in four-year colleges and universities primarily to other factors, such as overcrowded classrooms, underpreparation is clearly part of the story there as well.

WIDENING PREPARATION GAPS

College teachers can sympathize with the challenges faced by students who come to campus underprepared for the jump in expectations they encounter there, but they can also be frustrated by the weak academic skills many of these students bring to their classes. The surprise and frustration of teaching writing to college students who are not and never have been readers is captured well by the anonymous author of the 2011 memoir, *In the Basement of the Ivory Tower*. The author refers to himself "Professor X." X's standards were not particularly high. His fundamental principle was that writing should not "wobble": "We expect our houses to be plumb, our tables solid—why not our paragraphs?" However, many of his students had read fewer than ten books in their lifetimes. They had never studied grammar. Adherence to the sloppy, elliptical language of texting and tweeting had become an acceptable way for them to hide the fact that they were not capable of composing correct English sentences. They did not know how to use revision to come closer to the quality and depth of good writing because they did not have an archetype of good writing in their minds. Professor X wrote about the results of a first assignment:

> Out of about fifteen students, at least ten seemed to have no familiarity with the English language. There were words misspelled, rather simple words at that.... There was no overarching structure to the paragraphs... thoughts and notions were tossed at the reader haphazardly.... There were countless grammatical errors; sentences without verbs; sentences without subjects; commas everywhere, like a spilled dish of chocolate

sprinkles, until there were none, for paragraphs at a time; sentences that neither began with a capital letter nor ended with any punctuation whatsoever. . . . The vocabulary was not at a college level and perhaps not at a high school level. . . . Tenses wandered from present to past to past perfect back to present. (2011, 27–28)

Of course, it is up to teachers to take the challenges posed by the students in their classrooms and to help them understand subject matter; no quarter should be given to those who blame students and do not focus instead on what they are doing to help them learn. In chapter 8, I will discuss promising methods for improving college teaching. Here I will focus on what institutions have done to meet the needs of students like those who enrolled in Professor X's courses and the consequences for college curricula and conceptions of undergraduate education that the larger enrollments of the college-for-all period produced.

STUDENT SUCCESS INITIATIVES

As the variance in student abilities and motivations increased, so too did the number of interventions necessary to help keep students in college and on track to graduate. Colleges and universities have deployed dozens of new technologies and small armies of advisors and program staff to help students stick it out and complete their degrees.

Placement exams are the first tool employed, because they prevent students from taking on coursework beyond their current level of preparation. Prior to enrollment American college students are typically required to take English reading and writing placement tests. Those intending quantitative majors are also required to take mathematics placement tests. On the basis of test results students are enrolled in courses that suit their levels of preparation. Low placement slows students down—and indeed as many as half of community college students never make it out of their assigned remedial courses in mathematics.[11]

Beyond placement tests, campuses have provided funding for a variety of academic support services for students who are struggling in their courses—or would simply like to excel in them. These expenditures are up by one-third in public universities over the last two decades and by much more than that in private colleges and universities. The trend toward increasing academic support services is due, as higher education scholars Roger Geiger and Donald Heller put it, to "the increasing demands on universities to support a wide array of student abilities" (2011, 7)—and the perceived obligation of institutions to help every student succeed by staying in school and graduating. Student academic support services include summer preparatory courses, learning communities, tutoring, supplemental instruction, writing support, and academic advising. Many universities have developed special programs for students identified as most at risk for noncompletion.

At public universities, these programs were typically staffed by peer educators (undergraduate students who have achieved good grades), who are trained and supervised by professional staff. Peer educators are an ingenious approach to helping good students improve their own knowledge by becoming teachers of their peers who are struggling (there's no better way to learn a subject than to teach it), at a low cost (usually just above minimum wage), while reducing the intimidation factor that leads some shy or embarrassed undergraduates to avoid their professors' and teaching assistants' office hours. At private universities, the reliance on professional staff is greater.

Supplemental Instruction (SI) has proven to be one of the more effective programs that relies on peer educators. The underlying ideas are simple: repetition helps with retention of course materials and students are more likely to seek help from peers than from older adults. The approachability of peer educators appears to be a plus for many students who are too shy to ask questions of the professors or teaching assistants. The peer educators attend class and are trained on presenting material; they are expected not to depart from the professor's main points in lecture. Because SI is directed toward difficult courses, rather than at-risk students, it rarely creates a stigma for those who attend. Researchers have found that courses with SI support tend to show positive results; students who participate in SI achieve higher mean grades and persist longer in college than otherwise similar students (controlled for ethnicity and prior academic performance) who do not participate (Dawson et al. 2014). Other studies suggest that regular student attendance at SI sessions is necessary for the program to make a measurable difference in students' grades and that considerable course-level variation exists in the outcomes of SI (Coyne and Curran 2015).

It is worth noting a few of the other promising programs devised by colleges and universities to help less well-prepared students succeed. Georgia State University, for example, revamped its advising center and developed a predictive analytics program to rapidly intervene with students who were falling off track to timely graduation. Georgia State reports that it was able to raise its graduation rates by more than 10 percent over a four-year interval at the same time that the incoming academic qualifications of students declined (Georgia State University 2014). The University of Texas-Austin created the University Leadership Network, a program to support at-risk students by providing a four-year program of leadership training, experiential learning opportunities, and community and university service. In the first two cohorts studied, participating students had predicted four-year graduation rates 18 percent lower than other members of their entering classes, but UT assessments indicated that their persistence in the first two years nearly matched that of others in their entering cohorts (University of Texas-Austin 2017). The Virginia Tech Math Emporium is a space occupied by more than five hundred computers in which students can work on self-paced math instruction aided by math department teaching assistants who circulate to help students with problems. After introduction of the Math Emporium, introductory mathematics classes showed reductions of D and F grades and withdrawals by more than 10 percent, according to Virginia Tech assessments (Virginia Tech University 2016). Some of these programs, including the Math Emporium, appear to translate well across the campuses that adopt them (ibid.), but the scalability of most of these student success programs remains unproven.

Many campuses do not attempt to evaluate their student success programs. The model is more likely to be one that emphasizes providing service than evaluating whether the service is making a difference. The evaluations that are conducted could not pass muster among social scientists. They rely on post hoc matched samples rather than random assignment, missing potential motivational differences between those who do and do not seek services. It is difficult to know how much these unmeasured differences in student motivation—what social scientists call "self-selection bias"—contribute to positive outcomes.

A MISMATCH BETWEEN NEED AND RESOURCES

The bigger problem, however, is that the resources to run effective student success programs exist mainly at the universities that need them least. Georgia State, a minority-serving institution, is an exception in some ways, but it is not an exception when it comes to resources; the Georgia State program required the hiring of a fleet of new advisors and the acquisition of an expensive predictive analytics platform, totaling millions of dollars, and made possible only through a multimillion-dollar special grant from the state legislature. The University Leadership Network at the University of Texas provides $5,000 scholarships each year to participating students who keep their grades up, an expenditure of up to $250,000 per year. Virginia Tech received a $1.4 million grant from the Pew Foundation to open its Math Emporium and, even with that support, could not afford to build the structure on campus (it is located at a nearby shopping mall) (Virginia Tech University 2016).

Comprehensive regional universities and community colleges can compete for federal and state funds to build their student success programs, but many more proposals are rejected for funding than approved. Consequently, few of these institutions have the financial resources to undertake student success programs. Low staffing ratios are a major constraint on what can be accomplished in these institutions. One example helps to make the point: The national academic advising association recommends a student-to-advisor ratio of 300 to 1, and most research universities are able to maintain ratios within 100 students of that standard, but the average community college has advising caseloads of 1,000 to 1 and some run closer to 2,000 to 1 (Marcus 2012). The regional comprehensives fell somewhere in between.

The Rise of the "Practical Arts"

I now turn to changes in curriculum, academic engagement, and conceptions of the college experience that are, in one way or another, tied to the college-for-all system.

Higher education scholars assumed that one of the chief outcomes of the college-for-all system would be a dramatic shift toward more practical curricula and away from the liberal arts and sciences (see, e.g., Turner and Bowen 1990; Gumport 2002; Trow 2000, 2005; and, for a longer sociohistorical perspective, Frank and Gaebler 2006). The reasons for this prediction were straightforward: as colleges and universities enrolled larger numbers of students who were not academically inclined, it stood to reason that job-related curricula should gain ground. Indeed, in earlier work I argued that "the gradual shrinking of the old arts and sciences core of the university" and the expansion of occupational and professional programs meant that "activities considered ancillary in an earlier age have moved to the center and have become leading engines of growth" (Brint 2002, 231).

This conclusion turns out to require qualification. Occupational-professional (O-P) majors grew throughout the 1970s up until 1985, when they reached an apogee of two-thirds of all undergraduate degrees awarded. Business

TABLE 4.3. Empirical Core Curriculum, 1979–80 and 2010–11

1979–80 Degrees (rounded)		2010–11 Degrees (rounded)	
Academic Field (Share of Total Degrees)		*Academic Field (Share of Total Degrees)*	
Business	201,000 (22.1%)	Business	367,000 (21.4%)
Education	108,000 (12.0%)	Health Professions	164,000 (9.5%)
Engineering	64,000 (7.0%)	Psychology	109,000 (6.4%)
Health Professions	64,000 (7.0%)	Education	106,000 (6.2%)
Psychology	41,000 (4.5%)	Visual/Performing Arts	91,000 (5.6%)
Visual/Performing Arts	40,000 (4.5%)	Communications	84,000 (4.9%)
English	32,000 (3.5%)	Engineering	81,000 (4.7%)
Biological Sciences	31,000 (3.5%)	Biological Sciences	65,000 (3.8%)
Communications	29,000 (3.3%)	Criminal Justice	54,000 (3.1%)
Political Science	25,000 (2.8%)	English	54,000 (3.1%)
Liberal Studies/ Humanities	22,000 (2.4%)	Computer Science	47,000 (2.8%)
Agricultural Science	21,000 (2.4%)	Liberal Studies/ Humanities	47,000 (2.8%)
Economics	19,000 (2.0%)	Interdisciplinary Studies	46,000 (2.7%)
Consumer Science/ Home Ec.	18,000 (2.0%)	Political Science	40,000 (2.4%)
History	18,000 (2.0%)	Fitness/Recreation/ Leisure	39,000 (2.3%)
		History	35,000 (2.0%)

Source: Adapted from Bui 2014.

degrees led the way; about one in seven undergraduates majored in business at this high point and the dominance of business was even greater when scholars took into account the large number of students who took courses in subjects like accounting and marketing as a fallback in case their "Plan A" collapsed (Adelman 1999, 229). Following this high point, the ratio between occupational-professional and arts and sciences (A&S) degrees stabilized at 60:40 percent nationwide (Brint et al. 2005 and unpublished analyses by the author). The shift was not that dramatic because most students have been occupationally oriented most of the time—the 1960s were an aberration—and because the continued shift toward occupational programs did not continue into the 1990s and beyond.

Table 4.3 provides an overview of the empirical core curriculum in academic years 1979–80 and 2010–11, by focusing solely on the fields that awarded at least 2 percent of all baccalaureate degrees. Even at the beginning of the period, U.S. college students were far from embracing as preferred majors the traditional fields of the arts, humanities, social sciences, natural sciences, and mathematics. What we see instead is a potpourri of applied programs centered on business, health, education, and engineering together with basic programs in a handful of traditional fields such as psychology, English, biology, political science, and history. We also see the rapid rise of three new applied majors—computer science, criminal justice, and fitness, recreation, and leisure—and one new nominally basic major, communications, which nevertheless has many ties to the public relations and media industries.

GROWTH FIELDS

Beyond these mega-majors enrolling tens of thousands of students, we can see clear patterns of student choice among the fastest-growing fields. The fast-growing occupational-professional fields were nearly all connected to the power centers of the U.S. economy—that is, business, technology, government, health care, and mass media—as indeed were the very large applied fields listed above. They included fields like banking and finance; accounting; management information systems; civil engineering; mechanical engineering; allied health professions; and radio, television, and film production. The fast-growing arts and sciences fields included those related to understanding the building blocks of life (cell biology, molecular biology, cognitive/neuroscience), the environment (environmental science/studies, ecology), the arts (drama, studio art, and music), globalization (international relations, as well as many non-Western culture fields), and social inclusiveness (U.S. ethnic and women's studies). When we add the very large basic fields of psychology and communications to this mix, the shape of the future of the liberal arts and sciences looks creative, brainy, information centered, healthy, environmentally friendly, diversity conscious, and global in outlook. In other words, it looks quite a bit like the progressive and tech-minded culture of the upper-middle classes on the East and West coasts.[12]

When we examine institutional representation—how many colleges and universities adopted degree-granting fields as opposed to how many students graduated in them—two growth fields stand out for their extraordinary appeal to colleges and universities during the period: computer science and communications were both offered at fewer than a third of four-year colleges and universities in 1980–81, but by 2010–11 they were offered by more than 60 percent. Two other fields—accounting and drama—also started relatively

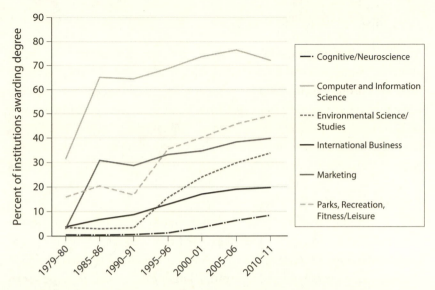

FIGURE 4.3. Sevenfold Growth Fields in Institutional Representation (selected fields), 1979–2011.

Source: Author's calculation from IPEDS online tool, 1979–2011.

small and grew to be offered by more than 50 percent of core institutions by the end of the period. The popularity of these fields reveals something about the ways in which students wanted to apply numeracy and literacy in the information age. In the growing but still incompletely institutionalized O-P fields (i.e., those without representation at 50 percent or more of IPEDS institutions), we see further evidence of the importance of five power centers in American society: (1) business (as represented by the growth in institutional representation of marketing, finance, international business, and human resources); (2) technology (numerous engineering fields); (3) media (radio/TV/film production, applied design, and, arguably, marketing); (4) health (nursing, allied health professions, public health, health administration); and (5) government (criminal justice, social work, and a miscellaneous category of "legal professions"). Among the A&S fields that were growing but still only incompletely institutionalized by 2010–11, we see further evidence of the importance of the environment (as represented by environmental science and ecology), understanding the building blocks of life (cognitive/neuroscience, cell and molecular biology), the arts (studio art, dance), globalization (anthropology and international relations, as well as many non-Western cultural studies fields), and social inclusiveness (U.S. ethnic studies and women's studies) (Brint et al. 2011) (see figure 4.3).

DECLINING FIELDS

As they observed "practical arts" fields growing, liberal arts educators mourned the decline of the humanities with an intensity that suggested they were the only fields with falling enrollments and declining institutional representation (see, e.g., American Academy of Arts and Sciences 2015; Berube and Nelson 1995; Delbanco 1999; Kernan 1997). As the English scholar Alvin Kernan put it, "[The] tectonic shifts in higher education have not, I think it is fair to say, been kind to the liberal arts in general, and to the humanities in particular. . . . The humanities, in plain words, have become a less and less significant part of higher education" (1997, 5–6).

But declining fields extended well beyond the humanities. Among the large fields that produced fewer degrees at the end of the period than at the beginning, three, it is true, were from the humanities (history, English, and Romance languages and literatures), but one other was from the social sciences (sociology), and one was typically categorized with the natural sciences (mathematics). Some smaller A&S fields, such as zoology and botany, were swept up in the reorganization of the life sciences from organism-centered study to study of basic life processes (see, e.g., Abir-Am 1997; Kay 1993). Many other declining A&S fields were the smaller European language fields (e.g., Germanic and Slavic languages and literatures), including the ancient languages of Greek and Latin that fall into classics programs. A few applied fields lost out to technology (library science) or to sociopolitical change (labor relations and home economics), and all other declining O-P fields slipped because of very low status.

When we look at declining fields in relation to institutional representation rather than degree production, the picture grows quite a bit darker for the arts and sciences. Of the larger fields—those represented at 50 percent or more of colleges and universities in 1970–71—nine of the ten that declined in representation were from the arts and sciences. These fields included four from humanities (Romance languages and literatures, history, philosophy, and English), three from the physical sciences (mathematics, chemistry, and physics), and two from the social sciences (economics and sociology). Romance languages and literatures (composed of French, Spanish, and Italian languages and literatures) showed the biggest declines; degrees in at least one of the Romance languages were offered at more than 60 percent of U.S. colleges and universities in 1980–81, but they were offered at barely 50 percent by 2010–11.

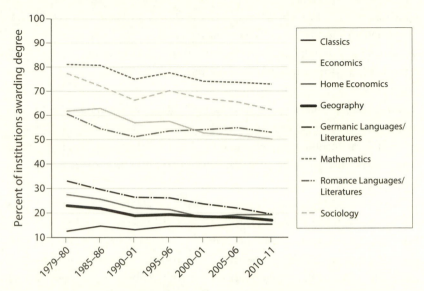

FIGURE 4.4. Declining Fields in Institutional Representation (selected fields), 1979–2011.
Source: Author's calculations from IPEDS online tool, 1979–2011.

Among the smaller fields that appeared at less than 50 percent of four-year colleges and universities in 1980–81, A&S fields were also hit comparatively hard. The loss in institutional representation of philosophy and physics is notable. Both fields grew a little in absolute representation but declined in relative terms as newly opened institutions failed to adopt them. Philosophy provides good preparation for law school, but it appeals to students who are comfortable with abstractions, a group that is in short supply at the occupationally oriented institutions that opened during the period. With less clear career prospects than engineering, physics may simply require too much mathematics for most non-engineering-bound undergraduate students at newer institutions (Brint et al. 2012a) (see figure 4.4).

The Outer-Directed Student

Growth also affected insiders' understandings of what college was for. At the turn of the twentieth century, Max Weber ([1921] 1946) wrote of the triumph of the "specialist type of man" over the "cultivated type of man." By this he meant that in the age of bureaucracy, qualifications and credentials indicating expertise in a specialized subject had displaced the older ideals of educating students more broadly for depth of understanding, judgment, a wide range of cultural knowledge, and the capacity to lead. The production of specialist types of men and women arguably remains the dominant goal of undergraduate education in the United States in our time—and clearly it remains the dominant objective in graduate and professional education. But it is at least equally likely that this goal is hedged in by other priorities to the extent that many undergraduate students—even a majority—may give lip service to career preparation as the primary goal while spending time primarily concerned with campus social life or with simply obtaining a credential that *may* prove valuable without expending an inordinate amount of effort on their studies.

The expansion of access to disadvantaged populations is directly related only to a few of the changes in student culture I will discuss. Low-income, first-generation, and underrepresented minority students are definitely *not* directly responsible for the reduced levels of study time or the higher levels of academic disengagement scholars have observed; indeed, ceteris paribus, they are marginally more likely to be engaged in their studies than students whose parents went to college (Brint and Cantwell 2014). Rather, the changes I will discuss are rooted in the growth of enrollments, which brings with it a wider range of student motivations and abilities.

COLLEGE STUDENT ORIENTATIONS

In the 1960s sociologists Burton Clark and Martin Trow (1966) proposed a typology of undergraduate student orientations. They divided undergraduate mentalities into four categories: (1) academically/intellectually oriented, (2) vocationally oriented, (3) collegiate social life oriented, and (4) credential seekers who had no strong commitment to a particular career goal. Their main concern was the challenge vocationally oriented students posed to the position of academically oriented students who were at the heart of the university's educational mission. They also recognized challenges to the academically and the occupationally oriented from two sides: first, those students who were primarily interested in what they called the "collegiate" life—fun, football, and parties—and, second, those who were primarily interested in obtaining credentials that could be helpful to them but did not require a high level of occupationally relevant skill development. Based on their observations of the University of California circa 1960, Clark and Trow considered these latter two orientations as small subcultures within an undergraduate student body primarily oriented to academics, to career preparation, or to both.

Today, higher education scholars take for granted that the intellectually oriented students represent a small minority on most American college campuses. In surveys of undergraduate students at some two dozen selective public universities taken at different years in the mid-2010s, 10 to 15 percent of students responded "often" or "very often" to the question: "This year— how often have you found your courses so interesting that you did more work than required?" (author's calculations from SERU data). One can imagine that the proportion would be lower at regional comprehensives and perhaps at least a little higher at selective private colleges and universities (see also College Board 2014).[13]

Because the premises of the Clark-Trow typology have broken down, more recent scholars have tended to think instead about other qualities that could be valuable indicators that students are getting something important out of college. A common recourse has been to look for students who are "engaged" in campus life as opposed to those who are "disengaged." There are many engaged personalities on campus; the academically engaged personality is only one. Outside of class, the engaged student brings a similar level of energy into community service activities, sports activities, campus social life, and other opportunities the campus offers.[14] Two leading researchers on college effects, social psychologists Ernest Pascarella and Patrick Terenzini, for example, concluded, "One of the most inescapable and unequivocal conclusions we can make is that the impact of college is largely determined by the individual's quality of effort and level of involvement in both academic and non-academic activities" (1991, 610). Other researchers have made distinctions between the various forms of engagement on campus—academic, club, and civic—and claim that high levels of participation on any one is indicative of an engaged student (see Douglass and Thomson 2017).

This sounds like a rationalization to me. After all, how many parents or state legislators would be willing to pay for students to be engaged solely or even primarily in campus social life, club activities, or community volunteering? Not many, I suspect. I will show in chapter 5 that social connections, club activities, and volunteering can contribute significantly to the educational power of the physical campus. Even so, they should be seen as secondary to the principal aims of higher education: the development of thinking abilities and occupationally relevant skills.

But what proportion of undergraduates *are* primarily engaged with academic study and/or career preparation, as opposed to these other options for engagement?[15] The answer is not self-evident. Different methodologies yield different results.

It is almost mandatory among college students to say that career preparation is a very important goal. About 85 percent of four-year college full-time freshmen in 2015 said that they were attending college to obtain a better job, 76 percent said they were in college to prepare for a specific career, and 70 percent said they were attending to make more money in their careers (HERI 2015). These figures do not vary much by institutional type. Among 14 major public research universities in 2012, for example, 85 percent or more of students on every campus said that "obtaining the skills I need to pursue my chosen career" was a "very important" college goal (author's calculations). These public university students were also interested in the social side of campus life. In 2012, 70 percent or more at every campus cited "meaningful friendships" as "very important," and more than half cited "enjoying my college years before assuming adult responsibilities" and "establishing social networks that will help further my career" as "very important" (author's calculations).

Time-use data tell a different story than survey responses, one that is more skewed to the social enjoyment side of college. Using a half century of time-use data, Philip Babcock and Mindy Marks (2010) showed that students' self-reported time attending and studying for class fell by nearly half between the early 1960s and the late 2000s and that these declines occurred at all levels of selectivity, in all majors, and among all demographic groups. At the University of California, students who responded to an undergraduate experiences survey in 2008 said they spent about forty hours a week enjoying and participating in campus social life and about twenty-seven hours a week studying or attending class (Brint and Cantwell 2010), the latter figure only slightly higher than Babcock and Marks (2010) found for their national sample in the late 2000s. Newer studies have used mechanical devices, such as Smartpen technologies that record time-stamped digitized pen strokes, to measure study time directly. These studies yield significantly lower estimates of actual time spent on study than do student self-reports—and the estimates are *not* highly correlated with student self-reports of study time (Rawson, Stahovich, and Meyer 2017). (It is gratifying, though, that these studies do find a link between study time and grades, a link that has been missing in most time diary studies.)

Allison Cantwell and I examined several dimensions of academic disengagement—the flip side of academic engagement—using survey data from University of California campuses compiled in 2012. We found that one-fifth of responding students said that they did half or less of the reading for their classes, and another one-fifth said they studied and attended class eighteen hours or less during an average week.[16] One-quarter of the survey respondents also reported rarely, if ever, participating in class or interacting with their instructors and teaching assistants. Students who complete the surveys tend to have somewhat higher grade-point averages than those who do not complete the survey (see Chatman 2007b), suggesting that these are conservative estimates of student academic disengagement. We know that the group that makes no significant progress in analytical and critical thinking during the college years may be somewhat larger. The leading studies suggest that 33 to 40 percent of entering college students fail to improve in a statistically significant sense on well-designed tests of analytical and critical thinking after four years of college (Arum, Roksa, and Cho 2011; Pascarella et al. 2011).[17]

Most college ethnographies have also emphasized the interests of students in campus social life or the divided consciousness of students who want to keep up good grades while at the same time fully enjoying the social side of the college experience. Some who have tried to develop typologies using the transcribed data from their interviews with college students find slight majorities on the social enjoyment side rather than the career preparation side of the undergraduate student body (see, e.g., Grigsby 2009). We know from these ethnographies that, at the very least, having fun with friends is a prominent part of the contemporary undergraduate experience. Mary Grigsby, for example, quotes a communications major who leaned strongly toward the social enjoyment side of college life:

> I definitely think there should be investment . . . work for whatever it is that you want to do, but most importantly, more than anything else, in college, you should have fun. It shouldn't necessarily come at the expense of your studies, [or] the overall goal of graduating, but if you're finding yourself at a point where this is no longer enjoyable, then something is wrong. Take this time to have fun and enjoy your youth! (2009, 54–55)

Many similar statements can be found in the ethnographies of college life by Armstrong and Hamilton (2013), Holland and Eisenhart (1990), Moffatt (1989), Mullen (2010), and Nathan (2005).[18] Relatively few of these students are part of the fun, football, and party scene. Instead the reference group for most socially oriented students is the circle of friends they see on a regular basis and, secondarily, the student clubs and organizations to which they belong. Could it be true, as the Stanford sociologist Mitchell Stevens and his colleagues have suggested, that first-generation college students are misled by their expectation that college is mainly about learning and skill development rather than the accumulation of potentially valuable social connections? (see Stevens, Armstrong, and Arum 2008, 133).

NEW IMAGES OF THE EDUCATED PERSON

Confronted by evidence of limited time investment in learning on college campuses, some economists have quietly stepped away from the emphasis of human capital theory on cognitive development—or specified its relevance to a relatively few high-demand and mainly quantitative fields (see, e.g., Arcidiacono 2004). They have focused instead on the development of communication skills and work-related attitudes such as deference to authority and capacity for what might be called organizationally bounded self-direction (Heckscher and Adler 2006). These are the traits that businesspeople themselves often mention when they are asked about desirable employee characteristics. Others have embraced MIT economist Lester Thurow's focus on the greater trainability of college-educated workers. For Thurow the labor market matches trainable individuals with training ladders:

> The function of education is not to confer skill and therefore increased productivity and higher wages; it is rather to certify . . . "trainability" and to confer . . . a certain status by virtue of this certification. Jobs and higher incomes are then distributed on the basis of this certified status. . . . The operative problem is to pick and train workers to generate the desired productivity with the least investment in training costs. (1972, 67, 69)

We can easily see how college articulates well with the production of trainable individuals: the requirements to show up for class, read assigned materials, listen carefully to professors, follow instructions, and turn in assignments regularly on many different subjects would surely seem to be directly related to trainability. The rotation of students across classrooms with very different teaching personalities and approaches to subject matter presumably also contributes to the flexibility required of a trainable person, as certified by a college degree.

Along similar lines, Martin Trow argued that degree holders are people who have the mental plasticity to succeed in complex environments. As Trow put it:

> In institutions marked by universal access, there is concern with the preparation of large numbers for life in an advanced industrial society; they are training not primarily elites . . . but the whole population, and

their chief concern is to maximize the adaptability of that population to a society whose chief characteristic is rapid social and technological change. (2005, 18)

Again, it is easy to see how a college campus, with its wide range of activities, both curricular and cocurricular, could help develop young people who are able to adapt quickly to new assignments, new opportunities, and changes in social relations and technology. The adaptable person can more or less smoothly glide from assignment to assignment and interaction to interaction, thanks to the four years of situational challenges embedded in their higher education experiences both inside and outside the classroom.[19] By putting students into many types of social situations, both in and out of class, these "person-reading" and "situation-reading" capacities are put to the test and can be developed and refined.

These ideas retain a connection between education and work, even if academic study recedes in importance. Other writers are skeptical of that connection, accept that students may not learn that much in college, and twist the contours of college socialization in surprising new directions. For the Stanford sociologist John W. Meyer, the most important product of undergraduate education is the provision of what he calls "cultural models of expanded actorhood." In Meyer's view, individuals in societies like the United States act on culturally legitimated scripts originating in the power centers of society, but the modern individual is nevertheless expected to have the subjective feeling that s/he is empowered to act. For these reasons, the socializing institutions of modern societies create the conditions for widespread feelings of empowerment. They do so by expanding human rights, ideologies of inclusion, and incentives for opinion giving. A major purpose of socializing institutions therefore is to develop, to use Meyer's formulation, "the posture of actorhood." As Meyer put it, "[character types typical of] passive old national state bureaucracies turn into actors filled with plans and strategies" (2008, 797). For these subjectively empowered actors, the idea or "myth" of rationality is important as a justification for opinions and plans—but actual knowledge may or may not exist or be important. The modern actor can and will produce opinions about issues and events about which s/he knows nothing, such as whether the United States should invade a country s/he has never heard of. It is the opinion generation itself that is important for the Meyer school. This posture may be misrecognized as engagement, when it is better described as a conforming reaction to environmental cues about how to declare oneself a modern person.

THE COUNTERFORCE: INCENTIVES
FOR POSTGRADUATE STUDY

It is not easy to come to a final conclusion from studies based on such different methodologies and premises, but I will nevertheless hazard an assessment: in the end, the wide variability in student motivations and aptitudes created by growth has not led to a collapse in undergraduate education, even though it has weakened the rigor of that education. It is true that academically disengaged undergraduates represent sizable minorities on many campuses and they are a majority on some, but they are not the dominant group on most campuses. Most full-time students at four-year colleges and universities are trying to develop skills they think will be useful to them in later life while at the same time enjoying "the college experience." They can be excited and stimulated by charismatic instructors, but they are prone to resist working hard in courses whose relevance to their academic interests or career goals they do not see. Many nominally full-time students are working too many hours for pay to allow themselves the opportunity to engage in an expansive way with their studies.

Apart from empirical misjudgments about the size of the academically disengaged population, scholars who depict college life as an Eden for slackers and hedonists also fail to account for the significant counterforce to academic disengagement arising from the growth of graduate degree aspirations. As I noted earlier, graduate enrollments have grown faster than undergraduate enrollments since the mid-1990s. More than 15 percent of college students enroll in graduate programs immediately following college and another several percent do so following a few years of work experience. These ambitions are driven in part by credential inflation. When faced with the choice of employing a young person with a graduate degree as compared to a young person with a baccalaureate only, employers in "knowledge-sector" industries will now typically opt for the more expensive but presumably better-trained and socialized person with graduate or professional degree credentials.

The rise of underemployment among college graduates is another source of students' heightened interest in advanced degrees. Using data from the Bureau of Labor Statistics, Richard Vedder and his associates (2013) have emphasized the high incidence of underemployment among college graduates. By underemployment, Vedder and his colleagues mean college graduates taking jobs that do not require college degrees and do not pay at the level of most occupations that do require college degrees. According to the

Bureau of Labor Statistics from 2010, of three million recent college graduates, more than 150,000 were in retail sales, 100,000 were providing services in restaurants, 80,000 were working as clerks, and 60,000 were working in blue-collar occupations.[20]

It is unlikely that the trend toward postgraduate studies will help reenergize undergraduate education across the board. For students who are not doing well in college or who are enrolled in majors with poor occupational prospects, the impact of underemployment could be to lower study effort further. Even so, the net effects of a booming graduate credentials market are likely to be salutary for study. Decent grades and letters of recommendation are necessary for graduate and professional school admission, and excellent grades and letters of recommendation are necessary for admission to top programs. These incentives may not keep the size of the disengaged undergraduate population from growing a little larger, but they should reinforce the commitment to study among the large proportion of college students—now more than half—who say they intend at some point to pursue graduate or professional degrees.

5

Multiplying Status Locations

In chapter 4, I showed how the commitments of colleges and universities to diversity and inclusion have been fuel for the advance of American higher education. In this chapter I will discuss how, in the college-for-all era, colleges and universities simultaneously maintained and expanded high-status tracks and locations. In most cases the mechanisms colleges used to encourage high-achieving and motivated students reinforced rather than redistributed family-related social advantages. These mechanisms ranged from increased levels of selectivity in the country's elite college and the maintenance of rigorous standards in quantitative majors to the addition of new honors and leadership programs. By multiplying status locations on campus, colleges and universities maintained and invented new hierarchies of privilege even as they accommodated intensifying demands for democratization and equity. These multiplying status locations are one reason why the white upper-middle-class students Natasha Warikoo (2016) interviewed at two Ivy League universities said they welcomed the diversification of the student body; diversity was desirable so long as it did not harm their own opportunities.

Table 5.1 compares characteristics of the access-oriented system of college for all and the status-oriented system of much better college for some. These are ideal types; actual institutions mix access and status concerns in complex ways.

TABLE 5.1. The Access and Status System of U.S. Undergraduate Education

	Access System	Status System
Principles	Opportunity Student Success	Institutionally Defined Merit Institutionally Defined Accomplishment Social Advantages
Key Mechanisms	Enrollment Growth	Selectivity Social Closure
Institutional Locations	Community Colleges Regional Comprehensives Lesser Universities Least Demanding Majors Newer Graduate Programs	Ivy League-like Institutions Selective Liberal Arts Colleges Public Flagship Universities Elite Graduate Programs Most Demanding Majors
Campus Locations	Academic Support Services Advising Services Learning Communities	Fraternities/Sororities Honors Programs Leadership Programs Restricted Majors

Desired Institutional
   Outcomes
	Retention
	Graduation
		Honors & Awards
		Prestigious Graduate School
		   Entry
		High-Status Careers

Campus Advocates	Progressive Faculty
	Community-Oriented Faculty
	Social Advocacy Groups
	First-Generation Students
	Administrators of Non-Elite
	   Institutions
		Eminent Older Faculty
		Professionally Oriented Faculty
		Campus Honors Societies
		Honors Students
		Administrators of Elite
		   Institutions
		Greek Life Councils

Supporting Institutions	Gates/Lumina Foundations Department of Education Higher Ed. Associations *Washington Monthly* ranks	Assoc. of Am. Universities (AAU) Consortium on Financing Higher Education (COFHE) *U.S. News & World Report* ranks College Board Educational Testing Service
Expectations of Students	Engaged Hardworking Seek Help as Required	High-Quality Performance Accumulation of Social & Cultural Capital
Desirable Traits of Graduates	Conscientious Flexible and Adaptable Sense of Agency Opinions and Plans Upwardly Mobile	Accomplished Knowledgeable Control of Situations Lifelong Intellectual Interests Well-Planned Career Strategy Well-Placed Friends

Persisting Advantages

Let me begin by discussing how the college sifting process works. Through each era of equal opportunity discourse and practice, one constant has remained: students from upper SES and racial-ethnic majority families have been far more likely than others to enroll in college, to enroll in selective colleges, to graduate from college, and to enter and complete graduate and professional programs. The advantages have been particularly great for whites and Asians whose fathers graduated from college and worked in professional or managerial occupations. The college-for-all system may have promoted "inclusive excellence," but the excellence it recognized and rewarded was not very equally distributed. Some sociologists refer to this pattern as "effectively maintained inequality" (Lucas 2001), and others go so far as to label it "maximally maintained inequality" (Raftery and Hout 1993).

Behind this social sifting lie the preexisting advantages that upper SES and racial-ethnic majority students bring with them to college. There are a large number of these advantages. Children whose parents have graduated college hear on average at least three times as many words during the day as students from families of high school dropouts (Hart and Risley 1995). Their parents are much more likely to read to them at night and to monitor their homework. Children of the highly educated are more likely to be exposed to cultural experiences, visiting museums and attending art performances, and to foreign travel. They are expected to do well in school, and their after-school lives are often carefully organized to develop skills in music or sport and to facilitate the juggling of many responsibilities (Lareau 2003). Opportunities for tutoring and test prep are available, as needed. These experiences and expectations weigh positively on the academic achievement of children from highly educated homes. Finances also matter. Pell Grants, which are intended to support lower-income families, have not kept up with the costs of college attendance. Low-income students consequently have increasing levels of unmet need. For some this means working fifteen to twenty hours or more a week while attending school, a workload that scholars have repeatedly shown negatively affects students' academic performance (see, e.g., Staff and Mortimer 2007).

The social sifting process works behind the scenes in the sense that its consequences are felt at every critical transition stage, as a proportion of students from lower-income, first-generation, and underrepresented minority groups come to believe that they lack the preparation, the motivation, and/

or the financial resources to persist. Family crises and work responsibilities also contribute to the tougher odds faced by these students. To call this process social sifting is sociologically accurate because individual decisions are rooted in broader social circumstances, but of course it fails to do emotional justice to the frustrations and sadness that decisions to withdraw from college bring to the lives of so many aspiring but socially disadvantaged college students. As a university administrator I attempted to comfort and sort out possibilities for some of these students whose lives had become a tangle of financial stress, romantic traumas, roommate problems, anxiety, depression, and declining grades.

WHO BENEFITS FROM COLLEGE?

The benefits of college degrees are very unequally distributed by social class and race. We might expect that this would be true for reasons related to financial wherewithal, levels of information about college, and students' academic preparation. But we would not necessarily expect that these gaps would grow wider during a period of enrollment expansion, as in fact they did. Divisions by social class were particularly wide—and were growing wider over time. By age twenty-five, approximately 80 percent of those born into the top income quartile will have received a postsecondary degree (including both baccalaureate and associate's degrees), but just 10 percent of those born into the bottom quartile will have done so (Bailey and Dynarski 2011; Mortenson 2010).[1]

Consistent with the great expansion during the period, more young people from each income level in the second cohort attended college than did those in the first, but the gaps between the top and the bottom also grew larger. For members of the birth cohort that attended college in the early 1970s, about 60 percent of students from top quartile families entered college, compared to about 20 percent of students from bottom quartile families, a 40 percent top-to-bottom gap. For members of the birth cohort that attended college in the late 1990s and early 2000s, by contrast, 80 percent of students from top quartile families entered college, compared to about 30 percent of students from bottom quartile families, a 50 percent gap (Bailey and Dynarski 2011, table 6.2). Moreover, unlike college access, virtually all the growth in college completion came from among students whose parents' earnings fell in the top quarter of the income distribution. More graduated from college in each income quartile, but the gap between the bottom and the top grew from about 30 percentage points for those who attended college in the 1970s to about 45 percentage points for those who attended college in the late 1990s and early 2000s (Bailey and Dynarski 2011, table 6.3).

By contrast, gaps in access to postsecondary education by race have remained relatively stable over time, even as gaps in completion grew wider. Among 2004 high school graduates who enrolled in postsecondary institutions immediately following high school, racial-ethnic gaps were not large. Seventy-three percent of Hispanics enrolled in postsecondary education—theirs was the lowest proportion—while 76 percent of African Americans, 82 percent of whites, and 90 percent of Asian Americans did so (NCES 2012b, 170). Entry rates did not change much in the following decade (Aud et al. 2012, table A-34-2); the black-to-white entry gap, for example, remained stable at about 7 percent (NCES 2016b, table 302.60).

The big issue is that minorities enrolled mainly in open-access two- and four-year colleges, while whites and Asians have enrolled disproportionately in colleges and universities that select among applicants. Since 1995, 82 percent of new white enrollments have gone to the 468 most selective colleges in the country, while 72 percent of Hispanic and 68 percent of African American enrollments have gone to two-year and four-year open-access institutions (Carnevale and Strohl 2013; see also Astin and Oseguera 2004; Bastedo and Jacquette 2011; Posselt et al. 2012). Graduation rates are low in open-access institutions, and successful transitions from two-year to four-year colleges occur for many fewer than half who intend to transfer (Dougherty and Kienzl 2006). Given these circumstances, it is not surprising that whites improved their six-year graduation rates from about 30 percent to over 40 percent between 1995 and 2015, while black graduation rates improved by just six points, from 15 to just over 20 percent, and Hispanics' graduation rates improved by only a little more than that of blacks (Kena et al. 2016, figure 4).

Black-white comparisons dominate the scholarly literature, but Asian American students were the big winners in the college-for-all system, together with white women. Asian graduation rates were notably higher than those of any other group throughout the period—exceeding those of whites by an impressive 20 percent in 2015 (NCES 2016b, table 322.20). Women's graduation rates exceeded men's by 7 percent (ibid.) It is the progress of these groups, in particular, that creates a significant challenge to the idea that college simply reproduces and legitimates preexisting group advantages, the position argued by Pierre Bourdieu and Jean-Claude Passeron (1977) and many other social scientists (see, e.g., Bowles and Gintis 1976; Lareau 2003; Raftery and Hout 1993). Clearly, new opportunities count when they are combined with high levels of motivation and follow through—and the capacity to locate financial resources to support success.

HAS DIVERSIFICATION CHANGED THE COMPOSITION OF THE UPPER-MIDDLE CLASS?

One way to examine the extent of the persisting advantage of traditionally advantaged groups is to look at the composition of people who have attained upper-middle-class incomes over time. In my view, such a focus on the upper-middle class is a good choice because it is reasonable to assume that most college students hope to leverage their educational credentials for access to incomes high enough to support a comfortable lifestyle (see, e.g., Bledstein 1976; Lamont 1992; Sobel 1983).

For purposes of this analysis, I defined the upper-middle class as the top quintile of earners. This is an imprecise definition, of course, because some people who do not have incomes at this level nevertheless are upper-middle class in lifestyle, either because of inherited wealth or because they benefit from regional differences in cost of living. Nevertheless, this is the best single-variable definition that public-use census data will allow. I looked at individual earners rather than households because household data are complicated by strong biases in favor of dual-earner couples.[2] By looking at the composition of the top quintile of individual earners over time, we can begin to answer the following question: How much did the push for greater diversity in higher education (and in the larger society) contribute to the diversification of the upper-middle class?

It is important to keep in mind that as the working population grows, so too does the size of the upper-middle class. This fact alone would allow for a larger absolute number of women and minorities in the upper-middle class, even if their relative proportions remained roughly constant. A stronger demonstration of the impact of the diversity era would be increasing relative proportions of women and minorities in the top quintile over time. But even increasing relative proportions need to be read in the context of the overall growth of the group in the adult population. If the size of a group, let's say hypothetically, doubled during the period from 10 to 20 percent, but its representation in the top income quintile grew by only 1 percent, members of the group would have legitimate reasons to feel frustration about their rate of progress in American society.

To answer questions about the changing composition of the top quintile over time, I examined Current Population Survey (CPS) data at five-year intervals from 1980 through 2015, with the assistance of a colleague, Kristopher Proctor. We limited this analysis to employed people who were age twenty-five or older. According to the CPS, in 1980, the top quintile was composed of nearly 33.5 million people; by 2015, the top quintile had grown to nearly 51 million people. This growth allowed for an expanded number of women and minorities in the top earning group. Blacks increased from 1.8 million to 3.7 million; Hispanics from 1.6 million to almost 4 million; and women made the largest gains of all, from 5.3 million to 17.3 million. The proportion of these groups in the top income quintile also grew during the period. Blacks increased by 1 percent, from approximately 6 to approximately 7 percent. Hispanics increased from nearly 5 to nearly 8 percent. And women's representation more than doubled, from 16 to 34 percent. The representation of blacks and Hispanics in the top income quintile did not, however, keep pace with their growth as a proportion of the U.S. adult population. The black proportion in the population increased by 2 percent, from 10 to 12 percent, and Hispanics more than doubled as a proportion of the population, from 7.5 to over 15 percent. Women, by contrast, remained roughly stable at 52 percent of the population, indicating impressive gains in upper-middle-class membership during the period, though gains that left them still well below their population proportion (see figure 5.1).

The other major change in the composition of the top quintile was in the distribution of educational attainments. The highly educated were over-represented in this upper-middle-income class throughout the period. But, where about one-third of the top income quartile had bachelor's or higher-level degrees in 1980, by 2015 that proportion was nearly two-thirds. The growing proportion of the highly educated in the upper-middle class closely paralleled their growth in the U.S. adult working population, which also nearly doubled during the period, from 17 percent to one-third of the total.

These figures provide not-too-subtle clues about the biggest relative losers during the period. They were poorly educated people (those with high school degrees or less), men, and whites—precisely the groups most prominent in the populist reaction that emerged in the 2010s under the banners of the Tea Party and white nationalism. Where white males had dominated the top quintile in 1980, holding nearly 80 percent of positions, they were down to a narrow majority (56 percent) by 2015. Only the growth of the stratum prevented the absolute numbers of white males in the top quintile from declining. In absolute numbers they barely held their own—adding two million top quintile earners during the period to an income stratum that grew by more than 86 million people over the period. The absolute number

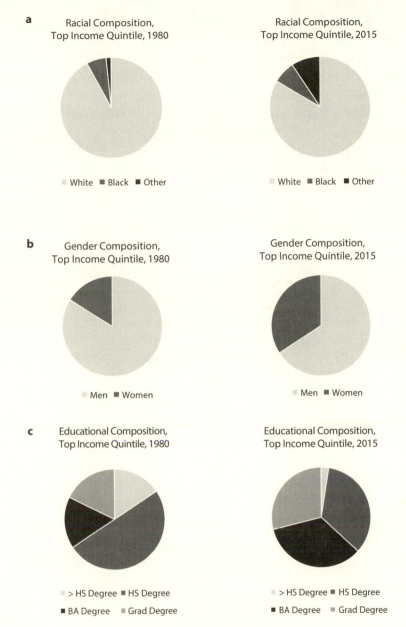

FIGURE 5.1. Changes in Top Quintile Composition, 1980–2015.
Source: Author's calculations from annualized Current Population Survey, 1980 and 2015.

of top quintile earners from every other demographic group (apart from those with less than high school degrees) grew in a robust way fueled by the population growth of the groups of which they were a part.

The conclusion I draw from this analysis is that expansion of the working population in the context of expanded higher education access and completion allowed more women and minorities to join the stratum of high earners, without negatively affecting the *absolute* size of the white male population in the top quintile. Population growth contributed to social peace by creating more places at the top, even if it did not greatly improve the relative opportunities of people from the most disadvantaged groups. The diversification of the top quintile has harmed the *relative* position of white men, but not to the extent that it posed a pressing problem for those who obtained college credentials. At the same time, the demographic and educational changes Proctor and I found were undoubtedly a problem for white men without college credentials who aspired to upper-middle-class (or higher) incomes.

White men may have experienced the most relative loss, but underrepresented minorities had reason for continued feelings of frustration as well. The foothold of blacks and Hispanics in the upper-middle class remained weak relative to their population share. One other conclusion is hard to avoid: in the absence of efforts to diversify and equalize opportunity in higher education and the labor force, the advantages of whites and Asian Americans would have, almost certainly, surpassed those they held.

High-Status Tracks

Like preexisting social advantages, tracking within higher education also limits the egalitarian consequences of diversification. Sociologists use the term "social closure" to describe efforts, conscious or unconscious, to monopolize valuable opportunities for the few through the effective maintenance of barriers to entry combined with disproportionate rewards for admission (see Murphy 1984; Parkin 1979). Closure mechanisms permeate higher education. In this section, I will discuss the four high-status tracks that have received the most attention from social scientists: (1) selective colleges and universities, (2) quantitative majors, (3) graduate degrees, and (4) high grade point averages.

Many people may feel uncomfortable discussing these high-status tracks as mechanisms for social closure because those who occupy them seem to have done so through the dint of valid individual accomplishments.

Admission to highly selective colleges, for example, is usually seen (especially by proud parents!) as symbolic of excellence, not as a mechanism of social closure. I do not deny that individual accomplishment counts; the great majority of students admitted to the most exclusive colleges have been top achievers in secondary school. At the same time, it is important to ask: Why do people compete to be admitted to these colleges? For most it is because they provide or are thought to provide unusually advantageous opportunities that others cannot access. This restriction that social scientists call "closure" is the other side of what most people count as "accomplishment." In much the same manner, one can say that admission to a prestigious private club is earned, but for social scientists its importance lies more often in the fact that acceptance as a member allocates valuable opportunities to some and not to others and that the barriers to admission are consequently carefully patrolled.[3]

We should also keep in mind that what institutions define as meritorious changes over time, and at any given time, represents a small subset of qualities that people can and do admire (see Guinier 2015; Karabel 2005, chap. 18). To choose just one example: in vying for college admissions applicants receive few, if any, points for demonstrations of courage, though this is a quality that most people say they greatly admire. Indeed, colleges have been regularly criticized for relying too heavily on standardized tests as indicators of "merit"—in part because of the strong correlation between test scores and socioeconomic status (see, e.g., Guinier 2015, 18–23; Lemann 1999, 271–77; Slack and Porter 1980). And of course preferences for legacy applicants can be justified as a way to maintain important relationships, but they are not otherwise consistent with the stated priorities of admission officers.

I will begin this section on high-status tracks by discussing why scholars expect these tracks to influence students' life chances—and, in the cases of selective colleges and high GPAs, also why doubts have been raised about their influence. I will then recount what the empirical literature tells us about the actual consequences of these tracks, once the advantages associated with social background and high school achievements have been taken into account. It is necessary to take these prior variables into account because we are interested in the net effects of high-status tracks—that is, their effects after we remove the impact of variables with which they are correlated. I will include here also the results of a previously unpublished study I conducted with two colleagues that contrasts the earnings outcomes for two cohorts of college students, one that graduated college in the 1970s and one that graduated in the 1990s.

SELECTIVE COLLEGES

For decades, social scientists argued that elite colleges were one linchpin in a status system that began with privileges at birth and ended for many in what C. Wright Mills called "the command posts" of society, the top business, political, and military positions (see Baltzell 1964; Domhoff 1971; Dye 1995; Mills 1956). Since that time, it has been more or less an article of faith among social scientists that highly selective colleges contribute to social stratification by admitting competitive classes, surrounding students with others of high social standing, providing an intellectually challenging education and unparalleled opportunities for the development of interpersonal skills, and creating contacts with faculty and alumni who are in a position to help advance careers (see, e.g., Hoxby 2009; Karabel 2005; Rivera 2012, 2015; Soares 2007, chap. 6).

At the top of the system are approximately 20 highly selective private research universities and nearly the same number of highly selective private liberal arts colleges. The average student at these schools scores at the level of the top 2 percent of college entrance test takers (1400 for the SAT/32 for the ACT) (see table 5.2). A few other institutions are very nearly as selective, extending the private sector elite institutions to as many as 50 total, or less than 1 percent of the total number of postsecondary institutions in the United States. The prestige of these institutions is constituted by the combination of great wealth (to take the extreme outlier, Harvard's endowment was over $32 billion in 2013), highly productive and eminent faculties (Harvard had more than 150 active members of the 2,200-member National Academy of Science in the same year), and very high levels of selectivity in admissions (just 5.8 percent of applicants were admitted to Harvard in 2012 and hundreds of valedictorians were rejected).

Among most of the elite private colleges and universities, entering class sizes have expanded by no more than 500 seats or so over the last thirty years. As the college-for-all system developed, elite privates increased the numbers of students they rejected dramatically over time. The eight colleges in the Ivy League collected more than 247,000 applications from America's top high school students (as well as many of the best students in the world), and they accepted 9 percent of them in 2013 (Hernandez College Consulting 2014). By contrast, in 1987, the eight Ivy League colleges received some 89,000 applications and accepted 26 percent (Persell and Cookson 1990). Stanford is now the most selective college in the United States, with 39,000 applicants for the class of 2017 and an acceptance rate of approximately 5 percent (Palo

TABLE 5.2. Endowments of Universities and Colleges Admitting Students with Average SAT Scores above 1400 or Average ACT Scores of 32 or Higher (2013)

Universities	2013 Endowment	Liberal Arts Colleges	2013 Endowment
Brown University	$2.7 b.	Amherst College	$1.8 b.
Cal Inst. Tech. (Cal Tech)	$1.8 b.	Barnard College	> $1 b.
Carnegie-Mellon University	$1.4 b.	Bowdoin College	$1.0 b.
Columbia University	$8.2 b.	Carleton College	> $1.0 b.
Cornell University	$5.3 b.	Claremont McKenna College	> $1.0 b.
Duke University	$6.0 b.	Dartmouth College	$ 3.7 b.
Emory University	$5.8 b.	Hamilton College	> $1.0 b.
Harvard University	$32.3 b.	Harvey Mudd College	> $1.0 b.
Johns Hopkins University	$3.0 b.	Haverford College	> $1.0 b.
Mass. Inst. Tech. (MIT)	$11.0 b.	Middlebury College	> $1.0 b.
Northwestern University	$7.9 b.	Olin College of Engineering	> $1.0 b.
Princeton University	$18.2 b.	Pomona College	$1.9 b.
Stanford University	$18.7 b.	Reed College	> $1.0 b.
Tufts University	$1.4 b.	Swarthmore College	$1.6 b.
University of Chicago	$6.7 b.	Washington and Lee College	$1.3 b.
University of Pennsylvania	$7.7 b.	Wellesley College	$1.6 b.
Univ. Southern California	$3.9 b.	Wesleyan University	> $1.0 b.
Vanderbilt University	$3.7 b.	Williams College	$2.0 b.
Washington University	$5.7 b.	Vassar University	> $1.0 b.
Yale University	$20.8 b.		

Sources: NACUBO 2013; Chronicle of Higher Education 2014.

Alto Online News 2013). Quite a bit of the falling admissions rates has to do with students applying to more schools now than they did in the past. But not all of it is due to this cause; many more top high school seniors are being urged to apply to selective colleges, and these applicants also now include tens of thousands of top students from outside the United States.

The opportunities available to students at elite private universities are unrivaled. They meet peers whose intellectual abilities place them in the top 1 to 3 percent of American students (and many who are in the top quarter of 1 percent). Some of these peers are from very wealthy backgrounds and are headed for positions of power in American society. Famous alumni visit their old college houses to give lectures and to provide advice (and potential contacts) to students. Students do not compete for internships only in their local areas but instead in multinational corporations, on Wall Street, in the leading national media outlets and cultural institutions, and as aides to top government officials. And there can be no doubt that alumni from these institutions tend to favor students who graduated from their own alma maters or those quite similar to them. Lauren Rivera described recruiters for major financial, consulting, and law firms looking more or less exclusively to Ivy League (and Ivy League–type) graduates for entry-level jobs. As one banking recruiter put it, "You are basically hiring yourself. This is not an objective process." Confidence comes from the recognition of people quite like oneself and the presumption that if they were admitted to these highly selective institutions "they must be good" (2012, 1014).

Although wealth gaps grew between the leading private and public universities (Barringer and Slaughter 2016; Newfield 2016), the thirty-five public flagship members of the Association of American Universities also dramatically increased their selectivity during the period. Between 1990 and 2010, during a time when average SAT scores held relatively steady around the established mean of 1000 for the verbal and quantitative reasoning tests combined, the average cumulative critical reading and math SATs at the AAU public research universities increased from 1100 to 1250. Students at these public flagships now score *on average* more than a standard deviation above the mean. Although student income data are not available for every major public research university, it is clear that students from upper quartile families took a larger share of places at these institutions over time. There is an obvious, but hardly novel, irony in nominally public institutions becoming the preserve of student elites. The Education Trust termed these public flagships "engines of inequality" and showed declining access trends for Pell Grant and minority students at the majority of these institutions between the early 1990s and mid-2000s (Haycock and Gerald 2006, 5–6). In a turnabout that early generations of elite theorists could not have predicted, the top public universities now produce slightly more senior business and political leaders than their elite private counterparts—albeit at far from the same rate (Brint and Yoshikawa 2017). In terms of undergraduate origins, the University of Michigan and the University of Illinois now produce approximately the same number of top business leaders as Stanford and they produce more than Yale or Princeton.

In spite of the opportunities they offer, some writers have raised doubts about how much—and even whether—highly selective colleges really had an impact on students' life chances. If these colleges were selecting the most academically gifted students and those who came from families and communities that invested most heavily in their children's success, perhaps they were more important for giving stamps of approval to students who would have succeeded with or without them. In the minds of these skeptical social scientists, whose work I will discuss below, it seemed likely that selective colleges were more important for legitimating social and cognitive advantages than for creating them.

QUANTITATIVE MAJORS

In contemporary academic life, scholars have emphasized that high-status tracks are also constituted by faculties of different rank. Where *philosophiae ratio* once in spirit reigned, *numerorum ratio* now in practice counts. For undergraduates, engineering and, to a lesser degree, health professions and business are considered the most marketable locations—even though the natural sciences and mathematics remain atop in the faculty pecking order of intellectual prestige. By contrast, the least desirable positions for undergraduates are occupied by the "soft" social sciences (such as cultural anthropology and counseling psychology), the humanities (with the notable exception of philosophy), and the arts, as well as the human services–oriented professional schools, such as education and social work. Many of these fields also rank low in the hierarchy of intellectual prestige, as do "business lite" fields like sports management and travel and tourism (see Armstrong and Hamilton 2013 on "business lite" curricula).

From the point of view of contributions to students' life chances, the most important division is the one between majors that require mathematical aptitude and skill and those that do not (see, e.g., Arcidiacono 2004; Carnevale, Rose, and Cheah 2011). The quantitative fields have developed a powerful market shelter constituted by the demand for quantitative credentials, and professors in these fields have cemented this market shelter by enforcing comparatively tough grading standards in comparatively rigorous curricula that large numbers of aspiring majors have been unable to master successfully. In addition, there are well-known gender and cultural biases in STEM fields (see, e.g., Chang et al. 2014).[4]

It is important to emphasize that rigorous curricula, with high failure rates, are not the only or even the primary reason why quantitative fields are able to erect market shelters. After all, Latin is another rigorous subject with high failure rates, but it would not be considered to constitute a market shelter within the university because Latinists are not in great demand by employers. Quantitative fields are able to erect market shelters because they are not easy to complete and because they are linked to desirable locations in the labor market. It is the combination that counts, not one or the other.

The curricula are built on introductory courses with high failure rates. Failure rates of 25 percent in introductory calculus courses (i.e., D, F, and NC grades) have been estimated for research universities (Bressoud et al. 2012), and we can safely assume that failure rates in introductory calculus are as high or higher in regional universities that attract less well-prepared students. The intent may be to ensure that students can master difficult bodies of knowledge; one consequence has been to create market shelters for those who are able to do so. Students who graduate from highly abstract and/or mathematical fields in the social sciences and humanities, such as economics and philosophy, are also relatively advantaged in the labor market.

A UCLA study that followed hundreds of thousands of first-year postsecondary students found that in 2004 nearly one-third of incoming postsecondary students declared an intention to study STEM fields, but five years later only about half this proportion had completed degrees in STEM (Hurtado, Eagan, and Chang 2010). The problem is not the level of students' interest in STEM majors; it is that many students cannot make it through the gateway courses in calculus, biology, chemistry, and physics. The loss has been especially high among underrepresented minorities; in the UCLA study only 22 percent of Latinos and 18 percent of African Americans and Native Americans who declared an interest in STEM as freshmen had completed degrees in STEM five years later (ibid.).[5]

It would seem that market forces, combined with federal support, should encourage higher enrollments in STEM majors, but that has not happened. Federal and state governments have been emphasizing recruitment and training in STEM fields since the end of World War II and have poured billions of dollars into these efforts, but the proportion of college students graduating in STEM fields has nevertheless declined, down from 21 percent in 1960 to 19 percent in 2016 (Snyder 1993; NCES 2016a). By contrast, the proportions graduating in business and health professions grew dramatically (see figure 5.2).

GRADUATE DEGREES

The academic demands of graduate education greatly exceed those of undergraduate education, and it is not surprising that graduate degrees have been associated in the minds of students and their parents with higher earnings. Studies by the Georgetown Center that do not control for potentially

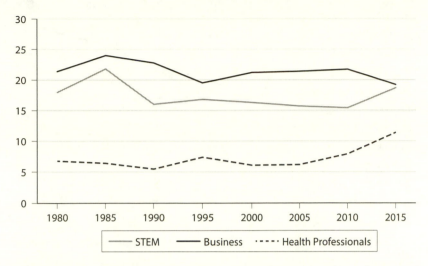

FIGURE 5.2. Undergraduate Degrees Awarded in STEM, Business, and Health Professions, 1980–2014.
Sources: Snyder 1993, table 29; NCES 2012b, table 282; NCES 2016b, table 318.20.

confounding prior variables find that expected lifetime cumulative earnings at the median for professional degrees in medicine and law were nearly twice as high as for the baccalaureate. Other master's degrees yielded cumulative average lifetime earnings at the median of about $500,000 above the bachelor's degree (Carnevale, Rose, and Cheah 2011, 3). Those with doctoral degrees fell in between but closer to the earnings expectations of doctors and lawyers. Those with doctoral degrees in computer science and engineering may now be very close to achieving incomes at the level of doctors and lawyers, or even to exceeding those levels (see figure 5.3).

Clearly students believe there is value to be gained in pursuing graduate education and employers believe there is value to be gained in employing them. Where fewer than 2 million students were enrolled in graduate and professional programs in 1980, some 3 million students were enrolled in them by 2015 and more than 900,000 graduate and professional degrees were awarded each year (NCES 2016a, Indicator 22). Beginning in 1990, the growth of graduate enrollments began to outpace that of undergraduate enrollments, with the proportion of graduate students to the total edging toward 15 percent by mid-decade (NCES 2015, tables 303.70 and 303.80). If current trends persist, considerably more than half of college graduates will at some point enroll in a graduate program (calculated from Okahana, Feaster, and Allum 2016 and NCES 2015, table 318.10).[6]

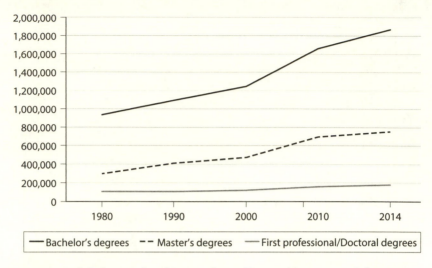

FIGURE 5.3. Bachelor's, Master's, and First Professional/Doctoral Degrees Awarded, 1980–2014. *Sources*: Snyder 1993, table 28; NCES 2012b, table 286; NCES 2016b, table 318.30.

Business and education continued to be the leaders in master's degrees awarded, with social sciences and humanities trailing (Posselt and Grodsky 2017, figure 1). In addition to professional credentialing requirements and advantages, the incentive to pursue graduate degrees was, for much of the period, particularly strong for students graduating from disciplines that did not provide as much guaranteed value in the labor market—those in interpretive fields, such as cultural anthropology, English, and history (Mullen, Goyette, and Soares 2003). The movement of high-achieving women from these fields into graduate and professional programs was an important driver of graduate school numbers (Roksa 2005). However, since the Great Recession, the largest gains in graduate program enrollments have been in the same fields that are associated with high incomes for undergraduates—namely, business, computer science, engineering, and health professions (Okahana, Feaster, and Allum 2016).

Graduate degrees matter; the question is whether these rewards hold up after statistical controls are introduced for family background and prior academic achievements. Studies have found that family socioeconomic status is a more important influence on graduate school attainments, at least for men, than it is for college graduation. It appears that high-status families are ahead of the curve in preparing their children to pursue advanced degrees. This raises the importance of statistically controlling for potentially confounding variables related to family socioeconomic status when examining graduate degree effects on students' life chances (Torche 2011).

HIGH GRADES

At the low end of the college GPA spectrum, grades act as a market shelter for successful college students by eliminating the unprepared and undermotivated (as well as those in financial hardship). The college wage premium is, in this sense, closely related to the maintenance of a GPA floor—typically students must achieve above a cumulative C average to remain in good standing. Above this floor, it is reasonable to assume that high grade point averages should be another high-status track. After all, grades have traditionally measured qualities such as conscientiousness and subject matter knowledge that many assume to be highly valued by employers. If grades have a powerful impact in the college labor market, the exclusion of academically average students from high grades can be considered a form of market sheltering for high achievers.

It may seem obvious to many that high grades are even more important than low grades in forming a stratification structure among college students. After all, they are the major mechanism that college instructors have at their disposal to create distinction among students. A high cumulative GPA leads to recognition on dean's honor rolls and makes students eligible for campus honors such as admission to Phi Beta Kappa and other academic honor societies. Graduate schools weigh college grades, together with test scores and letters of recommendation, when they admit students to master's and doctoral programs. How could college grades not matter as a high-status track?

Yet many scholars have wondered how effective grades really are as market shelters. One complication is that employers have consistently looked for interpersonal qualities when they make hiring and promotion decisions. These include the situationally appropriate mix of deference and assertiveness, as well as the capacity to engage effectively in teamwork and the ability to communicate clearly. Many of these qualities do not correlate strongly with the achievement of high college grades (Brown 1995; Heckscher and Adler 2007; Lusterman 1977; Squires 1979). Those who achieve high grades include people who enjoy learning as well as hardworking and determined "grinds," but not all of these people have the interpersonal skills to thrive in the workplace.

Grade inflation may also have rendered college GPAs a less-than-reliable quality guarantor. As work effort measured by average hours of study time has declined, grades have increased, leading to the paradoxical result that, unless students are now much smarter, less and less work is being rewarded with higher and higher grades (cf. Babcock and Marks 2011; Johnson 2003). Research by Stuart Rojstaczer and Christopher Healy (2012) on grading practices in more than 200 four-year colleges and universities reported that As represent 43 percent of all letter grades, an increase of 28 percent since 1960 and 12 percent since 1988. Moreover, selective private colleges and universities give, on average, significantly more As and Bs than do public universities of equal selectivity (see also Rojstaczer and Healy 2010).[7]

The situation is further complicated by the grading gap between quantitative and nonquantitative fields. The evidence is clear that, in general, it is more difficult to achieve high grades in STEM and STEM-related fields than in other fields (see Brint and Cantwell 2010). Simply in terms of the work effort required, a C+ in mechanical engineering is not equivalent to a C+, say, in communications. But it is difficult to know what the grade equivalence for a C+ in mechanical engineering would be in communications. Attempting to develop a correspondence table is not an inviting project: those who can grind through quantitative work in mechanical engineering may flounder in nonquantitative fields like communications where different mental operations and styles of expression are rewarded.

EMPIRICAL STUDIES OF HIGH-STATUS TRACKS

I have provided reasons why these four high-status tracks should matter for students' outcomes in life, but social scientists want to go beyond simple comparisons between those who have and have not attended elite colleges or have and have not majored in quantitative fields. They want to see whether the differences hold up after student social backgrounds and pre-college academic achievements are taken into account. It is possible that high-status tracks in college simply legitimate or reinforce these pre-college advantages.

We know from dozens of studies that family and academic background characteristics matter. All else equal, father's occupation and education have been consistently associated with higher earnings for both sons and daughters. Family income also shows modest net effects on early career earnings.[8] Similarly, ceteris paribus, men earn considerably more than women. Findings are less consistent with respect to race, once social background and academic achievement variables are taken into account. Some studies find race effects; others do not. The evidence on verbal test scores is mixed (and sometimes negative), but most studies find quantitative test scores to be positively related to early career earnings, and some find that high school grades are also predictive. These factors need to be taken into account before we can render a judgment about the net importance of selective colleges, quantitative majors, graduate degrees, or college grades. All of the studies discussed below include measures of student socioeconomic background and pre-college academic achievements as well as measures of the four high-status tracks.

Unfortunately, most of the studies examine earnings only—and usually only early career earnings. Earnings are an important outcome variable, of course, but additional measures of wealth, inventiveness, creative accomplishments, and life satisfactions would provide a more rounded picture, and these outcomes are only beginning to attract scholars' attention.

The larger share of the variation in early adult incomes is left unexplained in all of the studies discussed here, even after the full battery of social background and prior academic achievement variables are taken into account, and it continues to be left unexplained after high-status college tracks are taken into account. The trajectories of young people are simply too dependent on luck, timing, unobserved network ties, industrial upheavals, and the vagaries of the business cycle to predict outcomes with great accuracy. With that caution in mind, we can find support in the literature for the contribution of all four of the high-status college tracks I have discussed— albeit much less impressive support than one might expect in the cases of selective colleges and college grades.

Here is what we know from the studies:

Selective Colleges

When compared to findings about quantitative majors (discussed below), the findings for college selectivity have not been as consistent, and effect sizes have also tended to be quite a bit smaller. Many researchers have found relatively strong effects, but only between the most selective institutions and the least selective institutions (Brewer, Eide, and Ehrenberg 1999; Fox 1993; Hoxby 2001). Typical findings suggest that students who graduate from selective colleges can expect net income premiums on average of 5 to 10 percent compared to otherwise similar students who graduate from non-selective colleges. Similarly, cross-cohort studies examining students from the 1970s and 1980s found comparatively modest effects of college quality in both cohorts, net of covariates (Brewer, Eide, and Ehrenberg 1999; Hoxby 2001). At the same time, for men and women graduating from selective colleges and universities in the mid-1970s, William Bowen and Derek Bok

(1998) found sizable effects of selectivity level on mid-career earnings, suggesting that college quality may be slower than other high-status tracks to emerge as an influence on earnings.

The dissenters—those who minimize the effects of attending a selective college—have made provocative arguments. Stacy Dale and Alan Krueger (2002) attempted to take into account unobservable differences that could explain college selectivity effects by examining students who were admitted to selective colleges and universities but chose to attend less selective institutions. This is a clever approach because it avoids the problem of assuming that social background and high school academic performance fully account for possible differences in motivation or confidence that lead students to apply to selective colleges in the first place. Dale and Kruger then compared earnings outcomes of those who were admitted but did not attend selective institutions to otherwise comparable students who enrolled in selective institutions. They found no significant differences between the groups and argued that the actual impact of attending a selective college or university could be nil once unmeasured motivational and confidence differences were taken into account. In a later work, they went so far as to argue that the most selective college one applies to is a better predictor of adult earnings than the college one actually attends (Dale and Krueger 2011), a finding that surely could not sit well with Ivy League admissions officers. (Some economists have criticized this work on the grounds that those who do not accept offers to prestigious institutions may be too odd a group to support valid generalizations. See, e.g., Hoxby 2009.)

Other studies raise additional questions about the power of Ivy. While it is true that a relatively high proportion of top business and government leaders have degrees from selective institutions, the concentration is much greater among those with *graduate* business or law degrees than it is among those with high-status undergraduate degrees. In a sample of Fortune 1000 firms in 2014, Sarah Yoshikawa and I found that 18 percent of executives drawn from 15 industrial sectors (including government) had received their undergraduate degrees from the top 39 private colleges and universities. Interindustry variation was marked, with Ivy graduates more likely to populate industries like finance, Internet services, and entertainment, and very unlikely to populate industries like automotives, construction, and food production. By contrast, of the same executives with graduate degrees, more than 50 percent with graduate business degrees had obtained their degrees from the top 18 business schools and more than 40 percent with law degrees had obtained their degrees from the top 14 law schools. This study suggests that graduation from one of the most prestigious undergraduate colleges is simply not as important for eventual entry into the business and political elite as most people think—but the prestige of the graduate program attended is very important (Brint and Yoshikawa 2017).

However, one benefit of attending a prestigious college may be that it encourages the kind of creative intellectual activity that leads to new inventions and other cultural achievements. Alex Bell and his colleagues (2017) found that invention rates, as measured by patents, varied greatly by the college inventors attended, with science-oriented campuses like MIT and Georgia Tech producing many more inventors than others, net of all background covariates. Evidently, the exposure to creative people in college increases the likelihood of inventiveness. Elite college pedigrees also appear to be very important for achievements that gain recognition among the cultural elite of scientists, scholars, writers, and those who run the major foundations, think tanks, and arts organizations. My research group found a heavy over-representation of elite college graduates among members of the National Academies, the American Academy of Arts and Sciences, among prestigious journalists and writers—and among executives of major cultural institutions (see Brint et al. 2018). Perhaps these people should be considered members of a new postindustrial "power elite" whose influence derives not from political or economic power but from creations built on mastery of symbolic media.

Quantitative Majors

Studies including background characteristics as statistical controls have shown that college major is a strong, significant predictor of postgraduation earnings for college graduates, net of social background and academic achievements during high school. Perhaps surprisingly, it consistently shows stronger results than college selectivity. With rare exceptions (see Arcidiacono 2004; Song and Orazem 2004), engineering majors show up in the existing studies as earning the highest wage premiums (Berger 1988; Grogger and Eide 1995; James et al. 1989; Loury and Garman 1995; Rumberger and Thomas 1993; Thomas 2000), net of covariates. The studies are less consistent with respect to the rank order of other majors. In some earlier cohort studies (college graduates of the mid-1970s), social science majors performed quite well relative to other majors (James et al. 1989; Bowen and Bok 1998); in more recent cohort studies examining college graduates of the early 1990s, business, natural science, and health science majors have tended to earn more in early career than social science majors (Thomas

2000; Thomas and Zhang 2005), net of covariates. No studies have shown higher wage premiums for humanities, arts, education, or the residual category of "other" majors. Typically, education majors are found to earn less than others, and humanities majors differ insignificantly from education majors in early career earnings. Jeff Grogger and Eric Eide (1995) examined college graduate cohorts from the mid-1970s and mid-1980s. In both cohorts, they found higher wage premiums in early career associated with graduating in engineering, business, natural science, or social science than for graduating in arts, humanities, or education.

Following a review of nearly two dozen studies, the eminent higher education scholars Ernest Pascarella and Patrick Terenzini summarized the findings: the largest earnings go to majors with well-defined content knowledge, high levels of quantitative skill requirements, and close and direct functional relations to occupations with historically high average earnings. Most, but not all, of these majors are applied and have a history of being populated primarily by males (2005, 507).[9] Proponents of the liberal arts can, of course, take heart from the old saying that men and women do not live by bread alone—true enough, to the extent that the liberal arts enhance students' capacities for analysis, perception, and empathy.

Graduate and Professional Degrees

Net of covariates, graduate degrees are also consistently associated with higher incomes. Using the National Longitudinal Study of 1972 (NLS-72), Estelle James and colleagues (1989) found a significant postgraduate degree effect of approximately 10 percent on earnings measured in the mid-1980s, after extensive background and ability controls, as well as controls for major and college quality. Using another data set from the 1970s, Ralph Mueller (1988) found a similar effect for postgraduate degrees on earnings, using even more extensive controls, including measures for motivation and personality. One cross-cohort study comparing graduates from the 1970s and 1980s also showed postgraduate degree effects in both cohorts, net of an extensive battery of controls (Grogger and Eide 1995).

Differences among graduate degrees—for example, law versus medicine—have not been well studied. One valuable study was conducted by William G. Bowen and Derek Bok on graduates of selective colleges and universities in the mid-1970s. When they examined earnings twenty years after graduation for this sample of graduates, Bowen and Bok (1998) found strong effects of graduate degrees in medicine, business, and law and much weaker effects for all other graduate degrees. Medical degrees were worth an additional $77,000 in annual earnings for men on average, and business and law degrees were worth an additional $40,000 on average. (Women with these graduate degrees showed a similar pattern but at much lower earnings levels.) By contrast, those who pursued the doctorate were penalized in earnings, net of covariates.

These findings are now dated. Professors in marketable applied fields and doctoral-level engineers and computer scientists have likely gained ground, while the medical advantage may have declined a little since the time of Bowen and Bok's study. Graduate degree quality no doubt also influences incomes in fields where the spread of earnings is very large, as in the cases of law and business. Thus quite a bit more work needs to be done on the net effects of different types of graduate degrees and programs. For the time being the most we can say is that the evidence is strong that graduate degrees matter for adult incomes—and some professional degrees matter substantially more than others.

High Grades

Most well-controlled cross-sectional studies have also shown college grade effects on earnings in early career. In perhaps the best of these studies, James and her colleagues (1989) found an 8 percent premium for each full grade point increment in early career earnings of mid-1970s college graduates, holding major, college selectivity, and postgraduate degrees constant. In a comparable study, using Baccalaureate & Beyond data for graduates in the early 1990s, Scott Thomas (2000) found a change of a full grade point to be associated with a net 5 percent premium in earnings one year out of college.[10]

However, the validity of these findings has become more questionable over time with the mounting evidence on the spread of grade inflation and grade compression (Rojstaczer and Healy 2010, 2012). Peter Arcidiacono (2004) offered a first dissenting voice. He found that the positive effects of high grades for NLS-72 college graduates in early career dropped out for all majors but the education major once selection effects (i.e., the tendency of smarter students to complete harder majors and less able students to leave them) were statistically controlled through following student major switchers over the course of their college careers.

A NEW ORDER OF HIGH-STATUS TRACKS?

Research I conducted with two colleagues, Jacob Apkarian and Ron Kwon, helps fill in a gap in the literature: whether the high-status tracks that showed

significant effects on earnings for college graduates from the mid-1970s also
showed significant effects on earnings for college graduates from a more
recent cohort. This work suggests that graduate degrees may have become
more important over time and college grades less important as predictors
of early adult earnings. The contribution of this study is that it reveals, in
comparative perspective, the experience of a more recent cohort of college
graduates.

Apkarian, Kwon, and I examined the effects of high-status tracks on log of
earnings for a mid-1970s cohort of college graduates drawn from the National
Longitudinal Survey of 1972 (NLS-72) and an early 1990s cohort drawn from
Baccalaureate and Beyond (B&B).[11] NLS college graduates were studied
in 1976, at the time of their graduation, and again in 1986, ten years into the
labor force. B&B college graduates were studied in 1993, at the time of their
graduation, and again in 2003, also ten years into the labor force. The common ten-year time frame is obviously useful for comparative purposes. We
were also able to limit the samples in both cases to students who graduated
college within 4.5 years.

It is not possible to directly compare coefficients for high-status tracks
across time using these two data sets. One reason is that the variance—the
spread of values—in most variables is expanding as access expands. For example, if we have more students in the system, we are also going to have
more variation in student backgrounds and probably also more variation in
incomes. In a few cases, variance is decreasing. For example, we now have
more clustering of college GPAs near the high end of the scale. In cross-
cohort studies, we cannot know whether coefficients are higher because
the variable under consideration has actually become more important over
time or because there is more variance to explain in the parameters under
consideration (see Hauser and Featherman 1973; Johnson and Sell 1976). In
cross-cohort studies, the most we can say is that studies of college students
indicate that high-status tracks are important (or unimportant) predictors
of income in one or both periods.[12]

Like previous researchers, after controlling for respondents' background
characteristics, we found strong support for the influence of college major
in both cohorts. In the mid-1970s college cohort drawn from NLS-72, education and arts and humanities majors showed lower earnings than all other
major categories, net of covariates. Business and engineering showed significantly stronger effects on earnings than the other majors, with physical sciences, health professions, social sciences, and life sciences tightly bunched

behind. Similarly, in the early 1990s cohort drawn from B&B, education and arts and humanities majors showed significantly lower earnings than all other major categories, net of covariates. However, in the early 1990s cohort engineering and health professions majors showed stronger effects than the others, with business trailing, and physical sciences, social sciences, and life sciences tightly bunched behind. These findings suggest that being an engineering major retained value in the labor market across the nearly two decades studied, while education and arts/humanities created less value for graduates in early career. The rise of health professions and the (relative) decline of business majors cannot be proven with these data but bear further investigation.

Net of covariates, college selectivity, as measured by Barron's seven-point scale, showed limited influence on early career earnings for both mid-1970s and early 1990s graduates. Indeed, for the mid-1970s cohort, we had to group the first two selectivity levels in Barron's before we found a statistically significant variation by selectivity level using the middle level ("competitive") as the reference category. Lower levels were not distinguishable from the mid-rank in the Barron's scale. For the early 1990s graduates we had to descend further in the selectivity ranks, combining levels one through three before we found a statistically significant variation by selectivity level, again using the middle category as the reference point. The lower levels were not distinguishable from the mid-rank in Barron's. These findings lead us to conclude that either Barron's is an inadequate measure of college quality—something that is certainly possible—or, perhaps more likely, the important distinctions for early career earnings prospects are between several ranks of competitive colleges and all others. These results tend to support those who find that public flagship universities like UC Berkeley and the University of Michigan-Ann Arbor have joined the traditionally high-status private colleges and universities as important status locations.

In our study, graduate degrees were not a significant predictor of earnings for the mid-1970s NLS-72 cohort, but they provided, on average, a statistically significant net addition to earnings for the early 1990s B&B cohort. Standard errors for the effects estimates were high for the mid-1970s cohort, not surprising at a time when the proportion of the sample with graduate degrees was only 10 percent. By contrast, the standard error was much lower for the early 1990s cohort, at a time when the proportion of the B&B sample with graduate degrees was more than one-third. The differences we found could be due, in part, to the high standard errors in the early cohort or they could be due primarily to the increasing importance of graduate degrees for the later cohort. Unfortunately, the two data sets we analyzed did not make distinctions among types of graduate degrees.

Grades were a statistically significant predictor of earnings for the mid-1970s cohort but not for the early 1990s cohort. This finding is consistent with the doubts that have been raised by others about the discriminating power of grades in an era of grade inflation and grade compression. In the mid-1970s cohort, we see a linear drop-off in earnings between those with "As and Bs," those with "Bs and Cs," and those with "mostly Cs." In the early 1990s cohort, students who reported "Bs and Cs" tended to have lower incomes than other students, but otherwise we found no statistically significant results by self-reported college grades.[13] If they are accurate reflections of a changing reality, these findings will be very disappointing to college instructors whose primary instrument for recognizing distinction and encouraging harder work is the course grade!

When combined with the findings of other researchers, the evidence of our study suggests a period in which higher incomes in early career were strongly associated with the "STEM-plus" disciplines (including not only STEM majors but also quantitative majors in business, social sciences, and health professions), as well as a range of selective undergraduate colleges that extended well beyond the Ivy League, and at least the more marketable of the graduate and professional degrees. Advantaged social backgrounds and strong academic performance in secondary school also continued to count as important independent influences on early career earnings. What we do not see is a strong GPA effect. Given grade compression and grade inflation, it seems unlikely that a high college GPA will reemerge as an important independent influence in the labor market, apart from its influence on graduate school admissions.

Status Locations on Campus

The imagery of mass higher education conveys the sense of a faceless army marching off into a relatively featureless higher education landscape to be molded into relatively standardized material. Students, not surprisingly, want experiences and accomplishments that are recognizable for their distinctive qualities, and they want to march off into exciting circumstances that match their conceptions of themselves. If for this reason alone, colleges and universities experience as much pressure to expand status-conferring opportunities on campus as they do to expand the diversity of students they accept into their entering classes. Status-enhancing locations are of two types: those that are primarily connected to social distinction, as in the case of fraternities and sororities, and those that are primarily connected to academic or professional distinction, as in the case of honors and leadership programs. Some, like leading positions in student clubs and organizations, mix the two forms of distinction.

It is difficult to make generalizations about many of these on-campus status locations because they vary so much from campus to campus and because good statistical studies of their effects are scarce or nonexistent. They do not appear, for example, in the national data sets that scholars have used to examine the net effects of major, selectivity, graduate degrees, and grades. And yet they are important enough to highlight, because they are among the clearest indicators of the principal proposition of this chapter—that as colleges and universities become more inclusive, so too do they maintain and add to the number and types of status-conferring opportunities available to students. These campus status locations allow students to feel like they stand out from their peers. They also allow administrators to manage the contradictory pressures of expanding enrollments, important both for the promise of opportunity *and* for the bottom line, and the interests of ambitious students to stand out from the mass.

FRATERNITIES AND SORORITIES

Fraternities and sororities are the oldest and most important of the social-status-enhancing structures on college campuses, dating to the early nineteenth century—earlier if one counts forerunners such as the Phi Beta Kappa Society. Historically, most fraternity and sorority members have been white, Christian, and affluent—house fees put membership out of reach for the great majority of students. House voting on potential new pledges, including the practice of "black balling," where one negative vote ended a prospective member's candidacy, led to the exclusion of all but the most attractive students from lower-status backgrounds as "poor fits." Because they drew from the socially dominant group, it is perhaps not surprising that Greek letter fraternities were strongly associated with business and political success at the highest levels. Maria Konnikova (2014) reported that, in the twentieth century, a very high proportion of CEOs of Fortune 500 companies have been members of fraternities, as have been very large proportions of U.S. Supreme Court justices, U.S. senators, American presidents, and presidential cabinet members—more than 60 percent in every case.

Yet fraternity and sorority membership declined during the period, at least a little, as a proportion of a growing undergraduate student body. Of the 30,000 college graduates Gallup surveyed in 2014, 16 percent said they had been members of fraternities or sororities (Gallup Organization 2014); in the 1990s and early 2000s less than 10 percent of four-year college students had joined (Konnikova 2014; NSSE 2016). Those numbers began to swing back in the late 2000s. By 2015, nearly 14 percent of college freshmen said they were interested in joining fraternities or sororities (Ingraham 2015). Even so, there are many reasons to expect that Greek membership will fluctuate around a narrow band of undergraduate students. These reasons include the unsavory reputation of some campus chapters. But the most important reason is that fraternities and sororities have incentives to remain relatively exclusive in order to preserve their chapter's reputation as an attractive place to socialize. In spite of the diversification of college campuses, historically white fraternities and sororities have diversified only to a limited degree (Hughey 2010; Laird 2005). By remaining exclusive, the leading fraternities and sororities have also remained at the centers of elite social activity, and members spend considerable time planning and attending parties to maintain social preeminence. Elizabeth Armstrong and Laura Hamilton, for example, describe the elaborate planning that goes into party performances at "Midwestern University":

> For women . . . we classify as socialites or wannabes . . . partying was nothing short of a vocation. . . . Indeed, on Thursday through Sunday nights, after the flurry of hair dying, makeup applying and outfit borrowing died down, the silence on the floor was deafening. (2013, 84)

The negative academic consequences of fraternity and sorority life can be overstated (Pascarella, Flowers, and Whitt 2001). Even so, the members of Greek letter houses are not as well known for their accomplishments in classrooms and laboratories as for their weekend bashes. Nevertheless, university administrators often go out of their way to encourage the fraternity and sorority voice on campus and to develop majors in which the less academically inclined Greeks can succeed (Armstrong and Hamilton 2013). This solicitude is rational: the evidence suggests that alumni with Greek affiliations tend to give somewhat more to their colleges after graduation (for an overview, see Okunade and Wunnava 2011; see also Gallup Organization 2014, 9).

One might imagine that the absorbing party culture, the close bonding, and the verbal and physical hazing characteristic of Greek life is a kind of initiation into the interpersonal intensity and rough and tumble of powerful positions in American society. But lower proportions of corporate CEOs and political leaders in the last generation have been members of fraternities and sororities than in previous generations (Konnikova 2014). In 2014, the Gallup Organization found that college graduates who had been fraternity or sorority members were more likely than their non-Greek counterparts to say they felt financially secure, and the difference held up after the introduction of statistical controls for gender, race, and family socioeconomic status (the latter measured poorly). However, margins between Greeks and non-Greeks varied by only a few percentage points and may have been entirely due to unmeasured differences in social background.

INTERCOLLEGIATE ATHLETICS

About 3 percent of college students participate in intercollegiate athletics (calculated from NCAA 2017 and NCES 2016b). The revenue-generating sports of football and basketball receive most of the attention from the public, but athletes in these sports together make up only a little more than one-third of all male intercollegiate athletes. Track and field, soccer, and volleyball athletes were more numerous than basketball players among women. Other intercollegiate sports include lacrosse, cross country, swimming, tennis, golf, wrestling, ice hockey, and water polo—and softball and field hockey for women.

In the days when only men competed, athletes were often described as the "Big Men on Campus." In recent decades, the position of athletes has become more complicated. In a more pluralistic environment, student subcultures make a larger difference in the distribution of prestige on campus. Athletes remain highly prestigious among members of fraternities and sororities (Clotfelter 2011, 160), but other students may be indifferent to them. Athletes also tend to spend much of their free time with their teammates, strengthening bonds between themselves but separating them from interaction with nonathletes (Wolf-Wendel, Toma, and Morphew 2001). In revenue-producing sports like men's football and basketball, their status may be much higher off campus than on.

Again, few statistical studies exist of the impact of participation in intercollegiate athletics on later life success. The best of the U.S. studies found that males who participated in intercollegiate sports in the early 1980s were estimated to receive 4 percent higher incomes than otherwise similar nonathletes in early career earnings, though female athletes received no income advantage from their participation.[14] In this study, athletes were also more likely to graduate than otherwise similar nonathletes. According to the authors, for males "the findings suggest that athletic participation may enhance the development of discipline, confidence, motivation, competitive spirit and other subjective traits that encourage success" (Long and Caudill 1991, 531; see also Dewenter and Giessing 2014).[15]

STUDENT CLUBS AND ORGANIZATIONS

One way to stand out is to be a leader or featured member of a student club or organization. These organizations are a major part of campus social life. Only one-third of students from the 650 institutions with responses to the most recent National Survey of Student Engagement (NSSE) said they spent *no* hours on club activities (NSSE 2016). In academic year 2012–13, the average AAU public university campus supported one official student organization for approximately every 39 students, better than the faculty-to-student ratio in many of these students' courses. The average AAU private university campus showed a lower student-to-club ratio: one official student organization for every 18 students. (The top engineering schools were the most active of all, with student-to-club ratios of 8 or 9 to 1.) I also studied ratios at California State University (CSU) campuses to represent participation at comprehensive regional campuses. Fewer student organizations existed on the CSU campuses, but they were nevertheless numerous on many campuses; the average number of students per registered club or organization was 87:1 in AY 2012–13, with a range from 40:1 to 164:1 (author's calculations).

Given the number of student clubs and organizations, the opportunities to assume a leadership position are also great. In a sample of five large public research universities, my research team and I found that 38 percent of responding students said they were currently or had been officers of a student club or organization (Kwon et al. 2018). There are reasons to believe that this proportion is inflated; more conscientious and more active students tend to respond to campus surveys. A more probable estimate is that 15 to 25 percent of full-time four-year college students nationwide have the opportunity to serve as a club officer, a proportion that would certainly be higher at selective colleges and universities and lower at regional comprehensive universities.

Those who take leadership positions acquire a degree of social prestige, at least in the eyes of rank-and-file members. Participation in student clubs

TABLE 5.3. Frequency of Cocurricular Learning Experiences at Five Large Public Research Universities, 2014 (N = 3,161)

Activity	3 or more times (%)	1–2 Times (%)	Never (%)
Promoted an event	27.7	25.4	46.8
Recruited new members	25.7	27.2	47.1
Facilitated a discussion	23.4	23.9	52.7
Planned an event	23.7	26.8	49.5
Made a presentation that required research	20.0	26.5	53.6
Collected or analyzed data	18.9	19.3	61.9
Wrote a report or article	17.8	18.7	63.5
Chaired a meeting	15.6	13.3	71.2
Worked with another student as a peer educator or mentor	15.0	16.7	68.3
Engaged in an in-depth discussion about local, state, national, or international issues	15.2	15.5	69.3
Partnered with a community organization or organized community outreach	11.4	20.3	68.4
Created an artistic work or performance	10.7	14.0	75.3
Mediated a dispute	9.7	16.5	73.8
Created or updated a website or webpage	7.9	12.5	79.6
Invited or hosted a speaker	7.1	12.5	80.4
Designed or produced a product for sale	3.6	9.8	86.6
Wrote a constitution, bylaws, piece of legislation, or rules	2.6	11.5	85.9

Source: Author's calculation from the SERU Survey 2014.

may also help build skills that employers value. Approximately one-quarter of the respondents we studied said they had had three or more experiences planning events, promoting events, recruiting new members, and facilitating discussions as a result of their participation in student clubs and organizations. Nearly one-fifth of respondents reported three or more experiences chairing meetings. Three out of five respondents said their involvement in student clubs and organizations had been "very important" or "essential" in their development of listening skills, networking skills, and knowledge of how organizations work. Only slightly smaller proportions said that involvement in student clubs had been "very important" or "essential" in their development of teaching and oral presentation skills, in their development of emotional self-control, and in their capacity to maintain their ethical standards in challenging situations (see table 5.3).[16]

Not surprisingly, club officers were the most likely to report these experiences, followed by members who spent a comparatively high number of hours per week on club activities. Female students, students with high grade point averages, and upper-division students were somewhat more likely to report these skill development experiences and first-generation students a little less likely to do so.

Although we know something about the skill-developing opportunities associated with participation in student clubs, no well-controlled studies exist of the impact of student club membership on later life attainments for large samples of college graduates.

HONORS COLLEGES/PROGRAMS

Honors programs are the most common of the on-campus status tracks linked to academic and professional life. More than one thousand U.S. four-year colleges operate honors programs or honors colleges (as do hundreds of community colleges) (NCHC 2013a). Students become eligible for honors programs by virtue of their high school grades, test scores, and/or class rank. Many programs require students to write an essay as part of their application. The programs are intended to provide the small, intense liberal arts experience for academically ambitious students enrolled in large universities. They also provide a community of like-minded peers. Many offer honors housing and quite a bit more personal attention than most students on large universities can expect. Some programs require community service activities as part of civic engagement objectives. Nearly all honors programs require a senior thesis or capstone project.

I sampled forty-five programs at four-year colleges. These were not a random sample; I chose them from among the relatively few schools that published data on the number of students enrolled. The programs included both private and public campuses but were heavily weighted toward public universities. The most ambitious of the programs, such as those at Arizona State University, the University of Iowa, and Temple University, enrolled up to 7 percent of the student body. The documentation for these ambitious programs showed a high level of organization and esprit de corps, with many stories of students' achievements and a robust schedule of special events. Each of these programs had received endowments in support of the programs. More commonly, the sampled programs enrolled 2–6 percent of undergraduate students. Some small rural state universities and regional comprehensive universities ran very small honors programs, of 1 percent or less of the undergraduate student body.

Students are attracted to honors programs for a variety of reasons; some may simply want the priority registration that seems to be part of every program. But the status value of being part of an honors community is clearly part of the appeal. A banner headline on one of the honors websites included the invitation to "Distinguish Yourself." The statement on the honors website at one of the universities gives a sense of the qualities these programs seek to identify and develop: "Innovative ideas energize us. New challenges excite us. From curious thinkers to visionary creators, we set the standard on the quest to be more" (Oregon State University 2016).

Highly selective colleges and universities rarely operate honors colleges—they do not want to make distinctions among their undergraduates, all of whom are considered members of an honors program by virtue of admission. But at less selective colleges and universities, the growth of these programs has been steady; judging solely by membership in the national association, the programs have increased by more than 25 percent at four-year colleges over the last two decades and by 40 percent at community colleges. These programs vary in size and focus, but they all seek to provide "an Ivy League education at a state university price" (Seifert et al. 2007). As the national honors council puts it, "Honors programs are based on the belief that superior students profit from close contact with faculty, small courses, seminars, or one-on-one instruction, and course work shared with other gifted students, individual research projects, internships, foreign study, and campus or community service" (NCHC 2013b).

These programs create academically enriched experiences that have a positive influence on students' cognitive development. The most comprehensive study so far examined honors and otherwise similar non-honors students at eighteen four-year colleges in fifteen states. The honors students showed significantly higher positive gains between their first and fourth year in critical thinking, in mathematics, and in a composite score of performance on several skills tests relative to otherwise similar students who did not participate in honors programs (Seifert et al. 2007). It is plausible to think that honors students who complete their programs should be better prepared, on average, for graduate school because of the opportunities they have for debate and discussion with other motivated students in small seminar settings and because of the independent work and research on senior theses they are required to do. But currently no U.S. studies exist about whether honors programs produce unusually successful graduates compared to nonparticipants matched for social background and pre-college academic achievements.

RESTRICTED MAJORS

Restricted majors represent a close parallel on particular campuses to the market shelters provided by selectivity at Ivy League–type colleges. Departments and schools can restrict student numbers to improve the market position of those admitted. If the university can forge an identity for a program as having particularly high selectivity and demanding requirements its prestige can increase and the opportunities of graduates will accordingly be enhanced. It is surprising—and perhaps a testimony to the democratic ethos of public universities—that more programs do not attempt to impose them.

A review of campus websites suggests that selection processes are most commonly imposed in undergraduate business majors (which would otherwise be flooded with students), in top-rated arts programs, and in science and engineering programs that want to remain small and elite. Faculty in the arts, humanities, social sciences, and most occupational majors may add requirements to make progression to the upper division more difficult, but they typically only impose enrollment caps as a last resort if their popularity has greatly exceeded the teaching resources at their disposal.

The UC Berkeley undergraduate business major at the Haas School is exemplary of the characteristics typical of restricted majors. In 2012, 580 admitted Berkeley students applied for 267 places in the undergraduate program, and nearly 1,500 transfer students applied for fewer than 100 spaces. GPA requirements for transfer students were very high (a mean 3.8 GPA for those admitted). The admissions committee examined academic accomplishments, extracurricular activities, analytical ability through essay reads, and evidence of high moral character. In other words, they looked for students who could attend a top liberal arts college but were also a particularly good "fit" for the Bay Area business world. At a university admitting 5,000 freshmen every year, Haas students represent a very highly selected 5 percent of an already highly selected student body (UC Berkeley Haas School of Business 2013).

Architecture at Virginia Tech University, one of more than a dozen selecting majors on campus, illustrates several of the mechanisms that exist in the public university setting to create status islands by identifying talent, restricting numbers, and mobilizing student commitment. Prospective architecture students must maintain a 2.5 GPA throughout lower-division classes. If they are still interested in admission, they must then apply for the Summer Qualifying Design Lab and be interviewed for admission. They must pass this admission interview. They must also have their summer work reviewed both for admission to first-year lab and for admission to second-year lab. Being an architecture student at Virginia Tech is like making the football team: lots of tryouts and constant review of performance (Virginia Tech University 2013).

Auditions are an essential part of the creation of on-campus status tracks in the arts. Most students who wish to study theater at UCLA worry far more about their auditions than about anything else associated with admission to the campus. It is no wonder; by some (unpublished) reports UCLA accepts only 4 percent of the 2,000 students who apply for admission to the Department of Theater, an acceptance rate below that of Harvard or Stanford. Another famous example is the Indiana University Jacobs School of Music, which admits approximately 800 undergraduate students per year, based on auditions and interviews, from a self-selected applicant pool of more than 2,500. Competition is clearly not as stiff as it is for admission to conservatories like Juilliard, which admits about 7 percent of applicants, but it contrasts sharply with the open door of most university majors.

LEADERSHIP PROGRAMS

Leadership programs include at least one class for selected students, as well as continuing opportunities for interaction through retreats, workshops, and other activities. Longer-duration programs include a series of courses leading to a degree, certificate, or other campus recognition. Both Curt Brungardt and colleagues (2006) and John Dugan and Susan Komives (2007) estimated that more than one thousand colleges offered formal leadership programs by the mid-2000s, at least double the number from two decades before. Very few campuses offer degrees in leadership; certificates are far more common and represent the majority of even the more ambitious programs. Because these programs are selecting (or self-selecting) and are not found on all campuses, it seems unlikely that even 1 percent of students enroll in campus leadership programs.

The most expansive of these programs follow students throughout their college careers. The University of Virginia (UVA) has one of the more developed of such programs; the UVA leadership programs divide students into cohorts. "Emerging leaders" are exposed to famous alumni and faculty experts on leadership and read the literature on leadership and management with representatives from the dean's office while engaging in service-based projects. "Engaging leaders" work through a virtual network accessible by all students who occupy leadership positions on campus and participate in a half-day retreat for executive board members of student organizations. "Excelling leaders" attend a one-week summer program whose topics have in the past included case studies of leadership, effective and ethical decision making, diversity, delegation, motivation and empowerment, facilitation, and priority setting. During the week, students are introduced to university administrators and participate in discussions about the university's "goals, plans, and challenges." The university also runs leadership conferences and retreats for invited students and presidents of campus organizations, again focusing on networking and building identification with the university.

Claremont McKenna College in California offers another well-known leadership program. The requirements for the program, which runs as a non-degree-granting course sequence, include: a leadership foundation course, an ethics course, at least one other course on leadership from a liberal arts perspective, a leadership experiential requirement through an internship experience, and a leadership capstone experience. The program also includes an annual conference, prizes for leadership, intensive work at three-day retreats, a speaker series, and other activities. The goals of the program are characteristic of most: to understand leadership theories, concepts, and issues; to have knowledge of the methods by which leadership is studied; to understand cross-cultural and international issues related to leadership; to appreciate the importance of ethics; to develop critical thinking, analytical, and decision-making skills; to obtain awareness of one's own leadership potential and competencies; and to gain practical experience in applying leadership knowledge and principles (Claremont McKenna College 2016). Brungardt et al. (2006) found a similar sequence for the fifteen degree programs they studied in the mid-2000s.

Macalester College in Minnesota provides a contrasting example of a program attuned to the culture of inclusiveness. In the Sophomore Leadership Program, Macalester students "learn to view leadership as a process not just a position" and how to "empower [themselves] to be active member[s] of any team, community or organization." The program meets once a week for seventy-minute sessions throughout the fall semester. Students are expected to "begin to develop a personal philosophy of leadership"; "increase their self-awareness through assessments, discussion of values, beliefs, culture, and identity"; and "understand the multiple dimensions of individual and social group identities and how they affect interactions with others" (Macalester College 2013). Leadership programs like this one show how status locations on campus can adapt to a dominant ethos of egalitarianism and inclusivity.

Researchers have shown positive net associations between leadership programs and a range of civic values, including support for democratic institutions and, not surprisingly, interest in taking on leadership roles (Cress et al. 2001). Evidence of the influence of participation in leadership programs on adult economic success is, however, as yet missing.

ENTREPRENEURSHIP PROGRAMS

Of all the growing status locations on campus, the development of student entrepreneurship opportunities is the one most closely aligned with the trends toward academic innovationism I discussed in chapter 3. Student entrepreneurship programs include courses and degrees in entrepreneurship, participation in incubator and accelerator programs, and participation in business plan competitions.[17] The Ewing Marion Kauffman Foundation estimated that 400,000 students (or about 2 percent of all students) took one of 5,000 courses in entrepreneurship on American campuses in 2008. In 1975, colleges and universities offered around 100 formal majors, minors, and certificates in entrepreneurship. By 2006, they offered 500 of these programs. The proportion of students who said they wanted to own a business more than doubled between 1975 and 2008 to 3.3 percent (Morelix 2015).

The University of North Carolina-Chapel Hill offered one of the most comprehensive of the entrepreneurial programs for undergraduate students. UNC offered first-year seminars to give students a chance to explore commercial topics of interest in small groups with senior faculty members. The campus also provided a two-semester program for launching commercial and nonprofit ventures. The program included each of the phases adopted by university incubators and accelerators: a feasibility stage, in which ideas were refined and tested for commercial value; a launch phase where potentially viable ideas were exposed to experts and MBA students to help in the development of business plans; and a venture finance phase in which students learned about the varieties of private financing available to them and developed a plan to attract financing. UNC also held an annual student-led entrepreneurship business plan competition called the Carolina Challenge, in which teams competed by presenting their plans to panels of entrepreneurs, venture capitalists, philanthropists, and foundation executives. At

Washington University, St. Louis, students can apply for funds to run approved businesses in "prime-location, high-traffic, rental store fronts," with the proviso that they have to sell the equity in successful businesses to other students prior to graduation. At Georgetown, student entrepreneurs run virtually all campus businesses and services, including the campus ambulance service.

In 2013, according to one estimate, nearly 250 colleges and universities were operating business incubator and accelerator programs (AcceleratorInfo.com 2013). These programs helped students move from vague ideas to concrete business plans capable of attracting venture capital funding. Start X at Stanford University was the most famous of the campus accelerators. Open to anyone with a Stanford affiliation and supported by dozens of corporate investors, Start X proclaimed on its website that its founders' start-up companies had been acquired by large firms such as Twitter, Dropbox, Intuit, Apple, LinkedIn, Yahoo, Salesforce, and Instagram (Start X 2017). According to Stanford, the Start X fund invested $98 million in 200-plus Start X companies between 2013 and 2017. Student founders were required to find 30 percent or more initial capitalization from outside investors. To gain funding, students first applied and, if accepted, went through two rounds of interviews, receiving advice along the way from Start X staff and investors, with 8 to 10 percent of applicants eventually receiving funding to commercialize their ideas.

Business plan competitions, often described as "pitch contests," also proliferated in the years after 2000. These competitions were aimed primarily at undergraduate and graduate business students. In a few cases, winning competitors could receive as much as $200,000 in funding, but most of the better-known contests offered $25,000 to $30,000 to winners, together with thousands of dollars in services (such as staffing and legal assistance) and temporary office space (Farrell 2010). Successful competitors take the evidence of their wins into their negotiations with investors (Under30CEO 2018).

As in the case of leadership programs, university-based entrepreneurship programs have not received rigorous evaluations on results or cost-effectiveness. The number of successful businesses created by these programs, for example, remains unknown. Many students who are exposed to the programs undoubtedly come the conclusion that they do not have it in themselves to become entrepreneurs, but for the fraction of 1 percent of students who engage fully, the training received creates not only a status distinction but on rare occasion the beginnings of firms that will eventually produce substantial earnings.

Tensions between Status and Inclusion

How well have U.S. universities accomplished the seemingly contradictory feat of incorporating once-marginalized groups into a campus culture that continues to emphasize status differentiation at least as much as inclusiveness?

Sociologists identify four common outcomes of intergroup contact: assimilation, accommodation, competition, and conflict. I use the term "incorporation" in preference to assimilation because assimilation implies the adjustment of subordinate groups to the prevailing norms of dominant groups. This sort of adjustment is not common on university campuses, which maintain multiple norms and rarely require strict conformity to any of them. But previously excluded groups can, over time, be incorporated into the campus culture with little or no overt sense of competition or conflict.

INCORPORATION

The survey evidence suggests that efforts to create inclusive campus climates have been largely successful. Reviews of the campus climate literature by Jeni Hart and Jennifer Fellabaum (2008), Rankin and Associates (2014), and Darryl Smith (2009) indicate that a sizable majority of students, faculty, and staff on university campuses say they feel "comfortable" or "very comfortable" with the climate of inclusion on their campuses and in their departments. Rankin and Associates (2014) reported that 70 to 80 percent of those surveyed from each of these three groups on multiple campuses fall into one of the two "comfortable" categories. Yet as these findings indicated, comfort levels have not extended to all. Twenty to 25 percent of students, faculty, and staff who responded to these surveys reported that they have personally experienced "exclusionary, intimidating, offensive, or hostile conduct." Members of racial-ethnic minority groups, particularly African Americans and people of Middle Eastern descent, were more likely to report these experiences. In the same studies, 5–10 percent of women reported unwanted sexual contact (Rankin and Associates 2014).

These generally positive climate surveys are testament to the efforts faculty, staff, and students have made to create welcoming environments for all students. Administrators are usually quick to respond when intergroup tensions arise on campus, and their public remarks emphasize the importance of cultures of respect. Many campuses have introduced mechanisms such as required diversity training and general education courses that attempt to increase understanding of the disadvantages faced by historically marginalized groups. They have provided opportunities in the club structure and in residence halls for racial-ethnic and other affinity groups. Experiences on campus can reinforce climates of acceptance. According to college students surveyed by the UCLA Higher Education Research Institute, the experience of taking courses on intergroup relations and talking with students from different racial-ethnic and religious groups about their backgrounds and aspirations tended to improve intergroup understanding (Milem, Chang, and Antonio 2007).

Even departments that prioritize professional attainments usually do not want to seem uninterested in the democratization of the academy. All major scientific groups, including the National Academies of Science, Engineering, and Medicine, are on record as supporting the diversification of student bodies, faculty ranks, and administrative leadership (National Academies 2011a; see also NIH Office of the Director 2017; NSF Office of Diversity and Inclusion 2017). The sciences and engineering—and the disciplines that emulate them—remain bastions of traditional norms emphasizing academic merit, but they too are influenced by and responsive to the university's inclusionary aspirations—and most faculty members, at least most younger faculty members, do not see the two as in any way incompatible.

ACCOMMODATION

Campus climate surveys are based on quite general questions about relations on campus. They are incapable of examining intergroup relations in granular detail, and the generally positive image they convey consequently represents only part of the picture. On college campuses, accommodation is perhaps the most common of the outcomes of intergroup contact. Accommodation refers to the process by which powerful groups in a community make room for new groups without necessarily fully accepting them or equalizing their opportunities for status and power in the community. The multiplicity of microenvironments on campus eases the process of accommodation, even as they maintain inequalities. On multiethnic campuses, the sciences and engineering are heavily populated by Asians and whites, while the interpretive disciplines are disproportionately populated by African Americans,

Hispanics, and first-generation students. The divergent distribution of students helps maintain relatively peaceful intergroup relations, even as they allocate opportunities unequally. Similarly, cultural affinity organizations and ethnically themed residence halls provide structures and networks that support minorities without necessarily producing equalized opportunities.

The success of projects of inclusion depends on the perception that they are not costly to majority group students. As long as majority group students feel that opportunities are expandable rather than zero-sum, inclusivity has little downside and it can be embraced by the majority of faculty, staff, and students. Natasha Warikoo (2016) describes the "diversity bargain" on elite university campuses in the United States, which she defines as a willingness by majority group students to accept admissions preferences for minorities and pressures for inclusivity in college programs so long as this acceptance does not prevent majority group students from achieving their own ends in and beyond college. Certainly the same phenomenon exists in quantitative majors, which have become sites of multibillion-dollar government and foundation efforts to democratize STEM success.

Accommodation implies occasional, even frequent, friction. Majority group students must live with skepticism about their commitments to "social justice"—including occasionally harsh comments that these students should "check their privilege"—at the same time minority group students must battle the discomforts and insensitivities to which they remain subject. The many minority group students and women who stand out in their classes or their clubs provide constant demonstration that projects of inclusion are worthwhile and advantageous. Even if they sympathize with the ideals of inclusion and see evidence of its value, majority group students, faculty, and staff may resent what they perceive to be favoritism for minorities in particular cases. Minorities may feel that the disadvantages they have faced to join the campus community are not fully understood or accepted and that "excellence" and "merit" are simply ways of talking about the privileges of groups whose power on campus is greater than their own. These frictions are the price colleges and universities pay for trying to advance two overlapping, often mutually supportive, but not entirely congruent goals at once.

COMPETITION AND CONFLICT

A degree of competition and conflict is also evident in relations between majority and minority groups on campus. For conservatives this conflict has been engaged through accusations that university campuses are governed by a regime of "political correctness"—the prioritization of women's and minorities' issues, a high level of insensitivity to the values and opinions expressed by conservatives, and efforts to control the climate of conversation in ways that privilege politically liberal groups on campus. Conservatives have asserted that political correctness prevents the free flow of ideas and creates a "liberal bias" on campus. By contrast, college liberals assert that colleges and universities continue to neglect their responsibilities for creating a more socially just society. I discuss these issues at greater length in chapter 9.

Some forms of contestation are less visible to the public but no less consequential for the institutions. Perhaps the most important are efforts by progressive students and faculty members to redefine university norms and practices in a direction that favors the community minded over the intellectually accomplished. These redefinition efforts extend all the way from undergraduate admissions to faculty promotions—and even to denunciations of the possibility of objectivity in academic discourse. These are the most trying disputes of all because they strike at the core academic commitments of most well-established professors (and their allies among academically oriented university administrators).

Skepticism about test-based conceptions of meritocracy are common; several dozen colleges and universities have abandoned standardized tests because of their association with family socioeconomic status. The legal scholar Lani Guinier (2015) went a step further and proposed an alternative admissions framework. She argued that what she calls "test merit" should be replaced by "democratic merit." As she used the term, "democratic merit" includes at least the following qualities: leadership, collaboration, resiliency, and the drive to learn. Thus far the redefinition has had a limited impact. Efforts to redefine merit in a more community-minded way have also influenced evaluations of faculty members. Progressive faculty members in the arts, humanities, and social scientists are skeptical of standard measures of academic influence, such as journal impact factors, citation counts, and academic awards. They argue that new and creative work is often not recognized by the dominant journals or the professional associations. They lobby for a broad definition of merit to include publications that appear in low-impact journals or that involve community-based research. They sometimes argue that contributions to diversity should be taken into account in faculty merit evaluations, and at least one university system has made contributions to diversity an explicit criterion for hiring and promotion.[18]

The idea of scholarly objectivity itself has been under attack from the academic left since the early 1980s. Those who dislike the concept of objectivity were not primarily critical because of its changing historical meaning (cf. Daston and Galison 2007) but rather because they saw it as the characteristic stance of the powerful in a system rigged against those whose voices were rarely heard. As the feminist scholar Dorothy Smith put it,

> When you are outside and subservient to this [conceptual] structure of [nominally objective] sociology [women have] a very specific relation to it, which anchors them into the local and partial phase of [a] bifurcated world. . . . The governing conceptual mode [of objectivity] is appropriated by men and the world organized in the natural attitude, the home, is appropriated by [or assigned to] women. (1974, 9)

One alternative has been to examine the world from the standpoint of disadvantaged groups (see, e.g., Bell 1987; Delgado and Stefancic 2001; Harding 1993; Spivak 1988) or in relation to the intersection of identities—race, class, and gender—found among members of disadvantaged groups (Collins 1990). These conflicts over objectivity and standpoint are among the most fateful for disciplines that are far removed from the power centers of American society, and I will discuss them further in chapter 9.

WHO HAS POWER?

In situations of conflict between members of traditionally powerful groups and the advocates of increased diversity, who has power? The answer is not as straightforward as it might at first seem. On the surface, it would seem that the balance should be overwhelmingly in favor of those who come from advantaged backgrounds and occupy high-status positions. After all, star scientists and engineers are the dominant group on research university campuses, and most are white or Asian males from relatively privileged family backgrounds. Their orientation tends to be toward the promotion of academic accomplishments over other values. Arts, humanities, and social science disciplines are more divided over the priority of democratization as opposed to professional accomplishment, but the principles of meritocracy nevertheless hold in those departments in which professional attainments are prioritized.

Faculty members who are strongly oriented toward inclusivity and "social justice" do not lack power. Many members of the nominally dominant groups are sympathetic to campus progressives on ideological grounds. These people accept that injustices have been done to women and minorities and are interested in redressing the injustices. Many have encountered underrepresented students who have been standouts in their classrooms. Diversity-oriented faculty members also have the power to mobilize for change. Politically progressive networks can be a powerful pressure group, particularly when they do not face organized opposition—and they often do not. Most successful senior professors who are skeptical of the diversity-centered partisan politics of universities are too busy conducting their research and too involved with their professional lives to pay close attention (Hermanowicz 2013). University administrators will generally attempt to mollify mobilized groups on campus so as to avoid harming their school's reputation for inclusiveness. The positions of administrators reflect their institutional interests in campus peace and (sometimes also) higher enrollments. Indeed, the great majority of administrators are selected in part on the basis of their beliefs in diversifying the academy. The capacity to employ labels is the final power of social-justice progressives. Accusations of racial or gender bias are crippling labels in contemporary academic life, and even to be suspected of not appreciating the need for greater diversity in admissions and hiring can be a damaging insinuation. Because of these "powers of the weak," the proponents of academic excellence and the proponents of democratization are more evenly balanced when they come into conflict than facile analyses based on the presumption of "white male privilege" suggest.

The tensions between proponents of diversification and meritocracy have occasionally erupted into overt conflict. In divided departments leaders of the two sides are quick to deride the motives and values of the other. Yet from an institutional perspective, the tensions between the two do not begin to rival the benefits of providing space for both while recognizing the contributions that diversity can make to the identification of talented individuals and the contributions that academic merit criteria can make to the realization of a diversified community that is also high achieving.

6

The Priorities of Patrons

Standing above the everyday concerns of campus administrators, faculty members, and students are the large levers of government and private patronage. The Medicis were able to create a flowering in the arts and scholarship in fourteenth- and fifteenth-century Florence. Neither the renaissance of applied science nor the extensions of educational opportunity during the period could have occurred without multibillion-dollar investments by the federal government and the fifty states—the greatest of university patrons—as well as multimillion-dollar investments by thousands of contemporary Medici families. The major research universities, in particular, were showered with funds—never enough, of course, to do everything they wanted or hoped to do. The priorities of patrons strongly influenced the directions universities pursued—and those they avoided. Cancer therapies took off in large part because patrons poured money into them; American Studies languished in large part because it could find few patrons. This chapter analyzes the priorities that patrons expressed and the consequences of their largesse, focusing on the three giants of giving: the federal government, the fifty states, and million-dollar-plus donors.

Corporations are another important patron of universities, as I have argued in chapter 3. During the period they contributed 5 to 7 percent of funding to university R&D. And of course their engagement with universities extended far beyond funding for individual R&D projects. It ranged from the large-scale partnerships of prolific university-industry research

TABLE 6.1. Centers of Gravity in Preferences of Major Patrons to U.S. Higher Education

Actor	Research Orientation	Enrollment Orientation
Federal Patrons	Mixed, moving toward Academic Innovation	Mixed, tilted toward the Middle Class
State Patrons	Mixed, often Critical of Low-Enrollment Fields	Mixed, depending on State
Private Patrons	Academic Innovation	Status Conferral in Valued Fields and Activities
Corporations	Mixed, Academic Innovation but also Studies in Many Scientific Applied Fields	Training in High-Demand Business and Technical Occupations

centers, such as those discussed in chapter 3, all the way down to contracts to provide vending machines for residence halls. Companies also sometimes funded endowed professorships that were closely aligned with their industry interests, such as the Toyota Motor Company Endowed Professorship of Operations Management at New York University. At the same time, the involvement of corporations with specific departments and organized research units was more often episodic, piecemeal, and, frequently, low budget. In a careful study of corporate engagement with two colleges and four organized research units at Pennsylvania State University, Roger Geiger (2004, 186–93) found that typical involvements included donation of materials, use of specialized equipment for small fees, provision of testing services, sponsorship of research studies, consulting partnerships, and sponsorship of internships. At Penn State, Geiger found some 250 firms funded research studies and 200 more were involved in consortia. The absence of discussion of corporations in this chapter should not be interpreted to mean that I regard corporations as unimportant patrons. They are important, but the data on the multiplicity of their involvements are not as yet comprehensive enough to sustain generalizations.

I have described two polarities in academic life, one related to research, the other related to enrollment. The first divided discipline-based academic professionalism from science and technology-based academic innovationism; the second divided access-oriented social inclusion from merit-legitimated status confirmation. In this chapter, I will argue that the priorities of patrons tended to favor fields that were closely aligned with power centers in American society—many connected to technological innovation—and their financial aid preferences tipped decidedly in the direction of support for middle-class and affluent college students. Less well-connected fields and financially needy students were not neglected by patrons, but support for them failed to keep pace. By contrast, most professors identified with the structures of academic professionalism, and a large proportion also supported the universities' aspirations for wider social inclusion. This set up distinctively different coalitions within the higher education field, rallying different sets of actors, and creating, as I interpret it, a tension fruitful for the dynamism of the whole (see table 6.1).

Federal Support for Higher Education: An Overview

Through its expenditures on financial aid and research, the federal government has been the chief patron for colleges and universities. Without federal patronage, professors would have found their classrooms half full and their research labs filigreed with cobwebs. The volume of funding flowing from the two main federal spigots was not evenly balanced; financial aid expenditures ran nearly twice as high as R&D expenditures, and even this ratio requires an asterisk because it does not include student loan disbursements, a portion of which can reasonably be considered expenditures because they will eventually go into permanent default.

Looking only at grants-in-aid, federal expenditures on financial aid in 2015 consisted of Pell Grants to low-income students (encompassing the great majority of students from the bottom half of the family income distribution) and veteran's benefits yielding a total of $43.5 billion, with Pell Grants representing about three-quarters of this total. To these numbers we can add federal work-study funds and tax credits given to federal income tax filers for having a child or children in college, pushing the total to $65.1 billion. Both Pell Grants and veteran's benefits more than doubled in constant dollars from the mid-1990s to the mid-2010s, with the largest growth following the Great Recession. Federal student loan disbursements added another $100 billion in expenditures for financial aid by the end of the period. Ten to 20 percent of all loans were in default in any given year (Dynarski 2014). Calculations about whether the government makes or loses money on these loans are complicated by the difficulty of predicting how many students will fall behind or default on their loans and the exact costs of collecting outstanding loans. By one official estimate, the government sustained a loss of over $20 billion in 2016 on student loans (Lobato 2016). In this scenario, federal expenditures on financial aid could therefore be calculated, very roughly, at $80 to $85 billion in 2015 (including current Pell Grants, veteran's benefits, work-study, and tax credits, plus an estimate of loss for loan defaults and servicing).[1]

By contrast, the total university share of federally funded R&D in 2015 was $35.6 billion, less than half the financial aid total. Universities are a major player in federal R&D, but they are not *the* major player—that honor goes to the defense industry. In colorful prose, Florida congressman Buddy MacKay described federal R&D priorities as follows:

> First priority goes to things that explode and go fast. Second priority goes to projects that are huge and that generate Nobel Prizes. Third priority goes to projects that are supported by senior Members of Congress and that also bring new jobs into their state or district. Last priority goes to small projects that involve incremental change. (quoted in Morin 1993, 25)

MacKay's analysis can be faulted, but he was certainly right about priority number one. Defense R&D alone exceeded all other agency R&D combined throughout the 1980–2015 period, and the great majority of defense spending went for weapons and equipment development rather than research (AAAS 2016).[2]

Altogether, federal R&D spending on universities represented about one-quarter of total federal R&D spending. Universities were the primary beneficiaries only in the area of "basic" (as opposed to "applied") research. (Scare quotes are necessary because much of the research classified by the government as "basic" is better conceived as "use-inspired" basic research [see the discussion in Stokes 1997].) The ratio of federal funds going to universities for basic research, applied research, and development was about 8 to 3 to 1 in the later years of the period. Some $23.3 billion in federal funds were awarded to universities to support "basic science" research in 2015. "Applied research" garnered about $9 billion, and development a relative pittance at less than $3 billion (AAAS 2016).

No other federal expenditures rivaled financial aid or R&D as sources of federal support for higher education. Only two other budget categories exceeded $1 billion annually by the end of the period: the federal government provided general purpose appropriations of nearly $4 billion to the military academies, historically black colleges and universities, land grant institutions, and a few other specialized institutions (Pew Charitable Trusts

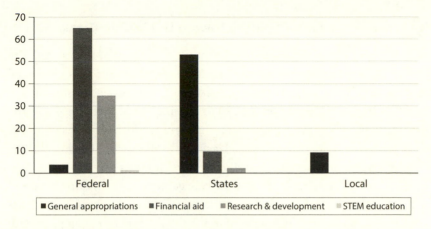

FIGURE 6.1. Federal, State, and Local Support for Higher Education by Expenditure Category, AY 2013–14 (in billions).
Sources: AAAS (2016) for federal R&D expenditures; American Institute of Physics (2015) for STEM education expenditures; the College Board (copyright © 2017 The College Board) for financial aid expenditures; the National Science Foundation (2016b) for state R&D expenditures; the Pew Charitable Trusts (2015) for state and local expenditures and federal general appropriations.

2015). The federal government also provided more than $1 billion annually for STEM education initiatives through programs operated primarily by the Department of Education and the National Science Foundation (American Institute of Physics 2015).

A comparison between federal and state support shows the extent to which the federal government is essential to the operational effectiveness of American colleges and universities. The total expenditures for the fifty states taken together represented only about two-thirds that of the federal government. The states' largest support stream was for general purpose funds, at $53 billion in 2015 (Pew Charitable Trusts 2015). These funds, also known as state appropriations or state subsidies, declined dramatically in constant dollars during the period. Together with tuition, general appropriations supported the educational and related plant operations of public colleges and universities. By the end of the period the fifty states also contributed approximately $10 billion a year in financial aid support (College Board 2016) and about $2 billion in research and development support (NSF 2016b), for a total of some $65 billion. The federal and state expenditures are summarized in figure 6.1 for academic year 2013–14, the last year in which data for all categories were available.

Student Financial Aid: Tilting toward the Middle Class

It is necessary to clear a few wide trails through the forest of federal policy to better understand the priorities and trajectories of this most important of all university patrons. I begin with the largest expenditure category, student aid.

The fiscal approach most helpful to low-income students is obviously one that combines low tuition charges and grants-in-aid in cases of unmet financial need, rather than loans. Such a policy would greatly fuel the social inclusion aspirations of college and university administrators, progressive-minded faculty members, and aspiring college students. Low tuition was not sustained during the period in either public or private universities. Grants-in-aid expanded, but the failure of federal Pell Grants to keep pace with costs encouraged the migration of low-income students from public flagship universities to lower and less expensive tiers in the public systems. By the 1990s federal financial aid policies were tipping decisively toward favoring middle- and upper-middle-class families.

Prior to 1980 two individuals were most important for the policy achievements of the federal government in student aid: President Lyndon Johnson, who built guaranteed student loans into the Higher Education Act of 1965; and Senator Claiborne Pell, who shepherded legislation providing grants to low-income students through Congress in 1972. The policy achievements of Johnson and Pell, together with their supporters in Congress, expanded federal financial aid opportunities and helped the United States become the world's leader in college graduation. In 1975–76 at the peak of financial aid funding and at a time when tuitions were not yet climbing, the average student received five times as much grant aid as he or she borrowed in loans.[3]

The availability of grant aid was only one of the reasons for the extension of equality of opportunity—and not the most important one. Instead, the low tuition costs typical of the period were the most important cause of heightened access. The most highly regarded public university system in the country, the University of California, required students to pay fees in the 1950s that would be equivalent to approximately $1,000 in 2015 dollars (Liaison Committee of the Regents of the University of California 1955, 405), and these fees increased only moderately through the 1970s. (As of 2017, tuition and fees totaled more than $14,000.) A few "thrifty" (i.e., low-tax) New England states required their public universities to operate mainly on tuition charges, but other states followed the California approach, albeit at lower levels of expenditure.

A TURN TOWARD LOANS AND TAX CREDITS

After 1980 the public resources available to support equality of opportunity declined relative to the amounts necessary to attend and complete college. Financial aid policy shifted toward favoring middle- and upper-middle-class students over working-class and poor students. This was true even though every time the Higher Education Act of 1965 was reauthorized, the size of the Pell Grant pool expanded. Between 1980 and 2005, Pell Grant allocations more than doubled in constant dollars from nearly $7 billion to more than $15 billion (College Board 2016, figure 18). But these increases were not enough to counter the more rapid increases in college tuition. At public universities, fees rose at nearly three times the rate of inflation after 1980, much faster than the incomes of all but the rich. As tuition increased, Pell Grants very nearly stagnated in real terms (CBO 2013). Every effort to raise Pell Grant minimums resulted in contentious disagreements between Republican social-spending skeptics and opportunity-conscious Democrats. The path of least resistance was to ease regulations on borrowing rather than to fight to keep grants proportionate to tuition (Mettler 2014, chap. 2).

Banks initially balked at becoming deeply involved in student loans, in large part because students lacked collateral to guarantee their loans. The problem of convincing banks to lend to students was solved by subsidizing student loans and by creating a government-sponsored entity, the Student Loan Marketing Association, better known as Sallie Mae, to warehouse loans that banks did not want on their books and to provide other services to lenders (Berman and Stivers 2016). By the mid-1980s, the average student borrowed as much as he or she received in grants, a ratio that persisted throughout most of the period. The takeoff point in the student loan market occurred in the early 1990s. With tuitions rising, most students increased their dependence on loans to finance their college educations (see figure 6.2).

By 1990, Sallie Mae had developed novel financial instruments for packaging loans and had entered the student loan market, quickly becoming the largest student lender, with approximately half of market share (U.S. Department of the Treasury 2006). In 1992, congressional amendments to the Higher Education Act supercharged the loan business. Congress made federal student loans available to all students regardless of income. They added unsubsidized loans for those with family expected contributions above qualifications for subsidized loans, and they added the so-called

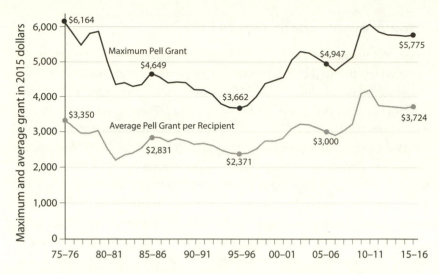

FIGURE 6.2. Total Federal Student Loan Volume and Average per FTE Student, FY 1971–2014. *Source*: Berman and Stivers 2016, figure 1. Republished with permission of Elsevier Science and Technology Journals; permission conveyed through Copyright Clearance Center, Inc.

PLUS loan with no limits on amounts that could be borrowed (Akers and Chingos 2016, 47). The price and service competition between Sallie Mae and the nascent government direct lending program also made borrowing more attractive to students and their families.[4] The size of the student loan market more than tripled between 1992 and 2005 (College Board 2016), as total borrowing increased from $12.5 billion in 1993 to $46.5 billion in 2005 (Berman and Stivers 2016, figure 1; College Board 2016, figure 7b). The availability of loans on relatively attractive terms may not have caused tuitions to rise, but it did *make it possible* for colleges and universities to charge more (Berman and Stivers 2016).

It was clear that student loans had spawned "a lucrative industry that yielded financial benefits for many banks that made or insured loans and especially for the federally-guaranteed loans made by . . . Sallie Mae" (Mettler 2014, 68–69). The Clinton administration retired Sallie Mae's government charter in 1996 so that it could trade stock on the New York Exchange. Ten years later it was managing more than $125 billion for 10 million borrowers. Even as a private entity, Sallie Mae retained government benefits in the form of guarantees for unpaid loans and high subsidies. Sallie Mae's profits, in turn, increased the financial incentive of other private financial institutions to engage in student lending. Low-income families tend to be loan-averse, raising the attractiveness of low-cost alternatives to four-year colleges.

A second policy change during the Clinton administration further enhanced the advantages of middle- and upper-middle-income families. Tax credits for parents with children in college had been rejected by generations of Democrats as a giveaway to middle-income taxpayers with money that could be better used to help the poor afford college. Tax credits were adopted by the Clinton administration as a prong in its strategy to triangulate the interests of Republicans and Democrats with those of the administration. However effective they may have been as a political tactic, tax credits drained funds from the Treasury that could have been used for student financial aid grants. And virtually all of this money went to middle- and upper-middle-class families—those who paid income tax—allowing them to deduct up to $1,500 from their tax bill in support of their children's college attendance.

BINGEING ON LOANS

From the early 1990s through 2010, federal student aid policy was dominated by the interests of the financial industry and the affluent, implicitly supported by colleges and universities whose regular increases in tuition were backstopped by the normalization of a student debt culture. Matthew Rotondi (2015) studied the culture of student debt and found that students at three Southern California colleges rationalized borrowing by seeing debt as an investment rather than a burden, by comparing their circumstances to those with higher levels of debt, and by putting off thinking about repayment until after college. Among four-year college graduates, average student debt increased from approximately $12,500 in 1992–93 to nearly $27,000 in 2011–12 (in constant dollars). The proportion of student borrowers also increased from just below 50 percent to just below 70 percent during the period (Fry 2014).

Surprisingly, researchers found that the increasing net costs of attending college explained only about one-third of the change in borrowing levels (Hershbein and Hollenbeck 2013).[5] Two other factors also loomed large: the growth of for-profits and the expansion of graduate enrollments. Average borrowing was much higher at the for-profits; in 2011–12, by one estimate, some 90 percent of students borrowed to finance college, and four-year degree recipients averaged nearly $40,000 in loan debt (Institute for College Access and Success 2014).[6] Graduate students also typically took out more loans than undergraduates; if we exclude the graduate students who took out no loans, the average graduate degree recipient took on $55,000 in debt in 2011–12 (Akers and Chingos 2016, 29).

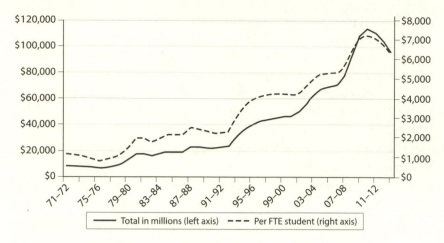

FIGURE 6.3. Average and Maximum Pell Grants, 1975–76 to 2015–16.
Source: College Board 2016, figure 17.

Grant aid benefited underrepresented minority students because they were disproportionately eligible for Pell Grants. In 2007–8, for example, 48 percent of white students had family incomes under $50,000, the approximate cut line for Pell eligibility, but 77 percent of African Americans and 71 percent of all minorities had family incomes below this level (Kantrowitz 2011). The declining relative purchasing power of Pell Grants impacted minorities disproportionately (see figure 6.3).

Pell Grant–eligible students have always been a rarity at prestigious private colleges, hovering, with few exceptions, at 5–15 percent of the undergraduate student body (see, e.g., Soares 2007, chap. 6). The distributional consequences of higher tuition and increased borrowing were, however, new to the public sector. Studies showed that this shift from grants to loans had little impact on high- and middle-income students but appreciably affected low-income students. Many low-income students felt that they needed to enroll in less expensive schools or drop out altogether (see, e.g., GAO 1995). At community colleges they were surrounded by part-time and vocationally oriented students and were not strongly encouraged by their peers or effectively enabled by their institutions to persist to a bachelor's degree (Brint and Karabel 1989; Dougherty and Kienzl 2006). Students also began to wait to attend college until they were older; in many cases they attended part-time while working twenty to thirty hours a week (Baker and Velez 1996). Fully adequate financial aid was hard to come by. Saunders (2015), for example, found that low-income students attending four-year colleges experienced a 59 percent increase in unmet need between 1995–96 and 2003–4, during a time when tuitions increased and Pell Grants flattened. Living expenses were a big problem for low-income students; even if they could afford tuition thanks to Pell Grants, other scholarships, and loans, they were often priced out of campus housing markets.

With Pell Grants unable to cover rising tuition costs, the proportion of lower-income students enrolled at flagship state universities declined significantly as a proportion of Pell-eligible students between 1992 and 2003 (Haycock and Gerald 2006) and declined again, albeit more moderately, between 2003 and 2007 (Haycock, Lynch, and Engle 2010). Between 1992 and 2003, 44 of 50 public flagships studied by the Educational Trust showed undergraduate enrollments marked by declining proportions of low-income students (Haycock and Gerald 2010, 15). Part of the reason had to do with the increasing admission standards of public flagship universities. But much of the change could be attributed to the declining purchasing power of federal aid grants in the face of higher tuition prices. A few states like California, New Jersey, New York, and Washington subsidized low-income students with generous state financial aid programs. But in most states, low-income students found themselves financially ill-equipped to attend the leading public universities. Donors added hundreds of millions of dollars to the grant pool through their contributions to scholarships, but these scholarships were most often intended to reward outstanding achievements in areas of interest to donors themselves—especially the fields in which they had themselves been successful—rather than to address issues of financial need (see the discussion of private philanthropy below).

THE SYSTEM ABIDES

The Obama administration passed several reforms to student financial aid. These reforms put the system on stronger financial and ethical footing but did not substantially alter its impact on students and their families. Following the Great Recession, banks became risk averse and were reluctant to make any loans, including student loans. This retreat threatened the continuation of financial aid at a time when colleges were being asked to enroll many more students who might otherwise have preferred to take jobs. In 2010, with the approval of Congress and against the opposition of conservatives tied to the banking industry, Deputy Secretary Robert Shireman and his colleagues at the Department of Education successfully ended the bank-based guaranteed student loan program, making direct lending by the federal government the source of an estimated 90 percent of student lending. (Private firms continued to be awarded contracts for servicing student loans.) This overhaul potentially saved the government billions of dollars, by some estimates (Berman and Stivers 2016), while ensuring continued borrowing.

Another reform cleaned up predatory lending in the for-profit sector. In 2015, after many years of ineffective efforts to regulate for-profits, Congress passed a gainful employment rule requiring institutions to provide data on the proportion of their graduates who were paying more than 12 percent of their income or more than 30 percent of discretionary income on student loans. Institutions with averages at this level or higher for two out of three consecutive years were no longer eligible for federal student aid for a minimum of three years. The gainful employment rule was aimed explicitly at the hard-sell lending practices of for-profit colleges, and it led, directly or indirectly, to the closing of hundreds of these colleges, including two of the largest for-profit chains, Corinthian and ITT Technical Institutes. By the end of the period, public and private nonprofit universities were ascendant in the online market and, with the exception of some well-established giants like the University of Phoenix, for-profit colleges were in retreat.

During the recovery from the recession loan volumes fell as jobs returned and more students chose to take their chances in the labor market. But neither the changes in policy nor the decline in loan volume altered the large role that student loans played in the lives of college graduates, and particularly in the lives of those who left college without degrees. For most, loans were manageable—according to the economists Beth Akers and Mark Chingos (2016, 33–36), the average student in 2013 who took loans paid back about $275 per month, approximately the same amount s/he spent on dining out. Nevertheless, the timing of repayments was uncomfortable. Repayments started at a time immediately following graduation or separation from college when young adults were least prepared to start making them. Income-contingent repayment plans were available, but many students did not know about them, and if they did, the red tape required to enroll in the plans led many give up the effort (see the discussion of financial aid reforms in chapter 9).

Research Funding: Aligning with National Priorities

If financial aid tipped toward students from the middle- and upper-middle classes, research and development awards flowed toward the dominant dis-

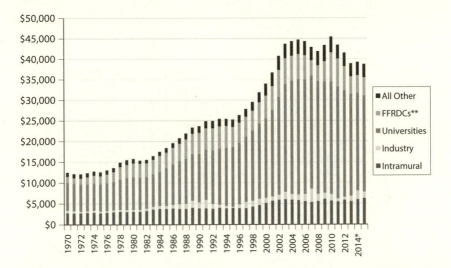

FIGURE 6.4. Federal Basic Research Funding by Performer, 1970–2015 (obligations in millions of constant FY 2016 dollars).
Source: AAAS 2016. National Science Foundation, National Patterns of R&D data series, available at http://www.nsf.gov/statistics/. *Preliminary Figures for FY14 and FY15. **FFRDCs = Federally funded research and development centers. Government-owned, contractor-operated laboratories.

ciplines and edged incrementally in the direction of government-defined national priorities and away from curiosity-driven research. The problem-identification and problem-solving interests of the disciplines remained important—and owed much to the federal government's continuing support. But science policies after 1980 created many new opportunities for the proponents of aligning universities more closely with identified national needs. Most of these priority areas were justified for their potential to bring new wealth and new jobs to communities, the foundational promise of academic innovationism.

Universities were the primary beneficiaries of the large increases in federal funding for science that began in the mid-1980s, escalated in the mid-1990s, and continued on a steep upward trajectory through the Great Recession period. This golden age of R&D funding was capped by the influx of American Recovery and Reinvestment Act (ARRA) expenditures in 2009–10, the first time that science funding had been used as a countercyclical economic policy instrument.

As figure 6.4 shows, university shares of federal basic science funding tripled during the period, at a time when the total funding for basic science

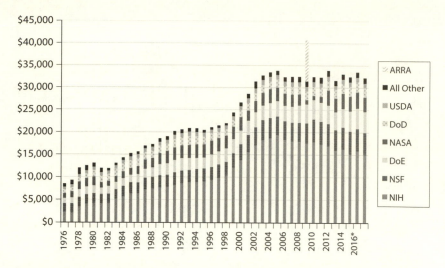

FIGURE 6.5. Trends in Basic Research by Agency, 1976–2017 (in billions of constant FY 2016 dollars).
Source: AAAS 2016. R&D analyses of OMB and agency R&D budget data. Includes conduct of R&D and R&D facilities. *Preliminary figures for FY16 and FY17.

(including grants to federal labs and industry) grew from $25 to $43 billion. The National Institutes of Health (NIH) have been the largest supporter of science research conducted at universities, at more than $15 billion in 2015. They were followed by the National Science Foundation (NSF) at approximately $5 billion, the Department of Energy (DOE) at $4.5 billion, the National Aeronautics and Space Administration (NASA) at approximately $3 billion, the Department of Defense (DOD) at nearly $2 billion, and the U.S. Department of Agriculture at a little less than $1 billion (AAAS 2016). All other agencies combined accounted for a little over $1 billion in 2015.[7]

Figure 6.5 shows the share of basic research funded by federal agencies during the period. The rapid advance of the National Institutes of Health beginning in the early 1990s is the most impressive feature of this time series. Near the end of the period the Department of Energy gained a larger share of federal "basic science" funding. Its work, once focused on national security, shifted toward new energy technologies, such as high-storage batteries and efficient solar conversion. It also became the lead agency for much of the work on new materials made possible by nanoscale technology. The growth of NSF funding near the end of the period is also noteworthy.

FUELING THE HIGH-OCTANE FIELDS

A fundamental trend of the period was the convergence of federal research patronage on fields that regularly contributed to new science and technology development. NIH funding went overwhelmingly to biomedical researchers and other life scientists. A significant portion of this work resulted in new therapeutic interventions in medicine. Bhaven Sampat and Frank Lichtenberg (2011) estimated that nearly half of drugs had patents that cited public sector patents and publications, a proportion that increased to two-thirds for the highest-impact drugs.[8] Another study found that NIH support was foundational in the discovery of eleven of the nineteen "most transformational" drugs produced between 1990 and 2015. They included drugs for treating cancer, blood disorders, nerve disorders, mental health problems, and pain—as well as contributions to improved anesthesia (Chakravarty et al. 2016). DOE funding went heavily to engineers and physicists who worked on clean energy sources and new materials with commercial applications. NSF maintained a wider net and was the largest government funder of computer science, mathematics, and social sciences. Some of its most celebrated work also contributed to the commercial economy, including the development of bar codes, computer-aided design, computer visualization techniques, data compression technologies, and edible vaccines (NSF 2017).

The social and behavioral sciences trailed far behind, and the arts and humanities were barely recognized. By end of the period, the social and behavioral science share ran at about 8 percent of the total (AAAS 2016). And both the National Arts and Humanities Foundations received funding at about the level of *0.4 percent* of NIH biomedical research alone, truly a pittance relative to the scale of funding provided to the R&D behemoths funding science and engineering.[9]

Scientists sometimes wrote a half dozen grant proposals a year to allow their labs to stay in business. Their access to funding came at a price. Nevertheless, this concentration of funding reinforced the high levels of creativity and accomplishment found in the science- and engineering-based high-tech economy and the sense of marginalization and indignation that spread through sections of the arts and humanities. The funding patterns of the period inflated Clark Kerr's puckish characterization of the "federal grant university" as composed of "scientists affluent, humanists militant" (1963, 60). If scientists were feasting on ample patronage, humanists were virtually starving for want of it (see figure 6.6).

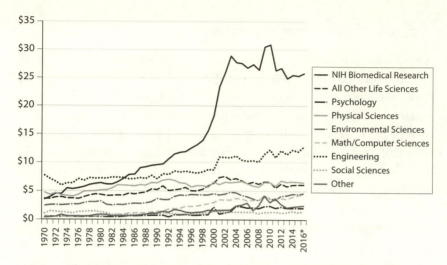

FIGURE 6.6. Trends in Federal Research by Discipline, 1970–2016 (obligations in billions of constant FY 2016 dollars).
Source: AAAS 2016; NSF 2016a. *FY 2015 and 2016 data are preliminary. Includes Recovery Act funding starting in FY09. "Other" includes research not elsewhere classified. Constant-dollar conversions based on GDP deflators from Budget of the U.S. Government FY 2017.

INCREASED FEDERAL DIRECTION

Beyond the windfall for fields that contributed to economic development, the second big story of the period was the slow-moving, incremental transformation of basic science funding away from the disciplines and individual investigators and toward state-defined science and technology opportunities and the funding of large teams to address these opportunities. In the traditional peer review system underlying federal research allocations, proposals are solicited by the science agencies and directorates and evaluated by academic experts. These evaluations focus on the scientific merit (and more recently also on the "broader impacts") of the proposal. Program managers recommend the highest-rated proposals for funding, sometimes requiring budget trimming in the process. The effectiveness of peer review enabled empaneled scientists to take a role beyond that of a mere interest group; instead, they exercised decision-making power within the constraints of the budgets allocated for peer-reviewed research grants. Traditional investigator-initiated projects remained an important feature of the federal government's research portfolio; at the same time, peer review was directed increasingly to programs identified by the agencies as big problems to tackle rather than remaining tied to the ideas of researchers hoping to advance knowledge in their disciplines.

I will discuss these incremental changes in relation to the three agencies responsible for most basic science research funding directed toward universities: the National Institutes of Health (NIH), the National Science Foundation (NSF), and the Department of Energy (DOE).

The National Institutes of Health

The NIH budget exceeded that of NSF by three to four times throughout most of the period, and doubled between 1998 and 2003.[10] Its research expenditures, running over $30 billion a year by 2015, represented the single most important reason why American universities excelled at biomedical research and have made disproportionate contributions to fundamental breakthroughs in the life sciences. Of this total, about half ($15 billion in 2015) was classified by NIH as basic scientific research. Although federal government statistics still use the familiar distinction between "basic" and "applied" research, in fact most of what is categorized as "basic research" at NIH and NSF is use-inspired and in that sense applied research, at least in aspiration. Many in the science policy community now use the term "curiosity-driven" to describe research that is conducted without potential applications in mind. This category of funded research is small relative to use-inspired basic research.

NIH was the most important federal funder of university scientific research, accounting for approximately 43 percent of the total in 2015 (AAAS 2016). When Congress pushed for greater focus on disease, as it often did, agency heads pushed back successfully by arguing that fundamental knowledge had wider applicability than disease-focused science and by emphasizing the serendipitous applications of basic science investigations. Harold Varmus, a NIH director in the 1990s, argued, for example, that basic scientific work, such as that leading to better understanding of genes and tissues, would ultimately form the basis for practical advances against any of several diseases (Varmus and Kirschner 1992).[11] And indeed a large proportion of new drugs associated with NIH funding were "first-in-class" therapies treating disease through novel mechanisms or molecular targets.

During the period covered in this book, research project grants (RPGs) accounted for 50–60 percent of the total agency budget (NIH 2017a). They declined a little from the late 1990s through 2010 (Sampat 2012) before rebounding to historic levels. RPGs include the classic individual and small-group investigator grants, the so-called R01 grants, as well as funding for a number of other NIH activity codes ranging from high-risk/high-reward discovery grants to longer-term multisite research grants. All RPGs are investigator initiated, peer reviewed, and competitively awarded. In addition to research project grants NIH funds a very large program of intramural research and a network of research centers focusing on translational and clinical medicine and public health issues. The share of funds allocated to intramural research and research centers now constitutes close to 20 percent of the total NIH budget, with research centers receiving about 10 percent (NIH 2017b).

NIH used a "Common Fund" mechanism to support cross-institute investments.[12] This is where we see the organization of science for a more centralized attack in national priority areas. Common Fund programs are intended to be "transformative, catalytic, synergistic, cross-cutting, and unique" (NIH 2017c). In 2015, the Common Fund supported thirty-one program areas at $546 million, a small fraction of its total research budget, and it had "graduated" fourteen other Common Fund projects. Most of these programs focused on curiosity-driven or use-inspired basic science research, but some, such as the regenerative medicine program and the druggable genome program, had obvious potential to generate economic activity. Each one reflected the growing interest in setting agendas for research scientists based on the judgment of agency heads and their advisors.

The National Science Foundation

NSF has often been maligned as the weak sibling of U.S. federal R&D (see, e.g., Morin 1993) because much of the space it was intended to occupy had already been absorbed by the federal mission agencies by the time it was finally founded in 1950. Nevertheless, the importance of the agency grew substantially during the period, and by 2015 it was managing a budget of $7 billion, reviewing more than 50,000 proposals a year, and awarding grants to about one-fifth of them. These figures were similar to the proposal and award volumes found at NIH, albeit with awards that were on average only about half the size (NIH 2015). Seventy-five to 80 percent of NSF funds have gone to university-based researchers and they accounted for about one-quarter of all extramural research on university campuses (NSF 2013, 2017).

Throughout the period, NSF allocated more than half of its budget to individual-investigator and small-team grants. And, indeed, during most of the period these allocations represented more than 60 percent of total expenditures, a ratio similar to that found at NIH.[13] Thus the basic structure of peer review prevailed against consistent pressures to link science funding to national priority areas as defined by agency bureaucrats, the president, or Congress. The large-scale facilities run by NSF, such as the Arctic Exploration Centers and the large telescope observatories, can reasonably be considered under the same rubric; they are common infrastructure available to support the work of hundreds of individual investigators and small teams.

Like the Common Fund at NIH, NSF's Cross-Foundation Investments offered a vehicle for the agency to focus scientific attention on government-identified national priority areas. In some cases, these cross-agency investments are connected to presidential initiatives, as in NSF's nanotechnology and brain science investments discussed in the next section. In other cases, they represent the agencies' own sense of national priorities or emerging opportunities for the advancement of science as identified by the National Academies and other advisors. Cross-Foundation Investments outside of facilities began in the mid-1980s with NSF support for the development of "NSFNET," the forerunner of the Internet (NSF 2000). In the 1990s and 2000s, the agency identified several other areas for cross-foundation investments, including in the science of learning, nanotechnology, and the ecology of infectious diseases.

Cross-Foundation Investments have absorbed a larger portion of the foundation's budget. In FY 2015, they included investments to contribute to clean energy technologies, to investigate new cyber-infrastructure, including safe and trustworthy cyberspace, to promote cyber-enabled materials manufacturing, to study sustainability in science, engineering, and education, to understand the brain, to conduct research at the interface of mathematics, biology, and the physical sciences, and to study risk and resilience in individuals and communities (NSF 2016d). Together these seven initiatives accounted for about one-seventh of the agency's total budget, a much larger fraction than the Common Fund absorbed at NIH. Some of these cross-agency investments have clear potential for economic spillovers, including, for example, clean energy and cyber-infrastructure, while others are primarily oriented to producing basic science breakthroughs.

The Department of Energy

The Department of Energy became a third important source of funding for academic science research during the period, and its strategy focused to a greater degree than that of NIH or NSF on work conducted by large-scale, multi-investigator teams working in designated national priority areas. At

DOE, universities competed for this funding with national laboratories, nonprofit organizations, and industry.

DOE reported $670 million in basic science research projects in 2013 (U.S. Department of Energy 2014a). Approximately one-third of this funding went to large-scale, multi-investigator projects through research center grants and grants to "innovation hubs." The department funded three Bio-energy Research Centers (BRCs) at $30 million, 46 Energy Frontier Research Centers (EFRCs) at $100 million, and five Innovation Hubs at $125 million (U.S. Department of Energy 2014b). Each of the BRCs and EFRCs is a partnership between more than one university and at least one national lab, and in most cases they also involved nonprofit organizations and industry. Of the 46 energy frontier centers operating in 2013, only 17 were headed by university researchers. Researchers from one of the 15 DOE-funded national labs headed the majority of the remainder. These centers built on the team science culture of the national weapons laboratories operated by the Atomic Energy Commission after World War II but focused on materials science, renewable energy, and chemical and biological processes underlying energy transfer.

Innovation hubs are also large-scale, multi-investigator initiatives but were intended to generate commercially viable technologies, as well as foundational knowledge. In 2013, they included the Fuels from Sunlight hub, the Energy Storage hub, the Joint Center for Artificial Photosynthesis hub, the Critical Materials Institute, and the Nuclear Engineering Modeling and Simulation hub. The DOE also ran a number of projects classified as "basic science" through the Energy Advanced Research Projects Administration (ARPA-E), intended for high-risk, high-reward research. The more than 350 ARPA-E projects were funded at $900 million in 2013, of which 35 percent went to academic researchers (U.S. Department of Energy 2014b). The government-directed approach to science funding at DOE, including requirements for industry partners, could be a harbinger of the future for the other agencies supporting basic science.

PRESIDENTIAL INITIATIVES

Presidential initiatives were another avenue for government-directed science policy, but they were used sparingly during most of the period, and, when they were not, Congress sometimes found them inviting targets for cost cutting or elimination.

The Rocky Reagan Record

The Strategic Defense Initiative (known by its critics as "Star Wars") was the most famous of the Reagan-era big-science initiatives. It was an attempt to protect the United States from intercontinental nuclear weapons through the construction of a defensive missile shield. After $30 billion in spending, the country was left with little more than hundreds of extended range guided missile projectiles, failing to achieve the impenetrable space shield Reagan had envisioned. The Reagan administration also sponsored the long-delayed and chronically overbudget space station and shuttle program. The space station cost an estimated $11.2 billion before it was canceled by the Clinton administration in 1998 and converted to an international space station, with contributions from Russia, Japan, Canada, and other countries.[14] Another disappointment of the Reagan era loomed large in the thinking of later presidents, the superconducting super-collider (SSC), described by Daniel Kevles as "a gargantuan machine to accelerate proton and antiprotons through circular tunnels, some 52 miles in circumference to an energy of 20 trillion electron volts" (1997, 269). SSC was intended to keep the United States in the forefront of high-energy physics. SSC was scrapped by Congress in 1992, with the acquiescence of then president Bill Clinton, after $2 billion of spending (in what had mushroomed to a projected $12 billion project). In high-energy physics, an era of international cooperation ensued, based at the Swiss super-collider site, CERN.

A Fainter Footprint after Reagan

Succeeding presidents appear to have been chastened by the rocky experiences of the Reagan administration with big-science projects. Each one, until Barack Obama, showed far more restraint than Reagan. President George H. W. Bush supported the Human Genome Project, planned during the Reagan administration and funded in 1990. The project had the goal of determining the sequence of the nucleotide base pairs that make up the human DNA and mapping all of the genes of the human genome. The completion of the project involved researchers at twenty universities in the United States and abroad. It was declared complete in 2003, under budget at $2.7 billion (of a projected $3 billion).

Bill Clinton was the first president during the period to use big-science projects as an economic driver outside of the national security and health sciences domains. Based on the results of an ongoing NSF cross-disciplinary project, "partnerships in nanotechnology," Clinton announced an anticipated decades-long federal R&D commitment to nanotechnology in early 2000. Science advisor Neal Lane's (1998) prediction that nanotechnology was the most likely new general purpose technology of the twenty-first century helped build momentum for the project comparable to the steam engine, the transistor, and the Internet (quoted in Lane and Kalil 2005). Nanotechnology is based on the ability to control and restructure matter at the atomic and molecular level in the range of 1–100 nanometers. (A human hair is about 80,000–100,000 nanometers wide.) Anticipated applications ranged from nanoscale manufacturing to molecular medicine. Clinton sponsored the National Nanotechnology Initiative (NNI) with an initial investment of $270 million in FY 2000. By 2015, the cumulative spending on NNI was $24 billion. Like the Human Genome Project, NNI was a highly decentralized, multi-investigator initiative involving twenty-five federal departments and agencies and thousands of researchers.

The George W. Bush administration was responsible for only one major big-science initiative, Project Bioshield, to protect Americans from chemical and biological weapons attacks through the creation of new vaccines and drugs as countermeasures to smallpox, anthrax, and other threats. Congress appropriated $5 billion for Project Bioshield in 2004, with the total cost growing to $50 billion by 2015. Bush also supported the American COMPETES legislation of 2007, a centerpiece of U.S. competitiveness policy discussed later in the chapter.

Obama's "Grand Challenges"

This relative circumspection in the use of presidential power to champion big-science projects changed with the election of Barack Obama. Obama came to office vowing to put science back into "its rightful place" (Obama 2009), and no president during the period did more to promote science initiatives—on the administration's terms.[15] The Obama administration changed the playing field, at least temporarily, supporting many large-scale investments in fields it defined as in the national interest, as well as funding new organizational mechanisms for delivering scientific breakthroughs. The organized scientific community lobbied for these concentrated investment strategies, backing a shift toward national science priorities so long as funding remained relatively widely distributed.[16]

Clean energy initiatives topped the list. By 2014, the Obama administration had invested more than $34 billion in loans for clean energy projects to jump-start energy transition (U.S. Department of Energy 2014a). By the end of the second Obama administration, the United States was generating three times the electricity from wind and thirty times as much from solar as it did in 2008, with large price drops in both of these renewable sources (Kalil and Dorgelo 2016). The Cancer Moonshot was another of the Obama era big-science initiatives. In 2016, Congress appropriated $1.8 billion over seven years to make more therapies available to more people, to improve treatments, and to facilitate early detection of cancers. The Precision Medicine initiative was intended to collect information on one million individuals in order to tailor medicine to individual variation in genetic composition, social environment, and individual lifestyle, as part of an effort to produce "the right treatment at the right time for the right person." Congress appropriated $215 million for the Precision Medicine initiative in 2015 and continued to support it beyond the Obama presidency. In 2013, Obama launched the Brain Research through Advancing Innovative Neurotechnology (BRAIN) initiative with $110 million in funding through the Defense Advanced Research Projects Agency (DARPA), NIH, and NSF and catalyzed by the end of his administration with $1.5 billion in public and private funds. The goal was to provide both a static and a dynamic model of brain function and thereby to identify treatments for neurological diseases and conditions. Like Precision Medicine, the initiative continued to gain congressional approval beyond the Obama presidency (Fox 2017).

Other national priority projects of the Obama administration included the National Robotics Initiative, which received $150 million in cumulative funding beginning in June 2011; the Big Data R&D Initiative, funded at $200 million in 2012; the National Network for Manufacturing Innovation, which generated $600 million in federal investment, matched by more than $1.2 billion in nonfederal funds following its launch in 2013; and acceleration of "next generation" broadband, created by an anticipated $40 billion spectrum auction starting in 2016 (Kalil and Dorgelo 2016). In most cases, small teams produced the research, but in all cases the federal government set the agenda.

Budget deficits, high levels of mandatory spending obligations, and sequestration created continuous difficulties for Obama's ambitions to put science "in its rightful place." Science agency budgets, other than those at DOE and NSF, were unable to grow beyond pre-Obama levels in constant dollars (Hourihan 2017, figure 1), and the successful big-science initiatives of the Obama administration consequently crowded out millions of dollars of small-science funding.[17] Without clear metrics to decide the right portfolio mix, scientists argued with one another about how to measure the gains and losses of the Obama era shift toward projects in administration-identified national priority areas.

WHY DID SMALL SCIENCE SURVIVE?

The shift of federal science funding toward national priorities generated its share of detractors among prominent scientists. Bruce Alberts, the former editor of *Science*, lamented that laboratory-based investigators were being crowded out of the decreasing funding pool in part because "the scale [of big-science projects] creates a constituency that makes these projects difficult to stop, even where there are clear signs of diminishing returns" (2012, 1583). Nobel laureates Joseph Goldstein and Michael Brown indicated concern about a possibly deeper impact on the development of scientific paradigms. They argued that "individual curiosity-driven science has been replaced by large consortia dedicated to the proposition that gathering vast amounts of correlative data will somehow provide the answer to life's fundamental questions" (2012, 1034). Acknowledging the shift toward big-science and grand-challenge projects, the economist Paula Stephan summarized the difficulty of making judgments when she wrote that "we just don't know" whether it is "better to spend $3 billion on the Human Genome Project or to support 6,000 researchers each to the tune of $500,000" (2012, 239).

Given the enthusiasm of the period for big projects in the national interest, a good question is: Why did small science continue to absorb the largest share of research funding at two of the three major sponsors of academic R&D, NIH and NSF? After all, each of the methods of funding science has a distinctive and appealing logic. Individual-investigator and small-team grants spread funding widely and allow the largest number of researchers to pursue their work. This expands the diversity of investigations beyond what other methods allow. Large-scale facilities allow access to scientific environments or instrumentation that would not be in the interest of any single institution or even a university consortium to fund. Centers of excellence allow top-flight scientists a larger canvas on which to work. They can create scientific synergies that small teams do not foster, and they can be mobilized for interdisciplinary problem solving. Cross-agency investments focus scientific attention on topics that may be ripe for solutions or issues of national moment. There were several attempts in Congress during the period to tie science funding more exclusively to research "in the national interest" as opposed to disciplinary interests. Well-orchestrated efforts along these lines by Senators Tom Coburn and Barbara Mikulski and Representative Lamar Smith all failed.[18]

That small science survived and thrived in this uncertain environment is a tribute to the resilience of inherited peer review structures, the record of accomplishment of individuals and small teams awarded through these structures, and the community-expanding logic of the individual-investigator model. Small science does create opportunities among a much wider group of researchers than big-science projects usually do. The interests of Congress and universities are another factor; Congress wants to fund science in every district if it can, and every university in every district also has an interest in expanding its share of the pie.

Competitiveness Policy

If science policy expanded to include specific attention to national priority initiatives, competitiveness policy was explicitly and directly devoted to these aims. As I showed in chapter 3, efforts to encourage the development and commercialization of new technologies became a dominant theme of U.S. R&D policy during the period. By the end of the period, the theme of commercialization permeated the R&D activities of government, recurring in the speeches of agency heads, in the language of grant solicitations, in the justifications for new initiatives, and in the reports of agency achievements. At the same time, competitiveness policy could not be described, except in its objective, as government-controlled R&D. Instead, it created a new policy theme in which numerous instruments of government were used to activate tens of thousands of organizations—small businesses, large corporations, and federal labs, as well as universities—on behalf of the singular goal of stimulating the development of new technologies with commercial potential.

THREE WAVES OF LEGISLATION

Congressional actions on competitiveness legislation formed in three waves, each of which directly affected universities' engagement with technology transfer and commercialization. I discussed these three waves briefly in chapter 3. Here I will show the extent to which each wave engendered strong bipartisan support—in marked contrast to the growing partisan discord surrounding most other legislative issues of the period.

The first wave, 1980–87, created incentives for universities and federal laboratories to transfer technology to the private sector. The Bayh-Dole Act of 1980 enhanced the incentives for universities to patent and license commercially viable ideas by easing restrictions on universities against patenting discoveries made in their laboratories with federal R&D support. Government lawyers and commerce officials, such as Norman Lasker and Betsy Acker Johnson, were primarily responsible for promoting the simplification of cumbersome government rules on university patenting (see Berman 2012, chap. 4). But universities were involved from the beginning in the lobbying that led to the act. Purdue University began lobbying Birch Bayh in 1978. Bayh-Dole passed the Senate 91–4 and the House by unanimous consent. Opposition to the Bayh-Dole was limited to a handful of Democrats led by Senator Russell Long, who feared that incentives for university patenting would restrict the free flow of knowledge and deplete the public treasury (Markel 2013). The two other major technology transfer bills focused on the federal laboratories. The Stevenson-Wydler Act of 1980 required that federal laboratories participate in and budget for technology transfer activities. It passed by voice vote in both chambers of Congress. The Federal Technology Transfer Act of 1986 amended Stevenson-Wydler to allow for formal cooperative research and development agreements, so-called CRADAs, between industry and federal laboratories and to create a Federal Technology Transfer Consortium to facilitate commercialization of inventions made in federal laboratories. It also passed by voice vote in both chambers.

The second wave, 1992–98, fostered technology development in small businesses. In 1976, an NSF staffer, Roland Tibbetts, was the first to propose shifting a portion of agency budgets to small business technology development. Tibbetts's approach found support, not surprisingly, in the small business community and in government research showing that high-tech small businesses were underappreciated engines of economic growth (BSTEP 2016). The Small Business Innovation Research (SBIR) Act of 1982 provided contracts and grants to small businesses to conduct R&D with commercial potential. It passed the Senate by a vote of 90–0 and the House by voice vote. University entrepreneurs were eligible for these awards, and most university-based start-ups competed for them. Research found that the university involvement with SBIR grew over time, and by the end of the period about 60 percent of the awards had a university connection of some kind, whether in an advisory or principal capacity (BSTEP 2016). The act was reauthorized and extended in 1997 and 2000 without significant opposition. Beginning in 1997, it required agencies whose R&D budget exceeded $100 million to set aside a percentage of the budget to fund grants and contracts through SBIR. This set-aside amount, originally 2.5 percent, grew to

3.2 percent by the end of the period, leading to annual expenditures of about $2.5 billion. Toward the end of the period, university lobbyists fought the proposed additional growth of set-asides as a threat to the funding of "basic science" research (Mervis 2016a).

The Small Business Technology Transfer Act of 1992 was intended to "bridge the gap" between discovery-oriented science and technological innovation by creating a new set of awards, the Small Business Technology Transfer (STTR) awards, requiring joint ventures with universities or other nonprofit research organizations. The 1992 act passed the Senate by voice vote and the House agreed without objection.[19] In practice, STTRs created thousands of small business–university partnerships (with federal laboratories also involved in some cases) in which small businesses were required to conduct at least 40 percent of the work. Only agencies with R&D budgets in excess of $1 billion were required to set aside funds for STTRs, 0.3 percent of their extramural budget, leaving the program with comparatively few sponsors and dwarfed in size by the seven to eight times larger SBIR program.

The third wave, 2007 and beyond, consisted of the sprawling America COMPETES Act of 2007 and its successors. America COMPETES was inspired by, and includes many of the specific recommendations of, the National Academies' report, *Rising above the Gathering Storm* (2005b), an effort to signal alarm about the status of American technological prowess in a competitive world economy and to provide policy direction for a response.[20] Among its many provisions,[21] America COMPETES called for doubling the budgets of the National Science Foundation, the National Institutes of Science and Technology (NIST), and the Department of Energy Office of Science; establishing the Energy Advanced Research Projects Administration (ARPA-E); providing provisions for preparing the STEM teaching workforce; creating funding for high school STEM academies; providing additional support for young researchers; expanding opportunities for women and minorities in science; and creating a Council on Innovation and Competitiveness. The bill authorized $33.6 billion in appropriations for these and other federal programs and activities. The act passed the House by a vote of 367–57. The 56 dissenting Republicans and one dissenting Democrat focused on the fiscal impact and potential wastefulness of several provisions of the bill. America COMPETES was never fully funded by Congress, and funding for the three designated science agencies, in particular, fell well below authorized levels (Gonzalez, Sargent, and Figliola 2010).

The 2010 reauthorization sought better coordination of federally supported STEM education and further improvements in STEM teaching and learning. It continued higher authorizations for NSF, the NIST laboratories, and DOE's Office of Science. It also created new programs to invest in "high risk/high reward" projects, with specific provisions for energy innovation, nanotechnology, and information technology. The COMPETES reauthorization passed the House 267–170, with majority Republican dissent, the first instance of a major crack in bipartisan support for competitiveness legislation. Opponents of the bill raised concerns about the cost of enacting the bill, the addition of new programs, and the length of the authorization period (ibid.). Bipartisanship was restored in the American Innovation and Competitiveness Act (AICA), the successor to America COMPETES, which did not set ambitious authorization targets for federal science agencies and passed with overwhelming bipartisan support. The enacted bill rebuffed Republican efforts to require NSF to fund research using explicit national interest criteria (Spady 2016).

START-UP AMERICA

An undercurrent of concern about the consequences of government-led commercialization of science persisted throughout the period, reflecting anxieties about both the future of curiosity-driven research and the traditions of open communication in scientific communities (see, e.g., Bok 2006; Caulfield, Harmon, and Joly 2012; Neal, Smith, and McCormick 2008, 142–43). Nevertheless, by the end of the period, the goal of commercializing research permeated the rhetoric and action of the federal government. The once top-secret Defense Advanced Research Projects Agency (DARPA) released a technology transition and commercialization fact sheet (DARPA, n.d.), and its parent agency, the Department of Defense, sponsored a defense innovation marketplace website (U.S. Department of Defense, n.d.). NIH listed available licensing opportunities and developed an electronic catalog for campuses to find unpatented biological materials (NIH 2014). Even the staid U.S. Department of Agriculture formed technology innovation partnerships with local, state, and regional economic development organizations to provide assistance to agriculture-related businesses (Walejko et al. 2012). Responding to congressional pressure, NSF began asking applicants to articulate how their projects served the national interest and formed an Innovation Corps to provide experiential entrepreneurial education to awardees (Cordova 2015). A National Research Council committee described the commercialization of scientific discoveries as "squarely within universities' core missions" (Merrill and Mazza 2010, 2). At a meeting of presidential science and technology advisors, Steven Chu, the secretary of energy, emphasized that his major focus was on turning scientific discoveries into practical, mass market application. "It's not about writing research papers anymore," he said. "You've got to deliver the goods" (quoted in American Physical Society 2009).

In his 2011 State of the Union, President Obama supercharged this theme by launching a "Start-up America" initiative in which he called on the research community to help structure the economy and praised entrepreneurs as the embodiment of "the promise of America." He characterized his "wealth and job creation plan" as "our generation's Sputnik moment" (Obama 2011). And indeed even the far reaches of space yielded to the spirit of the age when Congress's 2015 U.S. Commercial Space Launch Competitiveness Act authorized not only commercial space travel but the commercial mining of asteroids (Congress.gov 2015).

State-Centered, Elite-Biased Pluralism

Given the federal government's prominence as a patron of universities, the question of who governs federal higher education policy naturally arises. One can argue that in a capitalist economy government will attempt to serve the interests of business, even when business does not explicitly express its interests in the form of policy proposals, lobbying, or campaign contributions (Block 1977). It is clear that evaluations of science for its potential economic benefit increased during the period. Financial aid policy also shifted significantly to better reflect the interests of the affluent.

Even so, I am unconvinced by the idea that the formulation of federal higher education policy was dominated by the interests of business and affluent Americans. Though their influence waned somewhat during the period, curiosity-driven science and the financial aid needs of low-income students remained important forces in policy. Even state action explicitly in support of business registered a degree of autonomy, because the directions it took were not predetermined by a singular policy preference among business people. Take two examples: Policymakers during the period took opposed positions on the question whether government support of business was best achieved by cutting taxes and reducing regulation, as Republicans and their business allies often argued, or by investing in technology transfer through university-industry research centers and small business innovation grants, as Democrats and their business allies often preferred. Similarly, local and state policymakers came out on different sides on the question whether localities

should support traditional forms of economic development through industry recruitment strategies (aka "smokestack chasing") or through seeding
"grow-your-own" high-tech cluster development strategies. These decisions
reflected the preferences of shifting political coalitions, as well as prevailing
cultural frames for formulating policy. They were greatly influenced by the
convictions of policy entrepreneurs who lobbied for change – sometimes
for many fruitless years until problems or opportunities ripened sufficiently
to support the ideas they proposed (for other cases, see Kingdon 1984,
chap. 7).

Certainly economic elites played an important role in sounding the alarm
about American competitiveness, but the solutions most businesspeople
sought at first focused on tax breaks and regulation reforms rather than
higher education policy. Thereafter, business groups sponsored studies that
kept the heat up and served as cheerleaders for more aggressive government
action (see especially Berman 2012, chap. 2). Something similar occurred
in the arena of financial aid policy. Banks at first resisted student loans but
subsequently played a major role in the government's shift from grant to
loan funding of student financial aid, once they were assured of government
guarantees in the case of defaults. Yet their influence waned at the end of
the period when the government took over student lending. For the most
part, economic elites became deeply involved in policy only in the areas in
which they had a direct interest, and there typically as advocates of policy
directions rather than as authors of policy instruments or organizers of political coalitions.[22]

The admittedly cumbersome term "state-centered, elite-biased pluralism" is more descriptive of the power brokers of the period than any theories
emphasizing either the instrumental or structural influence of "the business
class" (see Slaughter and Rhoades 1996). By the term "state-centered," I
mean that the most prominent actors in federal policymaking were government employees—notably, federal agency heads and their senior staff, as well
as those who advised them. Those who advised agency heads were usually
closely connected to the academic world; they were either working scientists
themselves or scientists on leave for government service. Of course, presidents and Congresses exercised the ultimate power to embrace or reject
policies developed by agency heads and their advisors—and they also had
the power to propose new programs and initiatives. Members of Congress
used the power of the purse to cut programs they considered wasteful or
ineffective and to add programs and facilities they considered beneficial
for their constituents. By the term "elite-biased" I mean that the public was

rarely involved in policymaking, either directly or indirectly, that the key actors in policy debates were all part of elite circles. I also mean to indicate that adopted policy tended to tilt toward the interests of well-off Americans. By the term "pluralism" I mean that different constellations of actors exercised influence in different policy arenas at different times.

Case studies of federal higher education policymaking illustrate how apt a cumbersome phrase can be. Competitiveness policy originated in the work of academic economists, including Robert Solow, Kenneth Arrow, and Richard Nelson. It was later influenced by the studies of Bureau of Labor Statistics economist Michael Boretsky (1971, 1982) and Brookings Institution economist Edward Denison (1985), who found more receptive audiences than the earlier generation had for their studies showing slippage in U.S. global competitiveness and of the role played by innovation in economic growth (see Berman 2012, chap. 3). By the mid-1970s the leaders of business associations were lending full-throated support to the idea that government had a role to play in stimulating technological innovation.

The specific policy instruments adopted were in virtually every instance the brainchild of either government bureaucrats or leaders in the scientific community. The idea to remove obstacles to university patenting was promoted by government attorney Norman Lasker, policy analyst Jason Baruch, and assistant commerce secretary Betsy Ancker-Johnson (Berman 2012, chap. 5). Purdue University administrators led the early lobbying for easing restrictions on university patenting, convincing their home state senator, Birch Bayh, to draft legislation (Markel 2013). The idea for a federal role as catalyst to university-industry research centers originated in the director's office of the National Science Foundation under Richard Atkinson and was promoted aggressively by Atkinson's successor, Erich Bloch (Berman 2012, chap. 6). Roland Tibbetts, an official at NSF, came up with the idea for making grants and contracts available to small businesses through SBIR and later STTR arrangements (Tibbetts 2008). This idea gained traction following studies by academic economist David Birch and others showing that small businesses were responsible for most new job creation (Berman 2012, chap. 6). NSF scientist Mihail Roco, government science advisor Neal Lane, and presidential scientific advisor Thomas Kalil were among the most important proponents of the National Nanotechnology Initiative, each drawing on the original spark produced by the academic physicist Richard Feynman's paper urging scientific effort at the nanoscale level and the subsequent scientific progress it inspired (Lane and Kalil 2005). As I have noted, the National Academies' report, *Rising above the Gathering Storm* (2005b), provided many of the concrete policy recommendations adopted in the America COMPETES Act. Academic computer scientist Kenneth Wilson first used the concept of grand challenges in relation to his proposals to NSF to support the building of supercomputers (Wilson 1989). The idea was picked up and attached to a large number of priority science initiatives by Obama science and technology advisors John Holdren and Thomas Kalil (Hicks 2016). In some cases, government officials who had experience working in industry were important actors. Erich Bloch, a former research director at IBM, created a network of industry-oriented research centers at NSF, and Steven Chu, who championed big-science projects in the national interest at the Department of Energy, worked at Bell Labs before taking a professorship at UC Berkeley.[23]

Financial aid policy showed a similar pattern. The leading student lenders lobbied for the expansion of federal support for student loan programs and raised funds for politicians who supported higher student loan subsidies, but in other cases political officials were at the center of changes in financial aid policy. A Mississippi Democratic congressman, "Sonny" Montgomery, organized the coalition that extended benefits to GIs in the mid-1980s. Dick Morris, a political advisor to Bill Clinton, was a decisive voice on the income tax credit for college attendance, a policy long opposed by Democrats (Mettler 2014). And Obama administration officials, notably Assistant Secretary of Education Robert Shireman, were responsible for shifting student lending from private loan companies to the Department of Education through direct lending (Field 2010).

Agents of policy are not alone in the arena; veto groups are also important. The academic community has been the most important interest group in the higher education policy domain, and it repeatedly showed the capacity to mobilize through multiple organizational networks—the higher education associations, the national academies, the disciplinary associations, and the presidential science and technology advisors. It protected policy terrain that it valued, sponsored changes it endorsed, and killed most proposals it abhorred. Actions on the part of the academic community preserved peer review and small-science projects as the primary mechanisms for making awards in the two major science agencies funding academic researchers. Academic institutions encouraged competitiveness legislation they judged to be in the interest of research universities, lobbied effectively against additional increases in set-asides for small business grants and contracts through the SBIR and STTR programs, and quashed efforts to require science funding to be consistent with national interest priorities. The National Academies provided the primary recommendations for the America COMPETES Act, and the national higher education associations consistently supported congressional efforts to expand federal financial aid and philanthropic efforts to increase college graduation rates. Academics were the originators or primary sponsors of big-science projects that were based on decentralized funding models, including the Human Genome Project, the National Nanotechnology Initiative, the BRAIN initiative, and Precision Medicine. As I will show in chapter 8, the national higher education associations also preserved a high level of academic control over assessment of student learning outcomes. The community blocked efforts to create a stronger federal presence in accountability during the George W. Bush administration and fought successfully against the first Obama "college scorecard."

Retreats and Advances in the Fifty States

Collectively, the fifty states are the second most important patrons of higher education, and of course they are particularly important in the provision of general appropriations to support the educational activities of public universities. Critics of higher education policy during the period focused much of their fire on state disinvestment from public higher education (see, e.g., Aronowitz 2000; Newfield 2008, 2–16; Rhoten and Calhoun 2011; Tuchman 2009; Washburn 2000). As one of these critics, Christopher Newfield, wrote about the withdrawal of state funding, "Our public colleges have been cut, squeezed, trimmed, neglected, overstuffed, misdirected, kludged, and patched" (2016, 305). For these critics, the traditions of academic professionalism and social inclusion were both crippled by state negligence.

Were the critics right? Yes, if the focus is solely on state subsidies and, yes, in particular, if the focus is on students attending less prestigious public institutions. But a fair assessment must also include the success of the methods public universities used to survive and thrive during periods of declining state subsidies. These included the aggressive pursuit of new revenue streams through higher enrollments, stronger endowments, and recruitment of international students. And it must also include the advances many states made in their financial aid contributions, as well as the slow growth in state expenditures in support of university R&D. Most public flagship universities emerged from the period with vital signs intact, not just surviving but thriving. And many public regionals were able to capitalize on the strong interests of students in the occupational-professional programs that were their specialties. After 2012, the recovery from the Great Recession allowed states to raise their general appropriations expenditures significantly, and tuition costs as a proportion of total educational expenditures dropped for three years straight (SHEEO 2015). Undoubtedly, state disinvestment hurt the prospects of a great many students, but it did not gravely damage public universities *as institutions*. Instead, it made them more entrepreneurial and more attentive to the interests of students and their parents, and to government, industry, and nonprofit organizations outside their walls. Public universities proved that they could find the funds to retain strength, even as per-student state subsidies declined.

A CRISIS OF DISINVESTMENT?

States have long used universities as a balance wheel in state budgeting, pulling back in bad times and restoring funds in good times. They have done so because universities, uniquely among publicly supported entities, have alternative sources of funding (Hovey 1999). Michigan and some other deindustrializing states began to pull back in their funding of public universities beginning in the mid-1970s when the U.S. manufacturing economy was beginning its long slide into the doldrums. The 1980s were a relatively prosperous decade and state spending on higher education grew by a third in constant dollars. Tuition also grew, but at a slow rate, and states contributed more additional dollars to public higher education educational budgets than did students and their families (Geiger 2004, 43).

The balance began to tip in 1990. As Roger Geiger observed, "A pattern became established in which good economic times brought less restoration and bad times brought greater deterioration" (2004, 45). After the recession of 1990 many years passed before tax revenues grew sufficiently for states to expand their higher education budgets. The restoration of these budgets was weak, requiring universities to raise tuition to meet operating expenses. In Geiger's words, this pattern was "replayed with a vengeance" after the mild dot.com bust of 2001 (ibid.)—and it was replayed with a still greater vengeance following the Great Recession of 2007–8.

Between 1990 and 2015, educational appropriations increased by about $10 billion in constant 2015 dollars (SHEEO 2015), a 15 percent increase. Based on these figures alone one might wonder: Why all the fuss about state disinvestment? But these figures hide the mismatch between the slow growth in state appropriations and the rapid expansion of enrollments during the period. Once enrollment is taken into account, the scope of state disinvestment becomes clear. Average educational appropriations per full-time student decreased from about $8,500 in 1990 to about $7,000 in 2015, a decline of 20 percent. Moreover, universities were not able to control inflation-related increases for insurance, contracted services, staff salaries, retirement benefits, and other budget items. These cost increases exacerbated the effects of the slow growth in state educational expenditures. Net tuition per full-time student rose to cover the gap; across the states it more than doubled in constant 2015 dollars from just under $3,000 in 1990 to more than $6,000 in 2015 (SHEEO 2015, table 2).

Universities privatized to a significant degree, but it seems clear that this privatization put them in a stronger position than before. Many public flagship universities adopted "high-tuition, high-aid" pricing—a policy that took a part of the higher charges to subsidize low-income students (Turner 2006). By doing so, universities were able to retain at least the appearance of a commitment to social inclusion, even as they charged middle- and upper-middle-class students much more than they had before. As they raised tuition and increased their selectivity, most of the institutions actually lowered the chances that lower-income students would be admitted in spite of the aid they offered (Haycock, Lynch, and Engle 2010).

VARIATION AMONG THE STATES

The posturing of Republican governors during bad economic times led them to excoriate universities for wasteful spending and educationally dubious offerings, as well as for an overabundance of "political correctness," but research I conducted with Sarah Yoshikawa suggested that only two factors were statistically significant in explaining changes in state educational expenditures following the Great Recession: (1) the state's unemployment rate (an obvious correlate with tax revenues), and (2) the state's decision about whether to use stimulus funds in support of higher education expenditures. In addition, instead of regressing to the mean, states that spent relatively generously at the beginning of the period tended to increase their per capita state subsidy to public higher education institutions and those that spent little tended to reduce them further.[24] We were able to explain about 50 percent of the variation in changes in per capita state appropriations over the period using just these three variables. Republican governors were more inclined to spend state money on community colleges than on either research universities or regional comprehensives, but otherwise the influence of the consequential variables in the analysis did not vary greatly across research universities, regional comprehensives, and community colleges.

National averages mask the wide variation among the states in expenditures per student and in the share of educational costs borne by students. In academic year 2008–9, before the effects of the recession hit with full force, total expenditures per research university student (including tuition charges) ranged from over $25,000 in the wealthy and politically progressive states of Connecticut and Minnesota to less than half that amount in the poor states of South Dakota, Mississippi, Nebraska, Montana, and Arkansas (Desrochers and Wellman 2011, figure 15).[25]

Students' share of costs relative to states' share of costs varied still more widely. University students in New Hampshire and Vermont paid about 80 percent of the costs of their education (not including housing and meals), while students in Wyoming and Alaska bore less than one-quarter the cost. In general, New England states (and a few other tightfisted states such as Colorado and Oregon) required students to pay a larger share of educational costs while most mineral-rich Mountain states required students to pay a smaller share (Desrochers and Wellman 2011, figures 15 and A3). Low levels of state taxation went hand in hand with high shares of educational spending by students; low-tax states could not afford to spend as much on higher education. By contrast, high-subsidy states sometimes earmarked tax earnings on mineral rights, formally or informally, for the subsidization of higher education (Baum and Johnson 2016, 6).

WEAKENED REGIONALS?

In a 2011 essay the economist Daniel Hamermesh raised the specter of a growing gap between the public flagship campuses and the less favored regional comprehensives. "The long-term impacts of . . . budget cuts will not be minor at the broad array of lower-tier public institutions that account for the larger part of [the public] sector," he predicted.

> Many of them cannot raise tuition without reducing demand and thus their ability to spread their fixed costs. And many do not have an alumni base that is likely to generate endowment donations big enough to substitute for public revenues. In the end, those colleges will instead get by with fewer programs and larger classes; with fewer tenure-stream faculty members and still more adjuncts and temporary faculty; and with less-up-to-date facilities. (2011)

Tuition increases at the public regionals did sometimes have damaging effects on access and occasionally even on enrollment. At Adams State

University in Colorado, two hundred miles south of Denver, for example, state support declined by one-third in five years between 2007 and 2012. Tuition more than doubled to make up the gap. Like many of the regionals, Adams State is located in a low-income area; the region is heavily Hispanic and household income is about two-thirds the state average. More than 60 percent of its students received Pell Grants. After years of growing enrollments, the freshman class in 2012 shrank by nearly one-tenth. President David Salvi worried that the state had "priced some students out of the market" (quoted in Thurm 2012).

The Adams State experience was comparatively rare, however. Enrollments increased at most public regionals following the recession. Many students were attracted to occupational programs at the public regionals; in a bad economy, job-relevant credentials at a low price looked like a bargain. And the public regionals in most states were able to increase spending on instruction a little by raising tuition and in some cases by attracting higher levels of donor support (Desrochers and Wellman 2011). This experience was not universal. As the student body diversified in states like California, the students' educational experience suffered through reductions in staff and increases in class sizes—an indication of the limitations of universities' aspirations for greater social inclusion in the face of privatization (California Faculty Association 2017). Moreover, the regionals were state dependent to a greater degree than research universities, and none achieved much in the way of autonomy. In Pennsylvania, for example, low-enrollment programs in the state college system were subject to budgetary scrutiny from the state, but the high-tuition public research universities (Pennsylvania State University, Temple University, and the University of Pittsburgh) were exempted from this scrutiny because they had already won the status of "state-related" (but not "state-supported") institutions (Kelderman 2009).[26]

SURVIVING AND THRIVING

The pain of these cutbacks should not be minimized. Yet even during the depths of the Great Recession, the idea of a "crisis of the publics" was exaggerated. My research team and I analyzed IPEDS data between academic years 2007–8 and 2011–12 for all U.S. four-year colleges and universities (other than for-profits and specialized institutions) that reported during both years. In constant dollars, we found that mean faculty salaries for the ranks of assistant, associate, and full professor all increased during the recession (by 1–2 percent). We found that average staff size (measured as all full-time, nonfaculty, and non–medical school employees) increased by nearly 5 percent. Endowment, measured as institutional assets at the end of the fiscal year, increased by approximately 12 percent on average. Most important, mean expenditures per full-time student grew by about 6.5 percent (Brint et al. 2016).

Public universities were able to compete by expanding their revenue bases. Tuition increases were proportionately higher at public institutions—nearly double those of private institutions on average. Endowments also grew much faster proportionately, albeit from much lower bases. Enrollments also grew faster, including a sizable increase in the number of international students (up by 23 percent nationally). However, the dollar increases in private university tuitions were much larger, and they were only partly offset by increasing financial aid for low- and middle-income students (Chronicle of Higher Education 2015).

My research team also analyzed all of the Lexis-Nexis stories on a sample of three hundred colleges and universities. We found four strategies for surviving and thriving during the recession. Some small and mainly private institutions emphasized consumer service—giving students what they wanted whether this was a special travel abroad experience or streamlined student services. Another small group searched aggressively for new market opportunities, building new master's and online programs or leveraging their facilities for use by new sets of paying clients. A third, somewhat larger, and mostly public university group used stimulus funds to market themselves as green campuses while initiating optimistic building plans. The largest group—the one that included all of the more prestigious public and private universities—employed what we called the "full arsenal" to solve the problems created by the country's economic downturn: enrolling more students and, in particular, more international students; raising tuitions and fees; and seeking new government and industry partnerships at the same time that they reduced staff, tightened maintenance and IT budgets, and initiated temporary salary and hiring freezes (see Brint et al. 2016).

Not all indicators of the condition of public universities showed positive trends—here the critics were absolutely right; public universities lost a slightly higher proportion of tenured and tenure-track faculty than did private colleges and universities (albeit not by a statistically significant margin), and they added proportionally more adjunct faculty. With larger average enrollments, fewer tenured and tenure-track faculty to teach them, and not enough adjuncts to make up the gap, student-to-faculty ratios increased considerably faster in public universities than in private colleges and universities. Moreover, the modest growth in staff levels did not begin to keep pace with the rate of staffing improvement found in private colleges and universities.[27] Institutions that could not raise their revenue bases fast enough to keep up with state budget cuts struggled mightily to remain relevant to students.

But most *were* able to raise their revenue bases fast enough to counter state budget cuts. And in the recovering economy post-2012, the majority of states prevented additional tuition increases by restoring general appropriations at or beyond pre-recession levels (SHEEO 2015).

NEED-BASED VS. MERIT-BASED STATES

The assumption that state financial aid should be directed toward low-income families was universally accepted at the beginning of the period (College Board 2016). Sums allocated to students through state programs were not high, but they were explicitly directed to support equality of opportunity. This assumption did not hold throughout the period; even as need-based aid remained the dominant form of state financial aid support, merit aid grew to encompass more of the total.

Merit aid does not necessarily translate uniformly into a preference for white and middle-class students; many minority and low-income students are high achievers in secondary school and therefore eligible for merit aid. But the correlations between income, race, and achievement-based aid were high (Kantrowitz 2011). Merit aid consequently went disproportionately to middle-income and white or Asian students. State aid began to tip incrementally toward these groups beginning in the 1990s, paralleling the trajectory of federal financial aid. It was during this time that several southern states pioneered grant aid based on academic performance rather than need. Georgia's Hope Scholarships were the first and remained the most controversial of these programs because they shifted all aid to students who had received good grades in secondary school (or who qualified during college by maintaining good grades). The Hope Scholarships were introduced by conservative Democratic governor Zell Miller in 1993 and adopted in short order by several other southern states, including South Carolina, Tennessee, Kentucky, and Louisiana.

By the early 2000s, more than one-third of state aid was provided on the basis of merit rather than need (College Board 2016, 29), a sizable shift from the commitments of two decades before. Need-based aid continued to dominate, but it was being chipped away by states that had decided to go in a completely different direction. About half of the states considered financial need in more than 95 percent of cases—they remained fundamentally need based—while twelve states provided less than 40 percent of aid on the basis of need (ibid.). Only four states were relatively generous in providing grant aid per full-time student (offering $1,000 or more on average in 2014–15) *and* at the same time concentrated aid more or less exclusively on the neediest students. These states—California, New Jersey, New York, and Washington—were all comparatively wealthy and, except for the complicated case of New Jersey, politically progressive. The other nine states that provided generous state grants (i.e., over $1,000 per full-time student) concentrated higher proportions of aid on high-achieving students. These southern and Mountain states included South Carolina and Georgia, where little or no aid went to students on the basis of financial need (College Board 2016, 30), as well as each of the other Hope Scholarship states.

The extent to which unacknowledged racial preferences figured as a factor in the Hope Scholarship states remains unknown. Certainly that was not the stated intent. Instead, merit-based scholarships were promoted for their capacity to keep the best students attending college in state and for providing appropriate recognition to students who had shown they cared about good grades. But it is within the range of possibility that the governors who embraced merit-aid plans knew that most of the students who would receive scholarships were middle class and white. At the very least they may have been rewarding the members of their electoral coalitions with policies that they knew served their interests.

BIG-STATE BETS ON R&D

By 1994, all fifty states had engaged in some form of economic development activity involving university researchers or were in the final stages of planning for these activities (Berglund and Coburn 1995). These activities ran the gamut from the relatively high levels of spending on research parks, centers of excellence, and eminent scholars' programs discussed in chapter 3 to small-scale spending on equipment and facilities sharing or high-tech job training. In every one of the six states studied intensively by Dougherty and Etzkowitz (1995), corporatist networks composed of high-tech businesspeople, state government officials, and university administrators arose to promote and implement programs, shifting power away from legislators and the interest groups traditionally in their orbits. Dougherty and Etzkowitz (1995) found persistent "legislative doubt" about the efficacy of state science and technology policies, which took a long time to work and cost significant amounts in the meantime. Many states failed to provide the resources necessary to give the programs a chance to succeed, and others withdrew funding in the wake of gubernatorial transitions. The Texas Emerging Technologies Fund, for example, was closed in 2016 when a new governor arrived in office and criticized the lack of transparency and potential for political favoritism in awards made from the fund (Barnett 2015).

Altogether, R&D spending represented only a small portion of state allocations for higher education, climbing from about $500 million in 2006 to $950 million by the end of the period (NSF 2008, 2016b). Throughout most of the period state spending on R&D was dominated by a handful of populous states: California, Florida, Michigan, New York, Ohio, and Pennsylvania. These were not the only populous states in the union—Illinois was conspicuously missing—but they encompassed seven of the eight largest, and, together, they accounted for as much as two-thirds of total state R&D expenditures. Populous states with healthy tax bases bet that they could help leverage federal and institutional R&D expenditures in health, environmental safety, energy, information technology, transportation, and, in farm states, agriculture (NSF 2016b). The New York Centers of Excellence (Empire State Development, n.d.) and the California Institutes of Science and Innovation, discussed in chapter 3, were among the most prominent beneficiaries of state spending on R&D. By contrast, some sparsely populated largely rural states, such as Nevada, New Hampshire, Vermont, and Wyoming, spent next to nothing on state-funded university R&D (NSF 2008, 2016b).

Philanthropists and the Scientific Renaissance

Private philanthropy has played a role analogous to state subsidies in the financing of private colleges and universities. At the best-endowed private colleges, earnings from endowments accounted for more than one-third of educational expenses. These endowments have built up over many decades—in some cases over centuries. The wealthiest institutions managed endowments in the tens of billions. Many gifts to endowment came with strings attached, directed at particular fields, building projects, or types of students. Other funds—beloved by university presidents—were unrestricted and came with no strings attached.

The Medicis of the period were primarily interested in a scientific and technological, not an artistic or humanistic, Renaissance. And they were more interested in rewarding high achievers than giving a helping hand to the neediest students. I hasten to add the qualifying phrase, "in so far as we can tell from incomplete evidence," because, when the *Colleges & Universities 2000* research team looked into million-dollar-plus gifts, we collected data for two years only, 1990 and 2000. Combining data from the New York City–based Foundation Center and the IUPUI Center on Philanthropy, we counted more than 500 million-dollar or higher gifts in 1990 and more than 1,200 such gifts in 2000. Many of these gifts went to building renovations and other nondisciplinary purposes, but the majority of the gifts went toward the development of academic fields—about 55 percent in each of the two years. (We could not identify the purpose of about one-fifth of the gifts from the available records.)[28]

A sizable gap separated medicine from all other fields, both in the number and total size of gifts. Four other fields emerged as leading recipients of large gifts during the period: engineering, business, natural sciences, and the arts.[29] The arts are anomalous in this list that otherwise includes fields associated with power centers in American society. Educational giving clearly reflects the significance of cultural and spiritual aspirations, as well as material interests. Of the fields we coded, agriculture, social services, nursing, and cultural studies landed at or near the bottom in both years—for various reasons, all low-status fields. Two of the newer sciences were prominent recipients of gifts within the natural sciences: cognitive/neuroscience and environmental science. International relations represented a high proportion of the giving earmarked for the social sciences, one-third in 1990 and more than half in 2000 (see table 6.2).

Data on the very largest gifts to universities during the period confirm the significance of medicine, business, engineering, and natural sciences as the primary recipients of philanthropy. The most useful data for tracking these mega-donations come from a study of the fifty largest gifts to donors' alma maters. The study focused on gifts as a percentage of the alums' total wealth in an effort to measure generosity rather than the sheer size of gifts. These gifts typically ran to $100 million or more—in some cases above $300 million. Many of these very large donors gave to fields they had studied in college or to those in which they made their fortunes. More than one-fifth of these very large gifts went to business schools. The natural sciences followed with nine of the largest gifts. Again, a sizable number of the science gifts, six of nine, went to the rising fields of neuroscience and environmental science. Engineering, law/public policy, and social sciences followed with

TABLE 6.2. Million-Dollar-Plus Gifts by Field, 1990 and 2000

1990 Field	No. of Gifts	Total Amt.	2000 Field	No. of Gifts	Total Amt.
Medicine	54	$194.6 m.	Medicine	100	$696.7 m.
Engineering	28	$131.0 m.	Business	75	$500.4 m.
Natural Science	37	$141.6 m.	Engineering	41	$423.1 m.
Arts	33	$126.6 m.	Natural Science	77	$383.7 m.
Religion/Theology	13	$98.1 m.	Arts	59	$200.9 m.
Business	36	$86.5 m.	Public Health	29	$187.7 m.
Social Science	10	$35.1 m.	Education	55	$167.7 m.
Humanities	14	$32.4 m.	Computer Science	21	$141.7 m.
Law/Public Policy	18	$28.5 m.	Religion/Theology	47	$128.3 m.
Education	14	$27.5 m.	Social Science	50	$109.0 m.
Computer Science	9	$21.3 m.	Communications	25	$83.5 m.
Communications	8	$15.7 m.	Law/Public Policy	31	$74.4 m.
Human Services	7	$10.6 m.	Humanities	18	$69.6 m.
Agriculture	3	$8.1 m.	Human Services	17	$47.4 m.
Public Health	5	$7.2 m.	Agriculture	13	$45.8 m.
Cultural Studies	4	$4.6 m.	Nursing	18	$41.0 m.
Nursing	3	$4.0 m.	Cultural Studies	17	$36.5 m.
Academic Fields	295	$973.4 m.	Academic Fields	695	$3.33 b.
Nonacademic	122	$390.2 m.	Nonacademic	329	$1.52 b.
Unidentified	116	$497.0 m.	Unidentified	203	$380.7 m.
Total	533	$1.86 b.	Total	1,227	$5.23 b.

Source: Author's calculations from Foundation Center 2008, 2010; IUPUI Center on Philanthropy 2011.

four very large gifts each (The Best Schools 2017). Four out of five of these very large gifts went to the "Ivy League-plus" private universities or elite public flagships such as the University of Michigan and the University of Virginia. Thus the largest donors reinforced the dominance of the wealthiest and most productive universities, helping them maintain their wide lead over the competition.

The scientific renaissance of the period owes much to these very large donors. Financier Sanford Weill gave more than $200 million to the Cornell Medical School to "rapidly translate research breakthroughs into innovative treatments and therapies for patients" (Weill Medical Center 2013). A large gift from marketing executives Sandra and Ed Meyer created a new cancer center, also at Cornell. The publishing magnate Patrick McGovern jump-started brain research at MIT. Insurance executive Peter B. Lewis left tens of millions to Princeton to advance integrative genomics research. And, among many other bequests, steel company CEO David Dornsife and his wife, Dana, donated a state-of-the-art imaging center to the University of Southern California to allow neuroscientists to capture the brain's activity.[30]

Large donors spread their largesse widely—we classified two out of five gifts as serving nonacademic purposes. Renovations of dormitories and administration buildings, contributions to scholarship funds, and unrestricted gifts to endowment were among the favored targets of giving. So too were athletic programs. The T. Boone Pickens stadium at Oklahoma State University served as a fitting symbol of the state of the athletic arms race in 2010. Redesigned as part of the largest gift ever received by a university athletic department, the stadium included a 14,000-square-foot five-star locker room, complete with flat-screen televisions and upholsteries resembling a corporate boardroom more than a locker room. The sports medicine center included four hydrotherapy pools and a digital x-ray machine. The stadium also included a 20,000-square-foot gym and a team theater room appointed with more than 200 leather chairs. More than 100 party suites and 4,000 club seats ringed the top level of the stadium. Next on the agenda: a multimillion-dollar athletic village (Oklahoma State University Athletic Department 2012).

Cumulatively, smaller donors also contributed billions to colleges and universities during the period. Gifts under $100,000 are too numerous to count and represent a drop in the bucket at institutions with operating budgets in the hundreds of millions or billions of dollars, but gifts of $100,000 or more are enough to generate an endowment income for named professorships, new equipment for research labs, or support for specific studies. According to our study of giving in 1990 and 2000, medicine and the natural sciences received the largest volume of these smaller gifts (we counted those between $100,000 and $999,999). Fields concerned with public improvements also figured prominently among these smaller donors. Social sciences, education, public health, and human services were among the better-supported fields in both 1990 and 2000. By contrast, business, engineering, and the arts—each one among the pet fields of larger donors— lagged behind public service fields (see Brint et al. 2012b, table 5).

Scholarships were among the more popular targets for this level of giving. Some up-by-the-bootstraps entrepreneurs such as Columbia University alum John Kluge provided scholarships exclusively for needy students. But for the most part philanthropists gave scholarships to high-achieving students and to students participating in activities in which they had themselves excelled in college. Policy analyst Mark Kantrowitz's (2011) analysis of the National Postsecondary Student Aid Study of 2003–4 and 2007–8 showed that minorities represented about one-third of applicants for private scholarships in both years but received a smaller proportion of awards than they applied for. By contrast, white students applied for two-thirds of private scholarships and received more than 70 percent of them. Less than 10 percent of all scholarships explicitly considered students' race in making awards. As Kantrowitz observed,

> Scholarship sponsors tend to establish scholarships that select for characteristics, activities, and interests to them. . . . For example, African American students are much less likely to participate in equestrian sports . . . water sports . . . and winter sports . . . than Caucasian students. The sponsors of rodeo scholarships aren't motivated by a desire to indirectly discriminate against minority students; they just like to promote rodeo. But the net result is that private scholarships as a whole disproportionately select for Caucasian students. (2011, 18–19)

Other characteristics that made a difference in the distribution of private scholarships included national origins, geographical origins, religious affiliations, and specific fields of study. These qualifying criteria helped tilt private scholarships toward populations disproportionately composed of well-to-do and white students. The commitment of colleges and universities to social inclusion has been supported by Pell Grants, by grants-in-aid given by colleges and universities themselves from unrestricted funds (these were notably need based), and by the financial aid policies of a handful of progressive states. But private scholarships tilted sharply toward supporting students from advantaged groups (Kantrowitz 2011, 6).

The Conflicting Priorities of Professors and Patrons

The research interests of most professors during the period led them to favor investigations in which they worked alone or with small teams of colleagues, postdocs, and graduate students to solve problems defined by their disciplines. Their liberal politics led them to favor affirmative action and financial aid allocations tilted toward need-based criteria (see Gross 2013, 41–51; Gross and Simmons 2014). Patrons by and large harbored a different vision. Over the period, both governments and philanthropists leaned toward the identification of the most promising areas of inquiry and providing incentives to researchers to engage in these identified national priority challenges. Organizing professors, Stanford president John Hennessy said, was "like herding cats," adding that he was glad that he "had a lot of cat food to offer" (quoted in Labaree 2017, 188). Like Hennessy, major actors in the world of university patronage employed the incentives of grand challenge and national priority funding to organize professorial purposes. The balance in financial aid also shifted away from the preferences of professors and university administrators to advance diversity toward grants that favored the already advantaged.

Thus the professors' penchant for disciplinary professionalism and social inclusion was met by the patrons' yen for scientific and technological innovation and rewards to talent. It can be argued that the push and pull between the two conceptions of mission helped maintain the dynamism of the whole.

7

An Accumulation
of Administration

However much they may be influenced by public and private patronage, campuses remain at the heart of the institutional landscape of American higher education. They are the sites of research and educational production and the places in which institutional affiliations (or feelings of alienation) are rooted. For those less involved in professional networks—including the great majority of faculty members and virtually all students—they are the center of attention during the work day. They are the sites for informal friendship networks and community events. They are where learning happens.

As colleges and universities expanded and became more important features of the American institutional landscape, those who occupied senior managerial positions separated themselves more completely from the faculty. They developed features of a professionalized occupation—including separate training programs and formal knowledge bases—albeit one that remained influenced by traditions of shared governance. This separation led to many complaints by faculty members about the rise of a soulless corporate model of university administration. Professionalized management did not weaken the steering capacity of universities—quite the opposite. Yet bottom-line considerations did often intrude in ways that were counterproductive to the educational mission of the institutions.

No counterforce emerged as capable of protecting the integrity of this mission. Indeed, the separation of management was accompanied by further fragmentation of the faculty along the lines of rank, disciplinary centrality, institutional prestige, and, perhaps most important of all, security of employment. Expansion was used as a rationale to build administrative muscle and to restructure the instructional labor force. The institutions of academic professionalism slowed the advance of managerial influence, but they did not halt it. And these institutions of academic professionalism had little, if any, impact on the restructuring of the labor force. Instead, those lucky enough to be among the elect of tenured professors profited from the erosion in their ranks as teaching responsibilities were offloaded onto poorly paid adjunct instructors.

The Question of "Administrative Bloat"

In *The Fall of the Faculty*, the political scientist Benjamin Ginsberg satirized "the rise of the all-administrative university":

> Every year, hosts of administrators and staffers are added to college and university payrolls, even as schools claim to be battling budget crises that are focusing them to reduce the size of their full-time faculties. As a result, universities are filled with armies of functionaries—the vice presidents, associate vice presidents, assistant vice presidents, provosts, associate provosts, vice provosts, assistant provosts, deans, deanlets, deanlings, each commanding staffers and assistants—who, more and more, direct the operations of every school. Backed by their administrative legions, university presidents and other senior administrators have been able, at most schools, to dispense with faculty involvement in campus management, and, thereby, to reduce the faculty's influence in university affairs. (2011, 2)

Unquestionably, the ratio of managers and administrative staff to full-time faculty grew larger—and so too did the ratio of administrators to students. According to Ginsberg's figures, full-time faculty (including those off the tenure track) grew by 51 percent between 1975 and 2005, while administrators grew by 85 percent and professional staff by an impressive 240 percent. Where full-time faculty outnumbered administrators and staff in 1975 by nearly two to one, full-time faculty were outnumbered by administrators and staff thirty years later. Faculty-to-student ratios remained virtually unchanged, but staff-to-student ratios declined by half (ibid., 15–16). Management consulting firms (see, e.g., Denneen and Dretler 2012)

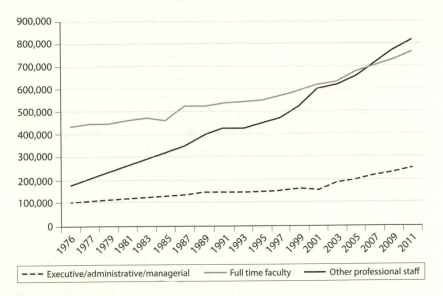

FIGURE 7.1. Administrative and Faculty Employees of U.S. Postsecondary Institutions, 1976–2011. *Source*: Author's calculation from U.S. Department of Education, Integrated Postsecondary Education Data System.

spoke of "administrative bloat," and the phenomenon continued to attract tart commentary by professors. The higher education economist Richard Vedder observed, "I wouldn't buy a used car from a university president. They say, 'We're making moves to cut costs,' and mention something about energy-efficient lightbulbs, and ignore the new assistant to the assistant to the associate vice provost they just hired" (quoted in Marcus 2014).

A fundamental distinction is between senior executives[1] and the administrative staff that support them. Administrative staff members outnumbered full-time faculty members, but the number of senior executives grew at a slower pace. Most critiques focused on upper administration. But such a focus is misplaced if the issue is "administrative bloat" because the real growth was in administrative support staff (see figure 7.1).

Was the growth of administrative staff warranted? Those who have looked at the issue tend to be in agreement about the impact of five of the six primary sources of staff growth. First, as institutions grew, they required more staff to conduct established administrative functions. A larger college or university will mean more accountants, student health professionals, maintenance people, and police officers—and those who supervise them. Second, a competitive environment required more staff to respond to critical resource dependencies. Most institutions added development staff, government affairs staff, recruitment staffs, and (in the case of research universities) research office staff and technology transfer and entrepreneurship staff in an effort to fight for resources to support campus operations. Third, students tended to demand new amenities that generate increases in staff. Preferences for larger recreation centers, new campus cuisine options, new technology infrastructure, online courses, or more plentiful off-campus study opportunities entailed a growth in staff in each of these areas—and of those to supervise them (Frank 2013). Fourth, universities became more highly regulated places, requiring more staff to fill out reports and to respond to inquiries. As Ginsberg himself noted,

> The federal government requires the reporting of mountains of data on everything from affirmative action through campus crime and the treatment of laboratory animals in university research facilities. Boards that accredit and license educational institutions require reams of reports and often make time-consuming site visits to inspect campus facilities. A variety of state agencies demand data and, in the case of public institutions, conduct extensive audits, reviews, surveys, and inspections. (2011, 29)

Fifth, colleges and universities felt it necessary to add some functions in an effort to help students and faculty succeed. They added academic support services such as advising and tutoring to help underprepared students. They added specialized offices to provide services to particular student groups, including minority students, LBGTQ students, veterans, and students with disabilities. They added teaching improvement centers to help faculty succeed in their instructional activities. Few foreign universities would consider adding such services, but in the American context these were necessary adjustments to support policies of inclusion.

What analysts have *not* agreed upon is the sixth source of growth: the extent to which administrators were prone to expand their own empires by thinking of new projects that require new assistants to implement. Ginsberg and other critics considered this an important reason for the growth of administration. "Most academics," Ginsberg wrote, "are familiar with the creativity . . . shown by administrators in inventing new tasks for themselves and the diligence they can demonstrate when endeavoring to capture established functions [from the faculty]" (2011, 33). Others were not so sure. Empire building no doubt occurs at every institution, but the extent to which it is a factor in universities cannot be easily determined because every administrative position can be justified by proponents for its contributions to one of the five other sources of staff growth.

Unfortunately, the standard reporting categories used by the federal government to describe college and university expenditures do not align very well with these explanations for the growth of administration. The categories break out spending on instruction, research, student services, academic support (such as IT, library, and advising), public service, operations and maintenance, auxiliary services (such as residence halls and restaurants), and institutional support. Institutional support is the category of greatest interest for critics of administrative bloat, although none of these categories other than instruction is irrelevant.

The economist Ronald Ehrenberg examined real changes in these expenditure categories during the period FY 1987 through FY 2008 (see table 7.1). The largest gains in real spending occurred in the areas of research and student services, with gains in student services particularly pronounced in private colleges and universities. The smallest gains were in operations and maintenance and auxiliary services. Instructional gains lagged behind gains in institutional support at every type of institution Ehrenberg studied, and the gaps were large at both public and private doctoral/research universities. Ehrenberg argued that the decreasing share of academic budgets going to instruction was *not* primarily the result of the growth of a "class of professional administrators who seek to 'feather their own nests'" (2012, 207). At the same time, he observed that it would be entirely wrong to think that academic institutions have rigorously controlled their administrative costs. Indeed, most of those who have looked carefully into the matter concluded that a rebalancing in the direction of administrative cost reduction and augmentation of instructional expenditures could have been possible—and would have benefited students (see Desrochers and Hurlburt 2016; Desrochers and Wellman 2011; Leslie and Rhoades 1995; Massy 2016).

Administrative bloat did not escape the attention of administrators themselves. The Great Recession led colleges and universities to undertake a number of cost-cutting measures, with a heightened focus on administrative costs. Relying on the advice of management consulting firms, they attempted to reduce whole layers of administration by increasing the number of direct reports each administrator supervised; made efforts to centralize procurement to achieve price concessions from providers; worked to achieve efficiencies in IT; and reorganized support services, often into centralized

TABLE 7.1. Annual Average Percent Real Changes in Expenditures per Full-Time Equivalent Students, FY 1987–2008

Institution Type	N	Instruction	Student Services	Academic Services	Research	Public Service	Instit. Support	Operations	Auxiliary
Public Doctoral	151	0.87	1.64	1.39	2.89	2.13	1.35	0.79	0.46
Private Doctoral	103	1.87	3.13	2.87	2.35	2.83	2.60	1.05	1.42
Public Master's	227	0.72	1.82	1.49	2.80	2.81	1.27	0.70	0.06
Private Master's	327	1.55	2.66	2.13	2.18	0.75	1.57	−0.33	0.11
Private Bachelor's	461	1.70	3.05	2.17	2.95	1.26	1.76	−0.23	0.52

Source: Ehrenberg 2012, 204. Calculations from IPEDS.

"shared services centers." Research by Desrochers and Wellman confirmed that administrative expenditures declined slightly during the depths of the recession in both public and private institutions, while instructional expenditures increased slightly in public universities only, and expenditures on student services ticked up slightly in both public and private institutions (2011, 25). Clerical and maintenance workers represented a declining share of employees (ibid., 30). Even so, in both private and public universities, "instructional shares of total spending were at or near ten-year lows" (ibid., 26).

The desire of many faculty members to focus on their research and teaching, rather than committee work, is a little-appreciated aspect of the debate about administrative bloat. Research on faculty job satisfaction suggests that the majority of faculty members would rather spend their time working on their next article or preparing their classes than advising and counseling students or serving on university committees (Finkelstein, Conley, and Schuster 2016, 265–89), a preference influenced by increases in the time faculty members spend in email correspondence with students (ibid.). Ginsberg (2011) asserted that faculty members could learn to reengage in these activities if reengagement resulted in the augmentation of tenured and tenure-track colleagues.[2] But heightened expectations for research output make this notion highly doubtful, at least for faculty members working in research universities. Clark (1987, 158–59) provided evidence that faculty members at research universities were content to let administrators do the work they preferred to avoid. More recent research confirms that male faculty members find ways to avoid committee work they do not welcome while female faculty members shoulder a disproportionate share of these responsibilities (Finkelstein, Conley and Schuster 2016, 537–38; Guarino and Borden 2017).[3]

The Separation of Management

Most senior administrators still rise from the ranks of the faculty, but the culture of senior administrators differs markedly from that of faculty members.[4] What I will have to say about this culture is not intended to encompass every senior campus leadership group. Some are far more dysfunctional than the portrait I will draw here, and some are more amenable to dissenters and the free flow of ideas. Even so, organizational theory suggests that college and university administrators should be among the most likely groups to close ranks and maintain corps discipline, simply because defections are dangerous for a group surrounded by empowered individual faculty members and their representative bodies, the academic senates. My experience talking with administrators at dozens of institutions reinforces these expectations of organizational theory.

Senior campus executive teams include presidents, vice presidents, and deans. As Robert Michels ([1911] 1962) argued long ago, every oligarchy must find ways to maintain power in spite of its small numbers. To maintain power, the senior administration recruits organizationally adept and politically able faculty members to join its ranks, sometimes co-opting potential dissidents. It exploits the disorganization of the faculty (and the students) through intense intragroup interaction and discipline within its own ranks. It uses its ties to influential outside parties to impress those without such ties. And it touts its achievements wherever possible through the communications media it controls and through its contacts with outside media. It is through these means that the senior administrative leadership can maintain control over the loosely organized mass of faculty members and the largely unorganized mass of staff and students.

Political effectiveness requires loyalty to the core group in interactions with the outside world. At a town hall meeting called by the president, the first rows of the auditorium are inevitably occupied by administrators, their loyalty expressed in physical space. One of the grave sins in administration is overt criticism of the senior leadership, a sin that can lead to excommunication. In my experience such expressions of disloyalty are a far more serious matter than simple incompetence, which can often be covered up by able junior staff. Public criticisms are indeed the equivalent of treason in managerial circles; they empower potential enemies while setting the individual's pride above the interest of the core group.

The modal personalities of senior administrators differ from those of the faculty, reflecting their positions and responsibilities. The typical senior administrator is highly conscientious and, at the very least, capable of extroversion, but s/he is not particularly open. Administrators restrict sensitive communications to a need-to-know basis. Among administrators, honesty is not always the best policy. Honest assessments encourage discontent among those criticized, and discontent can be communicable. Therefore, criticism is used sparingly and tactically. It is all but impermissible in a disciplined core group for members to express obvious stress, anxiety, or fear—and definitely not in public. Such expressions are acceptable among groups of faculty. Administrators develop skills of getting quickly to the heart of the matter, while faculty members are inclined to explore topics in a more roundabout way. Listening to a meeting of administrators is like driving on a freeway. Items are addressed at a good pace without many digressions. Listening to a faculty meeting can be like driving on a twisting country road, scenic and meandering, and occasionally leading into the woods. The schedules of senior administrators are packed with meetings. The expectation is that people will be on time and prepared. Meetings are conducted in a businesslike manner, with relatively little small talk or wasted time. Faculty members have greater liberty to come and go as they please and to speak at length off the cuff. University administrators do not have time for soliloquies, and they are not in any event inclined to value them. They tend to be much more interested in the data being used to support decisions and in crisp presentations.

Administrators interact with influential people on and off campus, and, like politicians in democracies throughout the world, they realize that today's opponent can be tomorrow's friend. Policy disagreements can be stated forcefully, but ad hominem attacks are avoided. Administrators attempt to convey the sense that they are problem solvers. Clear statements of objectives and clear directions forward are important. Many academic departments are also run in a businesslike way, but wide variation exists on this score. Faculty members are free to hold grudges for as long as they want. In poorly run departments, they can interrupt, grimace, and roll their eyes during faculty meetings without standing out among a gallery of equally expressive faces.

Administrators are a status group as well as a stratum with organizational authority. Their salaries are higher than those of all but a few of the faculty. They have larger offices and personal assistants. They have people to coordinate their schedules and to provide supporting materials for their meetings and speeches. When administrators dress as businesspeople, it is, in part, because they have an interest in differentiating themselves from other, scruffier individuals on campus. They recognize one another as having made sacrifices in personal freedom for the sake of the organization's well-being. The symbolic associations of business dress with efficiency, order, and productivity no doubt contribute to the attraction of this style of dress, as does the added expense required for such outfitting, indicative of the higher incomes of the administrative leadership.

THE CONDUCT OF UNIVERSITIES BY BUSINESSPEOPLE?

The most common complaint about the senior administrators of universities is that they have become indistinguishable from corporate executives. Critics point to the hefty salaries of senior administrators as indicators of their affinity with corporate executives. "When you have college presidents making $1 million, you are going to have $800,000 provosts, and $500,000 deans," policy analyst Patrick Callan observed. "This reflects a set of values that is not the way most people think of higher education" (quoted in Arum and Roksa 2011, 12). Others have drawn more direct parallels, typing university administrators as "capitalists" who seek to exploit knowledge products, such as new technologies and clinical trials facilities, for the pecuniary gain of their institutions (see, e.g., Aronowitz 2000; Slaughter and Leslie 1997) or as businessmen competing against other businessmen in a system in which "students tend to be seen as consumers rather than members of a campus community [and] the major responsibility for managers is to read the market . . . and attempt to reposition [their institutions] accordingly" to improve their comparative advantages (Gumport 2002, 55).

The critique is not entirely convincing. Opportunities to improve the financial situation of institutions must always be given serious attention, because higher education institutions are chronically in need of resources to do all of the things they would like to do. Senior administrators consequently become involved in assessing the viability of all proposals to increase revenues, whether these come from fund-raising campaigns, marketing and branding initiatives, new self-supporting master's degrees, technology transfer opportunities, the admission of more international and out-of-state students, expansion of the educational mission to incorporate students who want to take courses exclusively online, purchasing land, or renegotiating indirect cost rates with government rate setters.

At the better institutions these assessments are not based solely on prospects for revenue enhancement. Instead, they depend on the extent to which new resources are consistent with academic values. Some opportunities are too good to pass up; others too problematic to pursue. International and out-of-state students who are willing to pay higher tuitions are attractive to every institution, though not all have the reputation or the political flexibility to pursue them effectively. By contrast, donors who want to choose chair holders are attractive to very few, if any, self-respecting academic institutions because they compromise the fundamental principle that professors hold a monopoly on the expert judgments necessary to determine who should join their ranks.

When scholars talk about commercialization, they are generally talking about the willingness to compromise academic values for profit. Clearly, commercialization does occur. Big-time sports are largely commercial operations, opposed, as repeated scandals have shown, to the fundamental values of academe. Football-playing universities not only sanction activities that can injure players' brains; they often pay the orchestrators of this mayhem the largest salaries on campus. Technology transfer activities are commercial. Some cut-rate online degree programs (as well as low-quality on-campus programs) can be accurately described as diploma mills; many others are essentially commercial operations of varying quality. Revenue-hungry universities will add self-supporting master's programs whenever they think the market will support them—academic fit and quality may be an afterthought. Academic values, traditions of shared governance, and deference to professional expertise are the braking mechanisms that slow the advance of market logic. To survive, administrators must be attuned to the values characteristic of academic professionalism and accord at least occasional deference to them.

THE MAYORAL DISPOSITION

The depiction of senior administrators as corporate executives in academic robes is, in my view, tendentious and incomplete. The majority of college and university presidents might be better cast as politicians. The 2009 *Time*

magazine portrait of then Ohio State University president E. Gordon Gee
highlights this aspect of the presidential role:

> This is a thoroughbred politician. Gee shakes hands with gusto and ap-
> pears delighted by everyone he meets. Peering around the room, he cries
> out gleefully, "Where are our county commissioners?" A couple of hands
> go up, and he exults, "I love you guys!" What about state legislators?
> There's one in the corner. "I love you too!" giggles Gee. Everyone wants
> a word and a picture with him, and when the time comes to depart, he
> somehow radiates reluctance even as he quicksteps toward a waiting
> car. . . . There are 88 counties in Ohio, and Gee is in the process of barn-
> storming through every one of them. Again. (von Drehle 2009)

Like politicians, senior administrators act in an environment composed
of many vocal and mobilized constituencies. A very large number of constituency groups can help advance the mission or create unwelcome problems.
These constituencies include fellow senior administrators, a tenured faculty
jealous of its rights and prerogatives, students and their parents, alumni,
donors, key personnel at secondary school feeder institutions, staff (some of
whom may be unionized), outside pressure groups interested in using the university to advance their causes, regulators (such as the federal government
and regional accrediting bodies), and the active members of local communities surrounding the university. In public universities, these constituencies
also include state legislators and governors holding the purse strings and
interested in advancing educational initiatives. Building support, mollifying
pressure groups, and undermining real or potential opponents consequently
dominate the day-to-day activities of most senior administrators.

Presidents are the public face of their institutions. How they present the
institution matters. They consequently tend to be boosters and optimists in
their public presentations, however bleak they may feel about situations in
private. They focus on accomplishments, contributions, and bright futures.
Misguided policies, expensive mistakes, and wasted resources are kept out
of the public eye to the extent possible. Little good can come from their
exposure. By contrast, these missteps provide fodder for the faculty who
enjoy seeing themselves as better judges than those who manage. Administrators have other reasons to be uncomplaining and positive. When an
administrator complains, many on campus take note. Careful evasions or
nonrevealing answers are consequently necessary to avoid the dangers of

signaling too much or the risks of misinterpretation. Faculty members are at much greater liberty to speak their minds when they are unhappy because they enjoy academic freedom and because their opinions influence smaller circles.

Ceremonial occasions are important to university administrators because they place the focus of the community on institutional values and on administrators themselves as the official representatives of those values. Administrators gain the respect of the community for the respect they show to the institution on these occasions. The outstanding administrator is self-consciously a public person. Public people know how to charm and inspire when an audience is assembled on a ceremonial occasion. They know how to console in times of trouble. Even those who cannot charm and inspire follow the ground rules of ceremony. I have yet to see a senior administrator who is less than gracious and punctilious on ceremonial occasions, regardless of the many other matters on their minds (including the sometimes intense dislike they feel for those being honored).

Senior administrators must also have skills in conflict resolution. Senior administrators are protectors of the safety of the campus, the resources on which it relies, and the integrity of its research and teaching functions. They put in controls to monitor expenditures and committees to provide due process for those accused of misconduct. Universities are built on the foundations of tolerance and intellectual freedom; for this very reason they are beset by all manner of unsavory behavior: crimes perpetrated by students against one another, misappropriation of funds, explosively contentious hiring decisions, sexual harassment, bullying, scientific misconduct, and conflicts of commitment. Conflict abatement and resolution are consequently fundamental to the work of senior administrators. Patience wears thin quickly among these conscientious, busy people when they are confronted by scoundrels. When the time for action comes, they are inclined to act swiftly and surgically.

Administrators have the vices of their political virtues. Their need for optimism easily shades into self-interested "spinning." Their need for discipline encourages intolerance of those whose self-control is lower. They prefer to acquiesce with bad decisions than to appear disloyal to their superiors. Their need for certainty can mask a reliance on conventional thinking. Their busy schedules and dependence on personal ties for keeping abreast encourage their tendencies to follow the crowd. Their need to respond to politically connected individuals can lead them to press unjust causes. Professors feel superior to administrators as proponents of scholarly values and educational quality. They see administrators as careerists and interested only in the two "bottom lines"—revenues and (at least at the leading institutions) prestige. They feel superior to them in intellectual depth, outspokenness, sincerity, and independence. On balance, they are probably right to feel superior in these areas. It is the rare administrator who is paid for the qualities faculty members admire.

THE DECLINING QUALIFICATION OF INTELLECTUAL ACHIEVEMENT

Nevertheless, some administrators are intellectuals, as well as business-people and politicians. The Veblenian tradition of satirizing the conduct of universities by businessmen is unfair to the intellectual accomplishments of at least the leaders of the top research universities in the country. In the summer of 2017, I studied the biographies of the presidents of the top fifty research universities,[5] and the great majority of these biographies profiled individuals who had strong records of scholarly or scientific achievement in addition to the business and political skills required in their jobs. By my count, forty of the fifty had distinguished scientific or scholarly careers. The biographies included more than a dozen presidents who claimed to have published at least one hundred scientific or scholarly papers. They included one of the country's leading authorities on the First Amendment, an inventor of collaborating autonomous machines, a computer scientist who developed intelligent technologies to aid the disabled, the co-creator of the concept of emotional intelligence, and a finalist for the Pulitzer Prize. Only one of the fifty had pursued most of his career in business, and only two had pursued most of their careers in government service.

This level of intellectual achievement did not extend beyond the elite colleges and research universities. In teaching-centered institutions, presidents with important intellectual achievements were rare, and many did not even rise through the faculty ranks. Based on a sample of "top regional universities," virtually all private, from the 2016 *U.S. News & World Report* rankings, I found that that more than one-quarter had followed nontraditional career paths into the presidency—either through business or higher education administration or some combination of the two. Nonacademic career paths were still more common in public regional universities. My analysis of a random sample of fifty *C&U 2000* presidents from public regionals found that almost half (48 percent) came from nontraditional backgrounds; nearly one-quarter rose through a series of higher education administrative positions without ever having served on the faculty and another quarter were appointed following careers spent mainly in corporate legal or management positions, or in government service.[6]

TRACKS, TRAINING, AND SALARIES

The term "professionalized" refers to structural changes in how individuals are recruited into an occupation, the regulation of the occupation, and the practice norms for work in the occupation. Professions are characterized as based on formal training programs that limit access to the occupation, a formal body of knowledge that underlies practice, and an occupational community that creates and disseminates new knowledge related to practice and sanctions breaches of ethical conduct. Many professions, of course, also require licensing examinations prior to admission to practice.

Tracks and Training

In the case of university administrators, only some of these criteria of professionalization have been met—and then only partially. Senior administrators follow a variety of career paths. But the emergent patterns are clear: university management is becoming a separate career track independent of the faculty, occupied by people who have had limited ties to research and teaching and who interact primarily with those in their own occupational community. According to American Council of Education surveys going back to the mid-1980s, most college and university presidents have degrees in higher education administration and have spent their entire careers in academe. They have worked their way up in university management, typically beginning as deans, and their previous job was mostly likely to be provost/ academic affairs vice president (Cook 2012). As I have shown, others come to academe after successful careers in law, politics, or business.

A review of the top eleven higher education administration programs as determined by *U.S. News and World Report* (2017) reveals the outlines of a core curriculum for training as a university administrator, albeit in the midst of a wide range of program structures and considerable variation by degree level (master's, educational doctorate, or PhD).[7] The following courses were required at the master's or educational doctorate level by five or more of the top eleven programs at the end of the period: students and student development (in 9 programs); higher education policy (9); organizational theory/ governance (8); finance/economics of higher education (7); student access/diversity (7); planning, analysis, and/or institutional research (5); issues in higher education (5); and the history of higher education (5). Other common requirements (or electives) included: legal issues in higher education, organizational leadership/strategy, and research methods.

Faculty members who are considering a transition into university administration also have opportunities to apply for academic leadership programs sponsored by national higher education associations, summer executive training institutes at leading universities, or system-wide leadership development programs. The American Council of Education's (ACE) fellowship program provides opportunities for approximately forty successful applicants each year to shadow senior administrators for a semester or a year, while interacting with other fellows in multiday seminars and at national meetings. ACE boasts that of the two thousand fellows who have completed the program since its inception, 80 percent have served as presidents, chief academic officers, or other cabinet-level administrators, including deans (ACE 2017). The most famous of the university-run programs, the Harvard Institutes of Higher Education, has provided leadership seminars and networking opportunities during summers and interterms to ten thousand alumni since its inception in the late 1960s (Harvard Graduate School of Education 2017).

College and university administrators interact with their peers to discuss common interests at numerous invitation-only forums. Separate sessions for presidents, provosts, and deans are held at the national meetings of the American Council on Education, the Association of American Universities, the Association of Public and Land-Grant Universities, the Association of State Colleges and Universities, the Consortium for Financing Higher Education, the Education Advisory Board, the National Association of Independent Colleges and Universities, and other national associations, as well as system and regional associations of peer institutions.

Salaries

In the mid-1980s, the typical president of a doctoral-level university was paid about 70 percent more than the typical full professor. About one-third of that difference reflected the difference between the academic year (nine-month) salary of the professors and the calendar year (twelve-month) pay of the president (Davis and Davis 1999). However, by 1998, presidents were earning nearly twice as much as senior faculty (ibid.) and by 2015 they were earning 3.5 times as much on average in public universities and 4 times as much in private universities (calculated from Flaherty 2017). In 2014, more than three dozen private university presidents were earning $1 million or more in total compensation, and one year later eight public university presidents could count themselves in the same salary league (Bauman and O'Leary 2017).[8]

Tenure

Given Michels's "iron law of oligarchy," it is a wonder that administrations ever fall. Yet the average tenure of a college or university president dropped from 8.6 to 7 years between 2006 and 2011. Presidents of private colleges and universities tended to serve longer terms than presidents of public universities (Cook 2012). The most important reason for the declining average tenure of presidents is that the job has become harder. In the public sector conflicts with governors and state legislatures over funding can take a heavy toll. Athletic scandals can also consume the time of senior administrators at big-time athletics schools and can lead to their ouster.

It is also true that six or seven years is more than enough time for a president to wear out his or her welcome. Presidents make potential enemies on campus every time they pass over a candidate for an administrative position, deny a promotion, or fail to provide colleges with the attention they feel they deserve. Some studies suggest that faculty evaluations make little difference in presidential reappointments (Davis and Davis 1999), but the testimony of presidents themselves suggests that their perceptions of faculty disapproval can greatly discourage presidents and eventually lead to their resignations (Trachtenberg, Kauver, and Bogue 2016). Boards are another demanding group. Boards are angered when campus budgets are in the red, when fundraising campaigns fall short of their goals, and when the campus appears in the news for the wrong reasons. Decisions that touch on valued ties among board members can lead to conflict, as when a president denies admission to the son or daughter of a well-connected family. Moreover, the university board's expectations are likely to rise with the size of the president's compensation package. As Arthur Padilla and Sujit Ghosh put it, "Stellar compensation generates expectations of stellar performance" (1999, 3).

If they are ambitious to move into more prestigious positions, presidents will get to work fast on big projects; the founding of a new school or campus, a successful fund-raising campaign, dramatic growth in research funding, or progress in the diversification of the faculty can be used as evidence of leadership success. Of these, fund-raising success is the most likely to draw favorable attention. Again the case of E. Gordon Gee, who held six major university presidencies between 1981 and 2015, is instructive. In spite of numerous impolitic remarks over the years, Gee impressed search committees as a natural politician and demon fund-raiser. As journalist David von Drehle observed, "Gee's ceaseless and cunning campaign has him well on his way to a $2.5 billion fundraising goal, and it helped him emerge as a rare winner in Ohio's savage budget battle this year" (2009).

Steering toward the New Ends of Knowledge

University administrators wear many hats, and only some of their activities are closely related to the main themes of this book. But two of the challenges they experienced during the period were closely related. One was to find ways to pay for both increased enrollments and higher-level research expenditures. The other was to guide the disciplines into closer alignment with the university commitments to technological innovation and social inclusion.

I have discussed many of the conventional means that administrators have used to search for revenue to support educational and research endeavors. These included tuition increases, the development of new professional master's programs, the cultivation of donors, and the pursuit of research funding from federal and foundation patrons. In this section, I will focus on the use of cross-subsidies to meet the seemingly incommensurate demands for more teaching and more research. I have also discussed the responsiveness of universities to incentives in their environments for stronger contributions to economic development and social incorporation. Here I will focus on their use of interdisciplinary initiatives to circumvent the power of discipline-based departments and to direct teaching and research toward these new ends of knowledge.

CROSS-SUBSIDIES

Growth requires financial models that allow for responsiveness both to student enrollments and to research opportunities. The utilization of cross-subsidies is one of the tools that allows university managers to serve these two ends and to grow by doing so. Lower-division courses are a pivotal feature of cross-subsidization. Large lecture classes, full of first- and second-year students, are less expensive to teach than upper-division courses. These lecture classes are in this sense the "bread and butter" of universities, and they are even more cost-effective if they are taught by instructors or graduate students rather than by tenured faculty members. The revenues associated with them help subsidize more expensive small classes in upper-division and graduate programs. Unfortunately for students and their families, some universities will purposely enroll many more first-year students than they expect to complete because these new recruits are so inexpensive to teach. Cost accounting is one of the hidden economic drivers of the push for access.

The disciplines also carry differential value as subsidy providers. In general, social science, education, and business courses are inexpensive because they typically require only a white board, an instructor, and teaching assistants. They are the "cash cows" of universities and subsidize smaller-enrollment courses and courses that require lab techs and/or expensive materials (although materials fees are also common in universities).[9] One reason that university administrators allow the number of majors to float up in the always popular social sciences and business majors is that these high enrollments help fund low-enrollment but high-grant activity departments like physics and chemistry.

Research is, of course, a particularly expensive function of universities. Research-productive professors are expensive and so too is the equipment they need to do their work. And the expenses do not end there. A 2000 Rand Corporation study showed that federal indirect cost recovery rates do not cover the full indirect costs of research—so-called F&A (facilities and administration) costs (Goldman et al. 2000, 18–24). These F&A costs include allowances of depreciation of equipment, interest on debt associated with buildings and equipment, operation and maintenance expenses, library expenses, general administration expenses, departmental administration expenses, sponsored projects administration, and student services. Foundations pay much less in indirect costs, on average, than the federal government, making foundation research grants particularly costly for universities. Based on cost accounting from a sample of 102 universities, Rand researchers calculated that federal facilities and administration reimbursements failed to cover approximately 17 percent of total indirect costs (Goldman et al. 2000, 18–19).

The gap must be made up in some way. The savings accrued by hiring part-time faculty to teach lower-division courses can help defray the costs of research, even if this hiring contributes to widening the crevice that separates those who teach and do little research and those who research and do little teaching. In addition, increased enrollments in lower-division and "cash-cow" departments are also used to support research and to help subsidize F&A costs for research in many universities (Ehrenberg 2012). The students in large lecture courses bring in just as much money as the students in the small seminars, and this money can help pay the salaries of research-productive faculty members and make up for the shortfall universities experience in F&A research costs.

University budgeting took a turn during the period that seemed to threaten the elaborate cross-subsidies that permitted research to grow in tandem with (and sometimes on the back of) student demand. Responsibility-centered management (RCM) was based on the principle that the units responsible for revenue were entitled to retain these revenues, minus a "tax" to support central services such as the president's office, the police, and the library (see Curry, Laws, and Strauss 2013; Fuller, Morton, and Korschgen 2005; Goldstein and Meisinger 2005; Whalen 1991).[10] RCM models seemed to promise that enrollment-rich colleges and departments would at last become economically dominant after many years of subsidizing enrollment-poor but research-rich science and engineering units. RCM models became more popular during the period because of their apparent transparency and clear incentive structures (Hearn et al. 2006, 287), but without adjustments they would have threatened the intricate system of cross-subsidies that allowed universities to expand both enrollments and research by using the former to subsidize the latter.

In the end, the diffusion of RCM did not eliminate cross-subsidies. Multimillion-dollar subventions from colleges of social sciences, education, and business became necessary to keep science and engineering colleges operating at an acceptable quality level on most comprehensive campuses. (The reverse was true at technology-oriented campuses such as Stanford and MIT where liberal arts departments would have quite possibly disappeared if subventions were not provided to them by the high-enrollment science and engineering units.) RCM simply made more transparent transfers of income that were once hidden within the operating assumptions of centrally controlled accounting systems.[11]

INTERDISCIPLINARY INITIATIVES

Interdisciplinary initiatives contributed to the redirection of campus energies from the solution of problems in the disciplines to the search for new technologies and the incorporation of the experiences of women, minorities, and non-Western peoples. These interdisciplinary initiatives included the building of multidisciplinary research buildings, the identification of interdisciplinary centers of excellence on campus, the creation of strategic investment funds to seed interdisciplinary activities, and interdisciplinary cluster hiring to create areas of research strength in "cutting-edge" fields.

In the traditional approach to faculty hiring, deans make appointment lines available, but departmental faculty members are ultimately responsible for hiring the scholars who will provide excellent teaching and contribute to a department's standing in future decades. It is up to departmental faculty to determine the fields the department wishes to replace or develop (subject to the approval of deans). This traditional system of hiring leaves senior managers with comparatively little power over the long-term development of the university, except in so far as they are responsible for allocating faculty hiring lines differentially across departments.

During the period covered in this book, senior administrators found that they were capable of exercising stronger overall direction by aligning with the forces promoting interdisciplinary collaborations. The Beckman Institute for Advanced Science and Technology at the University of Illinois, founded in 1983, was the first large-scale multidisciplinary research building. Researchers with interdisciplinary grants were allowed to occupy space in the building for the period of their collaboration, ensuring a constant stream of new tenants. The building was designed to foster informal conversations among researchers working in different fields. The Beckman model inspired new building designs across a wide swath of academe: from wealthy campuses like Columbia and Stanford to struggling campuses like Howard University and the University of Texas-El Paso. The North Carolina State University Centennial Campus was a still more ambitious model along similar lines—in this case creating an entire community of university researchers and their actual or potential business partners on acreage near the university. Similar facilities were built at the Mission Bay campus of UC San Francisco and are anticipated for the Allston campus of Harvard University.

Duke University led the way in rethinking the disciplinary basis of university organization through its *Crossing Boundaries* report of 1988. This was shortly followed by an ambitious plan at the University of Southern California to develop a "more creative profile" by encouraging "innovative interdisciplinary research and teaching" (USC 1994). Dozens of universities used strategic development funds to seed interdisciplinary initiatives considered promising on either intellectual or revenue generation grounds (Sa 2008, 542–44). In these programs universities pooled resources and redistributed them competitively to form interdisciplinary "centers of excellence" in the hope that they would evolve into self-supporting structures.

The University of Wisconsin-Madison inaugurated the first large-scale cluster hiring program in 1989. A search of websites at the end of the period indicated that at least eighty-four universities had engaged in cluster hiring to build interdisciplinary strength in campus-identified fields (author's cal-culation).[12] In some cases, the clusters were proposed by the faculty, but they were ultimately chosen by senior administrators. Development oppor-tunities clearly influenced the choices of clusters, most of which centered on national science and engineering priority areas. As one vice chancel-lor of development told me, "Our donors do not want another study of Shakespeare. They want solutions to economic and social problems." But no comprehensive university campus could afford to focus exclusively on science and technology; the discontent generated by such a one-sided em-phasis could prove ruinous politically. Cluster hiring consequently usually included at least a few opportunities for the arts, humanities, and social sci-ences faculties. Many of these opportunities were related to social inclusion. They included such cluster themes as global arts, immigration, and African American disparities. Cluster hiring was also used explicitly to contribute to the diversity of the faculty; by making diversity a plus-factor in cluster hires university administrators were able to advance a social inclusion agenda, even as they steered their campuses into areas of national priority interest (see Urban Universities 2015).

My analysis of 69 planning documents from the early 2000s, supple-mented by interviews with 144 university leaders from the same institu-tions, revealed that virtually every one of the universities had taken a stance in favor of interdisciplinary collaboration and, by implication, against the continued dominance of discipline-based departments (Brint 2005, 26). Senior managers during the period fought to weaken the power of depart-ments, decrying the "siloing" of knowledge and the "artificial boundaries" created by overly specialized disciplinary communities. The difficulties of interdisciplinary collaboration were largely overlooked (cf. Dahlander and McFarland 2013; J. Jacobs 2013; Strober 2011). The investment of senior administrators in alternatives to departments helped institutionalize the idea that specialists should be aligned with solutions to large-scale economic and social problems rather than with the interests of their disciplines and should work as complements to a team rather than principally as agents of their own scholarly reputations.

Whatever merits they held as modes of intellectual progress—some were very successful, others busts—interdisciplinary initiatives served as a strategic instrument in the administrative counterrevolution against what Jencks and Riesman (1968) called the "academic revolution." Strategies to emphasize interdisciplinary creativity shifted a share of control from fac-ulty in departments who were experts in solving disciplinary problems to administrators who were experts in aggregating resources and planning and publicizing new large-scale initiatives. The role of university managers was to build the support on campus for interdisciplinary initiatives, to support them materially (if selectively) in projects ultimately chosen by management, and to draw them together under the same conceptual roof: creating the future through interdisciplinary problem-solving. In these efforts, they were typically joined by interdisciplinary enthusiasts among the leading scientists and progressive humanists on campus, two groups whose social networks crossed disciplinary boundaries (see Brint 2005).

Managerial or Dual Control?

The coming of an "all-administrative university" would mean the death knell of traditions of shared governance in academe—the expectation that faculty should be involved in the review of administrative initiatives and should have primary responsibility over matters of educational policy.[13] Another name for shared governance is "dual control." In the dual control model promulgated by the American Association of University Professors, senior administrators maintained primary responsibility for fund-raising, budgetary allocations, strategic planning, and administrative appointments, while faculty members maintained primary responsibility for curriculum, educational policies, and standards for professional evaluation (AAUP 1966; Corson 1960). Shared governance models further identified areas in which faculty and administrators should have joint responsibility for decision making because they required both the faculty's technical expertise and management's fiduciary responsibilities. These models suggested that faculty members and administrators should be jointly responsible for decisions in areas such as evaluation of professors for promotion and the launching of new programmatic emphases (see AAUP 1966; Kaplan 2001).

Beginning in the mid-1990s, critics questioned the continuing relevance of dual governance as norm and practice and offered an alternative image of academic governance that I will call "managerial control." These writers saw control and responsibility shifting toward administrators, even in areas in which the faculty had in the past held primary responsibility (see, e.g., Coopers & Lybrand 1995; Gumport 1997; Waugh 2003). The managerial control model follows from a conception of colleges and universities as increasingly adopting a corporate pattern of governance, replacing the collegial forms of earlier eras.[14] Scholars who identified this trend also focused on the consequences of managerial control, including actions that channeled academic development along managerially approved lines and restriction of faculty autonomy over teaching, curriculum, and conduct of research (Aronowitz 2006; Coopers & Lybrand 1995; Marginson and Considine 2000; Rhoades and Sporn 2002; Slaughter and Leslie 1997; Tuchman 2009; Washburn 2000). The combination of autocratic presidents, arbitrary boards, and professionalizing faculties created conditions in the early twentieth century for the development of norms of shared governance. But, Larry Gerber (2014) and others argued, the greater complexity of universities, the adoption of corporate business practices by university managers, and the employment of large numbers of adjunct faculty led to a steep decline in shared governance by the late twentieth century.

EVIDENCE ON CAMPUS DECISION MAKING

Were Gerber and others right about the decline of shared governance? Empirical studies examining governance in U.S. institutions of higher education have been largely interested in the level of faculty participation in governance and have not explicitly tested either the dual or the managerial control theory (Baldridge and Kemerer 1976; Kaplan 2004; Kissler 1997; Tierney and Minor 2003). Against the expectations of the critics of "corporatized management," all large-scale studies have found significant levels of faculty participation.[15] Each of the studies also showed the existence of some management-dominant institutions. Estimates of the size of this latter category varied, however, depending on question wording, from "roughly half" thinking their institutions were "administratively dominated" (Baldridge and Kemerer 1976) to approximately 25 percent seeing "most decisions as centralized" (Tierney and Minor 2003) to 20 percent seeing "hierarchy" as the best description of how decisions are made even in educational policy (Kissler 1997). In addition to relying on subjective descriptive language, none of the studies examined changes in decision making over time.

With the *Colleges & Universities 2000* research team, I examined the managerial control thesis by comparing the survey responses of provosts and academic vice presidents in two years—2000 and 2012—to questions about the actors "primarily involved" in decision making in thirteen campus policy areas (see Apkarian et al. 2014). The respondents to the surveys were, by virtue of their job responsibilities and the scope of their activities in academic affairs (Birnbaum 1988; Rosovsky 1990), the campus officials most likely to have adequate knowledge of decision making in their institutions across a wide range of decisions. We were interested to see whether the levels of perceived managerial control had increased over time in a constant sample of colleges and universities. We sent the survey out to all 385 *C&U 2000* sample institutions, but some provosts did not respond in one or both years, and others skipped the questions on governance. The final sample included responses from 139 institutions whose provosts responded in both years.[16]

The thirteen decisions we studied included six in which the dual control model, as we interpreted it using AAUP documents (see especially AAUP 1966; and Corson 1960), would predict primary administrative responsibility and limited or no faculty involvement: (1) selection of deans, (2) control of replacement positions for departing senior faculty, (3) control of replacement positions for departing junior faculty, (4) determination of departmental budgets, (5) decisions about program consolidations and closings, and (6) determination of faculty course loads. They included three decisions in which the dual control model would predict primary faculty responsibility and limited or no administrative involvement: (1) addition of new courses to the curriculum, (2) determination of program emphases at the departmental level, and (3) hiring of departmental support staff. They also included four decisions in which the dual control model would, as we interpret it, predict joint faculty-administrative responsibility: (1) selection of department chairs, (2) evaluation of faculty for promotions, (3) determination of new college- or university-wide academic initiatives, and (4) planning for new interdisciplinary programs. The surveys asked respondents to mark "at which level or levels decisions are primarily made," and it noted that respondents should mark as many levels as apply. The surveys emphasized that respondents should mark only those actors who shared "a primary role" in decision making.

In the responses to the 2000 survey we found nine of the thirteen decisions met our liberal fit criterion for adherence to the dual control model of governance (i.e., at least 50 percent of respondents identifying actors consistent with the expected pattern). Only adding new courses, determining course loads, allocating department budgets, and selection of chairs failed to conform to our predictions concerning the primary actors involved in decision making, following the dual control model. The dual control model provided a still better fit for the 2012 data. Eleven of the thirteen decisions fit our expectations using the 50 percent fit criterion. More than half of respondents listed only administrators as the primary decision makers on all six of the decisions expected to be decisions made by administrators. Two of the three expected faculty-only decisions met the criterion, as did three of the four expected joint responsibility decisions (see table 7.2).[17]

TABLE 7.2. Predictions and Results for 13 Academic Decisions by Year

	2000	2012
A. Predicted as Faculty-Only Primary		
Dept. Program Emphases[a] [†]	Faculty-only (54%)	Faculty-only (65%)
Hiring Dept. Staff	Faculty-only (50%)	**Faculty-only (46%)**
Adding New Courses	**Joint Resp. (49%)**	Faculty-only (55%)
B. Predicted as Administration-Only Primary		
Selection of Deans	Admin-only (78%)	Admin-only (81%)
Replacement of Sr. Faculty	Admin-only (59%)	Admin-only (69%)
Program Consolidations/Closings	Admin-only (56%)	Admin-only (62%)
Replacement of Jr. Faculty	Admin-only (57%)	Admin-only (68%)
Course Loads	**Admin-only (48%)**	Admin-only (60%)
Dept. Budgets[†]	**Joint Resp. (46%)**	Admin-only (57%)
C. Predicted as Joint Responsibility Primary		
Evaluation for Promotion	Joint Resp. (63%)	Joint Resp. (57%)
Planning Interdisciplinary	Joint Resp. (58%)	Joint Resp. (52%)
New Initiatives	Joint Resp. (57%)	Joint Resp. (50%)
Selection of Chairs	**Admin-only (53%)**	**Admin-only (61%)**

Source: *Colleges & Universities 2000* surveys. See Apkarian et al. 2014.

[a] Bold type indicates items in which responses varied from those predicted by the dual control model or failed to meet the 50 percent criterion.

[†] $p < 0.10$ (two-tailed)

By a strict measure of manager-only control—twelve or thirteen decisions made exclusively by administrators—only 1 percent of institutions could be characterized as managerially controlled in either year. Less stringent measures may be a more realistic guide to the incidence of manager-only control. In 2000 slightly more than one-fifth of the provosts (21 percent) said that administrators only were involved in eight or more of the thirteen decisions. In 2012 slightly more than one-fourth of provosts (27 percent) said that administrators only were involved in this many decisions. The change of 6 percent over the twelve-year period was *not* statistically significant at $p < 0.05$. When we raised the criterion for managerial control to nine decisions or more made by administrators only, the percentages in the managerially controlled category fell to 14 percent and 17 percent, respectively, and again the change over time was not statistically significant. On the bases of these findings, we characterized the support for the managerial control model as "very limited." Traditions of shared governance continued to matter for most provosts. By contrast, governing boards were only rarely mentioned (less than 2 percent of the time) as primary actors in any of these decisions. These decisions evidently did not rise to the level of board review at most institutions.

Of course, a study like this has limitations. It investigates provosts' cognitive maps of how decision making occurs, and these cognitive maps do not necessarily correspond to the ways decisions are actually made on campus. How one evaluates the data depends on how honest one feels provosts can be about matters of governance. The faculty may see decision making in a very different way. But the patterns of institutional variation we found certainly conform to expectations based on the documents that first attempted to define "shared governance" for university professors. In both years, liberal arts colleges were likely to have more areas of faculty participation in governance. Liberal arts colleges style themselves as communities, and this expectation requires that community members participate actively in governance. Faculty members in religiously affiliated institutions, perhaps believing in the just principles of established authorities, were more likely to teach in managerially controlled institutions. Administrators of large universities depend on "buy-in" from many actors, and the participation of multiple groups was common on large campuses on a wider variety of decisions than elsewhere; this was especially true on large research university campuses. Research university leaders become experts at building consensus through the formation of committees, working groups, and task forces. Through skillful delegation, administrators are able to harness at least small amounts of work effort from faculty colleagues, and by doing so they gain valuable allies for projects that may find resistance in some quarters on campus.

The Fragmented Faculty

The circumstances of the faculty affected their capacity to play a role in governance—and how big a role they could play. Near the beginning of the period, using interviews and 1984 survey data from the Carnegie Foundation for the Advancement of Teaching, the higher education scholar Burton Clark characterized the American academy as based on radically different arrangements of work—from "virtual think-tank settings at the top of the institutional hierarchy in such resource-rich fields as physics and biology to virtual secondary school conditions at the bottom where general teaching in introductory courses suppresses specialization" (1987, xxvii). Those at the top of this structure could exercise considerable leverage, those at the bottom little or none.

Clark identified institutional prestige and academic discipline as the structural bases for the "polymorphism" of the profession already evident at that time. These two structural coordinates together determined the central tendencies that most clearly divided academics: the amount of time spent on research as opposed to the amount of time spent teaching. Professors in resource-rich disciplines and located in resource-rich institutions spent little time teaching—and the most senior among them frequently only taught graduate students. At research universities, scientists and engineers might teach two or three courses a year, social scientists four courses a year, and humanities and arts professors five courses, with increasingly heavy emphasis on general courses for undergraduates rather than specialized courses for advanced undergraduates and graduate students.

Clark found little that unified the academic profession. In interviews with 170 faculty members drawn from six disciplines and diverse institutions, Clark's team found that intellectual values were the closest to defining an ideological core of the profession. Professors from all ranks, institutions, and fields spoke of "reaching for answers, "problem-solving," "intellectual curiosity," and "striving for understanding." Statements about the centrality of "intellectual honesty" followed closely. Clark's respondents emphasized their commitment to honest research, teaching, and advice and their abhorrence of plagiarism, falsification of data, and abuses of professorial power. But the differences in the working conditions of professors, he concluded, overwhelmed these common value commitments: "Diversification of teaching loads and tasks is a fundamental aspect of the institutional differentiation of the higher education system. It is also a primary component of the meaning of hierarchy" (89).

ACCELERATED POLYMORPHISM

The separation of management during the period was accompanied by the continuing fragmentation of the academic labor force. Differentiation along the lines of professorial rank, disciplinary status, institutional location, and job responsibilities were primary indicators of who held and lacked power among the faculty. The trends Clark identified accelerated, and new structures such as differentiated salary scales and teaching-only tracks developed to accommodate and rationalize the fracturing of the faculty. The shift from

professional organization to unionization at lower-tier institutions, anticipated by Clark, continued to be appealing for much of the period at public
regional universities and community colleges, and the steady shift in hiring from tenure track to non–tenure track was the most important development of all.

Rank

Full professors gained power during the period, and this was particularly
true of the most distinguished among them. They were disproportionately
the ones to whom university administrators looked for support and advice.
Distinguished senior professors were capable of decamping to other institutions and therefore required attention. Assistant professors had no
clout at all—they were not yet vested in any way—and it was a rare associate professor who had it. Salary data provide one indicator of fragmentation
by rank. Salary data collected by the American Association of University
Professors (AAUP) show a steady constant-dollar rise in the compensation
of full professors through the recession period when gains plateaued. The
gains for assistant and associate professors were much weaker, and those
of instructors and lecturers were all but nonexistent (Finkelstein, Conley,
and Schuster 2016, 328).

Discipline

Hierarchies of intellectual prestige align with perceptions about the cognitive demands for success in the various fields and the extent to which the
fields are producing important new fundamental discoveries. Physics and
mathematics, the heroic fields of the Atomic Age, once dominated the hierarchy of intellectual prestige, but molecular and cell biology rose in esteem
during the period because of the fundamental discoveries they generated
about life processes. Economics, the discipline closest to the natural sciences
in quantitative rigor, ranked highest in intellectual prestige in the social
sciences (Fourcade, Ollion, and Algon 2015). A humanities discipline like
philosophy also scored high in intellectual prestige because of its emphasis
on abstraction and rigorous logic.

The second and newer hierarchy was based on how much graduates in
different fields could expect to earn following graduation. This new hierarchy reflected the greater engagement of the university with the world
outside its walls and the rise of a market logic that affected administrators
and students alike. Here the professional fields of medicine, finance, law,
and engineering ranked higher than the natural sciences, while fields like

child development, counseling psychology, social welfare, and education ranked at or near the bottom. Although faculty members remained subject to the hierarchies of intellectual prestige—both disciplinary and personal—undergraduate students were attuned to the hierarchy of marketability and tended to consider it the far more important of the two.

The disciplines shaped the demeanor of faculty members and students because of their associations with the distinctive work settings students could expect to encounter following graduation. Carrie Yang Costello (2005) provided an illuminating picture of differences in the socialization of lawyers and social workers at the same prestigious West Coast research university campus. The soon-to-be lawyers were all-business. They dressed professionally, came to class prepared, and competed with one another openly for professorial recognition. They were not kind to students who failed to meet these norms. Their professors rarely allowed their political or personal beliefs to enter their teaching; they focused on the issues presented by the cases under discussion. By contrast, the social work students dressed casually, often in blue jeans, supported one another emotionally in class, embraced those who discussed personal problems or arrived to class late, and did not expect perfect answers or high levels of advanced preparation for class. Their professors occasionally wandered from topics to engage their personal feelings about political events and to emphasize that they were on the side of the disadvantaged rather than the privileged.

The practice of differentiating salary scales by a field's marketability outside of academe, in its infancy during the 1980s, became an increasingly accepted practice at research universities. Higher salary scales were introduced for faculties of business, engineering, law, and medicine and often extended to cognate fields such as computer science and economics. Average salaries also varied by the extent to which fields required quantitative skills and had ample opportunities to obtain external funding, though these differences paled in relation to perceptions about private sector marketability. The "community of fate" reinforced by relative equity in pay across disciplines dissolved at research universities, though it retained power at doctoral-granting and master's-granting regional universities, as well as liberal arts colleges.[18]

Institutional Locations

Prestigious institutions have more powerful faculties because these faculty members are in demand by other institutions. Job offers from prestigious institutions provide the necessary leverage, and faculty at elite institutions can more easily generate these offers. In addition, the leading departments reproduce network ties between themselves by ensuring that their top graduates are hired by other leading institutions (Burris 2004). Of course, the boost provided by location in a highly ranked department has to be accompanied by highly cited research output in order for these advantages to be realized in practice.

Salary data confirm the importance of institutional locations. Salaries at research and doctoral institutions increased faster than those at nondoctoral institutions, and the gap between private and public institutions grew considerably, particularly at the full professor level. In 1980, full professors at private and public doctoral institutions were paid on average nearly the same. By 2013–14, full professors at private institutions averaged more than $160,000 in annual salary, while those working at public institutions averaged just over $120,000 (AAUP 2014, table 4; Clark 1987, 332–33).

Job Responsibilities

Research is the foundation for faculty power because it provides the prestige on which institutions count and it gives the faculty leverage over administration owing to the capacity of researchers to decamp to other institutions: "Research is what makes the university something that is not replicable by off-the-shelf courses. [Research] also makes it impossible for [the university] bureaucracy to take over completely" (Clark 1987, 100). At enrollment-driven institutions where the great majority of faculty members do little or no research, professional leverage is limited and institutions become, in Clark's words, "client-driven."

Yet most full-time university faculty members spent little time on research during the week. In 2013–14, the modal university faculty member who responded to the Higher Education Research Institute survey said s/he spent 1–4 hours per week on research. The majority of research output was carried by the 30 percent of faculty members who said they spent more than 12 hours per week on research—and particularly by the one-sixth who said they spent more than 20 hours per week on research (Eagan et al. 2014, 33). Some high-grant departments were renowned for the absence of professors from undergraduate classrooms. The chair of a highly ranked psychology department told me, with considerable pride, that virtually none of his senior faculty colleagues taught undergraduates. In a study that covered the years 1992–99, James Fairweather (2005) demonstrated that hours spent in the classroom were significantly and negatively related to pay.

The Academic Proletariat

Aware of these trends, Burton Clark (1987) prophesied that the future professoriate might look more like that typical of medical school faculties in
the mid-1980s—that is to say, a welter of distinct and overlapping categories
of labor with tenured professors as a small, privileged minority. In medical
schools, regular faculty lines were rare except in biomedical science departments. Instead, one saw research professors who did no teaching; full-time
researchers working on grants; visiting assistant professors; clinical teaching faculty (who also took patients through their personal or group practices) with medical school appointments; part-time clinical teaching faculty
without regular appointments; residents who engaged in some instructional
activities; and staff members who organized clinical studies, thereby combining administrative, instructional, and research roles.[19] In some respects,
Clark's prophecy was realized during period. The relative size of the privileged group shrank, and new labor categories proliferated both in research
and teaching capacities, and in roles that mixed the two.

POSTDOCTORAL RESEARCHERS

Postdoctoral fellows were the most common type of full-time research
worker—and they were particularly common in biomedical and life science
labs where funding sources tended to be plentiful. The number of postdocs
grew by 150 percent between 2000 and 2015 alone, up to 40,000 individuals. The low salaries and greater experience of postdocs led many principal
investigators to prefer them as employees over the graduate students they
were nominally responsible for training. Postdocs contributed greatly to
the research productivity of science teams; much of the prolific output of
academic science during the period can be attributed to them (Cantwell
and Taylor 2015).

But postdocs who were aiming for academic careers found it hard to
get off the term-employment track. About 10 percent of the 40,000 postdocs in 2013 had been in their positions for six years or more—inspiring the
dispiriting coinage "permadoc" (Powell 2015). Postdocs were typically hired
solely as research workers, though some who coveted academic appointments volunteered to teach in order to gain experience. Some labs hired
long-term contract employees with specialized technical skills, and research
centers found ways to keep productive full-time researchers on their payrolls

through soft money, endowment income, and/or the acquiescence of senior administrators in support for long-term contracts.

Lecturers and Part-time Instructors

The low rungs of the teaching force were composed of two distinct strata: full-time lecturers and part-time instructors. Postdocs were typically grant supported and, as such, did not greatly affect the institutional bottom line. But lecturers and instructors did affect the institutional bottom line—in a very positive way. Indeed, a good case can be made that the growth of senior faculty salaries and perquisites was built, in large part, on the savings accrued through the employment of non-tenure-track faculty.

Full-time lecturers were hired on term contracts of varying length. These lecturers taught many more courses per term than the regular faculty—as many as four or five (but more often fewer than that). They accounted for 20 to 25 percent of the instructional force at four-year colleges and universities, with little change in their proportion over time. Some were given the title "visiting assistant professor." These people typically attempted to build research profiles that could catapult them into tenure-track positions while teaching on term appointments. Full-time lecturers were very common in mathematics, English, and foreign language departments where thousands of undergraduates passed through required introductory courses. Large professional schools of business and education also provided disproportionate employment opportunities for full-time lecturers, as did natural science and engineering departments in which many tenured and tenure-track faculty members were on leave and/or buying out teaching time with funds from grants.[20]

But the seismic change of the period was the growth of a large academic proletariat of part-time instructors, or adjuncts, as they were also known. By 2015, this class of part-timers, though it remained largely invisible to the public, claimed nearly half the instructional labor force in U.S. colleges and universities (Finkelstein, Conley, and Schuster 2016, 276). By 2000, the part-timers were the largest single category of academic workers, surpassing tenured and tenure-track professors, and by 2013, they represented more than two out of five in the instructional workforce. Among four-year colleges and universities, they were particularly prominent in private institutions, where they represented about half the labor force in 2013; by contrast, they represented fewer than 30 percent at public research universities (Finkelstein, Conley, and Schuster 2016, 61–62). But even at public research universities—the institutions most resistant to change—if full-time lecturers and graduate student instructors were added into the mix, fewer than half of faculty members were tenured or on tenure track by 2013 (ibid.).

The Plight of Part-Time Instructors

Because of their importance to the restructuring of labor in universities, a deeper dive is warranted into the circumstances and outcomes associated with the explosive growth of part-time instructors.

Part-timers came in a wide variety of types and with a variety of motivations. In professional schools, most were people who had professional practices or were retired from them and enjoyed the interchange with students when they had time to teach a course in their specialty area. These people were sometimes awarded the title "professor of practice" or "clinical professor." These experienced professionals added a desirable connection to "the real world." In arts and sciences, some part-timers fit the same mold; others were people who had unrelated professional or avocational interests—or family responsibilities—and preferred to supplement their incomes or home responsibilities with part-time piecework. A few were retirees or people on phased retirement who were trying out a potential new career. Most, however, were working toward more permanent statuses by teaching as many courses as possible at their preferred campuses. Most part-timers worked at a single campus and taught only a course or two each term (CAW 2012). The most discouraging conditions were suffered by the "freeway flyers" who pieced together an income by teaching multiple courses at multiple institutions. As one of these drive-by scholars put it, people like him "worked in the basement" of the great house of academe (Professor X 2011).

Working Conditions and Wages

The best source of data on adjunct faculty is the Coalition for the Academic Workforce (CAW) survey of 2010. The survey is far from perfect. It was not based on a sampling design; any academic worker who heard about it from one of the twenty-six sponsoring organizations was free to respond. The survey undersampled minorities and those teaching in the social and natural sciences while oversampling English and professional school instructors. It was fielded at the height of the recession when many colleges and universities were laying off staff, perhaps explaining the low number of courses most respondents reported teaching during the previous term. Nevertheless, the almost twenty thousand valid responses are the largest window we have onto the experiences of part-time academic workers.

According to respondents to the CAW survey, it is a myth that most part-timers preferred the flexibility of teaching piecework. Three-quarters of part-timers who responded to the survey said they were looking for, or would soon be looking for, tenure-track appointments. These were people who wanted a career in institutions that were failing to produce nearly the proportion of regular career paths necessary to accommodate them. Quite a few found themselves running into roadblocks with few skills that were transferable to other milieu. Over half of respondents said they had been teaching part-time for more than six years.

Throughout the period, their pay was miserable. According to CAW respondents, a typical course in 2010 paid about $2,500, up to about $3,400 in research universities. Those who could cobble together as many as eight courses in a year were still earning only $20,000 on average from their teaching pay. Even at the research university rate, an eight-course teaching load did not graze the $30,000 mark in 2010. Most supplemented their teaching income from other sources, but even so nearly three out of five of the CAW respondents reported personal incomes under $35,000 a year, an income significantly lower than beginning schoolteachers in most communities. "It is very poor pay," said one. "I have a daughter who is making more money and she is an exterminator" (quoted in Clark 1987, 206).

Working conditions were often equally appalling. Just over 10 percent of the CAW respondents reported access to health care benefits. Only 9 percent reported having private office space. Just 19 percent reported regular salary increases; only 16 percent reported tuition assistance; 12 percent travel support; and 11 percent access to institutional research grants. More than half said they shared computers with others, and just over half said they had a telephone available in their offices. Almost two-thirds said they had no secretarial assistance (CAW 2012). In some cases, adjuncts were not given access to library facilities or even course management systems.

The reasons are clear why college and university administrators went on adjunct hiring sprees during the period. Part-timers were much less expensive to hire than regular faculty, and they provided colleges and universities with great flexibility in responding to the ups and downs of undergraduate enrollments. The supply was also there; departments had a large reserve army of candidates looking for teaching jobs from which to choose. But the conditions that universities asked them to work under were often deplorable.

Problems of Instructional Quality

The costs to institutional integrity were also great, even if these costs were rarely discussed. Beginning in the 2000s, a string of studies documented the weaker teaching practices of part-time instructors as compared to tenured and tenure-track faculty members. Analysis of teaching practices in the 1994 National Study of Postsecondary Faculty showed that although many individual part-time instructors were excellent teachers, as a group they were significantly more likely to rely on multiple choice exams and less likely to use time-consuming assessments such as essays or term research papers. They were less likely to require multiple drafts of written work, to encourage oral presentations, or to employ student evaluations of one another's work as a learning device (Baldwin and Wawrzynski 2011). Part-time instructors were less accessible and less scholarly than regular faculty members (Schuster 2003; Schuster and Finkelstein 2006). They were much less likely to use email or websites to communicate with students (Baldwin and Wawrzynski 2011). They spent less time preparing for class, engaged in fewer interactions with students, had lower expectations for student performance, challenged students less often, and were less likely to use active and collaborative teaching techniques (Umbach 2007).

Many of these studies showed negative correlations between taking a high proportion of courses taught by part-time instructors and retention of students, both into second year and through graduation (Eagen and Jaeger 2008; Ehrenberg and Zhang 2005; Harrington and Schibik 2001; cf. Bettinger and Long 2005). The fault could hardly be placed on part-timers. Paid poorly, lacking access to facilities, often juggling a high teaching load, rarely mentored, and frequently taken for granted, they had every incentive to work as efficiently as possible. By contrast, the research evidence suggests that full-time lecturers followed teaching practices that were much more in line with those typical of regular faculty than those typical of part-timers (Baldwin and Wawrzynski 2011; Hagedorn, Perrakis, and Maxwell 2002; Umbach 2007).

UNIONIZATION

For a time, it seemed that collective bargaining would sweep through the lower rungs of academe to halt the worst abuses of hiring off the tenure track. In 1977, the national center studying faculty unionization reported

343 institutions with bargaining agents representing more than 100,000 faculty members (National Center 1977a, 1977b). In 1980, the Supreme Court's *Yeshiva* decision led to the decertification of many bargaining units among faculty members at private colleges on the grounds that their responsibilities included managerial work (for example, of teaching assistants) and therefore did not qualify for consideration under the National Labor Relations Board.[21] But public sector organizing continued and gained steam. By 1994 bargaining agents represented more than 242,000 faculty members on 1,057 campuses, about 22 percent of full-time faculty (and 26 percent of full- and part-time faculty). Through a close analysis of bargaining contracts, Gary Rhoades (1998) demonstrated that negotiated contracts were not antithetical to merit considerations and most included provisions for merit pay.

Yet the triumph of unionization never materialized. A 2005 AFL-CIO poll of full-time faculty at non-unionized colleges and universities showed limited support for unionization; a majority of faculty respondents said that they should have an association to represent them, but only 37 percent favored unions as representatives. One respondent commented, "Unionization does not fit intellectual activity very well" (quoted in Clay 2007, 30). This was, I suspect, the nub of the matter. Intellectual activity implies that the teacher/scholar is making independent and creative judgments about materials and their presentation. This accords poorly with the unions' focus on contractually stated job functions. Because their work requires expertise, faculty members like to think of themselves as professionals, even when their pay and work conditions are not commensurate with those of other professionals.[22]

A 2007 report estimated that 317,000 faculty members and 57,000 graduate student employees were represented by collective bargaining agents (National Center 2007). This amounted to the same proportion (26 percent) of faculty that had been represented a decade earlier but a higher proportion of graduate students. In 2012, the same organization estimated that the total of represented faculty members and graduate students continued to grow in absolute numbers over the five-year period, ticking up by 14 and 11 percent, respectively. But the broader population of faculty grew faster. The proportion of unionized faculty fell to 23.5 percent in 2012 and the proportion of unionized graduate students remained stable at just over 2 percent (calculated from National Center 2007, 2013 and NCES 2016b, tables 290 and 303.80). Collective bargaining continued to be more appealing at the bottom of the hierarchy, with 42 percent of public community college faculty represented by collective bargaining agents in 2012—and sharp drop-offs in four-year institutions as one moved up the prestige hierarchy (Finkelstein, Conley, and Schuster 2016, 305).[23]

The weak outcomes of unionization help explain the plateau. For adjunct faculty members, union membership had a demonstrated value. Although their wages were shockingly low whether they were unionized or not, adjuncts earned slightly higher per-course pay on unionized campuses than on otherwise similar campuses without unions. Health and retirement benefits were also more likely to be offered on unionized campuses (CAW 2012). But researchers found no statistically significant wage gains for unionized "regular" full-time faculty on four-year college campuses (Hendrick, Henson, and Krieg 2011; Wickens 2008), belying the fundamental promise of faculty unions that collective action would lead to improved wages and working conditions for those who joined.

OBVIOUS BENEFITS, HIDDEN COSTS

Economists such as Ronald Ehrenberg (2012) counseled that administrators should weigh the cost savings associated with hiring adjuncts against the retention losses of exposing undergraduates to a large number of part-time instructors. Although undoubtedly correct from a purely economic perspective, this trade-off could be interpreted differently: as short-changing students and risking the reputation institutions claimed they placed on educational quality.

University administrators have saved large sums by substituting part-time labor for full-time tenure-track lines. In research universities these savings have helped fund start-up packages, lab renovations, and departments that require subsidies. They have also been used to grow the size of the administrative staffs. The widespread employment of part-time faculty to teach lower-division undergraduate courses has materially reduced the quality of education in most of the institutions employing large numbers of part-timers, contributing to the crisis of limited learning during the undergraduate years. This hiring has also indirectly jeopardized the future well-being of graduate students who naively think that full-time jobs will be waiting for them at the end of their doctoral studies.

The time for administrative soul-searching and decisive action on the issues involving adjunct faculty was, by the end of the period, long overdue. The reforms that administrators could consider include the following: converting as many positions as possible into full-time ones with potential security of employment; reducing the use of adjunct instructors in introductory courses where first impressions of a field matter greatly; providing adequate office space, facilities, and library access; providing professional development opportunities such as travel grants; and encouraging departments to treat adjunct faculty members as "part of the family" by inviting them to departmental colloquia and social events. The architects of future accountability schemes might also consider including information about the proportion of classes taught by part-time instructors as part of required institutional profiles (see also the discussion in Baldwin and Chronister 2001).

8

Focus on the Classroom

In the next two chapters I take up the principal threats to the continued expansion and prominence of U.S. colleges and universities.[1] I devote the current chapter to the weakness that strikes at the core of academe's objectives and makes the triumph of online alternatives more plausible. The issue has been diplomatically described as "underachievement" in undergraduate education (Bok 2006), but it could be described equally well as the failure to inculcate professional standards and expectations for college teachers. I will analyze why the disparate efforts during the period to reform undergraduate teaching and to make colleges accountable for student learning failed to transform college classrooms. I will also show why the new sciences of learning have the potential to create the more powerful learning environments that earlier reformers failed to produce. In chapter 9, I discuss other major challenges to the U.S. higher education system: rising costs, online competition, and controversies over permissible speech.

I do not want to overstate the threat these challenges pose. The top one hundred or so research universities and the top thirty or so liberal arts colleges are in no danger from those who hope to disrupt the system; they are strong enough to weather any conceivable threat. Some other institutions, including "brand-name" religiously affiliated colleges and universities, such as Brigham Young University and the University of Notre Dame, can count on supporters who will not allow them to decline, and so can other campuses dear to alums. But a sizable proportion of poorly funded four-year public colleges and universities are at risk, not necessarily for closing their doors but rather for becoming industrialized online course distributors stripped of a campus culture and intellectual aspirations. At risk also are hundreds of low-enrollment, low-endowment private colleges.

Academic skill development is no longer considered the only important aim of undergraduate education, and some do not consider it the most important aim. In recent years respected social scientists have argued that the primary purpose of college is to provide a grounds for students to develop social network ties (Stevens, Armstrong, and Arum 2008) or to socialize them into the "posture of actorhood" (Meyer 2008). Others have focused on what they see as a rough equality among the multiple forms of engagement that undergraduates can pursue—academic, cocurricular, or civic engagement (Douglass and Thomson 2017). These ways of seeing the undergraduate experience reflect real changes in what students and their parents want out of college. Students and their parents tend to express greater interest in what happens outside than what happens inside the classroom (Clotfelter 2017, 179–85). One can take student-led tours of Ivy League institutions, as I have done, and hear florid, enthusiastically delivered testimonials to the opportunities that lie ahead in student clubs and organizations but hardly a word about what happens in classrooms.

In previous work I have argued that colleges' responsibilities for student development should ideally go beyond the classroom to include contributions to their personal development, interpersonal skill development, civic engagement, and preparation for economically secure employment (see Brint 2015b). At the same time, it seems implausible to me that colleges would want to argue for equality between academic and nonacademic forms of engagement. Other organizations from Toastmaster's to the Red Cross could perhaps do as well in nonacademic arenas of student development. But we do need colleges and universities to help students analyze and question complex texts, compose persuasive arguments, understand scientific concepts, sift evidence to come to conclusions, and weigh alternative explanations, as well as for many other academic skills that educators have reason to expect will lead to clearer and more effective thought.

Even so, it is a good question whether students' fates really depend on the development of their academic skills. I have already observed that many employers say they value qualities such as interpersonal skills, collaboration with peers, and responsiveness to authority as much as they value cognitive skills. Not all studies have found a strong relationship between academic gains in college and early adult earnings (see, e.g., Arum and Roksa 2014). Nevertheless, most of the evidence suggests that cognitive skills and economic well-being are related. A 2012 OECD program tested young adults (ages sixteen to thirty-four) on literacy, numeracy, and computer-aided problem-solving skills. Scores at a proficiency level were strongly associated with higher wages for young adults, with an average 22 percent gain in income for every standard deviation change in combined literacy and numeracy skills (OECD 2016). The results are compatible at the individual level with national-level findings on rates of GDP growth. Countries in which students score high on the OECD's Programme for International Student Assessment (PISA) tests at age fifteen tend to have significantly stronger growth rates in later years than countries in which students on average score low, even after controls are introduced to account for potentially confounding influences on GDP growth (Hanushek and Woessmann 2011, 160–87).

Not all successful countries require intensive periods of study during the college years. Japan, for example, is well known to demand little of college students who pass a pleasant, nearly study-free period between the intense competition of high school preparation and business employment. But unlike Japanese students most U.S. college students cannot claim that rigorous secondary school experiences have prepared them for experiences that require high levels of literacy, numeracy, or problem-solving skills after college. To the extent that higher education institutions are failing to contribute sufficiently to students' cognitive development, they can be considered to be failing in a fundamental way.

Students' Declining Commitment to Study

Concerns about undergraduate students' educational experiences go back many decades, but strong empirical evidence of the shortcomings of undergraduate education began to emerge only in the 2000s. The 2003 National Assessment of Adult Literacy showed that only 30 percent of college graduates could accurately interpret two competing editorials or make accurate inferences from a graph relating age, exercise, and blood pressure (Kutner et al. 2007).[2] A study of the analytical and critical thinking skills of 2,400 college students by Richard Arum and Josipa Roksa (2011) concluded that nearly half of the students studied made no significant gains in their reasoning capacity between freshman and the middle of sophomore year. A subsequent follow-up showed that more than one-third of these students made no statistically significant gains between freshman and the end of their senior year (Arum, Roksa, and Cho 2012). The study can be criticized; students had no clear incentives to put out maximum effort on the test. But the study has been replicated using alternative tests of analytical and critical thinking, with remarkably similar results (Pascarella et al. 2011). The aforementioned 2012 OECD assessment of young adults' skills also yielded an avalanche of disturbing information about the state of Americans' skills relative to those of young adults in the rest of the developed world. Americans ranked number 16 of 22 nations on the literacy test, and they tied for last place on both the numeracy and computer-aided problem-solving tests. Nor did the country's top achievers rank high internationally. The 90th percentile of scorers ranked sixteenth compared to their international counterparts; those with bachelor's degrees, twentieth; and holders of postgraduate degrees, nineteenth.

The social relations of learning in college classrooms help explain these disappointing test results. The economists Philip Babcock and Mindy Marks (2010) found a secular decline in study time from the early 1960s to the mid-2000s. In the early 1960s, students reported studying and attending class approximately forty hours per week. By the mid-2000s, study time had fallen to approximately twenty-seven hours per week. Babcock and Marks found comparable declines at every selectivity level, in every major, and among every demographic group, albeit from markedly different starting points (see figure 8.1). My own work with Allison Cantwell on time use among University of California students found that one-fifth of those responding to a census survey fielded in 2012 said they spent less than eighteen hours a week in class or studying for class. Another one-fifth reported that they read half or less of assigned reading for their classes. And one-quarter reported rarely, if ever, participating in class or being in touch with their instructors (Brint and Cantwell 2014). The findings were alarming, in part, because we know that more conscientious students are the ones more likely fill out a lengthy survey. These studies suggest that either teachers are not requiring much of their students or students are finding ways to minimize the time they spend on class with the acquiescence of their teachers.

The failure of instructors and administrators to attend to weaknesses in undergraduate teaching and learning can be considered the Achilles' heel of U.S. universities. I will focus on three persistent weaknesses: (1) teaching that encourages student passivity, (2) the limited accountability instructors expect of students, and (3) teaching for rote memorization rather than for understanding and mastery. These weaknesses are often interrelated as inadequately trained instructors dominate classroom air time without providing opportunities for students to interact with one another around course materials, fail to build in mechanisms to ensure that students are prepared

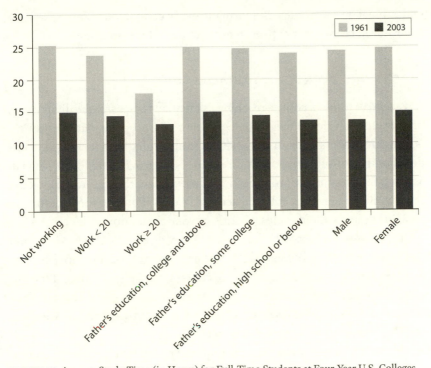

FIGURE 8.1. Average Study Time (in Hours) for Full-Time Students at Four-Year U.S. Colleges by Work Status, Parental Education, and Gender, 1961 and 2003.
Source: Babcock and Marks 2010, figure 2.

for and paying attention in class, and orient their courses toward an emphasis on what students need to know for tests rather than a mastery-level understanding of subject matter.

These problems do not, of course, plague every classroom. Expert and impassioned teachers such as Columbia English professor Andrew Delbanco have described the epiphanies that occur in discussions that "envelop the mind in multiple perspectives" and, quoting William James, lead to the "ideal vanishing point towards which we imagine that all our temporary truths will someday converge" (2012, 60). The opportunities for creating challenging, intensely engaging courses are at their maximum in small seminars in which students encounter skilled teachers and are inspired to be prepared—or feel they must be prepared for fear of disappointing their instructors and fellow students. Such experiences are the norm in doctoral education. The educational appeal of the country's best liberal arts colleges and private research universities is that they can provide a comparatively high number of these educational opportunities. But virtually every campus can point to at least a few dozen classes that approach or meet this educational ideal.

DIMENSIONS OF INSTRUCTIONAL EFFORT

It is useful to think of college teaching as involving at least three dimensions of instructional effort. One is to adequately convey subject matter. Another is to help students make the transition from inadequate to adequate understandings of subject matter. The third is to provide sufficient rigor in assignments to produce growth. One cannot expect that rigor will look the same at elite colleges as at broad access colleges, but every instructor can push his or her students at least a little beyond their comfort levels.

There are good reasons for doing so. Many years ago, Karen Miller and her colleagues (1985) measured the substantive complexity of schoolwork by examining the intellectual difficulty of courses, the length of time it took to complete work for them, and the complexity of out-of-class projects. They found that students who experienced greater substantive complexity in their work and less detailed supervision by teachers scored higher on "educational self-direction." These students were required to use more initiative, engage in deeper thought, and exercise more independent judgment. Unfortunately, the college-for-all system provides these deep-learning opportunities for only a minority of students.

University administrators can take their share of the responsibility for the limited learning that so often occurs in college classrooms. It is, after all, the institutional decision makers who have reduced the ratio of instructional staff per student and increased the ratio of administrative staff per student. They are also the ones responsible for bringing so many adjunct instructors into classrooms without providing them with adequate pay, working conditions, or supervision. The studies of the economist John Bound and his colleagues underscore the extent to which gaps between access and graduation are the result of institutional factors such as large class sizes and insufficient feedback on course work (see, e.g., Bound, Lovenheim, and Turner 2010). But the problems go beyond the "graduation gap"; the "throughput" models used to measure efficiency by charting rates of graduation and years to graduation do not capture anything about whether graduating students are learning skills of value while they are on campus. They are about input and output and nothing in between.

It is here that we see a fundamental tension between the university's value commitments and its financial drivers. Its desires to add value to students through effective teaching practices are consistently challenged by its financial incentives to maximize and optimize resources. The "competing logics" framework I developed in chapter 1 suggests that this tension can also be interpreted as a conflict between the logic of academic professionalism, which should embrace instructional quality (though it does not always), and the market logic of enrollment expansion. One reason for believing that undergraduate education will continue to underachieve is that institutional survival and well-being are inevitably more important to university administrators than difficult-to-measure values like educational quality. It follows that practices associated with student satisfaction will take precedence over practices that are related to educational quality but are not as closely associated with student satisfaction.

These administrative priorities do not necessarily create insuperable obstacles to the improvement of undergraduate teaching and learning. A robust research literature has developed on techniques that work to aid student learning. A much stronger teaching and learning environment is consequently on the horizon, if colleges and university faculty members have the will to adopt approaches that lead to better results for more students. Many are already doing so. Campuses such as Alverno College in Wisconsin, the University of Maryland-Baltimore County (UMBC), and the University of Texas-El Paso (UTEP) have gained reputations for teaching excellence over the years, either by focusing on rigorous assessments of student learning (the Alverno case) or through the extra efforts they have made to build scholars and scientists from among socioeconomically disadvantaged students (the UMBC and UTEP cases). University administrators can do their part by providing the resources to help faculty members become expert teachers and to make potentially transformative experiences like undergraduate research, study abroad, and skills-based learning communities available to more students.

THE CONTRADICTIONS OF POSTWAR ACADEME

By the mid-1960s, the trend toward populating academe with professional researchers was so noticeable that Christopher Jencks and David Riesman coined the term "the academic revolution" to mark what they assumed would be a permanent turning point in the shift of the profession from teaching to research (Jencks and Riesman 1968). For research university professors, the requirement to meet the exacting standards of colleagues evaluating articles and books warranted careful training; half-awake, half-interested undergraduates sitting in the back rows of large lecture halls were another matter.

In graduate training programs of the period, students were not required to demonstrate skills in pedagogy during their studies for the PhD, or understanding of the relation between types of pedagogy and subject matter content, or understanding of the aims or purposes of education. Rather, those who were not fortunate or promising enough to obtain research assistantships were thrown into teaching discussion sections without preparation, under the presumption that anyone smart enough to be in graduate school was smart enough to run a discussion section. For most would-be professors, teaching was an amateur activity, performed with limited regard to effectiveness, by people whose real training was for something else entirely.

Many observers within the university welcomed this era of the research-centered professoriate. For Clark Kerr, the new multiversity served the nation by providing greater access, scientific and scholarly progress, and expert advice to every constituency in its state and region. But, Kerr acknowledged, undergraduate teaching suffered:

> There seems to be a "point of no return" after which research, consulting, [and] graduate instruction become so absorbing that faculty efforts can no longer be concentrated on undergraduate instruction as they once were. (1963, 65)

Kerr provided no solution to the "cruel paradox that a superior faculty results in an inferior concern for undergraduate teaching," though he hoped that an escape from the paradox could eventually be found (ibid.).[3]

More astringent critics, like Columbia provost Jacques Barzun, pointed out the injustice of shortchanging undergraduate students:

> The student . . . is conscious [that his teachers] subject him to cavalier treatment . . . unpunctual, slipshod in marking papers, ill-prepared in lecture, careless about assignments. . . . To put it another way, the student sees and resents the fact that teaching is no longer the central concern of the university. . . . After making all due exceptions [for there are still thousands of devoted teachers and vigilant college heads], the students' complaint is justified. The great shift to research after 1945 would alone modify the university atmosphere sufficiently to warrant the impression of neglect, supported as it is by the reality of "publish or perish." (1968, 69)

Although Barzun and others (see, e.g., Schaar and Wolin 1965) expected a student uprising against desultory and negligent undergraduate teaching, these hopes were quickly disappointed. Instead, an ethic of consumerism emerged. This ethic reflected the growth of mass higher education, which brought many more ill-prepared and nonacademically oriented students to campus. Moreover, students now had the power, in the form of student evaluations, to register their desires in ways that affected teachers' expectations. The use of student evaluations of teaching became widespread in the 1970s (Riesman 1980). At large state universities, these forms became the primary method for evaluating performance in the classroom. Feedback from students about "too much reading" and "unfair tests" encouraged instructors to lower their expectations of student work in the hope of retaining high evaluations and in response to a declining academic ethos among students (Everett 1977; Grubb 1996; Johnson 2003; Riesman 1980).

TWO REFORM MOVEMENTS EMERGE

It is against this backdrop that two movements emerged during the period to address weaknesses in undergraduate education.[4] The limited success of these movements demonstrates how difficult it is to create meaningful change in undergraduate teaching and learning in a heterogeneous system lacking any semblance of coordination or any widely accepted standards for what constitutes effective instruction.

Sharing a critical stance toward the condition of undergraduate teaching and learning, the two movements otherwise shared little in common: *the teaching reform movement* worked on a doctrine for the improvement of teaching effectiveness, while *the outcomes assessment movement* focused on requiring institutions to assess how much students were learning in their classes. The higher education policy analyst Peter Ewell described the two movements as they emerged near the beginning of the period:

> Two antithetical "ideologies" . . . arose almost simultaneously in higher education discourse. The first came from inside the academy. . . . Its tenets were most clearly stated in an influential national report, *Involvement in Learning* [1984] . . . which argued that breakthrough improvements in undergraduate education could be achieved by establishing high expectations, deploying active and engaging pedagogies, and providing feedback about performance. . . . The second ideology had roots outside the academy based on strong state interest in pursuing [testing-based] educational reform. . . . Its tenets were embodied in a high visibility report by the National Governors Association, *A Time for Results* [1986]. . . . The report argued that colleges and universities should be held accountable for establishing clear standards for performance with respect to student

learning and that the results of student assessments should be publicly reported and coupled with consequential actions. (2005, 107)

It is clear that one strand of the teaching reform movement gained considerable ground during the period. Networks of teaching practitioners succeeded in disseminating selected principles of what I will call *the new progressivism*—specifically, those principles promoting student-centered learning, civic and community engagement, and sensitivity to the interests of diverse learners. In this way, they contributed to improvements in students' interactive engagement in the classroom, but not necessarily to their accountability for learning or their deeper understanding of course materials. By contrast, and perhaps surprisingly, the outcomes assessment movement failed to transform practice, even as it put learning outcomes more emphatically on the policy agenda.

The Teaching Reform Movement

The principal agents of the teaching reform movement were the great philanthropic foundations and foundation-sponsored advocacy organizations, such as the American Association of Colleges and Universities (AAC&U) and the Carnegie Foundation for the Advancement of Teaching (CFAT). Supported by the foundations, the principles of good teaching codified by leading educators of the period advocated active learning experiences, commitments to diversity and civic engagement, *and* challenging academic standards. Challenging academic standards were repeatedly extolled, based on evidence that learning improvement requires meeting high expectations. However, this advocacy of challenging academic standards proved to be no match for the consumerism and utilitarianism that came to dominate college student academic life. The trajectory of the teaching reform movement consequently mirrored the pattern of K–12 progressive education in the early twentieth century, when followers of John Dewey, such as William Heard Kilpatrick, deemphasized his mentor's insistence on rigor and frequent assessment and highlighted the student-centered, active learning, and community engagement themes in his work (Cremin 1961, 328; Labaree 2005).

"GOOD PRACTICES" IN COLLEGE TEACHING

The National Institute of Education's influential *Involvement in Learning* (NIE 1984) signaled both the growing importance of effective teaching and the challenges facing faculty in a system of mass higher education. This document, heavily influenced by UCLA higher education professor Alexander W. Astin, advocated movement away from the standard lecture format so that students could become inquirers—producers as well as consumers of knowledge. Following the lead of progressive educators, the report recommended the introduction of active modes of learning, such as faculty research projects and classes held in the field; internships and other forms of experiential learning; small discussion groups; in-class presentations and debates; individual learning projects; and supervised independent study. At the same time, in harmony with traditionalists, it also advocated timely feedback and more rigorous standards for evaluating student performance (National Institute of Education 1984, 27–28).

Arthur W. Chickering and Zelda Gamson's "Seven Principles for Good Practice in Undergraduate Education" promoted a similar set of recommendations. Their pithy opening sentence bears repeating for the sense of urgency it conveys: "Apathetic students, illiterate graduates, incompetent teaching, impersonal campuses—so rolls the drumfire of criticism" (1987, 3). Their easy-to-remember principles became a touchstone for reformers and formed a basis for subsequent national surveys of student engagement. As in the case of the National Institute of Education report, the seven principles offered something for both progressives (frequent faculty-student contact, collaborative and active learning experiences, and respect for the variety of students' talents and ways of learning) and traditionalists (focus on time spent on task, prompt feedback, and high expectations for performance).

SCHOLARSHIP RECONSIDERED

Ideologies provide blueprints for action, and by the end of the 1980s organizational changes had created the conditions for an ideological shift—from the research-centered hierarchy of the "academic revolution" to something new reflecting the variety of institutional missions found in U.S. higher education. That new ideology was formulated in Ernest L. Boyer's *Scholarship Reconsidered* (1990). As president of the Carnegie Foundation for the Advancement of Teaching, Boyer was well positioned to affect change in institutional practices.

Boyer's underlying goal was to install a confederation of interests in the place of academic hierarchy. To do so, he identified four legitimate forms of academic life: the scholarships of discovery, integration, application, and teaching. The use of the venerable term "scholarship" united academe under the idea of studiousness and learning rather than research and teaching. Boyer explicitly hoped to end debates about the relative value of research and teaching. "The most important obligation now confronting the nation's colleges and universities," he wrote, "is to break out of the tired old teaching versus research debate and define, in more creative ways, what it means to be a scholar. It's time [for the profession] to recognize the full range of faculty talent and the great diversity of functions higher education must perform" (xii).

The critical innovation in Boyer's work was the integration of teachers as equal partners in the confederation of scholars. Before Boyer, one rarely thought of teaching as scholarship, only as reflecting knowledge of scholarship. Although the term "scholarship" suggests the possibility of professionalizing the teaching function, for Boyer it remained the province of the inspired amateur, albeit one who thought deeply about subject matter and reflected often on the effectiveness of her practice. Yet the very naming of teaching as a form of scholarship encouraged steps in the direction Boyer himself initially failed to anticipate, toward research on teaching effectiveness that could be used to inform practice.

Boyer's work undoubtedly contributed to raising the stature of teaching as an object of concern and as a central identity for academics. In a national survey of postsecondary faculty conducted five years after the Boyer report, more than three-quarters identified teaching as the most important activity in their professional lives (Schuster and Finkelstein 2006, 87). The faculty as a whole reported that 60 percent of its work time was spent on average on teaching-related activities, as compared to 15 percent on research (ibid., 88). Only the natural and social sciences and engineering showed any reapportionment of effort in the direction of research (ibid., 91). In addition, institutions more often required evidence of "teaching excellence" in applications for positions following the Boyer report; such evidence was required in 60 percent of advertisements placed in the *Chronicle of Higher Education* (Meizlish and Kaplan 2008). These requirements grew at research universities, as much as baccalaureate- and master's-granting institutions, and particularly in the arts and humanities.

Ernest Boyer hoped to maintain scholarship at the center of the profession. Yet the American College Faculty surveys suggest that the centrality of scholarly contributions slowly eroded in the face of the participatory practices and eleemosynary goals of professors. Among full-time faculty in public doctoral-granting universities, interest in becoming an authority in one's field declined by 10 percent between 1989 and 2004, before increasing a bit in 2007. Interest in obtaining recognition from colleagues for scholarly achievements showed a similar rate of decline. Indeed, obtaining recognition from colleagues for one's scholarly contributions was no longer a goal held by a majority of faculty in public master's-granting institutions, even as helping others remained a primary goal. American college faculty outside of private universities were more likely to say in 2007 that helping others in difficulty was a more important goal than becoming an authority in one's field or obtaining recognition from colleagues for scholarly contributions (DeAngelo et al. 2007).

These data suggest that support for teaching did not preserve scholarship as the unifying feature of the academic profession but rather that college teaching in many institutions and fields was transformed from more of a scholarly profession into more of a helping profession. Academics who did not conduct much research began to develop their own norms of practice emphasizing active learning experiences, inclusive pedagogies, and social service goals. Boyer expected pluralism to strengthen the usefulness and unity of the profession. But the scholarship of teaching was not an intrinsic feature of the new progressivism that emerged out of the teaching reform movement.

THE NEW PROGRESSIVISM

A new progressivism emerged as the leading outcome of these reform movements. It focused more on student engagement and inclusive practices than on student performance. Practitioners found engagement activities easier to implement than challenging assignments—and less likely to create student discontent. For all of its successes, the new progressivism raised a central question: Can a strong academic profession be built around a teaching identity focused more on student engagement and social amelioration than on a commitment to the practices of scholarship and research?

The American Association of Colleges and Universities (AAC&U) is the organization most responsible for extending the good practices literature to include attention to the classroom climate for disadvantaged groups.[5] As I discussed in chapter 4, the initial work of the AAC&U was to create a warmer campus and classroom climate for women and minorities, first by publicizing their marginalization and then by connecting their full incorporation into the democratic project. This early work culminated in the American Commitments initiative (1993–2001), funded by the Ford Foundation, the

Hewlett Foundation, and the National Endowment for the Humanities. The connection between diversity and democracy provided a signal theme for this work. AAC&U drew on familiar images of pluralism but with a new twist: "Higher education," it wrote, "can nurture Americans' commitment and capacity to create a society in which democratic aspirations become democratic justice. Diversity proves a means of forging deeper civic unity" (Beckham 2000, 2). This conceptual link between diversity and democracy brought diversity thoroughly into the mainstream of liberal education, while updating the Deweyan tradition to incorporate the race- and gender-conscious movements on campus.

The National Survey of Student Engagement (NSSE) represented another powerful force in the institutionalization of the new progressivism. Led by George D. Kuh, a professor of higher education at Indiana University, NSSE was launched with Pew Foundation funding in 2000. NSSE built on decades of research by Kuh and his colleague Robert Pace on the College Survey of Educational Quality (CSEQ) (Kuh 2009). This work closely paralleled the precepts of *Involvement in Learning*. Conceived in part as an alternative to resources- and reputation-based college rankings of *U.S. News and World Report*, NSSE intended to measure more accurately the actual quality of undergraduate students' educational experiences. The five NSSE benchmarks, each addressed through scaling-related questions, probed levels of (1) student-faculty contact, (2) active and collaborative learning, (3) academic challenges, (4) educational enrichment activities, and (5) institutional climates conducive to learning.

In its inaugural year, NSSE was administered at more than 270 institutions; this number grew to more than 600 annually by the end of the decade (www.nsse.iub.edu). Institutions were soon comparing their engagement scores on the five key dimensions to national norms and norms for institutions of their type. NSSE generated an impressive number of reports detailing the distribution and consequences of engagement experiences, and it also championed case analyses of institutions that showed exceptional effectiveness in the production of engaged learning environments (Kuh et al. 2005). It developed a checklist of "high-impact" practices that found their way into the curriculum of hundreds of colleges. These included freshman seminars, senior capstone experiences, study abroad, undergraduate research, service learning experiences, and internships (Kuh 2008).

However, NSSE measured engagement, not learning,[6] and, although many college educators assumed that higher levels of engagement should register more or less directly in improved learning outcomes, empirical efforts to demonstrate this proposition were disappointing. Student scores on NSSE scales were, for example, only very weakly associated with scores on the Collegiate Learning Assessment (CLA), a test of analytical and critical thinking, and most factors failed to reach statistical significance once students' prior academic records (grade point average and SAT scores) were statistically controlled (Carini, Kuh, and Klein 2006). Other studies showed that high grades were common in humanities and social science courses in which the culture of engagement emphasized participation, interaction, and active learning experiences and were less common in the natural sciences and engineering where engagement typically meant long hours of study, usually with groups of peers, to master demanding quantitative material (Brint, Cantwell, and Hanneman 2008; Johnson 2003).

Changes in Classroom Practices

Classroom practices changed dramatically in the direction advocated by the new progressives, even as the more traditional-sounding parts of the Astin-Chickering teaching reform message, those focusing on high expectations and challenging assignments, were lost or ignored. Here the best evidence comes from the triannual studies of American faculty from the Higher Education Research Institute. From the late 1980s through the mid-2000s, extensive lecturing showed a marked decline as a teaching method, even in public research universities, and cooperative (small-group) learning opportunities a corresponding increase. Full-time college faculty increasingly said they were bringing their students into field settings; asking them to demonstrate their knowledge in front of class through oral presentations; relying on reflective writing and journaling; using real-life problems to illustrate lessons; and putting student-centered inquiry, rather than recitation of facts and concepts, at the center of their teaching work (Astin, Dey, and Korn 1991; DeAngelo et al. 2007; Dey et al. 1993; Lindholm et al. 2002; Lindholm et al. 2005; Sax et al. 1996; Sax et al. 1999).

These changes went together with an expanded conception of the goals of undergraduate education. Consistent with principles of the new progressivism, the American College Faculty studies also showed sharp increases in the centrality of social goals as well: reaching out to surrounding communities through community-based research; teaching appreciation of multicultural diversity; and interest in using undergraduate education as a vehicle for promoting social change. Just as the twentieth-century progressives socialized their ideals of citizenship through the elementary and secondary schools, so too do college faculty now overwhelmingly endorse the goals of diversity and community engagement. The main proponents of these changes were younger and female faculty members (DeAngelo et al. 2007, 5, 9, 11), suggesting that these trends are likely to continue as older faculty retire and college teaching faculties become increasingly populated by those brought up in the culture of the new progressivism.

Engagement versus Learning

The new progressives assumed that higher levels of engagement would lead more or less automatically to better student performance, as enhanced engagement triggered enhanced motivation to study. But the evidence indicates that challenging academic work and mechanisms to ensure accountability for learning are also very important influences on the motivation to study.[7] Looking at a sample of 2,400 students who took the CLA at the beginning of their freshman year and the middle of their sophomore year, Arum and Roksa (2011) found that students had improved their critical thinking, complex reasoning, and writings skills, as measured by the CLA performance task, by only 0.18 standard deviations, or an average seven percentile gain. Forty-five percent of students showed no change in their CLA scores. Arum and Roksa concluded that students' completion of three semesters of college had made a "barely noticeable" impact on the higher-level cognitive skills tested by CLA. They attributed the primary reason for this poor performance to the unwillingness of college instructors to give challenging assignments, which they measured, somewhat arbitrarily, as fewer than forty pages of course reading in a week and/or no assignment of papers of fifteen or more pages during the semester.

Trend data from NSSE confirm their conclusion. They showed that many active and collaborative learning activities grew more popular over time, while challenging requirements, such as the amount of time students spend studying per week and the number of twenty-page papers they wrote, remained static or declined (NSSE 2000, 2008). In the 2008 NSSE report, nearly two-thirds of seniors in NSSE sample institutions said they studied fifteen or fewer hours per week, and half said they had never written a paper of twenty pages or longer (NSSE 2008). In both cases, challenging requirements were less common in 2008 than those found eight years earlier.

One reason for this one-sided adoption of the "good practices" research is clear: underprepared and unmotivated students tended to penalize demanding teachers in their student evaluations (Babcock 2010), leading many instructors to worry that raising expectations would have negative consequences for their careers. The reliance on student evaluations of teaching as the sole measure of good teaching practice cemented student consumerism as an effective force in the classroom and one that tended to lower rather than raise expectations for learning, thereby undermining important planks in the good-practices platform.

The Triumph of Consumerism

The triumph of student consumerism is evident in these findings. Many students have effectively resisted professorial demands for higher levels of effort by simply refusing to engage their studies at a deep level. Ethnographic studies indicate students have relied on posted lecture notes, the prevalence of relatively easy courses to fill out their schedules, and teachers' openness to negotiations concerning work demands and grades (see, e.g., Grigsby 2009; Moffatt 1989; Nathan 2005). Arum and Roksa reported that more than 90 percent of students said they had talked to a professor about grades, but only one-quarter said they had talked to a professor about ideas presented in class. A majority of the 2,400 college students in the Arum and Roksa study said they had not taken a course during the previous term that required a total of twenty pages of written work, and 25 percent said they had not taken a course that required even forty pages of reading per week. Arum and Roksa concluded:

> Given the small amount of time students spend studying, it is no surprise that they are not learning much. This is partly a consequence of lax demands and expectations, but it is careless to think that simply increased faculty demands will produce greater learning in higher education. The college experience is perceived by many students at the core as a social experience. The collegiate culture emphasizes sociability and encourages students to have fun, to do all the things they have not had a chance to do before or may not have a chance to do after they enter "the real world" of the labor market. (2011, 131)

The system of low expectations existed because it served the interests of all major actors who were in daily contact with the classroom. A large proportion of college students—perhaps a near majority—saw college as a period of fun, friendship, and personal development before they began adult life. They hoped their investments in college-level training would pay off in the labor market, of course, but many assumed, perhaps quite realistically, that credentials themselves would add value, not what they learned in college. While faculty members were interested in making their classes lively and interesting, they also wanted to preserve time for research, correspondence, committee work, and other socioprofessional activities. Challenging requirements and multiple assessments added time to their preparation and created discontent among utilitarian-minded students. Nor were administrators particularly interested in adding more challenging material to the undergraduate curriculum. On the contrary, administrators were usually more interested in reaching enrollment targets and raising retention and graduation rates than in encouraging challenging course work or requiring students to demonstrate cognitive growth (Bok 2006; see also Arum and Roksa 2011, 141).

The climate of low expectations seems to have been particularly characteristic of occupational-professional programs outside of engineering where reading and writing requirements were weakest (Arum and Roksa 2011, 104–9). Yet some of the building blocks of cognitive gain may have been in short supply across the board. In a study of University of California undergraduates in 2008 my research team and I found that *no discipline* stood out in the frequency with which student majors reported analytical and critical thinking experiences in their classes, such as comparing two contrasting perspectives, assembling evidence to support an argument, or breaking down arguments into their component parts to assess the validity of each one (Brint, Cantwell, and Saxena 2012).

TEACHING FOR UNDERSTANDING

The forces of the new progressivism commanded impressive organizational tools and a relatively easy-to-implement checklist of reforms to attach to existing curricula. The same could not be said of the much more ambitious but less completely realized project of the Carnegie Foundation for the Advancement of Teaching under Ernest Boyer's successor, Lee S. Shulman. Under Shulman's leadership, the Carnegie Foundation embarked on a program to redefine and realize Boyer's vision of a scholarship of teaching. These efforts eventually steered the foundation away from the tenets of the new progressivism to a deeper inquiry into the aims and methods of undergraduate teaching. Shulman's approach came to share only part of the faith of the new progressivism in the power of student engagement. Engagement, he wrote, "is not enough." "Understanding is not independent [of engagement] but is an additional standard" (Shulman 2004, 56).

For Shulman, all good teaching was built, in the first instance, on subject matter mastery. Shulman emphasized, in addition, "pedagogical content knowledge"—the special materials and methods tied to knowledge-making in the disciplines, such as work with primary textual materials in history, surveys and ethnography in sociology, and diagnostic clinical rounds in medicine. Based on this knowledge and these disciplinary resources, teaching and learning could be conceived as an interactive process of bringing "something inside" of the teacher out in a methodical and powerful way—and of bringing "something outside" of the student, the lesson, into strong relief in students' consciousness. In all good teaching, methods of expression and bases of apprehension and understanding were consequently closely linked (Hutchings and Shulman 1999).

Shulman emphasized that the first obligation of the teacher is to determine what students know and can do, as well as their interests and passions. Working from these bases, Shulman and his associates (Huber and Hutchings 2005) advocated that teachers create "cognitive apprenticeships" in which students were asked to make their mental processes accessible to their fellow students and teachers and to work toward more expert understandings of course materials. Through a process of "uncoverage," teachers were encouraged to focus their first lessons on ideas and concepts that were both difficult to grasp and fundamental to subsequent learning in the class.

Teachers made their own thinking accessible to students by explicating the "intermediate processes" of understanding—the understandings that are employed habitually by expert learners but often hidden in the process of instruction. These could include, for example, explicit discussions of the flow of an argument, the translation of terms no longer in wide use, or a detailed, step-by-step interpretation of the architecture of a statistical table. Other techniques for making knowledge accessible included slowing down students' reading; eliciting students' descriptions of their thinking about passages in the text; administering oral rather than written midterms; employing structured online discussions to create learning communities oriented to key issues and ideas in a course; and posting examples of beginning, intermediate, and advanced understandings of texts with detailed explications of the major differences between these levels of mastery. Similar pedagogies were developed for mathematics—for example, in James Sandefur's "think alouds" in which math students were asked to describe, step by step, how they were thinking about a problem as they worked through its solution.

Shulman argued that students should demonstrate competence by performing skills in front of their teachers and classmates rather than by passively absorbing information. For Shulman, the pathologies of learning—amnesia (forgetting what was just learned), fantasia (misperceiving the lesson to reinforce existing knowledge), and inertia (inability to use knowledge in

TABLE 8.1. Characteristics Associated with Teaching for Rote Memorization and Teaching for Understanding

Teaching for Rote Memorization	Teaching for Understanding
Teaching is based on textbook coverage	Teaching begins with what students know often based on concept inventories
Instructor dominates class time	Student motivations/interests are assessed
Instructor emphasizes points students need to know for tests	Learning objectives are specified to students
Supplementary materials reinforce key points of lecture	Teaching builds from most fundamental theories/concepts/ideas
Review sheets consist of key points made in class that will appear on tests	Intermediate processes in understanding are discussed in step-by-step fashion
Students drill each other on what they think the instructor wants them to know	Instructors discuss the process by which concepts/models/principles developed
Assessments allow students to pass by repeating key points from lecture	Students are asked to give reasons for why they come to conclusions
	"Think alouds" and "difficulty papers" may be used to assess student understanding
	Detailed feedback is given on student work
	Students are encouraged to meet with the instructor to discuss their work
	Students have the opportunity to redo their work based on feedback
	Students are asked to perform what they know in class presentations, as well as on tests
	Post-test concept inventories are used to assess learning gains

new contexts)—were ultimately issues of ownership. Understanding implied ownership and the sense of ownership typically required performing what one knew.

Research on teaching for understanding has expanded beyond the ideas developed and promulgated by Shulman and his colleagues, as I will show in the concluding section of this chapter, but the Carnegie Foundation under Shulman's leadership deserves plaudits for introducing new insights about teaching for understanding and for popularizing early work in the sciences of learning that provided conceptual and evidentiary bases for these insights. Table 8.1 provides a partial list of elements of teaching for understanding as developed by the Carnegie Foundation and augmented by later researchers.

Growing out of the Carnegie program, Scholarship of Teaching and Learning (SoTL) colloquia sprouted on hundreds of college and university campuses, as did a number of impressive websites devoted to this scholarship. The colloquia took up such matters as visually effective presentation of lessons, new ways to assess student learning, uses of technology to improve pedagogy, the impact of learning communities, and other topics consistent with the Carnegie agenda under Shulman's leadership. The SoTL philosophy was not an industrial search for better systems but rather an apprenticeship system for craftsmen, based on sharing the distinctive visions of master teachers.[8]

Shulman's work was widely cited, but the organizational apparatus Carnegie used to spread these ideas showed neither the panache of the AAC&U campaigns nor the reach of NSSE. Instead, an artisanal model, built on networks of sympathetic practitioners, prevailed. This approach generated fresh insights about teaching and learning—insights with the potential to create more effective college teachers. But its insistence on "scaling down" through small-scale actions of unusually committed practitioners was destined to create islands of improved practice in a sea of relative indifference. According to Mary Taylor Huber and Pat Hutchings,

> The key is not the scale and scope but the care and thoughtfulness of the work, its capacity to change thought and practices, its generosity, even, perhaps, its power to surprise and delight. (2005, 30)

Whatever the merits of this argument, it led to relatively thin penetration of CFAT's "pedagogies of understanding."[9] Russell Edgerton, who did so much as a program officer at the Pew Foundation to promote the Carnegie program, concluded that more than two decades of reform activity resulted in "neither professional nor institutional transformation" (Edgerton, personal communication).[10] For all of its shortcomings as a campaign for change, CFAT's ideas about teaching for understanding, and vehicles such as the SoTL colloquia, did help build a cadre of researchers interested in applying the tools of inquiry to the problems of pedagogy.

The Outcomes Assessment Movement

In contrast to teaching reform, outcomes assessment can be defined as a response of state legislatures and regional accrediting bodies to the perception that colleges and universities had not done enough to ensure that students were learning course materials and essential academic competencies. Where the teaching reform movement took root in foundation-supported advocacy organizations, the outcomes assessment movement was promoted primarily by the states and the federal government, abetted by the regional accrediting associations.[11]

Fledgling efforts to encourage institutional assessment of learning outcomes began in the 1970s. The Educational Testing Service fielded the first open-response test of core skills, Academic Competencies in General Education, at 140 institutions, but it was later abandoned owing to the tendency of institutions to magnify small pre-/post-test differences and the test's unreliability in the mid-ranges of scoring (Adelman 2007). By the mid-1970s, twenty states had introduced minimal competency testing for graduating seniors, mirroring popular high school exit exams (Gilman 1978). Calls for action continued in the early 1980s, as the presidential report *A Nation at Risk* (1983) documented the shortcomings of U.S. primary and secondary education in the face of increasing competition from East Asia.

Three years later, the National Governors' Association took a stand. *A Time for Results* (1986), a key document of the period, stressed the same fears about the competency of U.S. college graduates and the same looming threat of Asian competition. It noted that U.S. higher education had set a new standard for access but observed that "access without quality is a cruel deception." In the document, a subcommittee of governors, led by John Ashcroft of Missouri, questioned assumptions about higher education: "Learning is assumed to take place as long as students take courses, accumulate [credit] hours and progress satisfactorily toward a degree." But, the subcommittee observed, "tests of elementary and high school teachers show that the BA is not a guarantee of even basic literacy, let alone competence." The report also cited, with little documentation, "substantial levels of dissatisfaction" among employers about the skills of college graduates. The report advocated systematic programs using multiple measures to assess undergraduate student learning, and it cited with approval institutions like Alverno College that had pioneered systematic assessment in the 1970s. It also applauded the Southern Accreditation Commission for being the first of the regional accrediting bodies to require an assessment component for reaccreditation.

PERFORMANCE FUNDING: THE FIRST WAVE

Between 1979 and 2007, twenty-five states enacted performance funding (though ten of those states dropped it over the years) (Burke and Minassians 2003; Dougherty and Reid 2007). In these states, financial resources were becoming conditioned upon institutional performance in specified areas. These areas included: student retention and graduation rates, student scores on licensing examinations, job placement rates, faculty research productivity, and measures of undergraduate access and campus diversity (McLendon, Hearn, and Deaton 2006). Performance funding proved costly to implement, susceptible to institutional manipulation of performance measures, and subject to reversal under new administrations or when unstable state finances caused deep cuts in regular higher education funding (Burke and Serban 1998; Dougherty and Natow 2009; Shulock and Moore 2002; Zumeta 2001).

Nevertheless, new demands for accountability, including direct assessment of student learning, gradually gained ground during this period. A 1987 report of the Education Commission of the States showed that two-thirds of states had initiated some form of required student assessment. However, many states used minimal competency measures at graduation, or even more indirect measures, such as graduation rates and pass rates on professional licensing examinations. Although assessment of student learning was in the air, few knew how to test directly for student learning outcomes in a cost-effective, relatively unobtrusive way. The large testing companies, ACT and ETS, thought they did know how to do it. They geared up for the new era by introducing or revamping multiple-choice tests, the Collegiate Assessment of Academic Proficiency (CAAP) and the Measure of Academic Proficiency and Progress (MAPP), respectively, that institutions could administer to their freshmen and seniors to determine the institution's "value added" to student academic competencies.

THE "LEARNING PARADIGM"

To the extent that a manifesto existed for the outcomes assessment movement, it was produced by two state college professors in California, Robert Barr and John Tagg. In a widely cited article from *Change* magazine, Barr and Tagg sought to shift thinking in academe from an "instruction paradigm" to a "learning paradigm":

> The paradigm that has governed our colleges is this: A college is an institution that exists to provide instruction. Subtly but profoundly we are shifting to a new paradigm: A college is an institution that exists to produce learning. This shift changes everything. (1995, 13)

The idea of a shift to a learning paradigm resonated strongly among state educational bureaucrats and in the world of higher education policy analysts.[12]

Over the next five years, a chorus of influential voices called for measurement of student learning outcomes and influential practitioners created demonstration projects to show how this measurement could be done. In 2000, the National Center for Public Policy and Higher Education, funded by several major foundations and led by the former governor of North Carolina and educational reformer James B. Hunt, began to publish report cards about state higher education performance, including "incomplete" grades for all states on student learning. In the same year, ABET, the accrediting agency for engineering schools, began its Engineering Criteria 2000 policy requiring outcomes measures and plans for continuous improvement based on results of outcomes assessments. In 2002, the Pew Trusts provided funding to two leaders of the assessment movement, Margaret Miller and Peter Ewell, to demonstrate the possibility of measuring college learning in six states for future incorporation into the National Center for Public Policy and Higher Education's "Measuring Up" reports (Ewell and Miller 2005). In 2003, the Carnegie Corporation of New York and the Teagle Foundation sponsored the development of a new type of test of core academic skills, the Collegiate Learning Assessment, based on the use of document libraries to solve "real-world" problems. In the same year, the national council of regional and disciplinary accrediting agencies, the Council for Higher Education Accreditation (CHEA), announced a policy of "mutual responsibility" between institutions and regional accrediting agencies for demonstrating student learning outcomes.

An opinion survey published by the Educational Testing Service (ETS) in 2003 discovered evidence of public concerns about educational quality, stronger among political conservatives and high school educated people than among liberals and those with college degrees. Primed by questions linking costs to quality assurance, a majority surveyed by ETS agreed that colleges should provide evidence that they were producing the learning results they promised, if they were going to continue to raise costs (ETS 2003). In 2004, the Business-Higher Education Forum argued for the first time in favor of assessments of student learning outcomes. Also in 2004, Miller and Ewell published their six-state report showing that states could demonstrate student learning outcomes through a variety of methods, including proficiency benchmarks. In 2004, the State Higher Education Executive Officers (SHEEO) launched a National Commission on Accountability in Higher Education, chaired by former secretary of education Richard Riley and former Oklahoma governor Frank Keating, both Republicans. The report they produced in 2005 concluded that most state systems "do not meet their intended purpose to improve and to provide evidence of student learning" and endorsed collection of data on student learning outcomes (National Commission on Accountability in Higher Education 2005).

THE ACCREDITING BODIES RESPOND

By the mid-1990s all six of the regional accrediting agencies had policies in place requiring institutions to demonstrate not only that they were tracking conventional measures of student success, such as four- and six-year graduation rates, but also that they had mechanisms in place to achieve established goals for student learning. In 1998, Congress formalized this commitment by making student achievement the first of nine areas in which the regional accrediting agencies were required to have standards.

While following federal directives for recognition, regional accrediting agencies have buffered institutions from state pressures for standardized testing. Some allowed institutions to take responsibility for assessing and achieving a unique set of learning outcomes that they establish for themselves. Others identified a core set of learning outcomes that ought to be examined by all institutions. These typically encompassed, at a minimum, critical and analytical thinking, written expression, and quantitative reasoning. Institutions and departments were granted considerable autonomy so long as they provide evidence that they are establishing learning objectives and developing ways to assess and report the achievement of these objectives. This permitted a variety of assessment approaches, ranging from the presentation of portfolios of student work to requirements for integrative research papers in senior capstone courses. Others built in learning objectives to required courses and required samples of work from these courses or adopted exit examinations as a way of determining whether learning objectives have been met.

Although the regional accrediting bodies developed elaborate procedures to ensure that institutions did more than pay lip service to their demands for evidence of student learning, accrediting requirements were nevertheless often treated by faculty members as an encumbrance requiring the appearance of compliance without deeper commitments to the goals of evaluating student learning in a more rigorous or consistent way at the programmatic rather than the course level. The limited resources and experience of accrediting agencies also encouraged high levels of institutional latitude; most, if not all, of the regional accreditors lacked experience in evaluating evidence of student learning or the qualifications to establish clear standards by which to do so (Ewell 2001a).

Even so, by fostering a common demand for evidence about student learning, the regionals created much more attention to student learning outcomes than had existed before. In 2009, the National Institute for

Learning Outcomes Assessment (NILOA), housed at the University of Illinois, fielded a study of the incorporation of assessment instruments. The study was funded by the Carnegie Corporation, the Lumina Foundation, and the Teagle Foundation. Officials at half of U.S. two- and four-year institutions responded to the survey, and the vast majority (92 percent) said they were engaged in institution-level assessments of student learning. Most said they were using survey instruments like NSSE or alumni surveys, weak measures of learning, but 39 percent said they were also using standardized tests of general knowledge and skill like CLA. At the program level, four of five respondents said they were assessing student learning outcomes in at least one program, and here portfolios of student work dominated. Most said that accreditation was the primary driver of their interest in assessment (Kuh and Ikenberry 2009; see also the follow-up study by Kuh et al. 2014).

THE SPELLINGS COMMISSION REPORT

In 2004, George W. Bush's secretary of education Margaret Spellings appointed a Commission on the Future of Higher Education, chaired by Texas businessman Charles Miller, to recommend reforms in higher education accountability. In 2006, the commission issued its final report, *A Test of Leadership*, which was highly critical of the performance of America's colleges and universities. The report dismissed previous efforts to bring accountability for student learning outcomes.

> Despite increased attention to student learning results by colleges and universities and accreditation agencies, parents and students have no solid evidence, comparable across institutions, of how much students learn in colleges or whether they learn more at one college than another. Similarly, policymakers need more comprehensive data to help them decide whether the national investment in higher education is paying off and how tax payer dollars could be used more effectively. (Spellings Commission 2006, 14)

The commission advocated measuring student achievement on a value-added basis that took into account students' previous achievements when assessing outcomes. It stated that this evidence should be made available to consumers and policymakers in an accessible, understandable way, and it proposed that "meaningful" interstate comparison of student learning be encouraged and implemented in all states (ibid., 4).

The specter of high-stakes testing haunted many in academe, who argued that such tests would yield little of value for students studying such a wide variety of disciplines (see, e.g., Chatman 2007a; Hawthorne 2008). The only way to test learning would be discipline by discipline, these educators argued, and this seemed an impossible task given the limited resources of colleges and universities and the limited capacity of state educational bureaucrats to grade such a wide variety of tests.[13] Leaders of the testing movement countered that tests of general skills were an important, if not the only important, measure of student achievement in college. Instead of relying on one test, they argued, multiple forms of assessment would be necessary—some to assess general skills, others to assess disciplinary knowledge, and still others to assess the "soft skills" required in leadership positions (see, e.g., Ewell 2004; Shulenberger 2008).

The Bush administration proposed that the federal government take a larger role in quality assurance. After extensive lobbying by the higher education associations, Senator Lamar Alexander, the chair of the committee responsible for reauthorization of the Higher Education Act, was convinced to allow the existing system of regional and professional accreditation to continue and to bar the federal government from prescribing standards that these agencies were required to use in assessing institutional effectiveness. But, in exchange for his support, Alexander insisted that higher education institutions themselves take on the responsibility to measure student learning outcomes in a serious way. Alexander's intervention led to the creation of the Voluntary System of Accountability (VSA), organized, with support from the Lumina Foundation, by two of the leading higher education associations. VSA set as an explicit goal the development of a system of accountability that would "facilitate comparisons of learning outcomes among institutions of higher education" (Millett et al. 2007, 2).

The VSA ultimately failed as an accountability mechanism. Of the more than 300 institutions participating in VSA as of fall 2009, less than one-third reported results of "core academic skills" using one of the three authorized testing instruments. Of the reporting institutions, the expected two-thirds reported results within a standard deviation of the mean for institutions with similar student academic ability profiles, but among the remaining institutions three times as many reported results "above" (one standard deviation above the mean) or "well above" (two standard deviations above) expected as those reporting results "below" or "well below" expected. Indeed, only five of 104 reporting institutions said that they were performing below expected levels, a statistical impossibility.

THE LIMITED OUTCOMES OF OUTCOMES ASSESSMENT

The states and the regional accreditors proved to be strong advocates of assessing student learning outcomes but weak implementers. By the end of the period, the states had been persuaded to defer to the regional and professional accrediting associations to provide quality assurance and to the VSA to experiment with the construct validity of several tests of general intellectual skills and to use these tests to monitor the "value added" of institutions.

Neither the regional accrediting bodies nor the VSA transformed the college classroom by demanding evidence of student learning outcomes. They encouraged richer discussions about learning objectives, but the regional accrediting agencies, for the most part, allowed institutions and departments to formulate their own objectives and to choose their own methods for demonstrating results. These requirements did not change practice as much as reformers hoped because they allowed departments to be their own prosecutors, judges, and juries. Similarly, the learning outcomes component of VSA continued to be slow to get off the ground. Thus, while national and transinstitutional actors succeeded in shaping the environment of discourse, their efforts met both passive and active resistance whenever they have attempted to prescribe tough standards for the assessment of student learning outcomes.

The sociologist Jal Mehta (2007) offered a plausible explanation for the fierce rhetoric but limited follow-through of the states in assessing student learning outcomes. In Mehta's view, higher education has been protected from accountability pressures by its reputation for quality and expertise, and by its larger private sector, which is practically immune from state accountability pressures. One might add political factors to this explanation. These political factors included the ability of higher education advocates to exploit doubts about the effectiveness of K–12 reform, as represented by the No Child Left Behind Act of 2000, partisan turnover in the governing coalitions of the states, and, in particular, the capacity of the higher education associations and regional accrediting bodies to assure key legislators that they would implement accountability measures responsive to public interest in quality assurance. Most state governments were, in the end, willing to accept these assurances, in part because they did not want to spend scarce state resources on enforcement mechanisms. The stakes were just not high enough to take policing out of the hands of the regional accreditors.

PERFORMANCE FUNDING: THE SECOND WAVE

Performance funding, however, continued to interest state policymakers, even after scholars and policy analysts identified persistent problems with its implementation and outcomes, including performance-based allocations that were too low to stimulate change and one-size-fits-all metrics that were not tailored to the circumstances of different types of colleges and universities. These findings led to changes in performance-funding formulas, with states raising the levels of funding based on performance and allowing institutions at different selectivity levels to adjust metrics to suit their student base (Li 2014). In spite of its rocky history, performance funding consequently gained momentum in the 2000s, winning the backing of the Gates and Lumina foundations and their networks. By 2014, twenty-five states either used performance funding or were planning to incorporate it. Tennessee continued to be its most persistent and aggressive advocate, allocating 100 percent of higher education funding based on performance indicators.

Even so, the expected outcomes failed to materialize. In a review of the extensive state-level literature on outcomes, the higher education policy analysts Kevin Dougherty and Vikash Reddy found "no statistically positive impacts of performance funding on six-year graduation rates in public four-year colleges" (2011, 27). In her examination of 467 institutions between 1997 and 2007, Jeong Cheol Shin (2009) reported similar results: no significant change after the introduction of performance funding. David Tandberg and Nicholas Hillman (2014) were among those who reported the most positive results; using sophisticated statistical techniques on state-level data from the period 1990 to 2010 they found small but statistically significant improvements in graduation rates in the seventh and eighth years after performance-funding implementation. Whether political winds would allow performance-funding stability up to eight years for these kinds of modest results remained an open question. And the unintended consequences of doing so also remained an open question; reports continued to trickle in of institutions adjusting graduation requirements downward in efforts to improve their performance profiles (Li 2014).

A Breakthrough Science of Learning?

Thus the most obvious consequences of two decades of reform were the diffusion of active learning pedagogies and surface-level adoption of relatively weak accountability measures to assess student learning outcomes. These limited achievements were clearly not enough to change the social relations of learning prevailing in most college classrooms.

But one development during the period did contain the potential to do so. The sciences of learning gained momentum in the 1990s and put new life into academe's self-examination of teaching practices. Little by little, change in teaching practices began to occur based on the creation and diffusion of new knowledge about effective teaching practices. Natural science educators, particularly physicists, took the lead in these efforts. Thanks to what now amount to thousands of research studies relating student learning to teaching practices, the techniques associated with learning gains in undergraduate science and mathematics courses are well known. Many of these practices have proven to be transferrable to courses outside the natural sciences, albeit not as often to the arts and humanities where pedagogies based on discussion and interpretation loom larger.

Slightly different emphases have emerged among the various groups that have sought to reform practice based on the results of research, but some broad commonalities are evident among them. The alignment of course content and course assignments with stated learning objectives is one such commonality. The use of active learning techniques is a second. The creation of high-energy and inclusive classroom environments is a third. The use of materials that require students to engage in analytical and critical thinking rather than rote memorization is a fourth. And the use of frequent assessments targeted to course learning objectives is a fifth. (For overviews, see Ambrose et al. 2010; Bransford, Brown, and Cocking 2000; Freeman et al. 2014; Froyd 2008; Wieman 2012.)

Teaching improvement became a policy priority by the end of the period, as indicated by the advocacy of the American Association for the Advancement of Science, the National Academies, the President's Council of Advisors on Science and Technology, and virtually all of the major higher education associations for the science of learning. Networks of expert practitioners sponsored by these organizations (and by some individual campuses) fanned out across academe to show how evidence-based teaching practices could be implemented to increase students' learning gains. Through these means, the principles developed by cognitive researchers were embedded in course redesign programs and in instructor certification programs such as the one cosponsored by the American Council on Education (ACE 2016), as well as in discipline specific efforts such as PULSE (Partnership for Undergraduate Life Science Education) with its heady roster of medical and federal sponsors (PULSE 2016).

In the following sections I will discuss the tools developed by learning scientists: those that are intended to increase student participation in learning, to improve students' accountability, and to help instructors teach more effectively for understanding rather than rote memorization.

PARTICIPATION TOOLS

The research literature showed that one strand of the new progressivism was entirely correct: students tended to learn more when they were actively engaged through classroom participation in the topics under discussion. Lecture halls had proven to be the bane of undergraduate education because of their tendency to bring out the worst aspects of mass higher education: the complete domination of classroom time and focus by instructors and the passivity of many students in the face of this control.

In a now classic article, the physicist Richard R. Hake (1998) compared traditional lecture-based classrooms in introductory mechanics courses to those based on what he called interactive engagement. Hake used two well-validated tests, the Halloun-Hestenes Mechanics Diagnostics test and the Force Concept Inventory. Instructors gave these tests to students prior to the beginning of class and then again at the end of class. Hake used changes in scores on the tests (pre- and post-test) to determine average gains for courses taught in the traditional lecture mode and those taught using interactive engagement techniques. The traditional classrooms were based on lectures typically followed by a short time for student questions. The interactive-engagement classrooms, by contrast, were based on mini-lectures or demonstrations followed by breakout sessions in which groups of students discussed a problem posed by the professor related to the topic under discussion. Some groups were then asked to report out on their conclusions. The professors corrected groups that had come up with wrong conclusions and elaborated on other groups' correct conclusions.

Hake compared pre- and post-test results on the Force Concept Inventory for more than 6,500 students in 67 introductory physics classes in 14 high schools, 16 colleges, and 32 universities. Average scores not surprisingly varied considerably from campus to campus, but the key comparative results were consistent and cumulatively persuasive; students in the interactive-engagement classes outperformed students in the traditional classrooms, with average gains almost two standard deviations above those achieved by students in traditional classrooms.[14] The time allowed for students to interact with one another around a problem and the professors' responses to their solutions evidently helped cement the learning of key concepts and relationships beyond what could be expected in a traditional lecture format. Concept inventories were subsequently developed for numerous fields, including astronomy, chemistry, engineering specialties, evolutionary science, geosciences, and statistics and applied in studies similar to the one reported by Hake (see, e.g., Smith, Wood, and Knight 2008). The results of studies using these concept inventories have confirmed the learning gains associated with interactive engagement as opposed to traditional lecturing.

The consistency of the advantage for interactive engagement helped lead a transformation in physics teaching and subsequently in many of the natural sciences and engineering. The physicist Eric Mazur (1997) was another leader in what he called the "peer instruction" movement. Mazur recounted that his sponsorship of new approaches to classroom instruction came from his realization that his introductory Harvard students were performing well on examinations because they could apply memorized equations appropriately to problems, but most did not have the foggiest idea about the underlying concepts and principles that made the equations work. They were dutifully working through difficult assignments without truly understanding what they were doing or why they were doing it.

During the period researchers focusing on interactive engagement developed a variety of techniques to foster student participation in class. The techniques built on and in some cases reconfigured the small-group discussions on which Hake and Mazur based their studies. One closely connected variation was the "think-pair-share" technique, which is based on teaming up two students to compare their ideas about a question posed by the professor and then having one of the students report out if the group is called upon. (Those who have used this technique emphasize the importance of allowing some silent time for more introverted students to compose their thoughts prior to the discussion with their partners.) Instructors also learned to begin their classes with a "hook" that produced discussion among the students. Polling for student responses to questions, either using electronic means or simply raised hands, allowed professors to question students on the reasons for their diverging responses.

Some professors with classes of students who were reluctant to answer questions walked the aisles of their lecture halls and offered extra points to students from different quadrants of the room who were willing to venture

TABLE 8.2. Teaching Practices Associated with Student Passivity and Student Participation

Student Passivity	Student Participation
More than 80 percent of class is lecture	Lecturing constitutes less than 60 percent of class time
Instructor stands at podium or in front of class	Instructor moves around the lecture hall asking questions
Instructor makes few efforts to engage students	Mini-lectures are followed by small group breakouts
Instructor plans few activities other than lecture	Instructor attempts to bring in all students by offering extra points for answers by students in all quadrants of the class
Videos/films are main supplementary materials	Other student discussion techniques are employed (e.g., think-pair-share, jigsaw, fishbowl)
Students are not called upon to answer instructor's questions	Demonstrations, simulations, and videos are used; students are first asked to predict outcome
Question time is limited to a few minutes at the end of class	Class includes opportunities to conduct hands-on research and/or to create a creative work and report on results
Slides on topics covered are available prior to class	Competitions may be employed (e.g., debates, best illustrations of concept, best posters)

an answer to a question. Others used the jigsaw technique in which each member of a group was tasked with learning one segment of a multipart assignment and segment experts from the several groups consulted one another prior to the presentation of the segment to other members of each of their jigsaw groups. Another colorfully named technique, the fishbowl, placed a group of students in front of the class to present a discussion of an assignment and permitted those outside the fishbowl to join those in it by asking questions or in some cases physically joining. Many more familiar approaches to interactive engagement also grew in popularity during the period, including debates, oral presentations, and contests for the best illustration of important concepts, ideas, or principles (see DeAngelo et al. 2007) (see table 8.2).

Studies I conducted of University of California students indicated that first-generation college students, particularly Asian American and Hispanic students, were less inclined than others to say that they participated in class (Brint, Cantwell, and Saxena 2012; Brint and Cantwell 2014). The sciences of learning underscore how important it is for instructors to encourage students to make the effort to participate actively in class, even in the face of their inhibitions. Increased learning has been the primary motivation to adopt peer instruction techniques, but greater equity in learning may be an important by-product.

ACCOUNTABILITY TOOLS

In the consumerist culture of the period, students complained regularly that too much was being required of them, but the truth seems to be that all too often little was being required of them. The time-on-task literature helps to show why low expectations matter. Time on task has been associated with stronger performance on tests in dozens of studies of K–12 classrooms. For similar reasons longer reading and writing assignments are associated with larger gains in analytical and critical thinking among otherwise similar students in higher education. The effort required to make sense of difficult prose, to wrestle with ideas, and to compose a longer paper can build cognitive capacity in much the same way that challenging workout regimens build the body's fitness.

Of course, students are regularly assessed on their class performance through paper assignments, quizzes, and examinations. Even so, the repertoire of assessment did not seem to be fully adequate to ensure student accountability for learning. Many students did not read for class and were unprepared to discuss reading materials. For this reason, college instructors turned to online reading quizzes, in-class reading quizzes, or brief responses to prompts about the assigned reading. One notable experimental study showed that daily online reading quizzes significantly improved student performance on final exams in an introductory psychology course while at the same time reducing achievement gaps between students from high- and low-income backgrounds (Pennebaker, Gosling, and Ferrell 2013). Dozens of similar findings have been reported elsewhere in the literature (see, e.g., Bell 1997; Johnson and Kiviniemi 2006; Marcell 2008; Padilla-Walker 2006).[15]

The disallowing of laptops and other electronic devices in the classroom has proven a more controversial approach to improving student accountability. Some students used their devices to take notes and to look up materials discussed in class online, but many others sat in the back rows of lecture halls and used them instead to post on social media, to catch up with the sports news, or to shop. Disallowing electronic devices made an emphatic statement about the priorities of the instructor, but it frequently also led to resentment. As an alternative, instructors ensured that electronic devices were being used for class-related purposes simply by walking the aisles while lecturing and

TABLE 8.3. Teaching Techniques Associated with Low and High Student Accountability for Learning

Low Accountability	High Accountability
No checks on whether students have done reading prior to class	Quizzes or prompts on reading are given prior to class
Attendance is not taken	Attendance is taken and points are reduced for nonattendance
Students are allowed to come in late and leave early without instructor's permission	Students are not allowed to come in late or leave early without instructor's permission
Laptops and devices are not monitored for class-related purposes	Laptops and devices are not permitted or are monitored for class-related purposes
Slides for class are available prior to class meeting	Many assessments are given
Assignments are not challenging	Assignments include relatively complex reading and lengthy papers
Few assessments are given	Feedback on assignments and exams is extensive
Feedback on assignments and exams is very limited	Students are required to attend office hours if grades are low
Students are not required to attend office hours to review work if grades are low	

docking points for those who were using their devices for non-class-related purposes. The elimination of screen-based distractions helped re-create the classroom as a "sacred space" in the Durkheimian sense, one that unlike normal life requires ritual respect for the "totemic" object of the subject under discussion and the focused attention of participants (see table 8.3).

The science of learning showed that student engagement and student accountability were both essential supports for the goals of teaching for understanding and cognitive development. The cultures of the disciplines, however, were divided so that instructors in more interpretive fields tended to emphasize high levels of classroom participation as the primary indicator of student commitment to learning and those in more quantitative fields tended to emphasize dutiful adherence to difficult work as the primary indicator of student commitment. With my colleagues Allison Cantwell and Robert Hanneman, I characterized these as the "two cultures" of student academic engagement (Brint, Cantwell, and Hanneman 2008), mirroring at the classroom level C. P. Snow's (1959) famous distinction between the two cultures of the humanities and the sciences. During the period, the two cultures slowly began to merge into one, as humanists looked for greater accountability and scientists began to incorporate higher levels of student participation.

TOOLS FOR UNDERSTANDING AND PROBLEM-SOLVING

Researchers in the science of learning built on many of the principles discovered by cognitive scientists and promoted by Lee Shulman and his colleagues at the Carnegie Foundation as "teaching for understanding." They demonstrated that effective learning objectives, such as showing the connection between course materials and students' career goals, can reinforce students' willingness to commit to cognitive mastery. They also emphasized the importance of showing students the process by which concepts, models, and principles were developed and something also about the personalities and conditions under which they were developed. They continued to emphasize the value of uncovering every step in students' thinking as they worked through problems. Researchers emphasized the importance of asking students why they came to particular conclusions and the necessity for quickly and considerately correcting those reasons when they were in error.

Learning scientists also emphasized the employment of exercises that can help students improve their analytical and critical thinking skills. These techniques have in fact been well known for decades, but many professors stopped using them in the face of increased student demand for easy-to-digest-and-remember content. They include assignments that require students to compare and contrast two or more perspectives on a topic of interest. To approach an assignment like this, students must first show that they understand the fundamentals of the analytical models under consideration. They must show that they can research the outcomes of cases in which each of the models was applied, and they must show that they can draw at least tentative conclusions from what their research has revealed. In this way, four essential elements of thinking come into play: definition of terms, evidence collection, application of concepts to new situations, and drawing conclusions based on evidence and analysis. The practice of preparing, performing, and analyzing experiments in science labs derives from the same tradition of deep thinking exercises, and it engages a similar set of mental operations: understanding the problem (definition), researching (through experimentation), analyzing results, and coming to conclusions based on results.

Researchers went beyond the precepts of teaching for understanding to consider also the teaching of problem-solving skills. Problem-based learning also has a long history (see, e.g., Bruner 1961), but it gained a new impetus from the market-related idea that students should show what they have learned in "real-world" situations. "Real-world" problem-solving exercises were intended to explicitly tie classroom learning to workplace dynamics. Many problems in workplaces resemble problem-based learning activities and call for the same work group engagement with problem definition, research on previous approaches, designs for interventions, and evaluation of the consequences of the enacted solutions. Problem-based learning approaches consequently focused on ambiguous problems that required students to attempt a variety of solutions, often using research to guide problem-solving, and sometimes also to design methods to determine whether the solution worked. An architecture class might, for example, work on building designs that maximize opportunities for inhabitants' interactions or an urban studies class might work on the best ways to determine the health care needs of a poor community and cost-efficient ways to provide for those needs once assessed. Well-designed problems of this type created a shared culture of learning and collaboration while at the same time engaging students' critical and analytical thinking skills.

Students exposed to problem-based learning exercises were required to go beyond the dutiful but surface work of repeating what teachers wanted them to know to the more challenging but also potentially more empowering work of applying what they had been learning to new problems that did not have immediately apparent solutions. These approaches required students to demonstrate persistence because they did not open themselves to readymade answers. As Shulman had argued, presentations of the work accomplished helped cement learning while providing students with the experience of receiving feedback on the approaches they had taken and the results of those approaches. In the professions, traditions such as medical rounds and moot court require public performance of knowledge because this performance is what counts in practice. Public performance can be a means of cementing knowledge ownership in the arts and sciences as well (Shulman 1997). It is one reason why posters and oral presentations became staples of the hundreds of undergraduate research symposia held annually on college and university campuses and why they have been adopted by some classroom instructors as well.

Given the new emphasis on problem-solving, it is not surprising that the trend toward student participation in undergraduate research advanced during the period. On many research university campuses, more than 50 percent of students engaged in an undergraduate research project under faculty and/or graduate student supervision at some point during their college careers either for credit, for pay, or as volunteers. Well-supervised undergraduate research could be a win-win for students and faculty. For students, it fostered deep engagement in problem-solving; for faculty members, it provided the opportunity to assist students by using the skills and passion that they brought to their own research projects. Dozens of research universities held spring undergraduate research symposia, with participation reaching 1,200 at the University of Washington-Seattle by the end of the period (University of Washington-Seattle 2018) and very high proportions of graduating seniors participating at institutions such as the U.S. Military Academy (Brian Keith, personal communication).

Indeed, many campuses adopted undergraduate research or creative activity experiences very early in the college career in order to capture student interest in the excitement of discovery and to make the drier learning in the classroom more interesting for its applicability. Advocates of early research experiences hoped that as students saw the payoff of these experiences, they would be more willing to spend time learning the concepts, principles, and tools that professional researchers brought to their work. The leaders in this area began to transform undergraduate education from a "sit-and-listen" experience into a "go-out-and-investigate" experience. One of these leaders, National Academy member Sue Wessler, merged bench and computational science with problem-based mini-lectures in a seamless whole for dozens of students in her first-year "Dynamic Genome" course (Warren 2018). In perhaps the most ambitious effort, the University of Texas-Austin started a program that involved more than seven hundred first-year science students in faculty-supervised research (University of Texas-Austin 2018).

Reflecting Mirrors for Instructors and Administrators

Since they were introduced in the 1960s, student evaluations of teaching have been used by instructors and universities as the primary means for providing evidence of teaching effectiveness. These evaluations provide valuable evidence on the elements of teaching that students are in a position to evaluate accurately. Those attributes include whether professors are on time, organized, clear, enthusiastic, and approachable. The biases of student evaluations of teaching are well known among researchers: less motivated students give lower evaluations; students sometimes focus on irrelevant features of teaching, such as an instructor's gender or appearance; and students are poor judges of whether they have learned much and whether teachers have been effective in producing deeper levels of understanding. One recent study, based on sophisticated statistical methods, concluded that "student evaluations of teaching (mostly) do not measure teaching effectiveness" (Boring, Ottoboni, and Stark 2016). This study joined a long line of research that came to similar conclusions. A good question is how this flawed system ever became institutionalized. Why would anyone expect students to have evidence-based knowledge of the techniques that can help them learn? It would be like asking hospitals to rate the effectiveness of doctors solely on the basis of what patients said about their bedside manner.

The Wieman-Gilbert (2014) Teaching Practices Inventory (TPI) emerged during the period as a promising approach to supplementing student evaluations with evidence-based knowledge about effective teaching.[16] The TPI was developed for science and mathematics courses, but it was used with minor modifications in social science and social science–related courses.[17] Following the completion of the course, instructors simply self-rated their use of research-based teaching practices using a point system developed by Wieman and Gilbert based on their assessment of the relative importance of the practices included in the inventory.[18] The inventory, which took ten to fifteen minutes to complete, included seventy-two items for self-evaluation.

The inventory included many items related to teaching for understanding: points for the specification of learning objectives, for lists of general competencies, and for topic-specific competencies instructors expected their students to gain from the class. It also included points for the specification of instructors' "affective goals" for the course, as well as for providing supplementary materials on websites or in handouts. It awarded points for including discussion of the process by which a concept, model, or principle was developed. It also allocated points for questions that required students to explain their reasoning for coming to a conclusion. It awarded points for assignments in which feedback was given and in which students were allowed to redo their work to improve their grades. It also allocated points for providing answer keys to students following grading of assignments and for encouraging students to meet with their instructor to discuss questions they answered incorrectly. It awarded points for the use of pre- and post-test concept inventories in which gain scores could be calculated for the class.

The TPI also awarded points for interactive engagement activities, including the number of small-group discussions during the term and the number of demonstrations, simulations, or videos where students were first asked to predict an outcome. It added points for the number of questions asked by the professor that were followed by student-to-student discussion. It also allocated points for lower fractions of the class given over to lecturing. Indeed, lecturing had to account for *less than 60 percent* of total class time during the term for instructors to gain a point on the TPI for good practice.

Recognizing the importance of student accountability, the inventory also awarded points for problem sets and assigned homework that contributed to the course grade. It included points for quizzes or prompts on the reading given prior to the class meeting to ensure that students were prepared for class. It included points for the assignment of papers or projects that gave students a degree of choice over topics. It also added points for the number of assessments used above a minimum of two, based on the principle that students learn more from multiple assessments of their performance.[19]

RESISTANCE TO REFORM

Faculty members who have not yet embraced evidence-based advances in teaching practice continue to express skepticism about the value of following *any* prescription for effective teaching. Part of this skepticism stems from traditions of academic freedom, which legislate against any interference in the classroom. Academic freedom protects the right of professors to express views that may flout conventional wisdom. On these grounds, some argue that expecting professors to use particular instructional methods impinges on academic freedom. And, of course, it is also true that different practices may be appropriate for different disciplines or different classes. Nevertheless, a distinction can be made between content and form. Academic freedom guarantees that the content of a course be left to the professor's expert judgment. But it is reasonable to expect that the forms of instruction be governed by professional standards based on well-established research findings.

Some have argued that efforts to pigeonhole faculty members into a particular teaching style robs them of their individuality and, further, that it is precisely the full expression of the individual personality that most affects students. For those who have argued this position, the conditions for human transformation are created by the match between the expression of the personality of an instructor and a student receptive to that particular personality. What needs to be weighed against this insight is the comfort that such a wide berth offers to instructors who are transforming no one, even as they dominate the great majority of classroom minutes. Teachers who are at the high end of the charisma scale should be left alone to work their magic. However, for the majority of professors who are not at the high end of the charisma scale, it is reasonable to expect that evidence-based practices should be given a tryout.

Another argument against the professionalization of teaching is resource driven; skeptics argue that instructors face severe resource and time shortages and any practices that add time to teaching should be rejected on pragmatic grounds. These objections are weighty when they come from instructors who have high teaching loads, large classes, and little institutional support. However, most of the teaching practices in the Wieman-Gilbert TPI require no more than a degree of forethought to put into effect. They are not onerous to adopt, particularly if universities were willing to reward those who made the effort. How difficult, for example, would it be for instructors to spell out learning objectives or to carefully align their course assignments with these objectives?

University administrators can use the same reflecting mirror discipline to determine whether the facilities they provide to instructors, the class sizes they sanction, the incentives they employ to improve teaching, and the metrics they use to measure effectiveness are better aligned with student learning or institutional interests in net tuition. Many institutions have found ways to enhance learning without imperiling the bottom line. I have mentioned a number of them in this chapter. These institutions can provide practical guidance on the way forward for administrators who are focused on monitoring body flow without sufficient concern for the cognitive development of the students flowing by.

THE MEDICAL COMPARISON

A comparison between education and medicine provides a sense of the distance to be traveled by college and university instructors. If doctors failed to use standard practices in the diagnosis and treatment of their patients, they would receive complaints from their patients and colleagues and could be sanctioned by their employing organizations. By contrast, students do not often complain about teachers who fail to use the teaching analog to standard medical treatment practices, provided they receive acceptable grades. And universities do not sanction instructors for their failure to employ them. But universities could easily decide to reward those who employ evidence-based teaching practices with higher marks on the teaching component of their reviews for salary increases and promotions. That would begin to make college teaching a professionalized activity, something that it cannot currently claim to be.

9

Other Challenges

COST, ONLINE COMPETITION, CONTENTIOUS SPEECH

The quality of undergraduate teaching was far from the only challenge that threatened the vitality of the American university system. Escalating costs were considered by many to be unsustainable and, even if sustainable, unjust to the millions of students who struggled financially to stay in school. Online entrepreneurs began to sense in the early 1990s that persistent quality concerns, together with rising costs, had created an inviting opportunity to disrupt business as usual on university campuses. These market opportunities led in time to an explosion of online learning alternatives and had many wondering whether the system of academic professionals working on physical campuses could in the long run withstand price and quality competition from online providers. The renowned management consultants Peter Drucker (quoted in Lenzer and Johnson 1997) and Clayton Christensen (quoted in Suster 2013) predicted the closing of thousands of colleges and universities by 2030. In addition, conflicts over permissible discourse drove wedges into the political culture of campus communities. Women and minorities protested against the indignities they suffered at the hands of insensitive white male students, while conservatives complained about the atmosphere for speech on campuses they considered to be governed by the stifling restrictions of "political correctness." In this chapter, I will examine the challenges of rising costs, online competition, and speech controversies—and evaluate the proposed solutions to them.

These challenges can be interpreted as problems of growth in the context of resource constraints. Cost problems were largely attributable to universities' requirements for sufficient revenues to support larger staffs and new responsibilities within the context of state disinvestment. Online competition was a result of the search for market alternatives to traditional, high-cost residential campuses within the context of an expanding system that included many low-income students. And the conflicts over speech were, in most cases, the by-product of tensions between students from comparatively privileged backgrounds and those from underrepresented groups in the context of competition for scarce status resources on campus.

The Affordability Conundrum

The cost "crisis" is easily exaggerated. No college affordability problem existed for most students during the period. To appreciate the truth of this assertion it is important to keep in mind three facts: First, college continued to be an exceptionally good investment for most students. College graduates earned more than $1 million more on average in their lifetimes than high school graduates. This amounted to a premium of about $25,000 per year in a forty-year work life. Toward the end of the period, the average public university student who took out loans acquired about $5,000 in annual debt, and the average private university student a little more than that. Graduate students tended to be more deeply in debt, but their labor market prospects were also more than proportionally better. Students who failed to achieve incomes 150 percent above the federal poverty line (i.e., approximately $18,000) struggled to make payments, but these students were a small minority among college graduates (ibid.). Instead, the students with unmanageable student debt loads were concentrated in three groups: (1) deeply indebted graduate students who had not located graduate-level employment opportunities; (2) students who attended for-profit colleges, where indebtedness was much higher on average; and (3) those who failed to complete their degree programs (Baum and Johnson 2016).

Colleges and universities offered hierarchical pricing: community college students paid least and elite private college students paid most. This contributed to a minimization of risks for students (although definitely not to reductions in income inequality across levels in the system). Moreover, net tuition was much lower than the sticker cost of attending college. Once federal, state, and institutional grants-in-aid and private college discounts on tuition were applied, the average public college student paid only about $500 more in tuition in 2011–12 than she had fifteen years before, and the average private college students paid only about $2,000 more (College Board 2015).

I do not mean to minimize the problem: even if the net price increases were not impressive, it is true that the costs of attendance continued to climb well above the rate of inflation throughout the period at a time when average family incomes were stagnating. This meant that families with children in college were paying a higher share of their incomes into college tuition. In the public sector, the higher tuition costs were, as I discussed in chapter 6, a direct response to declining state appropriations. Faced with a hole in their budgets, public universities turned to their most important alternative revenue stream, student tuition, to meet their payrolls. And, for families, net tuition and fees were only part of the total costs of college. These other expenses included living costs, transportation costs, meal plan costs, book costs, and hidden fees (such as materials fees in specific courses) (Goldrick-Rab and Kendall 2016). Taken together, they constituted a slightly heavier expenditure than tuition costs, at least at public four-year institutions. Policy discussions continued to focus, rather myopically, on tuition and fees only, when the distribution of these additional costs of college could have been front and center as well.

While the rising costs of attending college cannot properly be considered a crisis, they did introduce real strains in family finances, among both lower-income and middle-income families. When unexpected job losses or health emergencies occurred, these strains could turn into legitimate crises. Because states were on a roller coaster in funding public universities, neither families nor universities were able to develop stable expectations about college prices. Worse, tuition rose during recessionary periods, as states withdrew funding, at precisely the time that families were least prepared to deal with higher college prices.

For these reasons the affordability issue also cannot be dismissed as an issue only for students who had made a series of unfortunate choices or experienced unexpected problems in the labor market. Nor could it be dismissed as part of the sales pitch of tech entrepreneurs seeking to expand market share or of university administrators hoping to persuade state legislators to pass higher subsidies. The problems worsened during the Great Recession period; data from the SERU/UCUES surveys showed that about one in five students at leading public flagship universities said they had skipped meals occasionally for lack of money and more than three out of five said they had cut back on personal spending to help make ends meet. A number of other adjustments to financial hardships were reported, including taking more courses per term to graduate sooner, taking community college courses, buying fewer books, working longer hours in paid employment, and asking financial aid offices to renegotiate aid packages (Lapid and Douglass 2016, 7–8). If these behaviors were common at the country's leading public universities, it seems very likely that they were even more common at less well-funded institutions.

In contrast to the public sector, well-endowed private colleges and universities faced few affordability problems, even during recessionary periods when the market value of endowments tumbled. They were able to hold off for a year or two with hiring freezes and retain policies in which the great majority of students received some aid and those earning below upper-middle-class incomes received "full rides." However, less well-endowed private colleges were more tuition dependent and did face affordability issues, albeit of an entirely different type than those faced by public universities. Most of the private colleges discounted tuition deeply in order to attract large enough classes, a policy that proved over time to be a perilous path. NACUBO surveys showed a steady rise in the number of first-time, full-time freshmen receiving some form of financial aid—88 percent received some form of institutional aid—and average discount rates that reached nearly 50 percent by 2015–16 (Selzer 2016).

These colleges were trapped in a dilemma: they could not attract large enough classes without deep discounting. The trick was to raise tuition faster than discounts. But these continuous rises in tuition did scare away some families. Even with deeper-than-ever discounting, nearly half of the colleges responding to the NACUBO survey reported enrollment declines in 2015–16, continuing the pattern dating to the Great Recession (ibid.; Rivard 2014). A few colleges tried another approach, cutting tuition (and discounts) to show dramatically lower prices. This strategy also presented problems. Following the non-economic logic of status, students tended to identify high tuition charges as an indicator of institutional quality and high discounts as an indicator of the campus's special regard for them.[1]

Solutions to the affordability problem could, in theory, have been found in cost containment, in improvements to financial aid policies, or in higher (and more stable) state subsidies. I will argue that cost containment was a required part of any meaningful strategy to combat the affordability problem, but only improvements in financial aid policies promised a sustainable and durable path to reducing the severity of the problem. Federal policies began to change in the 1990s to reduce student exposure by allowing for income-contingent loan repayments and loan forgiveness options. As I will discuss later in the chapter, many problems existed with the design of these programs and with student levels of participation in them, but they provided a good start on a solution.

CAN COLLEGE COSTS BE CONTAINED?

One approach to the cost problem would be simply to cut expenditures in ways that did not harm core missions. During the period colleges and universities made strenuous efforts in this direction without making decisive progress. Some argued that this was partly due to the "cost disease" that afflicted labor-intensive industries (Baumol and Bowen 1966). Although education was one of the industries William Baumol and William Bowen had in mind when they coined the phrase, "cost disease" is a poor fit for understanding cost run-ups in colleges and universities, except in the most advanced graduate training situations. Colleges and universities can and do increase productivity by raising class sizes, sending more students off to study abroad, expanding summer term, hiring less expensive instructors, and in many other ways.

Better explanations of the cost run-up focus on the incentives universities face to expand staff and services. As I discussed in chapter 7, economists engaged in a lively debate about the role of "administrative bloat" in the increasing costs of attending college. It made sense that a larger number of senior managers with high salaries made a difference. And the expansion of administrative staff below senior management obviously contributed to payroll. But the best evidence suggested that increasing costs of administration have been offset at most institutions by the hiring of platoons of low-wage instructors. I discussed the deplorable consequences of this labor restructuring in chapter 7. Policy analysts have concluded that the costs of employing additional administrative staff amounts to a small proportion of universities' budgets and cannot account for tuition increases or costs that greatly exceed the inflation rate. Even at the most staff-heavy research universities administrative costs account for less than 10 percent of total expenditures (see Bowen 2013, 30–32).

Instead, the largest sources of cost increases at elite colleges and universities could be accounted for by efforts to increase quality by offering smaller classes or unique educational opportunities, to provide new services to students (such as state-of-the-art recreation centers and mental health services), to pay for large investments in new facilities and equipment (including IT), and to ensure access for low-income students through funding expensive financial aid packages (Clotfelter 1996). The costs of institutions are heavily driven by discipline and degree mix, with higher costs in the sciences than in the humanities and higher costs for graduate education than for undergraduate education (Middaugh, Graham, and Shahid 2003). Faculty members at these institutions contributed to cost increases less through salary demands than through lobbying for new research centers (requiring equipment and support staff) and for better support in research offices.

The more moderate cost increases at regional comprehensives and non-elite private colleges have derived from many of the same sources (notably new buildings, IT, and new services to meet the changing expectations of students). They are also driven by student preparation and course-taking behavior. When students fail to complete degrees or take many years to do so, productivity by definition declines and unit costs are higher than they would otherwise be. Very low four-year graduation rates are the norm at regional comprehensives—25 percent is considered a good showing—and even six-year graduation rates began to break 50 percent only at the end of the period.

College and university administrators found a number of ways to contain costs and they saved millions by doing so. Some of the more popular practices described by the National Association of Independent Colleges and Universities (NAICU) included renovating campuses for energy efficiency, consolidating administrative offices, outsourcing expensive campus services to outside vendors, centralizing procurement to put pressure on rates, and refinancing debt at lower market levels. Some campuses phased out very small classes and aggressively reduced administrative support costs. Some assigned administrative support services to less expensive student workers. By looking for inefficiencies and analyzing the value added of every administrative position, the University of Nebraska claimed to have cut administrative personnel costs by 5 percent (Rogers 2013) and New York University claimed a 7 percent saving (NAICU 2016). Many institutions recast their benefits offerings, reducing options or the value of benefits. (Some canny administrators introduced tiered systems so that only new employees found their benefits reduced, thereby limiting the outcry of veteran faculty members.)

Cost-cutting consortium arrangements also expanded during the period. Through banding together with institutions in their region, state, or quality stratum, institutions found that they were able to put downward pressure on insurance, procurement, and health care costs, eliminate duplicate courses, and provide new educational opportunities for students. The Wisconsin Association of Independent Colleges and Universities offered its twenty members more than forty-five cost-saving collaborations. These included joint administration of health plans, a study abroad consortium, professional development for faculty and departmental chairs, environmental safety audits, and data sharing and management. Between 2005 and 2010, it reported documented savings of $38 million (NAICU 2016). Dozens of other consortia following similar paths sprouted up during the period.[2]

However, these cost savings did not fully counterbalance cost increases— they only slowed them down. And even where they potentially allowed institutions to "bend the cost curve," few universities escaped the temptation to invest cost savings in new projects rather than passing them on to consumers in the form of lower tuition or living costs. The University of Chicago, for example, reported saving $75 million over three years; these savings were not used to make the university more competitive on price but rather allowed it "to invest in its core academic mission, including a continuing expansion of the faculty" (quoted in NAICU 2016). Tuitions held stable for several years at a time at institutions under state edict or governing board decree, but only a tiny handful of campuses reported actually lowering tuition after undertaking cost-saving measures (see AffordableColleges.com 2015).

FINANCIAL AID REFORMS

Improving students' chances of avoiding crippling debt can be considered a noncompeting alternative to reducing college costs. Congress and the banks began to search for ways to mitigate student debt burden beginning in the early 1990s. Over time these plans expanded to make more students eligible and to offer more generous terms. In 1998, Congress lengthened the amount of time available to students before loans were declared to be in default, extended the repayment period, and instituted new loan forgiveness plans for those who chose public service or teaching careers. The 2007 College Cost Reduction and Access Act allowed any remaining balance on direct loans (i.e., loans provided directly by the Department of Education) to be forgiven after students made 120 monthly payments working full-time for a qualified employer, provided that the employer was engaged in public service activities. A new income-based repayment plan was offered for all federal student loan borrowers in 2009, allowing students to fix repayment at 15 percent of calculated discretionary income. A series of similar income-based repayment plans were offered by banks in the 2010s with monthly payments reduced from a sum contingent on the loan amount and interest rate to a sum based on 10 percent of calculated discretionary income. In 2012, the Obama administration enacted a "Pay as Your Earn" plan, which offered reduced payments to borrowers in financial distress and loan forgiveness after twenty years of qualified monthly payments.

Student consumers and their parents often did not know about the plans because of the limited information provided about them by banks—and even by the federal government (Akers and Chingos 2016, 116–20). Nevertheless, use of income-based repayment plans increased; about one-quarter of undergraduate borrowers enrolled in them by the end of the period (College Board 2016, 17). The plans undoubtedly helped student borrowers avoid the worst outcomes of unmanageable debt.

Income-Contingent Repayment Plans

Nevertheless, economists found much to criticize in the federal loan repayment and forgiveness plans. Susan Dynarski argued that "there is no debt crisis" but rather "a repayment crisis." Students were being asked to repay loans at a time when their earnings were lowest and most variable from year to year. "As a result," she wrote, "there is a mismatch between the arrival of the benefits of college and its costs" (2014, 2). In particular, the standard of repayment in ten years' time was badly mismatched to adult earnings curves that peaked much later. Dynarski proposed an income-based repayment plan, with repayments rising with income. The federal policy Pay as You Earn, while recognizing financial duress, did not automatically adjust repayments to income. Some flexible repayment plans also existed, but the number of borrowers in these plans was much lower than in Pay as You Earn. Dynarski proposed that loan repayment could work in a manner parallel to Social Security, with loan payments automatically deducted from paychecks. She also proposed a longer time horizon for the repayment of loans.[3]

Sandy Baum and Martha Johnson (2016) offered a similar income-dependent repayment plan but one that targeted vulnerable borrowers explicitly and took a tougher stance toward colleges. Like Dynarski, they advocated simplification around a single plan designed to allow borrowers to postpone higher payments until their incomes could reasonably support these payments. They proposed that students be excluded from payments any time their incomes failed to reach 150 percent of the federal poverty level and that the proportion of all educational debt payments should never exceed 18 to 20 percent of discretionary income. For those outside these protected statuses, repayment assessments would vary by income, with higher earners paying a higher percentage of income on a sliding scale. Baum and Johnson advocated the principle that assessment rates should be set high enough and exclusions from repayment low enough to ensure that the great majority of borrowers repaid their loans. They opposed loan forgiveness on the grounds that it encouraged students not to repay loans and provided no check on the propensity of colleges to charge higher prices. They argued convincingly that loan forgiveness was expensive, estimating that half the costs of a universal income-dependent repayment plan would be due to loan forgiveness options set at twenty years out. They also recommended that colleges be held liable for financial consequences if high proportions of their students were unable to make loan repayments.[4]

By 2015, at least six countries were employing income-based repayment programs, showing that such programs were not beyond the ingenuity of governments, including those in Chile and Thailand commonly judged to be less developed administratively than the U.S. federal government. Each of the programs represented a variation on the themes advanced by policy analysts like Dynarski and Baum. In the United Kingdom, for example, all students paid a flat fee for college of £9,000 (approximately $14,000), and students began to repay their loans immediately after they found a job. Borrowers contributed 9 percent of any income that exceeded £21,000 (roughly $33,000). These funds came straight out of payroll. Both the assessment and the exclusion rates were quite generous by proposed American standards. And any remaining student loan balance was forgiven after thirty years.

To ensure the stability and expansion of higher education opportunities, a universal income-contingent loan repayment plan, one attentive to the employment realities experienced by students entering the labor force, seemed the most feasible and attractive recourse. In my view, Baum and Johnson offered a particularly well-designed approach, with attractive protections and incentives, that could be implemented should the political will develop to replace the current patchwork with a universal system of income-contingent loan repayment.

"Free-College" Plans

As tuitions climbed, seemingly more progressive "free-college" plans also proliferated. In 2016, the two leading Democratic Party presidential candidates introduced free-college plans, the more ambitious of the plans extending free college to public four-year universities as well as two-year colleges.

The term "free college" was a winner; it appealed to many politically progressive students, as its enthusiastic reception during the 2016 presidential election showed (Anderson 2016).

Someone had to pay for college; in the "free-college" plans that someone was the state and the taxpayers. By 2017, eight states had one or another form of free-college policies in place and others were considering proposals. Seven of the states limited free college to public community colleges and only one, New York, extended it to public four-year colleges and universities. The New York program consequently received the most attention. It provided tuition for all students attending New York State public colleges up to $100,000 in family income, with plans to raise the maximum eligibility to $125,000 (Campaign for Free College Tuition 2017), and it required students to reside in the state for as many years as they had received tuition funding. None of the plans addressed the costs of attending college apart from tuition—including room and board, health care, materials fees, and charges for extracurricular activities—leaving half or more of the affordability problem unattended for noncommuting students.

Each of the free-college plans identified revenue sources. These included lotteries, permanent endowments, irrevocable trusts, social impact bonds, college savings plans, and corporate donations (ibid.). Yet no one knew with certainty that these revenues would prove fully sustainable, and no one knew with certainty whether higher subsidies to individual students might in the end lead to lower appropriations for colleges and universities when states again came under financial pressure (Samuels 2017). Another unknown: How would turnover in governors' offices or state legislatures affect the plans? Not surprisingly, Republicans showed scant interest in them (Campaign for Free College Tuition 2017, 45).

Ironically, many of the free-college plans amounted to regressive taxation. For students fortunate enough to live in more politically progressive states, college tuition was already "free," or nearly free, because it was heavily subsidized through Pell, state, and institutional grants-in-aid. The same was true in the mineral-rich states that maintained very low tuition charges. Instead, free college subsidized students from middle- and upper-income families, who, under the existing system, paid, on average, a higher proportion of costs than their less advantaged peers (Chingos 2017). Even those plans that limited tuition freedom to community college created incentives for upper-income students to permit the state to pay for two of their college years, putting a burden on state finances while redistributing income to those least in need of it.[5]

A case could be made that free-college plans represented an electoral ploy aimed at college student voters to a greater degree than they represented a clearly sustainable and well-thought-out affordability policy.[6]

WILL THE STATES REINVEST?

State reinvestment would, of course, be another way to address the affordability problem, at least for the 70 percent of students who attended public higher education institutions. Before I consider what effect reinvestment would have, it is important to stipulate that state reinvestment is no panacea for an industry that is under strong pressure to add services and to maintain or improve facilities. Cost escalation is the single biggest source of the affordability problem and, as I have shown, it can be slowed significantly but it is only very rarely fully controlled. Cost escalation drives tuition much more than state disinvestment. Even if states raised their investment in public colleges and universities, they might have only a modest effect on expenditures and therefore on tuition—that is, unless they simultaneously forced tuition caps.

The most commonly used approach to examining the gap between college expenses and state appropriations is to count only "education and related" expenses and to plot them against state appropriations. As calculated by researchers responsible for the Delta Cost Study, education and related (E&R) expenses include spending on instruction and student services, plus a portion of spending on academic and institutional support and for operations and maintenance of buildings. These expenses are sometimes called "the full cost of education," even though, in fact, they gravely underestimate the full cost of education.[7]

Delta Cost Study researchers have been tracking the gap between E&R expenditures and state subsidies since the beginning of the Delta time series in the academic year 1987. Using Delta data, figure 9.1 shows the pattern of decline following recessions and shallow restorations during recoveries against the slow but nearly continuous increase in costs. (Figure 9.1 reports only on universities for which data were available for all years.) At the public research universities aggregated in panel A, the gap was only about $2,000 in the first year of the series but grew to more than $10,000 by AY 2015. At public master's-granting universities, a similar gap in the first year of the series grew to more than $8,000 by AY 2015. Restorations at the public research universities were barely noticeable following the Great Recession, even as costs grew at a faster pace.

a Public Research Universities (n=158)

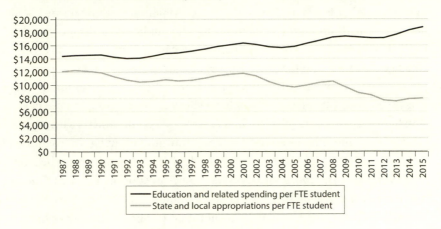

b Public Master's Granting Universities (n=228)

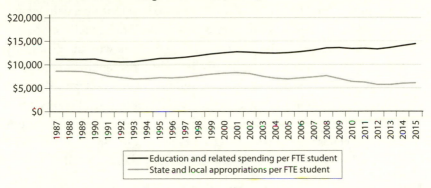

FIGURE 9.1. Education and Related Costs and State Appropriations per FTE Student,
AY 1987–AY 2015 (constant 2015 dollars).
Source: Calculations from Delta Cost Study Database provided by Steven Hurlburt of the
American Institutes of Research.

Should states raise their subsidy levels? Public goods theory suggests
they should, even if moderate increases in state funding will not fully solve
the problem of increasing costs. College education improves students'
economic opportunities. This can be considered a private good and consequently appropriately supported by students and their families. But, even
in the narrowest sense of the term "public good," higher education also
produces public goods. It produces many more adults who pay high taxes
and these taxes are used to support state programs that would otherwise

lack funding. Higher education is also strongly correlated with lower levels of crime, higher levels of civic participation (including volunteering), and better health. These have implications for the public purse, as much as for individual well-being. Areas with highly educated populations also attract strong employers who pay their employees competitive wages. These employees, in turn, buy goods and services from others in the community. As Enrico Moretti (2013) and others have shown, these spillover effects are substantial. Barbers and chefs in highly educated communities earn higher salaries than those in less-educated communities, allowing their families to achieve middle-class income more surely than would otherwise be true.

Few have raised more impassioned voices in support of an enhanced role for state investment than University of California professor Christopher Newfield (2008, 2016). Newfield argued that public defunding of higher education was American society's "great mistake."

> The great mistake was for our political system to give up on the democratization of intelligence. By that I mean the idea that, in a democracy, we must see the entire population as potentially intelligent if we educate them fully and fairly. The great mistake is to think we can advance by piling our best resources on a small elite—the 2 percent or so who go to Ivy-League-like private universities and liberal arts colleges. We have been trying this for many decades now—expanding enrollments while keeping everyday quality low. It is failing. I read the other day that political speeches were given at a 12th grade level in 1960, but are being delivered at a middle-school level today. (quoted in Lovy 2016)

Newfield (2016) argued that government had mistreated a public good as a private good, applied market rules where they were a poor fit (because the market underproduces public goods), and made higher education more expensive and more unequal than it needed to be.[8]

Perhaps, as higher education advocates like Newfield hope, the better angels of politicians' natures will eventually prevail, either because they find new revenue sources for universities or because they find alternative places to cut in their states' budgets. At some point a highly mobilized progressive public may demand these changes. Until that time, the empirical question is what state governors and legislators are likely to do, not what they should do.

As figure 9.1 shows, the prospects for substantial changes in the direction of more generous state subsidies are not promising. The pattern observed by Roger Geiger (2004) of large cuts during recessionary periods followed by shallow restorations below pre-recession levels continued during the recovery from the Great Recession but in a very weak way. With healthier tax bases and lower unemployment, most states raised subsidies but, in all but a few states, the raises were below pre-recession levels. And twelve states continued to cut their higher education budgets in AY 2015–16, well into the recovery period (Mitchell, Leachman, and Masterson 2016). Inundated by other priorities (including K–12 education, prisons, and the great expansion of Medicaid), unconvinced that the limits of elasticity of demand have been reached, and facing tax-averse populations, governors and legislators have made additional higher education spending a low priority.

The losses in state support were not related to lack of effort on the part of universities. Every state system has assigned well-connected staff or hired paid lobbyists to make the case for higher subsidies. These advocates developed solid, empirically grounded arguments responsive to the interests of state legislators. Republicans tend to be sympathetic to arguments about the contribution of universities to economic development, and Democrats tend to be sympathetic to arguments about the power of college to improve the life chances of disadvantaged students. University leaders consequently have every reason to continue to publicize the evidence of their institutions' contributions to innovation, entrepreneurship, and social mobility. Improvements in the efficiency of higher education, as measured by retention and graduation rates, are part of the case that can be made for state subsidies, and so too would be evidence of improved learning outcomes, should universities find meaningful ways to collect this evidence.

It is tempting in an era of accountability to suggest that performance funding agreements become more widely used, but in practice these agreements have tended to create as many problems as they have solved—from overinvestment in areas subject to performance funding formulas and underinvestment elsewhere to the manipulation of performance data to meet funding objectives. Nor have the formulas proven to be particularly durable; the turnover in state government ensures that some new administrations will want to undo much of what their predecessors have done (see Dougherty and Natow 2015).

In contrast, a worthwhile and potentially achievable policy goal would be to negotiate agreements about state subsidy levels over multiyear periods, so that both students and universities can plan ahead without having to face unexpected price increases to offset unexpected state budget cuts. Such compacts typically require agreements in return from universities about cost-cutting commitments and tuition caps. If costs are properly assessed and projected and tuition is set at realistic levels to meet legitimate cost increases, this approach can help stabilize expectations and planning for families and universities alike. It is an approach that was attempted in the State of California in the mid-2000s (Nicholas and Halper 2004) and adopted by both the State of California (Medina 2015) and the State of New York (SUNY 2017) in the mid-2010s. Universities may come to appreciate that the stability compacts allow is worth the restraints they require, but this will happen only if universities have partners who are interested in pursuing realistic approaches to understanding college costs and are trustworthy enough to follow through on their agreements.[9] It will also only happen if universities can project costs well and can provide a fair, lean accounting that universities do not, under normal conditions, have strong incentives to provide.

Online Juggernaut?

The rising costs of college attendance opened a market space for online entrepreneurs—some public and nonprofit, others for-profit—who saw the opportunity to provide equivalent or better educational products at a fraction of the cost. The limited effectiveness of face-to-face instruction in large lecture halls contributed to the attractiveness of the higher education market, as illustrated by the oft-repeated phrase, "Distance education begins in the tenth row." So too did the rise of "digital natives"—students socialized from an early age on the instantaneous pleasures and new social connections made possible through video games, Internet searches, and social media.

Beginning in the late 1980s, online entrepreneurs concluded that colleges and universities were suffering from uncontrolled costs leading to annual hikes in tuition and threatening the capacity of lower-income students to afford college. Worse, with professors more interested in scholarship and research than teaching, education quality improvements were difficult to detect. At a time when the United States needed more rather than fewer educated workers, the inability of colleges to control costs threatened not just poor students' mobility opportunities but the country's competitive position. The journalist Kevin Carey captured the essence of the indictment in the characteristically hyperbolic style of those who wanted to "reinvent" the university through the means of digital technology:

> The public universities that educate most students are in crisis. Rocked by steep budget cuts, they're increasing class sizes, cutting faculty salaries, and turning away tens of thousands of qualified students. Many of those universities offered mediocre, impersonal education to begin with.

Now they're getting worse, and nobody seems to know how to stop the bleeding. (2011, 226)

Software was "eating the world" and entrepreneurs envisioned higher education as the next fat target (Andreesen 2011).

Yet it was possible within a few years of the dot.com boom to draw a red line through most of the companies listed in Merrill-Lynch's *The Knowledge Web*, one of the bibles of the e-learning craze of the late 1990s (Merrill-Lynch 1999). Fathom.com, led by Columbia University and including such partner institutions as the London School of Economics, the Smithsonian Museum, and the New York Public Library, closed shop in 2003, $25 million in the red. The economist David Collis (2002) showed one reason why the revolution did not immediately materialize. The leading providers of online courses found the corporate training market easier to penetrate and navigate. Corporate expectations for quality were also higher, leading to quicker advances in attractive applications of online learning tools. Another reason was the "get-rich-quick" thinking of many of the early entrants, backed by abundant venture capital, but lacking interest in understanding how students learn.[10]

The pause did not last long. The for-profit University of Phoenix began offering online courses in 1989, long before most other universities conceived of comparable ventures. By the early 2000s, it was enrolling tens of thousands of students in accredited online courses and degree programs through its branches across the country. Other online-based for-profits, such as the Educational Management Corporation and the Kaplan Colleges, also showed strong growth in the 1990s. A few public universities, such as the University of Maryland University College and Southern New Hampshire University, were also beginning to build a market for broadly distributed online courses.

The best available data on online enrollments come from the federal IPEDS database.[11] Data from available years, beginning in AY 1999–2000, show that the number of students who took at least one of their courses online grew much faster than enrollments generally. More than five million college students were taking at least one online course by the end of the period, a number nearly five times higher than that recorded at the turn of the twenty-first century. A surprising one in four graduate students were taking courses in their programs exclusively online. Business, computer science, criminal justice, education, and health professions courses were the staples of online curriculum, and arts and humanities courses were offered comparatively rarely. Community college students were the primary participants in distance education in the early years of the time series, but four-year college and university students overtook them by 2010.

According to IPEDS data, seven in ten degree-granting institutions offered at least some online courses by 2015. About half of those courses were concentrated in less than 5 percent of reporting institutions. And 80 institutions enrolled 10,000 or more students in at least one online course, a 30 percent share of the total (Allen and Seaman 2016). The top providers were an assortment of aggressive for-profits (led by the University of Phoenix with more than 180,000 online students by the end of the period), evangelical Christian universities (Liberty University alone enrolled 90,000 online students), competency-based private nonprofits aimed at working adults (such as Western Governors University and Southern New Hampshire University), and military-friendly private nonprofits (Bellevue University and Park University were among the leading examples). A few public research universities were also heavily invested in the online market (including the University of Maryland University College, Arizona State University, and Pennsylvania State University) (Chronicle of Higher Education 2017a).

These online providers moved aggressively into new markets. Maryland signed multiple contracts with the military, and Arizona State signed contracts with Starbucks and the Mayo Clinic, among others. Purdue University, a late entry, purchased the entire for-profit Kaplan University platform. Most of the attention went to the giant for-profit operations—they were alternatively praised for attracting students who would otherwise remain underserved and castigated for misleading and abusive lending practices (for a comprehensive study, see United States Senate 2011). But, following enactment of the gainful employment rule, the for-profit share of online education shrank; by the end of the period most public universities were offering a sizable roster of online courses, and public university students had become the largest segment of the market. The legitimacy of nonprofit universities was simply higher than most for-profits could muster after a scandal-plagued era (see figure 9.2).[12]

WERE ONLINE COURSES JUST AS GOOD AS FACE-TO-FACE?

As online higher education caught on, a lively debate flared between those who reported no significant difference in learning between students enrolled in online as opposed to comparable face-to-face courses and those who doubted this could be true. Reviewing hundreds of studies from the 1990s, Thomas Russell (2001) found that the great majority of the studies

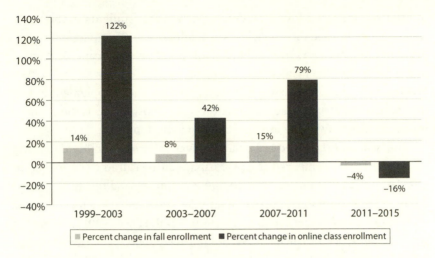

FIGURE 9.2. Percentage Change in Total Fall and All Online Enrollments, 1999–2015. *Source*: Author's calculation from IPEDS data.

showed no significant difference in learning between students enrolled in fully online courses, hybrid courses (combining online with some face-to-face interaction), and traditional classrooms. Russell's critics argued that the studies were systematically flawed—especially by their failure to control for the tendency of students who felt comfortable in online formats to take those courses and to perform better in them than a broader distribution of students would (see, e.g., Merisotis and Phipps 1999). Only designs based on random assignment of students between instructional modalities in equally well-designed courses could hope to answer the quality of learning question, they argued.

The cognitive scientists Marsha Lovett, Oded Meyer, and Candace Thille (2008) seemed to provide an answer when they randomly assigned volunteers to three modalities in introductory statistics courses at Carnegie Mellon University. The widely reported study found that students in the hybrid format performed better than those enrolled in the other two formats—with no significant differences between the latter two. In fact, the study suffered from some of the same flaws as others; Lovett and her colleagues selected students who indicated enough of a comfort level with online instruction to volunteer as guinea pigs in a study of this format. One might also wonder whether tech-savvy, high-achieving Carnegie Mellon students were the optimal subjects from which to generalize.

One of the better-designed studies of the period undertook a randomized control trial comparing face-to-face and fully online courses in microeconomics and found modest evidence that students in the traditional course learned more (Figlio, Rush, and Yin 2010). But another well-designed study using randomized control found no significant differences in outcome between hybrid and face-to-face only (see Bowen et al. 2013). Hybrid courses are expensive, of course, because they supplement online instruction with face-to-face instruction. When cost-saving is the primary incentive, few universities are interested in hybrid formats.

The issue was reopened in a troubling way by two Columbia University researchers who compared the performance (measured as course completion and grade) of more than 40,000 community and technical college students in Washington State over nearly 500,000 courses, a mix of online and face-to-face formats. Di Xu and Shanna Smith Jaggars (2014) seemed to solve the self-selection problem by looking at students' performance in the courses they themselves took in online and face-to-face formats. In other words, students were being judged against themselves, not against other students, for how well they performed in the two instructional modalities.[13] They found that all students tended to perform worse in the online courses, but performance was much more negative for males, African Americans, and those with lower GPAs than for females, whites and Asians, and those with higher GPAs. The study suggested that less prepared and less motivated students benefited from face-to-face instruction. The study raised equity issues about the bandwagon mentality surrounding online instruction. Just as statistics students at one of the nation's premier science universities may be a poor group from which to generalize, a good question is: How much do we want to generalize from the performance of community college students in Washington State? Researchers were digging in, but the question of the relative learning gains for students randomly assigned to online or face-to-face instruction remained in doubt.

SATISFIED STUDENTS, SKEPTICAL FACULTY

Students themselves expressed mixed but generally positive views about online courses. They liked the flexibility such courses provided—they could watch them anywhere, at any time, and in any state of dress and deportment. These were decisive advantages for working adults who needed to update their professional credentials or complete degrees required for career advancement. Students who were too shy to speak up in class often found online formats to be far more conducive to interaction than anxiety-producing face-to-face classes. They were able to polish their writing style on discussion boards, even if their oral communication abilities suffered some neglect. Others found that instructional quality, opportunities for interaction, and the reliability of the technology used all made a difference in their experiences of online courses; of course, these factors also influence the experience of face-to-face courses (Drennan, Kennedy, and Pisarski 2010; Inman, Kerwin, and Mayes 2010). Inquisitive adults often found online courses, even those they did not complete, to offer information that they could not otherwise easily obtain (see, e.g., A. Jacobs 2013). A sizable minority of students found online courses less engaging, and they tried to limit their online course-taking to those they found relatively easy or identified as necessary to "get out of the way." One of the students my research team interviewed said, "If there is a class you don't want to take, take it online and get it out of the way. That way you can save room for the courses you like or for your major. They aren't selling online courses because they are good education. They are selling them for convenience." Jaggars (2014) reported similar sentiments among a large sample of community college students.

Faculty members remained more skeptical than students. In 2009, the Association of Public and Land Grant Universities (APLU) found that 80 percent of those who taught face-to-face classes thought online courses were "inferior" or "somewhat inferior" to face-to-face instruction (McCarthy and Samors 2009). And for a dozen straight years through 2015, the proportion of university administrators responding to the Babson surveys who said that their faculties accepted the value and legitimacy of online education never topped one-third (Allen and Seaman 2016, 26). Where students valued convenience, faculty were concerned about quality—a concern bolstered for some by the survival instinct.

Some predictable differences emerged between those who had never taught online courses and those who had taught them, suggesting that experiences with online instruction might be enough to change instructors' views. But those who taught online also had distinctive interests that may have skewed their assessments. Some were technophiles—not the norm among the faculty at large. Others did not relish commuting to campus to teach their courses; they could put courses together and teach them far away from campus, sometimes in entirely different states. The enthusiasm of some instructors was undoubtedly related to the hope that canned online courses (with minimal updating) would eventually reduce their undergraduate teaching responsibilities.

In fact, online courses usually took more time to prepare and teach than face-to-face courses (Cavanaugh 2005). Bare-bones online courses—with camera fixed unblinkingly on a lecturing professor—were not engaging enough to hold most students' attention. At universities attempting to provide distance education at scale, online courses were expected to have production values, including multimedia presentations, libraries of online resources, and active discussion boards. Reading and responding to discussion board posts proved to be a consuming task for conscientious instructors, and email traffic also increased dramatically in online settings. Those who saw the possibility for cost or time savings were usually disappointed. Courses with high-quality production values ran up to $1 million or more to produce (McPherson and Bacow 2015). The new job titles "online course designer" and "instructional production specialist" proliferated as universities sought to raise the quality of their online offerings. Poorly resourced lower-tier campuses embraced the potential cost and convenience advantages of moving instruction online, but they could rarely hire staff with sufficient expertise to develop courses that were engaging enough for less-prepared students to value—or even complete.

Nevertheless, as online enrollments grew, the attitude of university officials seemed to shift from anxiety about the quality and effectiveness of online courses to a willingness to "let the market decide." As one of the corporate executives I interviewed put it, "The distance will tend to disappear between online and traditional campuses. There will be some of both and many types of partnerships between the two. Courses at universities that are not that good will disappear. Online providers will get those." Some of the executives I interviewed argued that students would prefer the convenience of online classes, while others said that many students would realize that they understood content better in a face-to-face course (see Brint, Paxton-Jorgenson, and Vega 2002). They would sort themselves out appropriately.

Elite universities continued to see market opportunities in fully online programs. The USC Rossier School of Education, the UC Berkeley School of Information, and the Computer Science Department at Georgia Tech were among the many campuses that offered fully online master's programs. For highly ranked universities, the certification requirements for adult professionals and the market rewards for universities meshed nicely on the Net.

MOOC EVOLUTION

An innovation released to fanfare in the early 2010s seemed to promise a solution to the problem of providing high-quality online courses for campuses that could not afford to produce them themselves. These were the so-called Massive, Open, Online Courses (MOOCs), promoted by two Stanford University spin-off companies, Coursera and Udacity, and edX, a nonprofit consortium of research universities including Harvard, MIT, and UC Berkeley. The two for-profit companies were able to raise tens of millions of dollars in venture capital, and they used these funds to recruit talented lecturers to enter a design process intended to deliver state-of-the-art online courses. In their first years of existence, some MOOCs enrolled as many as 150,000 students worldwide and courses enrolling tens of thousands of students were not uncommon.[14] These huge enrollments made MOOCs a sensation; the year 2012 was proclaimed the year of the MOOC by the *New York Times* (Pappano 2012).

Yet from the beginning, the MOOC providers faced criticism for their low completion rates. Hanan Khalil and Martin Ebner (2014) reported that the dropout rates of MOOCs offered by Stanford, MIT, and UC Berkeley professors were 80 to 95 percent. For example, only 7 percent of the 50,000 students who took the Coursera-UC Berkeley course on software engineering completed it, and only 2 percent of those who took Coursera's Social Network Analysis course earned a certificate for completion with minimal assessment. Some wondered why completing a MOOC should be any more likely than reading an entire issue of a magazine cover to cover. The motivation in both cases would be to pick and choose topics or articles that were of particular interest and to ignore the rest. Nevertheless, the low completion rates worried investors who hoped that the MOOCs would eventually storm the citadel of higher education, replacing many if not all face-to-face courses with the best-produced presentation by the best professor in the field.

Professors at less well-funded schools knew that they had something to fear. And they also spotted a vulnerability in the MOOCs: a one-size-fits-all philosophy. The MOOCs focused on preparing the optimal presentation by one of the most respected professors in a field without reference to the cultural backgrounds or academic preparation of the specific audiences the professor would be addressing. They relied on campus faculty to translate for students in the discussion sections following lectures. Members of the Department of Philosophy at San Jose University probed this weakness in their "Open Letter to Michael Sandel," after Sandel's MOOC titled "Justice," a famous course at Harvard, was adopted by San Jose State as a for-credit course:

> What kind of message are we sending our students if we tell them that they should best learn what justice is by listening to the reflections of the largely white student population from a privileged institution like

Harvard? Our very diverse students gain far more when their own experience is central to the course and when they are learning from our own very diverse faculty, who bring their varied perspectives to the content of courses that bear on social justice. (San Jose State University, Department of Philosophy 2013, 2)

The problem of how to sustain a viable financial model for MOOCs was not fully solved during the period, but the outlines of such a model did appear. MOOCs moved from open to all to behind a paywall for certificate seekers. In addition, Coursera contracted with some public university systems to offer courses for credit, with proceeds split between the college and the company, and they sold the names of students who had performed exceptionally well in their courses to corporate recruiters. The founder of one of the leading firms, Sebastian Thurn of Udacity, decided that the corporate training market had better short-term potential and shifted the attention of his company to that market, but the remaining U.S.-based firms and consortia were joined in the global MOOC market by two other major providers, one from Britain and the other from China.

In 2013, Coursera signed contracts with ten public university systems to partner in a variety of ways, not excluding the offering of courses for credit (Kolowich 2013). In the same year, a Gates Foundation–backed study led the American Council of Education to recommend that five Coursera courses be eligible for credit considerations at the 2,000 colleges and universities connected to its course crediting system (Coursera 2013). Although the period of infatuation with MOOCs had passed, the number of MOOCs offered worldwide continued to grow, passing the 4,000 mark in December 2015 and nearly doubling again to 7,500 by September 2017, up from just three in October 2011 (Chronicle of Higher Education 2017a, 41). Some of the problems bedeviling MOOCs also seemed to be on their way to solution, including protections against cheating on assessments, automatic essay grading (albeit without detailed feedback), and the introduction of self-paced courses.

A few faculty members who had signed up to give MOOCs as a way to reach larger audiences objected to Coursera's clear intent to make college and university professors into what the San Jose State philosophers called "glorified teaching assistants" or to eliminate them entirely. Princeton professor Mitch Duenier, a popular Coursera lecturer, severed ties with the company on the grounds that he did not want to participate in an operation giving state governors a reason to cut public university budgets further (Parry 2013).

Michael Sandel responded to the San Jose State philosophers with a brief statement that "the last thing in the world" he wanted would be to "undermine" other professors (quoted in Chronicle of Higher Education 2013b).

There are reasons to worry about the effects of technological displacement in an arena informed by teachers' assessments of student backgrounds, motivations, and abilities. I have personally witnessed the commitment of faculty at regional comprehensives to reaching and teaching their students. I recall one talk I gave on the campus of a California State University north of Los Angeles. In the discussion following the talk, I was immediately struck by the thought these instructors had put into their classroom practices and the creativity they showed in connecting with students at the level they found them. They spoke of how important it was to link their presentations to the backgrounds and interests of their students. Some had already adopted techniques advocated by leaders in the sciences of learning, and others were interested in learning how they could use or adapt them to their classrooms. Elite university professors might well have something to learn from such instructors. Research by Corbin Campbell and colleagues (Campbell, Jimenez, and Arrazol in press) suggested that instructors at lower-prestige universities in fact did a better job, on average, of scaffolding material for their students and helping them wrestle with new ideas.

Yet instead of lifting up the entire community of educators through sharing teaching practices that improved performance and fostered engaged learning, some presidents of elite universities concluded that it would be better to encourage the leveling of that community. At least one MOOC supporter, former Stanford president John Hennessy, was willing to acknowledge on the record that he wanted to put professors out of business—or at least into a diminished line of work:

> If elite universities were to carry the research burden of the whole system, less well-funded schools could be stripped down and streamlined. Instead of having to fund a fleet of ships, you'd fuel the strongest ones and let them tug the other boats along. (quoted in Heller 2013, 85)

The American Council on Education (ACE), the higher education association with the most inclusive membership, decided in 2013 to recommend that five Coursera courses be eligible for credit when students transferred to other institutions (Coursera 2013). The study of these courses proceeded with Gates Foundation funds, a far-from-disinterested party. From professors' point of view, the recommendation put the nose of the camel directly under the tent.

By the end of the period it appeared that MOOCs were poised to join the array of available creditable options in the labor market and, in a still quite limited way, on some public university campuses as well.

Thus the idea that for-profit companies would provide credit-worthy online courses was no pipe dream by the end of the period. The table was already set and universities like San Jose State were already experimenting with the introduction of MOOCs for credit. The quest of companies like Mozilla to introduce course- and sequence-level microcredentials as a substitute for degrees emerged as a parallel development. The "badges" promoted by Mozilla were analogous to those Boy Scouts wore for their outdoors accomplishments. They were stackable and presentable in an open image file. They recognized competencies, not programs of study. Adults could win badges for mastering specific skills such as multiple regression or computer visualization. Mozilla claimed that thousands of companies recognized the badges but provided little evidence that they had in fact made a significant dent in the credentials market (Mozilla Foundation 2017). Apart from a few instances, such as the Cisco Systems networking certifications for computer professionals, employers seemed to show little interest in microcredentials. Yet no one could deny their potential for disrupting the near monopoly colleges and universities held over higher-level educational credentialing (Olneck 2018).

QUESTIONS OF GOVERNANCE

In the end, there are two reasons why those who care about universities and their students have reasons to consider regulation of online offerings. The first is that not all students learn well in an online format. Based on the existing evidence, this appears to be particularly true for younger and less well-prepared students. But it is also true for students who need the immediate feedback of the classroom to feel engaged with their courses A good case can be made that going to class is similar to going to the gym for a workout. It is easier for most people to work out when they are surrounded by others who are doing the same thing. Highly motivated, busy adults often do just fine with a treadmill and weights in their homes, but most people are inspired by others who are physically co-present and working up a sweat together. Sociologists call this the power of collective rituals. Many classrooms provide analogous inspiration and discipline—and those that currently do not do so could.

This suggests that colleges and universities should look carefully at which students can perform well in online settings and which students are unlikely to perform well. One simple check, suggested by Xu and Jaggars (2014), would be to disallow online courses for first-year students and then to allow them only for students who have achieved a grade point average above an identified minimum—Xu and Jaggars suggest at least a B average. Before allowing students to enroll in online courses, advisors could also discuss with students the characteristics of those who tend to perform well and poorly in online settings. Further restrictions could then be imposed on those who fail or drop out of online courses. Colleges and universities prescribe what students can and cannot do in fulfilling degree requirements. Until the proof is in that lower-division students can appropriately self-regulate their exposure to fully online instruction, why should these courses be treated in a laissez-faire manner?

Beyond this, there is the issue of the broader educational value of the physical campus. Interactions on campus include not only the classroom but residence halls, coffee shops, and student clubs and organizations, and these interactions are important for students' commitment to campus life, including academic life (Astin 1993). As I showed in chapter 5, the experiences students have in their clubs and organizations include many closely aligned with adult jobs that require interpersonal skills. These interpersonal competencies cannot be developed easily behind a computer screen. Through their clubs and organizations, students gain experience running meetings, recruiting new members, hosting visitors, and working with others to plan and promote events. Students who are aspiring to leadership roles that require subtle interpersonal skills are unlikely to gain those skills if they are stuck behind a computer screen. Colleagues at the University of California have shown that the great majority of students are highly engaged in at least one of the learning environments provided by the physical campus, such as classrooms, research groups, and student clubs and organizations, or working in communities to solve civic problems, and a sizable minority are involved in more than one (Douglass and Thomson 2017).

For sheer information dissemination, online courses may be just as effective, at least for mature and motivated students, but that is less clear for other practices of high-quality teaching. We do not yet know the capacity of online courses to replicate the range of skill-building opportunities of face-to-face instruction. For the time being, most online courses are information deliverers, with feedback and discussion boards built in, but they do not necessarily excel as mechanisms for provoking students to stretch their critical capacities. Many face-to-face classrooms also fail in this way, of course. But this could be a comparative advantage of the face-to-face classroom, if more classrooms were designed for this purpose. Andrew Delbanco has made the point: "I don't think it is possible to overemphasize the distinction between instruction and provocation. It's a distinction that can be restated in many ways: facts versus knowledge, skill versus wisdom; discipline versus inspiration; information versus insight" (2012, 141). The face-to-face classroom, he suggested, can be the place where stakes are high enough for effective provocation to occur. The liberal arts curricula of companies like Minerva are attempting to provide comparable provocation; time will tell whether Delbanco is right.

The capacity to provoke is only one of the potential comparative advantages of face-to-face instruction. A short list would presumably also include: oral communication skills; persuasion of physically co-present classmates; providing and receiving impression-making mentoring; supervised field experiences; contributing to the quality of life of the campus and/or the surrounding community; participating in group problem-solving that requires weighing decisions in real time; creating a reputation for trustworthiness; reading verbal and nonverbal expressions accurately; and real-time discussions of scholarly and public issues. Of course, many classroom teachers utterly fail to fully utilize the comparative advantage of physical co-presence, but threats to job security could in the future lead to substantial improvements in their awareness of and practice in these areas of competitive advantage.

It is true that commuter and working students have more difficulty gaining the full value of the physical campus experience. But this should not imply that these students should be relegated to the periphery of campus life through a more or less exclusive diet of online courses, as so many "reinventing college" enthusiasts seem to suggest (see, e.g., Wildavsky, Miller, and Carey 2011), however reluctantly, as the only efficient solution. Instead, it means that universities should find ways to expand these opportunities and to fully integrate them into one or more of the powerful learning environments that only physical campuses can provide. It will require campuses to make an honest appraisal of the skills that cannot be easily developed online and then to ensure that opportunities to develop those skills are sufficiently plentiful on campus.

A second reason to consider regulation of online course-taking has to do with the vitality of the country's intellectual culture. This issue is obviously less visible in the day-to-day transactions on campus, but it is weightier in the long run. A world in which MOOCs or their successors dominate undergraduate education at less generously funded schools will not be a world that is hospitable to the survival of many fields and subfields of knowledge. Instead, it is a world in which the total intellectual horsepower of the country will be reduced. It is true that fewer than 5 percent of faculty members are responsible for the great majority of new knowledge produced in universities, but that new knowledge cannot find roots without the supporting structure of the much larger number of engaged faculty members who attend conferences, ask tough questions, read the literature, and teach consequential new work to their students.

A case can be made that intellectual diversity is at least as important from a cultural ecology perspective as biodiversity is in the natural world. The work of many different minds is necessary to foster the widest possible variety of potentially important intellectual developments, because it is rarely clear at first which new developments are most important. If serendipity and collision of ideas are essential features of productive and creative intellectual milieus, as I believe they are, it follows that larger numbers of "invisible colleges" working in fields and subfields are preferable to smaller numbers. The maximization of market power for a few celebrity professors would have negative repercussions for this diversity of intellectual life, an outcome that can be compared to farmers eating their own seed corn.

Peter Burgard, a Harvard professor of German, described how this process of knowledge retraction and flattening could occur in a future higher education landscape dominated by online courses:

> The fewer positions that are out there, the fewer PhDs get hired. The fewer PhDs get hired—well, you can see where that goes. It will probably hurt less prestigious graduate schools first, but eventually it will make it to the top graduate schools. . . . If you have a smaller graduate program, you can be assured the deans will say, "First of all, half of our undergraduates are taking MOOCs. Second, you don't have as many graduate students. You don't need as many professors in your department. . . ." And every time the faculty shrinks, of course, there are fewer fields and subfields taught. And when fewer fields and subfields are taught, bodies of knowledge are neglected and die. You can see how everything devolves from there. (quoted in Heller 2013, 89)

THE LEGAL EDUCATION MODEL

Some professional programs, including law, medicine, and dentistry, disallowed or limited the number of online courses students are permitted to take. Law presented a particularly interesting example of regulation based on assessment of student skill requirements. Forty-six states require degrees from accredited law schools. The law school accrediting body in turn requires at least 58,000 minutes of instructional time, 45,000 of which must be in regularly scheduled class sessions. No first-year courses can be taught online and no student in an accredited law school can take more than four units per semester online. A major reason for these restrictions is that law professors have concluded that it is impossible to replicate the Socratic method of ever-deeper probing questions outside of a classroom context in a public setting where the personal stakes are high. Legal scholars have also attempted to assess the skill requirements for proficient legal counsel. Some of the skills they have identified, such as teaching students to work effectively in small groups or to interpret complex legal codes, could arguably be taught as effectively through online courses with group projects and rigorous assessments, but others seem to require either face-to-face interaction or a public ritual focus (or both) to be successfully engrained in students' practices and habits of mind. They include: the confidence to speak publicly and to think on one's feet; practical skills such as interviewing, counseling, negotiating, and witness examination; development of a set of professional standards; inculcation of a sense of justice and understanding of competing concepts of justice; and instruction on different perspectives on the law (such as those of the litigator, the judge, the mediator, the arbitrator, and the legislator) (Schrag 2014, 121–24).

Like virtually every other domain of higher education, law programs have been under increasing pressure to allow more online education and, by the end of the period, the American Bar Association section responsible for legal education was beginning to chip away at its previous restrictions, recommending an increase from twelve to fifteen allowable credit hours online, eliminating the four-credit-hour limit on online credit per semester, and relaxing the standard that online courses provide "equal or excess" interaction as face-to-face courses, replacing it with the standard of "regular and substantive" interaction. Fully online programs for foreign students were also being offered by law schools at hefty fees. Surveying a changing landscape, the legal scholar Philip Schrag concluded:

> [Law schools] should give considerable thought to the elements of traditional legal education that should be preserved and how MOOCs can interact with and support rather than destroy within a few years a system

of legal education that the nation's universities have taken a century to develop. (2014, 134)

Schrag added that the current system had created a golden age of legal education, "which featured not only the transmission of knowledge but also the opportunity to hone skills in the classroom and the clinic and to explore values so that students could become critical thinkers and citizens" (ibid.). The underlying recommendation to assess and regulate the fit of online courses in relation to disciplinary (and related job) requirements is pertinent not only to law but to all academic programs.

Quandaries of Campus Speech

The last challenge I will discuss are the controversies over campus speech that erupted periodically during the period. College and university campuses found themselves caught between the persistence of insensitive and bigoted speech directed against minorities and the illiberal speech norms they tacitly allowed, in part, as a response to those instances of bias. These tensions over speech may seem trivial in relation to the more obviously challenging issues of educational quality, rising costs, and online competition. I disagree. Conservative media personalities and politicians ridiculed political correctness and identity politics on campus, and their criticisms contributed to undermining the confidence of Americans in their higher education institutions.

THE PERSISTENCE OF BIASED SPEECH AGAINST MINORITIES

There can be no doubt that incidents of bias and insensitivity continued to occur regularly on college campuses. These came in several forms: scandals that were sensational enough to hit the press; allegations of bias and hate crimes that were reported to police but may or may not have hit the press; and everyday incidents of wounding behavior as overt as an audible epithet or as difficult to interpret as a passing change in facial expression.

The existing evidence suggests that incidents with a profile high enough to be covered in the press were comparatively rare but became much more common during and after the presidential campaign of 2015–16. Reading through all Lexis-Nexis stories related to "racial incidents on campus," "homophobic" and "anti-gay" incidents on campus, and "anti-Semitic incidents on campus," I found what amounts to a steady trickle of reports on epithets shouted from dorm rooms, swastikas and "n-words" posted on residence hall white boards, bigoted flyers distributed on campus, and fraternity and sorority parties in blackface. There were also occasional incidents of harassment of African American professors, as in the famous case of William Cole at Dartmouth University in the mid-1980s.

Lexis-Nexis reported 260 total stories of racial incidents, 74 of anti-Semitic incidents, and 24 homophobic/anti-gay incidents on campuses between 1987 and 2017, with some stories repeated in multiple outlets. (Oddly, sexist incidents on campus were only rarely reported on Lexis-Nexis, though reports of sexual assaults numbered more than 2,400, again with some multiple reports.) Reports appeared more often from prestigious research universities, but this may reflect less about the rate of incidents than the urgency administrators felt to address them before the potential for protests escalated. It is not clear that these press reports are entirely trustworthy as a gauge of the actual number of bias incidents because some universities attempt to keep incidents out of the papers. Protected groups, on the other hand, will typically seek to publicize them. Whether entirely accurate or not, the press reports can be considered indicative of the instances of bigoted speech that occur with some regularity on college campuses.

More accurate data are available for a subset of years from the Federal Bureau of Investigation. A "hate crime" is defined by the FBI as "a criminal offense against a person motivated in whole or in part by an offender's bias against a race, religion, disability ethic origin, or sexual orientation" (FBI 2016). Campus hate crime statistics were collected beginning in 1992, following the passage of the Clery Act to improve campus security and crime reporting, but few campuses reported in the early years. As late as 1998, only 450 colleges reported these data to the FBI (Wessler and Moss 2001). Campuses were *required* to report hate crimes only in 2008 following a congressional amendment to the Clery Act. The data in table 9.1 from 2009 through 2014 come from approximately 4,700 two- and four-year colleges and universities. This amounted to one report for every six to seven campuses.

Most of the reported crimes consisted of destruction, damage, and vandalism. Acts of intimidation were the second most frequent of the categories used by the FBI, followed much less frequently by assaults. As in the case of press reports, typical crimes included racially derogatory email, anti-Semitic slurs, threatening messages left on answering machines, and KKK insignia posted on dorm white boards. According to 2012 data, a near-majority of these crimes were related to race. Crimes based on attacks on students'

TABLE 9.1. Campus Hate Crimes, 2009–14

Year	Reported Crimes
2009	672
2010	928
2011	761
2012	784
2013	778
2014	804

Source: NCES 2016b, table 329.30.

sexual orientation followed, and acts inspired by religious intolerance were third in prevalence (AIR 2015). Private, nonprofit colleges and universities were overrepresented in these statistics relative to public colleges and universities. Given the low proportion of students who attend private colleges, there are reasons to believe that racial tensions and FBI-defined hate crimes may in fact be higher on those campuses, though it may also be true that victimized students on these campuses are more likely to have the know-how and self-confidence to file a police report.[15]

The incidents of everyday wounding behavior that did not rise to the level of crimes or news stories is unknown and unknowable. Campus climate statistics reported in chapter 5 suggest that as many as one in four minority students throughout the period felt that the campus climate was at least somewhat unwelcoming to members of their group. As one Columbia University student said, "Just read the bathroom walls here and see if there's no race problem." There can be little doubt that some proportion of white college students will attempt to exclude minorities from mainstream academic and social networks and will treat these classmates with coldness and condescension. Some students have taken to calling such incidents "microaggressions" and claim that they are commonplace. Few social scientists discount the incidents of insensitivity and wounding exclusions that many students of color, many gay and lesbian students, many Muslim students, many Jewish students, and many outspoken feminists experience.

Yet it is also true that a potential exists for misinterpreting words of disagreement or ambiguous facial expressions as microaggressions. One of my former colleagues was notorious for questioning whether every statement with which she disagreed was a microaggression against her. These kinds of reactions, repeated in many variations, indicate that the term can be used as a tactic to halt conversation and to attempt to put members of putatively privileged groups on the defensive. It is also true that every student—not just minorities—encounters rebuffs, snubs, or disagreements that can feel wounding. Part of maturation is learning to interpret when these reactions are intended to be wounding and when they are unintentional or may be misinterpreted—and how to be resilient and assertive in the face of those that are intended to be wounding.[16]

With a few notable exceptions,[17] university administrators have been quick to address bias incidents out of legitimate concern for the well-being of minority students and because of their commitments to social inclusion. The entire panoply of administrative calming tools has been employed at one time or another to address incidents before they mushroom into angry protests that bring unwanted publicity. These include multiple listening sessions with disgruntled students, presidential town halls on issues of campus civility, workshops on political and social issues, establishment of new student centers to support minority students, and, in rarer cases, the implementation of requirements that students take a course on racial and ethnic and/or gender studies. Another indicator of concern: more than 350 colleges and universities passed hate speech codes during the period, though none that were challenged in court stood up to First Amendment objections (FIRE 2016).

CAMPUS THOUGHT POLICE?

The obverse side to biased speech is what has come to be known as "politically correct" speech. Political correctness can be defined as the attempt to suppress the expression of unwelcome beliefs and ideas and to penalize those who seem to express those beliefs and ideas. It can be interpreted as one of the accommodations that universities have made in their pursuit of social inclusion. In politically correct (PC) environments, students and faculty members were expected to speak the right words and to have the right attitudes. Denunciations of transgressors against politically correct speech were not uncommon. An Evergreen State University professor was accosted by students and colleagues after he protested that an announced "Day of Absence" without white people on campus was a form of coercive segregation in which he did not intend to participate. A Claremont McKenna College (CMC) dean resigned under pressure for saying that she was committed to working with students who "don't fit our CMC mold"—a sentiment that could have easily been interpreted as an (admittedly awkward) attempt at inclusivity. A Yale affiliate was pressured to resign over her advice that students not attempt to police Halloween costumes too minutely. These widely publicized events were the tip of the iceberg. On a day-to-day basis, the climate for speech could be chilling: one of William Deresiewicz's (2017) students told him that she had quickly learned to keep quiet about her Christian faith and her nonfeminist views about marriage. Another told him that she had to be quiet "about everything" because "she never knew when she might say something she was not supposed to say."

Reading all Lexis-Nexis stories between 1987 and 2017, I found 349 mentioning political correctness on campus (including multiples of cited articles). It was not difficult to find anecdotes that made college students (and the administrators who catered to them) sound ridiculously extreme. These messages included some truly surprising advice. A Scripps College orientation pamphlet observed that "white people are worthy of hatred and no one should feel bad for abhorring them" (Hoilman 2016). UC Berkeley administrators warned students not to say that "America is the land of opportunity" or "America is a melting pot" because it could be considered a microaggression against women and minorities (Volokh 2015). Politically correct speech was at times overtly bigoted against the members of putatively privileged groups, such as white males. Deresiewicz (2017), for example, described his experiences teaching humanities on liberal arts campuses: "If you are a white man, you are routinely regarded as guilty until proven innocent, the worst possible construction is put upon your words, and anything you say on a sensitive issue is received with suspicion at best."[18]

CONTEXTUALIZING THE ATTACKS ON PC CULTURE

Was PC a legitimate problem? There are ways to interpret at least one version of PC speech in a favorable light. This version—"PC-1," as Jonathan Zimmerman (2016a) called it—simply attempts to produce a more considerate and sensitive environment for student groups vulnerable to discrimination. There is nothing inherently wrong with such efforts—quite the contrary; they are one of the means by which social progress occurs. Some ideas that were once matters of contention become matters of socially accepted consensus with the passage of time. Only a vanishing number of ultra-right extremists, for example, believe that slavery is an acceptable form of social organization or that women should be denied the vote. Yet these were highly contested issues in the nineteenth century. It follows that some of what looks like political correctness today may look like humane attitudes and practices in the future. For this reason, many people on university campuses have stopped using the phrase "That's crazy" out of deference to the feelings of people with diagnosed mental health problems. We might consider this an overly intrusive form of censoring, but it can just as well be interpreted as evidence of a heightened sensitivity to the circumstances of others.

"PC-2," as Zimmerman called it, is something different: the attempt to impose a liberal orthodoxy and thereby to suppress dissenting views. Political conservatives rebelled against PC culture as coercive; they did not want their speech to be regulated by self-appointed campus thought police. Some of this was undoubtedly motivated by principled opposition to speech restrictions; some of it may have been motivated, more viscerally, by the desire to be granted a license to offend (see Binder and Wood 2014).[19]

Ridicule of extreme versions of political correctness became a staple in conservative media, and the recounting of cherry-picked anecdotes peaked when conservatives felt wind in their sails. Thus attacks on political correctness increased dramatically in the mid-1980s, during a period of conservative ascendance, as indicated by the popularity of books by Allan Bloom (1987), Dinesh D'Souza (1991), Bruce Kimball (1990), Page Smith (1990), and others who mocked the "illiberal education" provided by "tenured radicals." They spiked again with the rise of the Tea Party and the white nationalists of the 2010s (see, e.g., Horowitz and Laksin 2009). After presidential candidate Donald Trump said that "a big problem this country has is being politically correct," a national poll found that 53 percent of Americans agreed. When Trump's name was not used as part of the question stem, more than two-thirds of respondents agreed, including a majority of Democrats (Tumulty and Johnson 2016). You did not need to be a political conservative to find aspects of campus speech culture problematic.

But it was conservatives who jumped on the poll numbers to introduce legislation aimed at restricting speech on college campuses. Arizona enacted a law that schools "may restrict a student's right to speak, including verbal speech, holding a sign or distributing fliers or other materials, in a public forum" (Hardin 2018). And lawmakers in Michigan, Nebraska, South Carolina, and Wisconsin were considering similar legislation. Although these efforts seemed destined to fail the First Amendment test, they showed that reactions to campus speech issues were threatening to erode, as philanthropy executive John Hardin put it, "the foundation of free inquiry on which higher education is built" (ibid.).

WHAT THE EVIDENCE SUGGESTS

The contentious issues boiled down to whether nonconforming students felt inhibited to express views that some of their classmates might find to violate liberal orthodoxies; whether resort to politically correct norms reduced students' capacity to argue effectively for positions they favored; and, most fundamentally, whether the epistemologies supporting political correctness represented a threat to the principles of careful and critical discourse, the foundations on which scholarship and science rest.

An Open or Closed Door for Speech?

Survey questions provided a murky picture of college students' views about free speech because responses were not consistent across surveys and because responses depended greatly on question wording. The available evidence suggested that the climate for speech grew somewhat more restrictive during the period. Throughout the period, a majority of freshmen surveyed by UCLA's Higher Education Research Institute said that campuses should prohibit racist and sexist speech. The proportions increased from 60 percent in the early 1990s to more than 70 percent in the mid-2010s (Glinski 2016; Harper and Hurtado 2007). (Seniors were only a little less likely than freshmen to say that this speech should be banned.) Yet a survey of more than 3,000 students at 240 colleges and universities in 2016 showed that more than 75 percent of students said colleges should expose students to all types of speech, including those that some might experience as biased or offensive. Nearly the same proportion said that colleges should *not* attempt to limit speech that members of some groups might find upsetting or offensive (Gallup Organization 2016).[20]

The students in this Gallup survey were nevertheless concerned that speech conventions on campus may have felt overly constraining by some of their peers. More than half of students felt that the speech climate on their campus prevented some students from saying what they believed because others might find it offensive. Students who identified as Republicans were particularly likely to agree with the statement. Students also said they made little effort to listen to those with contrasting views: fewer than 20 percent said they did a good job of seeking out and listening to different views, a lower proportion than found among the adults surveyed by the same pollsters (ibid.).

Students also seemed less inclined over time to tolerate the views of invited speakers with whom they disagreed. About one-quarter of freshmen surveyed by UCLA said in 1986 that colleges should have the right to ban extreme speakers; by the mid-2000s more than 40 percent agreed (Harper and Hurtado 2007). The variations in responses to other surveys from the mid-2010s were sizable, ranging from about one-quarter to more than half of college students agreeing that offensive speakers should be banned. This wide variation suggested that the political leanings of the pollsters (or their funders) may have consciously or inadvertently influenced the findings (cf. Bowman 2017; Villasenor 2017).

Efforts to disinvite speakers perceived to be offensive were not uncommon. According to the Foundation for Individual Rights in Education, campus groups attempted to disinvite 342 speakers between 2000 and mid-2017 (FIRE 2017). Not all of these attempts were related to the political views of the speakers, but the majority were. Attempts from the Left were more than twice as common as those from the Right (by a margin of 209 to 102). The Left objected to speakers' views on race, gender, and foreign policy (particularly the Palestinian-Israeli conflict). The Right was more often concerned about abortion and contraception but also focused on immigration and foreign policy. Attempts to disinvite speakers crested after 2012, and throughout the 2000–2016 period nearly half of the attempts were successful (author's calculations). Some of the disinvited speakers had gained reputations as outrageous provocateurs; others were politicians whose actions in office offended campus groups; and a few, such as the geneticist James Watson and the social scientist Charles Murray, advanced ideas about race that students and faculty members found offensive. The idea of the university as a haven for free speech appeared to be in retreat, driven by students' unwillingness to countenance views with which they disagreed.

A Failure to Equip?

One of the more frequently heard arguments against PC culture was that it denied students the opportunity to learn to defend their views against the opposition of others. It did so, the critics argued, by permitting students to fall back on their feelings rather than encouraging them to think through and clarify their arguments against those of opponents (see, e.g., Lukianoff 2014). This position was well articulated by Geoffrey Stone, a law professor at the University of Chicago: "[A] university . . . should instill in its students and faculty the importance of winning the day by facts, by ideas, and by persuasion, rather than by force, obstruction, or censorship" (quoted in University of Chicago Law School 2016).

Did professors fail to equip their students to think through their assumptions and argue their positions with facts, ideas, and persuasion? In a survey of college faculty, Neil Gross found that politics rarely came up in science or engineering classrooms. Elsewhere, most professors he surveyed claimed to practice "political transparency": "If the topic on a given day calls for discussion of political issues, they may, if they deem it pedagogically helpful, reveal to students their own views while also working to ensure that this does not foreclose discussion" (2013, 206). Only a small minority said they practiced a more doctrinaire "critical pedagogy." Of course, one does not know how well these survey responses correspond to actual conduct in the classroom.[21]

If we narrow Geoffrey Stone's argument to focus solely on whether students are learning to wrestle with ideas they may find challenging, there are hints in the literature—though they are the barest of hints—that colleges and universities failed to achieve this educational aim as often as would have been desirable. A study I conducted with Allison Cantwell and Preeta Saxena, for example, suggests that college majors do not vary greatly in their expectations for analytical and critical thinking—and, further, that these expectations are not high. We found no significant variation between majors at University of California campuses in the frequency with which students said they experienced opportunities to develop their thinking skills through arguing positions with evidence, comparing and contrasting positions on a topic, or evaluating methods and conclusions. We did not find high mean scores on this scale, and we were surprised, in particular, that students in humanities and social science majors did not report more of these analytical and critical thinking experiences than students in natural science or engineering majors (Brint, Cantwell, and Saxena 2012).

An ambitious observational study by Corbin Campbell and colleagues reached similar conclusions. The Campbell team coded teaching behaviors in some six hundred classrooms on nine campuses of varying levels of prestige. Observers were trained for approximately thirty hours in the coding of behaviors linked to quality of teaching. One of the scales in the Corbin study is of particular interest: the extent to which teachers "prodded students to wrestle with new ideas." Campbell and her colleagues found mean scores on this scale closer to a rating of "ineffective" at high-prestige institutions and scores closer to a rating of "somewhat effective" at low-prestige institutions, with significantly higher scores for instructors working at the less prestigious institutions (Campbell, Jimenez, and Arrazol in press).

As I say, studies like these provide mere hints of a problem. More important, I think, are the logical problems with Geoffrey Stone's argument. One can learn to dissect competing arguments in a political theory class without this skill necessarily translating into the campus political arena. After all, the realm of politics is not only based on who has the better evidence and arguments. It is based as much on who has the more effective rhetoric and stronger passion and who can form the more motivated coalitions. These are skills that classroom debate minimizes or leaves out entirely. In highly politicized situations, convictions may seem situationally relevant in ways that winning the day by superior arguments does not.

The Campbell study is relevant to this point. In addition to comparing teaching practices across prestige levels, Campbell and her colleagues also compared instructors at comprehensive universities to those teaching at liberal arts colleges. Liberal arts college instructors scored on average close to an "effective" rating on the "wrestling with ideas" scale, as we might expect in these small, intellectually intense settings. Yet students at these colleges were also the ones who seemed to appear most frequently in stories about political correctness on college campuses. Recall, for example, the protests against the biology professor at Evergreen State College who refused to participate in "A Day of Absence" without white people, the students at Middlebury College who shouted down the controversial social scientist Charles Murray, and the Claremont McKenna College students who demanded their dean's resignation for advocating consideration of students who "don't fit our CMC mold." There is some indirect evidence here for the proposition that political convictions may overpower even very well-developed equipment for arguing when fundamental beliefs are felt to be under attack. The upshot may be that campus leaders would do better to depoliticize volatile situations than to worry about whether these situations show that they are failing to equip their students to argue dispassionately about politics.

Flawed Epistemology?

I now come to the most controversial topic of all: whether a connection existed between politically correct speech and epistemological attacks on traditional university norms of discourse. For a generation of left-leaning intellectuals, the new epistemological assumptions originated in the work of the *engagé* philosophers of the 1960s and 1970s—figures such as Pierre Bourdieu, Jacques Derrida, Michel Foucault, Richard Rorty, and, later, Judith Butler. These writers argued that truth was not discovered through the canons of rational discourse but was instead a feature of the hegemony of the powerful.

I will take as illustrative the example of Michel Foucault, among the most widely read and cited of the challengers to the rationalistic tradition.[22] What is essential to Foucault is how knowledge and power systems must combine to render an effect. Together epistemic regimes govern social life. Where madness, for example, was associated with religious mania in societies whose behavioral norms were governed by priests, it became, under the aegis of rising state bureaucrats, a threat to public order and a condition whose correction required confinement and confrontational rehabilitation in state-run asylums. Subsequently, it became a private disease whose treatment fell under the authority of the medical establishment. All of these approaches to madness were at once epistemic movements and movements of governance (Foucault [1961] 1964). By recognizing power as a determining force, the new epistemologies were inclined to see the university's pretensions to rational discourse as a mere sideshow or, worse, imbued with the assumptions of the powers of the age.

One of Foucault's critics, the philosopher John Searle, put it this way:

> The traditional university claims to cherish knowledge for its own sake and for its practical applications, and it attempts to be apolitical or at least politically neutral. The university [of the new philosophers] thinks that all discourse is political . . . and it seeks to use the university for beneficial rather than repressive political ends. (1994, 56)

The new epistemology took many humanities and some social science departments by storm. In the late 1980s, the heads of six nationally prominent humanities centers wrote, "As the most powerful modern philosophies and theories have been demonstrating, claims of disinterest, objectivity and universality are not to be trusted." Claims to objectivity, they argued, were usually no more than disguised forms of power seeking (ACLS 1989, 18).[23] Critique is essential to universities, and the new philosophers developed a powerful critique of existing cultural traditions and social relations.

Foucault and other power-centered philosophers were undoubtedly correct that knowledge must be adopted and enforced by a power structure to become an institutionalized force in social life. Yet the power of research to change practice also should not be discounted. Thousands of studies of mental illness—Foucault's madness—have led to pharmacological treatments for depression (see, e.g., Kramer 1993), better understanding of its triggers, cognitive-behavioral therapies that have shown measurable results (Hoffmann et al. 2012), coping strategies that help individuals prone to anxiety to remain on an even keel (Lazarus and Folkman 1984), and awareness of the psychological damage done by solitary confinement in prisons (Haney 2006).

There are good reasons to wonder whether the power-centered epistemologies served universities well, quite apart from their empirical shortcomings. As a counterpoint Searle (1994) laid out some of the basic tenets of what he provocatively called "the Western rationalistic tradition"[24] and others have called the university's norms of "careful and critical discourse":

> Knowledge is typically a mind-independent reality. It is expressed in a public language, it contains true propositions—these propositions are true because they accurately represent that reality—and knowledge is arrived at by applying, and is subject to, constraints of rationality and logic. The merits and demerits of theories are largely a matter of meeting or failing to meet the criteria implicit in this conception. (Searle 1994, 69)

Searle and others who supported the rationalistic tradition were not concerned with whether evidence and logic-based discourse had an effect in the world. They understood that it may or may not. They were concerned instead with its internal and external validity. Social movement organizations, state bureaucrats, political parties, and business networks are the vehicles of new power/knowledge systems more than universities usually are. But universities were nevertheless essential, Searle implied, for providing reasoned arguments for and against the aims of these organizations and networks. They were essential for knowing what scholars and scientists do not as yet know. And they were essential, at the deepest level, for upholding the principles of a world based on rational discourse that stretched beyond the confines of existing power/knowledge systems. Ironically, the university is founded on a belief in careful and critical discourse that reason itself cannot prove. But without the effective maintenance of this singular belief universities lose their capacity to shed new light, to criticize all that exists on the basis of new knowledge, to expand the consciousness of the powerful, and even at times to forge tools for dissenters.

A NEW FREE SPEECH MOVEMENT

A few universities emerged prior to the presidential campaign of 2016 to challenge the inclination of students to wall themselves off from speech they found threatening or offensive. One was the University of Chicago. After a series of interrupted events on campus, Robert Zimmer, the president of the University of Chicago, appointed a committee in 2014 to make recommendations on freedom of expression. The committee issued a statement the following year. It argued, in part:

> For members of the University community, as for the University itself, the proper response to ideas they find offensive, unwarranted and dangerous is not interference, obstruction, or suppression. It is, instead, to engage in robust counter-speech that challenges the merits of those ideas and exposes them for what they are. To this end, the University has a solemn responsibility not only to promote a lively and fearless freedom of debate and deliberation, but also to protect that freedom when others attempt to restrict it. (University of Chicago 2015)

The university's statement was adopted by more than half a dozen universities shortly after its release. The university's dean of students, John Ellison, referred to the committee's statement in a letter to incoming freshmen that he sent in August 2016.

> Our commitment to academic freedom means that we do not support so-called "trigger warnings," we do not cancel invited speakers because their topics might prove controversial, and we do not condone the creation of intellectual "safe spaces" where individuals can retreat from ideas and perspectives at odds with their own. (Ellison 2016)

These were outlying positions at the time. However, the climate of university opinion changed noticeably following the 2016 presidential election. This change may have been due to administrators' experiences with students who shouted down speakers or to the influence of high-profile articles on the negative consequences of overprotection (see, e.g., Lukianoff and Haidt 2015). More likely, it was a response to the public's expressed view that political correctness had become a "major problem"—and in some cases also to pressures from alumni donors to do something about it (see PEN America 2017, 2–3). The changing mood was evident in the higher education press where campuses like Purdue University, with a long history of supporting freedom of speech, were held up as models (Brown 2017). It was also evident in the appearance of the Heterodox Academy, an association of academics critical of restrictive campus speech practices, whose membership rose from 25 in fall 2015 to more than 1,250 two years later (Heterodox Academy 2017). Unlike previous critics of campus discourse, this group included professors and graduate students of all political persuasions.

The University of California-Berkeley's decision to invite a number of right-wing speakers to campus symbolized the new mood on campus (see, e.g., Schatz 2017). There was an undeniable fittingness in Berkeley's assumption of leadership in a second "free-speech" era, and an obvious irony in its sponsorship of radically conservative as compared to the leftist speakers it had tolerated during the first free speech movement. Yet the spectacle of professional provocateurs baiting Berkeley students and faculty without opportunities for dialogue and debate bore little resemblance to anyone's idea of an ideal speech situation. The Berkeley chancellor took a principled position that the "Year of Free Speech" she proclaimed would consist primarily of conversations among those holding opposed positions on topics such as whether colleges should ban offensive speech and how they should determine merit for purposes of admission. One hoped that academic leaders would follow Berkeley's example by moving, when they could do so, beyond the expensive spectacle of offering platforms to ethnonationalist demagogues as a concession to free-speech advocates of the Right.[25]

Academics who are genuinely committed to the value of free inquiry will want students to feel free to express views that do not conform to the majority opinion—and to feel empowered to challenge the majority opinion with evidence and arguments. The question for university administrators became how best to protect the gains for students (and universities) that flowed from their commitment to social inclusion in a political environment hostile to the norms that had so greatly influenced campus speech during the period. The attempt to roll back every feature of PC culture ran the risk of alienating students who were central to the universities' aspirations for social inclusion. It also raised the specter of a university callous to the injustices of American life. However, if universities desired to extend their bipartisan support, only one appealing, if potentially treacherous, path emerged: to provide consideration also for the experiences of lower-income and first-generation students, regardless of race, while reducing, to the extent possible, administratively condoned excesses of political correctness, and deepening *all* students' exposure to the liberating potential of the rationalistic tradition.

10

The Ends of Knowledge

Higher education historians often look to the 1950s and 1960s as the golden age of U.S. higher education (see, e.g., Geiger 1993; Labaree 2017; Neal, Smith, and McCormick 2008), but, by most measures, the appellation "golden age" is a better fit for the period covered in this book. During the period research expenditures from all sources grew by more than nine times through 2010 in constant dollars, and Web of Science publication and citation counts increased at nearly every one of the two hundred top U.S. research universities (Brint and Carr 2017). Both undergraduate and graduate enrollments nearly doubled (NCES 2016b, tables 303.70, 303.80). Instructional budgets per FTE student increased, even during the Great Recession period, nearly as fast at public universities as at private institutions (Brint et al. 2016, tables 1 and 2). The contribution of knowledge-sector industries also gained ground during the period, advancing up from about one-third in 1980 to about one-half of GDP in 2010 (Brint 2014). The proportion of the workforce with graduate degrees that provided some assurance of rigorous study and advanced cognitive skills edged up close to 15 percent of the adult population.[1] Many observers came to see universities as the cocreators of the future American economy, in collaboration with industry and government.

Yet the United States was still far from realizing the dream of theorists of postindustrial society: an economy dominated by knowledge-based industries and a social order directed by those who excel in cognitive rationality (cf. Baker 2014). College graduation certainly was no indicator of developed cognitive skills. Only a minority of college graduates were able to understand the differences in diametrically opposed editorials on the same subject or read a three-variable graph relating age, exercise, and blood pressure (Kutner et al. 2007). The gains of college students on tests of analytical and critical thinking were not impressive (Arum and Roksa 2011; Pascarella et al. 2011). Nor were universities the major producers of research in the United States. Business corporations had a presence that was at least twice as large, if we consider basic and applied research together (National Science Board 2016, chap. 4), and they conducted nearly as much basic research as universities. Universities did not have the capacity to fund their own work. The university share of academic research funding was about one-fifth of the total. Research universities would have collapsed without federal and state financial aid and research funding. Even in the sphere of training, colleges and universities competed with corporations. Firms offered on-the-job training activities that were at least equal in size to the educational endeavors of colleges and universities. Only in their power to issue the exchangeable currency of accredited degrees did colleges and universities stand out as a singularly important contributor to the American economy.

When considered in this light, the idea of a knowledge-based society, run by people with PhDs, seems a flight of fancy only professors at elite universities could project as a probable future. In a capitalist society, firms are the axial institutions, and the state endeavors, above all, to create a climate conducive to their profitability, while substituting for firms in areas like national security that are nonexcludable or have positive externalities that cannot be fully monetized. Universities fit in by certifying college graduates who are flexible and trainable and, at higher levels, have knowledge and skills that add substantial value to their employing organizations. They also contribute new technologies, other relevant research, and new ideas and concepts for public enlightenment. When I describe the possibility of a stronger contribution for universities in the future, as I will in what follows, I do not mean to suggest that they are on their way to becoming the central institutions of a knowledge-based society. I mean that the contributions they currently make can be greatly enhanced.

I have put forward a novel argument in this book, and I begin this concluding chapter by briefly reviewing the argument and its implications. The argument focuses on accommodation and conflict among three logics of practice influencing the development of contemporary universities. The first is the intellectual logic of disciplinary advance and education in the disciplines (including at the interstices of the disciplines). This logic takes root in the traditional structures of academe: the disciplinary associations, the respected journals, and the academic departments. The second is a market logic that encourages administrators and faculty members to pursue new sources of revenue wherever they can find them, so long as they can be justified on academic grounds. Technological innovation is a privileged element in this market logic, because it is the most dynamic source of economic development to which universities contribute. The third is a social inclusion logic that seeks to incorporate members of disadvantaged groups into the campus culture. The book has been an exploration of the ways that colleges and universities have woven together these competing, sometimes dissonant, but ultimately compatible principles: the search for as-yet undiscovered knowledge, the pursuit of new market opportunities, and the movement for greater social inclusion.

There can be no doubt that these three logics sometimes come into conflict. Universities' commitments to technological innovation have raised concerns about whether some schools and departments are becoming adjuncts of corporate research labs and are too close to business to serve as an independent source of innovation. They have led to conflicts of commitment and conflicts of interest. And they have raised questions about whether university researchers are abrogating their educational responsibilities and commitments to open science in pursuit of business ties. Universities' commitments to social inclusion have stirred controversies about who should be admitted to selective colleges, who should be hired and promoted—and the grounds that should be used to make these decisions. They have led to frequent dust-ups about the significance of the cultural achievements of consecrated thinkers working in the world's economic core countries as compared to dissidents and those living in its peripheries. And they have embroiled the university in controversies about the imposition of politically progressive speech norms. And yet the drive for technological innovations and the commitment to social inclusion have been engines not only of growth but of the growing prominence of universities.[2]

In the book, I have analyzed the often surprising consequences of expansion. As students and patronage poured into colleges and universities during the period, the institutions gained unexpected new powers together with gaping vulnerabilities. The growth of graduate populations created assembly lines for producing analytically competent personnel for the country's knowledge-intensive industries. These four dozen or so major industries—ranging from aeronautics to wireless communications—did not dominate the economy as theorists of postindustrial society predicted, but they did by the end of the period contribute as much as half of GDP. Those with graduate and professional degrees formed a cognitive resource of more than twenty-five million people, with PhDs alone outnumbering the citizens of Los Angeles. The expansion of this stratum of highly educated professionals helped create the conditions for more porous boundaries between universities and other institutional sectors. University researchers provided testing grounds for new ideas and new technologies developed outside their walls, even as they continued to produce their own at a startling rate.

The boom in undergraduate education created opportunities for mobility for many, a time for maturation for many more, and high-level skills for a motivated minority. It also had less salutary effects. Contained within the burgeoning enrollment statistics were hundreds of thousands of students who lacked either academic or developed professional interests. Colleges and universities accommodated these students by providing academic support services and often by expecting little of them. Expansion also encouraged the rise of the "practical arts"—especially applied fields of study connected to the power centers of the American economy: business, technology, health, media, and government. And it led to a flowering of new basic fields reflecting the culture of upper-middle-class progressives, raising enrollments in the arts, the environmental sciences, the brain sciences, fields with an international orientation, and those focusing on social inclusion. Traditional fields, including not only humanities but also fields like physics and mathematics, fared less well in the student marketplace.

The preferences of state and private patrons opened large opportunity gaps between the quantitative and interpretive disciplines, deepening a status division within the faculty ranks. The growing complexity of the environment surrounding higher education—marked by higher levels of regulation, new consumer demands, and incentives to strengthen constituency relations—created the conditions for a remarkable growth of administrative structures. The salaries of the administrative staff and the equipment and salary requirements of professors in privileged fields were offset by the hiring of armies of low-paid part-timers, an academic proletariat that comprised nearly half of the instructional workforce by the end of the period.

Storm Clouds, Gathering

Although expansion and growing prominence have been the touch points of this book, I am keenly aware that near the end of the period some of the institutional health indicators that looked so buoyant throughout most of the period began to tick in the opposite direction. Corporate support for university research continued to grow in constant dollars, but as a proportion of total R&D, this support hit a peak in 1999, at 7.4 percent, declined to below 5 percent in 2004 and then grew again to just under 6 percent, about the same proportion of support provided by nonprofits (National Science Board 2016, figure 5.1). Against the expectations and hopes of educators that corporations would eventually subcontract larger shares of R&D to universities, they instead absorbed a higher proportion of R&D in-house, including basic research. Corporate self-funding of basic research grew from the mid-2000s on, from about 10 percent to more than 25 percent of the total, while federal funding of basic research flattened during the same period and dipped below 50 percent by the end of the period (ibid., table 4-3; see also Mervis 2017). (Of course, these figures do not take into account other kinds of relationships with industry, including patenting and licensing, consulting relationships, and pipelines from graduate programs into corporate R&D.) Against this backdrop, the rise of university institutional spending in support of R&D could be considered a sign not just of increasing capacity but of the drying up of alternative sources of funding. And increased self-financing of research comes at least marginally at the expense of the institutions' educational missions; it takes away money that would otherwise be spent on education and is one cause of growing enrollments and class sizes (Ehrenberg, Rizzo, and Jakubson 2007).[3]

Annual patenting by U.S. universities rose exponentially from the late 1970s through the late 1990s, then plateaued for a decade before picking up again in 2008. However, the growth post-2008 is attributable almost entirely to foreign universities that maintain patent portfolios in the United States. Annual patenting by U.S. universities remained essentially flat (Leydesdorff, Etzkowitz, and Kushnir 2016). Licensing income has always been highly skewed toward a few strong producers. These trends continued throughout the period, with no uptick in the proportion of university technology transfer offices making a profit from licensing activities, and as many as 85 percent in the red (Valdivia 2013).

Nor did enrollments near the end of the period continue their decades-long upward climb. Total undergraduate fall enrollment fell for four consecutive years following 2010, before stabilizing in 2015 (NCES 2015, table 303.70). The decline in enrollments, concentrated at community colleges and for-profits, could be attributed to continuing high college costs and an economic recovery that made job seeking more attractive. Most lower-income young Americans knew people who had taken out large loans to finance college during the recession and had not found jobs that allowed them to repay their debts (Looney and Yannelis 2015). Graduate enrollments also declined slightly after decades of robust growth (NCES 2015, table 303.80) before stabilizing again in 2015. Access continued to improve for all groups, but graduation gaps by social class and race-ethnicity nevertheless opened wider than ever (Bailey and Dynarski 2011).

In the public sector, state subsidies in support of higher education did not return to pre-recession levels. Between 2008 and 2016, state spending was down an average of $1,600 per student, or 18 percent. Nine states showed declines of 30 percent or more, and only four states showed net gains in spending per student. Most states began to restore cuts made during the recession by 2015, but these restorations did not cover the losses sustained during the recession and immediate post-recession period. Tuitions increased on average by more than $2,000 during the period but, given the many mandatory spending increases, tuition increases did not cover the entire budget shortfall, requiring cuts in educational services to accompany higher tuition (Mitchell, Leachman, and Masterson 2016).[4] The growth of tenured and tenure-track faculty had slowed to a crawl as the size of the pool of contingent faculty members swelled (Finkelstein, Conley, and Schuster 2016).

The shift in public opinion about the effects of college "on the way things are going in the country" struck many in higher education as a particularly ominous sign. Through 2015, a slim majority of Republicans said that colleges and universities had a positive effect on the country. By 2017, only 36 percent of Republicans said college had a positive effect on the country, a 20 percent drop over two years (Pew Research Center 2017). Older and college-educated Republicans were the most negative demographic groups, suggesting that working-class resentment was not the principal factor driving these poll results. Instead, the rise of cultural populism in the 2016 presidential campaign pushed Republican opinion in a distrusting direction across a wide range of issues. In the case of higher education, the populist reaction built on the long history of anti-intellectualism among religious and business-oriented conservatives and the publicity given by conservative media to incidents that made colleges appear overly responsive to the identity politics of liberal professors and students. Of longer-term concern was the finding of another poll: that a majority of white working-class voters considered college more "a gamble that might not pay off" than "a smart investment in the future" (Graham 2017). The costs of college, the burdens of debt, and the growth of underemployment were by the end of the period beginning to chip away at the confidence Americans had historically shown in the power of education to improve their lot in life, regardless of their race or economic circumstances.

The changes in American higher education paralleled changes in American society. The top three dozen research institutions seemed to be in a class of their own, and other research universities struggled to keep up. As institutions competed with each other for faculty, top-achieving students, donors, grants, and the other resources that supported their reputations, they created great strength among themselves but little awareness of the situation of the sector as a whole. Salary gaps grew between senior administrators and senior faculty in marketable disciplines when compared to all others. An increasing number of presidents commanded multimillion-dollar salaries, while new assistant professors in the arts and humanities were hired at the pay of high school teachers. Salary divisions across the disciplines also grew. At an extreme, one could see instances like the following: after thirty years of employment and twenty published books, a distinguished social science professor at the University of California could be awarded the same pay as a freshly minted PhD assistant professor in the School of Business with just one published article to his name. Part-time and contingent labor made up a larger and larger share of hiring, allowing institutions to avoid paying benefits or feeling committed to security of employment. Although these instructors had every reason to complain, relatively few did, depending on their unions to fight for decent wages and working conditions and identifying with the liberal culture of academe. As in the broader society, both minority students and white working-class students showed signs of alienation. Many of the former saw their institutions as unresponsive to the economic challenges and social indignities they faced on a daily basis and many of the latter berated universities, often sotto voce, for capitulation to political correctness (Binder and Wood 2014) and for filling their time unnecessarily with "useless" general education requirements (Mullen 2010).

A Choice of Paths

By the end of the period, the leaders of American higher education faced a choice. One obvious possibility was to try to continue the generally successful course of the previous decades. Such a path would require fidelity to the policies that had worked so well through 2010: intensifying fundraising activities, trying to hold on to existing state subsidies, raising tuitions moderately, gradually expanding entering classes, providing online opportunities for many more, cultivating new categories of donors, encouraging new government spending on research and financial aid, and trying to cut costs where possible. These actions had created a vibrant higher education system during the period and had allowed institutions to make stronger contributions to the American economy and society.

A more ambitious path was also possible. To build a sector that contributed more and played a more central role in economy and society would require a growth strategy that made sense not only for individual campuses but for the system as a whole. It would require building creatively on current structures and accomplishments while mending the problems that had become all too obvious by the end of the period.

Such stronger future contributions would entail the development of at least two or three more centers of exceptional dynamism, such as those found in the Stanford-Berkeley-UC San Francisco complex in Northern California and the MIT-Harvard-Harvard Medical School complex in Cambridge and Boston (cf. Baker 2014, chap. 4). The most likely prospects for these super-university complexes were in New York City (whose center would be composed of Columbia University, New York University, and Cornell Tech), the Research Triangle (Duke University, the University of North Carolina-Chapel Hill, and North Carolina State University), Los Angeles (UCLA, USC, and their associated medical centers), and Atlanta (Georgia Tech, the University of Georgia, and Emory University). Such complexes require stronger connections with high-tech business firms, venture capitalists, and a donor base that greatly exceeds that currently found at least in the Atlanta and Research Triangle regions. It also requires many network ties between the academic institutions that make up the complex, ties that have not heretofore been particularly strong in Los Angeles or New York.

Increased dynamism would require concordant shifts to higher-level profiles of dozens of universities that ranked lower in the research hierarchy. Those located in regions with thriving high-tech businesses and medical centers could hope to develop along the lines of UC San Diego and UT Austin by "plugging into" an already existing ecology of potential partner firms, while at the same time encouraging start-ups that aligned with or complemented the capabilities of existing large firms. Those located in regions without such a favorable economic terrain would need to grow their own high-tech economies by engaging hundreds of more faculty and thousands of more students in entrepreneurship activities, a tall order for most universities, and one that requires access to an investment community to succeed. The experiences of the University of Colorado, the University of Michigan, and the University of Utah, discussed in chapter 3, showed that this strategy could work. Highly entrepreneurial presidents and provosts, very strong schools of engineering, first-rate medical centers, and a large donor base were important ingredients in this "grow-your-own" strategy.

Pursuing this second path would also require looking beyond the current meanings and policies of inclusion. Such a reconsideration could lead to the extension of admissions, student affairs support, and programming consideration to first-generation and low-income students, including whites, in the same way these considerations have been extended to minorities, women, and members of the LGBTQ community. Such an expansion is consistent with the commitment of universities to equality of opportunity. But it is not only a matter of consistency in mission. The political chasm between the two parties means that the future well-being of higher education may depend on how effectively colleges and universities extend their educational outreach activities into white lower-income and first-generation families, while simultaneously maintaining their commitments to building more inclusive environments for racial-ethnic and religious minorities. This will be no easy task, but some institutions, including a few research universities, such as Princeton and Stony Brook, are showing that it can be done.

In addition to deepening relations with industry and Americans in the bottom half of the income distribution, a phase shift in the quality of undergraduate teaching and learning will be required for colleges and universities to reach the higher levels of achievement that are within their reach. Colleges and universities provide experiences that increase students' conscientiousness, their adaptability, and their trainability. They were much less successful in academic skill building. During the period most college classrooms remained mired in a style of instruction that tested students' capacity to memorize presented material, and little else. Online courses can perform as well or better at such tasks. Public opinion showed doubts about the educational value of college courses. To overcome this skepticism, college classrooms would need to become places where students develop skills helpful to them in later life, including an interest in the life of the mind. They would need to become research-centered places where students are expected to bring evidence to bear to evaluate arguments, where they are presented information that allows them to explore hypotheses, where they are required to write and make oral presentations, where detailed feedback is given. In chapter 8, I described unobtrusive methods, such as the Wieman-Gilbert Teaching Practices Inventory, that allow instructors to supplement student evaluations of teaching with more valid measures of teaching effectiveness.

Two other issues bear heavily on the prospects of higher education in the coming decades. The first is online competition. Online courses can allow for the enrollment of students who otherwise could not attend college at all, and there are circumstances that make online course work the only feasible alternative to not attending college at all. Moreover, online courses can be as educationally challenging as face-to-face courses and show learning results that do not compare unfavorably with those of face-to-face classrooms. However, they often fail with immature students, and particularly with lower-division students who have not yet developed strong work habits. For more advanced students, online education works for creating specific knowledge or skill sets, but it is not an adequate substitute for students who aspire to professional or managerial occupations where diverse interactions, interpersonal skills, and public communications are required. The physical campus provides opportunities for building these capacities through meaningful chance encounters, mutual monitoring of nonverbal communications, and navigating uncomfortable situations that arise in face-to-face interaction. Student clubs and organizations contribute to the educational environment of the physical campus by providing students with opportunities to practice work-related skills like running meetings and facilitating discussions (Kwon et al. 2018). Universities should accordingly regulate the conditions under which enrolled students can waive requirements for face-to-face courses and time on campus. This would mean agreeing on and enforcing rules concerning the number of online credits that are permissible for students to take each year, a policy diametrically opposed to current market-driven trends in postsecondary provision. It would also mean articulating across the sector a much stronger rationale than currently exists for the superiority of the physical campus environment.

Cost is the other fundamental concern. State investment in higher education has shown declines during recession and partial restoration thereafter, and university administrators have depended on tuition increases (and enrolling more international and out-of-state students) to make up the balance. If tuition cannot be reduced because of states' disinclination to invest in higher education, the second-best scenario for maintaining and increasing enrollments is to marshal federal, state, and institutional support for low-income students and to use merit-based scholarships very sparingly. The states that have developed comparatively generous grant-in-aid programs (including California, New Jersey, New York, and Washington) are among the fastest-growing in the country and, with the exception of Georgia, those relying more heavily on merit scholarships are not. It should be clear from the analysis in chapter 9 that no general student debt crisis exists. Most students have not accumulated unmanageable debt, and college remains a good investment for the great majority of students, repaying many times over the costs of loans. However, repayment at a time when earnings are low *is* a burden for many students who have taken degrees in less remunerative fields or have had problems finding well-paying jobs. Well-designed and easy-to-use income-contingent loan repayment policies provide a sensible approach to the student debt problem (see Baum and Johnson 2016 and Dynarski 2014).

What Is Academic Autonomy?

Increased collaboration with industry and government will create new tensions between the ideals of service to society and the traditions of scholarly autonomy. So too will the continued growth in enrollment of low-income, first-generation, and underrepresented minority students.

In truth, neither scholars nor universities have ever been fully autonomous. In the United States, the colonial colleges were each affiliated with Protestant denominations, as were many of the private colleges that sprouted up as the country moved west,[5] and the public universities that began to be founded in the early nineteenth century were, quite obviously, creatures of their states. Trustees—many of them drawn from among the universities' wealthiest donors or the governor's closest political allies—exercised the right to hire and fire university presidents at will, and still do. Nor can faculty members accurately be described as autonomous thinkers. Employment depends on the judgment of colleagues and administrators. Problems are defined by the community of scholars, and the work of all scholars is rooted in the literature bearing on the problems he or she chooses to pursue. Reputations are made on the basis of what the community, through its various review and awards committees, determines about the quality of a scholar's work. The notion of autonomy is flattering to the maverick scholar, but not even the maverick survives without an approving coterie.

For these reasons, the term "relative autonomy" is a more accurate description of the type of independence universities and individual scholars can expect to attain. The term recognizes the extent to which campuses and individual scholars are embedded in relationships that put limits on them and provide incentives that shape their actions. The idea of relative autonomy, like that of autonomy itself, assumes significance only in contrast with the alternatives to it: in relation to universities, the alternative can be described as the encapsulation of action by the purposes, norms, and cultures of rival institutions. In relation to individuals, it can be described as the subordination of the thinking mind to organizational authorities inside and outside the confines of the university.

Autonomy depends in the first place on a diversity of funding sources. Most colleges and universities are in the fortunate position of drawing on multiple sources of revenue: state subsidies (if they are public institutions), student tuition, philanthropy, and federal and state research grants. Dependence on a single source of revenue reduces autonomy by providing leverage to the dominant suppliers of revenue. This is the reason why colleges and universities that are heavily dependent on tuition without other sources of revenue are said to be client-driven. The more sources of unrestricted funds and the more diverse these sources, the greater the potential autonomy of academic institutions and the more room administrators and faculty have for intellectual freedom.

Institutional leaders support this independence through the freedoms they allow, the regulations they enact, the reference points they emphasize, and the rituals they oversee. Table 10.1 provides a schematic overview of these supporting structures. The general meaning of freedoms and regulations should be clear enough. But the meaning of reference points and rituals may not be as clear. Reference points are the recurrent topics of speeches and conversations that reinforce the distinctiveness of academic institutions. Rituals are the community events that focus common attention on the symbols and values of academe.

Academic institutions, disciplinary associations, and individual academics are the co-creators of such independence as exists on college and university campuses. I will walk through the contributions of just one of these sets of actors—academic institutions—to provide a sense of why all four elements—freedoms, regulations, reference points, and rituals—should be of interest to those who see the advantages of maintaining a high degree of independence in institutions that are becoming more porous in relation to the outside world.

Colleges and universities support a high degree of independence, in the first instance, by protecting academic freedom. Academic freedom is the freedom to speak, write, and teach as one sees fit based on acquired expertise in one's field. Academic freedom in turn is conditioned by the awarding of tenure, the guarantee of lifetime employment for those whose produc-

TABLE 10.1. Structural Supports for the Relative Autonomy of Academe

	Freedoms	Regulations	Reference Points	Rituals
Organizational	Academic freedom (related to tenure) Choice of research Choice of courses	Against conflict of commitment Against conflicts of interest Scholarly merit Appt. qualifications Shared governance	Libraries Laboratories Classrooms Research Teaching evaluations Intellectual virtues Intellectual heroes Organizational saga	Regalia Processions Award ceremonies Honorary degrees Service
Professional/ Disciplinary	Academic freedom Choice of officers Choice of editors	Against conflicts of interest Publication Citation Investigation of misconduct claims Investigation of plagiarism claims Investigation of shoddy scholarship Review processes	Discipline Intellectual virtues Intellectual heroes Latest research Core concepts	Award ceremonies Featured speakers Conference sessions
Individual	Academic freedom Freedom of curiosity Freedom of experimentation Freedom of independent thought	Scholarly norms Scholarly ambitions Professional identity	The literature Theory Methods Hypotheses Findings Syllabi Instructional excellence Students	Class meetings Lab meetings Research group meetings Dept. meetings Senate meetings

tivity and performance as untenured professors are judged meritorious by colleagues (and senior administrators). Other freedoms are less fundamental but similarly reflect the trust bestowed on college faculty as a function of their scholarly expertise. These are the freedoms to choose the topics of one's research and (with the approval of department chairs) the courses one teaches, including how one teaches them. These choices contrast sharply with the assignment of tasks to professional staff by managers in other institutional spheres.

Colleges and universities impose boundaries between themselves and other institutional arenas through regulatory actions. Rules against conflicts of commitment are one of the most important of these regulatory mechanisms. Most colleges and universities regulate the amount of time professors can devote to outside commitments and many do not allow professors to consult with nonacademic organizations, including firms, more than one day a work week. While recognizing the value of outside relationships, these rules are intended to ensure that the primary responsibility of academics is to the university and their academic professions (Euben 2004). Enforcement of conflict of commitment is, however, notoriously weak because there are no offices for overseeing how professors actually use their time and the definition of a "day" is not clear for professors who regularly work many more than forty hours in a week. But those who do spend inordinate amounts of time away from the university can come under the scrutiny of their colleagues and in rare cases have been removed from tenured positions for conflicts of commitment. Colleges and universities also regulate conflicts of interest by requiring disclosures of organizations or individuals that have provided compensation or gifts. They have created standard contracts to regulate the period of time corporate partners can put restrictions on publication of results with commercial potential.

Evaluation is another side of regulation. Like other organizations, colleges and universities evaluate professors for their value added to the organization. But these evaluations differ appreciably from those found elsewhere. Contributions to the disciplines figure prominently because evaluations emphasize the quantity and quality of publications in scholarly and scientific journals and books. Such considerations are secondary elsewhere, worthy of note but (outside of a few public science oriented R&D shops) not primary criteria for evaluation. Colleges and universities reinforce the educational mission by requiring that professors and instructors work with students and submit evaluations of their teaching performance. Appointment files too are based on publications, teaching evaluations, and letters of recommendation from scholars in the field. In early career appointments, the reputation of the doctoral institution matters greatly, independent of scholarly qualifications, but that too can be considered a proxy for (as yet undemonstrated) academic merit (cf. Burris 2004). They also reinforce the research mission by making appointments depend on external review by scholars without reference to the preferences of senior administrators or donor communities.

As I discussed in chapter 7, shared governance is another regulatory mechanism that contributes to the autonomy of academe. A distinctive feature of shared governance is the control by the faculty of features of the organization that bear on the educational process, including courses and educational policy (and sometimes also including admissions). Consultation itself is not distinctive; mayors of big cities consult with a wide variety of constituency groups, but it is more continuous and may be better institutionalized on college and university campuses than elsewhere in American institutional life.

Reference points are the terms and topics of conversation that at once express and cement institutional identities. Nowhere else in American institutional life are references to libraries, laboratories, research offices, studios, and classrooms as common—certainly not as an ensemble of spaces. Nor do the actions of research, teaching, and service appear as regularly together as descriptors of mission. Talks at the most important awards ceremonies on campuses focus on academic accomplishments and intellectual virtues and highlight the deeds of those who have brought academic honor to the organization. When faculty members talk about their publications, their syllabi, their student evaluations, and the placements of their graduate students, they enter a community of discourse and a structure of identity that is distinctly different from that found elsewhere in American organizational life. If their conversations were filled instead with talk about their work with corporate partners, their consulting businesses, their service on boards, and their contributions to the profitability of their units, the institutional lines of demarcation would blur or become effaced entirely.

These of course are not the only words that matter. Colleges founded on religious principles will find ways to commemorate that aspect of mission, as will colleges founded on commitments to social mobility for underrepresented groups. The reference points of campus leaders matter because the centrality of academic commitments is always tenuous. Football rivalries, social justice considerations, and business partnerships consistently threaten to overshadow them. The institution that celebrates academic distinction is different than the institution that celebrates religious values, community engagement, social mobility, or partnerships with industry. The fidelity to the distinctive features of academe can be counted in the volume and centrality of the reference points articulated by university leaders and on university websites.

The rituals of academe can also help create a powerful focus on the fundamental animating principles of the institution. These ritual occasions include the procession of the faculty and administration in regalia at graduation ceremonies, the public recognition of faculty and student awards for scholarship, the introduction of new scholars into the community, and the awarding of honorary degrees. In some places, these ritual occasions are poorly attended and have lost their capacity to create feelings of commitment. In some cases, particular groups may split off from the community to express their own identities, as in the case of black student graduations. Where these ritual occasions remain intact and draw large crowds, they can bind the academic community as a distinctive entity, reinforcing boundaries between it and the outside world. They draw attention to the symbols of unity and hold these symbols up to a heightened level of respect through common focus and synchronized actions in relation to symbols of the community.

I will add only a few essential points about the other two supports for the independence of scholars: the disciplinary associations and individual scholars themselves. The leaders of the disciplinary associations shape scholarly communities by maintaining the quality of academic "currencies." By the term "currency" I mean the curriculum vitae items that are exchangeable for honors and positions and, indirectly, for research funding. The journals of the disciplinary associations are central to the publication and citation records of scholars and are in that sense the currency producers. By maintaining high academic standards in the journals they publish, the disciplinary associations also encourage good professional standards in the journals outside their orbits. They contribute to the regulation of academe by bestowing the association's most prestigious awards on exemplary works of scholarship and science, rather than for contributions to social mobility, economic innovation, or other worthy but secondary considerations. By recognizing individuals for their scholarly and scientific achievements, they hold up exemplary figures for community approbation. Beyond producing reputational currency, the disciplinary associations are responsible for the review committees that judge the quality of scholarly articles and books and the qualifications of scholars for appointments and promotions. The disciplinary associations also affirm the distinctiveness of academe through community "policing" actions. Journal editors can help shine a light on conflicts of interest by insisting that researchers report the source of funding for their studies. They can patrol the boundaries of research integrity by publicizing instances of scientific fraud, plagiarism, and shoddy scholarship, revelations that also engage the higher education press. They can encourage replications of research findings through the publication of data sets and computer code. They create meaningful boundaries also by choosing to keep their distance from political controversies of the day, maintaining focus on their community's recognized areas of expertise.

Ultimately, individuals are the carriers of professional identity, and neither organizational nor disciplinary supports can overcome the inducements of alternative identities when professional careers have stalled or ceased to be rewarding. Such alienation rarely occurs among scholars at the most prestigious colleges and universities. Individuals in these institutions are highly selected for their skills and commitment (as well as their pedigrees), and their accomplishments during their careers tend to reinforce lifelong investments in the profession and its institutions. Yet, as the sociologist Joseph Hermanowicz (1998) has demonstrated in a longitudinal study of physicists, less prestigious colleges and universities often recruit people with shallower ties to their disciplines, and they typically provide many alternative avenues for recognition within the local college community context. Hermanowicz described lower-ranked research universities as places where "identity pluralism" prevails. Most faculty members begin their careers with ambitions to make a professional mark. But those who are not successful in the professional path are prone to take up other causes—teaching innovation, social justice, senate service, college advising, or community engagements. At teaching-centered institutions, scholarship is a less important recruitment criterion than teaching, and the attractions of nonscholarly identities tend to be still stronger. Some faculty members, even if they meet their classes conscientiously, do not attend scholarly meetings, do not keep abreast of the literatures in their fields, and develop avocational interests that become more important to them than their professional identities.

The freedoms and regulations outlined in table 10.1 do not guarantee nobility in thought and action, and they are also far from complete in the scope of their coverage, even when their governance should in theory be absolute. Academic freedom, for example, is easily abused. It is a cover for lack of professionalism when professors shirk their teaching responsibilities or comment on public affairs based on their political prejudices rather than the expertise of their disciplines. It has also not proven to be an absolute right. Public or trustee opinion can restrict academic freedom and even pressure those who have exercised it to vacate their posts. Yet, in spite of these breaches, it remains a defining feature of academic independence because such freedoms are far more sharply curtailed in other institutional domains. Chemists in industry do not have the freedom to contradict or criticize their organizational superiors, at least not in public. Nor will government bureaucrats take public positions at odds with those of their departments or agencies.[6] The point is not that colleges and universities are valorous institutions and never violate their principles; it is only that these elements of independence *in so far as they are active* create distance between academic institutions and other institutions and define the distinctive expectations and commitments of the scholarly community qua scholarly community.

When the organizations and occupational associations involved in the co-production of academe fail to provide the distinctive freedoms and regulations of academic life, deemphasize distinctive reference points, and draw away from their affirming rituals, the professional identities and commitments of most scholars and scientists weaken. Similarly, even if these organizations and occupational associations do their part, individuals may begin to see themselves in ways that are at odds with the efforts of their employing organizations and occupational associations to maintain autonomy, and the independence fostered by these institutions weakens for lack of individuals' wholehearted engagement. Thus, for the autonomy of academe to be at its strongest, each of the elements of autonomy—academic freedoms, regulations, reference points, and rituals—requires maintenance at a high level. Similarly, each of the agents of autonomy—colleges and universities, disciplinary associations, and individuals in their roles as academics—must take responsibility for maintaining and strengthening, as necessary, these elements of autonomy.

The Ends of Knowledge

In thinking about the ends of knowledge, I do not principally mean the literal end of knowledge fields or the intellectual skills that allow them to prosper.[7] Instead, my intention is to highlight the purposes to which knowledge is attached: the ways that the patrons and proponents of colleges and universities can pull knowledge development in directions that reflect their ideal and material interests.

The disciplinary associations, of course, are very important patrons of knowledge, and they typically uphold the values of (relatively) disinterested scholarship, as defined by the members of disciplinary communities. The great force in academic life—its gravity, in both senses of the term—consists of the problem-identifying and problem-solving momentum of the disciplines—and of those who work between them. By analogy, we can consider universities as the most important lobe of the ever-expanding brain of humankind. However, unlike anything we see in a single lobe of the human brain, universities simultaneously preserve knowledge, generate new knowledge, and judge the validity of knowledge produced in other institutional domains. Even small steps build retrievable consciousness about the phenomena that constitute our own and other worlds. The continued centrality of the disciplinary associations and the journals they support is therefore essential for the independence of academe.

Much of the research conducted in the natural sciences and engineering—and some of it in the social sciences—has practical applications. And yet it is not easy to know what knowledge will have the most important practical implications. I can illustrate the difficulty by looking at the history of one current of ideas that proved central to the development of higher education during the period. Robert Solow's (1956, 1957) Nobel Prize–winning work on the role of innovation in economic growth had a long prehistory. This prehistory begins with the Austrian American economist Joseph Schumpeter (1942, 1947), who emphasized innovation and entrepreneurs as the dynamic elements in capitalism. Schumpeter's interest arose from his antipathy to Karl Marx, who, Schumpeter thought, had placed too much emphasis on the exploitation of labor by capital and too little emphasis on the entrepreneurial spirit and the development of technology as features of the means of production. Although Solow and his colleagues enjoyed a brief influence in the Kennedy administration, their ideas lay more or less dormant in policy circles until the slow growth and declining corporate profitability of the 1970s sparked interest in them again as a guide to possible governmental actions to stimulate the economy. The lags and slow progress in the development of new ideas, their inevitably contested character, the reputations that are won and lost in battling over them, the refinements that are made in them,[8] and the long latency before they may lead to change in the world outside of academe are all illustrated by the fate of Schumpeter's argument with the ghost of Karl Marx.

Secondarily, the missions of the federal government, the priorities of wealthy philanthropists, and the interests of business corporations and industries also shape the ends of knowledge. If the Office of Naval Research, for example, wants to understand how battles of the future will be fought by robots, we can be sure that many computer scientists will be engaged through requests for proposals to model these scenarios. If philanthropists believe that Asian societies are understudied, they can build a new empire of Asian studies with endowments for professors in these fields and scholarships for students willing to study them. In chapter 6, I discussed the impact of federal and philanthropic patronage and surely little more needs to be said at this point to affirm their influence on the ends of knowledge.

I have also emphasized two ideological currents that pulsed through academe during the period, expanding and deepening the volume of knowledge flowing in their directions. One was the innovation movement of the high-tech business community, which, with the assistance of the federal government, encouraged much greater attention to inventing and testing technologies with commercial potential. The other was the inclusion movement of progressive activists, which encouraged greater attention to issues of concern to women, minorities, and non-Western populations. The two combined to help stimulate the rise of interdisciplinary activity on campus (Brint 2005)—while simultaneously setting the two cultures of academe into newly divergent directions, one focusing on economic contributions and the other on social incorporation. It is not surprising that universities would seek to harness the energy and commitment of the high-tech business and progressive-activist communities into new organizational designs built on innovation and inclusion.

Relations with the outside world are essential, and every university and professional association that hopes to prosper will identify many ways to create bridges to the worlds outside of the university proper. Until recently we could be confident that the core of the university—its research and teaching missions—would be protected from the periphery of these community engagements. That expectation no longer holds. The exciting opportunities now seem to be with the institutions that purposely blur the lines between themselves and the high-tech business community, in particular. The goal of "new-design" universities like Arizona State (but also including large parts of Stanford, MIT, and many others) is to bring the business community closer into the research life of the university. Thus far, engagement with industry has been a net benefit to science. The universities that have invested most heavily in working with industry have also tended to fare comparatively well in the scholarly domains of publication and citation (see, e.g., Brint and Carr 2017). The melding is promoted by senior administrators, star professors, venture capitalists, and many others, but it also reflects the mirroring of social organization between the two institutional realms. Successful science and engineering labs have many of the characteristics of industrial R&D labs: large staffs, a hierarchy of staff, an emphasis on production, and the necessity to keep money flowing to stay in business. High-tech firms meanwhile strive to reproduce the intellectual culture of top research university campuses, and design their own campuses with those goals in mind.

The university's role in human capital development also fits this framework. As I have shown, the interests of universities and students alike have increasingly focused on professional programs closely associated with the power centers in American life. Business, engineering, health professions, government, and media degrees have led the way. The tremendous growth of professional master's degrees and science-based doctoral degrees has contributed to the creation of a powerful stratum of highly educated professionals who are in a position to provide both the skills necessary for an advanced capitalist society and, if they are willing to engage their liberal learning, the intellectual distance required for a conscience about the potential destructiveness of single-minded pursuits of profit and wealth. The universities' service to what can rightly be called a business-oriented civilization should not be underestimated and, if the university is to flourish in the future, it will continue to expand this service while maintaining the autonomy provided by a focus on the depth of intellect as least as much as the precision of training.

History is filled with examples of once-powerful institutions that failed to adapt to new circumstances in their environments. The railroads failed to see the potential of air travel as a competitor for their passenger business. Heavy steel manufacturers failed to anticipate the possibility of lightweight steel. French academies of art grew rigid and could not compete with independent art dealers whose shows attracted the creative elite. It is certainly possible that much of higher education could go the way of these institutional dinosaurs, effectively outflanked by nimbler and more engaging digital formats and modularized credentialing systems. To avoid this fate, it seems clear that higher education institutions will depend on closer ties both to industry and to families new to higher education. They will also need to find persuasive solutions to the issues of instructional quality, online competition, and cost that I have discussed here and in previous chapters.

The future of American higher education will depend on the exact nature in which traditional forms of independence and traditional understandings of scope are maintained, blurred, rebalanced, or, as in the future heralded by designs for a "New American University," perhaps overturned completely. Even as colleges and universities draw closer to the new engines of growth, encouraging them to help shape the ends of knowledge, it will be imperative for scientists and scholars to maintain sentry duty over what is more essential: teaching that adds substantial value to students' cognitive development and the rigorous review of research in all fields of formal and abstract knowledge that continue to provide illumination. By doing so professors can continue to follow the injunction that lies at the heart of the academic mission: Let there be light!

ACKNOWLEDGMENTS

This book has had a long germination, and I consequently have many people and institutions to thank for their support along the way. I would like to thank the following people for their collegiality and good suggestions as I worked through the ideas in this book: Andrew Abbott, Paul Alivisatos, Richard Arum, Trudy Banta, Craig Boardman, Barry Bozeman, David Brady, Henry Braun, George Breslauer, Steve Chatman, John Cheslock, Carol Christ, William Cummings, Scott Davies, Kevin Dougherty, John Aubrey Douglass, Judith Eaton, Russell Edgerton, Peter T. Ewell, Gil Eyal, David Fairris, MaryAnn P. Feldman, Irwin Feller, Neil Fligstein, Roger L. Geiger, David Grusky, Robert A. Hanneman, Heather Haveman, Joseph C. Hermanowicz, Mary Taylor Huber, Ron Huesman Jr., Jerry A. Jacobs, Thomas Kalil, Matthew Kaplan, Jerome Karabel, Wendy Katkin, Martin Kenney, Jud King, George Kuh, David Labaree, Michele Lamont, Erin Leahey, Matthew C. Mahutga, Simon Marginson, Mindy Marks, Daniel McFarland, Jal Mehta, James Miller, Margaret Miller, David Mowery, Christopher Oberg, Ernest T. Pascarella, Woody Powell, Craig Rawlings, Gary Rhoades, Creso Sa, Dick Scott, David Shulenberger, Lee S. Shulman, Mitchell Stevens, Ann Swidler, Gregg Thomson, Roger Waldinger, John P. Walsh, and Jane Wellman.

I would also like to thank the following people who responded to data requests: Jeff Bloem (Minnesota Population Center), Elizabeth Blue (National Science Foundation), Victor Borden (Indiana University), Richard Bryden (Harvard Business School), Cynthia E. Carr (for work on the Web of Science), Steven Hurlburt (American Institutes of Research), Kristopher Proctor (for work on the Current Population Survey), and Sarah R. K. Yoshikawa (for work on IPEDS).

Special thanks to colleagues who read and commented on chapters or sections of chapters: Elizabeth Berman, Kevin Dougherty, Roger Geiger, Jerry Jacobs, Michael Olneck, Gary Rhoades, Bob Samuels, Mitchell Stevens, Bill Tierney, and Jon Zimmerman. A conversation with Elizabeth

Dyson was pivotal to the development of the book's argument. Special thanks to others who helped me frame the argument of the book more clearly: Jerry Jacobs, Jerome Karabel, Gary Rhoades, and Michele Renee Salzman. My indefatigable and excellent research assistant Michaela Curran read through the manuscript to check facts and citations I queried and to flag missing references, and Komi German rechecked links to websites cited in the reference list.

My research on U.S. higher education has been supported for a decade and a half by three divisions of the National Science Foundation (Sociology, Science of Science Policy, and Education and Human Resources), by the Atlantic Philanthropies, and by the Spencer Foundation. I am grateful to these institutions for their support.

Among the talented students who have worked on the *Colleges & Universities 2000* research team include the following: Kayleigh Anderson, Jacob Apkarian, Quinn Bloom, Allison M. Cantwell, Gary Coyne, Michaela Curran, Kevin D. Curwin, Komi T. German, Ron Kwon, Lionel Lee, Charles S. Levy, John A. Maldonado, Kerry Mulligan, Scott Patrick Murphy, Katrina Paxton-Jorgenson, Kristopher Proctor, Mark Riddle, Tony Roberts, Matthew B. Rotondi, Zeinab Shukar, Lori Turk-Bicakci, Eric Vega, Tiffany Viggiano, Suki Wang, and Sarah R. K. Yoshikawa. Turk-Bicakci, Proctor, and Mulligan served as successive data managers on the project and performed this difficult role with great skill and cheerfulness.

I am grateful to have had the opportunity to present research from this project at professional meetings and university colloquia where I benefited greatly from the comments of colleagues. They include the annual meetings of the American Educational Research Association, the American Sociological Association, the Association for the Study of Higher Education, the International Sociological Association, the Reinvention Center, and the Sociology of Education Association. They also include colloquia and seminars at the Center for Studies in Higher Education (UC Berkeley), Harvard University, Hebrew University of Jerusalem, the Higher Education Institute (University of Georgia), the Higher School of Economics in Moscow, the Institute of Education (University College London), the New School for Social Research, the Radcliffe Institute, Stanford University, the University of California-Berkeley, the University of California-Irvine, the University of California-Merced, the University of Southern California, the University of Oslo, the University of Oxford, Uppsala University, and the VI Summer Institute in St. Petersburg.

I would like to thank Dallas L. Rabenstein for bringing me into a senior position in university administration, which allowed me to observe over a five-year period the workings of my own research university from a different and fruitful angle. I also want to thank the colleagues with whom I worked most closely during that time: John L. Briggs, Rena Burton, Richard A. Cardullo, Peter Graham, Gladis Herrera-Berkowitz, Bradley Hyman, JoAnn Javier, Michael A. McKibben, Debbie Pence, Thomas Perring, Chinya Ravishankar, Leonard Taylor, Beth Thrush, Michael Paul Wong, Victor Zordan, and the inestimable Christine Victorino.

Thanks also to Peter Dougherty of Princeton University Press, my most erudite and humane editor, for his enthusiasm and wise counsel, and to the staff at Princeton University Press for their careful work on the book, creative cover design, and help in every facet of production and distribution. These people include Jenn Backer, Mark Bellis, Bob Bettendorf, Chris Ferrante, and Jessica Yao.

As is true of all of my work, this book shows the imprint of colleagues with whom I debated decades ago at the Huron Institute's seminar on social theory and higher education, organized by Jerome Karabel. In addition to Karabel, these colleagues include Paul DiMaggio, Kevin J. Dougherty, David Karen, Katherine McClelland, David C. Stark, David Swartz, and Michael Useem.

I want to send out, in closing, lots of love to my brothers Armand and Michael Brint; their wives, Fran Resendez and Suzanne Brint; my glorious children, Juliana and Ben; Juliana's husband, Will Sommer; my inspiring mother and stepfather, Shirl and Wally Grayson; and especially to my wife, Michele Renee Salzman. This book was built on a foundation of love and could not have been built without it.

Chapter 1. The Universities Expansion Made

1. Bell, for example, extolled "the comprehensive numeracy" made possible by new intellectual technologies that formed the core of the emerging "knowledge society" (1973, 29–30), and he wrote of the university as the central institution of the emerging society: "Theoretical knowledge increasingly becomes the strategic resources, the axial principle, of a society. And the university research organizations, and intellectual institutions, where theoretical knowledge is codified and enriched, become the axial structures of the emergent society" (26). So far, Bell's prognostication has proven to be an exaggeration, but universities are clearly on the road to greater influence in society, if they can manage growth well and develop sustainable economic models.

2. This is an oversight Florida has been keen to correct in more recent work. In this more recent work, Florida has come to terms with the class divisions exacerbated by "the settlement patterns of the 'creative class.'" See, e.g., Florida et al. 2014.

3. These breakthroughs only scratch the surface of the contribution of university researchers to economic growth—Cole discusses many more in his book and on his website—but they establish that American research universities have been important contributors and, given the pace of breakthroughs, at an accelerating rate since 1980 (see Cole 2009, chaps. 8–9 and http:// university.discoveries.com).

4. Geiger argued that political choices also mattered; the "prevailing mood of suspicion" among governors and legislatures had been another factor constraining state spending on higher education (2004, 45)—and as a consequence propelling the privatization brought on by higher tuition charges. Some found evidence for differences among states dominated by Republicans and those dominated by Democrats (see, e.g., McLendon, Hearn, and Mokher 2009), but careful analyses over a longer time period found no statistically significant differences when Republicans were in control as compared to Democrats (Delaney and Doyle 2011). Other factors clearly mattered in overall state spending per capita. These included population size and total enrollment in higher education (positively associated with spending) and shifts from the public to the private sector within a state (negatively associated). Higher proportions of students attending community colleges were, not surprisingly, also negatively associated with state spending on higher education. See Delaney and Doyle 2011.

5. Neo-institutional scholars argue that as long as universities turn out graduates who are putatively rational and feel empowered to express opinions and plans, they are reproducing modern personalities whether or not much learning actually occurs in four years of college. In this view, learning and knowledge are secondary to the creation of modern personhood (see Meyer 2008). Similarly, some economists suggest that most of the equipment students need for success in the world is the product of home life and elementary and secondary education. For them, higher education mainly provides a stamp of approval on qualities developed prior to college

admission. Others look at college campuses as arenas for developing social connections that will be more important in life than whatever happens in the classroom. All of this can seem more than a bit cynical, and many state legislators, educators, and private citizens fault universities for paying too little attention to the learning experiences of students.

6. To be sure, the problems of undergraduate education reflected, to a large degree, system failures that began much earlier in students' life cycle. In the United States, the quality of elementary and secondary schools varies widely within and across communities. Fifteen-year-old students from Massachusetts have scored at the level of Taiwanese students—high by international standards—in recent tests of reading and mathematics. Students from Mississippi, by contrast, have scored at the level of countries from the developing world (Carnoy and Rothstein 2013). Average scores for the United States as a whole are in the middling range of the developed world, but standard deviations around the mean are, in comparative perspective, large (Han and Buchmann 2016). Within states, the social composition of secondary schools makes a large difference in the average preparation of graduates; students from schools located in affluent communities tend to be well prepared for college and those from schools located in poor communities tend to be ill-equipped (Palardy 2008).

7. Leading treatments of community colleges can be found in Brint and Karabel 1989; Dougherty 1994; Grubb 1996; Rosenbaum 2004; Rosenbaum, Ahearn, and Rosenbaum 2017; and Rosenbaum, Deil-Amen, and Person 2006.

8. The organizational sociologist W. Richard Scott (2015, 33) identified four pivot points that converged to push public colleges and universities along what he calls a "utilitarian trajectory" beginning in earnest after 1980. The first was the restratification of academic subjects and personnel based on the exchange value of particular forms of knowledge in the wider society. The second was the rise of consumerism among parents and students, marked by a concern with the market-value of degrees and by the ubiquity of student evaluations of courses and campus services. The third was the rise of academic managers who draw on business management ideas and performance metrics, such as returns on investment and opportunity costs, to inform and justify their decision making. The fourth was the view of the public and the state that academic training and research is primarily, if not solely, important for its capacity as an engine of economic growth. Scott explicitly draws here on the work of Berman (2012) and Gumport (2000).

9. Crow's intentions are captured in the list of eight "design aspirations" for the NAU model at his own institution: "(1) Leverage Place: ASU embraces its cultural, socioeconomic, and physical setting; (2) Transform Society: ASU catalyzes social change by being connected to social needs; (3) Value Entrepreneurship: ASU uses its knowledge and encourages innovation; (4) Conduct Use-Inspired Research: ASU research has purpose and impact; (5) Enable Student Success: ASU is committed to the success of each unique student; (6) Fuse Intellectual Disciplines: ASU creates knowledge by transcending academic disciplines; (7) Be Socially Embedded: ASU connects to communities through mutually beneficial partnerships; (8) Engage Globally: ASU engages with people and issues locally, nationally, and internationally" (Crow and Dabars 2015, 243).

10. It does not diminish Crow's achievement to note that ASU was on an upward trajectory prior to his presidency, having jumped from the 8th to the 5th decile in research and development expenditures between 1980 and 2000 among the top 190 research universities I studied with Cynthia E. Carr. Similarly, it had improved from the 5th to the 4th decile in publications and from the 6th to the 5th decile in citations between 1980 and 2000. This upward trajectory continued during Crow's presidency. By 2010 Arizona State University had jumped again to the 4th decile among this same set of universities in research and development expenditures. By 2010 it was in the 3rd decile in publications and the 4th decile in citations. See Brint and Carr 2017.

11. Although high, this proportion of part-time instructors is lower than that found at most large research universities (Finkelstein, Conley, and Schuster 2016, 64).

12. Crow and Dabars understood that the leading private research universities have little incentive to change and would in any event find many features of the NAU model unappealing. They recommended the NAU model to those seeking a more ambitious path, but they pulled up short of a general recommendation: "It would be counter-productive to profess the prescription of a set of design strategies applicable in all contexts . . . Rather . . . our intent has been to call attention to the potential for institutional innovation—or even massive change. . . . But any such reconceptualization must proceed according to its own intrinsic logic" (2015, 297).

13. This vision continues to have many adherents in both business and academe. The sociologist David P. Baker has argued: "The growth and intensity of science, rationalized inquiry, theory [and] empirical methods, all influenced and reinforced by [the] overarching [framework] of academic intelligence . . . are at the core of an epistemological revolution" (2014, 189–90). Yet for every person whose mind is changed by evidence-seeking and scientific methods, there are two or three who find these modes of thought incomprehensible, artificial, and alien. The social problems associated with stalled modernity are only slowly coming into focus.

14. Trow was not particularly interested in the causes of the early strength of higher education in the United States relative to other industrializing countries; others have covered that topic admirably, sometimes drawing selectively on Trow's work. The consensus is that four "key ingredients," to use the phrase of Graham and Diamond (1997, 200), are essential to an explanation. The first is the decentralization of the system following the failure of George Washington's plan for a national university and in the wake of the eagerness of each of the country's many religious denominations and town boosters to fund colleges in their communities, building on the model of the original colonial colleges. The second is the coincident development of well-funded state-chartered universities prior to the Morrill Acts and the subsequent founding of new universities from land grants provided by the Morrill Act and by wealthy industrialists, which expanded the number of high-performing institutions by the end of the nineteenth century. The third is the competition between this large decentralized population of institutions in a widening market for students, faculty, and financial resources, leading to the gradual upgrading of less well-resourced (and mainly public) institutions. If Berkeley and Michigan wanted to compete with Stanford and Harvard, they had to find the faculty and resources to do so. The fourth, and perhaps most important of all, is the influx of federal funding after World War II with multiple agency sponsorship and peer review that eventually created research prowess in some two hundred institutions and cemented American leadership in the production of basic research.

Chapter 2: The Academic Professions and American Society

1. As Stephen Turner observed, there is nothing logically essential about the ways the disciplines were constructed. Biology in the early days was a very expansive discipline, extending from the cellular to the ecological level; it is now dividing in ways that allow life scientists to focus on distinctive units of analysis in natural life processes. Rather than focusing on intellectual integrity, Turner focuses on the social closure advantages of disciplinary boundaries. He writes, disciplines "are cartels that organize markets for the production and employment of [new faculty] by excluding those job-seekers who are not products of the cartel" (2000, 51). The truth seems more likely to lie in the mix of intellectual developments, jurisdictional conflicts, and economic rewards for cartelization.

2. I include here NCES Classification of Instructional Programs (2010) at the four-digit level. These fields span those taught nearly exclusively at community colleges (such as machine repair) to those taught nearly exclusively in graduate programs (such as periodontics). See NCES 2010.

3. Among the four-million-copy sellers are Neil A. Campbell's *Biology*, H. W. Janson's *History of Art*, and Paul Samuelson's *Economics*. Stephen Hawkings's *Brief History of Time* has accumulated sales of ten million copies since its publication in 1988. The all-time leader among academic texts, however, may be William Strunk and E. B. White's *The Elements of Style*, which has sold more than twelve million copies since its publication in 1959.

4. Thirty institutions produced enough research to remain in the top 40 throughout the thirty-year period on all of the measures Carr and I used in this research (R&D expenditures, publications, and citations): the University of Arizona, the University of Colorado, the University of Florida, the Georgia Institute of Technology, the University of Illinois at Urbana-Champaign, the University of Michigan-Ann Arbor, the University of Minnesota-Twin Cities, Ohio State University, Pennsylvania State University, the University of Texas-Austin, Texas A&M University, UC Berkeley, UC Davis, UCLA, UC San Diego, UC San Francisco, the University of Washington-Seattle, and the University of Wisconsin-Madison, while the following private universities retained a similarly consistent standing: Columbia University, Cornell University, Duke University, Johns Hopkins University, Harvard University, the Massachusetts Institute of Technology, Northwestern University, the University of Pennsylvania, the University of Southern California, Stanford University, Washington University (St. Louis), and Yale University. A few small universities, such as the California Institute of Technology and Princeton University, produce at impressive levels relative to their size; and we can be completely certain that the research mentality also dominates in these institutions (author's calculations).

5. Cynthia Carr and I collected research expenditure data from the National Science Foundation (2015). We collected publication and citation data from the Web of Science created by Thomson-Reuters. We used whole counts of publications and citations, rather than fractional counts, meaning that all coauthors of papers were credited with the publication and the citations that accrued to the publication. See Brint and Carr 2017.

6. We began by taking all publications from 1980 and tracing citation counts on these publications through 2016, or thirty-six years in all. We then took the publications for 1985 and traced their citation counts through 2016, or thirty-one years in all. We continued this procedure through each fifth year, ending in 2005, resulting in an eleven-year collection span for 2005 publications. Our approach to studying citations required dropping 2010 because of immature data.

7. The gains in publications and citations were partly due to the more than threefold growth of journals in the WoS database between 1970 and 2005 (Larsen and von Ins 2010). I do not consider the productivity gains we observed to be simply an artifact of the changing sample base, however, because the growth in the number of high-quality journals catalogued is itself a function of a larger and more productive university labor force, capable of sustaining many more high-quality journals.

8. Carr and I found increasing dispersion in all three of our measures at the beginning of the period—during the first decade we studied, 1980–90 (Brint and Carr 2017). Geiger and Feller (1995) reported the same result for R&D expenditures only. They argued that dispersion principally benefited institutions of above-average quality, thereby adding to the nation's scientific prowess.

9. In federal FY 2014 funding, social science disciplines fell in the mid-range between natural sciences and arts and humanities: other social sciences (including criminology, demography, and area studies) ($717 million), economics ($344 million), education ($176 million), sociology ($157 million), anthropology ($26 million), and political science ($13 million) (NSF 2016a).

10. These achievements were threatened by the budget proposals of the Trump administration, which in 2017 proposed cuts of 22, 17, and 13 percent, respectively, to the basic science bud-

gets of the National Institutes of Health, the Department of Energy, and the National Science Foundation. See Science News Staff (2017). The proposed cuts were primarily to headquarters staff.

11. Other preoccupations in these leading social science articles and books included methodological developments to allow for more secure measurement and inferences, empirical tests of influential theories (including reformulations of theories based on these tests), and expositions of the consequences of important developments in society, such as the rise of information technology and the decline of spaces for informal discussion of public issues. Social scientific work is already beginning to explore the societal implications of such important recent developments as artificial intelligence, the rise of authoritarian populism in the developed world, and climate change.

12. In this probe of the occupations of people cited in *New York Times* reporting, I coded only those who were treated as objective and authoritative commentators in articles rather than as protagonists or antagonists. This distinction was not always easy to make. Politicians who are not yet protagonists but may become protagonists often assume the stance of the objective expert. I counted the occupations of authors of opinion pieces in the Sunday *New York Times* only, and not columnists who regularly appear in the newspaper. I did not count authors of books reviewed by the paper. Among other groups with more than a dozen counts were: journalists and editors; lawyers and judges; professional writers; and business service professionals (such as market analysts, management consultants, and corporate researchers).

13. Data and science do not necessarily exercise a strong influence on public opinion. Approximately one-third of Americans, for example, do not believe in evolution, despite the scientific consensus (Gross 2015). However, on issues that do not strike as closely to fundamental religious beliefs, the American public can be persuaded by science. By 2017, three out of five Americans believed that the effects of global warming had already started and a near-majority said that global warming was a "major concern," both sizable increases over a decade (Gallup Organization 2017).

14. For a more extensive and theoretically grounded analysis of knowledge exchanges involving university researchers and creators in other institutional sectors, see Brint 2018.

15. Ehrenberg and his colleagues (2010) showed that about half of those who entered graduate humanities programs at top-rated programs failed to complete their degrees. They typically ended up in professional or managerial occupations—not driving taxi cabs—but not necessarily in fields closely related to their studies. Many took up careers in teaching, editing, the arts, or managing small businesses.

16. Because different data sources use different industrial classification codes, the names of industries discussed in what follows vary depending on source.

17. My initial study used General Social Survey (GSS) data from 1972–1996 (Brint 2001). With the assistance of graduate student Jacob Apkarian, I later updated these data through 2010, again using the GSS (Brint 2014). I subsequently added an analysis of Bureau of Economic Analysis data for comparative purposes.

18. A process of aggregation and disaggregation was required to identify industries with high proportions of workers with advanced degrees. For that reason, Apkarian and I merged three- and four-digit North American Industrial Standard Codes to form the 180 industries included in this analysis.

19. Data on GDP contribution by industry were not available at the three-digit Standard Industrial Code level. In my first study of knowledge-sector industries, I consequently used two-digit industry codes relying on Yuskavage 1996.

20. The GSS is a sample survey, and it is likely that some of the small N industries at the bottom of table 2.4 would not meet the criterion of 5 percent with master's or higher-level degrees, if we drew a large number of samples from fictional alternative General Social Surveys.

21. These two unlisted industries are: Other Transportation and Support (seemingly a duplicate of Other Transportation) and Management of Companies.

22. By the mid-2010s, credential inflation (and perhaps also increasing cognitive work demands) had made the 5 percent criterion no longer a viable guide for identifying knowledge-sector industries. When I compared the list of industries drawn from the GSS to a recent (2016) estimate from the Current Population Survey (CPS), I found that by the mid-2010s, a 10 percent criterion was necessary to identify knowledge-sector industries. In the CPS data, I found 84 of 271 CPS industries (31 percent of the total) employed at least 10 percent of workers with master's or higher-level degrees. These industries showed a very high-level correspondence to those Apkarian and I identified for the period 1990–2010 using GSS data. Discrepancies were virtually all due to divisions in the CPS industrial codes that did not exist in the GSS industrial codes—for example, the GSS did not include outpatient clinics in its industrial coding, but the CPS did include them.

Chapter 3: The Rise of Academic Innovationism

1. Some scholars prefer the terms "academic entrepreneurship" (see, e.g., Mars and Rios-Aguilar 2010) or "academic capitalism" (see, e.g., Slaughter and Leslie 1997). Entrepreneurship typically implies business ownership or, at a minimum, the marketing of goods. Some of the practices of innovationism involved the training of graduate students and the open sharing of ideas for new technologies. The two unlisted industries in Table 2.5 clearly do not fit the concept of entrepreneurship and the former is a partial fit at best. Capitalism denotes a system in which the owners of private property compete on a market to gain profits—in the Marxian view, in part by exploiting labor and in part by adopting labor-saving technologies. Since most academic innovators do not own the means of production, the term seems a poor fit for the practices I have in mind.

2. The literature on the causes and consequences of the rise of a competitiveness agenda in U.S. research policy is extensive. For a sample of historical accounts and useful outcomes studies, see, in addition to those cited, Berman 2012; Croissant and Restivo 2001; Etzkowitz 1989; Fairweather 1988; Feller 1997; Geiger 2004, chap. 5; Slaughter 1990; and Waugaman and Porter 1992.

3. Much of the key legislation of the competitiveness era passed during the Reagan administration, and the Commission on Industrial Competitiveness was inaugurated in 1983 under the leadership of Reagan associate John A. Young of Hewlett-Packard. Near the end of the commission's work, Young and his colleagues founded the private U.S. Council on Competitiveness in 1986, including representatives of industry, academe, and labor. Congress established a complementary Competitiveness Policy Council in 1988. The Policy Council issued four reports aimed to improve the competitive position of the United States. In 1993, its "critical technologies" panel recommended increasing national investment in civilian and dual-use research and development, promoting commercialization of strategic technologies, incorporating universities to create a world-class technology base, and organizing government to produce high-impact results (Competitiveness Policy Council 1993).

4. British and Scandinavian scholars first formulated ideas about "national innovation systems" to focus on the importance of knowledge and learning in the generation of new technologies and products, and they saw a substantial role for the state in seeding industrial innovation (Freeman 1987; Lundvall 1988).

5. Competitiveness policy was not without influential critics. The Nobel Prize–winning economist Paul Krugman, writing in *Foreign Affairs*, argued that the policy posed "three real dangers." He wrote, "First, it could result in the wasteful spending of government money supposedly to enhance U.S. competitiveness. Second, it could lead to protectionism and trade wars.

Finally, and most important, it could result in bad public policy on a spectrum of important is-sues" because even issues that should not be interpreted through the lens of competitiveness policy may be interpreted through that lens (2004, 41).

6. Organized research units (ORUs) have been staples of university organization since the 1920s (Nash 1999), and most of these are interdisciplinary. Major research universities operated more than 100—sometimes several hundred—of these ORUs (J. Jacobs 2013). However, until the 1980s ORUs were never considered competitors with departments as vehicles for education or professional stature.

7. In a classic work, the sociologist Robert K. Merton (1942) identified four norms of sci-ence, each one of which distinguishes science as an ideal type of human social activity. *Univer-salism* denotes that scientific validity is established through rigorous methods independent of the sociopolitical status or personal attributes of participants. *Communalism* denotes that all sci-entists should have common ownership of intellectual property through publication of results. *Disinterestedness* means that scientific institutions are designed to benefit the scientific enterprise as a whole rather than to be used for the personal gain of individuals. *Organized skepticism* means that scientific claims are exposed to the critical scrutiny of other scientists before they are ac-cepted. Scientific claims should be treated as provisional until they are well confirmed by other members of the community.

8. The contributions of university systems can be nearly as impressive as those Cole (2009) recounts for American research universities as a whole. During the period of state disinvest-ment following the Great Recession, the historian Conrad Rudolph created a list of inventions produced by University of California faculty members. They included the discoveries of pho-tosynthesis, nuclear fission, and the depletion of the ozone layer through the emission of fluo-rocarbons. In medicine, they included the flu vaccine; cures for Hepatitis B, West Nile Virus, and Lyme Disease; and the creation of a hemostatic agent that facilitates immediate clot-ting and sealing of wounds. In agriculture, they included the development of new cultivars for fruits and vegetables; environmentally friendly pest control strategies; drought-resistant grains; and high-yield rice. They also included advances in information technology, from the mathematical theory that allowed for the development of the Internet, to the construction of the first modern central processing unit, to the production of the bar code scanner now used by virtually every commercial establishment. They included such practical technologies as metal sleeves to prevent the collapse of freeways during earthquakes, the wetsuit for exploring the oceans, and flame-retardant clothing for protecting firefighters (Rudolph 2016).

9. A particularity of the *PM* poll is that it includes household consumer goods as well as technological innovations that will seem to most readers to have had broader and more trans-formative impacts, such as the fiber optics, genetic engineering, the global positioning system, and the World Wide Web. The smoke detector, Velcro, and the waffle-sole running shoe (which contributed to the popularity of jogging) appear on the list, for example. The only instruction to panelists was to identify innovations that "have made the biggest impact" and constitute "the breakthroughs of our time" (Hutchinson 2005).

10. I developed a matrix for coding the involvement of researchers and funders from dif-ferent institutional arenas at four stages in the process of innovation: early research, refining research, development, and production. I included the following sets of actors: academic re-searchers, government researchers, corporate researchers, nonprofit/independent researchers, and foundation researchers. Under funders, I included government funding, corporate/invest-ment funding, foundation funding, and donor funding. I also included whether social movement activists were involved as a pressure group in the production of the innovation.

11. Researchers at Bell Labs alone made important contributions to seven of the fifty inven-tions—the cell phone, the charge-coupled device, communication satellites, lithium-ion batteries,

digital music, fiber optics, the laser) and an early contribution to an eighth in the form of the invention of the transistor that made semiconductors possible and eventually integrated circuits.

12. Zucker and Darby (2014) measured entry into a high-tech industry by the first time that a firm researcher published a paper in an area.

13. The four areas in which they found significant effects were: biology/chemistry/medicine (related to biotechnology), nanotechnology, and two catchall categories, "other science" and "other engineering." See Zucker and Darby 2014, table 2.

14. Do star scientists draw firms to a region, or does the region draw star scientists? Zucker and Darby (2014) attempt to examine the issue of causal direction by reestimating their regressions with location fixed effects and by lagging explanatory variables by one year. In these estimates, coefficients for the location of star scientists continued to be significant and positive in four of the six fields studied, both for the United States and for the top twenty-five science-producing countries.

15. According to the business strategist Michael Porter, clusters affect competition in three ways: first, by increasing the productivity of companies based in the area; second, by driving the direction and driving down the price of innovations; and third, by stimulating the formation of new businesses, which expands and strengthens the cluster itself. Clusters allow "each member to benefit as if it had greater scale, or as if it had joined with others formally, without requiring it to sacrifice its flexibility" (Porter 1998, 3).

16. Timothy Bresnahan and his coauthors (2001) argued that proximity to university researchers and their graduate students is not necessary to create high-tech clusters. Independent entrepreneurs or technically trained military veterans drove the development of clusters in Taiwan, South India, and Israel in locations distant from universities and with minimal initial interaction with university researchers. Nor was a highly trained labor force necessary to cluster formation, only sufficient knowledge, capital, and motivation to recruit well and to learn from co-producers.

17. Porter's theory of competitive advantage is often applied to regional economic development planning (Porter 1990, 1998). Consistent with the findings of case studies, universities play a supporting role in Porter's framework as compared to the main drivers: a preexisting industry base, high levels of demand for industry products, location of supporting up- and downstream industries, skilled labor, well-developed infrastructure, and government promotion for nascent agglomerations.

18. These judgments are provisional; failures to generate start-ups and industry clusters are rarely publicized by universities. Limited evidence exists on these cases. For the Boston University case, I have relied on materials from campus websites and Hofherr 2016. For the Emory case, see Market Street Services 2012. For the Princeton case, see PlanSmart NJ 2013. For the University of Chicago case, see University of Chicago, n.d. For the Vanderbilt case, see Read 2016.

19. For the Cornell case, see Cornell University 2011. For the Indiana University case, see Conover 2017. For the University of Illinois case, see Lauffer 2014. For the University of Massachusetts case, see Providence Business News 2014.

20. South Carolina appears to have been another exception to this rule. Originally founded in 1983, the South Carolina Centers of Excellence in Education program was reorganized in 2002 and closely modeled on the Georgia Research Alliance with centers focused on six industry-related clusters: advanced materials and nanotechnology, automotives and transportation, biomedical science, energy and alternative fuels, information science, and pharmaceuticals. The Centers of Economic Excellence are formed around 45 endowed chairs. Like GRA, SmartState claims strong returns on the $250 million state investments in the clusters, including the attraction of $6 in nonstate investment for every $1 in state investment. It also claims research grants

of $50 million, 89 patents, and 55 active licenses. It gives as examples 15 profitable start-up companies that began from state investments in the six clusters (State of South Carolina, n.d.).

21. Group dynamics probably also matter, although the research literature is not strong enough at this time to provide good tests of this premise. The existing literature, such as it is, suggests that interdisciplinary scholars working together on well-defined problems have higher probabilities of success than those who are pursuing interdisciplinary projects that are not tightly coupled in this way (Rhoten 2004). Groups that include people who can skillfully translate across disciplinary boundaries and have the interpersonal skills to foster collegiality seem also to have a higher probability of success (Collins, Evans, and Gorman 2010; Hollingsworth and Hollingsworth 2000; Rhoten 2004). The Hollingsworth study of Rockefeller University suggests that group success may be related to seminars or colloquia that require participants to employ methods or theories that cross disciplinary boundaries and to leaders who engage in mentoring and nurturing of junior colleagues (Hollingsworth and Hollingsworth 2000). And groups whose members regularly take part in community-building social activities may also enjoy a higher probability of sustained interaction (Severin 2013; Urban Universities 2015).

22. Academic statesmen have understood the dangers. "Altruism and idealism" are part of the ethos of the university, William Press (2013), a former president of the American Association for the Advancement of Science, observed, and the public, he argued, will lose regard for university scientists if these qualities become more difficult to discern. Former Harvard president Derek Bok also drew attention to the risks of losing public regard through a retreat from generosity in the service of institutional ideals: "Once the public begins to lose confidence in the objectivity of professors, the consequences extend far beyond the academic community. At a time when cynicism is so prevalent and the need for reliable information is so important, any damage to the reputation of universities, and to the integrity and objectivity of their scholars, weakens not only the academy but the functioning of our democratic, self-governing society. That is quite a price to pay for the limited, often exaggerated gains that commercialization brings" (2003, 114–15, 118).

Chapter 4: College for All

1. Completion rates for underrepresented minorities remained much lower than for Asians and whites. Of those who entered a four-year college in 2007, 70 percent of Asians completed in six years, compared to 58 percent of whites, 46 percent of Hispanics, and 39 percent of blacks (Carnevale and Strohl 2013).

2. Of course, medians do not capture much that is important about income distributions. At every educational level, women and non-Asian minorities earn less than men and whites or Asians/Asian Americans. (The gap for women is still about 25 percent below male earnings in all educational categories.) Moreover, a significant overlap exists among those with different levels of educational attainment; not all who achieve master's degrees do better than every college graduate and not all college graduates do better than every associate's degree holder. Indeed, two out of five of those with bachelor's degrees earn at or above the master's degree median, and the marketable 30 percent of those with associate's degrees earn at or above the bachelor's median. The Georgetown estimates also do not control for social background or academic achievement, variables that have proven important in sociological studies of status attainment.

3. Some university administrators *are* cynically motivated by the pecuniary interests of their institutions. In an unguarded moment, one senior administrator told me, "I want to bring in as many new freshmen as possible. Even if a large number of them fail out, they are cheap to teach, and I want to have their tuition fees and state subsidies while they are with us."

4. During the period, public universities with very high research activity grew considerably faster than their private counterparts at the undergraduate level, and the growth of privates occurred disproportionately at the graduate level.

5. Using financial data from 147 doctoral-granting institutions, De Groot, McMahon, and Volkwein (1991) revised the estimates on economies of scale and found substantial economies for public research universities enrolling as many as 50,000 students and for private universities enrolling as many as 17,000 students.

6. In addition to exercising the powers of the state through enforcement of nondiscrimination and affirmative action policies, the federal government has provided material incentives to colleges and universities to expand access and opportunity for underrepresented minority students. Title III of the Higher Education Act of 1965 set aside funds for institutions serving low-income and minority students. Amendments of 1998 to Title V of the Higher Education Act set aside funds to aid the institutional development of Hispanic-serving institutions. Title III of the Higher Education Act of 2008 extended categorical grants to institutions serving Asian Americans, Native Americans, and Pacific Islanders. The largest (and oldest) beneficiaries of these programs are the 106 historically black colleges and universities, which received more than $1.5 billion in federal grants in 2010 (Nelson 2012). In addition, 23 predominantly black colleges and universities received $10.8 million in 2010 (U.S. Department of Education 2010). Less developed are grants earmarked for Hispanic Serving Institutions (HSIs), amounting to more than $16 million in grants in 2010 to 29 institutions with Hispanic enrollments of 25 percent or more (Moltz 2010), and for Asian American Native American and Pacific Islander (AANAPI)-serving institutions ($8.6 million in grants in 2010 to nine institutions with at least 10 percent of undergraduate students in these categories) (White House Initiative 2012).

7. This type of atmosphere, Justice Powell believed, enhanced the training of the study body and better equipped the institution's graduates for civic engagement. Because such goals are essential to the nation's future and are protected by the First Amendment, Powell reasoned, race-conscious admissions policies, when narrowly tailored to meet these educational goals, served a compelling state interest (Chang, Chang, and Ledesma 2005).

8. A large scholarly literature on the intellectual benefits of diverse classes supported these commitments. Much of this literature was based on social psychological experiments purporting to show that diverse groups were more likely to come up with creative solutions to problems by yielding a broad range of options. This literature was summarized by Gurin (1999) as part of the University of Michigan's brief in support of its position in the *Grutter* case, a second major challenge to affirmative action in college admissions following *Bakke*. The extent to which these lab situations mirror problem solving in the real world remains an open question. See the discussion in Brint 2015a.

9. Citing a 2008 study by McKinsey and associates, the University Innovation Alliance founders argued that educational attainment gaps between rich and poor cost the country $1.3–2.3 trillion in lost gross domestic product because American workers were on average less able to master and adapt to the use of new technologies (Burns, Crow, and Becker 2015).

10. Policy analyst Richard Kahlenberg and colleagues (2010, 2015) provided empirical support for a shift from race-based admissions to class-based admissions. Kahlenberg's group reported that class-based affirmative action at ten public universities had succeeded not only in promoting greater economic diversity but in seven of ten cases had continued to deliver an equally or more racially diverse student body as well.

11. This roadblock was so severe that it led to calls by the Carnegie Foundation and other reformers to overhaul remedial mathematics education in community college by introducing non-calculus-based statistics rather than requiring the standard math sequence. Experiments with this change have shown higher pass rates, without demonstrating that the new approach

will work for students who wish eventually to complete baccalaureate degrees (Burdman 2012, 2015).

12. These figures are based on unpublished analyses by the author, with the assistance of Sarah R. K. Yoshikawa.

13. Very few students want to push themselves to take a full load of challenging courses. This means picking one or two relatively challenging classes a term and selecting among less challenging classes to fill out class schedules. "Guts" is the slang name for courses with light workloads, easy grading, or both. Guts include such famous courses in student lore as "animal planet" (conservation biology), "physics for poets" (introductory physics without the math), "rocks for jocks" (introduction to geology), "porn in the morn" (the sociology of sexuality), "heroes for zeroes" (Greek mythology), and even "frozen heroes for sub-zeroes" (Icelandic sagas). For an amusing guide to "guts" at Yale College circa the late 2000s, see "What Are the Gut Classes at Yale?" 2007.

14. The empirical evidence for the underlying "engagement" factor is hard to find, however, and indeed, research on University of California students has shown that the most socially and civically engaged students are typically *not* the most academically engaged students (see Brint and Cantwell 2010).

15. It is important to emphasize that efforts to determine the proportion of students who are primarily oriented in one way or another are bound to result in very rough approximations, because student orientations are not fixed across time and because multiple outlooks may exist simultaneously, or sequentially, taking precedence at different points in the academic career or the academic year. Even the most occupationally oriented students, for example, may have periods in which professional preparation is far from the most important thing on their minds.

16. Male students were much more likely than female students to be among the disengaged student populations, and students from wealthier families were marginally more likely to be so. Students majoring in arts, humanities, and social sciences were more likely to be among the disengaged populations, as were, not surprisingly, those with low grade-point averages (Brint and Cantwell 2014).

17. When students cannot see the justification for a course but are required to take it to fulfill distribution requirements, their common response is to expend as little effort as possible in mastering the subject matter—and in many cases to complain about how uninteresting they find the classes to be. Teachers in turn may reduce expectations and assign little material to their obviously disinterested or poorly prepared students. In the late 1990s, the Berkeley education professor W. Norton Grubb (1999) created a stir by observing that eight pages a week served as an average amount of reading required in many Northern California community college general education courses. Instructors felt that they could not assign more because students would not read more. More recently sociologists Richard Arum and Josipa Roksa reported that one-third of the more than 2,500 four-year college students in their 24 four-year college sample said they had not taken a single course in the prior semester that required as much as 40 pages of reading a week (2011, 71).

18. The superficiality and occasional unreliability of survey responses are clear, but ethnographies also have weaknesses as diagnostic instruments. Most of the college ethnographies are located in or focus on life in sororities and dorm floors where social life is the primary interest. They consequently miss what is happening in classrooms, libraries, and laboratories, opening the possibility that the balance is redressed to some degree in those locations.

19. Some critical observers of the college scene emphasize students' socialization not for work but for consumerism. Certainly consumerism figures prominently in the lives of many affluent students. For those in the Greek system this means paying the dues that allow upkeep on beautiful houses and lavish party giving, as well as the wardrobes, makeup, and accessories that

help sorority girls stand out in a sea of blue jeans (Armstrong and Hamilton 2013). For hipsters—at the other end of the taste (but not the social class) spectrum—this means vintage shirts and jackets, slim denims, hats, facial hair, thin ties, and offbeat experience hunting in bluegrass festivals, national parks, and art scenes (Kurutz 2013). Even for students who are not recognizably part of these highly visible campus subcultures, conscription into the consumer society is an almost mandatory part of the college social experience. It occurs through purchases of campus-branded gear, backpacks, handheld devices, computers, tickets to entertainment and sporting events, and the rest of the insignia and paraphernalia that mark a young person as someone who has achieved "college material" status in society.

20. Anthony P. Carnevale, the director of the Georgetown University Center on Education and the Workforce, engaged in a vigorous debate with another higher education economist, Richard Vedder, about the value of the college degree (see Lederman 2013). Carnevale emphasized the payoff to the college degree and Vedder the increasing levels of underemployment of college graduates. Part of the difference between the two turned on measurement issues. Carnevale did not always take into full account the opportunity costs associated with college education, and the Bureau of Labor Statistics on which Vedder relied does not have an airtight method for measuring the educational qualifications of jobs. Once the necessary adjustments are made to diminish the size of the college wage premium and to restrict the scope of BLS definitions of underemployment, we are left with the conclusion that both Carnevale and Vedder are correct: the college wage premium is high and has been growing, but underemployment among college graduates has also been growing. One reason why both are correct is that the market for high school–educated labor has greatly deteriorated, leading to bigger gaps between college graduates and high school graduates *and* a propensity for employers to hire college graduates (and those with some college education) for jobs once competently occupied by high school graduates.

Chapter 5: Multiplying Status Locations

1. The disparities are even greater among those attending elite colleges and universities. Three-quarters of those who attend Ivy League–type institutions come from the top SES quartile, and only 3 percent come from the bottom quartile. Indeed, at many elite private colleges a higher proportion come from the top 1 percent of families than from the entire bottom half of the income distribution (Chetty et al. 2017). One rung down, in less selective colleges and universities, the gap narrows, but nevertheless about half come from the top income quartile and just 7 percent from the bottom (Carnevale and Rose 2004).

2. One important advantage of attending a selective college not discussed here is that the likelihood of marrying someone who is interested in working and is a top earner him- or herself greatly increases. The top fifth of household income is dominated by dual-earning couples who have a baccalaureate or graduate education (see U.S. Bureau of the Census 2016b, HINC-01).

3. The potential arbitrariness of social closure mechanisms becomes apparent once we look into the discriminatory practices of many private clubs (and private universities). At one time, women and minorities were simply banned from private universities, and Jews were subject to pervasive discrimination (see, e.g., Karabel 2005, part 1).

4. We can gain a rough sense of the potential net impact of college major by examining rank order earnings. Groups from the Georgetown University Center on Education and the Workforce (Carnevale, Cheah, and Strohl 2012; Carnevale, Strohl, and Melton 2011) analyzed the Census Bureau's 2009 American Community Survey to understand the link between college majors and earnings. The Georgetown group focused on full-time working adults who had received their baccalaureates but had not obtained graduate degrees. The average earnings of engineer-

ing students topped the aggregated majors list ($75,000 per year average salary), followed by those of computer science and mathematics majors ($70,000 per year), business majors, health majors, and physical sciences majors (all in the $60,000 per year range). At the other end of the scale were humanities majors ($47,000 per year average salary) and arts majors ($42,000 per year), as well as education, psychology, and social work majors (all in the $42,000 per year range). The specific majors associated with the highest earnings were petroleum engineering, pharmaceutical sciences and administration, and mathematics and computer science (all in the $100,000–120,000 range). The specific fields with the lowest average earnings were counseling psychology ($29,000 average annual earnings), early childhood education, religious vocations, and social work ($38,000 average annual earnings or less).

5. The evidence suggests that with adequate institutional support, many more students from underrepresented groups could complete STEM majors successfully (see Chang et al. 2014).

6. It is impossible to know how much the increased demand for graduate degrees is produced by credential inflation and how much is produced by skills upgrading in occupations. Skill-biased technological change is clearly a factor. This term refers to the greater productivity that new technologies allow in professional occupations relative to manual occupations. Professors, for example, can produce many more papers with improvements in statistical packages and computer processing time and doctors can see more patients due to improvements in the accuracy and speed of medical technologies. But credential inflation undoubtedly also plays a role, at least in occupations that are not dependent on technology. Credential inflation is produced by employers who feel that their choices will be improved if they require higher-level qualifications at the same time that students see an interest in using higher-level credentials to stand out from their peers in crowded labor markets. Universities are happy to add degrees for which a market demand can be established and sometimes lead the charge to do so.

7. Grade inflation is highest at elite institutions. This can look like entitlement psychology. But it also reflects the results of a competitive reality. If one elite campus desires to make a change in the direction of rigorous grading and others maintain more generous grading standards, the students at the harder-grading campus will suffer in graduate school and job applications. To give a sense of the prevailing view of grades in elite institutions we need only to point to a saying common on the Stanford University campus: "A is for average, B is for bad." The sense of entitlement to high grades is apparent in the experience of the Princeton dean who attempted to reduce grade inflation during the mid-2000s by setting a 35 percent limit on As. She was the object of vitriolic attacks (see, e.g., Savage 2008), and the university eventually backed away from the policy (see Nieli 2014).

8. Family income shows a much larger impact on patenting: individuals whose families earned at the top 1 percent level were ten times more likely to patent new inventions than those whose families earned below the median (Bell et al. 2017).

9. Part of the advantage of business and engineering majors is connected to their greater likelihood of working in the private sector. Similarly, part of the disadvantage of education and social work majors is connected to their greater likelihood of working in the public or nonprofit sector (Roksa 2005).

10. The studies have been notably inconsistent with respect to who gains most from good grades. Using NLS-72 data, Loury and Garman (1995) found a much stronger effect of grades for African American students (25 percent) than whites (10 percent) in early career earnings. Examining mid-1970s graduates of selective colleges and universities, Bowen and Bok (1998) found similarly moderate effects of grades on earnings twenty years after graduation but with effects twice as large for men as for women. Looking at a broader stratum of college graduates in early career and using the 1987 Survey of Recent College Graduates data set, Rumberger and Thomas (1993) found initial wage premiums of 5 percent but this time for women only.

11. It is necessary to use the logarithm of earnings because the long tail of individuals at the high end of the income distribution typically leads to violations of the regression assumption that errors will be randomly distributed.

12. Studies of the effects of status variables are also plagued by problems of selection bias. Even when social scientists control for measured social background and academic achievements, they cannot know with certainty whether differences they find, for example, between Ivy League graduates and graduates of state universities, are due to the institution attended or to unmeasured individual differences in motivation, confidence, or resilience, as argued by Dale and Krueger (2002, 2011).

13. In part this may be due to the compression of grades in the later cohort. Some 53 percent reported either "mostly As" or "As and Bs" in the early 1990s cohort compared to 46 percent in the mid-1970s cohort. Those with "mostly Cs" or below dropped from 6 percent of the mid-1970s cohort to 2 percent of the mid-1990s cohort.

14. Nor is there much evidence for the proposition that athletes perform more poorly in the classroom than other students. Pascarella et al. (1999) found no significant net differences between student athletes and nonathletes with regard to cognitive development, grades in college, or time devoted to study. Umbach et al. (2006) found that athletes were not less likely to participate in effective educational practices, such as first-year seminars and undergraduate research, than other students, and where differences existed they tended to favor athletes.

15. Unmeasured motivational differences are, as always, issues in matched-sample studies like this one and, as I have indicated, threaten the validity of study findings.

16. Beyond these skill-building experiences in student clubs and organizations, it is important to keep in mind that student clubs and organizations create communities in ways that classes rarely do because they explicitly foster cooperative work on common causes. This is an influence compatible with success in adult life where competitive striving typically takes place within the context of cooperative efforts to achieve organizational goals.

17. Between 2003 and 2006, the Kauffman Foundation invested nearly $50 million in entrepreneurship programs on nineteen university campuses, including several I have highlighted in this chapter (Ewing Marion Kauffman Foundation 2008).

18. The University of California has institutionalized this contribution in its academic personnel manual; contributions to diversity are now official criteria in hiring and promotion (University of California, Office of the President 2015).

Chapter 6: The Priorities of Patrons

1. The more optimistic Congressional Budget Office (CBO) estimate is that the government made over $1.5 billion in student loans in 2016. But according to Lobato (2016), the CBO itself is skeptical of the assumptions behind this estimate, which government budget analysts are required by law to use when estimating the cost of the federal loan program. Similar to the more realistic CBO second estimation I have referred to in text, *Forbes* economist Preston Cooper (2016) calculated the amount of loan debt absorbed by the federal government each year at approximately $17 billion. See also College Board 2016, 20–21.

2. The research record of the Defense Advanced Research Projects Agency (DARPA) is nevertheless impressive and includes the early stage research and development of ARAPANET (the forerunner of the Internet), cloud computing, voice recognition software, street-level mapping, autonomous vehicles, and virtual reality. It also gets some credit for research and development of the global positioning system (GPS). See Cardinal 2011.

3. One reason for the emphasis on grants was that the banking industry at first opposed student loans; students had no collateral that could be repossessed and were therefore perceived by the industry as risky bets. The industry liked the idea that the federal government would offer subsidized loans, but they did not want the government to control loan rates or the terms of loans. Even government subsidies were not enough to convince bankers that these were good investments. As the financial aid policy analyst Suzanne Mettler put it, the voice of the financial sector was at first "much less powerful and persistent" than it became beginning in the 1980s (Mettler 2014, 60).

4. In 1990, a momentous change in accounting rules for federal expenditures—one that calculated student loans net of repayments rather than loan volume only—made it feasible for the first time for the government to lend directly to students rather than working solely through subsidies and guarantees to private lenders.

5. Net tuition costs are much lower than sticker prices. Net tuition is calculated after grants, other scholarship aid, and tuition credits are taken into account. Net tuition has climbed much more slowly than tuition sticker prices.

6. Default rates were also much higher among those who attended for-profits. According to a U.S. Senate report from 2011, at a time when about 10 percent of postsecondary students were attending for-profit colleges, these students were responsible for nearly half of student loan defaults (47 percent) (U.S. Senate 2011).

7. Throughout the period, six federal agencies supported 90 to 95 percent of federal R&D funding. After the Department of Defense (DOD) come the National Institutes of Health (NIH), the Department of Energy (DOE), the National Aeronautics and Space Administration (NASA), the National Science Foundation (NSF), and the U.S. Department of Agriculture (USDOA) in that order. Defense R&D exceeded nondefense R&D throughout the period—and continues to do so by about $10 billion annually. Defense R&D grew dramatically during the Reagan administration and then again during the period of the War on Terror. At $80 billion a year it is the behemoth of federal R&D. The great majority of these funds are spent on procuring weapons systems and military equipment.

8. This estimate is broadly consistent with other estimates using different methodologies. See, e.g., Cohen, Nelson, and Walsh 2002; Cockburn and Henderson 1996; and Mansfield 1998.

9. The National Endowments for the Arts and Humanities became easy targets for congressional conservatives because they both supported work that offended "Middle American" sensibilities. The "Piss Christ" and Robert Mapplethorpe exhibits of 1987 and 1989, respectively, were the most consequential of the flare-ups during the period. They were partly funded by the National Endowment for the Arts (NEA), and they ultimately led to deeper cuts and heightened Republican opposition to funding for the NEA. See Andrews 2017.

10. The concentration of science funding at NIH has often been questioned by those who believe that the balance between funding for the biomedical sciences and the physical sciences and engineering would benefit from growth in funding for the latter (see the discussions in Geiger 1993, 320–26; National Academies 2005; Neal, Smith, and McCormick 2008, 81–82; Stephan 2012, 141–45). President George W. Bush's commitment to double the size of the NSF budget was, in part, a response to the concerns of physical scientists and engineers about imbalance in federal support of science and engineering favoring the biomedical and life sciences.

11. At the same time, NIH has relied on "safety valves" to satisfy Congress, such as research centers located in key districts, contracts, and requests for applications concerning particular diseases (Sampat 2012). The progress of medical science has obviously been critical; without this progress, the influence of the health lobby and the political acumen of NIH directors would have become less material over time. NIH-funded research has contributed to great improvements in

public health, including the effective treatment of threats like the AIDS and Ebola epidemics, as well as a very large early stage discovery and development program for new drug therapies (Toole 2012).

12. Initiated in 2004 through the NIH Roadmap to Medical Discovery, the Common Fund was written into law by Congress in 2006 in the NIH Reform Act.

13. The current NSF portfolio of managed facilities includes three national observatories, located in Arizona, New Mexico, and Chile, equipped with giant optical and radio telescopes; a gravitational wave observatory that has successfully identified ripples in space and time emanating from black holes; three year-round research centers in the Antarctic, which have contributed to understanding climate change and other atmospheric and ecological phenomena; high-end computer facilities and ultra-high-speed network connections; and ships and submersibles used for ocean research. Approximately 15 percent of the NSF budget has been appropriated in recent years to support these projects (NSF 2017).

14. Although it was plagued by constant cost overruns and poor design decisions, the space station and shuttle nevertheless helped put the Americans back into the thick of space exploration, a goal also advanced by the Hubble telescope launched in 1990 and the *Mars Pathfinder* six years later.

15. In addition to the big-science initiatives discussed here, Obama created the first ever U.S. Chief Technology officer, the first-ever Chief Information Officer, as well as the first Chief Data Scientists and first Office of Digital Services (Holdren 2017). He also persuaded Congress to make the research and experimentation tax credit permanent and launched seven hundred "grand challenge" competitions throughout the federal government agencies (Kalil and Dorgelo 2016).

16. The Obama administration's initiatives began in interagency working groups, task forces, or subcommittees. These groups published more than ninety policy papers, many of which led directly to presidential initiatives (Kalil and Dorgelo 2016). Nearly all of the dozens of initiatives that emerged were structured as partnerships across government, industry, academe, and nonprofit organizations (Holdren 2017). Some of the proposals, such as investments in climate science, became objects of partisan disagreement, but most fared well in the congressional budget process.

17. For reviews of Obama administration science initiatives, see Holdren 2017; Hourihan 2017; Kalil and Dorgelo 2016; and Kramer 2016.

18. In the early 1990s, Senator Barbara Mikulski called on NSF to allocate 60 percent of its budget to projects in the national interest, but, in spite of her clout as chair of the Senate Appropriations Committee, she was unable to embed this preference in legislation (Neal, Smith, and McCormick 2008, 338). In 2011 Senator Tom Coburn published a blistering report criticizing NSF grant making (Coburn 2011), including proposals to radically reduce social science funding, but the report failed to gain traction. During the 2015 reauthorization of the America COMPETES Act, Representative Lamar Smith attempted to redirect NSF spending toward national priority areas in security, health, and economic development (Mervis 2015), and he too failed. In each case, the scientific community and sympathetic business groups lobbied to defeat congressional efforts to wrest control of science funding away from scientists. Coburn's 2011 report did lead to a new emphasis in NSF on "transformative" research, which was incorporated into its subsequent statements on intellectual merit.

19. The SBIR/STTR reauthorization of 2008 foundered on the lobbying of venture capital firms for access to government funds. Both programs were eventually reauthorized and extended in 2011 through 2017 with opportunities for limited participation of venture capitalist firms. Evaluations by the National Academies suggested that STTRs were more time consuming to generate and administer than SBIRs, because of their requirement for formal collaboration, but

were also more likely to have a transformative effect on small businesses and to generate new, commercially viable technologies (BSTEP 2016, chap. 6).

20. At least five other reports of the period helped generate a mood for action in Washington. See the reports of the Association of American Universities (2006), the Business Roundtable (2005), the Center for Strategic and International Studies (2005), the Education Commission of the States (2005), and the National Summit on Competitiveness (2005).

21. The original America COMPETES Act included eight titles containing more than one hundred sections that directed specific programs and policies in seven federal agencies (Gonzalez, Sargent, and Figliola 2010).

22. There were exceptions to the rule that businesspeople do not become directly involved in designing policy—Microsoft founder Bill Gates being the most important. In chapter 4 I discussed his role as a formulator and promoter of the "college completion agenda."

23. Elizabeth Berman (2012) has persuasively argued that the university-based competitiveness policies of the era—biotechnology deregulation, deregulation and simplification of technology transfer, and university-industry research centers—formed out of different constellations of government and university actors, but all were tied together by a common appeal to what she calls "the innovation frame"—the idea that government action in support of technological innovation can help improve the international competitiveness of the country while bringing new jobs and wealth to communities.

24. Five states—Louisiana, Arizona, Delaware, Pennsylvania, and Nevada—cut state expenditures on higher education by more than 20 percent between 2010 and 2015 (SHEEO 2015). Pennsylvania governor Tom Corbett initially proposed a 50 percent cut, one presumes as a negotiating position.

25. Expenditures per student at master's-granting public universities were about $4,000 lower on average in AY 2009, and they yielded a different order among the states, albeit with wealthier states still tending to spend more and poorer states still tending to spend less (see Desrochers and Wellman 2011, figure A3).

26. The efforts of the flagship campuses in Colorado, Oregon, and Wisconsin to break away from the less prestigious institutions in their states typified the movement from coordinated systems to loose confederations led by restive flagships and exemplified the gaps that were emerging as the elite- and broad-access sectors drifted further apart.

27. Student-to-faculty ratios increased by an average of 13 percent at public universities; the size of the tenured and tenure-track faculty decreased by approximately 8 percent; and the proportion of contingent faculty increased by 5 percent. In comparisons with private colleges and universities, each of these changes in mean values was significant at $p < .001$ (see Brint et al. 2016).

28. The million-dollar list includes gifts to a variety of organizations, not only colleges and universities. Work on this list required combing through each one to isolate gifts for colleges and universities and then classifying these gifts by academic field or other purposes. We received electronic files from the IUPUI Center on Philanthropy that had already been catalogued as pertaining only to higher education institutions. Records were spotty in relation to the purposes for the use of gifts; we found no information on uses in about one out of five cases. The data are also marred by a number of limitations. The most important is that not all pledges are actualized. Although the ordinal ranks among fields are likely correct, gift amounts should be treated with great caution. We do not have certainty that these lists are complete. We worked to eliminate duplications, but it is possible that some duplications exist between the two sources.

29. In 1990 religion and theology also ranked high thanks to a bequest of more than $38 million to two seminaries by the same individual.

30. Some large donations came with strings attached that universities (or their critics) considered susceptible to the corruption of unwarranted outside influence. A few notable cases

indicate the ways that donors seek to influence discourse or research in their own material or ideal interests. In 1995 Yale decided to give back a $20 million gift from the Bass family to fund Western Civilization because the family sought influence over the appointment of chairs whose funding derived from the gift (Steinberg 1995). The University of Michigan came under attack in 2012 when it was revealed that Dow Chemical's funding for a Sustainability Fellows program allowed a representative of the company to sit on the selection committee (Polsgrove 2012). Many libertarian magnates, including the Scaife and Olin families, have come under scrutiny for gifts to universities that required the adherence of chair holders to free-market principles. The latest to do so are the Koch brothers, who have donated nearly $20 million to 210 campuses in 46 states for purposes of advancing the principles of free-market economics (Levinthal 2015).

Chapter 7: An Accumulation of Administration

1. IPEDS' definition of "executive, administrative and managerial" personnel is as follows: employees holding titles such as top executives; chief executives; general and operations managers; advertising, marketing, promotions, public relations, and sales managers; operations specialties managers; administrative services managers; computer and information systems managers; financial managers; human resources managers; purchasing managers; postsecondary education administrators such as presidents, vice presidents (including assistants and associates), deans (including assistants and associates) if their principal activity is administrative and not primarily instruction, research, or public service, directors (including assistants and associates), department heads (including assistants and associates) if their principal activity is administrative and not primarily instruction, research, or public service, assistant and associate managers (including first-line managers of service, production and sales workers who spend more than 80 percent of their time performing supervisory activities); engineering managers; food service managers; lodging managers; and medical and health services managers.

2. A survey by Tierney and Minor (2003) of 2,000 department chairs, chief academic officers, and faculty senate leaders found that only 22 percent of respondents indicated the senate was an important governing body in their institutions, and more than half indicated that faculty at their institutions had low levels of interest in the senate. Dissatisfaction was especially high at doctoral/research universities, where only 19 percent of respondents said that faculty members had high levels of interest in the senate.

3. Self-reports suggest that the burden of committee work falls disproportionately on female faculty members, who may experience more ambivalence than their male colleagues about saying no to proposed committee assignments (Finkelstein, Conley, and Schuster 2016, 537–38; Guarino and Borden 2017).

4. This section is based on nearly a decade of observation of senior administrators at one research university and conversations with dozens of senior administrators. My observations and conversations accord with many of the findings of such classic works on managers and executives as Barnard 1938, Kanter 1976, and Whyte 1956.

5. I chose the fifty presidential biographies based on the total citation counts of universities and medical centers in 2010. Most of these institutions were top performers throughout the period 1980–2015. See Brint and Carr 2017 for a discussion of the methodology used for developing citation count data.

6. The *U.S. News* sample of presidents was drawn from their 2015 list. I chose twelve top schools from each of the four regions the magazine used for categorization: East, South, Midwest, and West. I added one each from the East and West to round out a top 50. Because I drew at random from the *C&U 2000* sample of public regional universities, this comparison group does

not constitute a top 50 list. It is almost certainly more representative than a top 50 list would be of the patterns of presidential careers lower in the hierarchy of four-year institutions.

7. According to *U.S. News and World Report* the top eleven higher education administration programs at the end of the period were as follows: University of Michigan-Ann Arbor, the University of Pennsylvania, Michigan State University, UCLA, Vanderbilt University, Pennsylvania State University, the University of Georgia, the University of Southern California, Indiana University, the University of Maryland-College Park, and Harvard University (USNWR 2017).

8. Presidential compensation, while sizable and growing, did not begin to match that of the top football and basketball coaches in major college athletic conferences—and at research universities they also sometimes fell short of that of the medical dean or leading surgeon on the faculty. Those who see university administrators as corporate CEOs in academic robes should also have another gap to contemplate: even though the institutions they run may be every bit as complex as corporations, the salaries of university presidents do not begin to match those of CEOs of large firms where $10 million or higher compensation packages are the norm. The gaps between presidents and front-line staff are also not as large as in industry; in industry those gaps can be as high as 1500 to 1 (McKenna 2015).

9. Some universities have introduced differential tuition for programs that are expensive or have better job prospects. A portion of these fee differences is held by the departments to fund the higher salaries for professors who teach in the "preferred" programs, and part can be used by the university to subsidize low-enrollment programs.

10. Responsibility-centered management (RCM) began in private universities in the 1970s and 1980s. Harvard coined the phrase "every tub on its own bottom" to describe the decentralized budgeting model it adopted. Among private universities, other early adopters included Cornell University, the University of Pennsylvania, the University of Southern California, and Vanderbilt University. The University of Indiana was the first public university to adopt RCM in 1989. The University of Michigan, the University of Minnesota, and the University of New Hampshire were among the early public university adopters. See Hearn et al. 2006.

11. RCM has had many critics. Critics point to the tendency of RCM to generate duplications as colleges attempt to draw away students in required or popular courses taught by other units. Enrollment chasing can also lead to lower-quality courses that will appeal to utilitarian-minded students. Critics also point out the incentives in RCM for revenue centers to seek to reduce spending on service units and subventions to less "prosperous" revenue-generating units. The idea that service units like student support services are not responsible for revenue strikes some critics as an arbitrary and invidious distinction (Hearn et al. 2006).

12. I would like to thank Michaela Curran for her work on this comprehensive web search.

13. The development of expectations for faculty input in governance followed the founding of the American Association of University Professors (AAUP) in 1915 and the Berkeley faculty revolt of 1919. The development of the dual pattern, often referred to as "shared governance," was greatly encouraged by the professionalization of the faculty in the post–world war period. The AAUP delivered an influential endorsement of dual governance in its 1966 "Statement on the Government of Colleges and Universities" (AAUP 1966). In this statement the AAUP and two other major higher education associations endorsed the principle that "differences in the weight of each (institutional) voice . . . should be determined by reference to the responsibility of each component for the particular matter at hand" (136) and allocated to the faculty "primary control" over "curriculum, subject matter and methods of instruction, research, faculty status, and aspects of student life that relate to the educational process" (139).

14. Many university administrators were highly critical of academic senates. They observed that senates made decision making slower and more cumbersome than it would otherwise have been. They pointed out that senates tend to attract faculty members who are less productive

scholars, lowering the quality of participation. They complained of an "us-versus-them" mentality that animated some senate members. They doubted that senate members could see the institutional interest above the interests of the departments or colleges they represented. (See Bowen and Tobin 2015; Duderstadt and Womack 2003, 166–69; Garland 2009, 81–103; Hirsch and Weber 2001.)

15. In Kaplan's (2004) survey, for example, 84 percent of respondents reported that faculty either made or directly influenced institutional policy, and this was most likely to be true in liberal arts colleges.

16. The survey was sent to chief academic officers (CAOs) of the 385 four-year colleges and universities in the *Colleges & Universities* 2000 sample. *C&U 2000* is based on a stratified random sample of U.S. four-year colleges and universities in the year 2000. The sample is weighted so that results are representative of the universe of four-year colleges and universities in 2000, excluding for-profits and specialized institutions. Response rates varied between the two survey years. In 2000, slightly over 300 responded; in 2012, slightly over 200 responded. Forty-eight percent (183) of CAOs responded to the survey both in 2000 and in 2012, allowing for a direct comparison of a matched sample of institutions across the two survey years. However, some CAOs did not respond to all items related to decision-making structures for both time points. These responses were excluded from the analysis, leaving responses from 139 CAOs in the matched sample.

17. Fit in this sample became much less satisfactory when we raised the criterion above 50 percent agreement. In 2000 only one of thirteen decisions received as many as two-thirds of responses in the normative category derived from the model, and only three of thirteen met this two-thirds level in 2012. We characterized the level of support we found for the dual control model as increasingly satisfactory with time at the 50 percent fit level but unimpressive using more stringent fit criteria.

18. The higher levels of dispersion found in faculty salaries and work conditions mirrored those found in other professions. The difference between partners in the largest corporate firms in New York or Washington, D.C., and solo attorneys working divorce cases in small towns are every bit as great as those between endowed professors at Harvard or Stanford and assistant professors in education schools at regional public universities. Top tertiary care neurosurgeons are separated by a similar gulf from internists working in rural clinics. National media figures are nominally in the same occupation as journalists reporting sports in small-town newspapers but live in different worlds. Perhaps the only difference between academe and these other professions is that the faculty, supported by the institutions of shared governance, held on longer to the ideal of collegial organization.

19. As Clark (1987) pointed out, medical school part-timers working in lucrative private or group practice had no economic incentive to seek the protections of tenure, given the heightened expectations for campus commitments required by a tenured appointment.

20. In some universities, full-time lecturers could gain security of employment. At the University of California, for example, lecturers with security of employment (LSOEs) or with potential security of employment (LPSOEs) became fixtures during the period. Lacking research expectations and rewarded solely for excellence in teaching, the LSOEs were members of the Academic Senate, with all the rights and privileges of this membership. Many were among the most engaged instructors on University of California campuses. Their rights to gain security of employment were guaranteed by collective bargaining agreements under which the lecturers operated.

21. The National Labor Relations Board reopened the door on private college and university collective bargaining in early 2015 when it offered a set of standards for determining whether faculty members were managerial (Jaschik 2015).

22. Nor did most faculty members consider themselves exploited by management. In spite of frequent comments about the lost souls working on "the dark side," relatively few faculty members saw themselves as an oppositional force. In the early 1990s less than 20 percent of full-time faculty members surveyed said that the statement "faculty are typically at odds with campus administration" was "very descriptive" of their campuses (Finkelstein, Conley, and Schuster 2016, 305). Faculty animus, as measured by agreement with this statement, increased a bit through the early 2000s and 2010s but never reached beyond one-quarter of respondents in *any* institutional sector among four-year college and university respondents (ibid.). At most institutions it took a well-publicized controversy or a long series of administrative blunders to engage the "silent majority" in issues of campus administration.

23. Republican Party opposition to unions made organizing more difficult. Some states, such as Wisconsin and Ohio, legislated limitations on collective bargaining by public employees.

Chapter 8: Focus on the Classroom

1. Sections of chapter 8 first appeared in my chapter "Focus on the Classroom: Movements to Reform College Teaching and Learning, 1980–2008," in *The Academic Profession: Transformation in Contemporary Higher Education*, ed. Joseph C. Hermanowicz (Baltimore: Johns Hopkins University Press, 2011): 44–91. © 2011 The Johns Hopkins University Press. Adapted and excerpted with permission of Johns Hopkins University Press.

2. Later administrations of the National Assessment of Adult Literacy to samples made up exclusively of recent college graduates showed no declines in literacy. The National Research Council concluded that the test as constructed could not detect who was proficient in literacy skills (NRC 2005), but one wonders whether recent college graduates are the right sample on which to base this judgment.

3. The evidence suggested that good practices in teaching, as defined by Chickering and Gamson (1987), remained a little stronger at highly selective institutions, but, as Ernest Pascarella and his colleagues (2006) put it, the net effect of institutional selectivity "may not count for much" (278).

4. It can be argued that the causes of this renewed focus on the classroom were similar to those that provoked rethinking of classroom teaching in secondary schools at the turn of the twentieth century: the construction of a mass system, fueled by the incorporation of working-class and immigrant students, in which a majority of students had limited preparation for learning and in which chronically underfunded institutions had limited resources to create powerful learning communities. Expansion, combined with continuing fiscal pressures in the public sector, encouraged concerns about the effectiveness of college teaching, while diversification led to concerns about the possibility of unequal results for women, minorities, and immigrants.

5. As early as 1969, it had issued a statement crediting minorities for "giving a fresh and compelling impetus to the movement for restoring relevance to academic programs" (AAC 1969). Its studies on the "chilly climate" for women in college classrooms received national attention in the 1970s and 1980s (see, e.g., Hall and Sandler 1982).

6. NSSE included student self-reports of learning gains in several skill areas. Self-reports showed modest correlations with objective tests of learning gains and cannot be taken at face value as evidence of student learning (see, e.g., Bowman and Seifert 2011).

7. A similar study with more elaborate controls on students' prior achievements also yielded modest or insignificant relationships between NSSE benchmarks and cognitive growth on the Collegiate Assessment of Academic Proficiency (Pascarella, Seifert, and Blaich 2009).

8. Other Shulman-inspired projects led to the creation of websites intended to spread pedagogical practices consistent with the "teaching for understanding" approach. Georgetown professor Randy Bass's *Visible Knowledge Project* website was the most important for advancing and codifying ideas about pedagogies of understanding. His website spotlighted techniques for slowing down and deepening knowledge transmission, for building on core ideas and concepts, and for making teachers' intermediate processes and performance standards visible to students, while revealing students' prior understandings and making their difficulties in understanding course materials visible to teachers.

9. The institution of the Carnegie Academy for the Scholarship of Teaching and Learning (CASTL) was the first of Shulman's organizational vehicles. Pew Foundation funds provided support for a summer academy located at the foundation where successful applicants, approximately fifteen a summer, met together to discuss and develop the ideas from their proposals for improvement of college teaching and learning. The total number of CASTL scholars topped out at fewer than one hundred. By contrast, SoTL colloquia emerged on campuses throughout the country, but they attracted only a minority of motivated teachers to their events. Even at such a highly engaged campus as Indiana University, only about one-quarter of tenured and tenure-track faculty had participated in a SoTL event by 2002, and fewer than sixty people attended these events, on average, on a campus of more than 2,000 faculty members. Some other Carnegie projects wound down by the end of Shulman's tenure as president. The Visible Knowledge Project ran out of funds in 2005 after a decade of pioneering work. Peer Review of Teaching remained operational but attracted a dwindling number of new portfolios after Pew funding ended. Carnegie's Knowledge Media Lab closed its electronic doors in September 2009, though its course portfolio software remained retrievable.

10. The objectives of the Carnegie Foundation changed dramatically with the selection of Anthony Bryk in 2007 to replace the retiring Shulman as president of the foundation. Bryk launched an ambitious effort to "scale up" R&D in education through well-supported industrial-style prototyping and mass diffusion, beginning with an assault on the low success rates of community college students in remedial mathematics. Even as the foundation moved into new areas, including "improvement science," this signature program remained controversial among math educators (Stigler, Givven, and Thompson 2013).

11. Outcomes assessment should be distinguished from the broader movement to increase accountability in higher education. Accountability has been linked to such performance indicators as graduation and job placement rates, and not only to learning outcomes. Performance funding, a popular approach to provide incentives for improved institutional performance, was one instrument of the broader accountability movement (see, e.g., Burke 2005; Dougherty and Natow 2009, 2015).

12. By 2001, ten states, concentrated in the South and Midwest, had experimented with or adopted standardized multiple-choice testing of student learning outcomes in publicly supported institutions (Ewell 2001b). Although the idea of demonstrating institutional value added to learning was gaining widespread appeal, few agreed on what types of learning should be measured or how it should be demonstrated. Some advocated discipline-specific knowledge, others more general cognitive skills (such as analytical thinking and writing), and still others wanted to focus on work-related skills. Some advocated multiple-choice tests for their cost-effectiveness, but others concluded that higher-level cognitive skills could not be demonstrated in this context and required the completion of more complex, "real-world" tasks.

13. An article by the assessment expert Trudy Banta summarized the experience of educators who had attempted to implement standardized tests of general intellectual skills, such as interpretation, critical analysis, and writing. Banta argued that such instruments primarily tested entering ability; were not content neutral and therefore privileged students specializing

in some disciplines more than others; contained questions and problems that did not match the learning experiences of all students at any given institution; and measured at best 30 percent of the knowledge and skills that faculty wanted students to develop. She also raised doubts about the reliability of gain scores at the individual level, the extent to which students took such tests seriously, and the dangers posed by high-stakes testing on the potential narrowing of the higher education curriculum to focus on the skills and content emphasized in the tests (Banta 2007).

14. It is important to allow for the possibility of instructor effects; it may be that better instructors are more inclined to use interactive-engagement techniques and they would also be more effective in traditional lecture formats. The consistency of the results achieved by Hake (1998) lead to the presumption that the format itself is at the very least a contributing factor to improvements in student learning.

15. The literature on quizzing is not entirely consistent. Some studies note that pre-class quizzes can contribute more to student stress than student learning if they are poorly designed or not well integrated with course learning objectives (see, e.g., Brothen and Wambach 2001). For this reason, some instructors preferred to ask students to write short answers to prompts about the reading as an alternative mechanism for ensuring that students are prepared for class.

16. Peer review of teaching has been the most common alternative to student evaluation of teaching, but peer reviewers need to be trained in evaluation and they need to have criteria and rubrics to use to evaluate their colleagues. They must then take time out of already crowded schedules to sit in on one or more classes. Without this training and these materials, peer evaluation can be as unreliable as student evaluation. Indeed, personal considerations can make it more unreliable. Colleagues in the same department may be inclined to give each other the benefit of the doubt for the sake of departmental peace. Colleagues in adjacent departments may be more even-handed, but it is difficult to convince colleagues in adjacent departments that they have the expertise to make informed judgments about teaching outside their own discipline.

17. As Wieman and Gilbert observed: "The large observed differences in the effectiveness of difference science teaching practices and the similarity of those differences across disciplines ... can be explained in terms of the basic principles of complex learning that have been established by the learning sciences. . . . These principles include such things as the need for intense, prolonged practice of the cognitive skills desired, with guiding feedback, and the importance of motivation and addressing the prior knowledge of the learner" (2014, 556).

18. The Teaching Practices Inventory does not begin to account for the quality of implementation of the practices it counts, a task Wieman and Gilbert consider "far more difficult" than simply assigning points for research-supported practices (2014, 561).

19. These were not the only prescriptions of the Teaching Practices Inventory. In courses that include teaching assistants, the TPI adds points for regular meetings with teaching assistants and for conversations with them about how to teach course materials. It also allocates points for what can be thought of as deep involvement in thinking about how to teach a course, including discussions with colleagues about how to teach the course, reading existing literature on approaches to teaching the course, and sitting in on the course when it is taught by colleagues.

Chapter 9: Other Challenges: Cost, Online Competition, Contentious Speech

1. At the 2013 annual meeting of the Council of Independent Colleges, a group of concerned private school presidents argued for reducing or eliminating merit aid to middle-class families and limiting aid to only those who needed it. According to one of the leaders of the group, Kenyon College president S. Georgia Nugent, many who agreed with the principle feared the policy

would lead to losses of enrollment and declines in prestige for their institutions (Gardner 2013). Although the pledge went nowhere, by the end of the recession period, many chief financial officers were questioning the sustainability of the high-tuition, high-discount policy. Yet none seemed to have attractive alternatives to recommend in its place (Rivard 2014).

2. Consortia of private nonprofit colleges are described in NAICU 2016. Another characteristic example is the "Ohio 5," which used its joint purchasing power to lower institutional costs on such things as computer equipment and software licensing, energy, and insurance. By sharing resources, the consortium worked to reduce administrative and academic redundancies; to offers students new learning opportunities and better services; to provide joint training and professional development workshops; and to participate collectively in peer review. The colleges also shared staff appointments in library storage and procurement.

3. Dynarski (2014) observed that modeling exactly how such a system would work in replenishing the Treasury would require a new individual-level longitudinal data base on student borrowing and earnings that followed students many years after college. However, before investing in such a database, it would be advisable first to examine results for countries like Australia, Canada, and England that have introduced repayment plans similar to the one Dynarski proposed.

4. Because loan defaults were much higher among students who left college without degrees, Baum (2005) also advocated programs that prepared at-risk students to be successful in college. In programs like the Indiana 21st Century Scholars, students on free or reduced lunch in eighth grade were eligible for academic support services that helped them complete a rigorous college prep curriculum. For those who succeeded, the program assured sufficient aid to guarantee that higher education would be within financial reach. Each eligible student's college fund built up as they achieved credits for progress toward college.

5. The alternative possibility of "white flight" from colleges with large concentrations of newly admitted low-income students also never entered calculations of the consequences of "free-college" plans.

6. In some cases, states enacted "free-college" plans with the stipulation that students who took advantage of them must work within the state for a specified amount of time. The hope was to prevent brain drain and to attract ambitious families into the state, but the policy literature showed no demonstration of the effectiveness of this strategy for low-growth states.

7. Education and related expenses formulas leave out many expenditure categories, such as running bookstores or research labs, because state appropriations are targeted for education expenses, not expenses fully funded, in theory, through other revenue sources (for example, through sales of books and merchandise or research grants).

8. Newfield and his colleagues calculated that Californians could restore their public higher education system to its former largely state-supported glory, at current enrollment levels, by paying a median amount of $48 more in an annual income tax surcharge. What was often left out in the promotion of this plan was that upper-income taxpayers would be assessed much more, as much as $40,000 per year.

9. One obstacle is that governors do not always abide by compacts, as in the famous case of Governor Arnold Schwarzenegger of California, who reneged in 2008 on a compact signed with the University of California in 2004. Universities too must be careful in negotiating such compacts. Many critics argued that the UC compact did not take funding losses following the dot. com bust into account and consequently locked the university into funding levels below those required to provide previous levels of quality (Paddock 2008).

10. As one of the corporate respondents to my research group's study of online education said, "Hungry Minds is an example. All they were in it for was the immediate payoff, and when it didn't look like it was going to happen they pulled the plug, leaving all their students out to

dry. That doesn't foster a good image for other privates" (quoted in Brint, Paxton-Jorgenson, and Vega 2002, 9).

11. The Sloan Foundation–funded surveys led by I. Edith Allen and Jeff Seaman were the better-known sources of data on online enrollments. However, comparisons with IPEDS data showed sharp divergence in estimates between the two. In 2013, the differences amounted to more than 2 million students. Allen and Seaman (2016) explain the difference as follows: In the Babson surveys, "online offerings were defined as broadly as possible—any offering of any length to any audience at any time. IPED[S] took a narrower view. It counted (only) offerings in a 4 or 5-year bachelor's program, an associate['s] degree program or a vocational or technical degree program below the baccalaureate. Non-credit courses, continuing education courses, courses for alumni, courses for students not registered for a degree program do not qualify for the IPED[S] definition. . . . In addition, many Babson respondents did not correctly remove students enrolled in more than one qualifying course, and therefore provided numbers that were too high" (40–41).

12. The agreement by Purdue University to purchase the financially battered for-profit Kaplan University in 2017 was symbolic of the relative strength of the two sectors at the end of the period. Kaplan was interested in finding a way out of a declining financial position due to lost enrollments, while Purdue indicated an interest both in serving students who might otherwise be abandoned and in jumping feet first into the online adult education market (Blumenstyk 2017).

13. This does not fully solve the self-selection problem, of course, because students may differentiate between courses they want to take or feel that they can succeed in online as compared to those they want to take or feel that they can succeed in face-to-face.

14. Sebastian Thurn, the founder of Udacity, reportedly saw the opportunity for a new firm when his early MOOC on artificial intelligence reached an audience of more than 160,000 participants worldwide (Heller 2013).

15. As in the case of press reports, there are reasons to suspect underreporting in FBI statistics due to resource limitations—community colleges hardly appear in these statistics—or the desire of university administrators to avoid unwanted publicity.

16. The psychologist Scott Lillienfeld (2017) reviewed the literature on microaggressions and found "negligible support" for any one of the five propositions researchers have studied: that microaggressions (1) are operationalized with sufficient clarity and consensus to allow rigorous scientific investigation; (2) can be interpreted explicitly by most or all minority group members; (3) reflect implicitly prejudicial and implicitly aggressive motives; (4) can be validly assessed using only respondents' subjective reports; and (5) lead to adverse effects for recipients' mental health. On the basis of this research, Lillienfeld has called for a moratorium on the use of the term and for the abandonment of campus advisories on microaggressions.

17. The University of Missouri became a cause célèbre in 2015 when the university president, Timothy M. Wolfe, seemed slow to respond to a series of incendiary, racially motivated incidents on campus. Wolfe resigned the following year, and university applications plummeted in the wake of the incidents. See Hartocollis 2017.

18. Alan Kors and Harvey Silverglate (1998) provided several case studies of these "worst possible constructions" including a well-publicized incident at the University of Pennsylvania of an intemperate plea for quiet being construed as a racial epithet.

19. For an engaging and insightful discussion of campus politics during the period, see Zimmerman 2016b.

20. Black students were much more likely than white students to support restrictions on speech that members of some groups might find offensive—two out of five did—and women

were somewhat more likely than men to support them—one out of three did (Gallup Organization 2017).

21. Some who claimed to take steps to foster dialogue may have unconsciously foreclosed it through the presentation of one-sided material or by telegraphing their own points of view. In these classrooms students may have felt that the social price for challenging prevailing opinion was simply too high to consider seriously.

22. The position can be traced directly to the work of the Italian Marxist philosopher Antonio Gramsci ([1948] 2011), if not to the work of Marx himself. It found an early anticolonialist exponent in Franz Fanon (1963). Of Foucault's contemporaries, Pierre Bourdieu (1977), Jacques Derrida (1981), and Richard Rorty (1991) were among the leading advocates of related positions.

23. The postmodern position, as described by Searle (1994), found an analog in the "alternative-facts" orthodoxies embraced by the Right in the mid-2010s.

24. I find Searle's term "the Western rationalistic tradition" unnecessarily limiting. Although this tradition has Western roots, it has been adopted by scholars and scientists worldwide and could consequently be better termed "the global rationalistic tradition."

25. The security costs for Berkeley's "free speech week" scheduled for September 2017 were estimated at well over $1 million (Schatz 2017). Some of the more prominent and controversial speakers cancelled prior to the event, reducing the cost significantly.

Chapter 10: The Ends of Knowledge

1. This knowledge-worker stratum included individuals with undergraduate STEM degrees and those with postgraduate degrees. And of course an uncounted number of college graduates with degrees in interpretive fields also had the experience of rigorous study and could demonstrate highly developed cognitive skills.

2. As should be evident from the discussion of postindustrial society at the end of chapter 2, I do not agree with the argument that technological innovation and social inclusion are recipes for equitable economic development across all states. It is true that nine of the ten states that rank highest in GDP per capita are politically liberal "blue" states that pay attention to technological innovation and social inclusion as well as business climate and industry strength. In 2015, these states were New York, Connecticut, Delaware, Massachusetts, New Jersey, Washington, California, Minnesota, and Maryland. Only one of the ten, Texas, was a conservative, or "red," state but it too showed a strong commitment to technological innovation, if not perhaps as much as the others to social inclusion (U.S. Department of Commerce, BEA 2017). Similarly, eight of the ten states that paid the highest per capita tax revenues to the federal government in 2015 were politically liberal blue states in which policy was attuned to business development, technological innovation, and social inclusion (IRS 2015, table 5). However, pre-transfer inequality and costs of living both tended to be higher in the high-GDP blue states, suggesting that the fruits of technological and business development were disproportionately enjoyed by the most affluent citizens and that problems of poverty were very far from having been solved. Thus the socioeconomic advantages of red states tend to include more equitable distributions of pre-transfer income and lower costs of living. Many high-GDP blue states redress these difficulties, to a greater or lesser degree, with higher state and local taxation and more generous social services.

3. Another indicator of stasis: the system of research universities reached a stable level of inequality in the distribution of R&D expenditures, publications, and citations by 2000 (Brint and Carr 2017). Considerable short-range mobility existed in this system but very little long-range mobility.

4. In the words of Center for Budget Policy researchers, "Cuts in state funding for public colleges and universities have driven up tuition and harmed students' educational experiences by forcing faculty reductions [and] fewer course offerings" (Mitchell, Leachman, and Masterson 2016, 1).

5. The nineteenth-century private colleges were overwhelmingly founded by religious groups whose leaders cared explicitly about culture and social betterment. Labaree (2017, chap. 2) provides evidence that, in addition, land speculators and railroad interests were in some cases influential proponents, acting on the assumption that new colleges would raise land prices in surrounding communities.

6. Academic freedom is not the only domain in which protections may come up short. Admissions rules, which nominally focus on academic qualifications, have been repeatedly violated when institutions feel that it is in their interest to admit marginally qualified (or unqualified) students whose parents or grandparents seem capable of making large donations (see Golden 2006).

7. Only a very few knowledge fields ended during the period, though more than a few declined in representation and some dropped out of the core curriculum, as in the case of the Romance languages and literatures. Many more fields and subfields have struggled to survive as market considerations continued to tilt universities in the direction of the power centers of the American economy and as online providers deemphasized low-enrollment fields. The threat that student utilitarianism poses to deep thinking experiences—even to bare information literacy—is an equally important consideration related to the ends of knowledge in the sense of a terminus.

8. The long history of revisions and refinements in any important strand of research is also well illustrated by the fate of Schumpeter's ideas. Economists such as Gerschenkron (1962) used Schumpeter's ideas to help explain why backward economies, burdened by few sunk investments, could make rapid gains over short periods of time. At the same time Solow's ideas were percolating, the economists Griliches (1957) and Ruttan (1956) were showing empirically how technological innovations in agriculture had greatly improved industry productivity, and the sociologist Rogers (1962) was demonstrating the processes of diffusion that allowed them to spread throughout the sector. Solow's work formalized the impact of innovation as a factor of production in sets of equations based on comparative statistical studies of national economic accounts, but his work did not end the discussion. Economists like Jorgenson (1966) contributed by emphasizing organizational characteristics of firms that impeded or facilitated innovation, and others such as Denison (1985) attempted to show the relative contribution of technological innovation and human capital development to growth, two concepts that Solow had lumped together in the idea of "technical change," broadly considered. More sophisticated modeling of endogenous economic growth continued in the work of Lucas (1988), Romer (1990), and others.

REFERENCES

Abbott, Andrew. 1988. *The System of Professions: An Essay on the Division of Expert Labor*. Chicago: University of Chicago Press.

———. 2001. *Chaos of Disciplines*. Chicago: University of Chicago Press.

AcceleratorInfo. 2013. "All University Programs." Retrieved from http://www.acceleratorinfo.com/see-all.html/.

Accreditation Board for Engineering and Technology (ABET). 2000. *Criteria for Accrediting Engineering Programs*. Baltimore: ABET.

Adelman, Clifford. 1999. *The New College Course Map and Transcript Files: Changes in Course Taking and Achievement, 1972–1993*. 2nd ed. Washington, DC: U.S. Department of Education, Office of Educational Research and Improvement.

———. 2007. "Death to Value Added." *Inside Higher Education*. January 26. Retrieved from www.insidehighered.com/views/2007/01/26/banta/.

Ad Hoc UMBI Review Committee (Ad Hoc Committee). 2010. *The Reorganization of UMBI and the Promise of Biotechnology in Maryland*. Retrieved from http://studylib.net/doc/7295725/the-reorganization-of-umbi-and-the-promise-of-biotechnology-in-maryland/.

Adler, Paul S. 2015. "Community and Innovation: From Tönnies to Marx." *Organization Studies* 36: 445–71.

AffordableColleges.com. 2015. "These 30 Colleges Are Reversing the Rise in Tuition." Retrieved from http://affordableschools.net/30-colleges-reversing-rise-tuition/.

Akers, Beth, and Matthew M. Chingos. 2016. *Game of Loans: The Rhetoric and Reality of Student Debt*. Princeton: Princeton University Press.

Alberts, Bruce. 2012. "The End of 'Small Science'?" *Science* 337: 1583.

Allen, I. Edith, and Jeff Seaman. 2016. *Online Report Card: Online Education in the United States*. Retrieved from https://onlinelearningsurvey.com/reports/onlinereportcard.pdf.

Allen, Thomas J., and Rory O'Shea. 2014. *Building Technology Transfer within Research Universities: An Entrepreneurial Approach*. Cambridge: Cambridge University Press.

Ambrose, Susan A., Michael W. Bridges, Michele DiPietro, Marsha C. Lovett, and Marie I. Norman. 2010. *How Learning Works: Seven Research-Based Principles for Smart Teaching*. San Francisco: Wiley.

American Academy of Arts and Sciences. 2015. *The State of the Humanities: Humanities Indicators*. Retrieved from https://www.amacad.org/multimedia/pdfs/publications/researchpapersmonographs/HI_HigherEd2015.pdf.

American Association for the Advancement of Science (AAAS). 2016. "Historical Trends in Federal R&D." *AAAS.org*. Retrieved from https://www.aaas.org/page/historical-trends-federal-rd/.

American Association of Colleges and Universities (AAC&U). 2002. *Greater Expectations: National Panel Report*. Washington, DC: AAC&U.

American Association of University Professors (AAUP). 1966. *Statement on Government of Colleges and Universities*. Washington, DC: AAUP.

——. 2014. *Annual Report on the Economic Status of the Profession*. Washington, DC: AAUP.

American Council of Learned Societies (ACLS). 1989. "Speaking for the Humanities." *ACLS*. Occasional Paper No. 7.

American Council on Education (ACE). 2016. "ACE and ACUE Announce Landmark Collaboration to Advance Student Success through Effective College Instruction." March 8. Retrieved from https://acue.org/wp-content/uploads/2016/03/ACE-Press-Release.pdf.

——. 2017. "ACE Fellows Program." Retrieved from http://www.acenet.edu/leadership/programs/Pages/ACE-Fellows-Program.aspx/.

American Institute of Physics. 2015. *FY 2016 Appropriation: STEM Education Programs Mostly Flat*. Retrieved from https://www.aip.org/fyi/2015/fy-2016-appropriations-stem-education-programs-mostly-funded-flat/.

American Institutes of Research (AIR). 2015. "College Hate Crimes, Compared by Category of Bias." July 9. Retrieved from http://www.air.org/resource/college-hate-crimes-compared-category-bias/.

American Physical Society. 2009. "Chu Lays Out Ambitious Plan for Energy Research." *APS News*. Retrieved from http://www.aps.org/publications/apsnews/200910/chu.cfm/.

American Student Assistance. 2014. "Student Loan Statistics." Retrieved from www.asa.org/policy/resources/stats/.

Abir-Am, Pnina G. 1997. "The Molecular Transformation of Twentieth-Century Biology." In *Companion to Science in the Twentieth Century*, eds. John Krige and Dominique Pestre. 495–524. New York: Routledge.

Anders, Lou. 2011. *Writing Excuses: The Hollywood Formula*. Retrieved from http://www.writingexcuses.com/tag/lou-anders/.

Anderson, Olga. 1988. "Austin Gives Big Welcome to SEMATECH." *The Scientist*. Retrieved from http://www.the-scientist.com/?articles.view/articleNo/9269/title/Austin-Gives-Big-Welcome-To-Sematech/.

Anderson, Tom. 2016. "Over 60 Percent of Americans Back Tuition-Free College." *CNBC*. August 1. Retrieved from https://www.cnbc.com/2016/08/01/over-60-of-americans-back-tuition-free-college-survey-says.html.

Andreesen, Marc. 2011. "Why Software Is Eating the World." *Wall Street Journal*. August 20. Retrieved from https://www.wsj.com/articles/SB10001424053111903480904576512250915629460/.

Andrews, Travis M. 2017. "Behind the Right's Loathing of the NEA: Two Exhibits from Nearly 30 Years Ago." *Washington Post*. March 20. Retrieved from https://www.washingtonpost.com/news/morning-mix/wp/2017/03/20/behind-the-loathing-of-the-national-endowment-for-the-arts-a-pair-of-despicable-exhibits-almost-30-years-ago/?utm_term=.1a8c10a167e5/.

Apkarian, Jacob, Kerry Mulligan, Matthew B. Rotondi, and Steven Brint. 2014. "Who Governs? Academic Decision-Making in U.S. Four-Year Colleges and Universities, 2000–2012." *Tertiary Education and Management* 20: 151–64.

Applebaum, Eileen, and Rosemary Batt. 1994. *The New American Workplace: Transforming Work Systems in the United States*. Ithaca: ILR Press.

Arcidiacono, Peter. 2004. "Ability Sorting and the Returns to College Major." *Journal of Econometrics* 121: 343–75.

Armstrong, Elizabeth A., and Laura T. Hamilton. 2013. *Paying for the Party: How College Maintains Inequality*. Cambridge, MA: Harvard University Press.

Aronowitz, Stanley. 2000. *The Knowledge Factory: Dismantling the Corporate University and Creating True Higher Learning*. Boston: Beacon Press.

Arrow, Kenneth. 1962. "Economic Welfare and the Allocation of Resources for Invention." In *The Rate and Direction of Inventive Activity*, ed. Committee on Economic Growth of the Social Science Research Council, 609–26. New York: Social Science Research Council.

Arum, Richard, and Josipa Roksa. 2011. *Academically Adrift: Limited Learning on College Campuses*. Chicago: University of Chicago Press.

———. 2014. *Aspiring Adults Adrift: Tentative Transitions of College Students*. Chicago: University of Chicago Press.

Arum, Richard, Josipa Roksa, and Esther Cho. 2012. *Improving Undergraduate Learning: Findings and Policy Recommendations from the SSRC-CLA Project*. New York: Social Science Research Council.

Ashkenas, Jeremy, Hayeon Park, and Adam Pearce. 2017. "Even with Affirmative Action, Blacks and Hispanics Are More Underrepresented at Top Colleges than 35 Years Ago." *New York Times*. August 24. Retrieved from https://www.nytimes.com/interactive/2017/08/24/us/affirmative-action.html/.

Association of American Colleges (AAC). 1969. *Racial Problems and Academic Programs*. Washington, DC: AAC.

Association of American Universities (AAU). 2005. *Report of the Interdisciplinary Task Force*. Washington, DC: AAU.

———. 2006. *National Defense Education and Innovation Initiative, Meeting America's Economic and Security Challenges in the 21st Century*. Washington, DC: AAU.

———. 2015. *AAU by the Numbers*. Retrieved from https://www.aau.edu/who-we-are/aau-numbers.

Astin, Alexander W. 1993. *What Matters in College? Four Critical Years Revisited*. San Francisco: Jossey-Bass.

Astin, Alexander W., Eric L. Dey, and William S. Korn. 1991. *The American College Teacher: National Norms for 1989–90 HERI Faculty Survey*. Los Angeles, CA: Higher Education Research Institute, University of California, Los Angeles.

Astin, Alexander W., and Leticia Oseguera. 2004. "The Declining 'Equity' of American Higher Education." *Review of Higher Education* 27: 321–41.

Attewell, Paul, and David E. Lavin. 2007. *Passing the Torch: Does Higher Education for the Disadvantaged Pay Off across the Generations?* New York: Russell Sage Foundation.

Aud, Susan, William Hussar, Frank Johnson, Grace Kena, Erin Roth, Eileen Manning, Xiolei Wang, and Jijun Zhang. 2012. *The Condition of Education 2012*. NCES 2012–045. Washington, DC: U.S. Department of Education.

Babcock, Philip. 2010. "Real Costs of Nominal Grade Inflation? New Evidence from Student Course Evaluations." *Economic Inquiry* 48: 983–96.

Babcock, Philip, and Mindy Marks. 2010. "Leisure College, USA: The Decline in Student Study Time." *American Enterprise Institute*. Retrieved from http://www.aei.org/publication/leisure-college-usa/.

———. 2011. "The Declining Time Cost of College: Evidence from a Half Century of Time Use Data." *Review of Economics and Statistics* 93: 468–78.

Bai, Zhaojun, Kuang-Jung Chang, Christopher S. Chen, P. W. Li, Kun Yang, and Iris Li. 2015. "Investigating the Effect of Transcendental Meditation on Blood Pressure: A Systematic Review and Meta-analysis." *Journal of Human Hypertension* 29: 653–62. Retrieved from https://www.ncbi.nlm.nih.gov/pubmed/25673114.

Bailey, Martha, and Susan Dynarski. 2011. "Inequality in Postsecondary Attainment." In *Whither Opportunity? Rising Inequality, Schools, and Children's Life Chances*, eds. Greg Duncan and Richard Murnane, 117–32. New York: Russell Sage Foundation Press.

Baker, David P. 2014. *The Schooled Society: The Educational Transformation of Global Culture*. Stanford: Stanford University Press.

Baker, Therese, and William Velez. 1996. "Access to and Opportunity in Postsecondary Education in the United States." *Sociology of Education* 69 (extra issue): 82–101.

Baldridge, J. Victor, and Frank R. Kemerer. 1976. "Academic Senates and Faculty Collective Bargaining." *Journal of Higher Education* 47: 391–411.

Baldwin, Roger G., and Jay L. Chronister. 2001. *Teaching without Tenure: Policies and Practices for a New Era*. Baltimore: Johns Hopkins University Press.

Baldwin, Roger G., and Matthew R. Wawrzynski. 2011. "Contingent Faculty as Teachers: What We Know, What We Need to Know." *American Behavioral Scientist* 55: 1485–1509.

Baltzell, Edward Digby. 1964. *The Protestant Establishment: Aristocracy and Caste in America*. New York: Random House.

BankBoston. 1997. *MIT: The Impact of Innovation*. Boston: BankBoston, Economics Department Special Report.

———. 2003. *Engines of Economic Growth: The Economic Impact of Boston's Eight Research Universities on the Metropolitan Boston Area*. New York: Appleseed.

Banta, Trudy. 2007. "A Warning on Measuring Learning Outcomes." *Inside Higher Education*. January 27. Retrieved from www.insidehighered.com/views/2007/01/26/banta/.

Barnard, Chester. 1938. *The Functions of the Executive*. Cambridge, MA: Harvard University Press.

Barnes, Brooks. 2013. "Solving Equation of a Hit Film Script, with Data." *New York Times*. May 5. Retrieved from http://www.nytimes.com/2013/05/06/business/media/solving-equation-of-a-hit-film-script-with-data.html?pagewanted=all&_r=0/.

Barnett, Melissa. 2015. "Texas Gov. Abbott Abolishes Rick Perry's Emerging Tech Fund." *Govt. Technology Magazine*. June 5. Retrieved from http://www.govtech.com/state/Texas-Gov-Abbott-Abolishes-Rick-Perrys-Emerging-Tech-Fund.html.

Barr, Robert B., and John Tagg. 1995. "From Teaching to Learning: A New Paradigm for Undergraduate Education." *Change* 27 (November/December): 13–25.

Barringer, Sandra N., and Sheila Slaughter. 2016. "University Trustees and the Entrepreneurial University: Inner Circles, Interlocks, and Exchanges." In *Higher Education, Stratification, and Workforce Development: Competitive Advantages in Europe, the U.S., and Canada*, eds. Sheila Slaughter and Barrett Jay Taylor, 151–73. London: Springer.

Barzun, Jacques. 1968. *The American University: How It Runs, Where It Is Going*. Chicago: University of Chicago Press.

Bastedo, Michael N., and Ozan Jacquette. 2011. "Running in Place: Low-Income Students and the Dynamics of Higher Education Stratification." *Educational Evaluation and Policy Analysis* 33: 318–39.

Baum, Sandy. 2005. "Approaching the Problem from Both Sides." *College Costs*. Retrieved from https://www.luminafoundation.org/files/publications/collegecosts/baum.pdf.

Baum, Sandy, and Martha C. Johnson. 2016. *Strengthening Federal Student Aid*. Washington, DC: Urban Institute.

Bauman, Dan, and Brian O'Leary. 2017. "Executive Compensation at Private and Public Colleges." *Chronicle of Higher Education*. Retrieved from http://www.chronicle.com/interactives/executive-compensation#id=table_private_2014/; http://www.chronicle.com/interactives/executive-compensation#id=table_public_2015/.

Baumol, William J., and William G. Bowen. 1966. *Performing Arts: The Economic Dilemma*. Cambridge, MA: MIT Press.

Beckham, Edgar F. 2000. *Diversity, Democracy, and Higher Education: A View from Three Nations*. Washington, DC: Association of American Colleges and Universities.

Bekelman, Justin E., Yan Li, and Cary P. Gross. 2003. "Scope and Impact of Financial Conflicts of Interest in Biomedical Research: A Systematic Review." *Journal of the American Medical Association* 289 (January 22/29): 454–65.

Bell, Alexander M., Raj Chetty, Xavier Jaravel, Neviana Petkova, and John van Reenen. 2017. "Who Becomes an Inventor in America? The Importance of Exposure to Innovation." *NBER Working Paper*. No. 24062. Retrieved from http://www.nber.org/papers/w24062.

Bell, Daniel. 1973. *The Coming of Post-Industrial Society: An Essay in Social Forecasting*. New York: Basic Books.

Bell, Derek. 1987. *And We Are Not Saved: The Elusive Quest for Racial Justice*. New York: Basic Books.

Bell, J. T. 1997. "Anonymous Quizzes: An Effective Feedback Mechanism." *Chemical Engineering Education (CEE)* 31 (1): 56–57. Retrieved from https://eric.ed.gov/?id=EJ540038.

Benson, Herbert, and Associates. 1975. *The Relaxation Response*. New York: HarperTorch.

Berg, Ivar E. 1970. *Education and Jobs: The Great Training Robbery*. New York: Praeger Publishers.

Berger, Mark C. 1988. "Predicted Future Earnings and Choice of College Major." *ILR Review* 41: 418–29.

Berglund, Dan, and Christopher Coburn. 1995. *Partnerships: Compendium of State and Federal Cooperative Technology Programs*. Columbus, OH: Batelle.

Berman, Elizabeth Popp. 2012. *Creating the Market University: How Academic Science Became an Economic Engine*. Princeton: Princeton University Press.

Berman, Elizabeth Popp, and Abby Stivers. 2016. "Student Loans as a Pressure on U.S. Higher Education." *Research in the Sociology of Organizations* 46: 129–60.

Bernhardt, Annette. 2012. "The Low-Wage Recovery and Growing Inequality." *National Employment Law Project Data Brief*. New York: National Employment Law Project. August.

Bernhardt, Annette, Martina Morris, Mark Handcock, and Marc Scott. 1999. "Trends in Job Instability and Wages for Young Adult Men." *Journal of Labor Economics* pt. 2, 17: S65–S90.

Berube, Michael, and Cary Nelson, eds. 1995. *Higher Education under Fire: Politics, Economics, and the Crisis of the Humanities*. New York: Routledge.

The Best Schools. 2017. "The Most Generous Alumni Donors to American Colleges and Universities." Retrieved from https://thebestschools.org/features/most-generous-alumni-donors/.

Bettinger, Eric, and Bridget Terry Long. 2005. "Help or Hinder? Adjunct Professors and Student Outcomes." Unpublished paper, Cornell University Institute of Labor Relations.

Bill and Melinda Gates Foundation. 2009. "Colleges Develop Innovative Models to Help Low-Income Adults Graduate." Retrieved from http://www.gatesfoundation.org/Media-Center /Press-Releases/2009/05/Colleges-Develop-Innovative-Models-to-Help-LowIncome-Adults -Graduate/.

Bills, David B. 2003. "Credentials, Signals, and Screens: Explaining the Relationship between Schooling and Job Assignment." *Review of Educational Research* 73: 441–70.

Binder, Amy J., and Kate Wood. 2014. *Becoming Right: How Campuses Shape Young Conservatives*. Princeton: Princeton University Press.

Birnbaum, Robert. 1988. *How Colleges Work: The Cybernetics of Academic Organization and Leadership*. New York: John Wiley.

Bizlistr. 2014. "Twin Cities Top Medical Devices Cos." Retrieved from http://bizlistr.com/com pany.php/id_10.

Bledstein, Burton. 1976. *The Culture of Professionalism*. New York: Norton.

Block, Fred. 1977. "The Ruling Class Does Not Rule." *Socialist Revolution* 3 (May–June): 6–28.

Bloom, Allan. 1987. *The Closing of the American Mind: How Higher Education Has Failed Democracy and Impoverished the Souls of Today's Students*. New York: Simon and Schuster.

Blumenstyk, Goldie. 2017. "In Purdue's New Vision, How Public Will Kaplan Be?" *Chronicle of Higher Education*. May 26. Retrieved from http://www.chronicle.com/article/In-Purdue-s -New-Vision-How/240017/.

Blumenthal, David, Nancyann Causino, Eric Campbell, and Karen Seashore Louis. 1996. "Relationships between Academic Institutions and Industry in the Life Sciences—An Industry Survey." *New England Journal of Medicine* 334: 368–73.

Blumenthal, David, Michael Gluck, Karen S. Lewis, Michael A. Stoto, and David Wise. 1986. "University-Industry Research Relationships in Biotechnology." *Science* 232: 1361–66.

Board on Science, Technology and Economic Policy; Policy and Global Affairs; National Academies of Sciences, Engineering, and Medicine (BSTEP). 2016. *STTR: An Assessment of the Small Business Technology Transfer Program*. Retrieved from https://www.ncbi.nlm.nih.gov /books/NBK338723/.

Boas, Taylor C., and Jordan Gans-Morse. 2009. "Neo-liberalism: From New Liberal Philosophy to Anti-Liberal Slogan." *Studies in Comparative International Development* 44: 137–61.

Bok, Derek. 2003. *Universities in the Marketplace: The Commercialization of Higher Education*. Princeton: Princeton University Press.

———. 2006. *Our Underachieving Colleges*. Princeton: Princeton University Press.

Boretsky, Michael T. 1971. "Concerns about the Present American Position in International Trade." *Technology and International Trade*. Washington, DC: National Academy of Science.

———. 1982. *The Threat to U.S. High Tech Industries: Economic and National Security Implications*. Washington, DC: U.S. Department of Commerce. Draft (March).

Boring, Ann, Kellie Ottoboni, and Philip B. Stark. 2016. "Student Evaluations of Teaching (Mostly) Do Not Measure Teaching Effectiveness." *Science Open Research*. Retrieved from https://www.math.upenn.edu/~pemantle/active-papers/Evals/stark2016.pdf.

Bossard, James H. S., and J. Frederic Dewhurst. 1931. *University Education for Business: A Study of Existing Needs and Practices*. Berlin: de Gruyter.

Boulder Economic Council. 2017. *Boulder's Innovation Economy*. Retrieved from http://boulder economiccouncil.org/boulder-economy/innovation-economy/.

Bound, John, Michael F. Lovenheim, and Sarah Turner. 2010. "Why Have College Completion Rates Declined? An Analysis of Changing Student Preparation and Collegiate Resources." *American Economic Journal: Applied Economics* 2 (3): 129–57.

Bourdieu, Pierre. 1977. *Outline of a Theory of Practice*. Cambridge: Cambridge University Press. Trans. Richard Nice. Originally published in French in 1972.

Bourdieu, Pierre, and Jean-Claude Passeron. 1977. *Reproduction in Education, Society, and Culture*. London: Sage.

Bowen, Howard. 1977. *Investment in Learning*. San Francisco: Jossey-Bass.

Bowen, William G. 2013. *Higher Education in the Digital Age*. Princeton: Princeton University Press.

Bowen, William G., and Derek Bok. 1998. *The Shape of the River: Long-Term Consequences of Considering Race in College and University Admissions*. Princeton: Princeton University Press.

Bowen, William G., Matthew M. Chingos, Kelly A. Lack, and Thomas I. Nygren. 2013. *Interactive Learning Online at Public Universities: Evidence from Randomized Trials. Journal of Policy Analysis and Management* 33: 94–111.

Bowen, William G., and Eugene M. Tobin. 2015. *Locus of Authority: The Evolution of Faculty Roles in the Governance of Higher Education*. Princeton: Princeton University Press.

Bowles, Samuel, and Herbert Gintis. 1976. *Schooling in Capitalist America: Educational Reform and the Contradictions of Economic Life*. New York: Basic Books.

Bowman, Karlyn. 2017. "Polls on Political Correctness." *Forbes*. June 5. Retrieved from https://www.forbes.com/sites/bowmanmarsico/2017/06/05/polls-on-political-correctness/#2081 79066093/.

Bowman, Nicholas A., and Tricia A. Seifert. 2011. "Can College Students Accurately Assess What Affects Their Learning and Development?" *Journal of College Student Development* 52: 270–90.

Boyer, Ernest L. 1990. *Scholarship Reconsidered: Priorities of the Professoriate*. Princeton: Carnegie Foundation for the Advancement of Teaching.

Branscomb, Lewis M., and James H. Keller, eds. 1999. *Investing in Innovation: Creating a Research and Innovation Policy That Works*. Cambridge, MA: MIT Press.

Bransford, John D., Ann L. Brown, and Rodney Cocking, eds. 2000. *How People Learn: Brain, Mind, Experience, and School*. Washington, DC: National Academies Press.

Braunerhjelm, Pontus, and Bo Carlsson. 1999. "Industry Clusters in Ohio and Sweden, 1975–1995." *Small Business Economics* 12: 279–93.

Brecher, Tony. 1989. *Academic Tribes and Territories: Intellectual Enquiry and the Culture of Disciplines*. Buckingham, England: Open University Press.

Bresnahan, Timothy, Alfonso Gambarella, and Annalee Saxenian. 2001. " 'Old Economy' Inputs for 'New Economy' Outcomes: Cluster Formation in the New Silicon Valleys." *Industrial and Corporate Change* 10: 835–60.

Bressoud, David M., Marilyn P. Carlson, Vilma Mea, and Chris Rasmussen. 2012. "Description and Selected Results from the MAA National Study of Calculus." *Mathematical Association of America*. Retrieved from https://www.maa.org/sites/default/files/pdf/cspcc/CSPCC4I JMEST-12-09-18.pdf.

Brewer, Dominic J., Eric R. Eide, and Ronald G. Ehrenberg. 1999. "Does It Pay to Attend an Elite Private College? Cross-Cohort Evidence on the Effects of College Type on Earnings." *Journal of Human Resources* 34: 104–23.

Brewer, Stephanie M., Jason M. Kelley, and James J. Jozefowicz. 2009. "A Blueprint for Success in the U.S. Film Industry." *Applied Economics* 41: 589–606.

Brint, Steven. 2001. "Professionals and the 'Knowledge Economy': Rethinking the Theory of Post-Industrial Society." *Current Sociology* 49 (4): 101–32.

———. 2002. "The Rise of the 'Practical Arts.' " In *The Future of the City of Intellect: The Changing American University*, ed. Steven Brint, 231–59. Stanford: Stanford University Press.

———. 2005. "Creating the Future: The 'New Directions' in U.S. Research Universities." *Minerva* 43: 23–50.

———. 2011. "Focus on the Classroom: Movements to Reform College Teaching and Learning, 1980–2008." In *The American Academic Profession: Transformation in Contemporary Higher Education*, ed. Joseph C. Hermanowicz, 44–91. Baltimore: Johns Hopkins University Press.

———. 2014. "Professional Responsibility in an Age of Experts and Large Organizations." In *Professional Responsibility: The Fundamental Issue in Education and Health Care Reform*, eds. Douglas E. Mitchell and Robert K. Ream, 89–107. London: Springer.

———. 2015a. "Merit Square-Off: The Fight over College Admissions." *Los Angeles Review of Books*. September 13. Retrieved from https://lareviewofbooks.org/article/merit-square-off-the-fight-over-college-admissions/.

———. 2015b. "Research University Spaces: The Multiple Purposes of an Undergraduate Education." *Research and Occasional Papers Series*. Centers for Studies in Higher Education, University of California, Berkeley. 9.16.

———. 2017. "New Concepts, Expanding Audiences: What Highly-Cited Texts Tell Us about the Future of Scholarly Knowledge in the Social Sciences." *Social Research: An International Quarterly* 84: 637–68.

————. 2018. "An Institutional Geography of Knowledge Exchange: Producers, Exports, Imports, Trade Routes, and Metacognitive Metropoles." In *Education in a New Society: Renewing the Sociology of Education*, eds. Jal Mehta and R. Scott Davies, 115–43. Chicago: University of Chicago Press.

Brint, Steven, Komi T. German, Kayleigh Anderson-Natale, Zeinab F. Shuker, and Siqi Wang. 2018. "Where Ivy Matters: The Educational Backgrounds of Members of the U.S. Cultural Elite." Unpublished paper, Department of Sociology, University of California, Riverside.

Brint, Steven, and Allison M. Cantwell. 2010. "Undergraduate Time Use and Academic Outcomes." *Teachers College Record* 112: 2441–70.

————. 2014. "Conceptualizing, Measuring and Analyzing the Characteristics of Disengaged Student Populations: Results from UCUES 2010." *Journal of College Student Development* 55: 808–23.

Brint, Steven, Allison M. Cantwell, and Robert A. Hanneman. 2008. "The Two Cultures of Undergraduate Academic Engagement." *Research in Higher Education* 49: 383–402.

Brint, Steven, Allison M. Cantwell, and Preeta Saxena. 2012. "Disciplinary Categories, Majors, and Undergraduate Academic Experiences: Rethinking Bok's 'Under-achieving Colleges' Thesis." *Research in Higher Education* 53: 1–25.

Brint, Steven, and Cynthia E. Carr. 2017. "The Scientific Productivity of U.S. Research Universities, 1980–2010: Continued Dispersion or Increasing Concentration?" *Minerva* 55: 435–57.

Brint, Steven, and Jerome Karabel. 1989. *The Diverted Dream: Community Colleges and the Promise of Educational Opportunity in America, 1900–1985*. New York: Oxford University Press.

Brint, Steven, Katrina Paxton-Jorgenson, and Eric Vega. 2002. "Online Courses and Degrees: Views from Corporate and University Providers." *Research and Occasional Papers series*. Center for Studies in Higher Education, University of California, Berkeley.

Brint, Steven, Kristopher Proctor, Robert A. Hanneman, Kerry Mulligan, Matthew B. Rotondi, and Scott Patrick Murphy. 2011. "Who Are the Early Adopters? The Institutionalization of Academic Growth Fields in U.S. Four-Year Colleges and Universities, 1975–2005." *Higher Education* 61: 563–85.

Brint, Steven, Kristopher Proctor, Kerry Mulligan, Matthew B. Rotondi, and Robert A. Hanneman. 2012a. "Declining Fields in U.S. Four-Year Colleges and Universities, 1970–2006." *Journal of Higher Education* 83: 582–613.

Brint, Steven, Kristopher Proctor, Scott Patrick Murphy, and Robert A. Hanneman. 2012b. "The Market Model and the Growth and Decline of Academic Fields in U.S. Four-Year Colleges and Universities, 1980–2000." *Sociological Forum* 27: 275–99.

Brint, Steven, Kristopher Proctor, Scott Patrick Murphy, Lori Turk-Bicakci, and Robert A. Hanneman. 2009. "General Education Models: The Changing Meaning of Liberal Education, 1975–2000." *Journal of Higher Education* 80: 605–42.

Brint, Steven, Mark Riddle, and Robert A. Hanneman. 2006. "Reference Sets, Identities, and Aspirations in a Complex Organizational Field: The Case of American Four-Year Colleges and Universities." *Sociology of Education* 79: 126–40.

Brint, Steven, Mark Riddle, Lori Turk-Bicakci, and Charles S. Levy. 2005. "From the Liberal Arts to the Practical Arts in American Colleges and Universities: Organizational Analysis and Curricular Change." *Journal of Higher Education* 76: 151–80.

Brint, Steven, and Sarah R. K. Yoshikawa. 2017. "The Educational Backgrounds of U.S. Business and Government Leaders." *Social Forces* 96: 561–90.

Brint, Steven, Sarah R. K. Yoshikawa, Matthew B. Rotondi, Tiffany Viggiano, and John Maldonado. 2016. "Surviving and Thriving: Adaptive Responses of U.S. Four-Year Colleges and Universities to the Great Recession." *Journal of Higher Education* 87: 859–89.

Brothen, Thomas, and Catherine Wambach. 2001. "Effective Student Use of Computerized Quizzes." *Teaching of Psychology* 28: 292–94.

Brown, David K. 1995. *Degrees of Control: A Sociology of Educational Expansion and Occupational Credentialism.* New York: Teachers College Press.

Brown, Sarah. 2017. "The Free-Speech Stronghold." *Chronicle of Higher Education.* September 22. A12–15.

Bruner, Jerome. 1961. "The Act of Discovery." *Harvard Educational Review* 31: 21–32.

Brungardt, Curt L., Justin L. Greenleaf, Christie J. Brungardt, and Jill R. Arensdorf. 2006. "Majoring in Leadership: A Review of Undergraduate Leadership Degree Programs." *Journal of Leadership Educators* 5: 4–24.

Bui, Quoctrung. 2014. "What's Your Major? 4 Decades of College Degrees in 1 Graph." *Planet Money* (for National Public Radio). Retrieved from http://www.npr.org/sections/money /2014/05/09/310114739/whats-your-major-four-decades-of-college-degrees-in-1-graph/.

Burdman, Pamela. 2012. *Changing Equations: How Community Colleges Are Re-thinking College Readiness in Math.* Oakland: Learning Works. Retrieved from http://www.learningworksca .org/changingequations/.

———. 2015. *Degrees of Freedom: Varying Routes to Math Readiness and the Challenge of Intersegmental Alignment.* Oakland: Learning Works. Retrieved from http://www.learningworksca .org/dof2/.

Burke, Joseph C., ed. 2005. *Achieving Accountability in Higher Education: Balancing Public, Academic and Market Demands.* San Francisco: Jossey-Bass.

Burke, Joseph C., and Andreea M. Serban, eds. 1998. "Performance Funding for Public Higher Education: Fad or Trend?" *New Directions for Institutional Research #97.* San Francisco: Jossey-Bass.

Burke, Joseph C., and Henrik Minassians. 2003. *Performance Reporting: "Real" Accountability or Accountability Lite.* Seventh Annual Survey. Albany: Rockefeller Institute of Government.

Burns, Bridget, Michael Crow, and Mark Becker. 2015. "Innovating Together: Collaboration as a Driving Force to Improve Student Success." *Educause Review.* Retrieved from https://er .educause.edu/articles/2015/3/innovating-together-collaboration-as-a-driving-force-to -improve-student-success/.

Burris, Val. 2004. "The Academic Caste System: Prestige Networks in Ph.D. Exchange Networks." *American Sociological Review* 64: 239–64.

Business Roundtable. 2005. *America's Potential: The Education for Innovation Initiative.* New York: Business Roundtable.

California Faculty Association. 2017. *Equity Interrupted: How California Is Cheating Its Future.* Retrieved from http://www.calfac.org/sites/main/files/file-attachments/equity_interrupted _1.12.2017.pdf.

California Institute for Telecommunications and Information Technology (CalIT2). n.d. "Research." Retrieved from http://www.calit2.net/research/index.php.

Campaign for Free College Tuition. 2017. *Making Public Colleges Tuition Free: A Briefing Book for State Leaders.* Retrieved from https://www.freecollegenow.org/briefing_book/.

Campbell, Corbin M., Marisol Jimenez, and Christine Arlene N. Arrozal. In Press. "Education or Prestige? The Teaching and Rigor of Courses in Prestigious and Non-Prestigious Institutions in the United States." *Higher Education.*

Cantwell, Brandon, and Barrett J. Taylor. 2015. "Rise of the Science and Engineering Postdoctorate and the Restructuring of Academic Research." *Journal of Higher Education* 86: 667–96.

Cardinal, David. 2011. "Changing the World: DARPA's Top Inventions." *Extreme Tech.* November 11. Retrieved from https://www.extremetech.com/extreme/105117-inventing-our-world -darpas-top-inventions/.

Carey, Kevin. 2011. "The Mayo Clinic of Higher Ed." In *Reinventing Higher Education: The Promise of Innovation*, eds. Ben Wildavsky, Andrew P. Kelly, and Kevin Carey, 225–38. Cambridge, MA: Harvard Education Press.

———. 2012. "The Siege of Academe." *Washington Monthly*. September/October. Retrieved from http://washingtonmonthly.com/magazine/septoct-2012/the-siege-of-academe/.

Carini, Robert M., George D. Kuh, and Stephen P. Klein. 2006. "Student Engagement and Student Learning: Testing the Linkages." *Research in Higher Education* 47: 1–32.

Carnevale, Anthony P., Ban Cheah, and Jeff Strohl. 2012. *Hard Times: College Majors, Unemployment and Earnings: Not All College Degrees Are Created Equal*. Washington, DC: Georgetown University Center on Education and the Workforce.

Carnevale, Anthony P., and Stephen J. Rose. 2004. "Socio-economic Status, Race-Ethnicity, and Selective College Admissions." In *America's Untapped Resource: Low-Income Students in Higher Education*, ed. Richard D. Kahlenberg, 101–56. New York: Century Foundation Press.

Carnevale, Anthony P., Stephen J. Rose, and Ban Cheah. 2011. *The College Payoff: Education, Occupation, Lifetime Earnings*. Washington, DC: Georgetown University Center on Education and the Workforce.

Carnevale, Anthony P., and Jeff Strohl. 2010. "How Increasing College Access Is Increasing Inequality, and What to Do About It." In *Rewarding Strivers: Helping Low-Income Students Succeed in College*, ed. Richard D. Kahlenberg, 71–83. New York: Century Foundation Press.

———. 2013. *Separate and Unequal: How Higher Education Reinforces the Intergenerational Reproduction of Racial Privilege*. Washington, DC: Georgetown University Center on Education and the Workforce.

Carnevale, Anthony P., Jeff Strohl, and Michelle Melton. 2011. *What's It Worth? The Economic Value of College Majors*. Washington, DC: Georgetown University Center on Education and the Workforce.

Carnoy, Martin, and Richard Rothstein. 2013. *What Do International Tests Really Show about U.S. Student Performance?* Washington, DC: Economic Policy Institute. Retrieved from http://www.epi.org/publication/us-student-performance-testing/.

Cartter, Allan M. 1966. *An Assessment of Quality in Graduate Education*. Washington, DC: American Council on Education.

Casper, Steven. 2014. "The University of California and the Evolution of the Biotechnology Industry in San Diego and San Francisco." In *Public Universities and Regional Growth: Insights from the University of California*, eds. Martin Kenney and David C. Mowery, 66–96. Stanford: Stanford Business Books.

Caulfield, Timothy, Shawn H. E. Harmon, and Yann Joly. 2012. "Open Science versus Commercialization: A Modern Research Conflict?" *Genome Medicine* 4. Retrieved from https://www.ncbi.nlm.nih.gov/pmc/articles/PMC3392762/pdf/gm316.pdf.

Cavanaugh, Joseph. 2005. "Teaching Online: A Time Comparison." *Online Journal of Distance Learning Administration Content* 8 (1). Retrieved from https://www.immagic.com/eLibrary/ARCHIVES/GENERAL/U_WGA_US/J050300C.pdf.

Center for Strategic and International Studies. 2005. *Waiting for Sputnik*. Washington, DC: Carnegie Center.

Chakravarty, Ranjana, Kristina Cotter, Joseph DiMasi, Christopher-Paul Milne, and Nils Mendel. 2016. "Public and Private Sector Contributions to the Research and Development of the Most Transformational Drugs of the Last 25 Years." *Therapeutic Innovation and Regulatory Science* 50: 759–68.

Chang, Mitchell J., June C. Chang, and Marica C. Ledesma. 2005. "Beyond Magical Thinking: Doing the Real Work of Diversifying Our Institutions." *About Campus*. Retrieved from http://onlinelibrary.wiley.com/doi/10.1002/abc.124/abstract/.

Chang, Mitchell J., Jessica Sharkness, Sylvia Hurtado, and Christopher B. Newman. 2014. "What Matters in College for Retaining Aspiring Scientists and Engineers from Under-represented Racial Groups." *Journal of Research in Science Teaching* 51: 555–80.

Chatman, Steve. 2007a. "Institutional Versus Academic Discipline Measures of Student Experience: A Matter of Relative Validity." *Research and Occasional Paper series*. Center for Studies in Higher Education, University of California, Berkeley.

———. 2007b. *Overview of University of California Undergraduate Experience Survey Response Rates and Bias Issues. SERU Project Technical Report*. Center for Studies in Higher Education, University of California, Berkeley.

Cheit, Earl. 1971. *The New Depression in Higher Education: A Study of Financial Conditions at 41 Colleges and Universities*. New York: McGraw-Hill.

Chen, Henry, Paul Gompers, Anna Kovner, and Josh Lerner. 2010. "Buy Local? The Geography of Venture Capital." *Journal of Urban Economics* 67: 90–102.

Chermack, Thomas J., Susan A. Lynham, and Wendy E. A. Ruona. 2001. "A Review of Scenario Planning Literature." *Futures Research Quarterly* 17 (2): 7–31.

Chetty, Raj, John N. Friedman, Emmanuel Saez, Nicholas Turner, and Danny Yagan. 2017. "Mobility Report Cards: The Role of Colleges in Intergenerational Mobility." *NBER Working Paper*. No. w23618. Retrieved from http://www.equality-of-opportunity.org/assets/docu ments/coll_mrc_slides.pdf.

Chickering, Arthur W., and Zelda F. Gamson. 1987. "Seven Principles for Good Practice in Undergraduate Education." *AAHE Bulletin* (March): 3–7.

Chingos, Matthew M. 2017. "There Is Actually Nothing for Low-Income Students in Cuomo's Free College Plan." *Washington Post*. January 4. Retrieved from https://www.washingtonpost .com/news/grade-point/wp/2017/01/04/there-is-actually-nothing-for-low-income-students -in-cuomos-free-college-plan/?utm_term=.682aa9e2f0a9/.

Christensen, Clayton M., Curtis W. Johnson, and Michael B. Horn. 2008. *Disrupting Class: How Disruptive Innovation Will Change the Way the World Learns*. New York: McGraw-Hill.

Christensen, Clayton M., and Henry J. Eyring. 2011. *The Innovative University: Changing the DNA of Higher Education from the Inside Out*. San Francisco: Jossey-Bass.

Chronicle of Higher Education. 2013a. "Table: Foundation Support for Higher Education Shares, Goals, and Recipients." January 14. Retrieved from http://www.chronicle.com/interactives /foundations-table/.

———. 2013b. "Michael Sandel Responds." May 2. Retrieved from http://www.chronicle.com /article/Michael-Sandel-Responds/139021/.

———. 2014. *2014 Almanac Issue*. Washington DC: Chronicle of Higher Education.

———. 2015. "Sortable Table: College and University Endowments, 2013–14." January 29. Retrieved from http://www.chronicle.com/article/Sortable-Table-College-and/151417/.

———. 2017a. "Almanac 2017–18." August 18. Washington, DC: Chronicle of Higher Education.

———. 2017b. "Colleges with the Highest Student-Mobility Rates." October 18. Retrieved from https://www.chronicle.com/article/Colleges-With-the-Highest/241450/.

Claremont McKenna College, Kravis Leadership Institute. 2016. "About." Retrieved from https://www.kravisleadershipinstitute.org/.

Clark, Burton R. 1987. *The Academic Life: Small Worlds, Different Worlds*. Princeton: Carnegie Foundation for the Advancement of Teaching and Princeton University Press.

———. 1998. *Creating Entrepreneurial Universities: Pathways to Transformation*. London: Oryx Press.

Clark, Burton R., and Martin Trow. 1966. "The Organizational Context." In *College Peer Groups*, eds. Theodore M. Newcomb and Everett K. Wilson, 17–70. Chicago: Aldine.

Clay, Rebecca. 2007. "The Union Label." *Monitor on Psychology* 38 (4): 30.

Clinton, Bill. 1992. "Technology: The Engine of Economic Growth. A National Technology Policy for America." September 18. Retrieved from https://www.ibiblio.org/nii/tech-posit.html.

Clotfelter, Charles T. 1996. *Buying the Best: Cost Escalation in Elite Higher Education*. Princeton: Princeton University Press.

———. 2011. *Big-Time Sports in American Universities*. Cambridge: Cambridge University Press.

———. 2017. *Unequal Colleges in an Age of Disparity*. Cambridge, MA: Harvard University Press.

Cluster Mapping Project (CMP). 2017. *US Cluster Mapping*. Retrieved from http://www.clustermapping.us/.

Coalition on the Academic Workforce (CAW). 2012. *A Portrait of Part-time Faculty Members*. June. Retrieved from http://www.academicworkforce.org/CAW_portrait_2012.pdf.

Coburn, Tom. 2011. *The National Science Foundation: Under the Microscope*. April. Retrieved from http://lcweb2.loc.gov/service/gdc/coburn/2014500020.pdf.

Cockburn, Ian, and Rebecca Henderson. 1996. "Public-Private Interaction in Pharmaceutical Research." *Proceedings of the National Academy of Science* 93: 12725–30.

Cohen, Wesley, Richard Nelson, and John Walsh. 2002. "Links and Impacts: The Influence of Public Research on Industrial R&D." *Management Science* 48: 1–23.

Cole, Jonathan R. 2009. *The Great American University: Its Rise to Preeminence, Its Indispensable National Role, Why It Must Be Protected*. New York: Public Affairs Publishers.

College Board. 2014. *The Tenth Annual AP Report to the Nation*. February 11. Washington, DC: The College Board. Retrieved from http://media.collegeboard.com/digitalServices/pdf/ap/rtn/10th-annual/10th-annual-ap-report-to-the-nation-single-page.pdf.

———. 2015. *Trends in Student Aid 2015*. Retrieved from https://trends.collegeboard.org/sites/default/files/trends-student-aid-web-final-508-2.pdf.

———. 2016. *Trends in Student Aid 2016*. Retrieved from https://trends.collegeboard.org/sites/default/files/2016-trends-student-aid.pdf.

College Factual. 2015. *Arizona State University*. Retrieved from www.collegefactual.com/colleges/arizona-state-university/academic-life/faculty-composition/.

Collinge, Allan M. 2010. *The Student Loan Scam: Inside the Most Oppressive Debt in U.S. History—And How We Can Fight Back*. Boston: Beacon Press.

Collins, Harry, Robert Evans, and Michael E. Gorman. 2010. "Trading Zones and Interactional Expertise." In *Trading Zones and Interactional Expertise*, ed. Michael E. Gorman, 7–24. Cambridge, MA: MIT Press.

Collins, Patricia Hill. 1990. *Black Feminist Thought: Knowledge, Consciousness, and the Politics of Empowerment*. New York: Routledge.

Collins, Randall. 1977. "Some Comparative Principles of Educational Stratification." *Harvard Educational Review* 47: 1–27.

———. 1979. *The Credential Society*. New York: Academic Press.

Collis, David J. 2002. "New Business Models for Higher Education." In *The Future of the City of Intellect*, ed. Steven Brint, 181–202. Stanford: Stanford University Press.

Colwell, Rita. 2002. "Rethinking the Rules to Promote Diversity." Paper presented at the Presidential Symposium on Diversity. Boston. August 18.

Commission on the Future of Higher Education (Spellings Commission). 2006. *A Test of Leadership: Charting the Future of U.S. Higher Education*. Washington, DC: Commission on the Future of Higher Education.

Competitiveness Policy Council. 1993. *A Competitiveness Strategy for America: Reports of the Subcouncils*. Retrieved from https://archive.org/details/ERIC_ED356390/.

Comte, Augustine. 1853. *The Positive Philosophy of Auguste Comte*. ed. Harriet Martineau. New York: Chapman.

Congress.gov. 2015. H.R. 2262—U.S. *Commercial Space Launch Competitiveness Act*. Retrieved from https://www.congress.gov/bill/114th-congress/house-bill/2262/.

Congressional Budget Office (CBO). 2013. *The Pell Grant Program: Recent Growth and Policy Options*. September. Retrieved from http://www.cbo.gov/sites/default/files/cbofiles/attachments /44448_PellGrants_9-5-13.pdf.

Conover, Jerry N. 2017. "Bloomington Forecast 2018." *Indiana Business Review*. Retrieved from http://www.ibrc.indiana.edu/ibr/2017/outlook/bloomington.html.

Cook, Bryan J. 2012. *The American College President Study: Key Findings and Takeaways*. Retrieved from http://www.acenet.edu/the-presidency/columns-and-features/Pages/The -American-College-President-Study.aspx/.

Cooper, Preston. 2016. "Federal Student Loans Will Cost Taxpayers $170 Billion." *Forbes*. April 10. Retrieved from https://www.forbes.com/sites/prestoncooper2/2016/04/10/federal-student -loans-will-cost-taxpayers-170-billion/#18cd18a562a9/.

———. 2017. "New York Fed Highlights Underemployment among College Graduates." *Forbes*. July 13. Retrieved from https://www.forbes.com/sites/prestoncooper2/2017/07/13/new -york-fed-highlights-underemployment-among-college-graduates/#5005111340d8.

Coopers & Lybrand. 1995. *Reinventing the University: Managing and Financing Institutions of Higher Education*. New York: John Wiley.

Cordova, France A. 2015. "Remarks at the FY 2016 NSF Budget Request Rollout." February. Re-trieved from https://www.nsf.gov/news/speeches/cordova/15/fc150202_fy16budget.jsp.

Cornell Tech. 2017. *Built to Make a 21st Century Impact*. Retrieved from https://tech.cornell.edu/.

Cornell University. 2011. *EDA University Center 2008–2011: A Community Economic Develop-ment Partnership for the Southern Tier. Final Report*. August. Retrieved from https://cardi .cals.cornell.edu/sites/cardi.cals.cornell.edu/files/shared/documents/RED/Cornell%20 EDA%20University%20Center%20Annual%20Report%20-%20Final%20Report%20%20 08-31-2011.pdf.

Cornwell, Grant H., and Eve Walsh Stoddard. 1999. *Globalizing Knowledge: Connecting Inter-national and Intercultural Studies*. Washington, DC: Association of American Colleges and Universities.

Corson, John Jay. 1960. *The Governance of Universities*. New York: McGraw-Hill.

Costello, Carrie Yang. 2005. *Professional Identity Crisis: Race, Class, Gender and Success at Profes-sional Schools*. Nashville: Vanderbilt University Press.

Coursera. 2013. "Five Courses Receive College Credit Recommendations." *Coursera Blog*. Feb-ruary 17. Retrieved from https://blog.coursera.org/five-courses-receive-college-credit/.

Coyne, Gary, and Michaela Curran. 2015. *Supplemental Instruction: Patterns of Student Use and Impact on Course Grades, Academic Year 2011–12*. Riverside: University of California, Riverside.

Cremin, Lawrence A. 1961. *The Transformation of the School, 1876–1957*. New York: Random House.

Cress, Christine M., Helen S. Astin, Kathleen Zimmerman-Oster, and John C. Burkhardt. 2001. "Developmental Outcomes of College Students' Involvement in Leadership Activities." *Journal of College Student Development* 42: 15–27.

Croissant, Jennifer, and Sal Restivo, eds. 2001. *Degrees of Compromise: Individual Interests and Academic Values*. Albany: State University of New York Press.

Crow, Michael M., and William B. Dabars. 2015. *Designing the New American University*. Balti-more: Johns Hopkins University Press.

Cuban, Larry. 1986. *Teachers and Machines: Classroom Use of Technology since 1920*. New York: Teachers College Press.

Curry, John R., Andrew L. Laws, and Jon C. Strauss. 2013. *Responsibility Centered Management: A Guide to Balancing Academic Entrepreneurship and Fiscal Responsibility.* 2nd ed. Washington, DC: National Association of College and University Business Officers.

Dahlander, Linus, and Daniel A. McFarland. 2013. "Ties That Last: Tie Formation and Persistence of Research Collaborations over Time." *Administrative Science Quarterly* 58: 69–110.

Dale, Stacy Berg, and Alan B. Krueger. 2002. "Estimating the Payoff to Attending a More Selective College: An Application of Selection on Observables and Unobservables." *Quarterly Journal of Economics* 117: 1491–1527.

———. 2011. "Estimating the Return to College Selectivity over the Career Using Administrative Earnings Data." *NBER Working Paper.* No. 17159. Cambridge, MA: National Bureau of Economic Research. Retrieved from http://www.nber.org/papers/w17159.

Daston, Lorraine, and Peter Galison. 2007. *Objectivity.* Cambridge, MA: MIT Press.

Davenport, Thomas H., and Laurence Prusak. 2000. *Working Knowledge: How Organizations Manage What They Know.* Boston: Harvard Business School Press.

Davis, James A. 1982. "Achievement Variables and Class Cultures: Family, Schooling, Job and Forty-Nine Dependent Variables in the Cumulative GSS." *American Sociological Review* 47: 569–86.

Davis, William E., and Douglas R. Davis. 1999. "The University Presidency: Do Evaluations Make a Difference?" *Journal of Personnel Evaluation in Education* 13: 119–40.

Dawson, Phillip, Jacques van der Meer, Jane Skalicky, and Kym Cowley. 2014. "On the Effectiveness of Supplemental Instruction: A Systematic Review of Supplemental Instruction and Peer-Assisted Study Sessions Literature between 2001 and 2010." *Review of Educational Research* 84: 609–63

DeAngelo, Linda, Sylvia Hurtado, John H. Prior, Kimberly R. Nelly, Jose Luis Santos, and William S. Korn. 2007. *American College Teacher: National Norms for the 2007–2008 HERI Faculty Survey.* Los Angeles: UCLA, Graduate School of Education, Higher Education Research Institute Graduate School of Education, University of California, Los Angeles.

Defense Advanced Research Projects Agency (DARPA). n.d. *Transition and Commercialization.* Retrieved from http://www.darpa.mil/work-with-us/for-small-businesses/commercialization -continued/.

de Groot, Hans, Walter W. McMahon, and J. Fredericks Volkwein. 1991. "The Cost Structure of American Research Universities." *Review of Economics and Statistics* 73: 424–31.

Delaney, Jennifer A., and William R. Doyle. 2007. "The Role of Higher Education in State Budgets." In *State Postsecondary Education Research: New Methods to Inform Policy and Practice,* eds. Kathleen M. Shaw and Donald E. Heller, 35–56. Sterling, VA: Stylus Publishers.

———. 2011. "State Spending on Higher Education: Testing the Balance Wheel over Time." *Journal of Education Finance* 36: 343–68.

Delbanco, Andrew. 1999. "The Decline and Fall of Literature." *New York Review of Books.* November 4. Retrieved from http://www.nybooks.com/articles/1999/11/04/the-decline-and-fall -of-literature/.

———. 2012. *College: What It Was, Is, and Should Be.* Princeton: Princeton University Press.

Delgado, Richard, and Jean Stefancic, eds. 2001. *Critical Race Theory: An Introduction.* New York: New York University Press.

Denison, Edward. 1985. *Trends in American Economic Growth, 1929–1982.* Washington, DC: Brookings Institution.

Denneen, Jeff, and Tom Dretler. 2012. "The Financially Sustainable University." *Bain & Company Insights.* July 6. Retrieved from http://www.bain.com/publications/articles/financially-sus tainable-university.aspx/.

Deresiewicz, William. 2017. "On Political Correctness." *American Scholar.* March 6. Retrieved from https://theamericanscholar.org/on-political-correctness/#.WdE7B2hSxaQ/.

Derrida, Jacques. 1981. *Positions*. Chicago: University of Chicago Press.

Desrochers, Donna M., and Steven Hurlburt. 2016. *Trends in College Spending, 2003–2013*. Washington, DC: American Institutes of Research.

Desrochers, Donna M., and Jane V. Wellman. 2011. *Trends in College Spending, 1999–2009*. Washington, DC: Delta Cost Project.

De Vany, Arthur, and W. David Walls. 1999. "Uncertainty in the Movie Industry: Does Star Power Reduce the Terror of the Box Office?" *Journal of Cultural Economics* 23: 285. Retrieved from http://pages.stern.nyu.edu/~wgreene/entertainmentandmedia/Devany&Walls.pdf.

Dewenter, Ralf, and Leonie Giessing. 2014. "The Effects of Elite Sports on Later Job Success." *SOEP Papers on Multidisciplinary Research Panel Data*. Retrieved from https://www.hsu-hh.de/fgvwl/wp-content/uploads/sites/572/2017/11/hsu-wp-vwl-152.pdf.

Dey, Eric L., Claudia E. Ramirez, William S. Korn, and Alexander W. Astin. 1993. *The American College Teacher: National Norms for the 1992–93 HERI Faculty Survey*. Los Angeles: Higher Education Research Institute, University of California, Los Angeles.

DiPrete, Thomas A., and Claudia Buchmann. 2013. *The Rise of Women: The Growing Gender Gap in Education and What It Means for American Schools*. New York: Russell Sage Foundation.

Dole, Robert. 2006. "Statement on the Bayh-Dole Act." House Committee Report 109–409. 109th Congress, 2nd Session.

Domhoff, G. William. 1971. *The Higher Circles: The Governing Class in America*. New York: Random House.

Dougherty, Kevin J. 1994. *The Contradictory College: The Conflicting Origins, Impacts, and Futures of the Community Colleges*. Albany: SUNY Press.

Dougherty, Kevin J., and Henry Etzkowitz. 1995. *The States and Science: The Politics of High Technology Industrial Policy at the State Level*. Riverdale, NY: Manhattan College. Final report to the National Science Foundation.

Dougherty Kevin J., and Gregory S. Kienzl. 2006. "It's Not Enough to Get through the Open Door: Inequalities by Social Background in Transfer from Community College to Four-Year Colleges." *Teachers College Record* 108: 452–87.

Dougherty, Kevin J., and Rebecca S. Natow. 2009. "The Political Origins of State-Level Performance Funding for Higher Education." Unpublished paper, Teacher's College, Columbia University.

———. 2015. *The Politics of Performance Funding in the United States*. Baltimore: Johns Hopkins University Press.

Dougherty, Kevin J., and Vikash Reddy. 2011. *The Impact of State Performance Funding Systems on Higher Education Institutions: Research Literature Review and Policy Recommendations*. New York: Columbia University, Teachers College, Community College Research Center. Retrieved from https://ccrc.tc.columbia.edu/publications/impacts-state-performance-funding.html/.

Dougherty, Kevin J., and Monica Reid. 2007. *Fifty States of Achieving the Dream: State Policies to Enhance Access to and Success in Community Colleges across the United States*. New York: Columbia University, Teachers College, Community College Research Center. Retrieved from http://files.eric.Ed.gov/fulltext/ED500216.pdf.

Douglass, John Aubrey, and Gregg Thomson. 2017. "Adrift or Engaged? A Multi-Engagement Model of the Student Experience Using SERU Data." Unpublished paper presented at the SERU Symposium on Undergraduate Education, Berkeley, CA. March.

Drennan, Judy, Jessica Kennedy, and Anne Pisarski. 2010. "Factors Affecting Student Attitudes toward Flexible Online Learning in Management Education." *Journal of Educational Research* 98: 331–38.

Drucker, Peter F. 1969. *The Age of Discontinuity: Guidelines to Our Changing Society*. New York: Harper and Row.

D'Souza. Dinesh. 1991. *Illiberal Education: The Politics of Race and Sex on Campus*. New York: Free Press.

Duderstadt, James J., and Farris Womack. 2003. *Beyond the Crossroads: The Future of the Public University in America*. Baltimore: Johns Hopkins University Press.

Dugan, John P., and Susan R. Komives. 2007. *Developed Leadership Capacity in College Students: Findings for a National Study: A Report for the Multi-Institutional Study of Leadership*. College Park, MD: National Clearinghouse for Leadership Programs.

Duke University. 1988. *Crossing Boundaries: Interdisciplinary Planning for the Nineties*. Durham: Duke University.

Durkheim, Emile. (1893) 1964. *The Division of Labor in Society*. Trans. George Simpson. New York: The Free Press.

Dye, Thomas. 1995. *Understanding Public Policy*. New York: Prentice-Hall.

Dynarski, Susan. 2014. "An Economist's Perspective on Student Loans in the United States." *The Brookings Institution ES Working Papers Series*. Retrieved from https://www.brookings.edu/wp-content/uploads/2016/06/economist_perspective_student_loans_dynarski.pdf.

Eagen, M. Kevin, and Andrea J. Jaeger. 2008. "Closing the Gate: Part-Time Faculty Instruction in Gatekeeper Courses and First-Year Persistence." *New Directions for Teaching and Learning* 115: 37–53.

Eagan, M. Kevin, Ellen B. Stolzenberg, Jennifer Berdan Lozno, Melissa C. Aragon, Maria Ramirez Suchard, and Sylvia Hurtado. 2014. *Undergraduate Teaching Faculty: The 2013–14 HERI Faculty Survey*. Los Angeles: Higher Education Research Institute Graduate School of Education, University of California, Los Angeles.

Edsall, Thomas B., and Mary Edsall. 1992. *Chain Reaction: The Impact of Race, Rights, and Taxes on American Politics*. New York: W. W. Norton.

Education Commission of the States (ECS). 2005. *Keeping America Competitive: Five Strategies to Improve Mathematics and Science Education*. Boulder, CO: Education Commission of the States.

Educational Testing Service (ETS). 2003. *Quality, Affordability, and Access: Americans Speak on Higher Education*. Retrieved from https://www.ets.org/Media/About_ETS/pdf/2003report.pdf.

Ehrenberg, Ronald G. 2000. *Tuition Rising: Why College Costs So Much*. Cambridge, MA: Harvard University Press.

———. 2012. "American Higher Education in Transition." *Journal of Economic Perspectives* 26: 193–216.

Ehrenberg, Ronald G., Michael J. Rizzo, and George H. Jakubson. 2007. "Who Bears the Growing Cost of Science at Universities?" In *Science and the University*, eds. Paula E. Stephan and Ronald G. Ehrenberg, 19–35. Madison: University of Wisconsin Press.

Ehrenberg, Ronald G., and Liang Zhang. 2005. "Do Tenured and Tenure-Track Faculty Matter?" *Journal of Human Resources* 40: 647–59.

Ehrenberg, Ronald G., Harriet Zuckerman, Jeffrey A. Goen, and Sharon M. Brucker. 2010. *Educating Scholars: Doctoral Education in the Humanities*. Princeton: Princeton University Press.

Ellison, John. 2016. "Letter to the Class of 2020." August. Chicago: University of Chicago, Office of the Dean of Students.

Empire State Development. n.d. "Centers for Advanced Technology." Retrieved from https://esd.ny.gov/centers-advanced-technology/.

Engel, Joel. 2015. "Madison's HealthTech Cluster: The Rise of EPIC and Everyone Else." *Xconomy*. August 17. Retrieved from http://www.xconomy.com/wisconsin/2015/08/17/madisons-health tech-cluster-epic-everybody-else/.

Engell, James, and Anthony Dangerfield. 1998. "The Market Model University: Humanities in an Age of Money." *Harvard Magazine* 3 (May–June): 48–55.

———. 2005. *Saving Higher Education in the Age of Money*. Charlottesville: University of Virginia Press.

Espenshade, Thomas, and Andrea Radford Walton. 2009. *No Longer Separate, Not Yet Equal: Race and Class in Elite College Admissions and Campus Life*. Princeton: Princeton University Press.

Etzkowitz, Henry. 1989. "Entrepreneurial Science in the Academy: A Case of the Transformation of Norms." *Social Problems* 36: 36–50.

Etzkowitz, Henry, and Loet Leydesdorff. 2000. "The Dynamics of Innovation: From National Systems and 'Mode 2' to a Triple Helix of University-Industry-Government Relations." *Research Policy* 29: 109–23.

Etzkowitz, Henry, Andrew Webster, and Peter Healey. 1998. *Capitalizing Knowledge: New Intersections of Industry and Academia*. Albany: SUNY Press.

Euben, Diane R. 2004. "Faculty Employment outside the University: Conflict of Commitment." Paper presented at the National Association of College and University Attorneys. Atlanta. March 5. Retrieved from http://pages.uoregon.edu/uosenate/dirsen089/COICOCC-AAUP-Conf.pdf.

Evans, Eliza. 2016. "Interdisciplinarity and Faculty Careers." Unpublished dissertation chapters. Graduate School of Education, Stanford University.

Everett, Michael. 1977. "Student Evaluations of Teaching and the Cognitive Level of Economics Courses." *Journal of Economics Education* 2: 100–103.

Ewell, Peter T. 2001a. *Accreditation and Student Learning Outcomes: A Proposed Point of Departure*. Washington, DC: Council on Higher Education Accreditation.

———. 2001b. "Statewide Testing in Higher Education." *Change* 33 (March–April): 50–70.

———. 2004. *Accreditation and the Provision Additional Information to the Public about Institutional and Program Performance*. Washington, DC: Council for Higher Education Accreditation.

———. 2005. "Can Assessment Serve Accountability: It Depends on the Question." In *Achieving Accountability in Higher Education: Balancing Public, Academic, and Market Demands*, ed. Joseph C. Burke and Associates, 104–24. San Francisco: Jossey-Bass.

Ewell, Peter T., and Margaret A. Miller. 2005. *Measuring Up on College-Level Learning*. San Jose, CA: National Center for Public Policy in Higher Education.

Ewing Marion Kauffman Foundation. 2008. *Entrepreneurial Education Comes of Age on Campus*. Retrieved from. http://www.kauffman.org/~/media/kauffman_org/research%20reports%20and%20covers/2013/08/eshipedcomesofage_report.pdf/.

Fairlie, Robert W., Arnobia Morelix, E. J. Reedy, and Joshua Russell. 2015. *The Kauffman Index. Start Up Activity*. Retrieved from http://www.kauffman.org/~/media/kauffman_org/research%20reports%20and%20covers/2015/05/kauffman_index_startup_activity_national_trends_2015.pdf/.

Fairweather, James S. 1988. *Entrepreneurship and Higher Education*. Washington, DC: Association for the Study of Higher Education.

———. 2005. "Beyond Rhetoric: Trends in the Relative Value of Teaching and Research in Faculty Salaries." *Journal of Higher Education* 76: 401–22.

Fanon, Franz. 1963. *The Wretched of the Earth*. New York: Grove Press.

Farrell, Maureen. 2010. "In Depth: 15 Big Small Business Contests." *Forbes*. January 26. Retrieved from https://www.forbes.com/2010/01/26/small-business-competition-entrepreneurs-finance-university_slide.html/.

Federal Bureau of Investigation (FBI). 2016. "What We Investigate; Civil Rights." Retrieved from https://www.fbi.gov/investigate/civil-rights/hate-crimes/.

Feldman, Maryann P. 1994. "The University and Economic Development: The Case of Johns Hopkins University and Baltimore." *Economic Development Quarterly* 8 (February): 67–76.

Feldman, Maryann P., and Pierre Desrochers. 2004. "Truth for Its Own Sake: Academic Culture and Technology Transfer at Johns Hopkins University." *Minerva* 42: 105–26.

Feller, Irwin. 1997. "Technology Transfer in Universities." In *Higher Education: A Handbook of Theory and Research*, ed. John C. Smart, 1–42. New York: Agathon Press.

Fethke, Gary C., and Andrew J. Policano. 2012. *Public No More: A New Path to Excellence for America's Public Universities*. Stanford: Stanford Business Books.

Field, Kelly. 2010. "Robert Shireman, Architect of Direct Loan Program's Triumph, Will Step Down at Ed Dept." *Chronicle of Higher Education*. May 17. Retrieved from https://www .chronicle.com/article/Robert-Shireman-Architect-of/65597.

Figlio, David N., Mark Rush, and Lu Yin. 2010. "Is It Live or Is It Internet? Experimental Estimates of the Effects of Online Instruction on Student Learning." *NBER Working Paper*. No. 16809. Retrieved from http://www.nber.org/papers/w16089.

Finkelstein. Martin J., Valerie Martin Conley, and Jack H. Schuster. 2016. *The Faculty Factor: Reassessing the American Academy in a Turbulent Era*. Baltimore: Johns Hopkins University Press.

Fitzgerald, Nancy, and Nancy Green Leigh, eds. 2002. *Industrial Revitalization: Cases and Strategies for Cities and Suburbs*. London: Sage.

Flaherty, Colleen. 2017. "The More Things Change." *Inside Higher Ed*. April 11. Retrieved from https://www.insidehighered.com/news/2017/04/11/aaup-faculty-salaries-slightly-budgets -are-balanced-backs-adjuncts-and-out-state.

Fleming, Lee, and David M. Waguespack. 2007. "Brokerage, Boundary Spanning and Leadership in Open Innovation Communities." *Organization Science* 18: 165–86.

Florida, Richard. 2002. *The Rise of the Creative Class: And How It's Transforming Work, Leisure, Community and Everyday Life*. New York: Basic Books.

Florida, Richard, Zara Matheson, Patrick Adler, and Taylor Brydges. 2014. "The Divided City and the Shape of the New Metropolis." September 6. Retrieved from http://martinprosperity .org/media/Divided-City.pdf.

Foucault, Michel. (1961) 1964. *Madness and Civilization: A History of Insanity in the Age of Reason*. New York: Vintage.

Foundation Center. 2008. "Grants of $100,000 or More to Higher Education circa 2000" (electronic data file). New York: The Foundation Center.

———. 2010. "Grants of $100,000 or More to Higher Education circa 1990" (electronic data file). New York: The Foundation Center.

Foundation for Individual Rights in Education (FIRE). 2016. *Spotlight on Speech Codes*. Retrieved from https://www.thefire.org/spotlight-on-speech-codes-2016/.

———. 2017. *Disinvitation Attempts*. Retrieved from https://www.thefire.org/resources/disinvita tion-database/.

Fourcade, Marion, Etienne Ollion, and Yann Algon. 2015. "The Superiority of Economists." *Journal of Economic Perspectives* 29: 89–114.

Fox, Maggie. 2017. "Congress Defies Trump, Gives Big Raise to NIH Medical Research." *NBC News*. May 1. Retrieved from https://www.nbcnews.com/health/health-news/congress-defies -trump-gives-big-raise-nih-medical-research-n753376/.

Fox, Marc. 1993. "Is It a Good Investment to Attend an Elite Private College?" *Economics of Education Review* 12: 137–51.

Frank, David John, and Jay Gabler. 2006. *Reconstructing the University: Worldwide Shifts in Academia in the 20th Century*. Stanford: Stanford University Press.

Frank, David John, Evan Schofer, and John Charles Torres. 1994. "Rethinking History: Change in the University Curriculum, 1910–1990." *Sociology of Education* 67: 231–42.

Frank, Robert H. 2013. "The Prestige Chase Is Raising College Costs." *New York Times*. March 10. Retrieved from http://www.nytimes.com/2012/03/11/business/college-costs-are-rising-amid -a-prestige-chase.html.

Freeman, Christopher. 1987. *Technology, Policy, and Economic Performance: Lessons from Japan*. London: Pinter.

Freeman, Scott, Sarah L. Eddy, Miles McDonough, Michele K. Smith, Nnadozie Okoroafor, Hannah Jordt, and Mary Pat Wenderoth. 2014. "Active Learning Increases Student Performance in Science, Engineering, and Mathematics." *Proceedings of the National Academy of Sciences* 111: 8410–15.

Freidson, Eliot. 1985. *Professional Powers: A Study of the Institutionalization of Formal Knowledge*. Chicago: University of Chicago Press.

Froyd, Jeffrey E. 2008. *White Paper on Promising Practices in Undergraduate STEM Education*. Washington, DC: National Academy of Science.

Fry, Richard. 2014. "The Changing Profile of Student Borrowers." *Pew Research Center Social Trends*. October 7. Retrieved from http://www.pewsocialtrends.org/2014/10/07/the-chang ing-profile-of-student-borrowers/.

Fuller, Bruce, and Richard Rubinson, eds. 1992. *The Political Construction of Education: The State, School Expansion and Economic Change*. New York: Praeger.

Fuller, Rex, D. Patrick Morton, and Ann Korschgen. 2005. "Incentive-Based Budgeting: Lessons for Public Higher Education." In *On Becoming a Productive University: Strategies for Reducing Costs and Increasing Quality in Higher Education*, eds. James E. Groccia and Judith E. Miller, 34–43. Bolton, MA: Anker Publishers.

Galbraith, John Kenneth. 1967. *The New Industrial State*. Boston: Houghton-Mifflin.

Gallup Organization. 2014. "Fraternities and Sororities: Understanding Life Outcomes." Retrieved from https://www.pikes.org/~/media/fraternities%20and%20sororities%20report .ashx.

———. 2016. "Free Expression on Campus: A Survey of College Students and U.S. Adults." Retrieved from https://www.knightfoundation.org/media/uploads/publication_pdfs/Free Speech_campus.pdf.

———. 2017. "Global Warming Concern at a Three-Decade High in U.S." Retrieved from http:// news.gallup.com/poll/206030/global-warming-concern-three-decade-high.aspx/.

Gammon, Katherine. 2016. "The Rise of Los Angeles Start-Up Ecosystem." *USC Trojan Family Magazine*. Retrieved from https://tfm.usc.edu/the-rise-of-las-startup-ecosystem/.

Gardner, Lee. 2013. "Private College Presidents Urge a Commitment to Need-Based Financial Aid." *Chronicle of Higher Education*. January 6. Retrieved from https://www.chronicle.com /article/Private-College-Presidents/136509.

Garland, James C. 2009. *Saving Alma Mater: A Rescue Plan for America's Public Universities*. Chicago: University of Chicago Press.

Gates, Bill. 2010. "Improving College Completion in the U.S." Retrieved from https://www.gates notes.com/Education/Improving-College-Completion-in-the-U-S.

Gates, Henry Louis. 1992. *Loose Canons: Notes on the Culture Wars*. New York: Oxford University Press.

Geiger, Roger L. 1993. *Research and Relevant Knowledge: American Research Universities since World War II*. New York: Oxford University Press.

———. 2004. *Knowledge and Money: Research Universities and the Paradoxes of the Marketplace*. Stanford: Stanford University Press.

Geiger, Roger L., and Irwin Feller. 1995. "The Dispersion of Academic Research in the 1980s." *Journal of Higher Education* 66: 336–60.

Geiger, Roger L., and Donald E. Heller. 2011. "Financial Trends in Higher Education: The United States." *Peking University Education Review* 1. Retrieved from https://ed.psu.edu/cshe/working-papers/wp-6.

Geiger, Roger L., and Creso Sa. 2008. *Tapping the Riches of Science: Universities and the Promise of Economic Growth.* Cambridge, MA: Harvard University Press.

General Accounting Office (GAO). 1995. "Higher Education Restructuring Student Debt Could Reduce Low-Income Dropout Rate." Retrieved from https://www.gao.gov/assets/230/220981.pdf.

Georgantzas, Nicholas C., and William Acar. 1995. *Scenario-Driven Planning: Learning to Manage Strategic Uncertainty.* Westport, CT: Quorum Books.

George, Bill. 2015. "Dow-DuPont Raises Even More Concerns America Is Abandoning Corporate Research." *Fortune.* December 12. Retrieved from http://fortune.com/2015/12/12/dow-dupont-corporate-research-america/.

Georgia Institute of Technology, Enterprise Innovation Institute. 2007. "Companies from Georgia Tech's Science & Technology Incubator Attract $1 Billion in Venture Funding." Retrieved from https://innovate.gatech.edu/entrepreneurs/1-billion-in-venture-funding/.

Georgia Research Alliance (GRA). n.d. "Georgia Research Alliance Brochure." Retrieved from http://gra.org/uploads/documents/2015/10/2015101414580948/GRABrochure_Final.pdf.

———. 2010. "The First 20 Years." Retrieved from http://gra.org/uploads/documents/2013/06/2013062411243236/GRA20thAnniversary.pdf.

Georgia State University. 2014. *GPS Advising at Georgia State University.* Retrieved from http://oie.gsu.edu/files/2014/04/Advisement-GPS.pdf.

Gerber, Larry G. 2014. *The Rise and Decline of Faculty Governance: Professionalization and the Modern American University.* Baltimore: Johns Hopkins University Press.

Gerschenkron, Alexander. 1962. *Backwardness in Historical Perspective: A Book of Essays.* Cambridge MA: Belknap Press of Harvard University Press.

Giancola, Jennifer, and Richard D. Kahlenberg. 2016. *True Merit: Ensuring the Brightest Students Have Access to Our Best Colleges.* Lansdowne, VA: Jack Kent Cooke Foundation. Retrieved from http://www.jkcf.org/assets/1/7/JKCF_True_Merit_Report.pdf.

Gibbons, Michael, Camille Limoges, Helga Nowotny, Simon Schwartzman, Peter Scott, and Martin Trow. 1994. *The New Production of Knowledge: The Dynamics of Science and Research in Contemporary Societies.* London: Sage.

Gilman, David A. 1978. "The Logic of Minimal Competency Testing." *NASSP Bulletin* 62: 56–63.

Ginsberg, Benjamin. 2011. *The Fall of the Faculty: The Rise of the All-Administrative University and Why It Matters.* New York: Oxford University Press.

Gladwell, Malcolm. 2006. "The Formula." *The New Yorker* October 16. Retrieved from https://www.newyorker.com/magazine/2006/10/16/the-formula.

Glazer-Raymo, Judith. 2005. *Professionalizing Graduate Education: The Master's Degree in the Marketplace.* San Francisco: Jossey-Bass.

Glinski, Theresa. 2016. "UCLA Study Shows Rise in Student Activism, Free Speech Approval Waning." *The FIRE.* February 12. Retrieved from https://www.thefire.org/ucla-study-shows-rise-in-student-activism-free-speech-approval-waning/.

Goetz, Thomas. 2003. "Open Source Everywhere." *Wired.* Retrieved from https://www.wired.com/2003/11/opensource/.

Golden, Daniel. 2006. *The Price of Admission: How America's Ruling Class Buys Its Way into Elite Colleges—and Who Gets Left outside the Gates.* New York: Crown Publishers.

Goldin, Claudia D., and Lawrence F. Katz. 2008. *The Race between Education and Technology.* Cambridge, MA: Belknap Press of Harvard University Press.

Goldman, Charles A., Traci Williams, David M. Adamson, and Kathy Rosenblatt. 2000. *Paying for University Research Facilities and Administration*. Santa Monica: Rand Corporation.

Goldrick-Rab, Sara, and Katharine M. Broton. 2015. "Hungry, Homeless and in College." *New York Times*. December 4. Retrieved from https://www.nytimes.com/2015/12/04/opinion/hungry -homeless-and-in-college.html?mcubz=0&_r=0/.

Goldrick-Rab, Sara, and Nancy Kendall. 2016. *The Real Cost of College*. New York: The Century Foundation.

Goldstein, Joseph L., and Michael S. Brown. 2012. "A Golden Era of Nobel Laureates." *Science* 338: 1033–34.

Goldstein, Larry, and Richard J. Meisinger. 2005. *College and University Budgeting: An Introduction for Faculty and Academic Administrators*. 3rd ed. Washington, DC: National Association of College and University Business Officers.

Gonzalez, Heather B., John F. Sargent, and Patricia Moloney Figliola. 2010. "America Competes Reauthorization Act of 2010 (H.R. 5116) and The America Competes Act (P.L. 110–69): Selected Policy Issues." *Congressional Budget Service*. Retrieved from http://www.ift.org /public-policyand-regulations/~/media/Public%20Policy/0728AmericaCompetesAct.pdf.

Gordon, Larry. 2015. "How the UC System Is Making Patents Pay Off." *Los Angeles Times*. October 10. Retrieved from http://www.latimes.com/local/education/la-me-uc-patents-20151011 -story.html/.

Gould, John D., and Clayton Lewis. 1985. "Designing for Usability: Key Principles and What Designers Think." *Association for Computing Machinery (ACM) Magazine* 28: 300–311.

Gouldner, Alvin. 1979. *The Future of Intellectuals and the Rise of the New Class*. New York: Seabury.

Gramsci, Antonio. (1948) 2011. *Prison Notebooks*. New York: Columbia University Press.

Graham, David A. 2017. "Why Do Republicans Suddenly Hate College So Much?" *The Atlantic*. July 13. Retrieved from https://www.theatlantic.com/politics/archive/2017/07/why-do -republicans-suddenly-hate-colleges-so-much/533130/.

Graham, Hugh Davis, and Nancy Diamond. 1997. *The Rise of American Research Universities: Elites and Challengers in the Postwar Era*. Baltimore: Johns Hopkins University Press.

Gray, Denis O., and S. George Walters, eds. 1998. *Managing the Industry/University Cooperative Research Center: A Guide for Directors and Other Stakeholders*. Columbus, OH: Battelle Press.

Green, Sally, Julian P. T. Higgins, Phillip Alderson, Mike Clarke, Cynthia D. Mulrow, and Andrew D. Oxman. 2011. "Introduction." In *Cochrane Handbook for Systematic Reviews of Interventions Version 5.1.0* [updated March 2011], eds. Julian P. T. Higgins and Sally Green, 3–10. Retrieved from http://handbook.cochrane.org/.

Greenberger, Phyllis. 2002. "University of Wisconsin Fosters Interdisciplinary Research on Sex Differences." *Journal of Women's Health and Gender-Based Medicine* 11: 334–40.

Grigsby, Mary. 2009. *Life through the Eyes of Students*. Albany: SUNY Press.

Griliches, Zvi. 1957. "Hybrid Corn: An Exploration in the Economics of Technological Change." *Econometrica* 25: 501–22.

Grogger, Jeff, and Eric Eide. 1995. "Changes in College Skills and the Rise in the College Wage Premium." *Journal of Human Resources* 30: 280–310.

Gross, Neil. 2013. *Why Are Professors Liberal and Why Do Conservatives Care?* Cambridge, MA: Harvard University Press.

Gross, Neil, and Solon Simmons. 2014. "The Social and Political Views of American College and University Professors." In *Professors and Their Politics*, eds. Neil Gross and Solon Simmons, 19–50. Baltimore: Johns Hopkins University Press.

Gross, Rachel E. 2015. "Evolution Is Finally Winning Out over Creationism." *Slate*. November 19. Retrieved from http://www.slate.com/articles/health_and_science/science/2015/11/polls _americans_believe_in_evolution_less_in_creationism.html/.

Grubb, W. Norton. 1996. *Working in the Middle: Strengthening Education and Training for the Mid-Skilled Labor Force*. San Francisco: Jossey-Bass.

———. 1999. *Honored but Invisible: An Inside Look at Teaching in Community Colleges*. New York: Routledge.

Guarino, Cassandra M., and Victor M. H. Borden. 2017. "Faculty Service Loads and Gender: Are Women Taking Care of the Academic Family?" *Research in Higher Education* 58: 672–94.

Guinier, Lani. 2015. *The Tyranny of Meritocracy: Democratizing Higher Education in America*. Boston: Beacon Press.

Gumport, Patricia J. 1997. "Public Universities as Academic Workplaces." *Daedalus* 126: 113–36.

———. 2000. "Academic Restructuring: Organizational Change and Institutional Imperatives." *Higher Education* 39: 67–91.

———. 2002. "Universities and Knowledge: Restructuring the City of Intellect." In *The Future of the City of Intellect*, ed. Steven Brint, 47–81. Stanford: Stanford University Press.

Gurin, Patricia. 1999. "Expert Reports in Defense of the University of Michigan: Expert Report of Patricia Gurin." *Equity and Excellence in Education* 32 (2): 36–62.

Hackett, Edward J. 2000. "Interdisciplinary Research Initiatives at the U.S. National Science Foundation." In *Practicing Interdisciplinarity*, eds. Peter Weingart and Nico Stehr, 248–59. Toronto: University of Toronto Press.

Hagedorn, Linda S., Athena I. Perrakis, and William Maxwell. 2007. "The Negative Commandments: Ten Ways Community Colleges Hinder Student Success." *Florida Journal of Educational Administration and Policy* 1. Retrieved from https://files.eric.ed.gov/fulltext/EJ902986.pdf.

Hake, Richard R. 1998. "Interactive-Engagement versus Traditional Methods: A Six-Thousand-Student Survey of Mechanics Test Data for Introductory Physics Courses." *American Journal of Physics* 66: 64–74.

Hall, Roberta, and Bernice R. Sandler. 1982. *The Classroom Climate: A Chilly One for Women?* Washington, DC: Project on the Status and Education of Women, Association of American Colleges.

Hall, Peter A., and Michele Lamont, eds. 2013. *Social Resilience in the Neo-liberal Era*. Cambridge: Cambridge University Press.

Hamermesh, Daniel S. 2011. "The Know-Nothing Assault on Higher Education." *Chronicle of Higher Education*. August 28. Retrieved from http://chronicle.com/article/The-Know-Nothing-Assault-on/128803.

Hamill, Sean. 2008. "Road Stirs Up Debate, Even on Its Name." *New York Times*. December 27. Retrieved from http://www.nytimes.com/2008/12/28/us/28highway.html.

Han, Siqi, and Claudia Buchmann. 2016. "Aligning Science Achievement and STEM Expectations for College Success: A Comparative Study of Curricular Standardization." *RSF: The Russell Sage Foundation Journal of the Social Sciences* 2 (1): 192–211.

Haney, Christopher. 2006. *Reforming Punishment: Psychological Limits to the Power of Prison*. Washington, DC: American Psychological Association Books.

Hanushek, Eric A., and Ludger Woessmann. 2011. "The Economics of International Differences in Educational Achievement." In *Handbook of the Economics of Education*, vol. 3, eds. Eric A. Hanushek, Stephen Machin, and Ludger Woessmann, 89–200. Amsterdam: North Holland.

Hardin, John. 2018. "You Can't Legislate Free Inquiry on Campus." *New York Times*. May 21. Retrieved from https://www.nytimes.com/2018/05/21/opinion/free-inquiry-campus.html.

Harding, Sandra. 1993. "Rethinking Standpoint Epistemology: What Is 'Strong Objectivity'?" In *Feminist Epistemologies*, eds. Linda Martin Alcoff and Elizabeth Potter, 49–82. New York: Routledge.

Harper, Shaun R., and Sylvia Hurtado. 2007. "Nine Themes in Campus Racial Climates and Implications for Institutional Transformation." In *Responding to the Realities of Race on Campus*, eds. Shaun R. Harper and Lori D. Patton, 7–24. San Francisco: Jossey-Bass.

Harrington, Charles, and Timothy Schibik. 2001. "Caveat Emptor: Is There a Relationship between Part-time Faculty Utilization and Student Learning Outcomes and Retention?" AIR 2001 Annual Forum. Long Beach, CA. Retrieved from https://eric.ed.gov/?id=ED512352.

Hart, Betty, and Todd Risley. 1995. *Meaningful Differences in the Everyday Experience of Young American Children*. Baltimore: Paul Brooks.

Hart, Jeni, and Jennifer Fellabaum. 2008. "Analyzing Campus Climate Surveys: Seeking to Define and Understand." *Journal of Diversity in Higher Education* 1: 222–34.

Hartocollis, Anemona. 2017. "Long after Protests, Students Shun the University of Missouri." *New York Times*. July 9. Retrieved from https://www.nytimes.com/2017/07/09/us/university-of-missouri-enrollment-protests-fallout.html.

Harvard Graduate School of Education. 2017. "Harvard Institutes of Education." Retrieved from https://www.gse.harvard.edu/ppe/programs/highered/.

Harvey, David. 2005. *A Brief History of Neo-liberalism*. New York: Oxford University Press.

Haug, P. 1995. "Formation of Biotechnology Firms in the Greater Seattle Region: An Empirical Investigation of Entrepreneurial, Financial, and Educational Perspectives." *Environment and Planning* A 27: 249–67.

Hauser, Robert M., and David L. Featherman. 1973. "Trends in the Occupational Mobility of U.S. Men, 1962–1970." *American Sociological Review* 38: 302–10.

Hawthorne, Joan. 2008. "Accountability and Comparability: What's Wrong with the VSA Approach?" *Liberal Education* 94 (2): 24.

Haycock, Kati, and Danette Gerald. 2006. *Engines of Inequality: Diminishing Equity in the Nation's Premier Public Universities*. Washington, DC: Education Trust.

Haycock, Kati, Mary Lynch, and Jennifer Engle. 2010. *Opportunity Adrift: Our Flagship Universities Are Straying from Their Public Mission*. Washington, DC: The Education Trust.

Hearn, James C., Darrell R. Lewis, Lincoln Kallsen, and Janet M. Holdsworth. 2006. "Incentives for Managed Growth: A Case Study of Incentives Based Planning and Budgeting in a Large Public Research University." *Journal of Higher Education* 77: 286–316.

Heckscher, Charles, and Paul S. Adler. 2006. *The Firm as a Collaborative Community*. Oxford: Oxford University Press.

Heller, Nathan. 2013. "Laptop U: Has the Future of College Moved Online?" *The New Yorker*. May 20. 80–91.

Hendrick, David W., Steven E. Henson, and John M. Krieg. 2011. "Is There Really a Faculty Union Salary Premium?" *ILR Review* 64: 558–75.

Hernandez College Consulting. 2014. *Ivy League Admission Statistics for the Class of 2018*. Retrieved from https://www.toptieradmissions.com/resources/college-admissions-statistics/ivy-league-admission-statistics-for-class-of-2018/.

Hermanowicz, Joseph C. 1998. *The Stars Are Not Enough: Scientists—Their Passions and Professions*. Chicago: University of Chicago Press.

———. 2013. "The Culture of Mediocrity." *Minerva* 51: 363–87.

Hershbein, Brad, and Kevin M. Hollenbeck. 2013. "The Distribution of College Graduate Debt, 1990 to 2008: A Decomposition Approach." Paper presented for the Upjohn/EPI/Spencer Conference on Student Loans. Ann Arbor, MI. October.

Heterodox Academy. 2017. "About Us." September 29. Retrieved from https://heterodoxacademy.org/about-us/.

Hicks, Diana. 2016. "Grand Challenges in U.S. Science Policy Attempt Policy Innovation." *International Journal of Foresight and Innovation Policy* 11: 22–42.

Higher Education Research Institute (HERI). 2015. *The American Freshman: National Norms for 2015*. Los Angeles: HERI. Retrieved from https://www.heri.ucla.edu/monographs/The AmericanFreshman2015.pdf.

Hirsch, Werner Z., and Luc E. Weber. 2001. *Governance in Higher Education: The University in a State of Flux*. London: Economica.

Hofherr, Justine. 2016. "Meet 23 Boston University Alumni behind Some of the City's Top Start-Ups." *BuiltinBoston.com*. September 8. Retrieved from https://www.builtinboston.com/2016/09/08/meet-boston-university-alumni-behind-some-city-top-startups/.

Hoffmann, Stefan G., Anu Asnaani, Imke J. J. Vonk, Alice T. Sawyer, and Angela Fang. 2012. "The Efficacy of Cognitive-Behavioral Therapy: A Review of Meta-Analyses." *Cognitive Therapy Research* 36: 427–40.

Hoilman, Carly. 2016. "College 'Unofficial Survival Guide' Lists 'Hatred of White People' as 'Legitimate Response to Oppression.'" *The Blaze*. April 27. Retrieved from http://www.theblaze.com/news/2016/04/27/colleges-unofficial-survival-guide-lists-hatred-of-white-people-as-legitimate-response-to-oppression/.

Holdren, John P. 2017. "Science in Its Rightful Place." June 12. Retrieved from https://obamawhitehouse.archives.gov/blog/2017/01/12/science-its-rightful-place/.

Holland, Dorothy C., and Margaret A. Eisenhart. 1990. *Educated in Romance: Women, Achievement, and College Culture*. Chicago: University of Chicago Press.

Hollingsworth, J. Rogers, and Ellen J. Hollingsworth. 2000. "Major Discoveries in Biomedical Research Organizations: Perspectives on Interdisciplinarity, Nurturing Leadership, Integrated Structures and Cultures." In *Practicing Interdisciplinarity*, eds. Peter Weingart and Nico Stehr, 215–44. Toronto: University of Toronto Press.

Horowitz, David, and Jacob Laksin. 2009. *One-Party Classroom: How Radical Professors at America's Top Colleges Indoctrinate Students and Undermine Our Democracy*. New York: Random House (Crown Forum).

Hourihan, Matt. 2017. "Science and Technology Funding under Obama: A Look Back." *AAAS News*. January 19. Retrieved from https://www.aaas.org/news/science-and-technology-funding-under-obama-look-back/.

Hout, Michael. 2012. "Social and Economic Returns to College Education in the United States." *Annual Review of Sociology* 38: 379–400.

Hovey, Harold A. 1999. *State Spending for Higher Education in the Next Decade: The Battle to Sustain Current Support*. San Jose: National Center for Public Policy and Higher Education.

Hoxby, Caroline M. 2001. "The Return to Attending a More Selective College: 1960 to the Present." In *Forum Futures: Exploring the Future of Higher Education, 2000 Papers*, eds. M. Devlin and J. Meyerson, 13–42. San Francisco: Jossey-Bass.

———. 2009. "The Changing Selectivity of American Colleges." *Journal of Economic Perspectives* 23: 95–118.

Huber, Mary Taylor, and Patricia Hutchings. 2005. *The Advancement of Learning: Building the Teaching Commons*. San Francisco: Jossey-Bass.

Hughey, Matthew. 2010. "A Paradox of Participation: Nonwhites in White Sororities and Fraternities." *Social Problems* 57: 653–79.

Hurtado, Sylvia, M. Kevin Eagan, and Mitchell J. Chang. 2010. "Degrees of Success: Bachelor's Degree Completion among Initial STEM Majors." *HERI Research Brief*. Los Angeles: Higher Education Research Institute Graduate School of Education, University of California, Los Angeles. Retrieved from https://www.heri.ucla.edu/nih/downloads/2010%20-%20Hurtado,%20Eagan,%20Chang%20-%20Degrees%20of%20Success.pdf.

Hutchings, Pat, and Lee S. Shulman. 1999. "The Scholarship of Teaching: New Elaborations, New Developments." *Change* 31 (September–October): 5, 10–15.

Hutchinson, Alex. 2005. "Top 50 Inventions." *Popular Mechanics* (December): 76–84, 135.

Hyman, Herbert, and Charles W. Wright. 1979. *The Enduring Effects of Education*. Chicago: University of Chicago Press.

Immerwahr, John. 2004. "Public Attitudes on Higher Education: A Trend Analysis, 1993 to 2003." *Public Agenda*. February.

Indiana University. 2016. *Innovate Indiana Initiatives*. Retrieved from http://innovateindiana.iu .edu/initiatives/business-formation.shtml/.

Indiana University Purdue University Indianapolis (IUPUI) Center on Philanthropy. 2011. *Million Dollar List*. Retrieved from www.milliondollarlist.org/.

Industrial Research Institute and R&D Magazine (Industrial Research Institute). 2016. "2016 Global R&D Funding Forecast." *R&D Magazine*. (Winter). Retrieved from https://www .iriweb.org/sites/default/files/2016GlobalR%26DFundingForecast_2.pdf.

Ingraham, Christopher. 2015. "A Decade of Bad Press Hasn't Hurt Fraternity Membership Numbers." *Washington Post*. March 9. Retrieved from https://www.washingtonpost.com/news /wonk/wp/2015/03/09/a-decade-of-bad-media-attention-hasnt-hurt-fraternity-membership -numbers/?utm_term=.3779730128a1/.

Inman, Elliot, Michael Kerwin, and Larry Mayes. 2010. "Instructor and Student Attitudes toward Distance Learning." *Community College Journal of Research and Practice* 6: 581–89.

Institute for College Access and Success. 2014. *Student Debt and the Class of 2013*. November 13. Retrieved from https://ticas.org/content/pub/student-debt-and-class-2013-0/.

Institute for Systems Biology. 2017. "Leroy Hood, MD, Ph.D." Retrieved from https://www.sys temsbiology.org/bio/leroy-hood/.

Integrated Post-Secondary Education Data Systems (IPEDS) Analytics. 2014. *Delta Cost Project Database 1987–2010 (STATA)*. Retrieved from https://nces.ed.gov/ipeds/Home/UseThe Data/.

Internal Revenue Service (IRS). 2015. *2015 Data Handbook*. Retrieved from https://www.irs.gov /pub/irs-soi/15databk.pdf.

Jacobs, A. J. 2013. "Two Cheers for Web U." *New York Times*. April 21. Retrieved from http:// www.nytimes.com/2013/04/21/opinion/sunday/grading-the-mooc-university.html.

Jacobs, Jerry A. 2013. *In Defense of Disciplines: Interdisciplinarity and Specialization in the Research University*. Chicago: University of Chicago Press.

Jaggars, Shanna Smith. 2014. "Choosing between Online and Face-to-Face Courses: Community College Student Voices." *American Journal of Distance Education* 28: 27–38.

James, Estelle, Nabeel Alasalam, Joseph C. Conaty, and Duc-Le To. 1989. "College Quality and Future Earnings: Where Should You Send Your Child to College?" *American Economic Review* 79: 247–52.

Jaschik, Scott. 2015. "A Big Union Win." *Inside Higher Ed*. January 2. Retrieved from https:// www.insidehighered.com/news/2015/01/02/nlrb-ruling-shifts-legal-ground-faculty-unions -private-colleges/.

Jencks, Christopher, and David Riesman. 1968. *The Academic Revolution*. New York: Anchor Books.

Johnson, Bethany C., and Mark T. Kiviniemi. 2006. "The Effect of Online Chapter Quizzes on Exam Performance in Undergraduate Social Psychology Classes." *Teaching of Psychology* 36: 33–37.

Johnson, Michael R., and Ralph R. Sell. 1976. "The Cost of Being Black: A 1970 Update." *American Journal of Sociology* 82:183–89.

Johnson, Valens. 2003. *Grade Inflation: A Crisis in College Education*. New York: Springer.

Jones, Daniel Stedman. 2012. *Masters of the Universe: Hayek, Friedman, and the Birth of Neo-Liberal Politics*. Princeton: Princeton University Press.

Jorgenson, Dale W. 1966. "The Embodiment Hypothesis." *Journal of Political Economy* 74: 1–17.

Kahlenberg, Richard D. 2010. *A Better Affirmative Action: State Universities That Created Alternatives to Racial Preference*. Washington, DC: The Century Foundation.

———. 2015. *Achieving Better Diversity: Reforming Affirmative Action in Higher Education*. Washington, DC: The Century Foundation. Retrieved from https://tcf.org/content/report/achieving-better-diversity/.

Kalil, Thomas, and Cristin Dorgelo. 2016. "100 Examples of Putting Science in Its Rightful Place." June 21. Retrieved from https://obamawhitehouse.archives.gov/blog/2016/06/21/100-examples-putting-science-its-rightful-place/.

Kamenetz, Anya. 2006. *Generation Debt*. New York: Riverhead Books.

———. 2010. *DIY U: Edupunks, Edupreneurs, and the Coming Transformation of Higher Education*. White River Junction, VT: Green.

Kanter, Rosabeth M. 1976. *Men and Women of the Corporation*. New York: Basic Books.

Kantrowitz, Mark. 2011. "The Distribution of Grants and Scholarships by Race," *Finaid.org*. September 2. Retrieved from http://www.finaid.org/scholarships/20110902racescholarships.pdf.

Kaplan, Gabriel. 2001. *Preliminary Results from the 2001 Survey on Higher Education Governance*. Washington, DC: American Association of University Professors and American Conference of Academic Deans.

———. 2004. "How Academic Ships Actually Navigate." In *Governing Academia*, ed. Ronald G. Ehrenberg, 165–208. Ithaca, NY: Cornell University Press.

Kaplan, Richard S., and David P. Norton. 1996. "Using the Balanced Scorecard as a Strategic Management System." *Harvard Business Review* 74 (January–February): 75–85.

Karabel, Jerome. 2005. *The Chosen: The Hidden History of Admission and Exclusion at Harvard, Yale, and Princeton*. New York: Houghton-Mifflin.

Kay, Lily E. 1993. *The Molecular Vision of Life: Caltech, the Rockefeller Foundation, and the Rise of the New Biology*. New York: Oxford University Press.

Kelderman, Eric. 2009. "Pa. State System Considers Consolidating Programs amid Financial Squeeze." *Chronicle of Higher Education*. September 14. Retrieved from https://www.chronicle.com/article/Pa-State-System-Considers/48361/.

Kena, Grace, William Hussar, Joel McFarland, Cristobal de Brey, Lauren Musu-Gillette, Xiaolei Wang, Jijun Zhang, Amy Rathbun, Sidney Wilkinson-Flicker, Melissa Diliberti, Amy Barmer, Farrah Bullock Mann, and Erin Dunlop Velez. 2016. *The Condition of Education 2016*. NCES 2016–144. Washington, DC: U.S. Department of Education, National Center for Education Statistics.

Kennedy, Joseph V. 2012. "The Sources and Uses of U.S. Science Funding." *New Atlantis* 36 (Summer): 3–22.

Kenney, Martin, and David C. Mowery, eds. 2014. *Public Universities and Regional Growth: Insights from the University of California*. Stanford: Stanford Business Books.

Kernan, Alvin W. 1997. "Introduction: Change in the Humanities and Higher Education." In *What's Happened to the Humanities?* ed. Alvin W. Kernan, 3–13. Princeton: Princeton University Press.

Kerr, Clark. 1963. *The Uses of the University*. Cambridge, MA: Harvard University Press.

Kevles, Daniel J. 1997. "Big Science and Big Politics in the United States: Reflections on the Death of the SSC and the Life of the Human Genome Project." *Historical Studies in the Physical and Biological Sciences* 27: 269–97.

Keyworth, George A. II. 1983. "Federal R&D and Industrial Policy." *Science* 220: 1122–25.

Khalil, Hanan, and Martin Ebner. 2014. "MOOC Completion Rates and Possible Methods to Improve Retention: A Literature Review." *Proceedings of the World Conference on Educational Multimedia, Hypermedia, and Telecommunications*, 1236–44. Chesapeake, VA: Association for the Advancement of Computing in Education.

Kimball, Bruce. 1990. *Tenured Radicals: How Politics Has Corrupted Our Higher Education*. New York: Harper & Row.

Kingdon, John. 1984. *Agendas, Alternatives, and Public Policies*. Boston: Little, Brown.

Kingston, Paul W., Ryan Hubbard, Brent Lapp, Paul Schroeder, and Julia Wilson. 2003. "Why Education Matters." *Sociology of Education* 76: 53–70.

Kirp, David L. 2003. *Shakespeare, Einstein, and the Bottom Line: The Marketing of Higher Education*. Cambridge, MA: Harvard University Press.

Kissler, Gerald R. 1997. "Who Decides Which Budgets to Cut?" *Journal of Higher Education* 68: 427–59.

Kolowich, Steve. 2013. "In Deals with 10 Public Universities, Coursera Bids for Role in Credit Courses." *Chronicle of Higher Education*. May 30. Retrieved from http://www.chronicle.com/article/In-Deals-With-10-Public/139533/.

Konnikova, Maria. 2014. "18 U.S. Presidents Were in College Fraternities: Do Frats Create Future Leaders, or Simply Attract Them?" *The Atlantic*. February 21. Retrieved from https://www.theatlantic.com/education/archive/2014/02/18-us-presidents-were-in-college-fraternities/283997/.

Kors, Alan Charles, and Harvey A. Silverglate. 1998. *The Shadow University: The Betrayal of Liberty on America's Campuses*. New York: The Free Press.

Kraatz, Matthew S., and Edward J. Zajac. 1996. "Exploring the Limits of the New Institutionalism: The Causes and Consequences of Illegitimate Organizational Change." *American Sociological Review* 61: 812–36.

Kramer, David. 2016. "Obama's Science Legacy Is Big on Climate Change and Clean Energy." *Physics Today*. December. Retrieved from https://physicstoday.scitation.org/doi/full/10.1063/PT.3.3390.

Kramer, Peter D. 1993. *Listening to Prozac*. New York: Penguin.

Krimsky, Sheldon. 2003. *Science in the Private Interest: Has the Lure of Profits Corrupted Biomedical Research?* Lanham, MD: Rowman & Littlefield.

Krimsky, Sheldon, and Lawrence S. Rothenberg. 2001. "Conflict of Interests Policies in Science and Medical Journals: Editorial Practices and Author Disclosure." *Science and Engineering Ethics* 7: 205–18.

Krugman, Paul. 1991. "Increasing Returns and Economic Geography." *Journal of Political Economy* 99: 483–99.

———. 2004. "Competitiveness: A Dangerous Obsession." *Foreign Affairs* 73: 28–44.

Kuh, George D. 2008. *High-Impact Educational Practices: What They Are, Who Has Access to Them, and Why They Matter*. Washington, DC: American Association of Colleges & Universities.

———. 2009. "The National Survey of Student Engagement: Conceptual and Empirical Foundations." In *Using Student Engagement Data in Institutional Research*, eds. Robert Gonyea and George D. Kuh, 5–20. San Francisco: Jossey-Bass.

Kuh, George D., and Stanley O. Ikenberry. 2009. *More than You Think, Less than We Need: Learning Outcomes Assessment in American Higher Education*. Champaign, IL: National Institute for Learning Outcomes Assessment.

Kuh, George D., Natasha Jankowski, Stanley O. Ikenberry, and Jillian Kinzie. 2014. *Know What Students Know and Can Do: The Current State of Learning Outcomes Assessment in U.S. Colleges and Universities*. June. Champaign, IL: National Institute for Learning Outcomes Assessment.

Kuh, George D., Jillian Kinzie, John H. Schuh, and Elizabeth J. Whitt. 2005. *Assessing Conditions to Enhance Educational Effectiveness: The Inventory for Student Engagement and Successes*. San Francisco: Jossey-Bass.

Kuhn, Thomas. 1962. *The Structure of Scientific Revolutions*. Chicago: University of Chicago Press.

Kurutz, Steven. 2013. "Caught in the Hipster Trap." *New York Times*. September 14. Retrieved from http://www.nytimes.com/2013/09/15/opinion/sunday/caught-in-the-hipster-trap.html?_r=0/.

Kutner, Mark, Elizabeth Greenberg, Ying Jin, Bridget Boyle, Young-chen Hsu, and Eric Dunleavy. 2007. *Literacy in Everyday Life: Results from the 2003 National Assessment of Adult Literacy*. Washington, DC: National Center for Education Statistics. Retrieved from http://files.eric.Ed.gov/fulltext/ED495996.pdf.

Kwon, Ronald, Steven Brint, Kevin D. Curwin, and Allison M. Cantwell. 2018. "Cocurricular Learning and the Physical Campus." Unpublished paper. Department of Sociology, University of California-Riverside.

Labaree, David F. 2005. "Progressivism, Schools and Schools of Education: An American Romance." *Paedagogica Historica* 41: 275–88.

———. 2011. "Adventures in Scholarship." In *Leaders in the Historical Study of American Education*, ed. Wayne Urban, 193–204. Rotterdam: Sense Publishers.

———. 2017. *A Perfect Mess: The Unlikely Ascendancy of American Higher Education*. Chicago: University of Chicago Press.

Laird, Thomas F. N. 2005. "College Students' Experiences with Diversity and Their Effects on Academic Self-Confidence, Social Agency, and Disposition toward Critical Thinking." *Research in Higher Education* 46: 365–87.

Lamont, Michele. 1992. *Money, Morals, and Manners: The Culture of the French and the American Upper Middle Class*. Chicago: University of Chicago Press.

———. 2009. *How Professors Think: Inside the Curious World of Academic Judgment*. Cambridge, MA: Harvard University Press.

Lane, Jason. 2011. "Global Expansion of International Branch Campuses: Managerial and Leadership Challenges." *New Directions for Higher Education* 155: 5–17.

Lane, Neal, and Thomas Kalil. 2005. "The National Nanotechnology Initiative: Present at the Creation." *Issues in Science and Technology* 21 (4). Retrieved from http://issues.org/21-4/lane/.

Langer Lab. 2017. "Professor Robert Langer." Retrieved from http://web.mit.edu/langerlab/langer.html/.

Lapid, Patrick A., and John Aubrey Douglass. 2016. "College Affordability and the Rise of Progressive Tuition Models." *Research and Occasional Papers Series*. Center for Studies in Higher Education, University of California, Berkeley.

Lapsley, James, and Daniel Sumner. 2014. "'We Are Both Hosts': Napa Valley, UC Davis, and the Search for Quality." In *Public Universities and Regional Growth: Insights from the University of California*, eds. Martin Kenney and David C. Mowery, 180–212. Stanford: Stanford Business Books.

Lareau, Annette. 2003. *Unequal Childhoods: Class, Race, and Family Life*. Berkeley: University of California Press.

Larsen, Paul Olesen, and Markus von Ins. 2010. "The Rate of Growth in Scientific Publication and Decline in Coverage by Science Citation Index." *Scientometrics* 84: 575–603.

Lauffer, Carol. 2014. *Identification of Technology Clusters for Economic Development*. Retrieved from http://www.urbanaillinois.us/sites/default/files/attachments/technology-clusters-presentation.pdf.

Lazarus, Richard S., and Sarah Folkman. 1984. *Stress: Appraisal and Coping*. New York: Springer.

Lecuyer, Christophe. 2014. "Semiconductor Innovation and Entrepreneurship at Three University of California Campuses." In *Public Universities and Regional Growth: Insights from the University of California*, eds. Martin Kenney and David C. Mowery, 20–65. Stanford: Stanford Business Books.

Lederman, Doug. 2013. "The College Grad/Employment Mismatch." *InsideHigherEd*. January 28. Retrieved from https://www.insidehighered.com/news/2013/01/28/are-college-graduates-underemployed-and-if-so-why/.

Lemann, Nicholas. 1999. *The Big Test: The Secret History of the American Meritocracy*. New York: Farrar, Straus and Giroux.

Lenzer, Robert, and Stephen S. Johnson. 1997. "Seeing Things as They Really Are." *Forbes*. March 10. Retrieved from https://www.forbes.com/forbes/1997/0310/5905122a.html/.

Leslie, Larry, and Gary Rhoades. 1995. "Rising Administrative Costs: Seeking Explanations." *Journal of Higher Education* 66: 187–212.

Levinthal, Dave. 2015. "Spreading the Free-Market Gospel." *The Atlantic*. October 30. Retrieved from https://www.theatlantic.com/education/archive/2015/10/spreading-the-free-market-gospel/413239/.

Leydesdorff, Loet, and Henry Etzkowitz. 1996. "Emergence of a Triple Helix of University-Industry-Government Relations." *Science and Public Policy* 25: 195–203.

Leydesdorff, Loet, Henry Etzkowitz, and Duncan Kushnir. 2016. "Globalization and Growth of U.S. Patenting (2009–2014)." Unpublished paper, University of Amsterdam, School of Communication Research.

Li, Amy. 2014. "Performance Funding in the States: An Increasingly Ubiquitous Public Policy in Higher Education." *Higher Education in Review*. Retrieved from http://sites.psu.edu/highered inreview/wp-content/uploads/sites/36443/2016/02/Li-2014.pdf.

Lillienfeld, Scott O. 2017. "Microaggressions: Strong Claims, Inadequate Evidence." *Perspectives on Psychology* 12: 138–69.

Lindholm, Jennifer A., Alexander W. Astin, Linda J. Sax, and William S. Korn. 2002. *The American College Teacher: National Norms for the 2001–02 HERI Faculty Survey*. Los Angeles: Higher Education Research Institute, University of California, Los Angeles.

Lindholm, Jennifer A., Katalin Szelenyi, Sylvia Hurtado, and William S. Korn. 2005. *The American College Teacher: National Norms for the 2004–2005 HERI Faculty Survey*. Los Angeles: Higher Education Research Institute, University of California, Los Angeles.

Link, Albert, and John T. Scott. 2003. "The Growth of Research Triangle Park." *Small Business Economics* 20: 167–75.

Lo, Clarence. 1990. *Small Property versus Big Government: The Social Origins of the California Tax Revolt*. Berkeley: University of California Press.

Lobato, Katie. 2016. "Is the Government Making Money Off Your Student Loans?" *CNN Money*. August 1. Retrieved from http://money.cnn.com/2016/08/04/pf/college/federal-student-loan-profit/index.html.

Loise, Vicki, and Ashley J. Stevens. 2010. "The Bayh-Dole Act Turns 30." *Science Transactional Medicine* 2. Retrieved from http://stm.sciencemag.org/content/2/52/52cm27.full.

Long, James E., and Steven B. Caudill. 1991. "The Impact of Participation in Intercollegiate Athletics on Income and Graduation." *Review of Economics and Statistics* 73: 525–31.

Looney, Adam, and Constantine Yannelis. 2015. "A Crisis in Student Loans? How Changes in the Characteristics of Borrowers and in the Institutions They Attend Contributed to Rising Defaults." *Brookings Paper*. Retrieved from https://www.brookings.edu/wp-content/uploads/2016/07/ConferenceDraft_LooneyYannelis_StudentLoanDefaults.pdf.

Loury, Linda, and David Garman. 1995. "College Selectivity and Earnings." *Journal of Labor Economics* 13: 289–308.

Lovett, Marsha, Oded Meyer, and Candace Thille. 2008. *The Open Learning Initiative: Measuring the Effectiveness of the OLI Statistics Course in Accelerating Student Learning*. Retrieved from https://oli.cmu.edu/wp-content/uploads/2012/05/Lovett_2008_Statistics_Accelerated_Learning_Study.pdf.

Lovy, Howard. 2016. "Author Says the 'Great Mistake' Was Running Universities Like Businesses." *Foreword Reviews*. September 1. Retrieved from https://www.forewordreviews.com /articles/article/author-says-the-great-mistake-was-running-universities-like-businesses/.

Lowery, Ann. 2014. "Changed Life of the Poor: Better Off but Far Behind." *New York Times*, May 1, A1ff.

Lucas, Robert E. 1988. "On the Mechanics of Economic Development." *Journal of Monetary Economics* 22: 3–42.

Lucas, Samuel R. 2001. "Effectively Maintained Inequality: Education Transition, Track Mobility, and Social Background Effects." *American Journal of Sociology* 106: 1642–90.

Luger, Michael I., and Harvey A. Goldstein. 1991. *Technology in the Garden: Research Parks and Regional Economic Development*. Chapel Hill: University of North Carolina Press.

Lukianoff, Greg. 2014. *Unlearning Liberty: Campus Censorship and the End of American Debate*. New York: Encounter Books.

Lukianoff, Greg, and Jonathan Haidt. 2015. "The Coddling of the American Mind." *The Atlantic*. September. Retrieved from https://www.theatlantic.com/magazine/archive/2015/09/the -coddling-of-the-american-mind/399356/.

Lundvall, Bengt-Ake. 1988. "Innovation as an Interactive Process: From User-Producer Interaction to the National System of Innovation." In *Technical Change and Economic Theory*, eds. Giovanni Dosi, Christopher Freeman, Richard R. Nelson, and Gerald Silverberg, 349–64. London: Pinter.

Lusterman, Seymour. 1977. *Education in Industry*. Ottawa: Conference Board in Canada.

Lyanages, Shanta. 2006. *Serendipitous and Strategic Innovation: A Systems Approach to Managing Science-Based Innovation*. Westport, CT: Greenwood.

Macalester College. 2013. "Sophomore Leadership Program." Retrieved from http://www.maca lester.edu/campuslife/leadership/sophomoreleadership.

Machlup, Fritz. 1962. *The Production and Distribution of Knowledge in the U.S.* Princeton: Princeton University Press.

MacLean, C. R. K., et al. 1997. "Effects of the Transcendental Meditation Program on Adaptive Mechanisms: Changes in Hormone Levels and Responses to Stress after 4 Months of Practice." *Psychoneuroendocrinology* 22: 277–95. Retrieved from https://www.ncbi.nlm.nih.gov /pubmed/9226731.

Mangan, Katherine. 2013. "How Gates Shapes State Higher Education Policy." *Chronicle of Higher Education*. July 14. Retrieved from https://www.chronicle.com/article/How-Gates-Shapes -State/140303.

Mansfield, Edwin. 1998. "Academic Research and Industrial Innovation: An Update of Empirical Findings." *Research Policy* 26: 773–76.

Marcell, Michael. 2008. "Effectiveness of Regular Online Quizzing in Increasing Class Participation and Preparation." *Journal for Scholarship on Teaching and Learning* 2: 1–19.

Marcus, John. 2014. "New Analysis Shows Problematic Boom in Higher Ed Administrators." *New England Center for Investigative Reporting*. February 6. Retrieved from https://www .necir.org/2014/02/06/new-analysis-shows-problematic-boom-in-higher-ed-administrators/.

Marcus, Jon. 2012. "Student Advising Plays a Key Role in Student Success—Just as It Is Being Cut." *Hechinger Report*. November 13. Retrieved from http://hechingerreport.org/student -advising-plays-key-role-in-college-success-just-as-its-being-cut/.

Marginson, Simon. 2011. "Imaging the Global." In *Handbook of Globalization and Higher Education*, eds. Roger King, Simon Marginson, and Rajani Naidoo, 10–39. Cheltenham, UK: Edward Elgar.

Marginson, Simon, and Mark Considine. 2000. *The Enterprise University: Power, Governance, and Reinvention*. Cambridge: Cambridge University Press.

Markel, Howard. 2013. "Patents, Profits, and the American People: The Bayh-Dole Act of 1980." *New England Journal of Medicine* 369: 794–96.

Market Street Services. 2012. *Economic Cluster Analysis: Atlanta Region*. June. Retrieved from http://atlantaregional.org/wp-content/uploads/2017/03/metro-atlanta-economic-cluster-review-2.pdf.

Mars, Matthew M., and Cecilia Rios-Aguilar. 2010. "Academic Entrepreneurship (Re)defined: Significance and Implications for the Scholarship of Higher Education." *Higher Education* 59: 44–60.

Massy, William F. 2016. *Re-Engineering the University: How to Be Mission-Centered, Market Smart, and Margin Conscious*. Baltimore: Johns Hopkins University Press.

Mazur, Eric. 1997. *Peer Instruction: A User's Manual*. Upper Saddle River, NJ: Prentice Hall.

McCarthy, Sally A., and Robert J. Samors. 2009. *Online Learning as a Strategic Asset*. Washington, DC: Association of Public and Land Grant Universities. Retrieved from https://files.eric.ed.gov/fulltext/ED517308.pdf.

McDuffie, Douglas B. 2012. "Evaluating the Factors of Gainesville's Innovation Economy." Master's thesis. University of Florida, Department of Urban and Regional Planning. Retrieved from http://ufdc.ufl.edu/UFE0045134/00001/.

McLendon, Michael K., James C. Hearn, and Russ Deaton. 2006. "Called to Account: Analyzing the Origins and Spread of State Performance-Accountability Policies for Higher Education." *Educational Evaluation and Policy Analysis* 28: 1–24.

McLendon, Michael K., James C. Hearn, and Christine G. Mokher. 2009. "Partisans, Professionals, and Power: The Role of Political Factors in State Higher Education Funding." *Journal of Higher Education* 80: 686–713.

McMurtrie, Beth. 2016. "The Promise and Perils of Cluster Hiring." *Chronicle of Higher Education*. March 13. Retrieved from https://www.chronicle.com/article/The-PromisePeril-of/235679/.

McPherson, Michael S., and Lawrence S. Bacow. 2015. "Online Higher Education: Beyond the Hype Cycle." *Journal of Economic Perspectives* 29 (4): 135–54.

Medina, Jennifer. 2015. "In California Budget Plan, Brown Wins Tuition Freeze for In-State Students." *New York Times*. May 14. Retrieved from https://www.nytimes.com/2015/05/15/us/in-california-budget-plan-brown-wins-deal-on-tuition-freeze-for-in-state-students.html?_r=0/.

Mehta, Jal. 2007. "Does Professional Status Affect Demands for Accountability? Comparing K–12 and Higher Education." Unpublished paper, Harvard University, Graduate School of Education.

Meizlish, Deborah, and Matthew Kaplan. 2008. "Valuing and Evaluating Teaching in Academic Hiring: A Multi-disciplinary, Cross-Institutional Study." *Journal of Higher Education* 79: 489–512.

Merisotis, Jamie. 2010. "Meeting the Big Goal: What Can Trustees Do?" August 30. Retrieved from https://www.luminafoundation.org/news-and-views/meeting-the-big-goal-what-can-trustees-do/.

Merisotis, Jamie, and Ronald A. Phipps. 1999. "What's the Difference? Outcomes of Distance versus Traditional Course-Based Learning." *Change* (May–June): 12–17.

Merrill, Stephen A., and Anne-Marie Mazza. 2010. *Managing University Intellectual Property in the Public Interest*. Washington, DC: National Academies Press.

Merrill-Lynch. 1999. *The Knowledge Web*. San Francisco: Merrill-Lynch.

Merton, Robert K. 1942. "The Normative Structure of Science." In Robert K. Merton, *The Sociology of Science: Theoretical and Empirical Perspectives*. Chicago: University of Chicago Press.

Mervis, Jeffrey. 2015. "Hate COMPETES? With New Bill, Rep. Smith Doubles Down on Pending NSF Legislation." *Science*. July 31. Retrieved from http://www.sciencemag.org/news /2015/07/hate-competes-new-bill-rep-smith-doubles-down-pending-nsf-legislation/.

———. 2016a. "U.S. Research Groups Going to War Again against Small Business Funding." *Science*. May 18. Retrieved from http://www.sciencemag.org/news/2016/05/us-research -groups-going-war-again-over-small-business-funding/.

———. 2016b. "Remembering Erich Bloch (1925–2016)." *Science*. December 1. Retrieved from http://www.sciencemag.org/news/2016/12/remembering-erich-bloch-1925-2016.

———. 2017. "Data Check: U.S. Government Share of Basic Research Funding Falls below 50 Percent." *Science*. March 9. Retrieved from http://www.sciencemag.org/news/2017/03/data -check-us-government-share-basic-research-funding-falls-below-50/.

Mettler, Suzanne. 2014. *Degrees of Inequality: How the Politics of Higher Education Sabotaged the American Dream*. New York: Basic Books.

Metz, Rebecca. 2012. "The Rise of the New York City Start-Up Scene." *MIT Technology Review*. August 2. Retrieved from https://www.technologyreview.com/s/428774/the-rise-of-the-new -york-startup-scene/.

Meyer, John W. 2008. "Reflections on Institutional Themes of Organizations." In *The Sage Handbook of Organizational Institutionalism*, eds. Royston Greenwood, Christine Oliver, Kerstin Sahlin, and Roy Suddaby, 788–809. London: Sage.

Michels, Robert. (1911) 1962. *Political Parties: A Sociological Study of the Oligarchical Tendencies of Modern Democracies*. New York: Free Press.

Middaugh, Michael F., Rosalinda Graham, and Abdus Shahid. 2003. *A Study of Higher Education Instructional Expenditures: The Delaware Study of Instructional Costs and Productivity*. Washington, DC: U.S. Department of Education, National Center for Education Statistics.

Milem, Jeffrey F., Mitchell J. Chang, and Anthony Lising Antonio. 2007. *Making Diversity Work on Campus: A Research-Based Perspective*. Washington, DC: American Association of Colleges & Universities.

Milken Institute. 2016. "State Technology and Science Index." Retrieved from http://statetechand science.org/.

Miller, Karen A., Melvin L. Kohn, and Carmi Schooler. 1985. "Educational Self-Direction and the Cognitive Functioning of Students." *Social Forces* 63: 923–44.

Millett, Catherine M., Leslie M. Stickler, David G. Payne, and Carol A. Dwyer. 2007. *A Culture of Evidence: Critical Features of Assessments for Postsecondary Student Learning*. Princeton: Educational Testing Service. Retrieved from https://www.ets.org/Media/Research/pdf /HED_COE2.pdf.

Mills, C. Wright. 1956. *The Power Elite*. New York: Oxford University Press.

Mitchell, Michael, Michael Leachman, and Kathleen Masterson. 2016. "Funding Down, Tuition Up: State Cuts to Higher Education Threaten Quality and Affordability at Public Colleges." *Center on Budget and Policy Priorities*. August 15. Retrieved from https://www.cbpp.org /research/state-budget-and-tax/funding-down-tuition-up/.

Mizruchi, Mark, Peter Mariolis, Michael Schwartz, and Beth Mintz. 1986. "Techniques for Disaggregating Centrality Scores in Social Networks." *Sociological Methodology* 16: 26–48.

Moffatt, Michael. 1989. *Coming of Age in New Jersey: College and American Culture*. New Brunswick, NJ: Rutgers University Press.

Moltz, David. 2010. "Hispanic-Serving Grants?" *Inside Higher Ed*. March 24. Retrieved from http://www.insidehighered.com/news/2010/03/24/titlev/.

Montieth, Gene. 2010. "Four Years Later, 315 Tech Corridor Powers On." Retrieved from http:// www.hivelocitymedia.com/features/3155_20_10.aspx/.

Morelix, Arnobia. 2015. *The Evolution of Entrepreneurship on College Campuses*. Kansas City, MO: Ewing Marion Kauffman Foundation.

Moretti, Enrico. 2013. *The New Geography of Jobs*. New York: Houghton-Mifflin.

Morin, Alexander J. 1993. *Science Policy and Politics*. Englewood Cliffs, NJ: Prentice-Hall.

Mortenson, Tom. 2010. "Family Income and Educational Attainment 1970 to 2009." *Postsecondary Opportunity* 221. Retrieved from www.postsecondary.org.

Mozilla Foundation. 2017. "Discover Open Badges." Retrieved from https://openbadges.org/.

Mueller, Ralph O. 1988. "The Impact of College Selectivity on Income for Men and Women." *Research in Higher Education* 29: 175–91.

Mullen, Ann L. 2010. *Degrees of Inequality: Culture, Class, and Gender in American Higher Education*. Baltimore: Johns Hopkins University Press.

Mullen, Ann L., Kimberly A. Goyette, and Joseph A. Soares. 2003. "Who Goes to Graduate School? Social and Academic Correlates of Educational Continuation after College." *Sociology of Education* 76: 143–69.

Murphy, Raymond. 1984. "The Structure of Closure: A Critique and Development of the Theories of Weber, Collins, and Parkin." *British Journal of Sociology* 35 (4): 547–67.

Musil, Caryn M. 1992. *The Courage to Question: Women's Studies and Student Learning*. Washington, DC: Association of American Colleges.

Musu-Gillette, Lauren, Jennifer Robinson, Joel McFarland, Angelina Kewal Ramani, Anlan Zhang, and Sidney Wilkinson-Flicker. 2016. *Status and Trends in the Education of Racial and Ethnic Groups 2016*. NCES 2016–007. Washington, DC: National Center for Education Statistics.

Narin, Francis, Kimberly S. Hamilton, and Dominic Olivastro. 1997. "The Increasing Linkage between U.S. Technology and Public Science." *Research Policy* 26: 317–30.

Nash, George H. 1999. *Herbert Hoover and Stanford University*. Stanford: Hoover Institution.

Nathan, Rebekah. 2005. *My Freshman Year: What a Professor Learned by Becoming a Student*. Ithaca, NY: Cornell University Press.

National Academies of Science, Engineering, and Medicine (National Academies). 2005a. *Facilitating Interdisciplinarity*. Washington, DC: National Academies Press.

———. 2005b. *Rising above the Gathering Storm: Energizing and Employing America for a Brighter Future*. Washington, DC: National Academies Press.

———. 2011a. *Expanding Underrepresented Minority Participation: America's Science and Technology Talent at the Crossroads*. Washington, DC: National Academies Press. Retrieved from https://grants.nih.gov/training/minority_participation.pdf.

———. 2011b. *Managing University Intellectual Property in the Public Interest*. Washington, DC: National Academies Press. Retrieved from https://www.nap.edu/read/13001/chapter/3/.

National Association of College and University Business Officers (NACUBO). 2013. *2013 NACUBO Commonfund Study of Endowments*. Retrieved from https://www.commonfund.org/2014/01/12/2013-nacubo-commonfund-study-of-endowments-viewpoint/.

National Association of Independent Colleges and Universities (NAICU). 2016. *Controlling Costs*. Retrieved from https://www.naicu.edu/research-resources/research-projects/controlling-costs/.

National Center for Education Statistics (NCES). 2010. *Classification of Instructional Programs (CIP)*. Retrieved from https://nces.ed.gov/ipeds/cipcode/Default.aspx?y=55.

———. 2012a. *Digest of Education Statistics 2012*. Washington, DC: NCES.

———. 2012b. *Condition of Education 2012*. Washington, DC: NCES. Retrieved from https://nces.ed.gov/pubs2012/2012045.pdf.

———. 2014. *Digest of Education Statistics*. Washington, DC: NCES. Retrieved from www.nces.Ed.gov/programs/digest/.

———. 2015. *Digest of Education Statistics.* Washington, DC: NCES. Retrieved from https://nces.Ed.gov/programs/digest/.

———. 2016a. *The Condition of Education 2016.* Washington, DC: NCES.

———. 2016b. *Digest of Educational Statistics.* Washington, DC: NCES. Retrieved from https://nces.ed.gov/pubs2017/2017094.pdf.

———. 2017. *Immediate College Enrollment Rate.* March. Retrieved from https://nces.ed.gov/programs/coe/pdf/coe_cpa.pdf.

National Center for the Study of Collective Bargaining in Higher Education and the Professions (National Center). 1977a. *Directory of Bargaining Agents and Contracts in Institutions of Higher Education.* April. New York: CUNY Hunter College.

———. 1977b. *Newsletter.* Retrieved from http://thekeep.eiu.edu/ncscbhep_newsletters/95/.

———. 2007. *Directory of U.S. Faculty Contractors and Bargaining Agents in Institutions of Higher Education.* New York: National Center.

———. 2013. *Directory of U.S. Faculty Contractors and Bargaining Agents in Institutions of Higher Education.* New York: National Center.

National Collegiate Athletic Association (NCAA). 2017. *Estimated Probability of Competing in Intercollegiate Athletics.* Retrieved from http://www.ncaa.org/about/resources/research/estimated-probability-competing-college-athletics/.

National Collegiate Honors Council (NCHC). 2013a. "Membership Survey and Institutional Database Summary." Lincoln, NE: NCHC.

———. 2013b. "What Is Honors?" Retrieved from http://nchchonors.org/public-press/what-is-honors/.

National Commission on Accountability in Higher Education. 2005. *Accountability for Better Results: A National Imperative for Higher Education.* Washington, DC: State Higher Education Executive Officers.

National Endowment for the Arts (NEA). 2016. "National Endowment for the Arts Appropriations History." Retrieved from https://www.arts.gov/open-government/national-endowment-arts-appropriations-history/.

National Endowment for the Humanities (NEH). 2017. "National Endowment for the Humanities (NEH) Funding Levels." Retrieved from http://www.humanitiesindicators.org/content/indicatordoc.aspx?i=75/.

National Governors' Association (NGA). 1986. *A Time for Results: The Governors' 1991 Report on Education.* Washington, DC: National Governors' Association.

National Institute of Education Study Group on the Conditions of Excellence in American Higher Education (NIE). 1984. *Involvement in Learning: Realizing the Potential of American Higher Education.* Washington, DC: NIE.

National Institutes of Health (NIH). 2014. "Licensing Opportunities." Retrieved from https://www.ott.nih.gov/opportunities.

———. 2015. "What Are the Chances of Being Funded?" Retrieved from https://nexus.od.nih.gov/all/2015/06/29/what-are-the-chances-of-getting-funded/.

———. 2017a. "Spending History by Institute/Center, Budget Mechanism, Etc. 1983–2017." Retrieved from https://officeofbudget.od.nih.gov/spending_hist.html/.

———. 2017b. "What We Do: Budget." Retrieved from https://www.nih.gov/about-nih/what-we-do/budget.

———. 2017c. "History of the Common Fund." Retrieved from https://commonfund.nih.gov/about/history/.

National Research Council (NRC). 2005. *Measuring Literacy: Performance Levels for Adults.* Washington, DC: National Academies Press.

National Science Board. 2016. *Science and Engineering Indicators 2016*. Washington, DC: National Science Board.

National Science Foundation (NSF). n.d. "Erich Bloch (1925–)." Retrieved from http://www.sciencemag.org/news/2016/12/remembering-erich-bloch-1925-2016.

———. 1989. *Industrial Participation in NSF Programs and Activities*. Washington, DC: NSF.

———. 2000. *America's Investment in the Future: NSF Celebrating 50 Years*. Retrieved from www.nsf.gov/about/history/nsf0050/pdf/aif.pdf.

———. 2007. "Broader Impacts Review Criteria." Retrieved from https://www.nsf.gov/pubs/2007/nsf07046/nsf07046.jsp.

———. 2008. "New NSF Survey Finds Six States Account for Nearly Half of State Agencies' R&D Expenditures." September. Retrieved from https://wayback.archive-it.org/5902/2016 0210222200/http://www.nsf.gov/statistics/infbrief/nsf08309/nsf08309.pdf.

———. 2013. *FY 2012 Report on the NSF's Merit Review Process*. Washington, DC: NSF. Retrieved from https://www.nsf.gov/nsb/publications/2013/nsb1333.pdf.

———. 2015. *Perspectives on Broader Impacts*. Washington, DC: NSF. NSF 15–008.

———. 2016a. *Survey of Federal Funds for Research and Development Fiscal Years 2014–2016*. April. Retrieved from https://ncsesdata.nsf.gov/fedfunds/2014/.

———. 2016b. "State Government R&D Expenditures Total More than $2.2 Billion in FY 2015." December. Retrieved from www.nsf.gov/statistics/2017/nsf17307/.

———. 2016c. *FY 2017 Budget Request to Congress*. February. Washington, DC: NSF. Retrieved from https://nsf.gov/about/budget/fy2017/pdf/fy2017budget.pdf.

———. 2016d. *FY 2016 Budget Request to Congress*. Washington DC: NSF. Retrieved from https://www.nsf.gov/about/budget/fy2016/pdf/fy2016budget.pdf.

———. 2017. "Major Multi-User Research Facilities." Retrieved from https://www.nsf.gov/about/budget/fy2017/pdf/33_fy2017.pdf.

National Science Foundation, Division of Science Resources Statistics. 2007. *Changing U.S. Output of Scientific Articles, 1988–2003*, eds. Derek Hill, Alan I. Rapaport, Rolf F. Lehming, and Robert K. Bell. Arlington, VA: National Science Foundation.

National Science Foundation, National Center for Science and Engineering Statistics. 2015. *Survey of Earned Doctorates*. Retrieved from www.nsf.gov/statistics/2017/nsf17306/data.cfm/.

National Science Foundation, Office of Diversity and Inclusion. 2017. "About Us." Retrieved from https://www.nsf.gov/od/odi/.

National Summit on Competitiveness. 2005. "Statement of the National Summit on Competitiveness: Investing in U.S. Innovation." December. Retrieved from https://www.aip.org/fyi/2005/national-summit-competitiveness/.

National Survey of Student Engagement (NSSE). 2000. *The NSSE 2000 Report: National Benchmarks of Effective Educational Practice*. Bloomington: Indiana University, Center for Postsecondary Research.

———. 2008. *Promoting Engagement for All Students: The Imperative to Look Within. 2008 Results*. Bloomington: Indiana University, Center for Postsecondary Research.

———. 2016. "2106 U.S. Survey Frequencies." Retrieved from http://nsse.indiana.edu/2016_institutional_report/pdf/Frequencies/Freq%20-%20Sex.pdf.

Neal, Homer A., Tobin L. Smith, and Jennifer B. McCormick. 2008. *Beyond Sputnik: U.S. Science Policy in the 21st Century*. Ann Arbor: University of Michigan Press.

Nelson, Libby A. 2012. "Funding Drop for Black Colleges." *Inside Higher Education*. September 26. Retrieved from http://www.insidehighered.com/news/2012/09/26/federal-funds-historically-black-colleges-drop/.

Nelson, Richard R. 1992. "National Innovation Systems: A Retrospective on a Study." *Industrial and Corporate Change* 1: 347–74.

Nester, William R. 1993. *American Power, the New World Order, and the Japanese Challenge*. London: Macmillan.

Newfield, Christopher. 2008. *Unmaking the Public University: The Forty-Year Assault on the Middle Class*. Cambridge, MA: Harvard University Press.

———. 2016. *The Great Mistake: How We Wrecked Public Universities and How We Can Fix Them*. Baltimore: Johns Hopkins University Press.

New York Times. 2017. "Economic Diversity and Student Outcomes at America's Colleges and Universities." *New York Times "The Upshot."* Retrieved from https://www.nytimes.com/interactive/projects/college-mobility/.

Nicholas, Peter, and Evan Halper. 2004. "Schwarzenegger, Colleges Reach Budget Agreement." *Los Angeles Times*. May 11. Retrieved from http://articles.latimes.com/2004/may/11/local/me-transfer10.

Nieli, Russell K. 2014. "Grade Inflation—Why Princeton Threw in the Towel." *Minding the Campus*. October 15. Retrieved from http://www.mindingthecampus.org/2014/10/grade-inflation-why-princeton-threw-in-the-towel/.

Norman, Donald A. 1988. *The Design of Everyday Things*. New York: Doubleday.

Oakley, Ann. 2005. *The Ann Oakley Reader: Gender, Women, and Social Science*. Bristol, UK: Polity Press.

Oakley, Francis. 1997. "Ignorant Armies and Nighttime Clashes: Changes in the Humanities Classroom, 1970–1995." In *What's Happened to the Humanities?* ed. Alvin W. Kernan, 63–83. Princeton: Princeton University Press.

Obama, Barack. 2009. "President Obama's Inaugural Address." January 20. Retrieved from http://media.washingtonpost.com/wp-srv/politics/documents/obama_inaugural_address.html?hpid=topnews/.

———. 2010. "Remarks by the President on Higher Education and the Economy at the University of Texas Austin." August 9. Washington, DC: The White House. Retrieved from https://www.whitehouse.gov/the-press-office/2010/08/09/remarks-president-higher-education-and-economy-university-texas-austin/.

———. 2011. "Remarks by the President in the State of the Union." January 20. Retrieved from https://obamawhitehouse.archives.gov/the-press-office/2011/01/25/remarks-president-state-union-address/.

O'Brien, S. E. 2016. "Northwest Austin Tech and Start-Up Corridor." Retrieved from https://seobrien.com/the-nw-austin-tech-startup-corridor/.

Office of Science and Technology Policy. 2013. *21st Century Grand Challenges*. Retrieved from https://obamawhitehouse.archives.gov/administration/eop/ostp/grand-challenges/.

Okahana, Hironao, Keonna Feaster, and Jeff Allum. 2016. *Graduate Enrollment and Degrees 2005 to 2015*. Washington, DC: Council of Graduate Schools.

Oklahoma State University Athletic Department. 2012. "Boone Pickens Stadium." Retrieved from http://www.okstate.com/facilities/boone-pickens-stadium.html/.

Okunade, Albert A. and Phanindra V. Wunnava. 2011. "Alumni Giving of Business Executives to the Alma Mater: Panel Data Evidence at a Large Metropolitan Research University." *IZA Discussion Paper*. Number 5428. Retrieved from http://ftp.iza.org/dp5428.pdf.

Olneck, Michael. 2018. "Digital Badges and Higher Education in a New Society." In *Education in a New Society: Renewing the Sociology of Education*, eds. Jal Mehta and Scott Davies, 229–70. Chicago: University of Chicago Press.

O'Mara, Margaret Pugh. 2005. *Cities of Knowledge: Cold War Science and the Search for the Next Silicon Valley*. Princeton: Princeton University Press.

Opidee, Ionna. 2015. "Supporting First-Gen College Students." *University Business.* Retrieved from https://www.universitybusiness.com/article/supporting-first-gen-college-students/.

Oregon State University. 2016. "Honors College." Retrieved from http://honors.oregonstate.edu/.

Organisation for Economic Cooperation and Development (OECD). 1996. *The Knowledge-Based Economy.* Paris: OECD. Retrieved from https://www.oecd.org/sti/sci-tech/1913021.pdf.

———. 2016. *Skills Matter: Further Results from the Survey of Adult Skills.* Paris: OECD.

Osborne, David, and Ted Gaebler. 1992. *Reinventing Government: How the Entrepreneurial Spirit Is Transforming the Public Sector.* New York: Penguin.

Owen-Smith, Jason, and Walter W. Powell. 2003. "The Expanding Role of University Patenting in the Life Sciences: Assessing the Importance of Experience and Connectivity." *Research Policy* 32: 1695–1711.

Paddock, Richard C. 2008. "Hardship Predicted for Students." *Los Angeles Times.* April 17. Retrieved from http://articles.latimes.com/2008/apr/17/local/me-cuts17/.

Padilla, Arthur, and Sujit Ghosh. 1999. "On the Tenure of University Presidents." *On the Horizon* 7 (5): 1–5. Retrieved from https://www.researchgate.net/profile/Sujit_Ghosh4/publication/259570857_On_the_Tenure_of_University_Presidents/links/55ccdd9408ae1141f6b9e862/On-the-Tenure-of-University-Presidents.pdf?origin=publication_detail/.

Padilla-Walker, Laura M. 2006. "The Effect of Daily Extra-Credit Quizzes on Exam Performance." *Teaching Psychology* 33: 236–39.

Palardy, Gregory J. 2008. "Differential School Effects among Low, Middle, and High School Class Composition Schools: A Multiple Group, Multilevel Latent Growth Curve Analysis." *School Effectiveness and School Improvement* 19: 21–49.

Palo Alto Online News. 2013. "Stanford Admits 2,210 for Class of 2013." April 1. Retrieved from http://www.paloaltoonline.com/news/show_story.php?id=29107/.

Pappano, Laura. 2012. "The Year of the MOOC." *New York Times.* November 2. Retrieved from http://www.nytimes.com/2012/11/04/education/edlife/massive-open-online-courses-are-multiplying-at-a-rapid-pace.html/.

Parkin, Frank. 1979. *Marxism and Class Theory: A Bourgeois Critique.* London: Tavistock.

Parry, Marc. 2013. "A Star MOOC Professor Defects—At Least for Now." *Chronicle of Higher Education.* September 3. Retrieved from http://www.chronicle.com/article/A-MOOC-Star-Defects-at-Least/141331/.

Parry, Marc, Kelly Field, and Beckie Supiano. 2013. "The Gates Effect." *Chronicle of Higher Education.* July 19. A18–28.

Partnership for Undergraduate Life Sciences Education (PULSE). 2016. *About the Partnership for Undergraduate Life Sciences Education.* Retrieved from http://www.pulsecommunity.org/page/about/.

Partovi, Hadi. 2015. "Is Seattle Silicon Valley's Next Favorite Stop?" *TechCrunch.* April 25. Retrieved from https://techcrunch.com/2015/04/25/is-seattle-silicon-valleys-next-favorite-stop/.

Pascarella, Ernest, Charles Blaich, Georgianna L. Martin, and Jana M. Hanson. 2011. "How Robust Are the Findings of Academically Adrift?" *Change* (May–June). Retrieved from https://www.tandfonline.com/doi/abs/10.1080/00091383.2011.568898.

Pascarella, Ernest T., Ty Cruse, Paul D. Umbach, Gregory C. Wolniak, George D. Kuh, Robert M. Carini, John Hayek, Robert M. Gonyea, and Chun-Mei Zhao. 2006. "Institutional Selectivity and Good Practices in Undergraduate Education: How Strong Is the Link?" *Journal of Higher Education* 77: 251–85.

Pascarella, Ernest T., Lamont Flowers, and Elizabeth J. Whitt. 2001. "Cognitive Effects of Fraternity and Sorority Membership: Additional Evidence." *NASPA Journal* 38: 280–301.

Pascarella, Ernest T., Tricia A. Seifert, and Charles Blaich. 2009. "Validation of the NSSE Benchmarks and Deep Approaches to Learning against Liberal Arts Outcomes." Paper presented at the annual meeting of the Association for the Study of Higher Education. Jacksonville, FL. November.

Pascarella, Ernest T., and Patrick T. Terenzini. 1991. *How College Affects Students.* San Francisco: Jossey-Bass.

———. 2005. *How College Affects Students.* Vol. 2, *A Third Generation of Research.* San Francisco: Jossey-Bass.

Pascarella, Ernest T., Rachel Truckmiller, Amaury Nora, Patrick T. Terenzini, Michael Edison, and Linda Serra Hagedorn. 1999. "Cognitive Impact of Intercollegiate Athletic Participation: Some Further Evidence." *Journal of Higher Education* 70: 1–26.

Patton, Carol. 2015. "Cluster Hiring: Fad or Best Practice?" *University Business.* August 1. Retrieved from https://www.universitybusiness.com/article/cluster-hiring-fad-or-best-practice/.

PayScale. 2016. *2016–2017 College Salary Report.* Retrieved from http://www.payscale.com/college-salary-report/majors-that-pay-you-back/.

Paytas, Jerry, Robert Gradeck, and Lena Andrews. 2004. *Universities and the Development of Industry Clusters.* Carnegie Mellon University Center for Economic Development. Retrieved from http://www.heinz.cmu.edu/center-for-economic-development/ced-pubs-projects/index.aspx/.

PEN America. 2017. *And Campus for All: Diversity, Inclusion, and Freedom of Speech at U.S. Universities.* June 15. Retrieved from https://pen.org/wp-content/uploads/2017/06/PEN_campus_report_06.15.2017.pdf.

Pennebaker, James W., Samuel D. Gosling, and Jason D. Ferrell. 2013. "Daily Online Testing in Large Classes: Boosting College Performance While Reducing Achievement Gaps." *PLOS One.* November. Retrieved from http://journals.plos.org/plosone/article?id=10.1371/journal.pone.0079774.

Persell, Caroline Hodges, and Peter W. Cookson Jr. 1990. "Chartering and Bartering: Elite Education and Social Reproduction." In *The High Status Track,* eds. Paul W. Kingston and Lionel S. Lewis. Albany: SUNY Press.

Pew Charitable Trusts. 2015. *Federal and State Funding of Higher Education: A Changing Landscape.* June 11. Retrieved from www.pewtrusts.org/en/research-and-analysis/issue-briefs/2015/06/federal-and-state-funding-of-higher-education/.

Pew Research Center. 2017. "Sharp Partisan Divisions in Views of National Institutions." July 10. Retrieved from http://www.people-press.org/2017/07/10/sharp-partisan-divisions-in-views-of-national-institutions/.

PlanSmart NJ. 2013. "What Will It Take to Support New Jersey's Industrial Clusters?" April. Retrieved from http://www.plansmartnj.org/wp-content/uploads/2013/05/IndustryCluster FinalReport4_30.pdf.

Polsgrove, Carol. 2012. "University of Michigan's Dubious Deal with Dow Chemical." *Huffington Post.* April 20. Retrieved from https://www.huffingtonpost.com/carol-polsgrove/university-of-michigans-dow-chemical_b_1439096.html/.

Ponomariov, Branco L., and P. Craig Boardman. 2010. "Influencing Scientists' Collaboration and Productivity Patterns through New Institutions: University Research Centers and Scientific and Technical Human Capital." *Research Policy* 39: 613–24.

Porter, Michael E. 1990. *The Competitive Advantages of Nations.* New York: The Free Press.

———. 1998. "Clusters and the New Economics of Competition." *Harvard Business Review* (November/December): 1–14. Retrieved from https://hbr.org/1998/11/clusters-and-the-new-economics-of-competition/.

Posselt, Julie R., and Eric Grodsky. 2017. "Graduate Education and Social Stratification." *Annual Review of Sociology* 43: 353–78.

Posselt, Julie R., Ozan Jacquette, Rob Bielby, and Michael N. Bastedo. 2012. "Access without Equity: Race and Ethnic Stratification in Higher Education." *American Educational Review Journal* 49: 1074–1111.

Powell, Kendall. 2015. "The Future of the Postdoc." *Nature*. April 7. Retrieved from http://www.nature.com/news/the-future-of-the-postdoc-1.17253/.

Powell, Walter W., Douglas R. White, Kenneth W. Koput, and Jason Owen-Smith. 2005. "Network Dynamics and Field Evolution: The Growth Interorganizational Collaboration in the Life Sciences." *American Journal of Sociology* 110: 1132–1205.

Press, William. 2013. "What's So Special about Science (and How Much Should We Spend on It?)" *Science* 342: 817–22. Retrieved from http://science.sciencemag.org/content/342/6160/817/.

Price, Robert M., and Laurie Goldman. 2002. *The Novartis Agreement: An Appraisal*. Administrative Review. University of California, Berkeley.

Professor X. 2011. *In the Basement of the Ivory Tower: Confessions of an Accidental Academic*. New York: Viking Penguin.

Providence Business News. 2014. "UMass Records Best-Ever Year for Start-Ups." *Providence Business News*. November 10. Retrieved from http://www.pbn.com/UMass-records-best-ever-year-for-startup-businesses,101336/.

Puri, Ankur, Ipek Demirsoy, Lucinda Woods, Mi Zhou, and Thongchai Rattanaruengyot. 2011. *The Minnesota Medical Devices Cluster: The Microeconomics of Competition*. Harvard Business School Project. Retrieved from https://www.isc.hbs.edu/resources/courses/moc-course-at-harvard/Documents/pdf/student-projects/USA_(MN)_Medical_Devices_2011.pdf.

Raftery, Adrian E., and Michael Hout. 1993. "Maximally Maintained Inequality: Expansion, Reform and Opportunity in Irish Education, 1921–75." *Sociology of Education* 66: 41–62.

Rankin and Associates. 2014. *University of California System: Campus Climate Final Report*. March. Retrieved from http://campusclimate.ucop.edu/_common/files/pdf-climate/ucsystem-full-report.pdf.

Rawlings, Craig, and Daniel A. McFarland. 2011. "Influence Flows in Academe: Using Affiliation Networks to Assess Peer Effects among Researchers." *Social Science Research* 40: 1001–17.

Rawlings, Craig, Daniel A. McFarland, Linus Dahlander, and Dan Wang. 2015. "Streams of Thought: Knowledge Flows and Intellectual Cohesion in a Multidisciplinary Era." *Social Forces* 93: 1687–1722.

Rawson, Kevin, Thomas F. Stahovich, and Richard E. Mayer. 2017. "Homework and Achievement: Using Smartpen Technology to Find the Connection." *Journal of Educational Psychology* 109: 208–19.

Read, Jan. 2016. "Successful Entrepreneur and Innovator Chosen to Lead New Innovation Center." *Vanderbilt R&D*. Retrieved from https://news.vanderbilt.edu/2016/02/01/robert-grajewski-chosen-to-lead-vanderbilt-innovation-center/.

Redden, Elizabeth. 2013. "Global Ambitions." *Inside Higher Education*. March 11. Retrieved from https://www.insidehighered.com/news/2013/03/11/nyu-establishes-campuses-and-sites-around-globe/.

Rhoades, Gary. 1998. *Managed Professionals: Unionized Faculty and Restructuring Academic Labor*. Albany: SUNY Press.

Rhoades, Gary, and Barbara Sporn. 2002. "New Models of Management and Shifting Modes and Costs of Production: Europe and the United States." *Tertiary Education and Management* 8: 3–28.

Rhodes, Frank Harold Trevor. 2001. *The Creation of the Future: The Role of the American University*. Ithaca, NY: Cornell University Press.

Rhoten, Diana. 2004. "Interdisciplinary Research: Trend or Transition?" *Items: Insights from the Social Sciences* 6–11. Retrieved from http://items.ssrc.org/interdisciplinary-research-trend-or -transition/.

Rhoten, Diana, and Craig Calhoun, eds. 2011. *Knowledge Matters: The Public Mission of the Research University*. New York: Columbia University Press.

Riesman, David. 1980. *On Higher Education: The Academic Enterprise in an Era of Rising Student Consumerism*. San Francisco: Jossey-Bass.

Riggle, James D., and Roger R. Stough. 2003. "Evaluating State Cooperative Technology Programs: With a Virginia Case Study and Comparative Data from Illinois." *Technological Forecasting and Social Change* 70: 639–51.

Rivard, Ry. 2014. "Discount Escalation." *Inside Higher Ed*. July 2. Retrieved from https://www .insidehighered.com/news/2014/07/02/prices-rise-colleges-are-offering-students-steeper -discounts-again.

Rivera, Lauren. 2012. "Hiring as Cultural Matching: The Case of Elite Professional Service Firms." *American Sociological Review* 77: 999–1022.

———. 2015. *Pedigree: How Elite Students Get Elite Jobs*. Princeton: Princeton University Press.

Roberts, Edward B., Fiona Murray, and J. Daniel Kim. 2016. *Entrepreneurship and Innovation at MIT: Continuing Global Growth and Impact*. Retrieved from https://gcase.files.wordpress .com/2016/01/mit-report-entrepreneurship-2015.pdf.

Roco, Mihail. 2011. "The Long View of Nanotechnology Development: The National Nanotechnology Initiative at 10 Years." *Journal of Nanoparticle Research* 13: 427–45.

Rogers, Everett. 1962. *The Diffusion of Innovations*. New York: Free Press of Glencoe.

Rogers, Jenny. 2013. "How Many Administrators Are Too Many?" *Chronicle of Higher Education*. January 17. Retrieved from http://www.chronicle.com/interactives/administrative_bloat/.

Rojstaczer, Stuart, and Christopher Healy. 2010. "Grading in American Colleges and Universities." *Teacher's College Record*. Retrieved from http://www.gradeinflation.com/tcr2010grad ing.pdf.

———. 2012. "Where A Is Ordinary: The Evolution of American College and University Grading, 1940–2009." *Teacher's College Record* 114 (7): 1–23.

Roksa, Josipa. 2005. "Double Disadvantage or Blessing in Disguise? Understanding the Relationship between College Major and Employment Sector." *Sociology of Education* 78: 207–32.

Romer, Paul. 1990. "Endogenous Technological Change." *Journal of Political Economy* 98: S71–S102.

Rorty, Richard. 1991. *Objectivity, Relativism, and Truth*. Cambridge: Cambridge University Press.

Rosenbaum, James E. 1998. "College-for-All: Do Students Understand College Demands?" *Social Psychology of Education* 2: 44–80.

———. 2004. *Beyond College for All: Career Paths for the Forgotten Half*. New York: Russell Sage Foundation Press.

Rosenbaum, James E., Caitlin E. Ahearn, and Janet E. Rosenbaum. 2017. *Bridging the Gaps: College Pathways to Career Success*. New York: Russell Sage Foundation Press.

Rosenbaum, James E., Regina Deil-Amen, and Ann E. Person. 2006. *After Admission: From College Access to College Success*. New York: Russell Sage Foundation Press.

Rosovsky, Henry. 1990. *The University: An Owner's Manual*. New York: W. W. Norton.

Rotondi, Matthew Baron. 2015. "Making Meaning of Student Debt: How Undergraduate Students Make Sense of Their Student Loan and Credit Card Debt." PhD diss., Department of Sociology, University of California-Riverside.

Rouse, William B. 2007. *People and Organizations: Explorations in Human-Centered Design*. New York: Wiley.

RTP Media Resources. 2013. *Triangle Universities Center for Advanced Studies, Inc.: A Brief History*. Retrieved from https://www.rtp.org/tucasi/.

Rudolph, Conrad. 2016. "UC We Gave You." Retrieved from http://escholarship.org/uc/item/3ww5g8jj/.

Rumberger, Russell W., and Scott L. Thomas. 1993. "The Economic Returns to College Major, Quality and Performance: A Multilevel Analysis of Recent Graduates." *Economics of Education Review* 12: 1–19.

Russell, Thomas. 2001. *The No Significant Difference Phenomenon*. Chicago: International Distance Education Certification Center.

Ruttan, Vernon W. 1956. "The Contribution of Technological Progress to Farm Output, 1950–75." *Review of Economics and Statistics* 38: 61–69.

Ryan, Camille L., and Kurt Bauman. 2016. *Educational Attainment in the United States: 2015*. Current Population Reports. March. Retrieved from https://www.census.gov/content/dam/Census/library/publications/2016/demo/p20-578.pdf.

Sa, Creso. 2008. "'Interdisciplinary Strategies' in U.S. Research Universities." *Higher Education* 55: 537–52.

Saenz, Emmanuel, and Gabriel Zucman. 2014. "Wealth Inequality in the U.S. since 1913: Evidence from Capitalized Income Tax Data." *NBER Working Paper*. No. 20625. Retrieved from https://gabriel-zucman.eu/files/SaezZucman2014.pdf.

Salmi, Jamil. 2009. *The Challenge of Establishing World-Class Universities*. Washington, DC: The World Bank.

Sampat, Bhaven N. 2012. "Mission Oriented Biomedical Research at the NIH." *Research Policy* 41: 1729–41.

Sampat, Bhaven N., and Frank R. Lichtenberg. 2011. "What Are the Respective Roles of the Public and Private Sectors in Pharmaceutical Innovation?" *Health Affairs* 30: 332–39.

Samuels, Bob. 2017. "What Makes for a Good Free College Plan?" *Inside Higher Education*. July 24. Retrieved from https://www.insidehighered.com/views/2017/07/24/key-questions-ask-about-free-college-plans-essay/.

San Jose State University, Department of Philosophy. 2013. "An Open Letter to Michael Sandel from the Department of Philosophy, San Jose State University." May 2. Retrieved from http://www.chronicle.com/article/The-Document-an-Open-Letter/138937/.

Sarfatti Larson, Magali. 1979. *The Rise of Professionalism: A Sociological Analysis*. Berkeley: University of California Press.

Saunders, Katherine. 2015. *Barriers to Success: Unmet Financial Need for Low-Income Students of Color at Community Colleges*. Washington, DC: Center for Law and Social Policy. Retrieved from https://www.clasp.org/publications/report/brief/barriers-success-unmet-financial-need-low-income-students-color-community.

Savage, Jacob. 2008. "And a Good Riddance to Princeton's Nancy Weiss Malkiel." March 3. http://www.ivygateblog.com/2008/03/and-a-good-riddance-to-princeton%E2%80%99s-nancy-weiss-malkiel/.

Sax, Linda J., Alexander W. Astin, Marisol Arrendondo, and William S. Korn. 1996. *The American College Teacher: National Norms for the 1995–96 HERI Faculty Survey*. Los Angeles: Higher Education Research Institute, University of California, Los Angeles.

Sax, Linda J., Alexander W. Astin, William S. Korn, and Shannon K. Gilmartin. 1999. *The American College Teacher: National Norms for the 1998–99 HERI Faculty Survey*. Los Angeles: Higher Education Research Institute, University of California, Los Angeles.

Saxenian, Annalee. 1994. *Regional Advantage: Culture and Competition in Silicon Valley and Route 128*. Cambridge, MA: Harvard University Press.

Schaar, Jack, and Sheldon Wolin. 1965. "A Special Supplement: Berkeley and the Fate of the Multiversity." *New York Review of Books*. March 11. Retrieved from www.nybooks.com/articles/13005/.

Schatz, Bryan. 2017. "Security for Far-Right's Free Speech Week Will Cost UC Berkeley More than $1 Million." *Mother Jones*. September 21. Retrieved from http://www.motherjones.com/politics/2017/09/security-for-the-far-rights-free-speech-week-will-cost-uc-berkeley-more-than-1-million/.

Schliefer, David, and Rebecca Silliman. 2016. "What's the Payoff? Americans Consider Problems and Promises of Higher Education." *Public Agenda Research Brief*. October. Retrieved from http://www.publicagenda.org/files/WhatsThePayoff_PublicAgenda_2016.pdf.

Schoen, Donald A. 1983. *The Reflective Practitioner: How Professionals Think in Practice*. New York: Basic Books.

———. 1987. *Educating the Reflecting Practitioner: Toward a New Design for Teaching and Learning in the Professions*. San Francisco: Jossey-Bass.

Schrag, Philip G. 2014. "MOOCs and Legal Education: Valuable Innovation or Looming Disaster?" *Villanova Law Review* 59: 83–134.

Schumpeter, Joseph. 1942. "The Creative Response in Economic History." *Journal of Economic History* 7: 149–59.

———. 1947. *Capitalism, Socialism, and Democracy*. New York: Harper and Row.

Schuster, Jack H. 2003. "The Faculty Make-Over: What Does It Mean for Students?" *New Directions in Higher Education* 123: 15–22.

Schuster, Jack H., and Martin J. Finkelstein. 2006. *The American Faculty: The Restructuring of Work and Careers*. Baltimore: Johns Hopkins University Press.

Schwartz, Peter. 1996. *The Art of the Long View: Planning for the Future in an Uncertain World*. New York: Doubleday.

Science News Staff. 2017. "What's in Trump's 2018 Budget Request for Science?" *Science*. May 23. Retrieved from http://www.sciencemag.org/news/2017/05/what-s-trump-s-2018-budget-request-science/.

Scott, W. Richard. 2015. "Higher Education in America: Multiple Fields Perspectives." In *Remaking College: The Changing Ecology of Higher Education*, eds. Michael W. Kirst and Mitchell L. Stevens, 19–38. Stanford: Stanford University Press.

Searle, John R. 1994. "Rationality and Realism: What Is at Stake?" In *The Research University in a Time of Discontent*, eds. Jonathan R. Cole, Elinor G. Barber, and Stephen R. Graubard, 55–83. Baltimore: Johns Hopkins University Press.

Seay, Brian. 2016. "CT's 'Seven Sisters' Launched State's Biosciences Golden Age." *Hartford Business.com*. December 5. Retrieved from http://www.hartfordbusiness.com/article/20161205/PRINTEDITION/312019936/cts-7-sisters-launched-states-bioscience-golden-age/.

Seifert, Tricia A., Ernest T. Pascarella, Nicholas Coangelo, and Susan Assouline. 2007. "The Effects of Honors Program Participation on Experiences of Good Practices and Learning Outcomes." *Journal of College Student Development* 48: 57–74.

Seligson, Hannah. 2012. "Hatching Ideas, and Companies, by the Dozens." *New York Times*. November 24. Retrieved from http://www.nytimes.com/2012/11/25/business/mit-lab-hatches-ideas-and-companies-by-the-dozens.html?pagewanted=all/.

Selingo, Jeff. 2013. *College (Un)bound: The Future of Higher Education and What It Means for Students*. New York: Houghton-Mifflin.

Selzer, Mark. 2016. "Discounting Reaches New Highs." *Inside Higher Ed*. May 16. Retrieved from https://www.insidehighered.com/news/2016/05/16/discount-rates-rise-yet-again-private-colleges-and-universities.

Severin, Laura. 2013. "Doing 'Cluster Hiring' Right." *Inside Higher Education*. September 30. Retrieved from https://www.insidehighered.com/advice/2013/09/30/essay-how-colleges -can-engage-cluster-hiring/.

Sewell, William H., and Vimal P. Shah. 1967. "Socioeconomic Status, Intelligence, and Attainment of Higher Education." *Sociology of Education* 40: 1–23.

Shiao, Jiannbin Lee. 2005. *Identifying Talent, Institutionalizing Diversity: Race and Philanthropy in Post–Civil Rights America*. Durham: Duke University Press.

Shin, Jeong Cheol. 2009. "The Impact of Performance-Based Accountability on Institutional Performance in the U.S." *Higher Education* 60: 47–68.

Shulenberger, David. 2008. *Measuring Core Educational Outcomes at Research Universities for Improvement and Accountability*. October. Washington, DC: National Association of State Colleges and Land-Grant Universities.

Shulman, Lee S. 1997. "Professing the Liberal Arts." In *Education and Democracy: Re-Imagining Liberal Learning in America*, ed. Robert Orrill, 151–73. New York: College Board Publications.

———. 2004. *Teaching as Community Property Essays in Higher Education*. San Francisco: Jossey-Bass.

Shulock, Nancy, and Colleen Moore. 2002. *An Accountability Framework for California Higher Education: Informing Public Policy and Improving Outcomes*. Sacramento, CA: Center for California Studies, Faculty Research Fellows Program.

Singer, Peter L. 2014. *Federally Supported Innovations: 22 Examples of Major Technology Advances that Stem from Federal Research Support*. Washington, DC: Information Technology and Innovation Foundation. Retrieved from http://www2.itif.org/2014-federally-supported -innovations.pdf.

Slack, Werner, and Douglas Porter. 1980. "The Scholastic Aptitude Test: A Critical Appraisal." *Harvard Educational Review* 50: 154–75.

Slaughter, Sheila. 1990. *Higher Learning and High Technology: Dynamics of Higher Education Policy Formation*. Albany: State University of New York Press.

Slaughter, Sheila, and Larry L. Leslie. 1997. *Academic Capitalism: Politics, Policies, and the Entrepreneurial University*. Baltimore: Johns Hopkins University Press.

Slaughter, Sheila, and Gary Rhoades. 1996. "The Emergence of a Competitiveness Research and Development Policy Coalition and the Commercialization of Academic Science and Technology." *Science, Technology, and Human Values* 21: 303–39.

———. 2004. *Academic Capitalism and the New Economy: Markets, States, and Higher Education*. Baltimore: Johns Hopkins University Press.

Smelser, Neil J. 1993. "The Politics of Ambivalence: Diversity in the Research Universities." *Daedalus* 122 (4): 37–53.

Smith, Burck. 2012. "Postsecondary Post-'Access.'" Paper presented at the American Enterprise Institute Conference, Stretching the Higher Education Dollar. August. Washington, DC.

Smith, Darryl. 2009. *Diversity's Promise for Higher Education: Making It Work*. Baltimore: Johns Hopkins University Press.

Smith, Dorothy E. 1974. "Women's Perspective as a Radical Critique of Sociology." *Sociological Inquiry* 44: 7–13.

Smith, Michele K., William B. Wood, and Jennifer K. Knight. 2008. "The Genetics Concept Inventory for Gauging Student Understanding of Genetics." *CBE Life Sciences Education* 7: 422–30.

Smith, Page. 1990. *Killing the Spirit: Higher Education in America*. New York: Vintage.

Snow, Charles Percy. 1959. *The Two Cultures*. Cambridge: Cambridge University Press.

Snyder, Thomas D., ed. 1993. *120 Years of American Education: A Statistical Portrait*. Washington, DC: National Center for Educational Statistics.

Soares, Joseph E. 2007. *The Power of Privilege: Yale and America's Elite Colleges*. Stanford: Stanford University Press.

Sobel, Michael. 1983. "Lifestyle Differentiation and Stratification in Contemporary U.S. Society." *Research in Social Stratification and Mobility* 2: 115–434.

Solow, Robert. 1956. "A Contribution to the Theory of Economic Growth." *Quarterly Journal of Economics* 70: 65–94.

———. 1957. "Technical Change the Aggregate Production Function." *Review of Economics and Statistics* 39: 312–20.

Song, Moohoun, and Peter F. Orazem. 2004. "Returns to Graduate and Professional Education: The Roles of Mathematical and Verbal Skills by Major." *Staff General Research Papers*. No. 12432. Iowa City: Iowa State University, Department of Economics.

Sorokin, Pitrim. 1927. *Social Mobility*. New York: Bedminster Press.

Spady, Tyrone. 2016. "Policy Update: Congress Passes American Innovation and Competitiveness Act." Washington, DC: Lewis-Burke Associates, LLM. Retrieved from https://blog.aspb .org/2016/12/19/policy-update-congress-passes-american-innovation-and-competitiveness-act/.

Spivak, Gayatri Chakravorty. 1988. "Can the Subaltern Speak?" In *Colonial Discourse and Post-Colonial Theory*, eds. Patrick Williams and Laura Chrisman, 46–111. New York: Columbia University Press.

Squires, Gregory D. 1979. *Education and Jobs: The Imbalancing of the Social Machinery*. New Brunswick, NJ: Transaction Publishers.

Staff, Jeremy, and Jeylan T. Mortimer. 2007. "Educational and Work Strategies for Adolescence to Early Adulthood: Consequences for Educational Attainment." *Social Forces* 85: 1169–94.

Stanback, Thomas M., Jr., Peter J. Bearse, Thierry J. Noyelle, and Robert A. Karasek. 1981. *Services: The New Economy*. Totowa, NJ: Allanheld, Osmun.

Stanford University. n.d. "Wellspring of Innovation." Retrieved from https://web.stanford.edu /group/wellspring/.

Start X. 2017. "Start X Accelerator Program." Retrieved from http://startx.com/accelerator/.

State Higher Education Executive Officers (SHEEO). 2015. *SHEF 2015: State Higher Education Finance FY 2015*. Washington, DC: SHEEO. Retrieved from http://www.sheeo.org/sites /default/files/SHEEO_SHEF_FY2015.pdf.

State of South Carolina. n.d. "About." *SmartState: SC Centers of Economic Excellence*. Retrieved from https://smartstatesc.org/introduction/.

State University of New York (SUNY). 2017. "Statement by SUNY Chairman H. Carl McCall and SUNY Chancellor Nancy L. Zimpher on New York State Budget Agreement." April 8. Retrieved from https://www.suny.edu/suny-news/press-releases/04–2017/4-8-17/statement -by-chairman-carl-mccall-and-chancellor-zimpher-on-budget-agreement.html/.

Steinberg, Jacques. 1995. "Yale Returns $20 Million to an Unhappy Patron." *New York Times*. March 15. Retrieved from https://www.nytimes.com/1995/03/15/us/yale-returns-20-million -to-an-unhappy-patron.html.

Stephan, Paula E. 2012. *How Economics Shapes Science*. Cambridge, MA: Harvard University Press.

Stevens, Mitchell L., Elizabeth A. Armstrong, and Richard Arum. 2008. "Sieve, Incubator, Temple, Hub: Empirical and Theoretical Advances in the Sociology of Higher Education." *Annual Review of Sociology* 34: 127–51.

Stigler, James, Karen B. Givven, and Belinda J. Thompson. 2013. "What Community College Developmental Mathematics Students Understand about Math." *Carnegie Foundation for the Advancement of Teaching Problem Solution Exploration Papers*. Retrieved from https:// www.carnegiefoundation.org/wp-content/uploads/2013/05/stigler_dev-math.pdf.

Stokes, Donald E. 1997. *Pasteur's Quadrant: Basic Science and Technological Innovation.* Washington, DC: Brookings Institution Press.

Stouffer, Samuel A. 1958. "The Student–Problems Related to the Use of Academic Ability." In *The Identification and Education of the Academically Talented Student in the American Secondary School*, ed. James B. Conant, 28–35. Washington, DC: National Education Association.

Strober, Myra H. 2011. *Interdisciplinary Conversations: Challenging Habits of Thought.* Stanford: Stanford University Press.

Suster, Mark. 2013. "In 15 Years from Now Half of US Universities May Be in Bankruptcy: My Surprise Discussion with @ClaytonChristensen." *Both Sides.* March 3. Retrieved from https://bothsidesofthetable.com/in-15-years-from-now-half-of-us-universities-may-be-in-bankruptcy-my-surprise-discussion-with-979f93bd6874.

Tandberg, David A., and Nicholas W. Hillman. 2014. "State Higher Education Performance Funding: Data, Outcomes, and Policy Implications." *Journal of Educational Finance* 39: 222–43.

Tibbetts, Roland. 2008. *Reauthorizing SBIR: The Critical Importance of SBIR and Small High Tech Firms in Stimulating and Strengthening the U.S. Economy.* Washington, DC: National Small Business Association. Retrieved from http://www.nsba.biz/docs/roland_tibbets_paper.pdf.

Tierney, William G., and James T. Minor. 2003. *Challenges for Governance: A National Report.* Los Angeles: Center for Higher Education Policy Analysis.

Thomas, Scott L. 2000. "Deferred Costs and Economic Returns to College Major, Quality, and Performance." *Research in Higher Education* 41: 281–313.

Thomas, Scott L., and Liang Zhang. 2005. "Post-Baccalaureate Wage Growth within 4 Years of Graduation: The Effects of College Quality and College Major." *Research in Higher Education* 46: 437–59.

Thurm, Scott. 2012. "Who Can Still Afford State U?" *Wall Street Journal.* December 14. Retrieved from https://www.wsj.com/articles/SB10001424127887323501404578163290734542674/.

Thurow, Lester. 1972. "Education and Economic Equality." *The Public Interest* 28 (Summer): 66–81.

Tobias, Sheila. 2009. "Professional Science Degrees May Be the 21st Century MBA." *Science News* 175 (13): 32.

Toole, Andrew A. 2012. "The Impact of Public Basic Research on Industrial Innovation: Evidence from the Pharmaceutical Industry." *Research Policy* 41: 1–12.

Torche, Florencia. 2011. "Is a College Degree Still the Great Equalizer? Intergenerational Mobility across Levels of Schooling in the United States." *American Journal of Sociology* 117: 763–807.

Trachtenberg, Stephen Joel, Gerald B. Kauver, and E. Grady Bogue. 2016. *Presidencies Derailed: Why University Leaders Fail and How to Prevent It.* Baltimore: Johns Hopkins University Press.

Trow, Martin. 1970. "Reflections on the Transition from Mass to Universal Higher Education." *Daedalus* (Winter): 1–42.

———. 1973. *Problems in the Transition from Elite to Mass Higher Education.* Berkeley: Carnegie Commission on Higher Education.

———. 2000. "From Mass Higher Education to Universal Access: The American Advantage." *Minerva* 37: 1–26.

———. 2005. "Reflections on the Transition from Elite to Mass to Universal Access: Forms and Phases of Higher Education in Modern Societies since WWII." *Institute of Governmental Studies Working Papers.* Institute of Governmental Studies, University of California, Berkeley. Later published in *International Handbook of Higher Education.* 18th ed., ed. James J. F. Forrest and Philip Altbach. London: Kluwer, 2007.

Tuchman, Gaye. 2009. *Wannabe U: Inside the Corporate University.* Chicago: University of Chicago Press.

Tumulty, Karen, and Jenna Johnson. 2016. "Why Trump May Be Winning the War on Political Correctness." *Washington Post*. January 4. Retrieved from https://www.washingtonpost.com/politics/why-trump-may-be-winning-the-war-on-political-correctness/2016/01/04/098cf832-afda-11e5-b711-1998289ffcea_story.html?utm_term=.97a4103ad383.

Turner, Sarah E. 2006. "Higher Tuition, Higher Aid and the Quest to Improve Opportunities for Low-Income Students in Selective, Public Higher Education." In *What's Happening to Public Higher Education?* ed. Ronald G. Ehrenberg, 251–74. Westport, CT: Greenwood Press.

Turner, Sarah E., and William G. Bowen. 1990. "The Flight from the Arts and Sciences: Trends in Degrees Conferred." *Science* 250: 517–21.

Turner, Stephen. 2000. "What Are Disciplines? And How Is Interdisciplinarity Different?" In *Practicing Interdisciplinarity*, eds. Peter Weingart and Nico Stehr, 46–65. Toronto: University of Toronto Press.

Umbach, Paul D. 2007. "How Effective Are They? Exploring the Impact of Contingent Faculty on Undergraduate Students." *Review of Higher Education* 30: 91–123.

Umbach, Paul D., Megan M. Palmer, George D. Kuh, and Stephanie J. Heinrich. 2006. "Intercollegiate Athletes and Effective Educational Practices: Winning Combination or Losing Effort?" *Research in Higher Education* 47: 709–33.

Under30CEO. 2018. "The Fifteen Largest Business Competition Plans." Retrieved from http://under30ceo.com/the-15-largest-college-business-plan-competitions/.

United States Bureau of the Census. 2016a. "Educational Attainment in the United States." Retrieved from https://www.census.gov/data/tables/2016/demo/education-attainment/cps-detailed-tables.html/.

———. 2016b. "Selected Characteristics of Households, by Total Money Income in 2015: HINC-01." Retrieved from https://www.census.gov/data/tables/time-series/demo/income-poverty/cps-hinc/hinc-01.html/.

United States Department of Commerce, Bureau of Economic Analysis (BEA). 2016. "Gross Domestic Product (GDP)-by-Industry Data: 1997–2015: 403 Industries." Retrieved from https://www.bea.gov/industry/gdpbyind_data.htm.

———. 2017. "Per Capita Real GDP by State (Chained 2009 Dollars)." Retrieved from https://www.bea.gov/newsreleases/regional/gdp_state/2017/pdf/qgsp0717.pdf.

United States Department of Defense. n.d. "Defense Innovation Marketplace." Retrieved from http://www.defenseinnovationmarketplace.mil/.

United States Department of Education. 2010. "US Department of Education Awards 23 Grants to Enhance Predominantly Black Institutions." Retrieved from https://www.ed.gov/news/press-releases/us-department-education-awards-23-grants-enhance-predominantly-black-institution/.

United States Department of Energy. 2014a. *Basic Energy Science Summary Report*. Retrieved from https://science.energy.gov/~/media/bes/pdf/reports/files/BES2014SR_rpt.pdf.

———. 2014b. *Task Force Report to Support the Evaluation of New Funding Constructs for Energy R&D in the DOE*. March 28. Retrieved from https://energy.gov/sites/prod/files/2014/04/f14/FINAL-Hubs%2Breport.pdf.

United States Department of Labor, Bureau of Labor Statistics (BLS). 2015. "Educational Attainment for Workers 25 Years or Older by Detailed Occupation." Retrieved from https://www.bls.gov/emp/ep_table_111.htm/.

———. 2016a. "Employed Persons by Detailed Occupation, Sex, Race, and Hispanic or Latino Ethnicity." Retrieved from http://www.bls.gov/cps/cpsaat11.pdf.

———. 2016b. "Gross Domestic Product by Industry Data." Retrieved from http://www.bea.gov/industry/gdpbyind_data.htm.

United States Department of the Treasury. 2006. *Lessons Learned from the Privatization of Sallie Mae*. Washington, DC: U.S. Department of the Treasury. Retrieved from www.treasury.gov /about/organizational-structure/offices/Documents/SallieMaePrivatizationReport.pdf.

United States President's Commission on Higher Education (Truman Commission). 1947. *Higher Education for American Democracy*. New York: Harper Brothers.

United States Senate, Committee on Health, Education, and Welfare (United States Senate). 2011. *Senate Report on For-Profit Colleges—Executive Summary*. Retrieved from https:// www.help.senate.gov/imo/media/for_profit_report/ExecutiveSummary.pdf.

University of California, Berkeley, Haas School of Business. 2013. "Admissions Criteria." Retrieved from http://www.haas.berkeley.edu/Undergrad/.

University of California, Office of the President. 2015. *APM-210–1-d. Appointment and Promotion, Review and Appraisal Committees*. Oakland: University of California. Retrieved from https://www.ucop.edu/academic-personnel-programs/_files/apm/apm-278-210-6-2nd-sys -rev/apm-210-6-2rev-clean.pdf.

University of Chicago. n.d. "Economic Impact and Jobs." Retrieved from http://civicengagement .uchicago.edu/anchor/economic-impact-and-jobs/.

———. 2015. *Report of the Committee on Freedom of Expression*. Chicago: University of Chicago. Retrieved from https://freeexpression.uchicago.edu/sites/freeexpression.uchicago.edu/files /FOECommitteeReport.pdf.

University of Chicago Law School. 2016. "Professor Geoffrey Stone Discusses Free Speech at the American Law Institute." June 6. Retrieved from https://www.law.uchicago.edu/news /prof-geoffrey-stone-discusses-free-speech-campus-american-law-institute/.

University of Pennsylvania. 2014. "Community and Economic Development." Retrieved from http://aese.psu.edu/graduateprograms/cedev.

———. 2015. "Impact: Powering Philadelphia and Pennsylvania." Retrieved from http://www .evp.upenn.edu/pdf/Penn_Economic_Impact_Powering_PHL_PA.pdf.

University of Southern California (USC). 1994. *The Strategic Plan of the University of California*. June 8. Los Angeles: University of Southern California.

———. 1998. *Four-Year Report on the 1994 Strategic Plan*. Retrieved from https://about.usc.edu /files/2011/07/USC_strategicplan_1994_4year_report_optimized.pdf.

University of Texas-Austin. 2017. "University Leadership Network." Retrieved from https://stu dentsuccess.utexas.edu/uln.

———. 2018. "Freshman Research Initiative." Retrieved from https://cns.utexas.edu/fri.

University of Washington-Seattle. 2018. *Undergraduate Research Symposium*. Retrieved from https://www.washington.edu/undergradresearch/symposium/.

University of Wisconsin-Madison. 2003. *Report of the Provost's Ad Hoc Advisory Committee to Evaluate the Cluster Hiring Initiative University of Wisconsin-Madison*. November. Madison: Office of the Provost. Retrieved from https://provostfacstaff.wiscweb.wisc.edu/wp-content /uploads/sites/208/2017/05/ClusterReport2003.pdf.

———. 2008. *Report of the Cluster/Interdisciplinary Advisory Committee to Evaluate the Cluster Hiring Initiative*. July. Madison: Office of the Provost. Retrieved from https://provostfac staff.wiscweb.wisc.edu/wp-content/uploads/sites/208/2017/07/ClusterReport_2008.pdf.

Urban Universities for HEALTH (Urban Universities). 2015. *Faculty Cluster Hiring for Diversity and Institutional Climate*. April. Retrieved from http://urbanuniversitiesforhealth.org /media/documents/Faculty_Cluster_Hiring_Report.pdf.

US News and World Report (USNWR). 2017. *Best Higher Education Administration Programs*. Retrieved from https://www.usnews.com/best-graduate-schools/top-education-schools /higher-education-administration-rankings/.

Useem, Michael, and Jerome Karabel. 1986. "Pathways to Top Corporate Management." *American Sociological Review* 51: 184–200.

UStar. 2017. "UStar—the University of Utah: Strengthening Utah's Economy." Retrieved from http://www.ustar.utah.edu/.

Valdivia, Walter D. 2013. "University Start-Ups: Critical for Improving Technology Transfer." Washington, DC: Brookings Institution, Center for Technology Innovation. Retrieved from https://www.brookings.edu/wp-content/uploads/2016/06/Valdivia_Tech-Transfer_v29_No -Embargo.pdf.

Van de Vord, Rebecca, and Korolyn Pogue. 2012. "Teaching Time Investment: Does Online Really Take More Time than Face-to-Face?" *International Review of Research in Open and Distributed Learning* 13: 132–46.

Van der Heijden, Kees. 1997. *Scenarios: The Art of Strategic Conversation*. New York: John Wiley & Sons.

Van Noorden, Richard. 2014. "Global Scientific Output Doubles Every Nine Years." *Nature.com*. May 7. Retrieved from http://blogs.nature.com/news/2014/05/global-scientific-out put-doubles-every-nine-years.html/.

Varmus, Harold, and Marc W. Kirschner. 1992. "Don't Undermine Basic Research." *New York Times*. November 29. Retrieved from http://www.nytimes.com/1992/09/29/opinion/don-t -undermine-basic-research.html/.

Varum, Cecilia. A., and Carla Melo. 2010. "Directions in Scenario Planning Literature: A Review of the Past Decades." *Futures* 42: 355–69. Retrieved from https://www.sciencedirect.com /science/article/pii/S0016328709001955.

Veblen, Thorstein. 1918. *The Higher Learning in America: A Memorandum on the Conduct of Universities by Businessmen*. New York: Hill and Wang.

Vedder, Richard, Christopher Denhart, and Jonathan Robe. 2013. *Why Are Recent College Graduates Underemployed?* Washington, DC: Center for College Affordability and Productivity.

Villasenor, John. 2017. "Views among College Students Regarding the First Amendment: Results of a New Survey." *FixGov Blog, Brookings Institution*. September 18. Retrieved from https:// www.brookings.edu/blog/fixgov/2017/09/18/views-among-college-students-regarding-the -first-amendment-results-from-a-new-survey/.

Virginia Tech University. 2013. "Restricted Majors." Retrieved from www.registrar.vt.edu/pro spective/majros/restricted-majors.html/.

Virginia Tech University, Department of Mathematics. 2016. "Honors and Awards." Retrieved from https://www.emporium.vt.edu/emporium/home.html.

Vogel, Ezra. 1979. *Japan as Number One: Lesson for America*. Cambridge, MA: Harvard University Press.

Volokh, Eugene. 2015. "UC Teaching Faculty Members Not to Criticize Race-Based Affirmative Action, Call America 'Melting Pot' and More." *Washington Post*. June 6. Retrieved from https://www.washingtonpost.com/news/volokh-conspiracy/wp/2015/06/16/uc-teaching -faculty-members-not-to-criticize-race-based-affirmative-action-call-america-melting-pot -and-more/?utm_term=.e03a23c28764/.

Von Drehle, David. 2009. "Big Man on Campus." *Time*. November 11. Retrieved from http:// content.time.com/time/specials/packages/article/0,28804,1937938_1937934_1937914,00.html.

Wacquant, Loïc. 2009. *Punishing the Poor: The Neoliberal Government of Social Insecurity*. Durham: Duke University Press.

Walejko, Gina K., Mary E. Hughes, Susannah V. Howieson, and Stephanie S. Shipp. 2012. "Federal Laboratory-Business Commercialization Partnerships." *Science* 337: 1297–98.

Wallace, Dawn, and Phyllis King. 2013. "EEOC vs. Higher Education: Recent Laws and Interpretations Impacting Faculty Discrimination." *Journal of Legal, Ethical and Regulatory Issues* 16: 1–6.

Wallach, Dieter, and Sebastian C. Scholz. 2012. "User-Centered Design: Why and How to Put Users First in Software Development." In *Software for People*, eds. Alexander Madche, Achim Botzenhardt, and Ludwig Neer, 11–38. Berlin and Heidelberg: Springer-Verlag.

Walshok, Mary, and Joel West. 2014. "Serendipity and Symbiosis: UCSD and Local Wireless Industry." In *Public Universities and Regional Growth: Insights from the University of California*, eds. Martin Kenney and David C. Mowery, 127–52. Stanford: Stanford Business Books.

Ware, Mark, and Michael Mabe. 2009. *The STM Report: An Overview of Scientific and Scholarly Publishing*. Oxford: International Association of Scientific, Technical and Medical Publishers. Retrieved from https://www.stm-assoc.org/2009_10_13_MWC_STM_Report.pdf.

———. 2015. *The STM Report: An Overview of Scientific and Scholarly Journal Publishing*. Oxford: International Association of Scientific, Technical and Medical Publishers. Retrieved from http://www.stm-assoc.org/2015_02_20_STM_Report_2015.pdf.

Warikoo, Natasha K. 2016. *The Diversity Bargain: And Other Dilemmas of Race, Admissions, and Meritocracy at Elite Universities*. Chicago: University of Chicago Press.

Warner, John. 2015. "ASU: Teaching as a Luxury." *Inside Higher Education*. June 18. Retrieved from https://www.insidehighered.com/blogs/just-visiting/asu-teaching-luxury/.

Warren, J. D. 2018. "$1 m. Gift Empowers Next Generation of Scientists." *UCR Today*. March 5. Retrieved from https://ucrtoday.ucr.edu/52014.

Washburn, Jennifer. 2000. *University, Inc.: The Corporate Corruption of Higher Education*. New York: Basic Books.

Waugaman, Paul G., and Roger J. Porter. 1992. "Mechanisms of Interaction between Industry and the Academic Medical Centre." In *Biomedical Research: Collaboration and Conflict of Interest*, eds. Roger J. Porter and Thomas Malone, 93–118. Baltimore: Johns Hopkins University Press.

Waugh, William L., Jr. 2003. "Issues in University Governance: More 'Professional' and Less Academic." *ANNALS of the American Academy of Political and Social Science* 585: 84–96.

Weber, Max. (1921) 1946. "Bureaucracy." In *From Max Weber*, ed. Hans H. Gerth and C. Wright Mills, 196–244. New York: Oxford University Press.

Weddle, Rick L., Elizabeth Rooks, and Tina Valdecanas. 2006. "Research Triangle Park: Evolution and Renaissance." Retrieved from http://www.rtp.org/sites/default/files/RTP_History_0.pdf.

Weill Medical Center. 2013. "Weill Cornell Reaches $1.3 Billion Goal for Its Pioneering Discoveries to Make a Difference Campaign." April 30. Retrieved from https://news.weill.cornell.edu/news/2013/04/weill-cornell-reaches-13-billion-goal-for-its-pioneering-discoveries-that-make-a-difference-campaign/.

Wessler, Stephen, and Margaret Moss. 2001. *Hate Crimes on Campus: The Problem and What to Do About It*. October. Washington, DC: U.S. Department of Justice. Retrieved from https://www.brookings.edu/blog/fixgov/2017/09/18/views-among-college-students-regarding-the-first-amendment-results-from-a-new-survey/.

Whalen, Edward L. 1991. *Responsibility Centered Budgeting: An Approach to Decentralized Management for Institutions of Higher Education*. Bloomington: Indiana University Press.

"What Are the Gut Classes at Yale?" 2007. Retrieved from http://gawker.com/297435/what-are-the-gut-classes-at-yale.

White House Initiative on Asian American and Pacific Islanders (White House Initiative). 2012. "Fact Sheet: Asian American and Native American Pacific Islander Serving Institutions." Retrieved from https://www2.ed.gov/about/inits/list/asian-americans-initiative/aanapisi-fact-sheet.doc.

Whyte, William Foote. 1956. *The Organization Man*. New York: Simon and Schuster.

Wickens, Christine M. 2008. "The Organizational Impact of University Labor Unions." *Higher Education* 58: 545–64.

Wieman, Carl. 2012. "Applying New Research to Improve Science Education." *Issues in Science and Engineering* (Fall): 25–37.

Wieman, Carl, and Sarah Gilbert. 2014. "The Teaching Practices Inventory: A New Tool for Characterizing College and University Teaching in Mathematics and Science." *CBE Life Sciences Education* 13: 552–69.

Wildavsky, Ben, Andrew Miller, and Kevin Carey. 2011. *Reinventing Higher Education.* Cambridge, MA: Harvard Education Press.

Wilensky, Harold. 1964. "The Professionalization of Everyone?" *American Journal of Sociology* 70: 137–58.

Wilson, Ian D., Edward R. Adlard, Michael Cooke, and Colin F. Poole, eds. 2000. *Encyclopedia of Separation Science.* Ann Arbor: University of Michigan.

Wilson, Kenneth G. 1989. "Grand Challenges to Computational Science." *Future Generation Computer Systems* 5: 171–89.

Wolf-Wendel, Lisa E., J. Douglas Toma, and Christopher C. Morphew. 2001. "How Much Difference Is Too Much Difference? Perceptions of Gay Men and Lesbians in Intercollegiate Athletics." *Journal of College Student Development* 42: 465–79.

Wolfle, Dael. 1958. "Educational Waste." *Bulletin of Atomic Scientists: Science and Education* (November): 364–68.

Worley Wanda L., and Lee S. Tesdell. 2009. "Instructor Time and Effort in Online and Face-to-Face Teaching: Lessons Learned." *IEEE Transactions on Professional Communication* 52: 138–51.

Wu, Weiping. 2005. "Dynamic Cities and Creative Clusters." *World Bank Policy Research Working Paper.* No. 3509. February. Retrieved from http://documents.worldbank.org/curated/en/441151468762563308/pdf/WPS3509.pdf.

XPrize. n.d. *Active Prize Competitions.* Retrieved from http://www.xprize.org/prizes/.

Xu, Di, and Shanna Smith Jaggars. 2014. "Performance Gaps between Online and Face-to-Face Courses: Differences across Types of Students and Academic Subject Areas." *Journal of Higher Education* 85: 633–59.

Young, Jeffrey R. 2012. "Badges Earned Online Post Challenge for Traditional College Diplomas." *Chronicle of Higher Education.* January 8. Retrieved from http://www.chronicle.com/article/Badges-Earned-Online-Pose/130241/.

Yuskavage, Robert E. 1996. "Improved Estimates of Gross Product by Industry, 1959–94." *Survey of Current Business* (August): 133–55.

Zabusky, Jonathan. 2015. "NYC Start-Ups: The Growth of Silicon Alley." *Huffington Post.* June 30. Retrieved from http://www.huffingtonpost.com/jonathan-zabusky/nyc-tech-start-up-b-318 5826.html.

Zamarra, John W., Robert H. Schneider, Donald K. Robinson, and John W. Salerno. 1996. "Usefulness of the Transcendental Meditation Program in the Treatment of Patients with Coronary Artery Disease." *American Journal of Cardiology* 77: 867–70. Retrieved from https://www.ajconline.org/article/S0002-9149(97)89184-9/fulltext.

Zimmerman, Eilene. 2013. "Austin's 'Silicon Hills' Builds on Its Infrastructure." *New York Times.* July 17. Retrieved from https://boss.blogs.nytimes.com/2013/07/17/austins-silicon-hills-builds-on-its-infrastructure/.

Zimmerman, Jonathan. 2016a. "The Two Kinds of PC." *Inside Higher Education.* June 16. Retrieved from https://www.insidehighered.com/views/2016/06/16/examination-two-kinds-political-correctness-essay/.

———. 2016b. *Campus Politics: What Everyone Needs to Know.* London: Oxford University Press.

Zoghi, Cindy, Alec Levenson, and Michael Gibbs. 2005. "Why Are Jobs Designed the Way They Are?" *BLS Working Papers.* Working Paper 385. Washington, DC: U.S. Department of Labor, Bureau of Labor Statistics. Retrieved from https://www.bls.gov/ore/pdf/ec050080.pdf.

Zucker, Lynne G., and Michael R. Darby. 1996. "Star Scientists and Institutional Transformation: Patterns of Invention and Innovation in the Formation of the Biotechnology Industry." *Proceedings of the National Academy of Sciences* 93: 12709–16.

———. 2014. "Movement of Star Scientists and Engineers and High-Tech Firm Entry." *Annals of Economics and Statistics* 115/116 (special issue): 125–75.

Zucker, Lynne G., Michael R. Darby, and Jeff Armstrong. 2002. "Commercializing Knowledge: University Science, Knowledge Capture, and Firm Performance in Biotechnology." *Management Science* 48: 138–53.

Zucker, Lynne G., Michael R. Darby, and Marilynn B. Brewer. 1998. "Intellectual Human Capital and the Birth of U.S. Biotechnology Enterprises." *American Economic Review* 88: 290–306.

Zumeta, William. 2001. "Public Policy and Accountability in Higher Education: Lessons from the Past and Present for the New Millennium." In *The States and Higher Education Policy: Affordability, Access, and Accountability*, ed. Donald E. Heller, 155–97. Baltimore: Johns Hopkins University Press.

INDEX

A NOTE ON THE TYPE

This book has been composed in Adobe Text and Gotham.
Adobe Text, designed by Robert Slimbach for Adobe,
bridges the gap between fifteenth- and sixteenth-century
calligraphic and eighteenth-century Modern styles.
Gotham, inspired by New York street signs, was designed
by Tobias Frere-Jones for Hoefler & Co.